Morningside
Heights
and Harlem ⑫

D0491198

★ **Cathedral of
St. John the Divine** ⑫
See pages 224 – 5

Upper
West
Side

⑨

Central
Park

⑩

⑪

Upper
East
Side

★ **Solomon R. Guggenheim Museum** ⑪
See pages 186 – 7

④

⑤

Upper
Midtown

⑥

⑧

Lower
Midtown

★ **Metropolitan Museum** ⑩
See pages 188 – 95

EAST RIVER

N

★ **United Nations** ⑧
See pages 158 – 61

★ **St. Patrick's
Cathedral** ⑤
See pages 176 – 7

★ **Grand Central Terminal** ⑥
See pages 154 – 5

0 kilometers		2
0 miles	1	

STAR SIGHTS FARTHER AFIELD

★ **The Cloisters** *See pages 234 – 7*

★ **Botanical Garden** *See pages 240 – 41*

★ **Bronx Zoo** *See pages 242 – 3*

★ **MoMA Queens** *See page 245*

★ **Brooklyn Museum** *See pages 248 – 51*

EYEWITNESS *TRAVEL GUIDES*

NEW YORK

EMPIRE STATE

DK EYEWITNESS *TRAVEL GUIDES*

NEW YORK

Main contributor:
ELEANOR BERMAN

DK

DORLING KINDERSLEY
LONDON • NEW YORK • MUNICH
MELBOURNE • DELHI
www.dk.com

A DORLING KINDERSLEY BOOK

www.dk.com

PROJECT EDITOR Fay Franklin
ART EDITOR Tony Foo
EDITORS Donna Dailey, Ellen Dupont
DESIGNERS Steve Bere, Louise Parsons, Mark Stevens
EDITORIAL ASSISTANT Fiona Morgan

CONTRIBUTORS
Lester Brooks, Patricia Brooks, Susan Farewell

PHOTOGRAPHERS
Max Alexander, Dave King, Michael Moran

ILLUSTRATORS
Richard Draper, Robbie Polley, Hamish Simpson

This book was produced with the assistance of
Websters International Publishers.

Reproduced by Colourscan (Singapore)
Printed and bound by South China Printing Co. Ltd., China

First published in Great Britain in 1993
by Dorling Kindersley Limited
80 Strand, London WC2R 0RL
**Reprinted with revisions 1994, 1995 (twice),
1997, 1999, 2000, 2001, 2002**

Copyright 1993, 2002 © Dorling Kindersley Limited, London
A Penguin Company

CONTENTS

**Baseball star,
Babe Ruth
(1895–1948)**

INTRODUCING
NEW YORK

South Manhattan skyline

Vesuvio Bakery, SoHo

Trump Tower, Upper Midtown

The New York City Ballet

Tug boat at the North Wind
Undersea Institute Museum

TRAVELLERS'
NEEDS

Bagel from a New York deli

SURVIVAL GUIDE

Solomon R Guggenheim Museum, Upper East Side

HOW TO USE THIS GUIDE

THIS EYEWITNESS TRAVEL GUIDE helps you get the most from your stay in New York with the minimum of practical difficulty. The opening section, *Introducing New York*, locates the city geographically, sets modern New York in its historical context and describes the highlights of the year. *New York at a Glance* is an overview of the city's attractions. Section two, *New York Area by Area*, guides you through the city's sightseeing areas. It describes all the main sights with maps, photographs and detailed illustrations. In addition, five planned walks take you step-by-step through special areas.

Well-researched tips on where to stay, eat, shop, and on sports and entertainment are in section three, *Travelers' Needs. Children's New York* lists highlights for young visitors, and section four, *Survival Guide*, shows you how to do everything from mailing a letter to using the subway.

NEW YORK AREA BY AREA

Manhattan has been divided into 15 sightseeing areas, each described separately. Each area opens with a portrait, summing up the area's character and history and listing all the sights to be covered. Sights are numbered and clearly located on an *Area Map*. After this comes a large-scale *Street-by-Street Map* focusing on the most interesting part of the area. Finding your way around each area is made simple by the numbering system. This refers to the order in which sights are described on the pages that follow.

Sights at a Glance lists the sights in the area by category, including: Historic Streets and Buildings, Modern Architecture, Museums and Galleries, Churches, Monuments, and Parks and Squares.

The area covered in greater detail on the *Street-by-Street Map* is shaded red.

Numbered circles pinpoint all the listed sights on the area map. Trump Tower, for example, is ❷

1 The Area Map

For easy reference, the sights in each area are numbered and located on an Area Map. *To help the visitor, the map also shows subway stations, heliports and ferry embarkation points.*

Photographs of facades and distinctive details of buildings help you locate the sights.

Color-coding on each page makes the area easy to find in the book.

Travel tips help you reach the area quickly by public transportation.

2 The Street-by-Street Map

This gives a bird's-eye view of the heart of each sight-seeing area. The most important buildings are illustrated, to help you spot them easily as you walk around.

A locator map shows you where you are in relation to surrounding areas. The area of the *Street-by-Street Map* is shown in red.

Trump Tower ❷ is also shown on this map.

A suggested route for a walk takes you past some of the area's most interesting sights.

Red stars indicate the sights that no visitor should miss.

NEW YORK AT A GLANCE

Each map in this section concentrates on a specific theme: *Museums, Architecture, Multicultural New York*, and *Celebrated New Yorkers*. The top sights are shown on the map; other sights are described on the two pages following and cross-referenced to their full entries in the *Area by Area* section.

Each sightseeing area is color-coded.

The theme is explored in greater detail on the pages following the map.

3 Detailed information on each sight
All important sights in each area are described in depth here. They are listed in order, following the numbering on the opening Area Map. Practical information is also provided.

4 New York's major sights
These are given two or more full pages in the sightseeing area in which they are found. Important buildings are dissected to reveal their interiors; museums have color-coded floor plans to help you find particular exhibits.

PRACTICAL INFORMATION
Each entry provides all the information needed to plan a visit to the sight. The key to the symbols is inside the back cover.

Map reference to Street Finder at back of book

Address   **Sight Number**

Trump Tower ❷

725 5th Ave. **Map** 12 F3.

(832-2000. M *5th Ave-53rd St.* **Garden level, shops open** 10am–6pm Mon–Sat. **Building open** 8am–10pm daily. **Adm free**. See **Shopping** p311. 📷 ♿ **Concerts.** 🍴 💻 🔲

Opening hours   **Services and facilities available**

Telephone number   **Nearest subway station**

The Visitors' Checklist provides the practical information you will need to plan your visit.

The facade of each major sight is shown to help you spot it quickly.

Red stars indicate the most important exhibits or works of art on display inside, or the most interesting architectural details of the building.

A color key helps you find your way easily around the collection.

Floors are referred to in accordance with American usage, ie the "first floor" is at ground level.

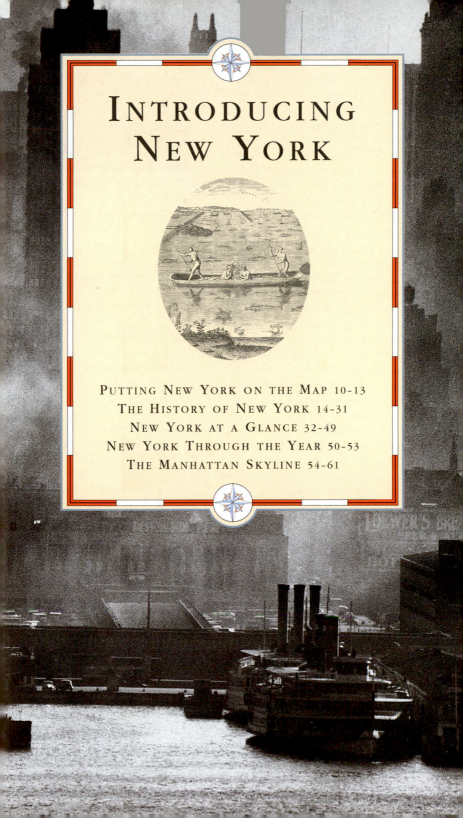

Introducing
New York

Putting New York on the Map

New York is a city of eight million people, covering 301 sq miles (780 sq km). The city gives its name to the state of New York, the capital of which is Albany, 156 miles (251 km) to the north. New York is also a good base from which to visit the historic towns of Boston and Philadelphia, as well as the nation's capital, Washington, DC.

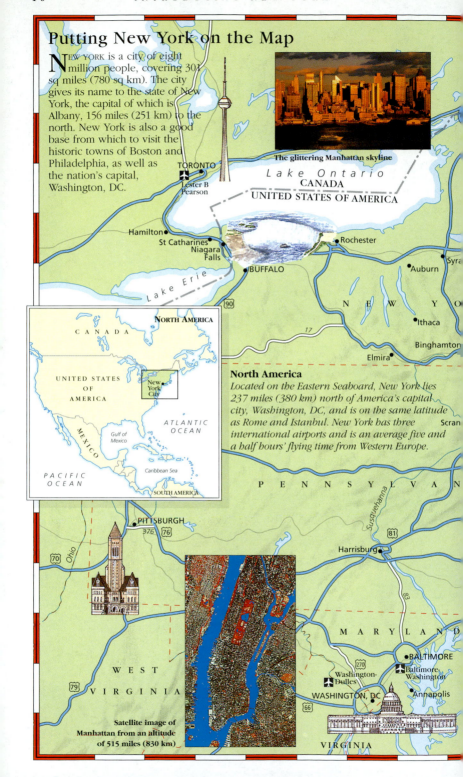

The glittering Manhattan skyline

TORONTO
Lester B Pearson

Lake Ontario

CANADA
UNITED STATES OF AMERICA

Hamilton
St Catharines
Niagara Falls
BUFFALO

Rochester
Auburn
Syra

Lake Erie

90

N   E   W   Y   O

Ithaca

Binghamton

Elmira

NORTH AMERICA

C A N A D A

UNITED STATES
OF
AMERICA

New York City

ATLANTIC
OCEAN

M E X I C O
Gulf of Mexico

PACIFIC
OCEAN

Caribbean Sea

SOUTH AMERICA

North America

Located on the Eastern Seaboard, New York lies 237 miles (380 km) north of America's capital city, Washington, DC, and is on the same latitude as Rome and Istanbul. New York has three international airports and is an average five and a half hours' flying time from Western Europe.

Scran

P E N N S Y L V A N

Susquehanna

81

PITTSBURGH
376   76

Harrisburg

70   Ohio

83

M A R Y L A N D

BALTIMORE

Baltimore-Washington

270

Washington-Dulles

WASHINGTON, DC

66

Annapolis

W E S T
79
V I R G I N I A

Satellite image of Manhattan from an altitude of 515 miles (830 km)

VIRGINIA

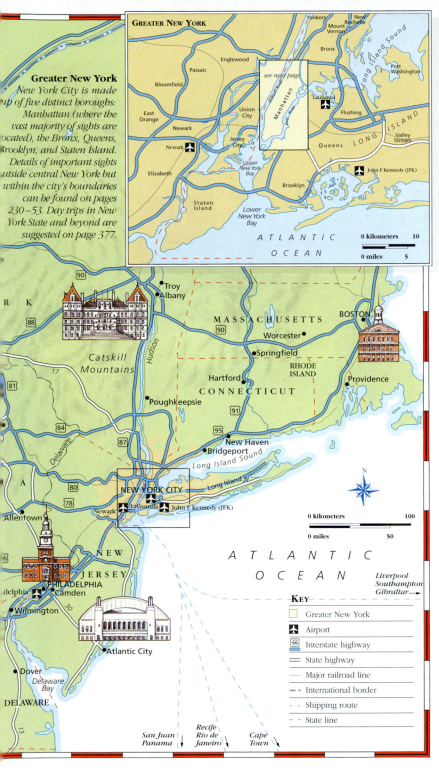

Greater New York

New York City is made up of five distinct boroughs: Manhattan (where the vast majority of sights are located), the Bronx, Queens, Brooklyn, and Staten Island. Details of important sights outside central New York but within the city's boundaries can be found on pages 230–53. Day trips in New York State and beyond are suggested on page 377.

GREATER NEW YORK

Yonkers
New Rochelle
Mount Vernon
Englewood
Bronx
Passaic
Port Washington
Bloomfield
LaGuardia
Flushing
East Orange
Union City
Newark
Jersey City
Valley Stream
Newark
Queens
LONG ISLAND
LONG ISLAND SOUND
Manhattan
Hudson River
East River
Elizabeth
Upper New York Bay
John F Kennedy (JFK)
Brooklyn
Staten Island
Lower New York Bay
see next page

ATLANTIC OCEAN

| 0 kilometers | 10 |
| 0 miles | 5 |

Troy
Albany

88
90

MASSACHUSETTS
Worcester
BOSTON

90
Springfield

Catskill Mountains
Hudson

17
81

RHODE ISLAND

Hartford
CONNECTICUT
Providence

Poughkeepsie

84
87
91

95
New Haven
Bridgeport

80
Long Island Sound
Long Island

NEW YORK CITY
78
Newark   LaGuardia   John F Kennedy (JFK)

Allentown

N

6
NEW JERSEY
PHILADELPHIA
Camden
delphia
Wilmington
30

ATLANTIC OCEAN

Liverpool
Southampton
Gibraltar →

Atlantic City

Dover
Delaware Bay
DELAWARE

13

San Juan
Panama

Recife
Rio de
Janeiro

Cape
Town

KEY

	Greater New York
✈	Airport
66	Interstate highway
═══	State highway
──	Major railroad line
─ ─	International border
····	Shipping route
- - -	State line

Manhattan

MOST OF THE SIGHTS described in this book lie within 15 areas of Manhattan. Each of these has its own section in the book. If you are short of time, you could restrict your sightseeing to one or two areas. Many of New York's oldest and newest buildings rub shoulders in Lower Manhattan. It is from here, too, that you can take the Staten Island ferry for breathtaking views of the famous skyline and the Statue of Liberty. Midtown includes the Theater District and Fifth Avenue's glittering shops as well as museums, entertainment and such landmark skyscrapers as the glorious Chrysler Building. Museum Mile on the Upper East Side is a cultural paradise and, since it runs alongside Central Park, you can rest en route and watch New Yorkers at play.

PAGES 138–47
*Street Finder maps
8, 11–12*

PAGES 128–37
*Street Finder maps
7–8*

PAGES 106–13
*Street Finder maps
3–4*

PAGES 100–105
*Street Finder map
4*

PAGES 64–79
*Street Finder maps
1–2*

PAGES 80–91
*Street Finder maps
1–2*

PAGES 92–9
*Street Finder maps
4, 5*

Chelsea and
the Garment
District

Gramercy
and the
Flatiron
District

Greenwich
Village

East
Village

SoHo
and
TriBeCa

Lower
East Side

Lower
Manhattan

Seaport
and the
Civic
Center

PAGES 208–17
*Street Finder maps
11–12, 15–16*

PAGES 218–29
*Street Finder maps
19–20*

Morningside
Heights and
Harlem

Upper
West Side

Central
Park

Upper East
Side

Theater
District

Upper
Midtown

Lower
Midtown

EAST RIVER

PAGES 180–201
*Street Finder maps
12–13, 16–17*

PAGES 202–7
*Street Finder maps
12, 16*

PAGES 164–79
*Street Finder maps
12, 13–14*

PAGES 148–63
*Street Finder maps
9, 12, 13*

PAGES 114–19
*Street Finder maps
4, 5*

PAGES 120–27
*Street Finder maps
8, 9*

0 kilometers   2

0 miles   1

THE HISTORY OF NEW YORK

FROM ITS FIRST sighting almost 500 years ago by Giovanni da Verrazano, New York's harbor was the prize that all of Europe wanted to capture. The Dutch first sent fur traders to the area in 1621, but they lost the colony they called New Amsterdam to the English in 1664. The settlement was re-christened New York and the name stayed, even after the English lost the colony in 1783, at the end of the Revolutionary War.

A shell-work cloak worn by an Indian chief

THE GROWING CITY

In the 19th century, New York grew rapidly and became a major port. Ease of shipping spawned manufacturing, commerce was king and great fortunes were made. In 1898, Manhattan was joined with the four outer boroughs to form the world's second-largest city. From 1800 to 1900, the population grew from 79,000 to 3 million people. New York City became the country's cultural and entertainment mecca as well as its business center.

THE MELTING POT

The city continued to grow as thousands of immigrants came seeking a better life. Overpopulation meant that many at first lived in slums. Today, the mix of cultures has enriched the city and become its defining quality. Its eight million inhabitants speak some 100 languages.

Manhattan's skyline took shape as the city grew skyward to make space for its ever-increasing population. Throughout its history, the city has experienced alternating periods of economic decline and growth, but in both good times and bad, it remains one of the world's most vital cities.

The following pages illustrate significant periods in New York's history.

A deed signed by New Amsterdam's last Dutch governor, Peter Stuyvesant, in 1664

The southern half of Manhattan and part of Brooklyn in 1767

Early New York

Indian husk mask

Mᴀɴʜᴀᴛᴛᴀɴ ᴡᴀs a forested land populated by Algonquian-speaking Natives when the Dutch West India Company established a fur trading post called New Amsterdam in 1625. The first settlers built houses helter-skelter, so even today the streets of Lower Manhattan still twist. Broadway, then called by the Dutch name *Breede Wegh*, began as an Indian trail known as the Week-quaesgeek Trail. Harlem has also kept its Dutch name. The town was unruly until Peter Stuyvesant arrived to bring order. But the colony did not produce the expected revenues, and in 1664 the Dutch let it fall to the English, who renamed it New York.

GROWTH OF THE METROPOLIS
☐ 1664   ☐ Today

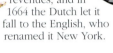

Seal of New Netherland
The beaver pelt and wampum (Indian shell beads) on the seal were the currency of the colony of New Netherland.

FIRST VIEW OF MANHATTAN (1626)
The southern tip of Manhattan resembled a Dutch town, down to the windmill. Although shown here, the fort had not yet been built.

Dutch ships

The First New Yorkers
Algonquian-speaking Natives were the first inhabitants of Manhattan.

Iroquois Pot
Iroquois Indians were frequent visitors to early Manhattan.

Indian Village
Some Algonquians lived in longhouses on Manhattan before the Dutch arrived.

Native canoe

TIMELINE

1524 Giovanni da Verrazano sails into New York harbor

1626 Peter Minuit buys Manhattan from the Natives

1653 Wall is built for protection from attack; adjacent street is called Wall Street

1625 Dutch establish first permanent trading post

| 1600 | 1620 | 1640 |

1609 Henry Hudson sails up the Hudson River in search of the Northwest Passage

1625 First black slaves brought from Africa

1643–45 Indian skirmishes end with temporary peace treaty

1647 Peter Stuyvesant becomes colonial governor

1654 First Jewish settlers arrive

Dutch Delftware
Colonists brought this popular tin-glazed earthenware pottery from Holland.

Manhattan Skyline
The Strand, now Whitehall Street, was the site of the city's first brick house.

Tiger timbers

WHERE TO SEE DUTCH NEW YORK
Dug up by workmen in 1916, these remnants of a Dutch ship, the *Tiger*, which burned in 1613, are the earliest artifacts of the period and are now in the Museum of the City of New York *(see p197)*. Rooms in this museum, as well as in the Morris-Jumel Mansion *(see p233)* and the Van Cortlandt House Museum *(see p238)*, display Dutch pottery, tiles and furniture.

Purchase of Manhattan
Peter Minuit bought the island from the Natives in 1626 for $24 worth of trinkets.

Dutch windmill

Fort Amsterdam

Peter Stuyvesant
The last Dutch governor was a tyrant who imposed strict laws – such as an edict closing all the city's taverns at 9 o'clock.

1660 First city hospital established

1664 British forces oust Dutch without a fight and change name to New York

1676 Great Dock built on East River

1698 Trinity Church dedicated

1660

1680

1700

The surrender of New Amsterdam to the British

1680s Bolting Laws give New York exclusive right to process and ship grain

1683 First New York city charter established

1689 Merchant Jacob Leisler leads revolt against taxes and takes over the city for two years

1693 Ninety-two cannons installed for protection; area becomes known as the Battery

1691 Leisler sentenced to death for treason

Colonial New York

UNDER BRITISH RULE, New York prospered and the population grew rapidly. The bolting of flour (grinding grain) was the main commercial enterprise. Shipbuilding also flourished. As the city prospered, an elite emerged that could afford a more refined way of life, and fine furniture and household silver were made for use in their homes during the Colonial period. During more than a century of governing New York, Britain proved more interested in profit than in the welfare of the colony. The Crown imposed hated taxes, and the spirit of rebellion grew, although especially in New York, loyalties were divided. On the the eve of Revolution, New York was the second-largest city in the 13 colonies, with 20,000 citizens.

Colonial gentleman

Colonial currency

GROWTH OF THE METROPOLIS
🟧 *1760*   ⬜ *Today*

Bedroom

Colonial Street
Pigs and dogs roamed free on the streets of Colonial New York.

Dining room

Kas
This Dutch-style pine wardrobe was made in New York's Hudson River valley around 1720.

Shipping
Trade with the West Indies and Britain helped New York prosper. In some years, 200 or more vessels visited the port.

TIMELINE

1702 Lord Cornbury appointed Colonial governor; he often wore women's clothes

1711 Slave market set up at the foot of Wall Street

1720 First shipyard opens

| 1700 | 1710 | 1720 | 1730 |

1710 Iroquois chief Hendrick visits England

1732 First city theater opens

1725 *New York Gazette*, city's first newspaper, is established

Captain Kidd

The English pirate William Kidd was a respected citizen, lending a block and tackle to help build Trinity Church (see p68).

VAN CORTLANDT HOUSE

Frederick Van Cortlandt built this Georgian-style house in 1748 on a wheat plantation in what is now the Bronx. Today a museum (see p238), it shows how a well-to-do Dutch-English family once lived.

West parlor

WHERE TO SEE COLONIAL NEW YORK

Colonial buildings are open to the public at Historic Richmond Town on Staten Island (*see p252*). Fine examples of Colonial silver and furniture are on display at the Museum of the City of New York (*see p197*).

Richmond Town General Store

Colonial Kitchen

Plain white cheese, called "white meat," was often served in place of meat. Waffles, introduced by the Dutch, were popular. Fresh fruit was rare, but preserved fruits were eaten.

Pewter baby bottle   Cheese mold   Waffle iron

Decorative Carvings

A face carved in stone peers over each of the front windows.

Sucket fork, for eating preserved fruits

1734 John Peter Zenger's libel trial upholds freedom of the press

1741 Slave uprising creates hysteria; 31 slaves are executed, 150 imprisoned

1754 French and Indian War begins; King's College (now Columbia University) founded

British soldier

1759 First jail built

1740   **1750**   **1760**

King's College

1733 Bowling Green becomes first city park; first ferries to Brooklyn

1762 First paid police force

1763 War ends; British gain control of North America

Revolutionary New York

George Washington, Revolutionary general

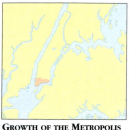

GROWTH OF THE METROPOLIS

▢ *1776*   ▢ *Today*

DUG UP INTO TRENCHES for defense, heavily shelled by British troops and scarred by recurring fires, New York suffered during the American Revolution. But despite the hardships, many continued to enjoy cricket games, horse races, balls and boxing matches. After the British took the city in 1776, it became their headquarters. The Continental army did not return to Manhattan until November 25, 1783, two years after the fighting ended.

American soldier

Battle Dress
The Continental (Patriot) army wore blue uniforms, while the British wore red.

British soldier

Soldier's Haversack
American soldiers in the War of Independence carried their supplies in haversacks.

TOPPLING THE KING
New Yorkers tore down the statue of King George III in Bowling Green and melted it down to make ammunition.

Battle of Harlem Heights
Washington won this battle on September 16 , 1776. But he did not have enough troops to hold New York so retreated, leaving it to the British.

Patriot

Death of a Patriot
While working behind British lines in 1776, Nathan Hale was captured and hanged by the British without trial for spying.

TIMELINE

1765 British pass Stamp Act; New Yorkers protest; Sons of Liberty formed

1767 New duties imposed with Townshend Act; after protests, the act is repealed

1770 Sons of Liberty fight British in the "Battle of Golden Hill"

1774 Rebels dump tea in New York harbor to protest taxes

1760

1770

1780

St. Paul's Chapel

1766 St. Paul's Chapel completed; Stamp Act repealed; Statue of George III erected on Bowling Green

General William Howe, commander in chief of the British troops

1776 War begins; 500 ships under General Howe assemble in New York harbor

Fire Fighters

Fires had long threatened the city, but during the war a series of fires nearly destroyed it. In the wake of the patriot retreat, on September 21, 1776, a devastating fire razed Trinity Church and 1,000 houses.

Leather fire bucket

Statue of George III

Flags of the Revolution

Washington's army flew the Continental colors, with a stripe for each of the 13 colonies and a Union Jack in the corner. The Stars and Stripes became the official flag in 1777.

First Stars and Stripes

Continental colors

General Washington Returns

Washington received a hero's welcome when he reentered New York on November 25, 1783, after the British withdrawal.

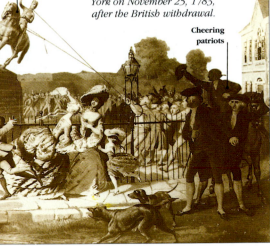

Cheering patriots

WHERE TO SEE THE REVOLUTIONARY CITY

In 1776, George Washington used the Morris-Jumel Mansion in upper Manhattan as a headquarters (see p233). He also slept at the Van Cortlandt House (see p19 and p238). After the war he bade farewell to his officers at Fraunces Tavern (see p76).

Morris-Jumel mansion

1783 Treaty of Paris signed, US wins independence; British evacuate New York

1789 George Washington inaugurated as first president at Federal Hall

1790 US capital is moved to Philadelphia

1801 *New York Post* founded by Alexander Hamilton

1794 Bellevue Hospital opens on the East River

1790

1800

1785 New York named US capital

1784 Bank of New York chartered

1792 Tontine Coffee House built – first home of the Stock Exchange

1791 New York Hospital, city's oldest, opens

Washington's inauguration

1804 Vice President Aaron Burr kills political rival Alexander Hamilton in a duel

New York in the 19th Century

Governor De Witt Clinton

Fırmly established as the nation's largest city and preeminent seaport, New York grew increasingly wealthy. Manufacturing increased due to the ease of shipping; tycoons like John Jacob Astor made millions. The rich moved uptown; public transportation followed. With rapid growth came fires, epidemics and financial panics. Immigrants from Ireland, Germany, and other nations arrived. Some found prosperity; others crowded into slums in Lower Manhattan.

GROWTH OF THE METROPOLIS
- 1840
- Today

Sheet Music
The Stephen Foster ballad Jeanie With the Light Brown Hair *was popular at this time.*

Keeping Fit
Gymnasiums such as Dr. Rich's Institute for Physical Education were established in New York in the 1830s and 1840s.

Croton Distributing Reservoir was built in 1842. Until then, New Yorkers had no fresh drinking water – they relied on deliveries of bottled water.

Omnibus
The horse-drawn omnibus was introduced for public transportation in 1832 and remained on New York streets until World War I.

TIMELINE

1805 First free state schools established in New York

1811 Randel Plan divides Manhattan into grid pattern above 14th Street

1812–14 War of 1812; British blockade New York harbor

The Constitution, most famous ship in War of 1812

1835 Much of old New York razed in city's worst fire

1810

1820

1830

1807 Robert Fulton launches first steamboat, on the Hudson River

1822 Yellow fever epidemic; people evacuate to Greenwich Village

1823 New York surpasses Boston and Philadelphia to become nation's largest city

1827 New York abolishes slavery

1837 New Yorker Samuel Morse sends first telegraph message

The Brownstone
Many brownstone row houses were built in the first half of the century. The raised stoop allowed separate entry to the parlor and ground-floor servants' quarters.

Crystal Palace was an iron and glass exhibition hall erected for the 1853 World's Fair.

THE PORT OF NEW YORK
New York's importance as a port city grew by leaps and bounds in the early 19th century. Robert Fulton launched his first steamboat, the *Clermont*, in 1807. Steamboats made travel much quicker – it now took 72 hours to reach Albany, which was both the state capital and the gateway to the West. Trade with the West by steamboat and canal boat, and with the rest of the world by clipper ship, made the fortunes of many New Yorkers.

The steamboat *Clermont*

NEW YORK IN 1855
Looking south from 42nd Street, Crystal Palace and the Croton Distributing Reservoir stood where the main public library and Bryant Park are today.

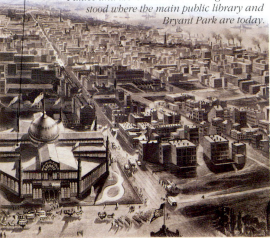

Crystal Palace in Flames
On October 5, 1858, New York's Crystal Palace exhibition hall burned to the ground, just as its predecessor in London did.

Grand Canal Celebration
Ships in New York harbor lined up to celebrate the 1825 Erie Canal opening. In connecting the Great Lakes with Albany, the state capital, on the Hudson River, the canal opened a water link between the Midwest and the Port of New York. New York realized huge profits.

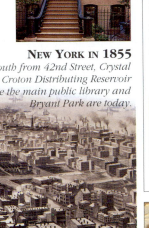

1849 Astor Place riots; ships set sail for California Gold Rush

1851 *New York Times* first published

1853 New York hosts first World's Fair

1861 Civil War begins

1857 Financial panic and depression

1863 Draft riots last four days, many die

1865 Abraham Lincoln lies in state in City Hall

1840

1850

1860

Early baseball player

1845 New York Knickerbockers, first organized baseball team chartered

Clipper ship card

1858 Vaux and Olmsted design Central Park; Macy's founded

Crowds in Central Park

1842 Croton Reservoir built

FOR SAN FRANCISCO

FREE TRADE

The Age of Extravagance

**Industrialist
Andrew Carnegie**

As New York's merchant princes grew ever wealthier, the city entered into a gilded era during which many of its most opulent buildings went up. Millions were lavished on the arts with the founding of the Metropolitan Museum, Public Library and Carnegie Hall. Luxury hotels like the Plaza and the original Waldorf-Astoria were built, and elegant department stores arose to serve the wealthy. Such flamboyant figures as William "Boss" Tweed, political strongman and king of corruption, and circus man Phineas T. Barnum were also larger than life.

GROWTH OF THE METROPOLIS

▬ *1890*   ▢ *Today*

Overlooking the Park
*The Dakota (1880) was
the first grand luxury
apartment house on
the Upper West Side
(see p216).*

Palatial Living
*Mansions lined
Fifth Avenue.
When it was built
in 1882, W.K.
Vanderbilt's
Italianate palace
at 660 Fifth
Avenue, was one
of the farthest
north.*

Fashion City
*Lord & Taylor
built a new store
on Broadway's
Ladies' Mile; 6th
Avenue between
14th and 23rd
streets was
known as
Fashion Row.*

BATHING SUITS.

A GREAT SPECIALTY AT
LORD & TAYLOR'S, Broadway and 20th Street, N.Y.
CHEAPEST AND BEST QUALITY OF BATHING SUITS IN THE CITY.

THE ELEVATED RAILROAD
*By the mid 1870s, elevated railroads
or "Els" ran along 2nd, 3rd, 6th and
9th avenues. They made travel faster,
but left noise, grime and
pollution in their wake.*

TIMELINE

1870 J.D. Rockefeller founds Standard Oil

1867 Brooklyn's Prospect Park completed

1868 First elevated railroad built on Greenwich Street

1871 The first Grand Central Depot opens on 42nd St.; "Boss" Tweed is arrested and imprisoned

1877 A.G. Bell demonstrates the telephone in New York

1865   **1870**   **1875**

1869 First apartment house built on 18th Street; Black Friday financial crisis hits Wall Street

*The interior of
the Stock Exchange*

1873 Banks fail: Stock Exchange panics

1872 Bloomingdale's opens

1879 St. Patrick's Cathedral completed; first city telephone exchange opened on Nassau Street

Mark Twain's Birthday
Mark Twain, whose 1873 novel The Gilded Age *portrayed the decadent lifestyle of New Yorkers, celebrated his birthday at Delmonico's.*

WHERE TO SEE THE AGE OF EXTRAVAGANCE

The Gold Room in the Henry Villard Houses *(see p174)* is a good place to experience the city's past. Formerly the Music Room, it is now a venue for afternoon tea. The Museum of the City of New York also has two period rooms *(p197)*.

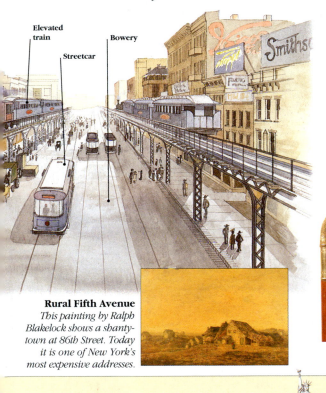

Elevated train
Streetcar
Bowery

Rural Fifth Avenue
This painting by Ralph Blakelock shows a shanty-town at 86th Street. Today it is one of New York's most expensive addresses.

The Tweed Ring
William "Boss" Tweed led Tammany Hall, which dominated city government. He stole millions in city funds.

Nast's cartoon of "Boss" Tweed

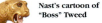

Tammany Tiger
The Museum of the City of New York has "Boss" Tweed's cane, which sports a gold Tammany Tiger mascot on its handle.

1880 Canned fruits and meats first appear in stores; Metropolitan Museum of Art opens; streets lit by electricity

1883 Metropolitan Opera opens on Broadway; Brooklyn Bridge completed

1886 Statue of Liberty unveiled

1891 Carnegie Hall opens

1880

1885

1890

1888 Great Blizzard dumps 22 in (56 cm) of snow

1890 First moving picture shows appear in New York

Grand display of fireworks over Brooklyn Bridge, 1883

1892 Cathedral of St. John the Divine begun; Ellis Island opens

New York at the Turn of the Century

Horse-drawn carriage

By 1900, NEW YORK was a hub of American industry: 70% of the country's corporations were based there, and the port handled two-thirds of all imported goods. The rich got richer, but in the crowded slums, disease spread. Even so, immigrants kept their rich traditions alive, and political and social reform emerged. In 1900, the International Ladies' Garment Workers' Union was founded to battle for the rights of the women and children who toiled in dangerous factories for low wages. The Triangle Shirtwaist Factory fire in 1911 also sped reform.

GROWTH OF THE METROPOLIS

□ 1914   □ Today

Gateway to America
Almost five times as crowded as the rest of New York, the Lower East Side was the most densely populated place in the world.

Crowded Conditions
Tenements were unhealthy and overcrowded. They often lacked windows, air shafts or proper sanitary facilities.

WHERE TO SEE TURN-OF-THE-CENTURY NEW YORK
The Lower East Side Tenement Museum (see p97) has exhibits on tenement life.

Tailor's scissors

Hip bath

Inside a Sweatshop
Workers toiled long hours for low wages in the overcrowded sweatshops of the garment district. This view of Moe Levy's shop was taken in 1912.

Streetcars on Broadway

TIMELINE

1895 Olympia Theater is first to open in the Broadway area

1898 Five boroughs merge to form world's second-largest city

1901 Macy's opens Broadway department store

1895

1900

1896 First bagel served in a Clinton Street bakery

1900 Mayor Robert Van Wyck breaks ground for city's first subway with silver shovel

1903 Lyceum Theater opens – oldest Broadway house still in use

1897 Waldorf-Astoria Hotel opens: the largest hotel in the world

FLATIRON BUILDING

Overlooking Madison Square where Broadway, Fifth Avenue and 23rd Street meet, the 21-story tower was one of the city's first skyscrapers (1902). Triangle-shaped, it was dubbed the Flatiron Building (see p125).

Underlying steel structure

Elaborate limestone facade

Only 6 ft (185 cm) wide at apex of triangle

Supper in the Saddle
Decadent parties were all the rage. C.K.G. Billings's horseback dinner at Sherry's restaurant in 1903 was the talk of all New York.

Plaza Promenade
The section of Fifth Avenue in front of the Plaza Hotel was considered the most elegant in the city.

Ventilated hairpiece

High Fashion
In 1900 styles were stiff, with wire hoops and bustles worn beneath ornate dresses. Later, clothes became softer and more practical.

Long bustle

Wire hoops

1906 Architect Stanford White shot at Madison Square Garden, which he had built in 1890

1909 Wilbur Wright flies first plane over New York

1910 Pennsylvania Station opens

1913 Woolworth Building is world's tallest; new Grand Central Terminal opens; Harlem's Apollo Theater opens

1905

1910

1905 First crossing of the Staten Island Ferry

1907 First metered taxicabs; first Ziegfeld Follies

1911 Triangle Shirtwaist Factory fire kills 146 sweatshop workers; New York Public Library completed

Woolworth Building

New York Between the Wars

Entrance card to the Cotton Club

T HE 1920s WERE a time of high living for many New Yorkers. Mayor Jimmy Walker set the pace, whether squiring chorus girls, drinking in speakeasies or watching the Yankees. But the good times ended with the 1929 stock market crash. By 1932, Walker had resigned, charged with corruption, and one-quarter of New Yorkers were unemployed. With Mayor Fiorello La Guardia's 1933 election, New York began to recover and thrive.

GROWTH OF THE METROPOLIS
■ *1933*   □ *Today*

Exotic Costumes
Chorus girls were a major Cotton Club attraction.

THE COTTON CLUB
This Harlem nightclub was host to the best jazz in town, as first Duke Ellington and then Cab Calloway led the band. People flocked from all over the city to hear them.

Defying Prohibition
Although alcohol was outlawed, speakeasies – semi-secret illegal drinking dens – still sold it.

Home-Run Hitter
In 1927, baseball star Babe Ruth hit a record 60 home runs for the Yankees. Yankee Stadium (see p239) became known as "the house that Ruth built."

Sawed-off shotgun concealed in violin case

Gangsters
Dutch Schultz was the kingpin of an illegal booze racket.

TIMELINE

1918 End of World War I

1919 18th Amendment bans alcohol, launches Prohibition Era

1920 US women get the vote

Opening of the Holland Tunnel

1926 Jimmy Walker becomes mayor

1931 Empire State Building becomes world's tallest

1920	1925	1930

1924 Novelist James Baldwin is born in Harlem

1925 *The New Yorker* magazine is launched

1927 Lindbergh flies across the Atlantic; first talking movie, *The Jazz Singer*, opens; Holland Tunnel opens

1929 Stock market crash; Great Depression begins

1930 Chrysler Building completed

Big Band Leaders
Banned from many downtown clubs, black artists like Cab Calloway starred at the Cotton Club.

Broadway Melodies
The 1920s were the heyday of the Broadway musical, with a record number of plays opening.

THE GREAT DEPRESSION
The Roaring Twenties ended with the stock market crash of October 29, 1929, which set off the Depression. New York was hard hit: squatters' shacks sprang up in Central Park and thousands were out of work. But art flourished as artists went to work for the Works Projects Administration (WPA), creating outstanding murals and artworks throughout the city.

Waiting to receive benefits in 1931

Breakfast menu

Lindbergh's plane,
Spirit of St. Louis

Lindbergh's Flight
New Yorkers celebrated Lindbergh's nonstop solo flight across the Atlantic in 1927 in a variety of ways, including a breakfast in his honor.

Rockefeller Center
Millionaire John D. Rockefeller drives the final rivet to celebrate the opening of Rockefeller Center on May 1, 1939.

Mass Event
Forty-five million people visited the 1939 World's Fair in New York.

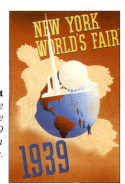

1933 Prohibition ends; Fiorello LaGuardia begins three terms as mayor

1940 Queens-Midtown Tunnel opens

1942 Times Square blacked out during World War II; Idlewild International Airport (now JFK) opens

1935

1940

1945

1936 Parks Department headed by Robert Moses; new parks created

1939 Rockefeller Center is completed

1941 US enters World War II

1944 Black leader Adam Clayton Powell elected to Congress

Postwar New York

Since World War II, New York has seen both the best of times and the worst. Although established as the financial capital of the world, the city itself almost went bankrupt in the 1970s. Wall Street hit its peak in the 1980s, then experienced its worst crash since 1929. Since the early 1990s, New York has seen a dramatic drop in the crime rate and an increase in the restoration and renewal of such landmarks as Grand Central Terminal and the "new" Times Square. This constant rebuilding is emblematic of the city's position at the cultural and financial hub of the United States.

BILTMORE THEATER

1967 Hippie musical *Hair* opens on Off-Broadway, then transfers to the Biltmore Theater

1953 Merce Cunningham founds dance company

1963 Pennsylvania Station razed

1971 Pop artist Andy Warhol has a retrospective show of his work at the Whitney Museum

1959 Guggenheim Museum opens

1966 Newspaper and transit strikes

1970 John Lindsay starts second term as mayor

1945 End of World War II

1946 UN headquarters established in New York

1954 Ellis Island closes

1945	1950	1955	1960	1965	1970
MAYORS:	IMPELLITERI	WAGNER	LINDSAY	LINDSAY	LINDSAY
1945	1950	1955	1960	1965	1970

One of the most popular bands of the "swinging '60s" – The Beatles

1964 New York World's Fair; race riots in Harlem and Bedford-Stuyvesant; Verrazano Narrows Bridge links Brooklyn and Staten Island; Beatles play at Shea Stadium

1947 Jackie Robinson, first black baseball player in the major leagues, signs with Brooklyn Dodgers

Souvenir scarf

1968 20,000 anti-establishment hippies gather in Central Park; student sit-ins at Columbia University

Andy Warhol with actresses
Candy Darling and Ultra Violet

Donald Trump

1983 Economic boom: property prices
skyrocket; Trump Tower completed by real
estate tycoon Donald Trump, who symbolizes
the "yuppie" wealth of the 1980s

2001
World Trade
Center destroyed
in a terrorist
attack. The
Pentagon, in
Washington, also
suffers major
damage. President George
W Bush declares
war on terrorism

1975 Federal
loan saves New
York from
bankruptcy

1981 New York
regains solvency

1988 Twenty-
five percent of
New Yorkers live
below the
poverty line

1990 David Dinkins,
New York's first black
mayor, takes office; Ellis
Island reopens as an
immigration museum

1977 New York
power blackout
lasts 25 hours

1987 Stock
market crash

1993 Rudolph Giuliani
takes office as mayor

1975	1980	1985	1990	1995	2000
BEAME	KOCH	KOCH	DINKINS	GIULIANI	GIULIANI
1975	1980	1985	1990	1995	2000

1973 World
Trade Center
completed

1986 Shock of corruption scandals
rock Mayor Koch's administration;
Centennial
of Statue
of Liberty

2000
Population
reaches just
over 8
million

1995 The
neglected
Chelsea Piers
are renovated
and open as a
mammoth
sports and
entertainment
complex
(see p136)

NEW YORK AT A GLANCE

THERE ARE ALMOST 300 places of interest described in the *Area by Area* section of this book. They range from the bustling New York Stock Exchange *(see pp70–71)* to Central Park's peaceful Strawberry Fields *(see p206)* and from synagogues to skyscrapers. The following 16 pages are a time-saving guide to New York's most interesting sights. Museums and architecture each have a section, and there are guides to the people and cultures that have given the city its unique character. Each sight is cross-referenced to its own full entry. Below are the top ten tourist attractions to start you off.

NEW YORK'S TOP TEN TOURIST ATTRACTIONS

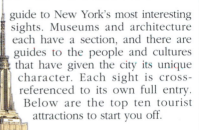

Ellis Island
See pp78–9.

Empire State Building
See pp134–5.

South Street Seaport
See p84.

Rockefeller Center
See p142.

Museum of Modern Art
See pp170–73.

Central Park
See pp202–7.

Metropolitan Museum of Art
See pp188–95.

Statue of Liberty
See pp74–5.

Brooklyn Bridge
See pp86–9.

Chinatown
See p96.

Park Avenue's relentless flow of traffic

New York's Best: Museums

New York's museums range from the vast scope of the Metropolitan Museum to the personal treasures of financier J. Pierpont Morgan's own collection. Several museums celebrate New York's heritage, giving visitors an insight into the people and events that made the city what it is today. This map features some highlights, with a detailed overview on pages 36 and 37.

Museum of Modern Art
The world's most comprehensive collection of modern art includes such gems as Picasso's Goat (1950).

Intrepid Sea-Air-Space Museum
Situated on a large aircraft carrier on the Hudson River, this naval museum also traces the progress of flight and undersea exploration.

Pierpont Morgan Library
One of the world's finest collections of manuscripts, prints and books includes this rare French Bible from 1230.

Merchant's House Museum
This perfectly preserved 1820s house belonged to a wealthy trader.

Ellis Island
This museum vividly re-creates the experiences of many millions of immigrant families.

Theater District

Upper West Side

Chelsea and the Garment District

Lower Midtown

Greenwich Village

Gramercy and the Flatiron District

SoHo and TriBeCa

East Village

Lower East Side

Lower Manhattan

Seaport and the Civic Center

Ellis Island

HUDSON RIVER

EAST RIVER

0 kilometers   2

0 miles   1

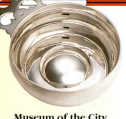

American Museum of Natural History
Dinosaurs, meteorites, and much more have fascinated generations of visitors here.

Morningside Heights and Harlem

Central Park

Upper East Side

Upper town

Museum of the City of New York
Costumes, works of art and household objects (such as this 1725 silver dish) create an intricate and detailed picture of New York's past.

Cooper-Hewitt Museum
A wealth of decorative arts is displayed in industrialist Andrew Carnegie's former Upper East Side mansion.

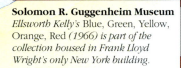

Solomon R. Guggenheim Museum
Ellsworth Kelly's Blue, Green, Yellow, Orange, Red *(1966) is part of the collection housed in Frank Lloyd Wright's only New York building.*

Metropolitan Museum of Art
Of the millions of works in its collection, this 12th-dynasty Egyptian faïence hippo is the museum's own mascot.

Frick Collection
The collection of 19th-century railroad magnate Henry Clay Frick is displayed in his former home. Masterpieces include St. Francis in the Desert *(about 1480) by Giovanni Bellini.*

Whitney Museum of American Art
This exceptional collection includes many views of New York. One of the best is Brooklyn Bridge: Variation on an Old Theme *(1939), by Joseph Stella.*

Exploring New York's Museums

Richmond Town tobacco tin

YOU COULD DEVOTE an entire month to visiting New York's museums and still not do them justice. There are more than 60 museums in Manhattan alone, half that number again in the other boroughs. The wealth of art and the huge variety of offerings – from old masters to old fire engines, dinosaurs to dolls, Tibetan tapestries to African masks – is equal to that of any city in the world. Note that some museums may be closed on Monday as well as on another day. Many stay open late one or two evenings a week, and some have one evening when admission is free. Not every museum charges for admission, but donations are always welcome.

PAINTING AND SCULPTURE

NEW YORK is best known for its art museums. The **Metropolitan Museum of Art** houses an extensive collection of American art as well as world-famous masterpieces. **The Cloisters**, a branch of the "Met" in Upper Manhattan, is a treasury of medieval art and architecture. The **Frick Collection** has a superb display of Old Masters. In contrast, the **Museum of Modern Art (MoMA)** has some of the world's most famous Impressionist and modern paintings. **The Whitney Museum of American Art** and the **Solomon R. Guggenheim Museum** also specialize in modern art, the Whitney's biennial show being the foremost display of contemporary work by living artists. The cutting edge of today's art is to be seen at the **New Museum of Contemporary Art**, and the work of untrained artists can be seen at the **American Folk Art Museum**. The **National Academy of Design** displays a collection of 19th- and 20th-century art, donated by its members. In Harlem, the **Studio Museum** shows the work of black artists.

CRAFTS AND DESIGN

IF YOU ARE interested in textiles, porcelain and glass, embroideries and laces, wallpaper and prints, visit the **Cooper-Hewitt Museum**, the decorative arts outpost of Washington's Smithsonian Institution. The design collections at **MoMA** are as well known as the paintings, tracing the history of design from clocks to couches. The **American Craft Museum** offers the finest work of today's skilled artisans in mediums from furniture to art glass, and the **American Folk Art Museum** presents folk forms, from quilts to canes. Silver collections are notable at the **Museum of the City of New York**. The fine displays of native art at the **National Museum of the American Indian** include jewelry, rugs and pottery.

PRINTS AND PHOTOGRAPHY

THE excellent **International Center of Photography** is the only museum in New York totally devoted to this medium. Collections can also be seen at the **Metropolitan Museum of Art** and **MoMA**, with many examples of early photography at the **Museum of the City of New York** and **Ellis Island**.

Prints and drawings by such great book illustrators as Kate Greenaway and John Tenniel are featured at the **Pierpont Morgan Library**. The **Cooper-Hewitt Museum** has examples of the use of prints in the decorative arts.

FURNITURE AND COSTUMES

THE ANNUAL exhibition of the Costume Institute at the **Metropolitan Museum of Art** is always worth a visit. Also impressive is the American Wing, with its 24 rooms of original furnishings tracing life from 1640 to the 20th century. Period rooms depicting New York in various settings, beginning with the 17th century Dutch, are on display at the **Museum of the City of New York**. There are also some house museums that give a realistic picture of furnishings and life in old New York. The **Merchant's House Museum**, a preserved residence from the 1820s, was occupied by the same family for 98 years. **Gracie Mansion**, the residence of the mayor, was the 1799 country house of a wealthy shipping merchant and is open periodically for public tours. The **Theodore Roosevelt Birthplace** is the brownstone where the 26th president of the United States grew up, and the **Mount Vernon Hotel Museum** was an early 19th-century resort.

Corn husk doll, American Museum of Natural History

The Peaceable Kingdom (c.1840–1845) by Edward Hicks, at the Brooklyn Museum

HISTORY

Palm pistol at the Police
Academy Museum

AMERICAN HISTORY unfolds at **Federal Hall**, the first US capital: George Washington took his oath as America's first president on the balcony in April 1789. Visit the **Fraunces Tavern Museum** for a glimpse of colonial New York. **Ellis Island** and **Lower East Side Tenement Museum** re-create the hardships faced by immigrants. The new **Museum of Jewish Heritage** in Battery City is a living memorial to the Holocaust. The **NYC Fire Museum** and the new **Police Museum** chronicle heroism and tragedy, while the **South Street Seaport Museum** re-creates early maritime history.

TECHNOLOGY AND NATURAL HISTORY

Forest-dwelling bonga, American Museum of Natural History

SCIENCE MUSEUMS hold exhibitions from nature to space-age technology. The **American Museum of Natural History** has vast collections covering flora, fauna and cultures from around the world. Its Rose Center/Hayden Planetarium offers a unique view of space. The *Intrepid* Sea-Air-Space **Museum** is a repository of technology that chronicles military progress. It is based on the decks of an aircraft carrier.

If you missed a classic Lucille Ball sitcom or footage of the first man on the moon, the place to visit is the **Museum of Television and Radio**, which holds these and many other classics of TV and radio.

ART FROM OTHER CULTURES

Egyptian mummy, Brooklyn Museum

ARTWORK of other nations is the focus of several special collections. Oriental art is the specialty of the **Asia Society** and the **Japan Society**. The **Jewish Museum** features major collections of Judaica and has changing exhibitions of Jewish life. **El Museo del Barrio** is dedicated to the arts of Puerto Rico, including many pre-Columbian artifacts. For an impressive review of African-American art and history, visit the **Schomburg Center for Research in Black Culture**. Finally, the **Metropolitan Museum of Art** excels in its multicultural displays of art, ranging from ancient Egypt to contemporary Africa.

LIBRARIES

NEW YORK'S notable libraries, such as the **Pierpont Morgan Library**, offer some superb art collections as well as a chance to view pages from rare books. The **New York Public Library** shows a collection that includes manuscripts of many famous works.

BEYOND MANHATTAN

OTHER MUSEUMS worth a visit include the **Brooklyn Museum,** with its one and a half million paintings. The

American Museum of the Moving Image in Queens has a unique collection of motion-picture history. The **Jacques Marchais Museum of Tibetan Art** is a rare find on Staten Island as is **Historic Richmond Town**, a well-restored village dating from the 1600s.

New York's Best: Architecture

EVEN WHEN FOLLOWING world trends, New York has given its own twist to the turns of architectural fashion, the style of its buildings influenced by both geography and economy. An island city, with space at a premium, must look upward to grow. This trend was reflected early on with tall, narrow town houses and later with the city's apartment buildings and skyscrapers. Building materials such as cast-iron and brownstone were chosen for their local availability and practical appeal. The result is a city that has developed by finding flamboyant answers to practical needs. A more detailed overview of New York's architecture is on pages 40 to 41.

Apartment Buildings
The Majestic is one of five Art Deco twin-towered apartment buildings on Central Park West.

Cast-Iron Architecture
Mass-produced cast-iron was often used for building facades. SoHo has many of the best examples, such as this building at 28–30 Greene Street.

Post-Modernism
The quirky, yet elegant, shapes of buildings like the World Financial Center, built in 1985 (see p69), mark a bold departure from the sleek steel-and-glass boxes of the 1950s and 1960s.

Map labels:
HUDSON RIVER
Theater District
Chelsea and the Garment District
Greenwich Village
Gramercy and the Flatiron District
SoHo and TriBeCa
East Village
Lower East Side
Lower Manhattan

Brownstones
Built from local sand-stone, brownstones were favored by the 19th-century middle classes. India House, built in a Florentine palazzo style on Wall Street, is typical of many brownstone commercial buildings.

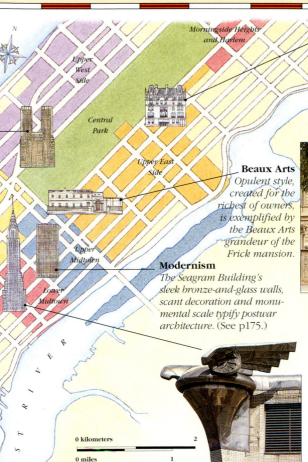

Morningside Heights and Harlem

Upper West Side

Central Park

Upper East Side

Upper Midtown

Lower Midtown

19th-Century Mansions
The Jewish Museum (see p184), formerly the home of Felix M. Warburg, is a fine example of the French Renaissance style that typified these mansions.

Beaux Arts
Opulent style, created for the richest of owners, is exemplified by the Beaux Arts grandeur of the Frick mansion.

Modernism
The Seagram Building's sleek bronze-and-glass walls, scant decoration and monumental scale typify postwar architecture. (See p175.)

0 kilometers   2
0 miles   1

The Skyscraper
The glory of New York architecture, these buildings expressed a perfect blend of practical engineering skill together with fabulous decoration, such as this gargoyle on the Chrysler Building.

EAST RIVER

Federal Architecture
Federal style was popular in civic architecture of the 19th century; City Hall combines it with French Renaissance influences.

Tenements
Constructed as an economic form of housing, for many these buildings were a stark introduction to new lives. Mainly built on the Lower East Side, the apartments were hopelessly overcrowded. In addition, the buildings' design, with inadequate air shafts, resulted in apartments with little or no ventilation.

Exploring New York's Architecture

IN ITS FIRST 200 YEARS, New York, like all of America, looked to Europe for architectural inspiration. None of the buildings from the Dutch colonial period survive in Manhattan today; most were lost in the great fire of 1776 or torn down to make way for new developments in the early 1800s. Throughout the 18th and 19th centuries, the city's major architectural trends followed those of Europe. With the advent of cast-iron architecture in the 1850s, the Art Deco period and the ever-higher rise of the skyscraper, New York's architecture came into its own.

A Federal-style front door

FEDERAL ARCHITECTURE

THIS AMERICAN adaptation of the Neoclassical Adam style flowered in the early decades of the new nation, featuring square buildings two or three stories tall, with low hipped roofs, balustrades and decorative elements – all carefully balanced. **City Hall** (1811, John McComb, Jr. and Joseph François Mangin) is a blend of Federal and French Renaissance influences. The restored warehouses of **Schermerhorn Row** (c1812) in the Seaport district are also in Federal style.

BROWNSTONES

PLENTIFUL AND CHEAP, the brown sandstone found in the nearby Connecticut River Valley and along the banks of the Hackensack River in New

A typical brownstone with stoop leading up to the main entrance

Jersey was the most common building material in the 1800s. It is found all over the city's residential neighborhoods, used for small homes or small

apartments – some of the best examples of brownstone can be found in **Chelsea**. Because street space was limited, these buildings were very narrow in width, but also very deep. A typical brownstone has a flight of steps, called a stoop, leading up to the living floors. Separate stairs lead down to the basement, which was originally the servants' quarters.

TENEMENTS

TENEMENTS WERE built to house the huge influx of immigrants who arrived from the 1840s up to World War I. The six-story blocks, 100 ft (30 m) long and 25 ft (8 m) wide, offered very little light and air except from tiny side-wall air shafts and windows at each end, leaving the middle rooms in darkness. The tiny apartments were called railroad flats after their similarity to railroad cars. Later designs had air shafts between buildings, but these helped the spread of fire. The **Lower East Side Tenement Museum** has scale models of the old tenements.

CAST-IRON ARCHITECTURE

AN AMERICAN architectural innovation of the 19th century, cast iron was cheaper than stone or brick and allowed ornate features to be prefabricated in foundries from molds and used as building facades. Today, New York has the world's largest concentration of full and partial cast-iron facades. The best, built in the 1870s, are in the **SoHo Cast-Iron Historic District**.

The original cast-iron facade of 72–76 Greene Street, SoHo

BEAUX ARTS

THIS FRENCH school of architecture dominated public buildings and wealthy residential properties during New York's gilded age. This era (from 1880 to about 1920) produced many of the city's most prominent architects, including Richard Morris Hunt (**Carnegie Hall**, 1891; **Metropolitan Museum**, 1895), who in 1845 was the first American architect to study in Paris; Cass Gilbert (**Custom House**, 1907; **New York Life Insurance**

ARCHITECTURAL DISGUISES

Some of the most fanciful forms on the New York skyline were devised by clever architects to disguise the city's essential but utilitarian – and rather unattractive – rooftop water tanks. Look skyward to discover the ornate cupolas, spires and domes that transform the most mundane of features into veritable castles in the air. Examples that are easy to spot are atop two neighboring Fifth Avenue hotels: the Sherry Netherland at 60th Street and the Pierre at 61st Street.

Standard water tower

The Dakota Apartments, built in 1884, on the Upper West Side across from Central Park

buildings resembled castles and châteaux, and were built around courtyards not visible from the street. Favorite landmarks are the **five Twin Towers** on Central Park West, the San Remo, Eldorado, Century, the Beresford, and the Majestic. Built during the peak of Art Deco (1929 to 1931), they create the distinctive skyline seen from the park.

Empire State Building (1931) was completed. Both are Art Deco classics, but it was Raymond Hood's **Group Health Insurance Building**, formerly the McGraw-Hill Building, that represented New York in 1932 in the *International Style* architectural survey.

The World Trade Center *(see p72)* was New York's tallest building until September 2001 *(see p54)*. It represented the "glass box" Modernist style, now superseded by the Post-Modern style, such as the **Citigroup Center** (1977).

Building, 1928; the **US Courthouse**, 1936; the teams of Warren & Wetmore (**Grand Central Terminal**, 1913; **Helmsley Building**, 1929); Carrère & Hastings (**New York Public Library**, 1911; **Frick mansion**, 1914); and McKim, Mead & White, the city's most famous firm of architects (**Villard Houses**, 1884; **United States General Post Office**, 1913; **Municipal Building**, 1914).

APARTMENT BUILDINGS

A S THE CITY'S population grew and space became ever more precious, family homes in Manhattan became much too expensive for most New Yorkers, and even the wealthy joined the trend toward communal living. In 1884 Henry Hardenbergh's Dakota *(see p216)*, one of the first luxury apartment buildings, started a spate of turn-of-the-century construction on the Upper West Side. Many of the

SKYSCRAPERS

A LTHOUGH CHICAGO gave birth to the skyscraper, New York has seen some of the greatest innovations. In 1902 Daniel Burnham, a Chicago architect, built the **Flatiron Building**, so tall at 300 ft (91 m) that skeptics said it would collapse. By 1913, the **Woolworth Building** had risen to 792 ft (241 m). Soon, zoning laws were passed requiring "setbacks" – upper stories were stepped back to allow light to reach street level. This suited the Art Deco style. The **Chrysler Building** (1930) was the world's tallest until the

Art Deco arched pattern on the spire of the Chrysler Building

245 Fifth Avenue (Apartment Building)

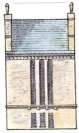

60 Gramercy Park North (Brownstone)

Hotel Pierre (Beaux Arts)

Sherry Netherland Hotel (Beaux Arts)

Multicultural New York

WHEREVER YOU GO in New York, even in pockets of the hectic high-rise city center, you will find evidence of the richly ethnic flavor of the city. A bus ride can take you from Madras to Moscow, Hong Kong to Haiti. Immigrants are still coming to New York, though numbers are fewer than in the peak years from 1880 to 1910, when 17 million people arrived. In the 1980s, a million newcomers, largely from Caribbean countries and Asia, arrived and found their own special corner of the city. Throughout the year you will encounter crowds celebrating one of many festivals. To find out more about national celebrations and parades, see pages 50 to 53.

Hell's Kitchen
Renamed "Clinton" to reflect a new residential mix, this neighborhood was the first home of Irish immigrants.

Little Ukraine
Services are held at T. Shevchenko Place as part of the May 17 festivities to mark the Ukrainians' conversion to Christianity.

Little Korea
Not far from Herald Square, a small enclave of Koreans has made a niche.

Little Italy
For ten days in September, the Italian community gathers around the Mulberry Street area, and the streets are taken over by the celebrations of the Festa di San Gennaro.

Chinatown
Every year, in January or February, Mott Street is packed as residents celebrate the Chinese New Year.

Theatre District

Chelsea and the Garment District

Gramercy and the Flatiron District

Greenwich Village

SoHo and TriBeCa

East Village

Seaport and the Civic Center

Lower East Side

Lower Manhattan

The Lower East Side
The synagogues around Rivington Street reflect the religious traditions of this old Jewish area.

0 kilometers 2

0 miles 1

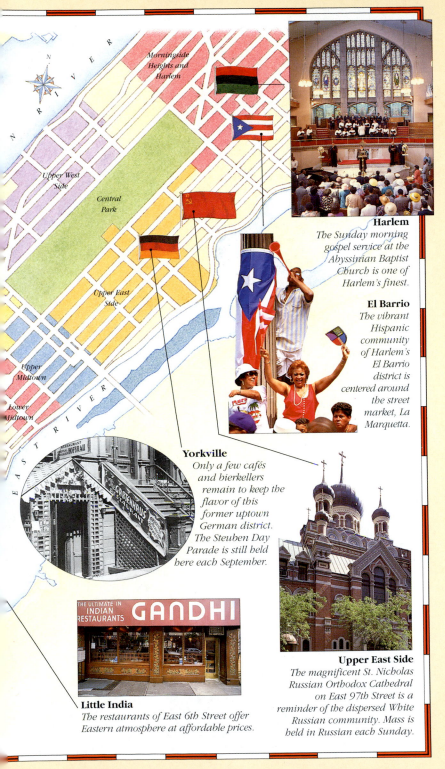

Morningside
Heights and
Harlem

Upper West
Side

Central
Park

Upper East
Side

Upper
Midtown

Lower
Midtown

HUDSON RIVER

EAST RIVER

Harlem
The Sunday morning gospel service at the Abyssinian Baptist Church is one of Harlem's finest.

El Barrio
The vibrant Hispanic community of Harlem's El Barrio district is centered around the street market, La Marquetta.

Yorkville
Only a few cafés and bierkellers remain to keep the flavor of this former uptown German district. The Steuben Day Parade is still held here each September.

Upper East Side
The magnificent St. Nicholas Russian Orthodox Cathedral on East 97th Street is a reminder of the dispersed White Russian community. Mass is held in Russian each Sunday.

Little India
The restaurants of East 6th Street offer Eastern atmosphere at affordable prices.

Exploring New York's Many Cultures

Stained glass at the Cotton Club

EVEN "NATIVE" NEW YORKERS have ancestral roots in other countries. Throughout the 17th century, the Dutch and English settled here, establishing trade colonies in the New World. Soon America became a symbol of hope for the downtrodden elsewhere in Europe. Many flocked across the ocean, some penniless and with little knowledge of the language. The potato famine of the 1840s led to the first wave of Irish immigrants, followed by German and other European workers displaced by political unrest and the Industrial Revolution. Immigrants continue to enrich New York in countless ways, and today an estimated 100 languages are spoken.

Turkish immigrants arriving at former Idlewild Airport in 1963

THE JEWS

THERE HAS BEEN a Jewish community in New York since 1654. The first synagogue, Shearith Israel, was established by refugees from a Dutch colony in Brazil and is still active today. These first settlers, Sephardic Jews of Spanish descent, included such prominent families as the Baruchs. They were followed by the German Jews, who set up successful retailing enterprises, like the Straus brothers at Macy's. Russian persecution led to the mass immigration that began in the late 1800s. By the start of World War I, there were 600,000 Jews living on the Lower East Side. Today, this area is more Hispanic and Asian than Jewish, but it holds reminders of its role as a place of refuge and new beginnings.

THE GERMANS

THE GERMANS began to settle in New York in the 18th century. From Peter Zenger onward (see p19), the city's German community has championed the freedom to express ideas and opinions. It has also produced giants of industry, such as John Jacob Astor, the city's first millionaire.

THE ITALIANS

ITALIANS FIRST came to New York in the 1830s and 1840s. Many came from northern Italy to escape the failing revolution at home. In the 1870s, poverty in southern Italy drove many more Italians across the ocean. In time, they became a potent political force in the city, exemplified by Fiorello La Guardia, one of New York's finest mayors.

THE CHINESE

THE CHINESE were late arrivals to New York. In 1880, the population of the Mott Street district was a mere

Eastern States Buddhist Temple, in central Chinatown (see pp96–7)

700. By the 1940s, they were the city's fastest-growing and most upwardly mobile ethnic group, extending the old boundaries of Chinatown and establishing new neighborhoods in parts of Brooklyn and Queens. Once a closed community, Chinatown now bustles with tourists exploring the streets and markets, and sampling the restaurant food.

THE HISPANIC AMERICANS

Hispanic religious carving at El Museo del Barrio (see p229)

PUERTO RICANS were in New York as early as 1838, but it was not until after World War II that they arrived in large numbers in search of work. Most live in El Barrio, formerly known as Spanish Harlem. Professionals who fled Fidel Castro's Cuba have moved out of the city itself but are still influential in Hispanic commerce and culture. Parts of Washington Heights have large Dominican and Columbian communities.

THE IRISH

THE IRISH, who first arrived in New York in the 1840s, had to overcome harsh odds. Starving and with barely a penny to their names, they labored hard to escape the slums of Five Points and Hell's Kitchen (now Clinton), helping to build the modern city in the process. Many joined the police and fire-fighting forces, rising to high rank through dedication to duty. Others set up successful businesses, such as the Irish bars that act as a focus for the now-scattered New York Irish community.

THE AFRICAN AMERICANS

PERHAPS the best-known black inner-city community in the Western world, Harlem is noted for the Harlem Renaissance of writing *(see pp28-9)* as much as it is for great entertainment, gospel music and soul food. The move of black African Americans from the South to the North began with emancipation in the 1860s and increased markedly in the 1920s, when Harlem's black population rose from 83,000 to 204,000. Today Harlem is undergoing revitalization in many areas. The African American population has also dispersed throughout the city.

THE MELTING POT

OTHER NEW YORK cultures are not distinctly defined but are still easily found. Ukrainians gather in the East Village, around St. George's Ukrainian Catholic Church on East 7th Street. Little India can be spotted by the restaurants along East 6th Street. Koreans own many of the small grocery stores in Manhattan, but most tend to live in the Flushing area of Queens. The religious diversity of New York can be seen in the Islamic Center on Riverside Drive, the

A woman celebrating at the Greek Independence Day parade

Russian Orthodox Cathedral on East 97th Street *(see p197);* and the new Islamic Cultural Center on 96th Street – Manhattan's first major mosque.

THE OUTER BOROUGHS

BROOKLYN IS by far the most international borough. Caribbean newcomers from Jamaica and Haiti are one of the fastest-growing immigrant groups. West Indians tend to cluster along Eastern Parkway between Grand Army Plaza and Utica Avenue, the route of the lavish, exotically-costumed West Indian Day Parade in September. Recently arrived Russian Jewish immigrants have turned Brighton Beach into "Little Odessa by the Sea," and the Scandinavians and Lebanese have settled in Bay Ridge and the Finns in Sunset Park. Borough Park and Williamsburg are home to Orthodox Jews, and Midwood has an Israeli – Middle East accent. Italians live in the Bensonhurst area. Greenpoint is little Poland, and Atlantic Avenue is home to the largest Arab community in America.

The Irish were among the earliest groups to cross the Harlem River into the Bronx. Japanese executives favor the more exclusive Riverdale area. One of the most distinctive ethnic areas is Astoria, Queens, which has the largest Greek population outside the motherland. Jackson Heights is home to a large Latin American quarter, including 300,000 Colombians. Indians also favor this area and neighboring Flushing. But it is the Asians who have transformed Flushing, so much so that the local train is known as "The Orient Express."

The New York police, a haven for Irish Americans

NEWCOMERS WHO MADE THEIR MARK *See also pp46–9.*

The dates mark the year these immigrants entered the US via New York.

1890	1895	1900	1905	1910	1915	1920	1925	1930	1935	1940

1932 George Balanchine (Russia), ballet choreographer

1906 "Lucky" Luciano (Italy), gangster (deported 1946)

1893 Irving Berlin (Russia), musician

1908 Bob Hope (England), comedian

1921 Bela Lugosi (Hungary), star of *Dracula*

1933 Albert Einstein (Germany), scientist

1894 Al Jolson (Lithuania), singer

1909 Lee Strasberg (Austria), theater director

1896 Samuel Goldwyn (Poland), movie mogul

1904 Hyman Rickover (Russia), developer of nuclear submarine

1913 Rudolph Valentino (Italy), film star

1923 Isaac Asimov (Russia), scientist and writer

1902 Joe Hill (Sweden), labor activist

1903 Frank Capra (Italy), film director

1912 Claudette Colbert (France), film star

1938 von Trapp family (Austria), singers

Celebrated Visitors and Residents

Nearly all New Yorkers have immigrant roots if you go back far enough. Indeed, many of the city's most prominent residents have migrated here, coming to New York to find creative freedom and sometimes fleeing from constraints or repression in their native countries. As a result, some of the most brilliant contributions to New York's colorful history and culture have been made by first-generation immigrants and visitors.

George Balanchine *(1904–83)*
The ballet choreographer migrated from Russia in 1933 and formed the New York City Ballet.

Dylan Thomas *(1914–53) The Welsh poet drank himself to a tragically early death; he frequented the White Horse Tavern in Greenwich Village.*

Marcel Duchamp *(1887–1968) In 1917 the French Dadaist climbed Washington Square arch to protest against US partici- pation in World War I.*

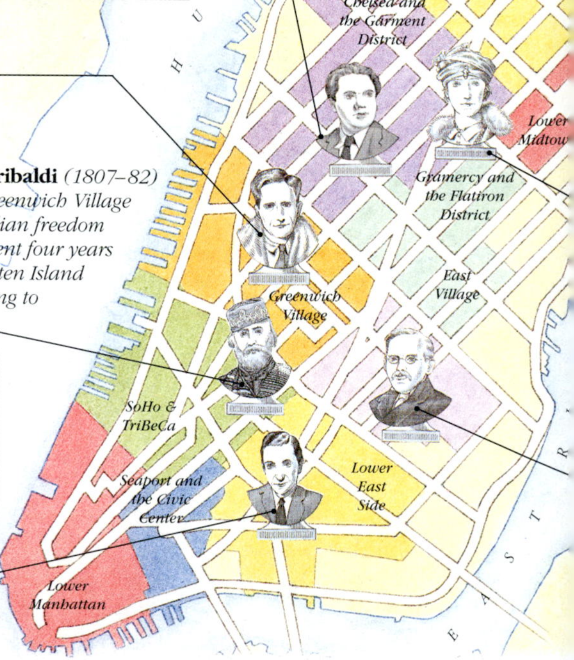

Giuseppe Garibaldi *(1807–82) A statue in Greenwich Village honors the Italian freedom fighter who spent four years in exile on Staten Island before returning to unify Italy.*

Irving Berlin *(1888–1989) Born Israel Baline in Siberia, he grew up on the Lower East Side and composed the hit tune "White Christmas."*

Theater District

Chelsea and the Garment District

Lower Midtown

Gramercy and the Flatiron District

East Village

Greenwich Village

SoHo & TriBeCa

Lower East Side

Seaport and the Civic Center

Lower Manhattan

HUDSON RIVER

EAST RIVER

Isaac Bashevis Singer (1904–91) The Polish Jewish novelist lived on West 86th Street for many years.

John Audubon (1785–1851) America's most famous ornithologist grew up in France. His New York estate was in Washington Heights.

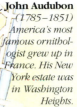

Morningside Heights and Harlem

Upper West Side

Central Park

Marcus Garvey (1887–1940) During the 1920s Jamaican-born Garvey lived in Harlem, where he was an influential black leader.

John Lennon (1940–80) The Liverpool-born musician and his wife, Yoko Ono, made their home on the Upper West Side.

Upper East Side

Harry Houdini (1874–1926) The escape artist from Budapest had a vision of his death at age 52 and left his West 113th Street house weeping.

Upper Midtown

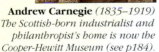

Andrew Carnegie (1835–1919) The Scottish-born industrialist and philanthropist's home is now the Cooper-Hewitt Museum (see p184).

Sarah Bernhardt (1844–1923) The French actress attended services at the Little Church Around the Corner (see p127) during her time in New York.

0 kilometers 2

0 miles 1

Jacob Riis (1849–1914) A Danish immigrant, he slept in Bowery doorways before writing How the Other Half Lives, which helped alleviate New York's squalor.

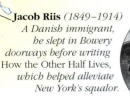

Remarkable New Yorkers

NEW YORK HAS NOURISHED some of the best creative talents of this century. Pop art began here, and Manhattan is still the world center for modern art. The alternative writers of the 1950s and '60s – known as the Beat Genèration – took inspiration from the city's jazz clubs. And since it is the financial capital, many leading world financiers have made New York their home.

Pop artist Andy Warhol

WRITERS

Novelist James Baldwin

MUCH GREAT AMERICAN literature was created in New York. *Charlotte Temple, A Tale of Truth*, first published in 1791 by Susanna Rowson (c1762 – 1824), was a tale of seduction in the city and a best-seller for 50 years.

America's first professional author was Charles Brockden Brown (1771–1810), who came to New York in 1791. The novels of Edgar Allan Poe (1809 – 49), the pioneer of the modern detective story, expanded the thriller genre. Henry James (1843–1916) published *The Bostonians* (1886) and became the master of the psychological novel, and his friend Edith Wharton (1861–1937) became known for her satirical novels about American society.

American literature finally received international recognition with Washington Irving's (1783–1859) satire, *A History of New York* (1809). It earned him $2,000. Irving coined the names "Gotham" for New York and "Knickerbockers" for New Yorkers. He and James Fenimore Cooper (1789–1851), whose books gave birth to the "Western" novel, formed the Knicker-

bocker group of US writers. Greenwich Village has always attracted writers, including Herman Melville (1819–91) whose masterpiece, *Moby Dick* (1851), was very poorly received at first. Jack Kerouac (1922–69), Allen Ginsberg and William Burroughs all went to Columbia University and drank at the San Remo Café in Greenwich Village. Dylan Thomas (1914–53) lived at the Chelsea Hotel (*see p137*). Novelist Nathanael West (1902– 40) worked in the Gramercy Park Hotel, and Dashiell Hammett (1894–1961) wrote *The Maltese Falcon* while living there. James Baldwin (1924– 87), born in Harlem, wrote *Another Country* (1963) on his return to New York from Europe.

ARTISTS

THE NEW YORK School of Abstract Expressionists founded the first influential American art movement. It was launched by Hans Hofmann (1880–1966) with Franz Kline and Willem de Kooning, whose first job in America was as a house-painter. Adolph Gottlieb, Mark Rothko (1903–70) and Jackson Pollock (1912–56) went on to popularize this style. Pollock, Kline and de Kooning all had their studios on the Lower East Side.

Pop art began in New York in the 1960s with Roy Lichtenstein and

Andy Warhol (1926–87), who made some of his cult films at 33 Union Square. Keith Haring (1958–90) was a very prolific graffiti artist whose work as a pop artist is now receiving recognition.

Robert Mapplethorpe (1946–89) acquired notoriety for his homoerotic photos of men. Jeff Koons has now superseded him as the *bête noire* of the art establishment.

The illusionistic murals by Richard Haas enliven many walls throughout the city.

ACTORS

IN 1849 the British actor Charles Macready started a riot by saying Americans were vulgar. A mob stormed the Astor Place Opera House, where Macready was playing Macbeth, police opened fire, and 22 rioters were killed. In 1927 Mae West (1893–1980) spent 10 days in a workhouse on Roosevelt Island and was fined $500 for giving a lewd performance in her Broadway show *Sex*. Marc Blitzstein's radical pro-labor opera *The Cradle Will Rock* produced by Orson Welles (1915–85) and John Houseman (1902–88), was immediately banned and the show had to move to

Vaudeville actress Mae West

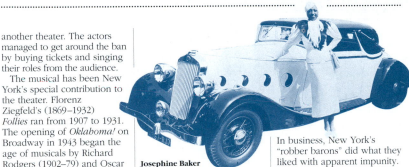

another theater. The actors managed to get around the ban by buying tickets and singing their roles from the audience.

The musical has been New York's special contribution to the theater. Florenz Ziegfeld's (1869–1932) *Follies* ran from 1907 to 1931. The opening of *Oklahoma!* on Broadway in 1943 began the age of musicals by Richard Rodgers (1902–79) and Oscar Hammerstein, Jr. (1895–1960).

Off Broadway, the Provincetown Players at 33 MacDougal Street were the first to produce Eugene O'Neill's (1888–1953) *Beyond the Horizon* (1920). His successor as the major innovative force in US theater was Edward Albee, author of *Who's Afraid of Virginia Woolf?* (1962).

MUSICIANS AND DANCERS

LEONARD BERNSTEIN (1918–90) followed a long line of great conductors at the New York Philharmonic, including Bruno Walter (1876–1962), Arturo Toscanini (1867–1957) and Leopold Stokowski (1882–1977). Maria Callas (1923–77) was born in New York but moved to Europe.

Carnegie Hall *(see p146)* has featured Enrico Caruso (1873–1921), Bob Dylan and the Beatles. A record concert attendance was set in 1991 when Paul Simon drew a million people for his free concert in Central Park.

The legendary swinging jazz clubs of the 1930s and 1940s are now gone from 52nd Street. Plaques on "Jazz Walk" outside the CBS building honor such

Josephine Baker

famous performers as Charlie Parker (1920–55) and Josephine Baker (1906–75).

Between 1940 and 1965, New York became a world dance capital with the founding of George Balanchine's (1904–83) New York City Ballet and the American Ballet Theater. In 1958, choreographer Alvin Ailey (1931–89) started the American Dance Theater, a showcase for modern dance works by a multiracial troupe.

INDUSTRIALISTS AND ENTREPRENEURS

Tycoon Cornelius Vanderbilt

THE RAGS-TO-RICHES story is an American dream. Andrew Carnegie (1835–1919), "the steel baron with a heart of gold," started with nothing and died having given away $350 million. His beneficiaries included public libraries and universities throughout America. Many other foundations are legacies of wealthy philanthropists. Some, like Cornelius Vanderbilt (1794–1877) tried to shake off their rough beginnings by patronizing the arts.

In business, New York's "robber barons" did what they liked with apparent impunity. Financiers Jay Gould (1836–92) and James Fisk (1834–72) beat Vanderbilt in the war for the Erie Railroad by manipulating stock. In September 1869 they caused Wall Street's first "Black Friday" when they tried to corner the gold market, but fled when their fraud was discovered. Gould died a happy billionaire, and Fisk was killed in a fight over a woman.

Modern entrepreneurs include Donald Trump *(see p31)*, owner of Trump Tower, and Leona and the late Harry Helmsley. Despite Leona's imprisonment for tax evasion, their property empire remains intact and includes such New York sites as the Helmsley Building *(see p156)*.

ARCHITECTS

CASS GILBERT (1858–1934), who built such Neo-Gothic skyscrapers as the Woolworth Building of 1913 *(see p91)* was one of the men who literally shaped the city. His caricature can be seen in the lobby, clutching a model of his masterpiece. Stanford White (1853–1906) was as well known for his scandalous private life as for his fine Beaux Arts buildings, such as the Players Club *(p126)*. For most of his life, Frank Lloyd Wright (1867–1959) spurned city architecture. When he was persuaded to leave his mark on the city, it was in the form of the Guggenheim Museum *(pp186–7)*. German-born Ludwig Mies van der Rohe (1886–1969), who built the Seagram Building, did not believe in "inventing a new architecture every Monday morning," although some might argue that this is just what New York has always done best.

Musical producer Florenz Ziegfeld

NEW YORK THROUGH THE YEAR

SPRINGTIME IN NEW YORK sees Park Avenue filled with blooms, while Fifth Avenue goes green for St. Patrick's Day, the first of the year's many big parades. Summer in the city is hot and humid, but it is worth forsaking an air-conditioned interior to step outside, where parks and squares are the setting for free open-air music and theater. The first Monday in September marks Labor Day and the advent of comfortable temperatures and the orange-red colors of autumn. Then, as Christmas nears, the shops and streets begin to sparkle with dazzling window displays.

Dates of the events on the following pages may vary. For details consult the listings magazines *(see p353)*. The New York Convention and Visitors Bureau *(see p352)* also issues a useful quarterly free calendar of events.

SPRING

EVERY SEASON in New York brings its own tempo and temptations. In spring, the city shakes off the winter with tulips and cherry blossoms in the parks and spring fashions in the stores. Everyone window shops and gallery hops. The hugely popular St. Patrick's Day Parade draws the crowds, and thousands don their finery for the Easter Parade down Fifth Avenue.

Inventive Easter bonnets in New York's Easter Parade

MARCH

St. Patrick's Day Parade
(Mar 17), Fifth Ave, from 44th to 86th St. Green clothes, green flowers – even green beer.
Greek Independence Day Parade *(Mar 25)*, Fifth Ave, from 49th to 59th St. Greek dancing and food.
New York City Opera Spring Season *(Mar– mid-Apr)*, Lincoln Center *(p338)*.
Ringling Bros and Barnum & Bailey Circus *(late Mar– end May)*, Madison Square Garden *(p133)*.

EASTER

Easter Flower Show *(week before Easter)*, Macy's department store *(pp132–3)*.
Easter Parade *(Easter Sun)*, Fifth Ave, from 44th to 59th St. Paraders in costumes and outrageous millinery gather around St. Patrick's Cathedral.

APRIL

Cherry Blossom Festival *(late Apr– May)*, Brooklyn Botanic Garden. Famous for Japanese cherry trees and beautifully laid out ornamental gardens.
Annual Earth Day Festival Activities *(varies)*.
Baseball *(Apr– May)*, Major league season starts for Yankees and Mets *(p344)*.
New York City Ballet Spring Season *(Apr– Jun)*, New York State Theater and Metropolitan Opera House in Lincoln Center *(p212)*.

MAY

Martin Luther King Jr. Parade *(third Sun)*, Fifth Ave, from 57th to 79th St. A parade to honor the memory of the black civil rights leader who was assassinated in Memphis in 1968.

Parading in national costume on Greek Independence Day

Ninth Avenue Street Festival *(mid-May)*, from W 37th to W 57th St. A feast of ethnic foods, music and dance.
Washington Square Outdoor Art Exhibit *(last week-end May, first weekend Jun)*.
Memorial Day Activities *(last weekend)* A parade down Fifth Ave, festivities at South Street Seaport.

Yellow tulips and cabs shine on Park Avenue

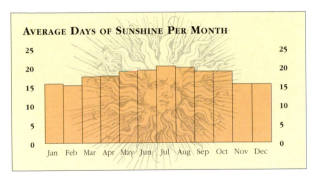

AVERAGE DAYS OF SUNSHINE PER MONTH

Jan Feb Mar Apr May Jun Jul Aug Sep Oct Nov Dec

Days of Sunshine
New York enjoys long hours of summer sun from June to August, with July the month of greatest sunshine. The winter days are much shorter, but many are clear and bright. Autumn has more sunshine than spring, although both are sunny.

SUMMER

NEW YORKERS escape the hot city streets when possible, for picnics, boat rides and the beaches. Macy's fireworks light up the Fourth of July skies, and more sparks fly when the New York Yankees and Mets baseball teams are in town. Summer also brings street fairs, outdoor concerts, and free Shakespeare and opera in Central Park.

Policeman dancing in the Puerto Rican Day Parade

JUNE

Puerto Rican Day Parade
(first Sun), Fifth Ave, from 44th to 86th St. Floats and marching bands.
Museum Mile Festival
(second Tue), Fifth Ave, from 82nd to 105th St. Free entry to museums.
Central Park Summerstage
(Jun–Aug), Central Park. Music and dance of every variety, almost daily, rain or shine.
Metropolitan Opera Parks Concerts. Free evening concerts in parks throughout the city *(pp338–9)*.
Goldman Memorial Band Concerts *(Jun–Aug)*, Lincoln Center *(p212)*. Traditional band concerts.

Shakespeare in the Park
(Jun–Sep). Broadway stars take on the bard at Delacorte Theater, Central Park *(p335)*.
Lesbian and Gay Pride Day Parade *(mid Jun)*, from Columbus Circle along Fifth Ave to Washington Sq *(p113)*.
JVC Jazz Festival *(late Jun–early Jul)*. Top jazz musicians perform in various halls in the city *(p341)*.

JULY

Macy's Firework Display
(Jul 4), East River. High point of the city's Independence Day celebrations, featuring the best fireworks in town.
American Crafts Festival
(late June–early July), Lincoln Center *(p212)*. High-quality crafts.
Mostly Mozart Festival, *(mid-Jul–end Aug)*, Avery Fisher Hall, Lincoln Center *(pp338-9)*.
NY Philharmonic Parks Concerts *(late Jul–early Aug)*. Free concerts in parks

Festivities at a summer street fair in Greenwich Village

throughout the city *(p339)*.
Lincoln Center Festival
(Jul), Dance. opera, other performing arts from around the world.

AUGUST

Harlem Week *(mid-Aug)*. Films, art, music, dance, fashion, sports and tours.
Out-of-Doors Festival *(mid-Jul–early Sep)*, Lincoln Center. Free dance and theater performances *(p334)*.
US Open Tennis Championships *(late Aug–early Sep)*, Flushing Meadows *(p345)*.

Crowds of spectators flock to the US Open Tennis Championships

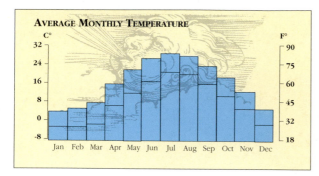

AVERAGE MONTHLY TEMPERATURE

C° ... F°

Jan Feb Mar Apr May Jun Jul Aug Sep Oct Nov Dec

Temperature
The chart shows the average minimum and maximum temperatures for each month in New York. With top temperatures averaging 84° F (29° C), the city can become hot and humid. In contrast, the months of winter, although rarely below freezing, can seem bitterly cold.

AUTUMN

LABOR DAY marks the end of the summer. The Giants and the Jets kick off the football season, the Broadway season begins and the Festa di San Gennaro in Little Italy is the high point in a succession of colorful neighborhood fairs. Macy's Thanksgiving Day Parade is the nation's symbol that the festive season has arrived.

SEPTEMBER

Richmond County Fair
(Labor Day weekend), in the grounds of Historic Richmond Town *(p252)*. New York's only authentic county fair.
West Indian Carnival
(Labor Day weekend), Brooklyn. Parade, floats, music, dancing and food.
Brazilian Festival *(early Sep)*, E 46th St, between Times Sq and Madison Ave.

Exotic Caribbean carnival costume in the streets of Brooklyn

Brazilian music, food, and crafts.
New York is Book Country *(mid-Sep)*, Fifth Ave, from 48th to 59th Sts. Book fair.
Festa di San Gennaro *(third week)*, Little Italy *(p96)*. Ten days of festivities and processions.
New York Film Festival *(mid-Sep – early Oct)*, Lincoln Center *(p212)*. American films and international art films.
Von Steuben Day Parade *(third week)*, Upper Fifth Ave. German-American celebrations.
American Football *(season begins)*, Giants Stadium, home to the Giants and the Jets *(p344)*.

OCTOBER

Columbus Day Parade *(2nd Mon)*, Fifth Ave, from 44th to 86th Sts. Parades and music to celebrate Columbus's first sighting of America.
Pulaski Day Parade *(Sun closest to Oct 5)*, Fifth Ave, from 26th to 52nd Sts. Celebrations for Polish-American hero Casimir Pulaski.
Halloween Parade *(Oct 31)*, Greenwich Village. Brilliant event with fantastic costumes.
Big Apple Circus *(Oct – Jan)*, Damrosch Park, Lincoln Center. Special themes are presented each year *(p349)*.
Basketball *(season begins)*, Madison Square Garden. Local team is the Knicks *(p344)*.
New York City Marathon *(last Sun Oct or first Sun Nov)*. From Staten Island through all the city boroughs.

Huge Superman balloon floating above Macy's Thanksgiving Day Parade

NOVEMBER

Macy's Thanksgiving Day Parade *(fourth Thu)*, from Central Park West and W 79th St to Broadway and W 34th St. A joy for children, with floats, huge balloons and Santa.
Rockefeller Center Ice Skating Rink *(Nov– Mar)*, Open to the public. You can skate beneath the famous Christmas Tree.
Magnificent Christmas Spectacular *(Nov–Jan)*, Radio City Music Hall. Variety show, with the Rockettes.

Revelers in Greenwich Village's Halloween Parade

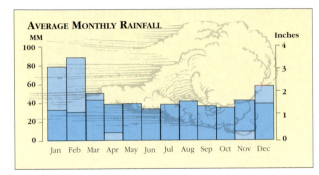

AVERAGE MONTHLY RAINFALL

| MM | | | | | | | | | | | | Inches |

Jan Feb Mar Apr May Jun Jul Aug Sep Oct Nov Dec

Rainfall
March and August are the months of heaviest rainfall in New York. Rainfall in spring is unpredictable, so be prepared. Sudden heavy snowfalls in winter can cause chaos in the city.

■ Rainfall

■ Snowfall

WINTER

NEW YORK is magical at Christmas – even the stone lions at the Public Library don wreaths for the occasion, and shops become works of art. From Times Square to Chinatown, New Year celebrations punctuate the season, and Central Park becomes a winter sports arena.

Statue of Alice in Wonderland in Central Park

DECEMBER

Tree-Lighting Ceremony *(early Dec)*, Rockefeller Center *(p142)*. Lighting of the giant Christmas tree in front of the RCA Building.
Messiah Sing-In *(mid-Dec)*, Lincoln Center *(p212)*. The audience rehearses and performs under the guidance of various conductors.
Hanukkah Menorah *(mid–late Dec)*, Grand Army Plaza, Brooklyn. Lighting of the huge menorah (candelabra) every night during the eight-day Festival of Lights.
New Year's Eve. Fireworks display in Central Park *(pp204–5)*; festivities in Times Square *(p145)*; 5-mile (8-km) run in Central Park; poetry reading in St. Mark's Church.

JANUARY

National Boat Show *(mid-Jan)*, Jacob K. Javits Convention Center *(p136)*.
Chinese New Year *(late Jan/Feb)*, Chinatown *(pp96–7)*. Dragons, fireworks and food.
Winter Antiques Show *(late Jan)*, Seventh Regiment Armory *(p185)*. NYC's most prestigious antiques fair.

FEBRUARY

Black History Month. African-American events take place throughout the city.
Empire State Building Run-Up *(early Feb)*. Runners race to the 102nd floor *(pp134–5)*.
Lincoln and Washington Birthday Sales *(Feb 12–22)* Big department stores sales throughout the city.
Westminster Kennel Club Dog Show *(mid-Feb)*, Madison Square Garden *(p133)*. Major dog show.

Chinese New Year celebrations in Chinatown

PUBLIC HOLIDAYS

New Year's Day (Jan 1)
Martin Luther King Day (3rd Mon, Jan)
President's Day (mid-Feb)
Memorial Day (end May)
Independence Day (Jul 4)
Labor Day (1st Mon, Sep)
Columbus Day (2nd Mon, Oct)
Election Day (1st Tue, Nov)
Veterans Day (Nov 11)
Thanksgiving Day (4th Thu, Nov)
Christmas Day (Dec 25)

The giant Christmas tree and decorations at Rockefeller Center

The Southern Tip of Manhattan

Tʜɪs ᴠɪᴇᴡ of Lower Manhattan, seen from the Hudson River, encompasses some of the most striking modern additions to the New York skyline, including the distinctively topped quartet of the World Financial Center. You will also catch glimpses of an earlier Manhattan: Castle Clinton set against the green space of Battery Park and, behind it, the noble Custom House building. From 1973 until September 2001 the area also boasted the World Trade Center, in its day the city's tallest building. Its landmark towers were destroyed in a terrorist attack on the city.

DESTRUCTION OF THE WORLD TRADE CENTER

On September 11, 2001, two planes bound for Los Angeles were hijacked and targeted at the World Trade Center. Hundreds of people died in the impact, but thousands more were killed when the twin towers collapsed. Two other planes were also hijacked that morning; the first struck the Pentagon, while the second came to ground near Pittsburgh. The death toll exceeded the number of troops killed in the Revolutionary War *(see pp20–21)*, and comparisons were made with the bombing of Pearl Harbor. Images of the destruction were seen across the world, drawing wide support for a "war against terrorism."

World Financial Center
At the heart of this complex is the Winter Garden – a place to shop, dine, be entertained or just enjoy the Hudson River views (see p69).

World Trade Center
Twin 110-story towers dominated the sky-line (see p72).

Detail from the *Upper Room*

The Upper Room
This walk-around sculpture by Ned Smyth is one of many works of art in Battery Park City (see p72).

An Earlier View
This 1898 photograph shows a skyline now changed beyond recognition.

Downtown Athletic Club

The Heisman Trophy for football is kept in this fine Art Deco building.

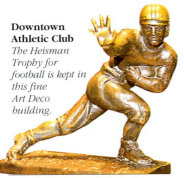

US Custom House

This magnificent 1907 Beaux Arts building now houses the Museum of the American Indian (see p73).

East Coast War Memorial

In Battery Park, a huge bronze eagle by Albino Manca honors the dead of World War II.

26 Broadway

The tower of the former Standard Oil Building resembles an oil lamp. The interior is still decorated with company symbols.

Bank of New York

17 State Street

26 Broadway

1 Liberty Plaza

Liberty View

Castle Clinton

US Custom House

American Merchant Mariners' Memorial (1991)

This sculpture by Marisol is on Pier A, the last of Manhattan's old piers. The pier also has a clock tower that chimes the hours on ships' bells.

Shrine of Mother Seton

The first US-born saint lived here (see p76).

Lower Manhattan from the East River

AT FIRST SIGHT, this stretch of East River shoreline, running up from the tip of Manhattan Island, is a seamless array of 20th-century office buildings. But from sea level, streets and slips are still visible, offering glimpses of old New York and the Financial District to the west. On the skyline itself, a few of the district's early skyscrapers still proudly display their ornate crowns above their more anonymous modern counterparts.

LOCATOR MAP

☐ *East River View*

India House
The handsome brownstone at One Hanover Square is one of the finest of its kind.

Vietnam Veterans Plaza
An engraved green-glass memorial dominates the former Coenties Slip, a wharf filled in to make a park in the late 19th century (see p76).

Hanover Square
A statue of one of the Dutch mayors, Abraham De Peyster, sits near the house where he was born in 1657.

One New York Plaza

55 Water Street

Barclay's Bank Building

Battery Maritime Building
This historic ferry terminal serves only Governors Island (see p77).

Downtown Heliport
Air-Sea Rescue and sightseeing flights operate from here.

Delmonico's
High society dined here a century ago.

New York Stock Exchange
Although hidden from view by more modern edifices, this is still the hub of the hectic Financial District (see pp70–71).

40 Wall Street
In the 1940s, the pyramid-topped tower of the former Bank of Manhattan was hit by a light aircraft.

70 Pine Street
Replicas of this elegant Gothic-style tower can be seen near the Pine and Cedar Street entrances.

Bank of New York
This serene 1928 interior is part of the bank set up in 1784 by Alexander Hamilton (see p21).

Morgan Bank
Columns from lobby to rooftop are the theme of this striking modern building.

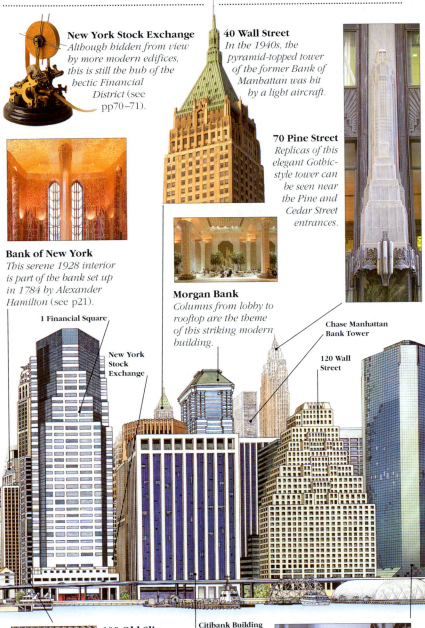

1 Financial Square

New York Stock Exchange

Chase Manhattan Bank Tower

120 Wall Street

Citibank Building

100 Old Slip
Now in the shadow of One Financial Square, the small palazzo-style First Precinct Police Department was the city's most modern police station when it was built in 1911.

Carved medallion, 100 Old Slip

***Queen Elizabeth* Monument**
The ocean liner that sank in 1972 is remembered here.

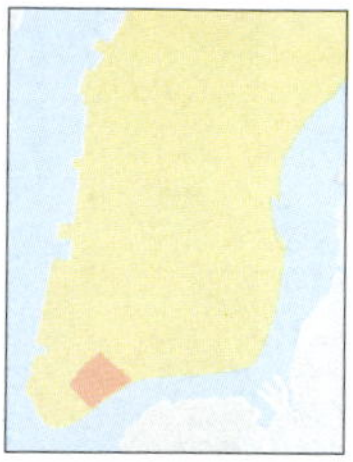

South Street Seaport

(see pp82–3)

As THE FINANCIAL DISTRICT ends, the skyline, as seen from the East River or Brooklyn, changes dramatically. The corporate headquarters are replaced by the piers, low-rise streets and warehouses of the old seaport area, now restored as the South Street Seaport *(see pp82–3)*. The Civic Center lies not far inland, and a few of its monumental buildings can be seen. The Brooklyn Bridge marks the end of this stretch of skyline. Between here and midtown, apartment blocks make up the majority of riverside features.

LOCATOR MAP

South Street Area

Stonework on the Woolworth Building

Pier 17

A focal point of the Seaport, this traditional-style leisure pier is packed with exciting shops, vendors and restaurants.

Woolworth Building

The handsomely decorated spire marks the headquarters of F.W. Woolworth's empire. It is still the finest "cathedral of commerce" ever built (see p91).

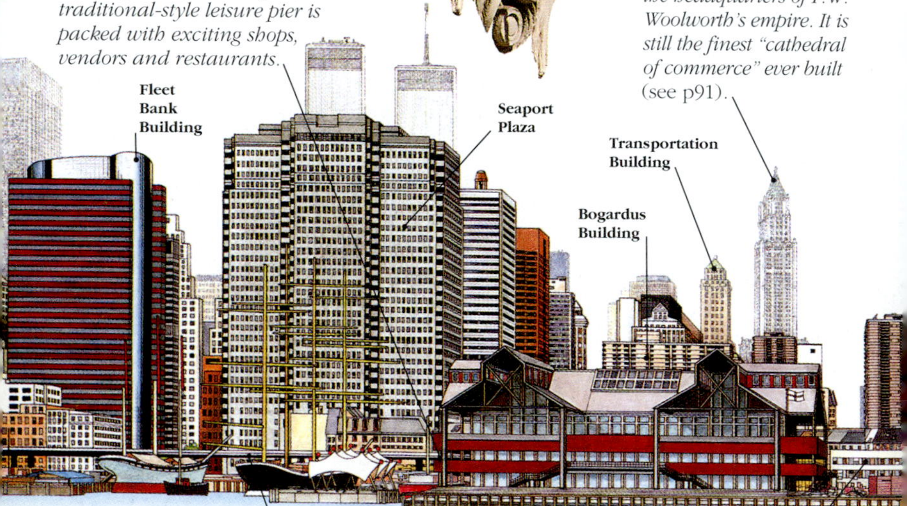

Fleet Bank Building

Seaport Plaza

Transportation Building

Bogardus Building

Maritime Crafts Center

At Pier 15, craftspeople demonstrate traditional seafaring skills such as woodcarving and model-making.

Fulton Fish Market

This is the largest wholesale fish market in the US and takes place at the Seaport before dawn.

Police Plaza

Five in One (1971–4), in Police Plaza, is a sculpture by Bernard Rosenthal. It represents the five boroughs of New York.

United States Courthouse

The Civic Center is marked on the skyline by the golden pyramid of architect Cass Gilbert's courthouse (see p85).

Municipal Building

Among the offices of this vast building is the Marriage Chapel, where weddings "at City Hall" actually take place. The copper statue on the skyline is Civic Fame *by Adolph Weinman (see p85).*

Surrogate's Court and Hall of Records

Archives dating back to 1664 are stored and displayed here (see p85).

Verizon Telephone Company

Police Plaza

Pace University

Southbridge Towers

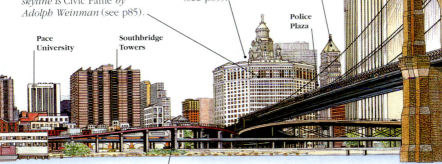

Con Edison Mural

In 1975, artist Richard Haas re-created the Brooklyn Bridge on the side wall of a former electrical substation.

Brooklyn Bridge

Views of, and from, the bridge have made it one of New York's best-loved landmarks (see pp86–9).

Midtown Manhattan

LOCATOR MAP
◻ Midtown

THE SKYLINE OF midtown Manhattan is graced with some of the city's most spectacular towers and spires – from the familiar beauty of the Empire State Building's Art Deco pinnacle to the dramatic wedge shape of Citicorp's modern headquarters. As the shoreline progresses uptown, so the architecture becomes more varied; the United Nations complex dominates a long stretch, and then Beekman Place begins a strand of exclusive residential enclaves that offer the rich and famous some seclusion in this busy part of the city.

LOCATOR MAP
◻ Midtown

Chrysler Building
Glinting in the sun by day or lit up by night, this stainless-steel spire is, for many, the ultimate New York skyscraper (see p153).

Grand Central Terminal
Now dwarfed by its neighbors, this landmark building is full of period details, such as this fine clock (see pp154–5).

Empire State Building
At 1250 ft (381 m), this was the tallest building in the world for many years (see p134–5).

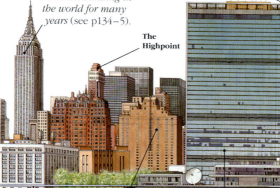

The Highpoint

MetLife Building

United Nations
Works of art from member countries include this Barbara Hepworth sculpture, a gift from Britain (see pp158–61).

Tudor City
Built in the 1920s, this complex is mock Tudor on a grand scale, with over 3,000 apartments (see p156).

1 and 2 UN Plaza
Angular glass towers house offices and the UN Plaza Hotel (see pp156 and 280).

General Electric Building
Built of red brick in 1931, this Art Deco building has a tall spiked crown that resembles radio waves. (see p174).

Citigroup Center
St. Peter's Church nestles in one corner of the Citigroup Center, with its raked tower (see p175).

Waldorf–Astoria
Twin copper-capped towers rise high above one of the city's finest hotels. The interior is also splendid (see p175).

Rockefeller Center
The outdoor skating rink and walkways of this complex of office buildings are a great place to people watch (see p142).

General Electric Building

The Nail, by Arnoldo Pomodoro, St. Peter's Church, Citicorp Center

866 UN Plaza

100 UN Plaza

St. Mary's Garden
The garden at Holy Family Church is a peaceful haven.

Japan Society
Japanese culture, from avant-garde plays to ancient art, can be seen here (see p156–7).

Beekman Tower
Now an all-suite hotel, this Art Deco tower was built in 1928 as a hotel for women who were members of US college sororities.

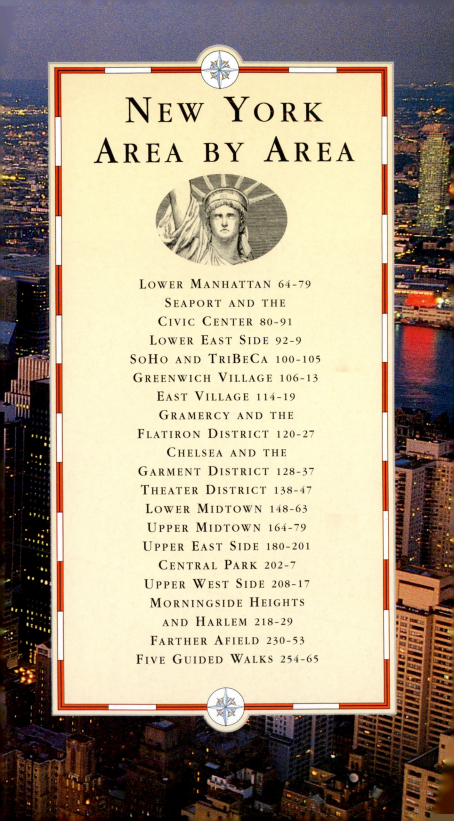

New York Area by Area

LOWER MANHATTAN

THE OLD AND THE NEW converge at Lower Manhattan, where Colonial churches and early American monuments stand in the shadow of skyscrapers. New York was born here, and this was the site of the nation's first capitol. Commerce has flourished since 1626, when Dutchman Peter Minuit purchased the island of Man-a-hatt-ta from the Algonquian Indians for goods valued at $24 *(see p17)*. At the time of revising this guide a number of landmark buildings in the area were destroyed *(see p54)*. The full extent of the damage was not known, so visitors are advised to call all sights to check opening and transportation information.

Minuit memorial on Bowling Green

Trinity Church at the foot of Wall Street

SIGHTS AT A GLANCE

Historic Streets and Buildings
Federal Reserve Bank **1**
Federal Hall **2**
New York Stock Exchange pp70–71 **3**
Downtown Athletic Club **8**
Cunard Building **9**
Fraunces Tavern Museum **13**
Battery Maritime Building **16**

Museums and Galleries
US Custom House **11**
Ellis Island pp78–9 **18**

Castle Clinton National Monument **20**
Museum of Jewish Heritage **21**

Monuments and Statues
Statue of Liberty pp74–5 **17**

Parks and Squares
Bowling Green **10**
Vietnam Veterans' Plaza **14**
Battery Park **19**

Boat Trips
Staten Island Ferry **15**

Churches
Trinity Church **4**
Shrine of Saint Elizabeth Ann Seton **12**

Modern Architecture
World Financial Center **5**
World Trade Center Site **6**
Battery Park City **7**

Bronze statue of a bull, symbol of Wall Street, near the Custom House

GETTING THERE
The best subway routes to the tip of Manhattan are the Lexington Ave 4 or 5 trains to Bowling Green; N or R to Whitehall St; or the 7th Ave 1 or 9 trains to South Ferry. For Wall St, take subways 2, 3, 4 or 5 to Wall St, or N or R to Rector St. The M1, M6 and M15 buses and the M22 crosstown route all serve the area.

SEE ALSO
- *Street Finder,* maps 1, 2
- *Where to Stay* pp274–5
- *Restaurants* pp290–92

0 meters 500
0 yards 500

KEY
Street-by-Street map
M Subway station
Ferry boarding point
Heliport

Street by Street: Wall Street

No intersection has been of greater importance to the city, past or present, than the corners of Wall and Broad streets. Three important sites are located here. Federal Hall National Monument marks the place where, in 1789, George Washington was sworn in as president. Trinity Church is one of the nation's oldest Anglican parishes. The New York Stock Exchange, founded in 1817, is to this day a financial nerve center whose ups and downs cause tremors around the globe. The surrounding buildings are the very heart of New York's famous financial district.

The Marine Midland Bank rises straight up 55 stories. This dark, glass tower occupies only 40% of its site. The other 60% is a plaza in which a large red sculpture by Isamu Noguchi, *Cube*, balances on one of its points.

Trinity Building, an early 20th-century Gothic skyscraper, was designed to complement nearby Trinity Church.

The Equitable Building (1915) deprived its neighbors of light, prompting a change in the law: skyscrapers had to be set back from the street.

★ **Trinity Church**
Built in 1846 in a Gothic style, this is the third church on this site. Once the tallest structure in the city, the bell tower is now dwarfed by the skyscrapers that surround it. Many famous early New Yorkers are buried in the churchyard ❹

Wall Street subway (lines 4, 5)

The Irving Trust Company, built in 1932, has an outer wall patterned to look like fabric. In the lobby is an Art Deco mosaic in shades of flame and gold.

26 Broadway was built as the home of the Standard Oil Trust. An oil lamp rests on top of it.

BROADWAY

NEW STREET

BROAD STREET

EXCHANGE PLACE

New York Stock Exchange ★
The hub of the world's financial markets is housed in a 17-story building constructed in 1903. Its visitors' center explains the history and workings of the Stock Exchange ❸

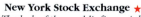

The Liberty Tower is clad in white terra-cotta and is in the Gothic style. It was later turned into apartments.

The Chamber of Commerce is a fine Beaux-Arts building of 1901.

STAR SIGHTS

★ **Federal Hall National Monument**

★ **Federal Reserve Bank**

★ **New York Stock Exchange**

★ **Trinity Church**

LOCATOR MAP
See Manhattan Map pp12–13

KEY

– – – Suggested route

| 0 meters | 100 |
| 0 yards | 100 |

Chase Manhattan Bank and Plaza has the famous Jean Dubuffet sculpture, *Four Trees*, located in the plaza.

★ **Federal Reserve Bank**
In the style of a Renaissance palace, this is a bank for banks. US currency is issued here ❶

Louise Nevelson Plaza is a park containing Nevelson's sculpture *Shadows and Flags*.

Wall Street is named for the wall that kept enemies and warring Indians out of Manhattan – the street is now the heart of the city's business center.

Wall Street in the 1920s

★ **Federal Hall National Monument**
Originally the US Custom House, this classical building now houses an exhibit about the Constitution ❷

Federal Reserve Bank ❶

33 Liberty St. **Map** 1 C2. ☎ 720-6130.
Ⓜ *Wall St.* ◯ *8:30am–5pm Mon–Fri.* ⬤ *public hols.* ✗ ♿ ✔ *every hour 9:30am–2:30pm. Reserve in advance.* Ⓦ www.ny.frb.org.

Entrance to Federal Reserve Bank

THIS IS A GOVERNMENT bank *for* banks – it is one of the 12 Federal Reserve banks, and therefore issues US currency. You can identify bank notes originating from this branch by the letter B in the Federal Reserve seal on each note.

Below ground is a five-story vault that serves as the largest storehouse for gold owned by the nations of the world. Each nation's gold is stored in its own compartment within the subterranean vault, guarded by 90-ton doors. Payments between nations used to be made by physical transfers of gold, but this is no longer so.

Designed by York & Sawyer, the building was completed in 1924. It occupies a full block and is liberally adorned with fine wrought-iron grillwork. It was inspired by the palaces of the Italian Renaissance.

Federal Hall ❷

26 Wall St. **Map** 1 C3. ☎ 825-6870.
Ⓜ *Wall St.* ◯ *9am–5pm Mon–Fri; Sat, Sun in Jul & Aug.* ⬤ *public holidays.* 📷 ♿ ✔ 📖
Ⓦ www.nps.gov.feha

A BRONZE STATUE of George Washington on the steps of Federal Hall marks the site where the nation's first president took his oath of office in 1789. Thousands of New Yorkers jammed Wall and Broad Streets for the occasion. They roared their approval when the Chancellor of the State of New York shouted, "Long live George Washington, President of the United States."

The present imposing structure, built between 1834 and 1842 as the US Custom House, is one of the finest Classical designs in the city. Display rooms off the Rotunda include the Bill of Rights Room and an interactive computer exhibit about the Constitution.

New York Stock Exchange ❸

See pp70–71.

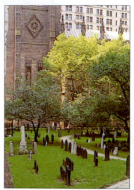

Trinity Churchyard

Trinity Church ❹

Broadway at Wall St. **Map** 1 C3. ☎ 602-0872. Ⓜ *Wall St, Rector St.* ◯ *7am–6pm Mon–Fri, 8am–4pm Sat, 7am–4pm Sun.* ✝ *9am, 11:15am Sun.* 📷 *except during services.* ✔ *2pm daily.* **Concerts** *Thu.* 📖 📱
Ⓦ www.trinitywallstreet.org

THIS SQUARE-TOWERED Episcopal church at the head of Wall Street is the third one on this site in one of America's oldest Anglican parishes, founded in 1697. Designed in 1846 by Richard Upjohn, it was one of the grandest churches of its day, marking the beginning of the best period of Gothic Revival architecture in America. Richard Morris Hunt's design for the sculpted brass doors was inspired by Ghiberti's *Doors of Paradise* in Florence.

Restoration has uncovered the original rosy sandstone, long buried beneath layers of city grime. The 280-ft (86-m) steeple, the tallest structure in New York until the 1860s, still commands respect despite its towering neighbors.

Many prominent early New Yorkers were members of Trinity parish. Statesman Alexander Hamilton; steamboat inventor Robert Fulton; and William Bradford, founder of New York's first newspaper in 1725, are among those buried in the graveyard.

Marble-columned rotunda within Federal Hall

World Financial Center ❺

West St. **Map** 1 A2. ☎ 945-0505.
Ⓜ 1, 2, 3, 9, A, C, E to Chambers St,
1, 9, N, R to Cortlandt St. 🚌 M1, M6,
M9, M10, M22. 📷 ♿ 🍴 🛍 🛗
Ⓦ www.worldfinancialcenter.com

A MODEL OF URBAN design by
Cesar Pelli & Associates,
this development is a vital
part of the revival of Lower
Manhattan. Four office towers
soar skyward, housing the
headquarters of some of the
world's most important financial companies. At the heart
of the complex lies the dazzling Winter Garden, a vast
glass-and-steel public space,
flanked by 45 restaurants and
shops, opening onto a lively
piazza and marina on the
Hudson River. The sweeping
marble staircase leading
down to the Winter Garden
often doubles as seating for
free arts and events, varying
from the classic to the contemporary in music, dance
and theater. Sixteen 50-ft
(15-m) palm trees from the
Mojave Desert make this a
1990s version of the "palm
court" of yesteryear.

Main floor of the Winter Garden

The atrium is a sparkling vault of
glass and steel, 120 ft (36 m) high.

**The "hourglass"
staircase** is used as
extra seating during
concerts in the
Winter Garden.

An esplanade borders the Hudson.

Cafés and shops line the atrium.

Inaugurated in 1988, this is a
place designed for people
and for pleasure, and it has
been hailed as the Rockefeller
Center of the 21st century.

In September 2001, the
Center was damaged in a terrorist attack which destroyed
the World Trade Center (see
p54). The damaged area, including the Winter Garden,
is currently being restored.

World Financial Center viewed from the Hudson River

New York Stock Exchange ❸

IN 1790, TRADING in stocks and shares took place haphazardly on or around Wall Street, but in 1792, 24 brokers who traded under a buttonwood tree at 68 Wall Street signed an agreement to deal only with one another, and the basis of the New York Stock Exchange was formed. Membership is strictly limited. In 1817, a "seat" cost $25; today costs more than two million dollars, and a rigorous test of suitability is required. Visitors can watch the bustle of the trading posts from a gallery overlooking the trading floor. The NYSE has weathered slumps ("bear markets") and booms ("bull markets"), and has seen advances in technology, from tickertape to microchip, turn a local marketplace into a global one.

Ticker-tape Machine
Introduced in the 1870s, these machines printed out up-to-the-minute details of purchase prices on ribbons of paper tape.

Public entrance, Broad Street

Computerized stock tickers flash a steady stream of prices as fast as the human eye is able to read them.

WHAT A TRADING POST DOES

The 17 trading posts each consist of 22 groups or "sections" of traders and technology, each trading the stock of up to 10 listed companies. Commission brokers work for brokerage firms, and rush between booth and trading post, buying and selling securities (stocks and bonds) for the public. A specialist trades in just one stock at a time, quoting bids to other brokers, and independent floor brokers handle orders for busy brokerage firms. Clerks process the orders that come into the trading post via SuperDOT computer into the Exchange's Market Data System. The supervisor's job is to monitor the smooth and legal running of the post. The pages help on the busy exchange floor,

Trading post

bringing orders from the booths to the brokers and specialists. Post display units show stock prices, and flat screens show prices and trades for the specialist.

The 48-Hour Day

During the 1929 Crash, stock exchange clerks worked nonstop for 48 hours. Their mood stayed cheerful despite the panic outside.

Public viewing gallery

Trading post

Trading Floor

On the busiest days, some 2 billion shares are traded for more than 2,000 listed companies. The advanced electronics that support the Designated Order Turnaround (SuperDOT) computer are carried above the chaos of the trading floor in a web of gold piping.

Great Crash of 1929

On Tuesday, October 29, over 16 million shares changed hands as the stock market crashed. Investors thronged Wall Street in bewilderment but, contrary to popular myth, traders did not leap from windows in panic.

Members' entrance, Wall Street

TIMELINE

1792 Buttonwood Agreement signed on May 17

1844 Invention of the telegraph allows trading nationwide

1867 Ticker-tape machines introduced

1903 Present Stock Exchange building opens

1976 DOT system replaces ticker-tape

1987 "Black Monday" crash, October 19. Dow Jones Index drops 508 points

1750	1800	1850	1900	1950	2000

1817 New York Stock & Exchange Board created

1863 Name changed to New York Stock Exchange

1865 New Exchange Building opens at Wall and Broad Streets

1869 "Black Friday" gold crash, September 24

1929 Wall St. Crash, October 29

1981 Trading posts upgraded with electronic units

2001 After 8 years of bull markets, economy starts to sink after Bush election

Crowds gather outside during the 1929 Crash

World Trade Center Site ⑥

Map 1 B2. Ⓜ *Chambers St, Rector St.* Ⓦ *www.wtc-top.com*

IMMORTALIZED by countless film-makers and photographers, the twin towers of the World Trade Center dominated the skyline of Manhattan for 27 years, until September 2001, when they collapsed following a terrorist attack on America *(see p54)*. The enormous weight of each building was supported by an inner wire cage, which melted when two passenger aircraft were flown into the towers.

They were originally part of a complex of buildings consisting of six office blocks and a hotel, connected by a vast underground concourse lined with shops and restaurants. A bridge also linked the complex to the World Financial Center *(see p69)*, which survived the attack.

The World Trade Center was home to some 450 companies from all over the world, employing 50,000 workers.

Large numbers of visitors came to see the unparalleled views from the observation deck or the rooftop promenade at Two World Trade Center. The express elevator took just 58 seconds to reach the 107th floor. At One World Trade Center, this speedy ascent could be taken to the 107th floor for drinks or dining at the Windows on the World restaurant.

One of the Center's most memorable days came on August 7, 1974, when Philippe Petit

The tightrope act in progress

stepped out onto a tightrope between the two towers and entertained crowds of amazed office workers for almost an hour with the ultimate high-rise balancing act.

The future of the site is uncertain, but the construction of a group of smaller office blocks is being discussed. A memorial to the thousands of people who died here is also being planned. At the time of going to press, access to the area was restricted.

Philippe Petit about to step out between the two towers in 1974

Battery Park City ⑦

Map 1 A3. Ⓜ *1,9 to Cortland St.* 🅿 ♿ 🚻 🛗 Ⓦ *www.batteryparkcity.org*

Battery Park City esplanade

GOVERNOR MARIO CUOMO set the tone for this project in 1983 when he urged the developers, "Give it a social purpose – give it a soul." The city's newest neighborhood is an ambitious development on 92 reclaimed acres (37 ha)

along the Hudson River. The offices, buildings, restaurants, apartments, sculptures and gardens emphasize quality and are built very much on a human scale.

Battery Park City will house over 25,000 people. The most visible part is the World Financial Center, four towers centered around the Winter Garden, with its huge atrium lined with palm trees. The total cost has been estimated at $4 billion.

The 1.2 mile walk along the river offers unobstructed views of the Statue of Liberty.

Downtown Athletic Club ⑧

19 West St. **Map** 1 B4. 🄲 *425-7000.* Ⓜ *4, 5 to Bowling Green. Lobby open to visitors.* Ⓦ *www.dacnyc.org*

ONE OF DOWNTOWN's most striking buildings, this 1926 Art Deco creation features a front arcade of

arches with a Moorish flavor and a facade of patterned salt-glazed tiles in a range of colors from burnt orange to brown. The tiles have kept their fresh look, thanks to a natural glaze that has resisted the city soot. The rooms of the club, open to members and their guests, have the calm, sleek atmosphere of an old-fashioned ocean liner.

Downtown Athletic Club facade

Ornate ceiling of the Cunard Building's Great Hall

Cunard Building ❾

25 Broadway. **Map** 1 C3. ⒞ *363-9490* Ⓜ *Bowling Green.* ⓞ *post office hours (see p361.)* **NYC Police Museum** ⒞ *301-4440* ⓞ *10am–6pm Mon–Fri, 10am–4pm Sat, Sun.* Ⓦ *www.nycpolicemuseum.org*

Go PAST the ornate facade, the brass doors, and wrought-iron gates of the US Post Office to see the elaborate, domed Great Hall of this 1921 building. Here, tickets were booked on classic liners such as the *Queen Mary* and the original *Queen Elizabeth*, when the Cunard Line was the largest passenger ship company in the world. The hall has magnificent murals and frescoes, and an ornately decorated ceiling. Paintings by Ezra Winter on the vaulting show the ships of early explorers. The building now houses the new **Police Museum**. The exhibits includes NYPD artifacts, interactive displays, an old station house muster room, seminars and special events.

Bowling Green ❿

Map 1 C4. Ⓜ *Bowling Green.*

THIS TRIANGULAR plot north of Battery Park was the city's earliest park, used first as a cattle market and later as a bowling ground. A statue of King George III stood here until the signing of the Declaration of Independence, when, as a symbol of British rule, the statue was hacked to pieces and smelted for ammunition *(see pp20–21).* The wife of the governor of Connecticut is said to have melted down enough pieces to mold 42,000 bullets.

The fence, erected in 1771, is still standing, but minus the royal crowns that once adorned it. They met the same fate as the statue. The Green was once surrounded by elegant homes. Beyond it is the start of Broadway, which runs the length of Manhattan and, under its formal name of Route 9, all the way north to the State capital in Albany.

Top of a column at the US Custom House

US Custom House ⓫

1 Bowling Green St. **Map** 1 C4. ⒞ *668-6624.* Ⓜ *Bowling Green.* ⓞ *10am–5pm daily, 10am–8pm Thu.* ● *Dec 25.* ⓞ & Ⓦ *www.si.edu/nmai*

ONE OF NEW YORK's finest Beaux Arts designs, this 1907 granite palace by Cass Gilbert is a fitting monument to the city's role as a great seaport, incorporating the talents of the best sculptors and artists of the time. Forty-four stately Ionic columns stand guard, adorned with an ornate frieze. Four heroic sculptures by Daniel Chester French depict four continents as seated women: Asia (contemplative), America (facing optimistically forward), Europe (surrounded by symbols of past glories) and Africa (still sleeping).

Inside, murals by Reginald Marsh decorate the fine marble rotunda, showing the progress of ships into the harbor. Look to your right, opposite the entrance, to see a portrait of movie star Greta Garbo giving a press conference on board ship. In 1973 the US Customs Service moved out, leaving the building empty but for a small bankruptcy court.

The Custom House took on a new function in 1994, when the George Gustav Heye Center of the National Museum of the American Indian was finally unveiled on three floors of the building. The museum's outstanding collection of about a million artifacts along with an archive of many thousands of photographs, spans the breadth of the native cultures of North, Central and South America.

Exhibitions include works by contemporary Native American artists as well as changing displays drawn from the permanent collection.

Fountain at Bowling Green

Statue of Liberty ⓱

A GIFT FROM THE FRENCH to the American people, the statue was the brainchild of sculptor Frédéric-Auguste Bartholdi and has become a symbol of freedom throughout the world. In Emma Lazarus's poem, which is engraved on the base, Lady Liberty says: "Give me your tired, your poor,/ Your huddled masses yearning to breathe free." The statue loomed over Paris before its home on Bedloe's Island (now called Liberty Island) was ready. Unveiled by President Grover Cleveland on October 28, 1886, the statue was restored in time for its 100th anniversary in 1986.

★ **Golden Torch**
In 1986, a new torch replaced the corroded original. The replica's flame is coated in 24-carat gold leaf.

The crown is the highest level open to visitors.

The frame was designed by Gustave Eiffel, who later built the Eiffel Tower. The copper shell hangs on iron bars from a central iron pylon.

A central pylon anchors the 225-ton statue to its base.

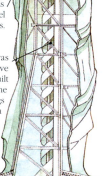

From Her Toes to Her Torch
Three hundred molded copper sheets riveted together make up Lady Liberty.

354 steps lead from the entrance to the crown.

Observation deck and museum

THE STATUE
With a height of 305 ft (93 m) from ground to torch, the Statue of Liberty dominates New York harbor.

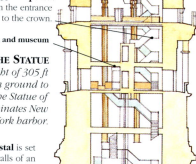

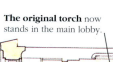

★ **Statue of Liberty Museum**
Posters featuring the statue are among the items on display.

The pedestal is set within the walls of an army fort. It was the largest concrete mass ever poured.

The original torch now stands in the main lobby.

★ **Ferries to Liberty Island**
Ferries cross New York Harbor to Liberty Island, where the Statue offers some of the city's finest views

Portrait of Liberty
Bartholdi's mother was the model for Liberty. The seven rays of her crown represent the seven seas and seven continents.

Making the Hand
To mold the copper shell, the hand was made first in wood, then plaster.

A Model Figure
A series of graduated scale models enabled Bartholdi to build the largest metal statue ever constructed.

FRÉDÉRIC-AUGUSTE BARTHOLDI

The French sculptor who designed the Statue of Liberty intended it as a monument to the freedom he found lacking in his own country. He said "I will try to glorify the Republic and Liberty over there, in the hope that someday I will find it again here." Bartholdi devoted 21 years of his life to making the statue a reality, even traveling to America in 1871 to talk President Ulysses S. Grant and others into funding it and installing it in New York's harbor.

Restoration Celebration
On July 3, 1986, after a $69.8 million clean-up, the statue was unveiled. The $2 million fireworks display was the largest ever seen in America.

STAR FEATURES

★ **Golden Torch**

★ **Statue of Liberty Museum**

★ **Ferries to Liberty Island**

St. Elizabeth Ann Seton Shrine ⓬

7 State St. **Map** 1 C4. 📞 269-6865.
Ⓜ Whitehall, South Ferry. 🕐 6:30am–
5pm Mon–Fri; services. ✝ frequent.
📷 Ⓦ www.setonshrine.org

Elizabeth Ann Seton

Eᴌɪᴢᴀʙᴇᴛʜ ᴀɴɴ Seton (1774–1821), the first native-born American to be canonized by the Catholic Church, lived here from 1801 to 1803. Mother Seton founded the American Sisters of Charity, the first order of nuns in the United States.

After the Civil War, the Mission of Our Lady of the Rosary turned the building into a shelter for homeless Irish immigrant women – 170,000 passed through on their way to a new life in America. The adjoining church was built in 1883. The Mission established and maintains the shrine to Mother Seton.

The house itself was built in 1793, and in 1806 a Federal wing was added, with a curved, columned porch. The Georgian-style and Federal facades have been carefully restored according to an 1859 print. They are all that survives of the early mansions of Lower Manhattan.

Fraunces Tavern Museum ⓭

54 Pearl St. **Map** 1 C4. 📞 425-1778.
Ⓜ South Ferry, Bowling Green.
🕐 10am–4:45pm Tue–Fri. ● public hols, day after Thanksgiving. 🚫 🎦
Lectures, films. 🍴 🛒

Nᴇᴡ York's only full remaining square block of 18th-century commercial buildings contains an exact replica of the Fraunces Tavern, originally built in 1719, where George Washington said farewell to his officers in 1783. The tavern had been an early casualty of the Revolution: the British ship *Asia* shot a cannonball through its roof in August 1775. The building was purchased in 1904 by the Sons of the Revolution in the State of New York. Its restoration in 1907 was one of the nation's first efforts to preserve its heritage.

The restaurant on the ground floor has wood-burning fireplaces and great charm. Upstairs is a museum, with changing exhibits of paintings, prints and decorative arts that interpret the history and culture of early America.

Vietnam Veterans Plaza ⓮

Between Water St and South St.
Map 2 D4. Ⓜ Whitehall, South Ferry.

Tʜɪs ɴᴇᴡʟʏ ʀᴇɴᴏᴠᴀᴛᴇᴅ multilevel brick plaza has an upscale shopping mall below. However, in its center is a huge wall of translucent green glass, engraved with excerpts from speeches, news stories and moving letters to families from servicemen and women who died in the war.

Staten Island Ferry – one of the city's best bargains

Staten Island Ferry ⓯

Whitehall St. **Map** 2 D5.
📞 487-5761 or 487-5766. Ⓜ
South Ferry. 🕐 24 hrs. **Free.** 📷 ♿
See **Practical Information** p353.

Tʜᴇ ғɪʀsᴛ business venture of a promising Staten Island boy named Cornelius Vanderbilt, who later became the railroad magnate, the ferry has operated since 1810, carrying island commuters to

The 18th-century Fraunces Tavern Museum and restaurant

and from the city and offering visitors an unforgettable close-up of the harbor, the Statue of Liberty, Ellis Island and Lower Manhattan's incredible sky-line. The fare is still the city's best bargain: it's free.

Battery Maritime Building 16

11 South St. **Map** 2 D4. M *South Ferry.* ● *to the public.*

FROM 1909 TO 1938, the municipal terminal for ferries to Brooklyn operated here on the site of a small wharf known as Schreijers Hoek, from which Dutch Colonial ships once set sail for the mother country. At the height of the ferry era, 17 lines made regular runs from these bustling piers, which are used now only by the Coast Guard service for Governors Island.

The building was designed in 1907. Arriving boats face 300-ft (91-m) arched openings guarded by tall, ornately scrolled columns and adorned with latticework, molding and rosettes typical of the Beaux Arts period. This is actually a false front of sheet metal and steel, painted green to resemble copper.

Ironwork railing on the Battery Maritime Building

Statue of Liberty 17

See pp74–5.

Ellis Island 18

See pp78–9.

Castle Clinton National Monument in Battery Park

Battery Park 19

Map 1 B4. M *South Ferry, Bowling Green.*

NAMED FOR the cannons that once protected the harbor, the park is wedged between the water and the crush of buildings, and is one of the best places in the city for gazing out to sea. Over the years, landfill has extended the greenery far beyond its original State Street boundary.

Beaux Arts subway entrance at the corner of Battery Park

The park is rimmed with statues and monuments, such as the Netherlands Memorial Monument and memorials to New York's first Jewish immi-grants and the Coast Guard. Others honored are Giovanni da Verrazano, the first explorer to see these shores, and also the poet Emma Lazarus.

Castle Clinton National Monument 20

Battery Park. **Map** 1 B4. ☎ 344-7220. M *Bowling Green, South Ferry.* ◯ *8:30am–5pm daily.* ● *Dec 25.* ◉ ㅤ ⟟ *Concerts.* ⟟ W www.nps.gov.cacl

CASTLE CLINTON WAS built in 1807 as a defense post for the artillery. Originally, it stood about 300 ft (91 m)

offshore, connected to Battery Park by a causeway; but landfill gradually linked it to the mainland. None of its 28 guns was ever used in battle.

The fort was enclosed in 1824 and became a fashion-able theater known as Castle Garden. Phineas T. Barnum introduced "Swedish nightin-gale" Jenny Lind here in 1850. It later preceded Ellis Island as the city's immigration center in 1855, processing 7.5 million newcomers. In 1896, the building was remodeled by McKim, Mead & White to become the New York Aquar-ium, a popular attraction that later moved to Coney Island in 1941 *(see p247)*.

Now it is a monument and the main visitors' center for the National Park Service sites in Manhattan, with exhibits featuring panoramas of New York history. The complex is also the departure point for the Statue of Liberty–Ellis Island ferry *(see p353)*.

Museum of Jewish Heritage 21

18 First Place. **Map** 1 B4. ☎ 968-1800. M *Bowling Green.* ◯ *9am–5pm Sun–Wed, 9am–8pm Thu, 9am–3pm Fri.* ● *Sat, Jewish holidays.* ⬚ ㅤ ⟟ ⟟ *Lectures.* W www.mjhnyc.org

THE MUSEUM OF Jewish Heritage, which opened in 1997, has powerful exhibits telling the story of 20th century Jewish life and serves as a monument to the Holocaust. There are three main themes: pre-Nazi times, the horror of the War, and the hope and renewal of the present day. Photographs, artifacts and films bring the story to life.

Ellis Island ⑱

Half of America's population can trace its roots to Ellis Island, which served as the country's immigration depot from 1892 until 1954. Nearly 17 million people passed through its gates and dispersed across the country in the greatest wave of migration the world has ever known. Today the site is a national museum. Exhibits such as *Through America's Gate* retrace the steps through the entry inspections. *Peopling of America* places Ellis Island within the context of 400 years of US immigration history. Much of this story is told with photos and the voices of actual immigrants. No other place or museum explains so well the "melting pot" that formed the unique character of New York and the nation.

Main building

Rail Ticket
A special fare for emigrants led many on to California.

The railroad office sold tickets onward to the final destination.

★ **Dormitory**
There were separate sleeping quarters for male and female detainees.

THE RESTORATION

Ellis Island lay in ruins until 1990. A $189 million renewal project replaced the copper roof domes, cleaned the mosaic tiles and restored the interior using any surviving original fixtures.

The ferry office sold tickets to New Jersey.

★ **Baggage Room**
The immigrants' meager possessions were checked here on arrival.

Great Hall ★
Immigrant families were made to wait for "processing" in the Registry Room. The old metal railings were replaced with wooden benches in 1911.

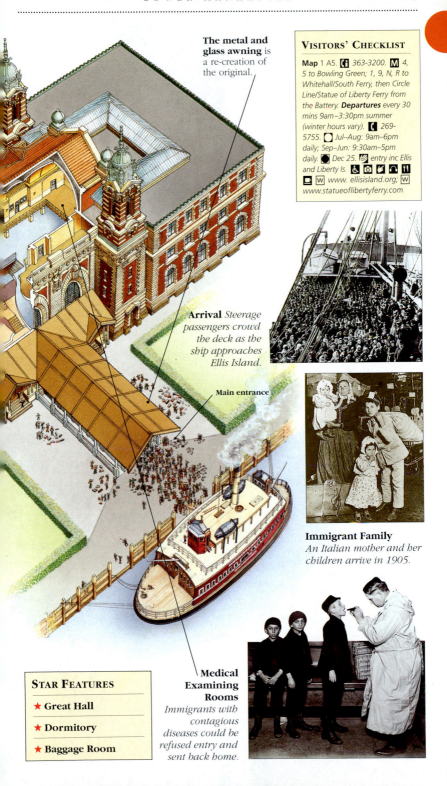

The metal and glass awning is a re-creation of the original.

Arrival *Steerage passengers crowd the deck as the ship approaches Ellis Island.*

Main entrance

Immigrant Family
An Italian mother and her children arrive in 1905.

STAR FEATURES

★ **Great Hall**

★ **Dormitory**

★ **Baggage Room**

Medical Examining Rooms
Immigrants with contagious diseases could be refused entry and sent back home.

SEAPORT AND THE CIVIC CENTER

ANHATTAN'S BUSY Civic Center is the hub of the city, state and federal governments' court systems and the city's police department. In the 1880s it was the heart of the newspaper publishing business as well. The area is still a handsome enclave of imposing architecture with fine landmarks from every period in the city's history, from the 20th-century Woolworth Building to 19th-century City Hall and 18th-century St. Paul's

Ship's figurehead, South Street Seaport

Chapel, New York's oldest building in continuous use. Nearby is South Street Seaport. Called the "street of sails" in the 19th century because of the many ships that were moored there, the seaport underwent a decline when sailing ships became unprofitable. The area has now been restored and is home to a museum and many shops and restaurants. The Brooklyn Bridge, once the largest suspension bridge in the world, lies to the north.

SIGHTS AT A GLANCE

Historic Streets and Buildings
South Street Seaport **1**
Schermerhorn Row **2**
Brooklyn Bridge pp86–9 **3**
Criminal Courts Building **4**
New York County Courthouse **5**
United States Courthouse **6**
Municipal Building **7**
Surrogate's Court, Hall of Records **8**
Old New York County Courthouse **9**
City Hall **10**
Woolworth Building **12**
AT&T Building **14**

Churches
St. Paul's Chapel **13**

Parks and Squares
City Hall Park and Park Row **11**

GETTING THERE
Many subway lines serve the area: the 7th Ave/Broadway 2 and 3 trains to Park Pl; the Lexington Ave 4, 5 and 6 to Brooklyn Bridge; the 8th Ave A, C and E to Chambers St and the N and R to City Hall. By bus take the M1, M6, M9, M10, M15, M101/102 or the M22 crosstown.

SEE ALSO
• *Street Finder,* map 2
• *Restaurants* pp290–92
• *Lower Manhattan Walk* p257

KEY
▨ Street-by-Street map
Ⓜ Subway station
⛴ Riverboat boarding point

0 meters		500
0 yards		500

South Street Seaport

Street by Street: South Street Seaport

PART COMMERCIAL, part historical, the development of South Street Seaport has turned the former heart of the 19th-century port of New York, which had long been neglected, into a lively part of the city. Shops and cafés abound; tall ships are once again moored here. The South Street Seaport museum tells the story of New York's maritime past through craft demonstrations, ship tours and river cruises. Workers from Wall Street come here to eat and drink.

★ **South Street Seaport**
Once full of sailors and sailing ships, the seaport is now a lively complex of shops, restaurants and museums ❶

Cannon's Walk is a 19th- and 20th-century block of buildings, with an outdoor café, shops and a very lively marketplace.

The Titanic Memorial is a lighthouse built in 1913 in memory of those who died on the *Titanic*. It now stands on Fulton Street.

To Fulton St. subway (4 blocks)

Schermerhorn Row
Built as warehouses (1811–13), the buildings now house several businesses, including the North Star Pub (see p308) and Brookstone ❷

The Boat-Building Shop lets you watch as skilled craftspeople build and restore small wooden vessels.

At the Maritime Crafts Center woodcarvers and painters can be seen at work on models, ship carvings and figureheads.

Ship in a bottle

The Pilothouse was originally from a steam tugboat built in 1923 by New York Central. The Seaport's admission and information center is to be found here.

★ **South Street Seaport** (see p308)

STAR SIGHTS

★ **Brooklyn Bridge**

★ **South Street Seaport**

The Consolidated Edison
electrical substation, built in 1975, has an illusionistic mural of the Brooklyn Bridge by Richard Haas on one side to help it blend in with its historic neighbors.

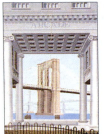

LOCATOR MAP
See Manhattan Map pp12–13

KEY

- - - Suggested route

0 meters   100
0 yards   100

Meyer's Hotel, built in 1873, became a hotel in 1881. Now a bar, it retains a feel of days gone by when markswoman Annie Oakley stayed here.

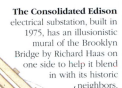

★ Brooklyn Bridge
An engineering wonder when it was built in 1883, the bridge is still remarkable. From the pedestrian walkway there are fine views of the city and the bridge itself **3**

The Fulton Fish Market has been here for over 150 years. Once sold fresh from the boat, the fish now come in by road. The market is open only in the early morning hours *(see p347).*

Pier 17 offers three floors of shops, restaurants and food stands, with great views from the top floor of the Brooklyn Bridge and historic ships.

The schooner
Pioneer is used for river cruises from the Seaport. The 1908 *Ambrose* lightship, which guided ships into port, is also moored here.

The Ambrose lightship at a South Street Seaport pier on the East River

South Street Seaport ●

Fulton St. **Map** 2 E2. 🅲 732-7678. Ⓜ
Fulton St. ⬤ *10am–9pm Mon–Sat,*
11am–8pm Sun. 📷 ♿ ✓ *Concerts.*
🍴 ⬛ **South Street Seaport**
Museum 207 Front St. 🅲 748-8600.
⬤ *May –Sep: 10am–6pm daily; 8pm*
Thu; Oct –Apr: 10am–5pm. ⬤ *Tue; Jan*
1, Thanksgiving, Dec 25. 📷 ♿
✓ *Lectures, exhibits, films.* 🍴 ⬛
Ⓦ www.southstseaport.com; Ⓦ
www.southstseaport.org (for museum)

THE HEART of New York's
19th-century seaport has
been given an imaginative
new lease on life. Glitzy
stores and restaurants sit
harmoniously beside seafaring
craft, historic buildings and
museum exhibits, with spectacular views of Brooklyn
Bridge and the East River
from the cobblestone streets.

The historic ships docked
alongside the piers range from
the little tugboat *W.O. Decker*
to the grand four-masted bark
Peking, the second-largest
sailing ship in existence. Mini-
sailing trips on the schooner
Pioneer are a great way to see
the Seaport from the river.

Fulton Fish Market at dawn

The Fulton Fish Market has
been here since 1821. Though
fish are no longer delivered
from boats but arrive in refrig-
erated trucks, many still find
the busy morning action an
exciting sight, but you'll need
to be there before dawn.

The Museum, founded in
1967, covers the 11 blocks of
what was the country's leading port. In addition to the six
historic ships, the Museum has
more than 10,000 artifacts, artworks, and documents from
the 19th- and early 20th-
century maritime world, as well
as a wealth of archaeological
items from local urban sites.

Schermerhorn Row ●

Fulton and South Sts. **Map** 2 D3.
Ⓜ *Fulton St.*

THIS IS THE architectural
showpiece of the seaport.
Built in 1811 by shipowner
and chandler Peter Schermerhorn on land reclaimed from
the river, the buildings were
originally warehouses and
counting-houses. The opening
of the Brooklyn Ferry termi-
nus in 1814 and of
Fulton Market in
1822 made the block
desirable property.

The Row has been
restored as part of
the South Street
Seaport develop-
ment, and it now
houses a visitors'
center, shops,
restaurants, and an
ice-skating rink.

Brooklyn Bridge ●

See pp86–9.

Criminal Courts Building ●

100 Centre St. **Map** 4 F5.
Ⓜ *Canal St.* **Open** *9am–5pm*
Mon–Fri. **Closed** *public hols.*

THIS 1939 BUILDING is Art
Moderne in style, with
towers reminiscent of a
Babylonian temple. The
three-story-high entrance is
set back in a court, behind
two huge, square free-
standing granite columns –
an intimidating sight for the
accused. The building also
houses the Manhattan
Detention Center for Men,
which was formerly across
the street in a building known
as "The Tombs" because of its
Egyptian-style architecture.
The nickname has stuck,
although the original is long
gone. An aerial walkway, or
"bridge of sighs," links the
courts with the correctional
facility across Centre Street.

The building also houses
the night courts, where cases
are heard from 5pm to 1am
on weekdays.

Entrance to the Criminal
Courts Building

New York County Courthouse ●

60 Centre St. **Map** 2 D1.
Ⓜ *Brooklyn Br-City Hall.* **Open** *9am–*
5pm Mon–Fri. **Closed** *public hols.*

BUILT TO REPLACE the Tweed
Courthouse *(see p90)*, this
new county courthouse was
completed in 1926.

The fluted Corinthian portico at the top of a wide staircase is the main feature of the hexagonal building. The austere exterior is offset by a circular-columned interior rotunda featuring Tiffany lighting fixtures and a series of rich marble and ceiling murals by Attilio Pusterla on themes of law and justice. Six wings radiate from the rotunda, each housing a single court and its facilities.

The courtroom drama *Twelve Angry Men,* starring Henry Fonda, was filmed here.

New York County Courthouse

United States Courthouse **6**

40 Centre St. **Map** 2 D1. **M** Brooklyn Br-City Hall. ◯ 9am–5pm Mon-Fri. ● public hols.

THIS COURTHOUSE is the last work by noted architect Cass Gilbert, designer of the Woolworth Building. Begun in 1933, the year before his death, it was finished by his son. The 31-story structure is

United States Courthouse

a pyramid-topped tower set on a classical temple base. The bronzework on the doors is handsome, but the interior lacks the colorful decoration Gilbert had outlined in his sketchbooks. Aerial walkways link the building with its Police Plaza Annex.

Municipal Building **7**

1 Centre St. **Map** 1 C1. **M** Brooklyn Br-City Hall. ◙ ♿

THE MUNICIPAL Building, constructed in 1914, dominates the Civic Center and straddles Chambers Street. It was McKim, Mead & White's first skyscraper and houses government offices and a marriage chapel. The exterior, in harmony with City Hall, has no excess detail to detract from the earlier building. The most notable feature is the top, a fantasy of towers capped by Adolph Wienman's statue *Civic Fame.*

A railway passage (no longer in use) through the base, and the plaza joining the building to the IRT subway station entrance were built as concessions to modern transportation needs. The building has had a far-reaching influence on architectural style; the main building at Moscow University is said to have been modeled on its design.

Surrogate's Court, Hall of Records **8**

31 Chambers St. **Map** 1 C1. **M** City Hall. ◯ 9am–5pm Mon–Fri. ● public hols. ◙ ♿ ✔

A BEAUX ARTS triumph, the original Hall of Records was begun in 1899 and completed in 1911. The elaborate columned facade is of white Maine granite, with a high mansard roof. The figures by Henry K. Bush-Brown in the roof area represent life's stages from childhood to old age; the statues by Philip Martiny over the colonnade are of notable New Yorkers

Municipal Building

such as Peter Stuyvesant. Martiny also made the representations of New York in its infancy and New York in revolutionary times at the Chambers Street entrance.

The Paris Opéra was the inspiration for the twin marble stairways and painted ceiling of the dazzling central hall. The ceiling mosaic by William de Leftwich Dodge features the signs of the zodiac as well as symbols of record keeping.

The Hall of Records holds public records dating back to 1664. A permanent exhibition, *Windows on the Archives*, features historical papers, drawings, letters and photographs illustrating what life was like in New York from 1626 to the present.

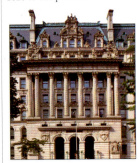

Surrogate's Court

Brooklyn Bridge ❸

Completed in 1883, the Brooklyn Bridge was the largest suspension bridge and the first to be constructed of steel. Engineer John A. Roebling conceived of a bridge spanning the East River while ice-bound on a ferry to Brooklyn. The bridge took 16 years to build, required 600 workers and claimed over 20 lives, including Roebling's. Most died of caisson disease (known as "the bends") after coming up from the underwater excavation chambers. When finished, the bridge linked Manhattan and Brooklyn, then two separate cities.

Souvenir medal cast for
the opening of the bridge

BROOKLYN BRIDGE
From making the wire to sinking the supports, the bridge was built using new techniques.

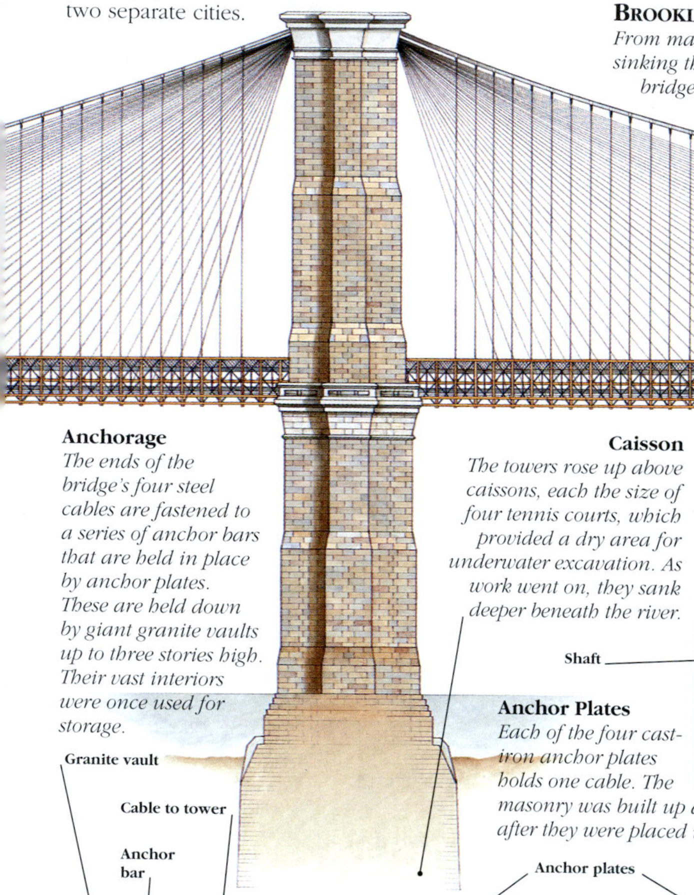

Anchorage
The ends of the bridge's four steel cables are fastened to a series of anchor bars that are held in place by anchor plates. These are held down by giant granite vaults up to three stories high. Their vast interiors were once used for storage.

Granite vault

Cable to tower

Anchor bar

Anchor plate

Vault

Caisson
The towers rose up above caissons, each the size of four tennis courts, which provided a dry area for underwater excavation. As work went on, they sank deeper beneath the river.

Shaft

Anchor Plates
Each of the four cast-iron anchor plates holds one cable. The masonry was built up around them after they were placed in position.

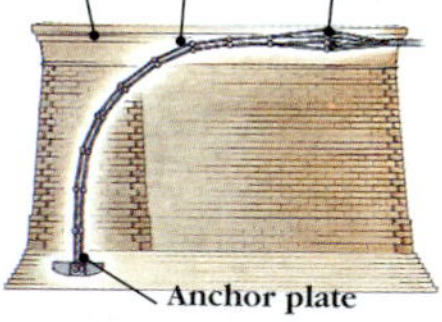

Anchor plates

Central span is 1,595 ft (486 m) long

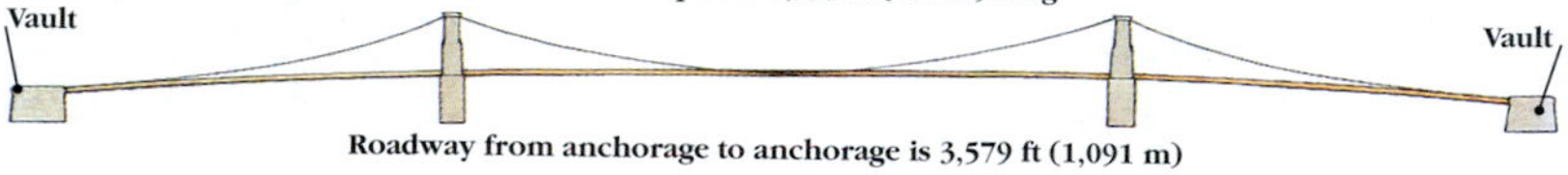

Roadway from anchorage to anchorage is 3,579 ft (1,091 m)

Vault

First Crossing
Master mechanic E.F. Farrington in 1876 was the first to cross the river on the bridge-in-progress, using a steam-driven traveler rope. His journey took 22 minutes.

VISITORS' CHECKLIST

Map 2 D2. **M** 4, 5, 6 to Brooklyn Bridge-City Hall (Manhattan side); A, C to High St, Brooklyn Bridge (Brooklyn side). M9, M22, M101, M102.

Steel Cable Wire
Each cable contains 3,515 miles (5,657 km) of wire, galvanized with zinc for protection from the wind, rain and snow.

Brooklyn Tower (1875)
Two Gothic double arches, each 277 ft (84 m) high, one in Brooklyn, the other in Manhattan, were meant to be the portals of the cities.

JOHN A. ROEBLING
The German-born Roebling designed the bridge. In 1869, just before construction started, his foot was crushed between an incoming ferry and the ferry slip. He died three weeks later. His son, Washington Roebling, finished the bridge, but in 1872 he was taken from a caisson suffering from the bends and became partly paralyzed. His wife, under his tutelage, then took over.

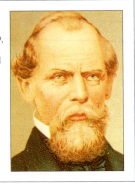

Inside the Caisson
Immigrant workers broke up rocks in the riverbed.

MAKING THE CABLES

Thickness of steel wire (actual size)

End of wire

How the Cables Were Made

Each of the four main cables has 19 strands, each made of 278 steel wires. The wires were not twisted, but laid parallel.

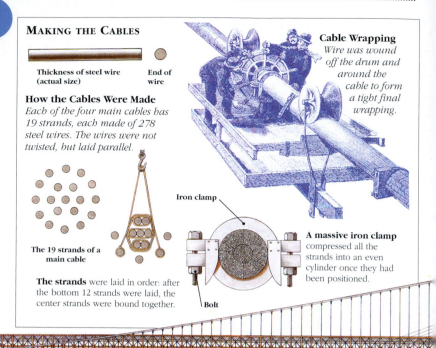

Cable Wrapping

Wire was wound off the drum and around the cable to form a tight final wrapping.

The 19 strands of a main cable

The strands were laid in order: after the bottom 12 strands were laid, the center strands were bound together.

Iron clamp

A massive iron clamp compressed all the strands into an even cylinder once they had been positioned.

Bolt

Bustling Bridge

This 1883 view from the Manhattan side shows the original two outer lanes for horse-drawn carriages, two middle lanes for cable cars and the elevated center walkway.

1983 Centennial Fireworks over the Brooklyn Bridge
Celebrating the bridge's 100th year, this display was awesome.

Panic of May 30, 1883

After a woman tripped on the bridge, panic broke out. Of the estimated 20,000 people on the bridge, 12 were crushed to death.

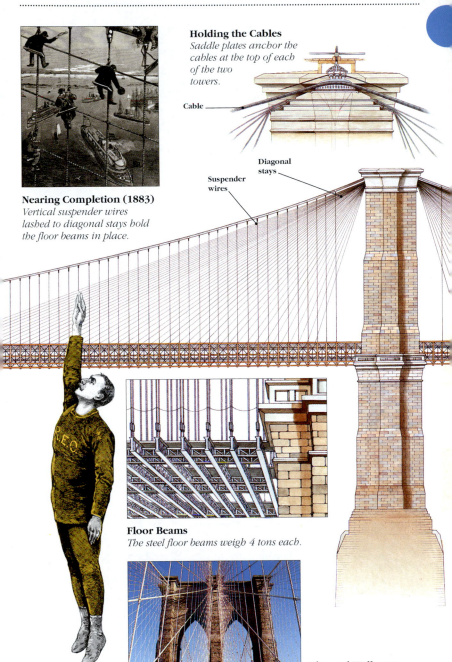

Holding the Cables
Saddle plates anchor the cables at the top of each of the two towers.

Cable

Diagonal stays

Suspender wires

Nearing Completion (1883)
Vertical suspender wires lashed to diagonal stays hold the floor beams in place.

Floor Beams
The steel floor beams weigh 4 tons each.

Odlum's Jump
Robert Odlum was the first to jump off the bridge, on a bet, in May 1885. He later died from internal bleeding.

Elevated Walkway
Poet Walt Whitman said that the view from the walkway – 18 ft (5.5 m) above the road – was "the best, most effective medicine my soul has yet partaken."

Old New York County Courthouse ❾

52 Chambers St. **Map** 1 C1.
Ⓜ *Chambers St-City Hall.* ◑ *for renovation*.

THIS BUILDING is best known for the scandal it caused. It is nicknamed the "Tweed Courthouse" after the political boss who spent 20 times the budget for the building and pocketed $9 million of the total $14 million cost. "Boss" Tweed even bought a marble quarry and sold materials to the city at huge profit. Public outrage eventually led to his downfall in 1871 – ironically, he was tried in his own courthouse and died in a New York jail *(see p25)*.

After an $85 million restoration, including the 85-ft (26-m) rotunda and the grand staircase, this vibrant 19th-century landmark will be the new home of the Museum of the City of New York.

City Hall's imposing early 19th-century facade

City Hall ❿

City Hall Park. **Map** 1 C1. ☎ 788-6865. Ⓜ *Brooklyn Br-City Hall.* ◑ *for prearranged tours only.* ◙ ♿ 📠 788-6865.

CITY HALL, has been the seat of the New York city government since 1812, and is one of the finest examples of early 19th-century American architecture. A stately Federal-style building (with a bit of French Renaissance influence), it was designed by John McComb, Jr., the first prominent American-born architect, and French emigré Joseph Mangin.

Marble cladding was not used for the building's rear, since it was not expected that the city would ever develop farther to the north. In 1954, a program of restoration remedied this and the interior was refurbished.

Mangin is usually given credit for the exterior, McComb for the beautiful interior with its fine domed rotunda encircled by 10 columns. The space beneath it opens onto an elegant marble stairway, leading to the splendid second-floor City Council chambers and the Governor's Room, which houses a portrait gallery of early New York leaders. This magnificent entrance has welcomed rulers and heroes for nearly 200 years. In 1865 Abraham Lincoln's body lay in state in this hall.

Stand on the steps and look to your right to see a statue of Nathan Hale, a US soldier hanged by the British as a spy in September 1776 during the Revolutionary War. His last words – "My only regret is that I have not more lives than one to offer in the service of my country" – won him a permanent place in the history books and hearts of America.

P.T. Barnum's museum blazes as crowds watch from City Hall Park

City Hall Park and Park Row ⓫

Map 1 C2. Ⓜ *Brooklyn Br-City Hall.*

THIS WAS New York's village green 250 years ago, complete with stocks and whipping post. It was the scene of pre-Revolution protests against English rule, and there is a memorial to the "Liberty Poles" (symbols of revolt) on City Hall's west lawn. The Declaration of Independence was read to George Washington and his troops here on July 9, 1776.

Later, Phineas T. Barnum's American Museum at the park's southern tip drew crowds from 1842 until it burned down in 1865. The Park Row building was the site of the Park Theater. From 1798 to 1848, the best actors of the day, such as Edmund Kean and Fanny Kemble, performed there. Park Row runs along the east side of City Hall Park. Once called "Newspaper Row," it was lined with the lofty offices of the *Sun*, *World*, *Tribune* and other papers. Printing

Statue of Benjamin Franklin in Printing House Square

House Square has a statue of Benjamin Franklin with his *Pennsylvania Gazette*.

In 1999 City Hall Park underwent major renovations; its clean, open space is a fine place to sit and relax.

Woolworth Building ⑫

233 Broadway. **Map** 1 C2. Ⓜ *City Hall.* ⬜ *office hours.*

Bas-relief caricature of architect Gilbert in the Woolworth lobby

In 1879, SALESCLERK Frank W. Woolworth opened a new kind of store, where shoppers could see and touch the goods, and everything cost five cents. The chain of stores that followed made him a fortune and changed the face of retailing forever.

The 1913 Gothic headquarters of his empire was New York's tallest building until 1930. It set the standard for the great skyscrapers.

Architect Cass Gilbert's soaring two-tiered design, adorned with gargoyles of bats and other wildlife, is topped with a pyramid roof, flying buttresses, pinnacles and four small towers. The marble interior is rich with filigree, sculptured reliefs and painted decoration, and has a high glass-tile mosaic ceiling that almost seems to glow. The lobby is one of the city's treasures. Gilbert showed his sense of humor here, in bas-relief caricatures of the founder counting out his fortune in nickels and dimes; of the real estate broker closing a deal; and of Cass Gilbert himself cradling a large model of the building. Paid for with $13.5 million in cash, the building has never had a mortgage. Woolworth's went out of business in 1997. The building is now owned by the Witkoff Group.

St. Paul's Chapel ⑬

209-11 Broadway. **Map** 1 C2. 📞 602-0874. Ⓜ *Fulton St.* ⬜ *9am–3pm Mon–Fri, 7am-3pm Sun.* ⬛ *most public hols.* 🕐 *8am Sun.* 📷 *by appt.* **Concerts**.*1pm Mon.* Ⓦ *www.trinitywallstreet.org*

In THE LONG SHADOW of the World Trade Center stands Manhattan's only remaining

The Georgian interior of St. Paul's Chapel

church built before the Revolutionary War. It is a Georgian gem. The colorful interior, lit by Waterford chandeliers, is the setting for free concerts. The pew where newly inaugurated George Washington prayed has been preserved. In the churchyard, the Actor's Monument commemorates George F. Cooke, who played many great roles at the Park Theater; he drank himself to death at the Shakespeare Tavern on Fulton Street.

AT&T Building ⑭

195 Broadway. **Map** 1 C2. Ⓜ *Broadway-Nassau.* ⬜ *office hours.*

COLUMNS, columns everywhere mark this former headquarters designed by Welles Bosworth from 1915 to 1922. The facade is said to have more columns than any other building in the world, and the interior of the building is a forest of marble pillars. The whole edifice looks like a gigantic square-topped layer cake.

A sea sprite above the door of the AT&T (American Telephone and Telegraph) Building

LOWER EAST SIDE

19th-century tin, Lower East Side Tenement Museum

Nowhere does the strong ethnic flavor of New York come through more clearly than in Lower Manhattan, where many immigrants first settled. Here Italians, Chinese and Jews established distinct neighborhoods, preserving their languages, customs, foods and religions in the midst of a strange land. New immigrants from many nations now occupy some of these neighborhoods of low-rise buildings, but the old flavor remains. The area brims with restaurants, some of the city's greatest bargains and a spirit found nowhere else. The composer Irving Berlin grew up here. Looking back on those days he said: "Everybody ought to have a Lower East Side in their life."

SIGHTS AT A GLANCE

Historic Streets and Buildings
Home Savings of America ❶
Police Headquarters Building ❷
Little Italy ❸
Chinatown ❹
Orchard Street ❽
Delancey Street ❿

Puck Building ⓬
Engine Company No. 31 ⓮

Parks and Squares
Columbus Park ❺

Museums and Galleries
Lower East Side Tenement Museum ❼

Churches and Synagogues
Eldridge Street Synagogue ❻
Bialystoker Synagogue ❾
Old St. Patrick's Cathedral ⓭

Landmark Stores
Schapiro's Winery ⓫

GETTING THERE

Chinatown and Little Italy can be reached by subway on the N and R or the Lexington Ave 4, 5 and 6 trains to Canal St, or by taking the M101/102 bus. The Lower East Side is served by the B and D trains to Grand St, the F train to Delancey St or the M15 bus.

SEE ALSO

0 meters 500
0 yards 500

KEY

▨ Street-by-Street map

Ⓜ Subway station

Dragon puppet in Chinatown at Chinese New Year

Street by Street: Little Italy and Chinatown

NEW YORK'S LARGEST and most colorful ethnic neighborhood is Chinatown, which is growing so rapidly that it is overrunning nearby Little Italy as well as the Lower East Side. Streets here teem with grocery stores, gift shops and hundreds of Chinese restaurants; even the plainest offer good food. What is left of Little Italy can be found at Mulberry and Grand streets, where old-world flavor abounds.

★ **Little Italy**
The scents of Italy still waft from the restaurants and bakeries of this area, once home to thousands of immigrants. ❸

★ **Chinatown**
Home to a thriving – and still expanding – community of Chinese immigrants, this area is famous for its restaurants and hectic street life. The area truly comes alive around the Chinese New Year in January or February ❹

The Market on Canal Street has a wide range of bargains in new and used clothes and fresh produce.

Ⓜ **Canal Street subway (lines N, R, 4, 5, 6)**

The Eastern States Buddhist Temple at 64b Mott Street contains over 100 golden Buddhas.

The Wall of Democracy on Bayard Street is covered with newspapers and posters describing the situation in China.

Columbus Park ❺
This park was once the site of 19th century New York's worst slum.

Confucius Plaza is marked by sculptor Liu Shih's monument to the Oriental philosopher.

Chatham Square has a memorial to Chinese-American war dead.

Police Headquarters Building
The dome of this Baroque civic building towers over the City Hall area. In 1973, the police moved out; ten years later the building was turned into apartments ❷

LOCATOR MAP
See Manhattan Map pp12–13

Umbertos Clam House
serves Italian seafood. It is also known as the place where Mafia boss Joey Gallo was shot in 1972.

KEY

— — — Suggested route

0 meters 100
0 yards 100

Home Savings of America
Stanford White designed this in 1894 for the old Bowery Savings Bank ❶

★ **Eldridge Street Synagogue**
Now restored, this is the first temple of its size built in the US by European Jews ❻

Bloody Angle, where Doyers Street turns sharply, was the gruesome site of many gangland ambushes during the 1920s.

STAR SIGHTS

★ **Eldridge Street Synagogue**

★ **Chinatown**

★ **Little Italy**

Home Savings of America ❶

130 Bowery. **Map** 4 F4. **M** *Grand St, Bowery.* ○ *banking hours.*

Imposing inside and out, this Classical Revival building was built for the Bowery Savings Bank in 1894. Architect Stanford White designed the ornamented lime-stone facade to wrap around the rival Butchers' and Drovers' Bank, which refused to sell the corner plot. The interior is decorated with marble pillars and a ceiling scattered with gilded rosettes.

By the middle of the 20th century, the bank was a contrast to the Bowery with its vagrants and flophouses.

Detail from Home Savings of America

Police Headquarters Building ❷

240 Centre St. **Map** 4 F4. **M** *Canal St.* ● *to the public.*

Completed in 1909, this was a fitting home for the city's new professional police force. Corinthian columns line the main portico and the end pavilions, and the dome dominates the skyline. However, lack of space meant the headquarters had to conform to an awkward, wedge-shaped site in the midst of Little Italy.

For nearly three-quarters of a century, this was where "New York's finest" came to

work. During Prohibition, Grand Street from here to the Bowery was known as "Bootleggers' Row," and alcohol was easily obtained except when a police raid was due. The liquor merchants paid handsomely for a tip-off from inside police headquarters.

The police moved to new headquarters in 1973, and in 1985 the building was converted into a luxury cooperative apartment project.

Little Italy ❸

Streets around Mulberry St. **Map** 4 F4. **M** *Canal St.* Ⓦ *www.littleitalynyc.com*

The southern Italians who came to New York in the late 19th century found themselves living in the squalor of "dumbbell" apartments. These were built so close together that sunlight never reached the lower windows or back-yards. With over 40,000 people living in 17 small, unsanitary blocks, diseases such as tuberculosis were rife.

Despite the privations of life on the Lower East Side, the community that grew up around Mulberry Street was lively with the colors, flavors and atmosphere of its homeland. These have lingered on, although the Italian population has

dwindled to a mere 5,000 and the boundaries of Chinatown have encroached on the traditional "Little Italy."

The most exciting time to visit is during the Feast of San Gennaro, which is held around September 19 *(see p52)*. For nine days each year, Mulberry Street is renamed Via San Gennaro. On the saint's day, his shrine and relics are paraded through the streets. Throughout the feast the milling crowds enjoy music, dancing, fairground sideshows and stalls selling every conceivable kind of Italian food and drink, as well as other ethnic cuisines.

Little Italy's restaurants offer simple, rustic food served in friendly surroundings at reasonable prices.

Italian café in Little Italy

Chinatown ❹

Streets around Mott St. **Map** 4 F5. **M** *Canal St.* **Eastern States Buddhist Temple** ○ *9am–8pm daily.*

The chinatown of the early 20th century was primarily a male community, made up of immigrants who had first gone to California. Wages were sent home to their families in China who were prevented from joining them by US immigration laws. The men relaxed by gambling at mahjong. The community remained isolated from the rest of the city, financed and controlled by its own secret organizations, the Tongs.

Some of the Tongs were simply family associations who provided loans. Others, such as the On Leong and the Hip Sing, who were at war with one another, were criminal fraternities. Tiny, crooked Doyers Street was called "Bloody Angle"; enemies were lured there and set

Stonework figures adorning the Police Headquarters Building

A Chinese grocer tending his shop on Canal Street

upon by gang members waiting around the bend.

A truce between the Tongs in 1933 brought peace to Chinatown. By 1940 it was home to many middle-class families. Immigrants and businesses from Hong Kong also brought postwar prosperity to the community. Today over 80,000 Chinese-Americans live here.

Many people visit the neighborhood simply to feast on Chinese cuisine, but there is more to do here than eat. There are also galleries, antiques and curio shops, and Oriental festivals *(see p53)*. To glimpse another side of Chinatown, step into the incense-scented dimness of the Eastern States Buddhist Temple at 64b Mott Street, where offerings are piled up and over 100 golden Buddhas gleam in the candlelight.

Columbus Park ❺

Map 4 F5. **M** *Canal St.*

THE TRANQUILLITY of Columbus Park today could not be further removed from the scene near this site in the early 1800s. The area, known as Mulberry Bend, was a red-light district, part of the infamous Five Points slum. Gangs with names like the Dead Rabbits and the Plug Uglies roamed the streets. A murder a day was commonplace; even the police were afraid to pass through. Partly as a result of the writings of reformer Jacob Riis *(see p47)*, the slum was finally taken down in 1892. Now the park is the only open space in all of Chinatown.

Eldridge Street Synagogue ❻

12 Eldridge St. **Map** 5 A5.
C *219-0888.* **M** *East Broadway.*
◯ *11am-4pm Sun.* **✦** *Fri at sundown, Sat 10am onward* ◲ Ø
✦ *11am & 2:30pm Tue, Thu, and by appt.* **◻** **W** *www.eldridgestreet.org*

WHEN THIS HOUSE of worship was built by the Orthodox Ashkenazi from Eastern Europe in 1887, it was the most flamboyant temple in the neighborhood. But many immigrant Jews saw the Lower East Side as just the beginning of a new life, and later moved out of this massive synagogue.

In the 1930s, the huge sanctuary, rich with stained glass, brass chandeliers, marbleized wood paneling and fine carving, was closed. Three decades later a group of citizens raised funds for preservation, and restoration is now complete. A brief audiovisual presentation recounts the history of the synagogue and its renovation.

Even after years of neglect, the facade, with touches of Romanesque, Gothic and Moorish designs, is impressive. Inside, the Italian hand-carved ark and sculpted wooden balcony show why this building was the pride of the area.

Lower East Side Tenement Museum ❼

90 Orchard St. **Map** 5 A4.
C *431-0233.* **M** *Delancey, Grand St.*
◯ for ◲ *only, 11am–5:30pm, (every 20 mins) daily.* **●** *Jan 1, Thanksgiving, Dec 25.* ◲ Ø
▣ ***Lectures, films, videos.***
W *www.tenement.org*

Street vendor's pushcart (1890s) from the museum

THE INTERIOR of this building was restored to re-create apartments as they appeared in the late 1870s, in 1916, 1918, and 1935. There were no regulations on tenement living conditions until 1879. Many rooms had no windows, and indoor plumbing was rare. The rooms give a sense of the cramped and deplorable conditions in which so many lived. The museum program includes the newest exhibit "The Sweatshop Apartment" and offers excellent walking tours of the area.

Stained glass from the Synagogue

Orchard Street 8

Map 5 A3. **M** *Delancey, Grand St.
See **Shopping** p312.*
W www.lowereastsideny.com

JEWISH IMMIGRANTS founded the New York garment industry on Orchard Street, named after the orchards that once stood here on James De Lancey's colonial estate. For many years the street was filled with pushcarts loaded with goods for sale, many of which were made at home in the teeming tenements of the neighborhood.

The pushcarts are long gone and not all the shopkeepers are Jewish, but the flavor remains and the stores still close on Saturday, the Jewish Sabbath. On Sunday there is an outdoor market, and shoppers fill the street from Houston to Canal, looking for clothing bargains.

Zodiac mural from the synagogue

Bialystoker Synagogue 9

7–11 Willett St. **Map** 5 C4.
C 475-0165. **M** *Essex St.*
★ *frequent services.* **O**

THIS 1826 Federal-style building was originally the Willett Street Methodist Church. It was bought in 1905 by Jewish immigrants from the Bialystok province in Poland, who converted it into a synagogue. For this reason, it faces west instead of the traditional east. It has a beautiful interior, with lovely stained-glass windows, a

Canal Street Market vegetable stall

three-story carved wooden ark and murals representing the signs of the zodiac and views of the Holy Land.

Delancey Street 10

Map 5 C4. **M** *Essex St. See **Shopping** p312.*

ONCE A MAJESTIC boulevard, Delancey Street today is little more than an obligatory entrance to the Williamsburg Bridge. The street was named for James De Lancey, whose farm was situated here during colonial days. De Lancey remained loyal to George III during the Revolution and fled to England after the war, before his land was seized.

Most of the stores on this once-grand shopping street are now run-down, but you can still buy an authentic English bowler hat (not to mention an authentic American Stetson cowboy hat, or almost any other kind of hat) at the Buranelli Hat Company at 101 Delancey.

Schapiro's Winery 11

126 Rivington St. **Map** 5 B3.
C 674-4404. **M** *Essex St.* **O**
11am–5pm Mon–Thu, 10am–5pm Sun. **●** *Jewish hols, Fri.* **O** **&**
● *hourly, Sun only. Reservations necessary.* **W** www.shapiro-wine.com

SCHAPIRO'S was founded in 1899 so that Jewish immigrants to New York could have their traditional kosher wines for the Sabbath

and holidays. It has survived Prohibition, the Depression and the dwindling numbers of local Jewish residents. The owner swears it will still be in business when his grandchildren have grandchildren.

Today, Schapiro's produces 32 different types of wine. Though the grapes are now crushed in upstate New York, fermenting and bottling are still done on the premises. The operation can be seen on "quickie" tours; afterward, you can taste the sweet, thick wine that gave rise to Schapiro's motto: "You can almost cut it with a knife!"

Farther east along Rivington Street at No. 150, Streit's Matzoh is another long-established neighborhood landmark, where visitors can

Schapiro's kosher wine

watch the freshly baked unleavened bread rolling off conveyor belts behind the sales counter.

Puck Building 12

295–309 Lafayette St. **Map** 4 F3.
M *Lafayette.* ○ *to the public during business hours.* **C** *274-8900.*

Puck statue on building's north-east corner

THIS BLOCK-SQUARE architectural curiosity was built in 1885 by Albert and Herman Wagner. It is an adaptation of the German *Rundbogenstil*, a mid-19th-century style characterized by horizontal bands of arched windows and the skillful use of molded red brick.

The building is part of the city's publishing history. Situated on the edge of Manhattan's old printing district, from 1887 to 1916 it housed the satirical *Puck*, a magazine similar to the British *Punch*. At the turn of the century it was the largest building in the world devoted to lithography and publishing.

Today it is used as the site of some of New York's most stylish parties and artiest fashion-photography shoots. The only connection remaining to the mythical Puck is the gold-leaf statue on the third-floor corner of Mulberry and Houston, and the smaller version over the entrance on Lafayette Street.

Walk half a block and you will see a display of *Puck* covers in Bars and Backbars at 49 East Houston.

Old St. Patrick's Cathedral 13

263 Mulberry St. **Map** 4 F3.
C *226-8075.*
M *Prince St.* ○ *daily 8am–1pm, 3:30–9pm* ●
Wed. ✝ *9:00am, Mon-Sat, 5:30pm Sat, 9:30am Sun, Spanish 11:00am Sun.*
W *www.oldsaintpatricks.org*

THE FIRST St. Patrick's was begun in 1809 – one of the oldest churches in the city. When fire destroyed the original in the 1860s, it was rebuilt much as it is today. When the archdiocese moved the cathedral uptown *(see pp176–7)*, it became the local parish church, and has flourished despite a constantly changing ethnic congregation.

Below the church are vaults containing the remains of, among others, one of New York's most famous families of restaurateurs, the Delmonicos. Pierre Toussaint was also buried here. In 1990 his remains were moved from the old graveyard beside the church to a more prestigious burial place in a crypt in the uptown St. Patrick's. Born as a slave in Haiti in 1766, Toussaint was brought to New York, where he became

Old St. Patrick's Cathedral

a prosperous wig-maker as a free man. He later devoted himself to the poor, tending cholera victims and using his money to build an orphanage. The Vatican is now considering him for sainthood.

Engine Company No. 31 14

87 Lafayette St. **Map** 4 F3.
C *966-4510.* **M** *Canal St.*
○ *to the public.*

IN THE 19TH CENTURY, fire stations were considered important enough to merit a building of architectural importance and the Le Brun firm was the acknowledged master of the art. This 1895 station is one of their best. The building resembles a Loire château, with its steep roof, dormers and towers, seeming almost fairy tale-like in this location.

The present-day tenant is the Downtown Community Television Center, which offers courses and workshops to members but which is no longer open to the public.

Facade of Engine Company 31, in the style of a French château

SoHo and TriBeCa

ART AND architecture are the twin lures that have transformed these formerly industrial districts. SoHo (south of Houston) was threatened with demolition in the 1960s until preservationists drew attention to the rare cast-iron architecture. The district was saved, and artists began to move into the loft spaces.

Storefront of a SoHo bakery

Galleries, cafés, shops and designer boutiques followed. Brunch and gallery hopping in SoHo is now a favorite weekend outing. As rents rose, many artists were priced out of SoHo and moved to TriBeCa (triangle below Canal). Now, trendy TriBeCa not only attracts galleries but also has many of the city's newest restaurants.

SIGHTS AT A GLANCE

Historic Streets and Buildings
Haughwout Building ❶
St. Nicholas Hotel ❷
Greene Street ❸
Singer Building ❹

Harrison Street ❾
White Street ❿

Museums and Galleries
Guggenheim Museum SoHo ❺
Museum for African Art ❼

New Museum of Contemporary Art ❻
New York City Fire Museum ❽

GETTING THERE
Take the 6th Ave D or F subway to Broadway-Lafayette; the Lexington Ave 6 to Bleecker St; or the N or R to Prince St. For Canal St, take the 7th Ave/Broadway 1 or 9; the 8th Ave A, C or E; or the Lexington Ave 4, 5, 6, N or R. Bus routes are the M1, M6, and the M21 Houston St crosstown.

SEE ALSO
• **Street Finder,** map 4
• **SoHo Walk** pp260
• **Restaurants** pp290–92

0 meters 500
0 yards 500

KEY
Street-by-Street map
M Subway station

Cast-iron facades on Greene Street

Street by Street: SoHo Cast-Iron Historic District

THE LARGEST concentration of cast-iron architecture in the world *(see p40)* survives in the area between West Houston and Canal streets. The heart of the district is Greene Street, where 50 buildings erected between 1869 and 1895 are found on five cobblestoned blocks. The intricately designed facades were mass-produced in a foundry but are now rare works of industrial art, well suited to the character of the district.

West Broadway, as it passes through SoHo, combines striking architecture with a string of art galleries, art shops, designer boutiques, and small restaurants.

Zona at 97 Greene Street stocks original and imaginative items for the home.

Creature from the Enchanted Forest

72–76 Greene Street, the "King of Greene Street," is a splendid Corinthian-columned building. It was the creation of Isaac F. Duckworth, one of the masters of cast-iron design.

Enchanted Forest casts a magic spell, just as its name suggests, selling children's toys and books in a fairy-tale forest setting. *(See p314.)*

Performing Garage is a tiny experimental theater that pioneers the work of avant-garde artists.

★ **Greene Street**
Of all Greene Street's fine cast-iron architecture, one of the best is 28–30, the "Queen," which was built by Duckworth in 1872, and has a tall mansard roof ❸

Canal Street-Broadway subway (2 blocks)

10–14 Greene Street dates from 1869. Note the glass circles in the risers of the iron stoop, which allowed daylight to reach the basement.

15–17 Greene Street is a late addition from 1895, in a simple Corinthian style.

Pace-Wildenstein Gallery is one of a group of galleries housed in a Tuscan-style cast-iron building by Henry Fernbach. *(See p324.)*

LOCATOR MAP
See Manhattan Map pp12–13

KEY

– – – Suggested route

Guggenheim Museum SoHo
Museum Mile's modern giant has branched out into the heart of SoHo, to rapturous acclaim ❺

★ **Singer Building**
This terra-cotta beauty was built in 1904 for the famous sewing machine company ❹

New Museum of Contemporary Art
This museum is dedicated to showing innovative work by living artists ❻

Prince Street subway station (lines N, R)

Dean & DeLuca is one of the best gourmet food stores in New York. Its range includes a global choice of coffee beans. *(See p326.)*

Richard Haas, the prolific muralist, has transformed a blank wall into a convincing cast-iron frontage.

101 Spring Street, with its simple, geometric facade and large windows, is a fine example of the style that led to the skyscraper.

St. Nicholas Hotel
During the Civil War, this former luxury hotel was used as a headquarters for the Union Army ❷

0 meters 100
0 yards 100

Haughwout Building
In 1857 this was an elegant store, featuring the first Otis safety elevator ❶

Haughwout Building ❶

488–492 Broadway. **Map** 4 E4.
Ⓜ *Canal St.*

Haughwout Building facade

THIS CAST-IRON building was
erected in 1857 for the
E.V. Haughwout china and
glassware company, which
once supplied the White
House. Beneath the grime,
the design is superb: rows of
windows are framed by arches
set on columns flanked by
taller columns. Mass-produced
sections repeat the pattern
over and over. The building
was the first to use a steam-
driven Otis safety elevator, an
innovation that made the
skyscraper a possibility.

St. Nicholas Hotel ❷

521–523 Broadway. **Map** 4 E4.
Ⓜ *Prince St.*

ENGLISH PARLIAMENTARIAN
W.E. Baxter, visiting New
York in 1854, reported of the
recently opened St. Nicholas
Hotel: "Every carpet is of velvet
pile; chair covers and curtains
are made of silk or satin
damask … and the embroidery
on the mosquito nettings itself

**St. Nicholas Hotel in its heyday in
the mid-19th century**

might be exhibited to royalty."
It is small wonder, then, that
it cost over $1 million to build
– and with profits of over
$50,000 for that year it must
have seemed money well
spent. Its glory was short-lived,
however. In the Civil War it
served as a Union Army headquarters. Afterward, the better
hotels followed the entertainment district uptown, and by
the mid-1870s the St. Nicholas
had closed. There is little left
on the ground floor to attest
to its former opulence, but
look up to the remains of its
once-stunning marble facade.

Greene Street ❸

Map 4 E4. Ⓜ *Canal St.*

Haas mural on Greene Street

THIS IS THE HEART of SoHo's
Cast-Iron District. Along
five cobblestoned blocks are
50 cast-iron buildings dating
from 1869 to 1895. The block
between Broome and Spring
streets has 13 full cast-iron
facades and from 8–34 is
the longest row of cast-
iron buildings anywhere.
Those at 72–76
are known as
the "King of
Greene Street,"
but 28–30, the
"Queen," is
considered to
be the finest.
The architecture
is best appreci-
ated as a
streetscape, with row
upon row of
columned facades.
Walk into any
of the galleries housed
within to see the
spacious interior lofts.

At the corner of Greene and
Prince streets, the illusionistic
muralist Richard Haas has
created an eye-catching work,
disguising a plain brick side
wall as a cast-iron frontage.
Look for the detail of the little
gray cat, which sits primly in
an "open window."

Singer Building ❹

561–563 Broadway. **Map** 4 E3.
Ⓜ *Prince St.*

THE "LITTLE" Singer Building
built by Ernest Flagg in
1904 is the second and
smaller Flagg structure by this
name, and many critics think
it superior to the 41-story
tower on lower Broadway
that was torn down in 1967.
The charmingly ornate
building is adorned with
wrought-iron balconies and
graceful arches painted in
striking dark green. The 12-
story facade of terra-cotta,
glass and steel was advanced
for its day, a forerunner of
the metal and glass walls to
come in the 1940s and 1950s.
The building was an office
and warehouse for the Singer
sewing machine company,
and the original Singer name
can be seen cast in iron
above the entrance to the
store on Prince Street.

**Early electric-powered
Singer sewing machine**

Guggenheim Museum SoHo ⑤

575 Broadway. **Map** 4 E3.
🄲 423-3600. Ⓜ Prince St.
🄾 11am–6pm Thu–Mon. ♿
🅆 www.guggenheim.org.

THIS DRAMATIC gallery opened in 1992 to critical acclaim. Designed by architect Arata Isozake, it features displays that complement those at the main Guggenheim Museum *(see p186)*.

New Museum of Contemporary Art ⑥

583 Broadway. **Map** 4 E3. 🄲 219-1222. Ⓜ Prince St. 🄾 noon–6pm Wed, Sun, noon–8pm Thu, Fri, Sat. 🄻 **Lectures, readings.** 🄿 🅆 www.newmuseum.org

Les Enfants de Dijon by Christian Boltanski, at the New Museum

MARCIA TUCKER left her post as the Whitney Museum's Curator of Painting and Sculpture in 1977 to found this museum. Jeff Koons and the late John Cage are among those whose work has been featured in thematic shows. Tucker exhibits the kind of work she feels is missing from more traditional museums.

Museum for African Art ⑦

593 Broadway. **Map** 4 E3. 🄲 966-1313 Ⓜ Prince St. 🄾 10.30am–5.30pm Tue–Fri, noon–6pm Sat.. 🄾 (free Sun). 🄿 🅆 www.africanart.org

ONE OF ONLY two American museums devoted to African art, these galleries have been ingeniously designed by architect Maya Lin, creator of Washington's Vietnam Veteran's Memorial. The high-caliber changing shows often tour to major museums in the US and abroad. The museum also offers lectures, music and dance performances, and includes an excellent shop.

1901 La France horse-drawn steam pumper in the City Fire Museum

New York City Fire Museum ⑧

278 Spring St. **Map** 4 D4. 🄲 691-1303. Ⓜ Spring St. 🄾 10am–4pm Tue–Sun. 🄾 ♿ 🅆 nycfiremuseum.org

THIS SPLENDID museum is housed in a Beaux Arts–style 1904 firehouse. New York city's unsurpassed collection of fire-fighting equipment and memorabilia from the 18th century to 1917 includes scale models, bells and hydrants. Upstairs, fire engines are neatly lined up for an 1890 parade. A new interactive fire simulation exhibit is great for kids.

Harrison Street ⑨

Map 4 D5. Ⓜ Chambers St.

SURROUNDED BY modern high-rise blocks, this rare row of eight beautifully restored Federal town houses, with their pitched roofs and distinctive dormer windows, almost seems like a stage set. The houses were constructed in the late 1700s and early 1800s. Two of the buildings were designed by John McComb, Jr., New York's first major native-born architect, and were moved from Washington Street, their original site, for preservation purposes. The houses had previously been used as warehouses and were about to be razed to the ground, when, in 1969, the Landmarks Preservation Commission intervened and helped secure the necessary funding to enable them to be completely restored. They are now privately owned.

On the other side of the high-rise complex is Washington Market Park. this area was formerly the site of New York city's wholesale produce center. The market moved from this historic district and relocated to the Bronx at the beginning of the 1970s.

White Street ⑩

Map 4 E5. Ⓜ Franklin St.

WHILE NOT as fine and intricate as some of the SoHo blocks, this sampling of TriBeCa cast-iron architecture shows a considerably wide range of styles. The house at No. 2 has carefully balanced Federal features and a rare gambrel roof, in contrast with the mansard roof of No. 17 (the Alternative Museum). Numbers 8 to 10 White, designed by Silesian-born Henry Fernbach, in 1869, have impressive Tuscan columns and arches, with Neo-Renaissance shorter upper stories to give an illusion of height. In contrast, 38 White is the home of neon artist Rudi Stern's gallery, Let There Be Neon.

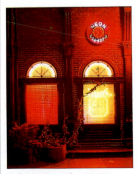

Rudi Stern's Let There Be Neon gallery in White Street

GREENWICH VILLAGE

NEW YORKERS call it simply "the Village," and it did indeed begin as a country village, an escape for city dwellers during the yellow fever epidemic of 1822. The crazy-quilt pattern of streets, reflecting early farm boundaries or streams, could not be made to conform to the city's grid plan, and Greenwich Village has

Jazz club flag on West 3rd Street

remained an enclave apart, a bohemian haven that has been home to many celebrated artists and writers. A popular gay district is here, but on the whole the area has become mainstream and very high-priced. Near Washington Square, it is dominated by New York University students. Nonconformists tend to live in the cheaper East Village.

SIGHTS AT A GLANCE

Historic Streets and Buildings
St. Luke's Place ❶
75½ Bedford Street ❷
Isaacs-Hendricks House ❸

Grove Court ❹
Jefferson Market Courthouse ❻
Patchin Place ❼
Salmagundi Club ❾
Washington Mews ⓬
New York University ⓭

Museums and Galleries
Forbes Magazine Building ❽

Churches
First Presbyterian Church ❿
Church of the Ascension ⓫
Judson Memorial Church ⓮

Parks and Squares
Sheridan Square ❺
Washington Square ⓯

GETTING THERE

By subway, take lines A, B, C, D, E, F or Q to West 4th St-Washington Sq, the 7th Ave 1 and 9 to Christopher St-Sheridan Sq or the R to 8th St. By bus take the M1, M5, M6 or the M8 crosstown.

0 meters   500
0 yards   500

SEE ALSO

• **Street Finder,** maps 3–4

• **Village Walk** pp260–61

• **Where to Stay** pp274–5

• **Restaurants** pp290–92

KEY

Street-by-Street map

M Subway station

Billboards on the corner of Christopher Street and Seventh Avenue South

Street by Street: Greenwich Village

ASTROLL THROUGH HISTORIC Greenwich Village is a feast of unexpected small pleasures – charming row houses, hidden alleys and leafy courtyards. The often quirky architecture suits the bohemian air of the Village. Many famous people, particularly artists and writers, such as playwright Eugene O'Neill and actor Dustin Hoffman, have made their homes in the houses and apartments that line these old-fashioned narrow streets. By night, the Village really comes alive. Late-night coffeehouses and cafés, experimental theaters and music clubs, including some of the best jazz venues, beckon you at every turn.

The Lucille Lortel Theater is at 121 Christopher Street; it opened in 1955 with *The Threepenny Opera*.

Christopher Street, a part of New York's gay community, is lined with all kinds of shops, bookstores and bars.

Twin Peaks at 102 Bedford Street began life in 1830 as an ordinary house. It was rebuilt in 1926 by architect Clifford Daily to house artists, writers and actors. Daily believed that the quirky house would help their creativity flourish.

Grove Court
Six houses dating from 1853 to 1854 are set at the back of a leafy courtyard ❹

Chumley's at 86 Bedford Street *(see p309),* once a speakeasy, now a restaurant, still seems secret. There is no sign outside, just a small menu.

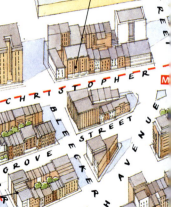

75½ Bedford Street
Built in 1873 in an alley, this is the city's narrowest house ❷

★ **St. Luke's Place**
This beautiful row of Italianate houses was built in the 1850s ❶

To Houston Street subway (2 blocks)

The Cherry Lane Theater was founded in 1924. Originally a brewery, it was one of the first of the Off-Broadway theatres.

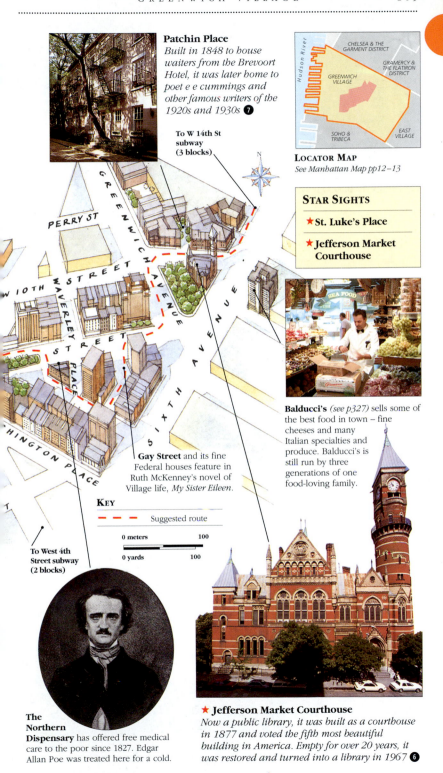

Patchin Place
Built in 1848 to house waiters from the Brevoort Hotel, it was later home to poet e e cummings and other famous writers of the 1920s and 1930s **7**

To W 14th St subway (3 blocks)

CHELSEA & THE GARMENT DISTRICT

Hudson River

GRAMERCY & THE FLATIRON DISTRICT

GREENWICH VILLAGE

SOHO & TRIBECA

EAST VILLAGE

LOCATOR MAP
See Manhattan Map pp12–13

STAR SIGHTS

★ **St. Luke's Place**

★ **Jefferson Market Courthouse**

Balducci's *(see p327)* sells some of the best food in town – fine cheeses and many Italian specialties and produce. Balducci is still run by three generations of one food-loving family.

PERRY ST

GREENWICH AVENUE

W IOTH STREET

WAVERLEY STREET

PLACE

SIXTH AVENUE

HINGTON PLACE

Gay Street and its fine Federal houses feature in Ruth McKenney's novel of Village life, *My Sister Eileen.*

KEY

– – – Suggested route

0 meters 100
0 yards 100

To West 4th Street subway (2 blocks)

The Northern Dispensary has offered free medical care to the poor since 1827. Edgar Allan Poe was treated here for a cold.

★ **Jefferson Market Courthouse**
Now a public library, it was built as a courthouse in 1877 and voted the fifth most beautiful building in America. Empty for over 20 years, it was restored and turned into a library in 1967 **6**

Row houses on St. Luke's Place

St. Luke's Place **1**

Map 3 C3. **M** *Houston St.*

FIFTEEN ATTRACTIVE row houses, dating from the 1850s, line the north side of this street. The park opposite is named after a previous resident of St. Luke's Place, Mayor Jimmy Walker, the popular dandy who ran the city from 1926 until he was forced to resign after a financial scandal in 1932. In front of No. 6 are the lamps that always identify a mayor's home in New York. In recent years, the most recognizable house on the block has been No. 10, shown on television as the home of the Huxtable family in *The Cosby Show* (although the series sets it in Brooklyn). This is also the block where *Wait Until Dark* was filmed, starring Audrey Hepburn as a blind woman living at No. 4. Theodore Dreiser was one of several writers, including the poet Marianne Moore, who lived here. He wrote *An American Tragedy* while living at No. 16. One block north, the corner of Hudson and Morton Streets marked the edge of the Hudson River three centuries ago.

Mayor's lamp at No. 6

75½ Bedford Street **2**

Map 3 C2. **M** *Houston St.* ○ *to the public.*

NEW YORK'S narrowest home, just 9½ ft (2.9 m) wide, was built in 1893 in a former passageway. The poet Edna St. Vincent Millay lived here briefly, followed by the actor John Barrymore, and later Cary Grant. The three-story building has been recently renovated and is marked by a plaque.

Just around the corner, at 38 Commerce Street, Miss Millay founded the Cherry Lane Theater in 1924 as a site for avant-garde drama. It still premieres new works. Its biggest hit was the 1960s musical *Godspell*.

Cottage on Bedford Street

Isaacs-Hendricks House **3**

77 Bedford St. **Map** 3 C2. **M** *Houston St.* ○ *to the public.*

THIS IS THE OLDEST surviving home in the Village, built in 1799. The old clapboard walls are visible on the sides

Isaacs-Hendricks House

and rear; the brickwork and third floor came later. The first owner, John Isaacs, bought the land for $295 in 1794. Next came Harmon Hendricks, a copper dealer and associate of revolutionary Paul Revere. Robert Fulton, who used copper for the boilers in his steamboat, was a customer.

Grove Court **4**

Map 3 C2. **M** *Christopher St/ Sheridan Sq.*

AN ENTERPRISING grocer named Samuel Cocks was responsible for this group of six town houses, fitting snugly into an area formed by the bend in the street. (The bends in this part of the Village originally marked divisions between colonial properties.) Cocks reckoned that having residents in the empty passage between Nos. 10 and 12 Grove Street would help his business at No. 18.

But residential courts, now prized as exclusive private addresses, were not considered respectable in 1854, and the lowbrow residents attracted to the area soon earned it the nickname "Mixed Ale Alley." O. Henry later used this block as the setting for his 1902 work *The Last Leaf*.

The mid-19th-century town houses at Grove Court

Sheridan Square ❺

Map 3 C2. Ⓜ *Christopher St–Sheridan Sq.*

THIS IS THE HEART of the Village, where seven streets come together in such a maze that early guidebooks called it "the mousetrap." It was named after the Civil War General Philip Sheridan who became commander in chief of the US Army in 1883. His statue stands in nearby Christopher Park.

The Draft Riots of 1863 took place in the square, when mobs revolting against army service tried to lynch freed slaves. More than a century later, another famous disturbance rocked the

Sheridan Square scene

square. The Stonewall Inn on Christopher Street was a gay bar that had stayed in business (it was then illegal for gays to gather in bars) by paying off the police. However, on June 28, 1969, the patrons rebelled, and the pitched close combat that resulted found police officers barricaded inside the bar for hours while crowds taunted them from outside. It was a landmark moral victory for the budding Gay Rights movement. The inn still stands but is no longer a bar. The Village remains a focus for the city's gay community. The spirited gay Halloween Parade *(see p52)* through the Village, noted for its outrageous costumes, brings thousands out.

Pointed tower of "Old Jeff"

Jefferson Market Courthouse ❻

425 6th Ave. **Map** 4 D1. Ⓒ 243-4334. Ⓜ *W 4th St–Washington Sq.* ◻ *10am–6pm Mon, noon–6pm Tue, Thu, Fri, 12–8pm Wed, 10am–5pm Sat.* ⬤ *Sun, public hols.* ♿ Ⓦ *www.nypl.org*

PERHAPS THE MOST treasured Village landmark, "Old Jeff" was saved from the wrecking ball and converted into a branch of the New York Public Library through a spirited campaign that began at a local Christmas party in the late 1950s.

The site became a market in 1833, named after former president Thomas Jefferson. Its fire lookout tower had a giant bell that alerted the neighborhood's volunteer fire fighters. In 1865, the founding of the municipal fire department made the bell obsolete, and the Third Judicial District, or Jefferson Market, Courthouse was built. With its Venetian Gothic–style spires and turrets, it was named one of the 10 most beautiful buildings in the country when it opened in 1877. The old

Statue of General Sheridan in Christopher Park

fire bell was installed in the tower. Here, in 1906 Harry Thaw was tried for Stanford White's murder *(see p124)*.

By 1945, the market had moved, court sessions were discontinued, the four-sided clock had stopped and the building was endangered. In the 1950s, preservationists campaigned first to restore the clock and then the whole building. Architect Giorgio Cavaglieri has preserved many original details, including the stained glass and a spiral staircase that now leads to a dungeonlike reference room.

Facade and an ailanthus tree at Patchin Place

Patchin Place ❼

W 10th St. **Map** 4 D1. Ⓜ *W 4th St–Washington Sq.*

ONE OF MANY delightful unexpected pockets in the Village is this tiny block of small residences, lined with ailanthus trees planted in order to "absorb the bad air." The houses were built in the mid-19th century to house Basque waiters from the Fifth Avenue Brevoort Hotel.

Later the houses became fashionable addresses, with many writers living here. The poet e e cummings lived at No. 4 from 1923 until his death in 1962. English poet laureate John Masefield also lived on the block. So did playwright Eugene O'Neill and John Reed, whose eyewitness account of the Russian Revolution, *Ten Days That Shook The World* was filmed by Warren Beatty as *Reds*.

Toy battleship from the Forbes Magazine Collection

Forbes Building and Galleries ⑧

62 5th Ave. **Map** 4 E1. 206-5548. **M** 14th St–Union Sq. **Galleries** 10am–4pm Tue, Wed, Fri, Sat (times may vary). No strollers ⊘ Thu.

Sᴏᴍᴇ ᴀʀᴄʜɪᴛᴇᴄᴛᴜʀᴀʟ critics have called this 1925 limestone cube by Carrère & Hastings pompous. It was originally the headquarters of the Macmillan Publishing Company. When Macmillan moved uptown, the late Malcolm Forbes moved in with his financial magazine, *Forbes*. The Forbes Magazine Galleries show Forbes's diverse tastes, with Fabergé eggs made for the last Russian czar; over 500 antique toy boats; 12,000 toy soldiers; and a signed copy of Abraham Lincoln's Gettysburg Address, among other presidential memorabilia. There are also exhibitions of paintings, ranging from French to American Military works.

Salmagundi Club ⑨

47 5th Ave. **Map** 4 E1. 255-7740. **M** 14th St–Union Sq. 8:30am–midnight Mon–Fri, 8am–5pm Sat, noon–5pm Sun. ⊘

Aᴍᴇʀɪᴄᴀ'ꜱ ᴏʟᴅᴇꜱᴛ artists club resides in the last remaining mansion on lower Fifth Avenue. Built in 1853 for Irad Hawley, it now houses the American Artists' Professional League, the American Water-color Society and the Greenwich Village Society for Historic Preservation. Washington Irving's satiric periodical, *The Salmagundi Papers*, gave the club its name. Founded in 1871, the club moved here in 1917. Periodic art exhibits open the late 19th-century interior to the public.

Exterior of the Salmagundi Club

First Presbyterian Church ⑩

5th Ave at 12th St. **Map** 4 D1. 675-6150 **M** 7th Ave–Union Sq. noon–12:45pm Mon, Wed, Fri, 11am–12:30pm Sun. www.firstpresnyc.org

Dᴇꜱɪɢɴᴇᴅ ʙʏ Joseph C. Wells in 1846, this Gothic church was modeled on the Church of Saint Saviour in Bath, England. The church is noteworthy for its brownstone tower. The carved wooden plaques on the altar list every pastor since 1716. The south transept by McKim, Mead & White was added in 1893. The fence of iron and wood was built in 1844 and then restored in 1981.

Church of the Ascension ⑪

5th Ave at 10th St. **Map** 4 E1. 254-8620. **M** 14th St–Union Sq. noon–2pm, 5–7pm daily. 6pm daily, 9am, 11am, 6pm Sun. (not during services). www.ascensionnyc.org

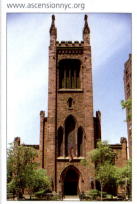

Church of the Ascension

Tʜɪꜱ ᴇɴɢʟɪꜱʜ Gothic Revival church was designed in 1840–41 by Richard Upjohn, architect of Trinity Church. The interior was redone in 1888 by Stanford White, with an altar relief by Augustus Saint-Gaudens. Above the altar hangs *The Ascension*, a mural by John La Farge, who also designed some of the stained glass. The belfry tower is lit at night to show off the colors.

In 1844 President John Tyler married Julia Gardiner here; she lived in nearby Colonnade Row (*see p118*).

Washington Mews ⑫

Washington Sq N at E 8th St. **Map** 4 E2. **M** W 4th St.

Bᴜɪʟᴛ ᴀꜱ ꜱᴛᴀʙʟᴇꜱ, this hidden enclave was turned into carriage houses around 1900. The south side was added in 1939. Gertrude Vanderbilt Whitney, founder of the Whitney Museum, lived and worked here.

On the corner of University Place is NYU's French House, remodeled in a French style, where movies, lectures and classes in French are held.

New York University ⑬

Washington Sq. **Map** 4 E2.
📞 998-1212, 998-4636. Ⓜ
W 4th St. ⬤ 8:30am–8pm
Mon–Fri. W www.nyu.edu

Originally called the University of the City of New York, NYU was founded in 1831 as an alternative to Episcopalian Columbia University. It is now the largest private university in the US and extends for blocks around Washington Square.

Construction of the school's first building on Waverly Place sparked the Stone-cutters' Guild Riot of 1833: contractors protested the use of inmates from a state prison to cut stone. The National Guard restored order. The original building no longer exists, but a memorial with a piece of the original tower is on a pedestal set into the pavement on Washington Square South. Samuel Morse's telegraph, John W. Draper's first-ever photographic

Bust of Sylvette by Picasso, between Bleecker and West Houston streets

portrait and Samuel Colt's six-shooter were invented here.

The Brown Building, on Washington Place near Greene Street, was the site of the Triangle Shirtwaist Company. In 1911, 146 factory workers died in a fire here, leading to new fire safety and labor laws.

A 36-ft (11-m) enlargement of Picasso's *Bust of Sylvette* is in University Village.

Judson Memorial Church ⑭

55 Washington Sq S. **Map** 4 D2.
📞 477-0351. Ⓜ W 4th St. ⬤
10am–1pm, 2pm–6pm Mon–Fri.
✝ Sun 11am. W www.judson.org

Built in 1892, this McKim, Mead & White church is an impressive Romanesque building with stained glass by John La Farge. Designed by Stanford White, it is named after the first American missionary sent to foreign soil, Adoniram Judson, who served in Burma in 1811. A copy of his Burmese trans-lation of the Bible was put in the cornerstone when the building was dedicated.

It is the unique spirit of this church, not the architecture, that makes it stand out. Judson Memorial has played an active role in local and world concerns and has been the site of activism on issues ranging from AIDS to the arms race. It is also home to avant-garde art exhibitions and off-Off Broadway plays.

Arch on the north side of Washington Square

Washington Square ⑮

Map 4 D2. Ⓜ W 4th St.

Now one of the city's most vibrant open spaces, Washington Square was once marshland through which the quiet Minetta Brook flowed. By the late 1700s, the area had been turned into a public cemetery – when excavation began for the park, some 10,000 skeletal remains were exhumed. The square was used as a dueling ground for

a time, then as a site for public hangings until 1819. The "hanging elm" in the northwest corner remains. In 1826 the marsh was filled in and the brook diverted under-ground, where it still flows; a small sign on a fountain at the entrance to Two Fifth Avenue marks its course.

The magnificent marble arch by Stanford White, completed in 1895, replaced an earlier wooden version that had spanned lower Fifth Avenue to mark the centenary of George Washington's inaugur-ation. A stairway is hidden in the right side of the arch. In 1916, a group of artists led by Marcel Duchamp and John Sloan broke in, climbed atop the arch, and declared the "free and independent republic of Washington Square, the state of New Bohemia."

Across the street is "the Row." Now part of NYU, this block was once home to New York's most prominent families. The Delano family, writers Edith Wharton, Henry James and John dos Passos, and artist Edward Hopper all lived here. Number 8 was once the mayor's official home.

Today students, families and free spirits mingle and enjoy the park side by side. A few drug dealers frequent the park, but it is safe by day.

Window on the corner of West 4th Street and Washington Square

EAST VILLAGE

ETER STUYVESANT had a country estate in the East Village, and in the 19th century, the Astors and Vanderbilts lived here. But around 1900, high society moved uptown and immigrants moved in. The Irish, Germans, Jews, Poles, Ukrainians and Puerto Ricans all left their mark in the area's churches, landmarks and the city's most varied

Mosaic, facade of St. George's Ukrainian Catholic Church

and least expensive ethnic restaurants. In the 1950s low rents attracted the "beat generation." Later, Hippies were followed by punks. The area's experimental music clubs and theaters still feature the latest styles. Astor Place buzzes with students. To the east are Avenues A, B, C and D, an area known as "Alphabet City," which is slowly being redeveloped.

SIGHTS AT A GLANCE

Historic Streets and Buildings
Cooper Union **1**
Colonnade Row **3**
Bayard-Condict Building **8**

Museums and Galleries
Merchant's House Museum **4**

Churches
St. Mark's-in-the-Bowery Church **5**
Grace Church **6**

Parks and Squares
Tompkins Square **7**

Famous Theaters
Public Theater **2**

SEE ALSO

• *Street Finder*, map 4, 5

• *Where to Stay* pp274–5

• *Restaurants* pp290–92

GETTING THERE

By subway, the Lexington Ave 6 train stop at Astor Pl is the most convenient; the area is also served by the M15 and M101/102 buses and the M8 crosstown bus.

0 meters	500
0 yards	500

KEY

▨	Street-by-Street map
M	Subway station

Gothic bas-relief on the facade of Grace Church

The interior of McSorley's Old Ale House

Street by Street: East Village

AT THE SPOT WHERE Tenth and Stuyvesant streets now intersect, Peter Stuyvesant's country house once stood. His grandson, also named Peter, inherited most of the property and had it divided into streets in 1787. Among the prize sites of the St. Mark's Historic District are the St. Mark's-in-the-Bowery Church, the Stuyvesant-Fish house and the 1795 home of Nicholas Stuyvesant, both on Stuyvesant Street. Many other homes in the district were built between 1871 and 1890 and still have their original stoops, lintels and other architectural details.

Astor Place saw rioting in 1849. English actor William Macready, playing *Hamlet* at the Astor Place Opera House, criticized American actor Edwin Forrest. Forrest's fans revolted and there were 34 deaths.

Alamo is the title of the 15-ft (4.5-m) steel cube in Astor Place designed by Bernard Rosenthal. It revolves when pushed.

Astor Place subway (line 6)

ASTOR PLACE
LAFAYETTE STREET
STABLE COURT
BOWERY
FOU

Colonnade Row
Now in shabby disrepair, these buildings were once expensive town houses. The houses, of which only four are left, are unified by one facade in the European style. The marble was quarried by Sing Sing prisoners ❸

Public Theater
In 1965 the late Joseph Papp convinced the city to buy the Astor Library (1849) as a home for the theater. Now restored, it sees the opening of many famous plays ❷

★ **Merchant's House**
This museum contains the house's original Federal, American Empire and Victorian furniture ❹

STAR SIGHTS

★ **Cooper Union**

★ **Merchant's House Museum**

★ **Cooper Union**
Founded by self-made man Peter Cooper in 1859, it still provides a free education to its students ❶

The Stuyvesant-Fish House
(1803–4) was constructed out of brick. It is a classic example of a Federal-style house.

St. Mark's-in-the-Bowery-Church
The church was built in 1799 and the steeple added in 1828 ❺

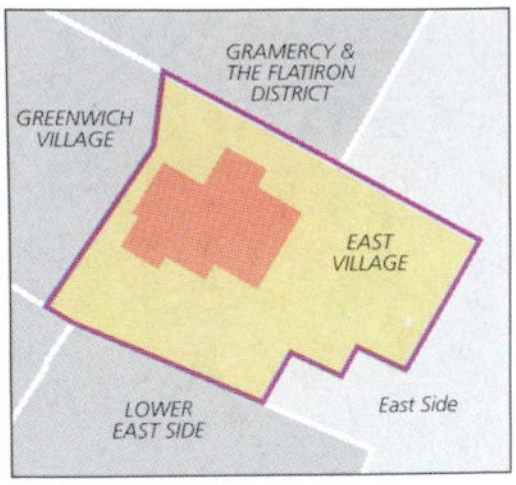

LOCATOR MAP
See Manhattan Map pp12–13

Renwick Triangle
is a group of 16 houses built in 1861 in the Italianate style.

Stuyvesant Polyclinic
was founded in 1857 as the German Dispensary, and it is still a health clinic. The facade is decorated with the busts of many famous physicians and scientists.

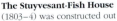

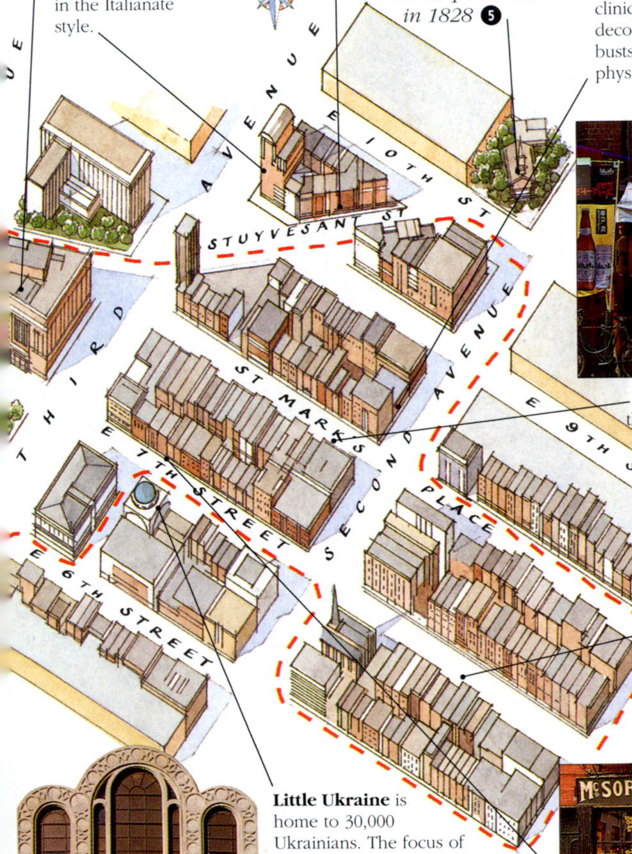

St. Mark's Place was once the main street of hippie life. It is still the hub of the East Village youth scene. Funky shops now occupy many of the basements.

Little India, the row of Indian eateries on the south side of East Sixth Street, offers a taste of India at budget prices.

Little Ukraine is home to 30,000 Ukrainians. The focus of the community is St. George's Ukrainian Catholic Church.

KEY

- - - - Suggested route

0 meters   100
0 yards   100

McSorley's Old Ale House still brews its own ale and serves it in surroundings seemingly unchanged since it opened in 1854. (*See p309.*)

Great Hall at Cooper Union, where Abraham Lincoln spoke

Cooper Union ❶

30 Cooper Sq. **Map** 4 F2.
📞 353-4100. Ⓜ Astor Pl.
🕐 by appointment only, and for
lectures and concerts in Great Hall.
⬤ Jun–Aug, public hols. 🚫 ♿
🌐 www.cooper.edu

PETER COOPER, the wealthy
industrialist who built the
first US steam locomotive,
made the first steel rails and
was a partner in the first trans-
atlantic cable venture, had no
formal schooling. He founded
New York's first free, nonsectarian and coeducational
college specializing in design,
engineering, and architecture.
Still free, the school inspires
intense competition for
places. The six-story building
was the first with a steel
frame, made of Cooper's own
rails. The building was renovated in 1973–74. The Great
Hall was inaugurated in 1859
by Mark Twain, and Lincoln
delivered his "Right Makes
Might" speech there in 1860.
Cooper Union continues to
sponsor a Public Forum.

Public Theater ❷

425 Lafayette St. **Map** 4 F2. 📞 260-
2400 (box office). Ⓜ Astor Pl.
See also **Entertainment** p332. 🌐
www.publictheater.org

THE LARGE redbrick and
brownstone building that
is the home of the New York
Shakespeare
Festival

began its life in 1849 as the
Astor Library, the city's first
free library, now part of the
New York Public Library. It is
a prime American example of
German Romanesque Revival
style. When the building was
threatened with demolition in
1965, Joseph Papp, founder of
the Shakespeare
Festival,
persuaded
New York City to buy
it as a home for the
company. Renovation
began in 1967,
and much of the
handsome interior
was preserved
during conversion
into six theaters.
Although much of
the work shown is
experimental, the
Public Theater was
the original home
of hit musicals *Hair*
and *A Chorus Line*.
The latter moved
uptown to become a long-
running Broadway production.

Colonnade Row ❸

428–434 Lafayette St. **Map** 4 F2.
Ⓜ Astor Pl. ⬤ to the public.

THE CORINTHIAN columns
across these four buildings
are all that remain of a once-
magnificent row of nine Greek
Revival town houses. They
were completed in 1833 by
developer Seth Geer and
were known as "Geer's Folly"
by skeptics who
thought no one
would live so far
east. They were
proved wrong
when the houses
were taken by
such eminent
citizens as John

Jacob Astor and Cornelius
Vanderbilt. Washington Irving,
author of *Rip Van Winkle* and
other classic American tales,
lived here for a time, as did
two English novelists, William
Makepeace Thackeray and
Charles Dickens. Five of the
houses were lost when the
John Wanamaker Department
Store razed them in the early
20th century to make room
for a garage. The remaining
buildings are falling to ruin.

Merchant's House Museum ❹

29 E 4th St. **Map** 4 F2. 📞 777-1089.
Ⓜ Astor Pl. 🕐 1–5pm Thu–Mon and
by appt. 📷 🚫 (no flashes permitted)
📅 **Lectures** 🚻
🌐 www.merchantshouse.com

**The original 19th-century iron stove in the
kitchen of the Merchant's House Museum**

THIS REMARKABLE Greek
Revival brick town house,
improbably tucked away on
an East Village block, is a
time capsule of a vanished
way of life. It still has both its
original fixtures and its
kitchen, and is filled with the
actual furniture, ornaments
and utensils of the family that
lived here for almost 100
years. Built in 1832, it was
bought in 1835 by Seabury
Tredwell, a wealthy merchant,
and stayed in the family until
Gertrude Tredwell, the last
member, died in 1933. She
had maintained her father's
home just as he would have
liked it, and a relative
opened the house as a
museum in 1936. The first-
floor parlors are very grand,
a sign of how well New
York's merchant class lived
in the 1800s.

The Public Theater on Lafayette Street

St. Mark's-in-the-Bowery Church  ❺

131 E 10th St. **Map** 4 F1. ☎ 674-6377. Ⓜ *Astor Pl.* ⏰ 8:30am–4pm *Mon–Fri.* ✝ 6:30pm Wed, 10:30am *Sun* 🚫 Ⓦ www.stmarkschurch.org

ONE OF New York's oldest churches, this building, dating from 1799, replaced a 1660 church on the *bouwerie* (farm) of Governor Peter Stuyvesant. He is buried here with seven generations of his descendants and many other prominent early New Yorkers. Poet W.H. Auden, who was a member of the parish, is also commemorated here.

In 1878, a grisly kidnapping took place in the churchyard, when the remains of department store magnate A.T. Stewart were removed and held for $20,000 ransom.

The church rectory at 232 East 11th Street is a little-known work, from 1900, by Ernest Flagg. He achieved renown for his Singer Building (*see p104*).

Grace Church ❻

802 Broadway. **Map** 4 F1. ☎ 254-2000. Ⓜ *Astor Pl.* ⏰ 10am–5:30pm *Mon–Fri,* noon–4pm Sat. 🔵 *public hols.* ✝ 7:30am, noon, Mon–Fri, 6pm Wed, 9am, 11am, 6pm Sun. 🚫 ♿ *Concerts.* Ⓦ www.gracenyc.org

JAMES RENWICK, JR., the architect of St. Patrick's Cathedral, was only 23 when he designed this church, yet many consider it his finest achievement. Its delicate early Gothic lines have a grace befitting the church's name. The interior is just as beautiful, with Pre-Raphaelite stained glass and a handsome mosaic floor.

The church's peace and serenity were briefly shattered in 1863, when Phineas T. Barnum

Tom Thumb and his bride at Grace Church

staged the wedding of midget General Tom Thumb here; the crowds turned the event into complete chaos.

The marble spire replaced a wooden steeple in 1888 amid fears that it might prove too heavy for the church – and it has since developed a distinct lean. The church is visible from afar, because it is on a bend on Broadway. Henry Brevoort forced the city to bend Broadway to divert it around his apple orchard.

Grace Church altar and window

Tompkins Square ❼

Map 5 B1. Ⓜ *2nd Ave, 1st Ave.*

THIS ENGLISH-STYLE park has the makings of a peaceful spot, but its past has more often been dominated by strife. It was the site of America's first organized labor demonstration in 1874, the main gathering place during the neighborhood's hippie era of the 1960s and, in 1991, an arena for violent riots when the police tried to evict homeless people who had taken over the grounds. The square also contains a poignant monument to the neighborhood's greatest tragedy. A small statue of a boy

and a girl looking at a steamboat commemorates the deaths of over 1,000 local residents in the *General Slocum* steamer disaster. On June 15, 1904, the boat caught fire during a pleasure cruise on the East River. The boat was crowded with women and children from this then-German neighborhood. Many local men lost their entire families and moved away, leaving the area and its memories behind.

Bayard-Condict Building ❽

65 Bleecker St. **Map** 4 F3. Ⓜ *Bleecker St.*

THE GRACEFUL columns, elegant filigreed terra-cotta facade and magnificent cornice on this 1898 building mark the only New York work by Louis Sullivan, the great Chicago architect who taught Frank Lloyd Wright. He died in poverty and obscurity in Chicago in 1924.

Sullivan is said to have objected vigorously to the sentimental angels supporting the Bayard-Condict Building's cornice, but he eventually gave in to the wishes of Silas Alden Condict, the owner.

Because this building is squeezed into a commercial block, it is better appreciated from a distance. Cross the street and walk a little way down Crosby Street for the best view.

The Bayard-Condict Building

GRAMERCY AND THE FLATIRON DISTRICT

FOUR SQUARES were laid out in this area by real estate developers in the 19th century to emulate the quiet, private residential areas in many European cities. Gramercy Park, still mainly residential, was one of them. The townhouses around the square were designed by some of the

Lizard on a statue in Union Square

country's best architects, such as Calvert Vaux and Stanford White, and occupied by some of New York's most prominent citizens. Today, not far away, boutiques, trendy cafés, and high-rise apartments have taken over the stretch of lower Fifth Avenue just south of the famous Flatiron Building.

SIGHTS AT A GLANCE

Historic Streets and Buildings
New York Life Insurance Company **2**
Appellate Division of the Supreme Court of the State of New York **3**
Metropolitan Life Insurance Company **4**
Flatiron Building **5**
Ladies' Mile **6**
National Arts Club **8**
The Library at the Players **9**
Block Beautiful **11**
Gramercy Park Hotel **12**
Con Edison Headquarters **14**

Museums and Galleries
Theodore Roosevelt Birthplace **7**

Churches
The Little Church Around the Corner **16**

Parks and Squares
Madison Square **1**
Gramercy Park **10**
Stuyvesant Square **13**
Union Square **15**

SEE ALSO
- *Street Finder,* maps 8, 9
- *Where to Stay* pp274–5
- *Restaurants* pp290–92

GETTING THERE
The closest subway station is at 23rd St, where the Lexington Ave No. 6 train stops. Buses to the area include the M101/102 on 3rd Ave, and the M1, M2 or M3 on 5th and Madison Avenues. The crosstown bus is the M26.

0 meters   500
0 yards   500

KEY
Street-by-Street map
M Subway station

◁ **Con Edison Headquarters by night**

Street by Street: Gramercy Park

GRAMERCY PARK AND nearby Madison Square tell a tale of two cities. Madison Square is ringed by offices and traffic and is used mainly by those who work nearby, but the fine surrounding commercial architecture and statues make it well worth visiting. It was once the home of Stanford White's famous pleasure palace, the old Madison Square Garden, a place where revelers always thronged. Gramercy Park, however, retains the air of dignified tranquility it has become known for. Here, the residences and clubs remain, set around New York's last private park, for which only those who live on the square have a key.

Statue of Diana atop the old Madison Square Garden

★ **Madison Square**
The Knickerbocker Club played baseball here in the 1840s and was the first to codify the game's rules. Today office workers enjoy the park's many statues of 19th-century figures, among them Admiral David Farragut ❶

23rd Street subway (lines N, R)

★ **Flatiron Building**
The triangle made by Fifth Avenue, Broadway and 23rd Street is the site of one of New York's most famous early skyscrapers. When it was built in 1903, it was the world's tallest building ❺

A sidewalk clock found in front of 200 Fifth Avenue marks the very end of the once-fashionable shopping area, known as Ladies' Mile.

Ladies' Mile
Broadway from Union Square to Madison Square was once New York's finest shopping area. ❻

Theodore Roosevelt Birthplace
The house is a replica of the one in which the 26th American president was born ❼

KEY

– – – Suggested route

0 meters   100

0 yards   100

National Arts Club
This is a private club for the arts, on the south side of the park ❽

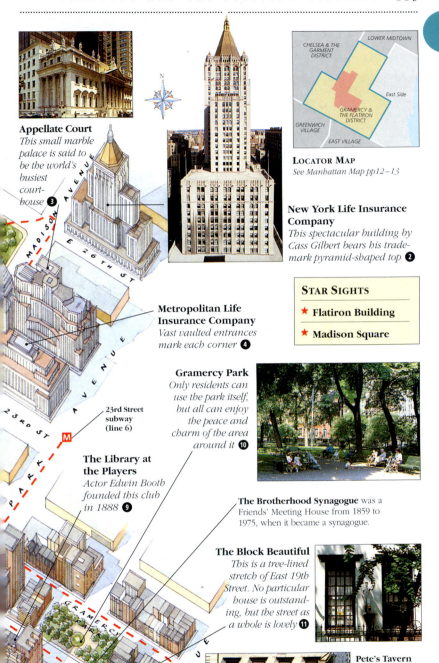

Appellate Court
This small marble palace is said to be the world's busiest courthouse ❸

LOCATOR MAP
See Manhattan Map pp12–13

New York Life Insurance Company
This spectacular building by Cass Gilbert bears his trademark pyramid-shaped top ❷

Metropolitan Life Insurance Company
Vast vaulted entrances mark each corner ❹

STAR SIGHTS

★ **Flatiron Building**

★ **Madison Square**

Gramercy Park
Only residents can use the park itself, but all can enjoy the peace and charm of the area around it ❿

23rd Street subway (line 6)

The Library at the Players
Actor Edwin Booth founded this club in 1888 ❾

The Brotherhood Synagogue was a Friends' Meeting House from 1859 to 1975, when it became a synagogue.

The Block Beautiful
This is a tree-lined stretch of East 19th Street. No particular house is outstanding, but the street as a whole is lovely ⓫

Pete's Tavern
has been here since 1903. Short story writer O. Henry, a well-known chronicler of the city, wrote "The Gift of the Magi" in the second booth.

Madison Square ❶

Map 8 F4. **M** 23rd St.

Farragut's statue, Madison Square

PLANNED AS the center of a fashionable residential district, this square became a popular entertainment center after the Civil War. It was bordered by the elegant Fifth Avenue Hotel, the Madison Square Theater and Stanford White's Madison Square Garden. The torch-bearing arm of the Statue of Liberty was exhibited here in 1884.

Quiet once again, it is a lunchtime spot for neighborhood office workers, and a place to stroll and admire the sculptures. The 1880 statue of Admiral David Farragut is by Augustus Saint-Gaudens, with a pedestal by Stanford White. Farragut was the hero of a Civil War sea battle; figures representing Courage and Loyalty arising from the waves are carved on the base. The statue of Roscoe Conkling commemorates a US senator who died of exposure during the great blizzard of 1888. The Eternal Light flagpole, by Carrère & Hastings, honors the soldiers who fell in France during World War I.

New York Life Insurance Company ❷

51 Madison Ave. **Map** 9 A3.
M 28th St. ◻ office hours.

THIS IMPOSING building was designed in 1928 by Cass Gilbert of Woolworth Building fame. The interior is a masterpiece, adorned with enormous hanging lamps, bronze doors and paneling, and a grand staircase leading, of all places, to the subway station.

Other famous buildings have stood on this site. Barnum's

Hippodrome was here in 1874, then the first Madison Square Garden opened in 1879. A wide range of entertainments were put on, including the prizefights of heavyweight boxing hero John L. Sullivan in the 1880s. The next Madison Square Garden – Stanford White's legendary pleasure palace – opened on the same site in 1890. Lavish musical shows and social events were attended by New York's elite, who paid over $500 for a box at the prestigious annual horse show.

The building had street-level arcades and a tower modeled on the Giralda in Seville. A gold statue of the goddess Diana stood atop the tower. Her nudity was shocking, but far more scandalous was the decadent life and death of White himself. In 1906, while watching a revue in the roof garden, he was shot dead by millionaire Harry K. Thaw, the husband of White's former mistress, showgirl Evelyn Nesbit. The headline in the journal *Vanity Fair* summed up popular feeling: "Stanford White, Voluptuary and Pervert, Dies the Death of a Dog." The ensuing trial's revelations about decadent Broadway high society leave modern soap operas far behind.

New York Life Insurance Company's golden pyramid roof

Appellate Division of the Supreme Court of the State of New York ❸

E. 25th St. at Madison Ave. **Map** 9 A4. ◐ 340 0400. **M** 23rd St. ◻ 9am–5pm Mon–Fri (court in session from 2pm Tue, Wed, Thu, from 10am Fri). ● public hols. ⊘

APPEALS RELATING TO civil and criminal cases for New York and the Bronx are heard here, in what is widely considered to be the busiest court of its kind in the world. James Brown Lord designed the small yet noble Palladian Revival building in 1900.

Statues of *Justice* and *Study* above the Appellate Court

It is decorated with more than a dozen handsome sculptures, including Daniel Chester French's *Justice* flanked by *Power* and *Study*. During the week, the public is invited to step inside to admire the fine interior, designed by the Herter brothers, including the courtroom when it is not in session. Among the elegant details worth looking for are the fine stained-glass windows and dome, the murals and the striking cabinetwork.

Displays in the lobby often feature some of the more famous cases that have been heard in this court. Among the celebrity names that have been involved in appeals settled here are Babe Ruth, Charlie Chaplin, Fred Astaire, Harry Houdini, Theodore Dreiser and Edgar Allan Poe.

Clock tower of the Metropolitan Life Insurance Company

Metropolitan Life Insurance Company 4

1 Madison Ave. **Map** 9 A4. *578-2211.* *23rd St.* *to the public, except lobby.*

IN 1909, THE ADDITION of a 700-ft (210-m) tower to this 1893 building ousted the Flatiron as the tallest in the world. The huge four-sided clock has minute hands said to weigh 1000 lb (454 kg) each. The building is lit up at night, and is a familiar part of the evening skyline. It served as the company symbol "the light that never fails."

A series of historical murals by N.C. Wyeth, the famed illustrator of such classics as *Robin Hood*, *Treasure Island* and *Robinson Crusoe* (and the father of painter Andrew Wyeth), once graced the walls of the cafeteria. They are now on display in the lobby.

Flatiron Building 5

175 5th Ave. **Map** 8 F4. *23rd St.* *office hours.*

ORIGINALLY NAMED the Fuller Building after the construction company that owned it, this building by Chicago architect David Burnham was the tallest in the world when it was completed in 1902. One of the first buildings to use a steel frame, it heralded the era of the skyscrapers.

It soon became known as the Flatiron for its unusual triangular shape, but some called it "Burnham's folly," predicting that the winds created by the building's shape would knock it down. It has withstood the test of time, but the winds along 23rd Street did have one notable effect. In the building's early days, they drew crowds of males hoping to get a peek at women's ankles as their long skirts got blown about. Police officers had to keep people moving along, and their call, "23-skidoo" became slang for "scram."

The stretch of Fifth Avenue to the south of the building was, until recently, rather run down but is fast coming to life with chic shops such as Emporio Armani and Paul Smith, giving the area new cachet and a new name, "the Flatiron District."

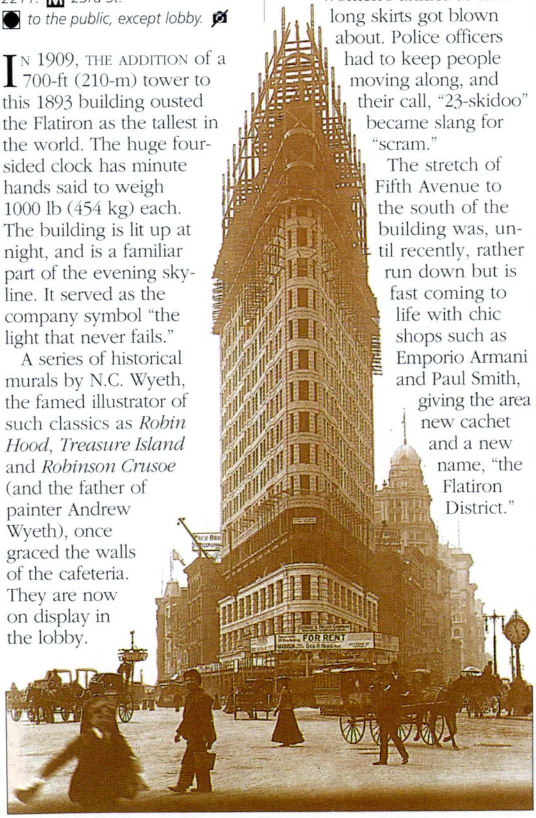

Flatiron Building during its construction

Ladies' Mile 6

Broadway (Union Sq. to Madison Sq.). **Map** 4 E1 to 8 F4. *14th St, 23rd St.*

Arnold Constable store

IN THE 19TH CENTURY, the "carriage trade" came here in shiny traps from their town houses nearby, to shop at stores such as Arnold Constable (Nos. 881–887) and Lord & Taylor (No. 901). The ground-floor exteriors have changed beyond recognition; look up to see the remains of once-grand facades.

President Teddy Roosevelt

Theodore Roosevelt Birthplace 7

28 E. 20th St. **Map** 9 A5. *260-1616* *14th St.-Union Sq.* *9am–5pm Mon–Fri (last adm: 4pm).* *public hols.* ***Lectures, concerts, films, videos.*** www.nps.gov/thrb

THE RECONSTRUCTED boyhood home of the colorful 26th president displays everything from the toys with which the young Teddy played to campaign buttons and emblems of the trademark "Rough Rider" hat that Roosevelt wore in the Spanish-American War. One exhibit features his explorations and interests; the other covers his political career.

Bas-relief faces of great writers at the National Arts Club

National Arts Club **8**

15 Gramercy Pk S. **Map** 9 A5. 475-3424. **M** 14th St-Union Sq, 6 to 23rd St. noon–5pm for exhibitions. www.nationalartsclub.org

DESIGNED BY Calvert Vaux in 1881–84, this large brownstone was the residence of New York governor Samuel Tilden, who condemned "Boss" Tweed (see p25) and established a free public library. The National Arts Club bought the home in 1906 and kept the original high ceilings and stained glass. Members have included most of the leading American artists of the late 19th and early 20th century, who were asked to donate a painting or sculpture in lieu of a subscription for life membership; these gifts form the permanent collection. The club is open to the public for exhibitions.

The Library at the Players **9**

16 Gramercy Pk S. **Map** 9 A5. 228-7610. **M** 14th St-Union Sq, 6 to 23rd St. exc for pre-booked group tours.

THIS TWO-STORY brownstone was the home of actor Edwin Booth, brother of John Wilkes Booth, President Lincoln's assassin. Architect Stanford White

remodeled the building as a club in 1888. Although intended primarily for actors, members have included White himself, author Mark Twain, publisher Thomas Nast and Winston Churchill, whose mother, Jennie Jerome, was born nearby. A statue of Booth playing Hamlet is across the street in Gramercy Park.

Decorative grille at The Players club

Gramercy Park **10**

Map 9 A4. **M** 23rd St.

GRAMERCY PARK is one of four squares (with Union, Stuyvesant and Madison) laid out in the 1830s and 1840s to attract society residences. It is the city's only private park, and residents in the surrounding buildings have keys to the park gate as the original owners once did. Look through the railings at the southeast corner to see Greg Wyatt's fountain, with giraffes leaping around a smiling sun.

The buildings around the square were designed by some of the city's most famous architects, including

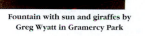

Fountain with sun and giraffes by Greg Wyatt in Gramercy Park

Stanford White, whose house was located on the site of today's Gramercy Park Hotel. Particularly fine are 3 and 4, with graceful cast-iron gates and porches. The lanterns in front of 4 serve as symbols marking the house of a former mayor of the city, James Harper. Number 34 (1883) has been the home of the sculptor Daniel Chester French, the actor James Cagney and circus impresario John Ringling (who had a massive pipe organ installed in his apartment).

Block Beautiful **11**

E. 19th St. **Map** 9 A5. **M** 3rd Ave, 14th St-Union Sq, 6 to 23rd St.

House facade on the Block Beautiful on East 19th Street

THIS IS A SERENE, tree-lined block of 1920s residences, beautifully restored. None of them is exceptional on its own, but together they create a wonderfully harmonious whole. Number 132 had two famous theatrical tenants: Theda Bara, silent movie star and Hollywood's first sex symbol, and the fine Shakespearean actress Mrs. Patrick Campbell, who originated the role of Eliza Doolittle in George Bernard Shaw's Pygmalion in 1914. The hitching posts outside 141 and the ceramic relief of giraffes outside 147-149 are two of the many details to look for as you walk along the block.

Gramercy Park Hotel **⑫**

2 Lexington Ave at 21st St. **Map** 9 B4.
C 475-4320. **M** 14th St-Union Sq.
W www.gramercyparkhotel.com

Located on the site of Stanford White's house, this hotel has, for more than sixty years, been a home away from home for many international visitors and New Yorkers alike. The hotel's delightfully old-fashioned bar, with its antique sconces, candles, and wood-slat windows, is one of New York's best-kept secrets and seems made to order for romantic or clandestine trysts. Here, you might well find yourself seated next to a wealthy, very old matron or a wealthy, very young rock star. The hotel itself is right next to the only private park in Manhattan. If you want to go into the park and pretend you live in this rarified neighborhood, ask at the reception desk for a guest key to the park.

Stuyvesant Square **⑬**

Map 9 B5. **M** 14th St-Union Sq.

This oasis, in the form of a pair of parks divided by Second Avenue, was part of Peter Stuyvesant's original farm in the 1600s. It was still in the Stuyvesant family when the park was designed in 1836; Peter G. Stuyvesant sold the land to the city for the nominal sum of $5 (much to the delight of those living nearby, who saw real estate values jump). A statue of Stuyvesant by Gertrude Vanderbilt Whitney stands in the park. The park separated the Stuyvesant area from the poorer Gas House district.

Con Edison Headquarters **⑭**

145 E 14th St. **Map** 9 A5.
M 3rd Ave, 14th St-Union Sq.
● to the public.

The clock tower of this building, which dates

The towers of Con Edison (right), Metropolitan Life and the Empire State

from 1911, is a local landmark. Originally conceived by Henry Hardenbergh, the architect best known for such buildings as the Dakota (see p216) and the Plaza (see p179). the 26-story tower was built by the same firm who designed Grand Central Terminal. Near the top of the tower, a 38-ft (11.6-m) bronze lantern was built as a memorial to Con Ed's employees who died in World War I. The tower itself is not as tall as nearby Empire State Building, but when it is lit up at night, it makes an attractive showpiece, in addition to a potent symbol of the company that keeps Manhattan and the other four boroughs shining.

Union Square **⑮**

Map 9 A5. **M** 14th St-Union Sq.
Farmers' Market Mon, Wed, Fri, Sat.

Greenmarket day at Union Square

Opened in 1839, this park joined Bloomingdale Road (now Broadway) with the Bowery Road (Fourth Avenue or Park), and hence its name. Later, the center of the square was lifted up for a subway to run beneath it. The park became popular with soapbox orators. During the Depression in 1930, more than 35,000 unemployed people rallied here, before marching on to City Hall to demand jobs. The square hosts a popular greenmarket where farmers from all over New York State sell their fresh produce.

The Little Church Around the Corner **⑯**

1 E 29th St. **Map** 8 F3.
C 684-6770. **M** 28th St. **○** 9am–5pm daily. **↑** 8, 9, 11am Sun. **◉**
& **✓** Sun after 11am service.
Lectures, concerts, recitals. **✓**
www.littlechurch.org

Built from 1849 to 1856, the Episcopal Church of the Transfiguration is a tranquil retreat. It has been known by its nickname since 1870 when Joseph Jefferson tried to arrange the funeral of fellow actor George Holland. The pastor at a nearby church refused to bury a person of so lowly a profession. Instead, he suggested "the little church around the corner." The name stuck and the church has had special ties with the theater ever since. Sarah Bernhardt attended services here.

The south transept window by John La Farge, shows Edwin Booth playing Ham Jefferson's cry of "God b the little church around corner" is commemora window in the south

CHELSEA AND
THE GARMENT DISTRICT

THIS WAS OPEN farmland in 1750, but by the 1830s it was a city suburb, and in the 1870s, with the coming of the elevated railroads *(see pp24–5)*, it had become quite commercial. Music halls and theaters lined 23rd Street. Fashion Row grew in the shadow of the El, with department stores serving middle-class New York. But, as fashion moved uptown, Chelsea drifted farther downhill. It became a warehouse district, until the Els were removed and New Yorkers rediscovered the charming 19th-century town houses. While Chelsea's fortunes were waning, Herald Square to the north was thriving as Macy's arrived, and New York city's retailing and garment districts grew up around it.

Statue of garment worker, at 555 7th Avenue

a's Empire Diner

SIGHTS AT A GLANCE

Historic Streets and Buildings
Empire State Building
pp134–5 ❷
General Post Office ❼
General Theological
Seminary ⓫

Chelsea Historic District ⓬
Hugh O'Neill Dry Goods
Store ⓮

Churches
Marble Collegiate Reformed
Church ❶
St. John the Baptist Church ❺

Modern Architecture
Madison Square Garden ❻
Jacob K. Javits Convention
Center ❽

Chelsea Piers Sports and
Entertainment Complex ❾

Monuments
Worth Monument ⓯

Parks and Squares
Herald Square ❸

**Landmark Hotels and
Restaurants**
Empire Diner ❿
Chelsea Hotel ⓭

Landmark Stores
Macy's ❹

Medallion
celebrating technology
at the Empire State Building

| 0 meters | | 500 |
| 0 yards | | 500 |

SEE ALSO
• *Street Finder*, maps 7–8
• *Where to Stay* pp274–5
• *Restaurants* pp290–92

GETTING THERE
To Chelsea, take the 7th Ave/
Broadway 1 or 9 subway trains
to 18th or 23rd St. The 8th Ave
A, C and E trains go to 23rd St.
Buses include the M10 and
M11, M14 or the M23
crosstown. To reach the area
around Macy's, take the 1 or 9
or the 2 or 3 express trains to
34th St/Penn Station. The 8th
Ave trains also stop at 34th St.

KEY

🟥	Street-by-Street map
Ⓜ	Subway station
🛳	Heliport

Street by Street: Herald Square

HERALD SQUARE is named for the New York *Herald*, which had its office there from 1894 to 1921. Today full of shoppers, the area was once one of the raunchiest parts of New York. During the 1880s and '90s, it was known as the Tenderloin District and was filled with dance halls and bordellos. When Macy's opened in 1901, the focus moved from flesh to fashion. New York's Garment District now fills the streets near Macy's on and around Seventh Avenue, also known as Fashion Avenue. To the east on Fifth Avenue is the Empire State Building, with the city's best eagle's-eye views from the observation deck.

Manhattan Mall, the site of Gimbel's, Macy's former archrival, holds 90 stores, a huge food court, and a floor for children's wares.

Fashion Avenue is another name for the stretch of Seventh Avenue around 34th Street. This area is the heart of New York's garment industry. The streets are full of men pushing racks of clothes and furs.

34th Street-Penn Station subway (1, 2, 3, 9, A, C, E)

The Ramada Hotel Pennsylvania was a center for the 1930s big bands – Glenn Miller's song "Pennsylvania 6-5000" made its telephone number famous.

St. John the Baptist Church
A beautiful set of carved Stations of the Cross is hung on the walls of the white marble interior of this church ❺

The SJM Building is at 130 West 30th Street. Mesopotamian-style friezes adorn the outside of the building.

The Fur District is at the southern end of the Garment District. Furriers ply their trade between West 27th and 30th streets.

The Flower District, around Sixth Avenue and West 28th Street, hums with activity in the early part of the day as florists pack their vans with their highly scented, brightly colored wares.

28th Street subway (lines N, R)

★ Macy's
The biggest department store in the world has something for everyone ❹

The Greenwich Savings Bank (now the HSBC) is a Greek temple to banking with huge columns on three sides.

34th Street subway (lines B, D, F, N, Q, R)

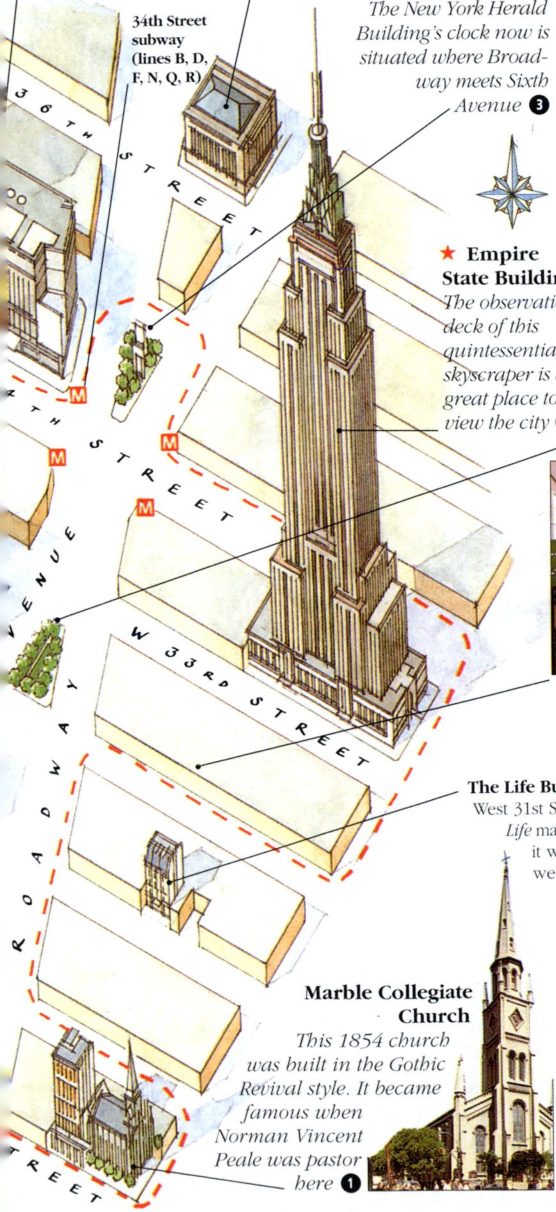

Herald Square
The New York Herald Building's clock now is situated where Broadway meets Sixth Avenue ❸

LOCATOR MAP
See Manhattan Map pp12–13

KEY

– – – Suggested route

0 meters 100
0 yards 100

★ Empire State Building
The observation deck of this quintessential skyscraper is a great place to view the city ❷

Greeley Square is more of a traffic island than a square, but it does have a fine statue of Horace Greeley, founder of the New York *Tribune*.

Little Korea is an area of Korean businesses. In addition to shops, there are restaurants nearby on West 31st and 32nd streets.

The Life Building at 19 West 31st Street housed *Life* magazine when it was a satirical weekly. Carrère & Hastings designed the building in 1894. It is now a hotel (*see p276*).

Marble Collegiate Church
This 1854 church was built in the Gothic Revival style. It became famous when Norman Vincent Peale was pastor here ❶

STAR SIGHTS

★ **Macy's**

★ **Empire State Building**

Marble Collegiate's Tiffany stained-glass windows

Marble Collegiate Reformed Church ❶

1 W. 29th St. **Map** 8 F3. 686-2770. **M** 28th St. 10am–4pm Mon–Sun. Sep–Jun: 11:15am Sun; Jun–Sep: 10:30am Sun. during services. **w** marblechurch.org

T his church is best known for its former pastor Norman Vincent Peale, who wrote *The Power of Positive Thinking*. Another positive thinker, ex-president Richard M. Nixon, attended services here when he was a lawyer in his pre–White House days.

The church was built in 1854 using the marble blocks that give it its name. At that time, Fifth Avenue was nothing more than a dusty country road, and the cast-iron fence around the church was there to keep livestock out.

The original white and gold interior walls were replaced with a stenciled gold *fleur-de-lis* design on a soft rust background. Two stained-glass Tiffany windows, depicting Old Testament scenes, were placed in the south wall in 1893.

Empire State Building ❷

See pp134–5.

Herald Square ❸

6th Ave. **Map** 8 E2. **M** 34th St-Penn Station. See **Shopping** p313.

N amed after the New York *Herald*, which occupied a fine arcaded, Italianate Stanford White building here from 1893 to 1921, the square was the hub of the rowdy Tenderloin district in the 1870s and 1880s. Theaters, such as the Manhattan Opera House, dance halls, hotels and restaurants kept the area humming with life until reformers clamped down on sleaze in the 1890s. The ornamental Bennett clock, named for James Gordon Bennett Jr., publisher of the *Herald*, is now all that is left of the Herald Building.

The Opera House was razed in 1901 to make way for Macy's and, soon after, other department stores followed, making Herald Square a mecca for shoppers. One such store was the now-defunct Gimbel Brothers Department Store, once arch rival to Macy's. (The rivalry was affectionately portrayed in the New York Christmas movie *A Miracle on 34th Street*). In 1988 the store was converted into a vertical mall with a glittery neon front. Although most of the old names have gone, Herald Square is still a key shopping district.

Macy's ❹

151 W. 34th St. **Map** 8 E2. 695-4400. **M** 34th St-Penn Station. 10am–8:30pm Mon–Sat; 11am–7pm Sun. See **Shopping** p311. public hols.

T he "world's largest store" covers a square block, and the merchandise inside covers just about any item you could imagine in every price range.

Macy's was founded by a former whaler named Rowland Hussey Macy, who opened a small store on West 14th Street in 1857. The store's red star logo came from Macy's tattoo, a souvenir of his sailing days.

By the time Macy died in 1877, his little store had grown to a row of 11 buildings. It was to expand further under two brothers, Isidor and Nathan Straus, who had operated Macy's china and glassware department. By 1902 Macy's had outgrown its 14th Street premises, and the firm acquired its present site. The eastern facade has a new

Macy's 34th Street facade

The nave of St. John the Baptist Church

entrance but still bears the bay windows and Corinthian pillars of the 1902 design. The 34th Street facade still has its original caryatids guarding the entrance, along with the clock, canopy and lettering. Inside, many of the original wooden escalators are still in good working order.

The sea featured again in Macy's history in 1912 – a plaque by the main entrance commemorates the death of Isidor and his wife in the sinking of the *Titanic*.

Macy's sponsors New York's renowned Thanksgiving Day parade and the Fourth of July fireworks. The store's Spring Flower Show draws thousands of visitors.

St. John the Baptist Church ❺

210 W. 31st St. **Map** 8 E3. 🗌 *564-9070*. Ⓜ *34th St-Penn Station.* 🗌 *6:45am–6pm daily.* ✝ *throughout the day.* 📷 ♿ 🚻

FOUNDED IN 1840 to serve a congregation of newly arrived immigrants, today this small Roman Catholic church is almost lost in the heart of the Fur District. The exterior has a single spire. Although the brownstone facade on 30th Street is dark with city soot, many treasures lie within this dull exterior. The entrance is through the modern Friary on 31st Street.

The sanctuary by Napoleon Le Brun is a marvel of Gothic arches in glowing white marble surmounted by gilded capitals. Painted reliefs of religious scenes line the walls; sunlight streams through the stained-glass windows. Also off the Friary is the Prayer Garden, a small, green and peaceful oasis with religious statuary, a fountain and stone benches.

Madison Square Garden ❻

4 Pennsylvania Plaza. **Map** 8 D2. 🗌 *465-6741.* Ⓜ *34th St-Penn Station.* 🗌 *Mon–Sun, times vary according to shows.* 🎟 *See* **Entertainment** *p344.* ⓦ *www.thegarden.com*

THERE'S ONLY ONE good thing to be said for the razing of the extraordinarily lovely McKim, Mead & White Pennsylvania Station building in favor of this undistinguished 1968 complex: it so enraged city preservationists that they formed an alliance to ensure that such a thing would never be allowed to happen again.

Madison Square Garden itself, which sits atop underground Pennsylvania Station, is a cylinder of precast concrete, functional enough as a 20,000-seat, centrally located home for the famous New York Knickerbockers (the Knicks) basketball and New York Rangers hockey teams. It also has a packed calendar of other events: rock concerts, championship tennis and boxing, outrageously staged wrestling, the Ringling Bros. and Barnum & Bailey Circus, an antiques show, a dog show and more. There is also a 5,600-seat theater.

In spite of some recent renovation work, Madison Square Garden lacks the panache of its earlier location, which combined a truly stunning Stanford White building with equally extravagant entertainment *(see p124).*

The massive interior of Madison Square Garden

General Post Office ❼

421 8th Ave. **Map** 8 D2. 🗌 *967-8585.* Ⓜ *34th St-Penn Station.* 🗌 *24 hrs a day, every day, (incl public hols).* See **Practical Information** *p361.*

DESIGNED BY McKim, Mead & White in 1913, in a style to complement their 1910 Pennsylvania Station across the street, the Post Office is a perfect example of a public building of the Beaux Arts period. The imposing, two-block-long structure has a broad staircase leading to a facade with 20 Corinthian columns and a pavilion at each end. The 280-ft (85-m) inscription across it is based on a description of the Persian Empire's postal service: "Neither snow nor rain nor heat nor gloom of night stays these couriers from the swift completion of their appointed rounds."

There are plans to convert it to the "new" Penn Station.

The Corinthian colonnade of the General Post Office

Empire State Building ❷

Empire State Building

T HE EMPIRE STATE BUILDING, once overshadowed by the World Trade Center *(see p72)*, is the tallest skyscraper in New York. Construction began only weeks before the Wall Street Crash of 1929, and by the time it opened in 1931, space was so difficult to rent that it was nicknamed "the Empty State Building." Only the immediate popularity of the observatories saved the building from bankruptcy – to date, they have attracted more than 100 million visitors – but the building soon became a symbol of the city the world over.

102nd-floor observatory

The Empire State was planned to be 86 stories high, but a then 150 ft (46 m) mooring mast for zeppelins was added. The mast, now 204 ft (62 m), transmits TV and radio to the city and four states.

Colored floodlighting of the top 30 floors marks special and seasonal events.

Symbols of the modern age are depicted on these bronze Art Deco medallions placed throughout the lobby.

CONSTRUCTION

The building was designed for ease and speed of construction. Everything possible was prefabricated and slotted into place at a rate of about four stories per week.

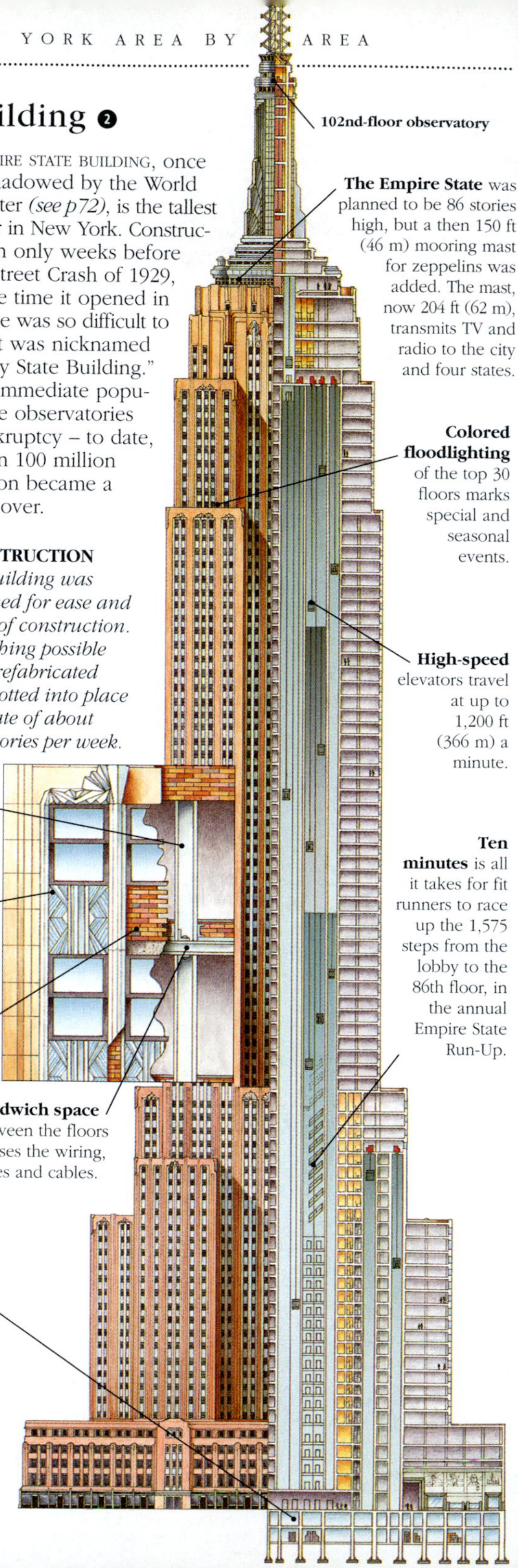

High-speed elevators travel at up to 1,200 ft (366 m) a minute.

The framework is made from 60,000 tons of steel and was built in 23 weeks.

Aluminum panels were used instead of stone around the 6,500 windows. The steel trim masks rough edges on the facing.

Ten million bricks were used to line the whole building.

Ten minutes is all it takes for fit runners to race up the 1,575 steps from the lobby to the 86th floor, in the annual Empire State Run-Up.

Sandwich space between the floors houses the wiring, pipes and cables.

Over 200 steel and concrete piles support the 365,000-ton building.

STAR FEATURES

★ **Fifth Avenue Entrance Lobby**

★ **Views from 86th- and 102nd-floor Observatories**

VISITORS' CHECKLIST

350 5th Ave. **Map** 8 F2. 736-3100. B, D, F, N, Q R to 34th St. Q32, M1, M2, M3, M4, M5, M16, M34. **Observatories** 9:30am– midnight daily (last adm: 11:30pm); 9am–5pm Dec 24; 11am–7pm Dec 25; 11am–7pm Jan 1. www.esbnyc.com

★ **Views from the Observatories**
The 86th floor has outdoor observation decks for bird's-eye views of Manhattan. From the 102nd floor, 1,250 ft (381 m) high, you can see more than 80 miles (125 km) on a clear day, but check the visibility rating in the lobby first.

Sky Boy
Photographer Lewis Hine documented the workers' bravery during the 1930s construction. Here, a worker climbs up a cable. The wide Hudson River appears small in the background.

Empire State 1454 ft (443 m) with mast

Eiffel Tower 1045 ft (319 m)

Great Pyramid 350 ft (107 m)

Big Ben 220 ft (67 m)

Pecking Order
New Yorkers are justly proud of their city's symbol, which towers above the icons of other countries.

Lightning Strikes
The Empire State is a natural lightning conductor, struck up to 500 times a year. The outside deck is closed during storms, the inside viewing area open.

★ **Fifth Avenue Entrance Lobby**
A relief image of the skyscraper is superimposed on a map of New York State in the marble-lined lobby.

ENCOUNTERS IN THE SKY
The Empire State Building has been seen in many films. However, the finale from the 1933 classic *King Kong* is easily its most famous guest appearance, as the giant ape straddles the spire to do battle with army aircraft. In 1945 a real bomber flew too low over Manhattan in fog and struck the building just above the 78th floor. The luckiest escape was that of a young elevator operator whose cabin plunged 79 floors to the basement. The emergency brakes saved her life.

Jacob K. Javits Convention Center **8**

655 W. 34th St. **Map** 7 B2. *216-2000.* **M** *34th St-Penn Station.* **Opening times** *vary with shows.* *on non-show days.* **W** www.javitscenter.com

The Convention Center – modern New York architecture at its best

STRIKINGLY MODERNISTIC in appearance, this glass building facing the Hudson, which opened in 1986, was designed by I.M. Pei to give New York the space for large-scale expositions. The 15-story building is constructed of 16,000 panes of glass, the two main halls can accommodate thousands of delegates and the lobby is high enough to hold the Statue of Liberty. In 1989 the final completion of the Galleria River Pavilion added another 40,000 sq ft (3,750 sq m) of open space and two outdoor terraces overlooking the river.

Chelsea Piers Complex **9**

11th Ave (17th & 23rd Sts) **Map** 7 B5. *336-6666.* **M** *14th St, 23rd St.* **M23.** *daily.* **W** www.chelseapiers.com

THIS MAMMOTH complex, which opened in 1995, has converted four neglected piers into a center for a vast range of sports and leisure activities *(see p31).* The facilities include skating rinks, running tracks, a golf driving range, a marina, and 11 TV and film production sound stages.

Empire Diner **10**

210 10th Ave. **Map** 7 C4. *243-2736.* **M** *23rd St.* *24hrs daily.* *4–8am Tue. See* **Restaurants and Bars** *p306.*

THIS ART DECO beauty is a faithful refurbishing of a classic 1929 American diner, complete with stainless steel bar and black and chrome trim. Bette Davis reputedly declared it her favorite diner. Its cuisine and clientele are up-to-date New York style.

A 15th-century music manuscript from the Seminary's collection

General Theological Seminary **11**

20th–21st Sts. **Map** 7 C4. *243-5150.* **M** *23rd St. or 34th St.-Penn Station.* *noon–3pm Mon–Fri, 11am–3pm Sat.* **W** www.gts.edu

FOUNDED IN 1817, this block-square campus accepts 150 students at a time to train for the priesthood. Clement Clarke Moore, a professor of Biblical Learning, donated the site, officially known as Chelsea Square. The earliest remaining building dates from 1836; the most modern, St. Mark's Library, was built in 1960 and holds the largest collection of Latin Bibles in the world.

The campus can be entered from Ninth Avenue only. Inside, the garden is laid out in two quadrangles like an English cathedral close: it is especially lovely in spring.

The Empire Diner before hungry club-goers arrive for breakfast

Chelsea Historic District ⓬

From 9th to 10th Aves. and from W. 20th to 21st Sts. **Map** 8 D5. **M** *18th St.*

A LTHOUGH HE is more well-known as the author of "A Visit from St. Nicholas" than as an urban planner, Clement Clarke Moore owned an estate here and divided it into lots in the 1830s creating handsome rows of town houses. Restoration has since rescued many of the original buildings.

Of these, the finest are seven houses known as Cushman Row, running from 406– 418 West 20th Street, which were built from 1839–1840 for Don Alonzo Cushman. He was a merchant who also founded the Greenwich Savings Bank. He joined Moore and James N. Wells in the development of Chelsea. Rich in detail and intricate ironwork, Cushman Row is ranked with Washington Square North as supreme examples of Greek Revival architecture. Look for cast-iron wreaths around attic windows and the pineapples on the newel posts of two of the houses – old symbols of hospitality.

Farther along West 20th Street, from 446–450, there are fine examples of the Italianate style for which Chelsea is also renowned.

A house on Cushman Row

The detailed brickwork arches of windows and fanlights subtly implied the wealth of the owner, being able to afford this expensive effect.

Hugh O'Neill Dry Goods Store

Chelsea Hotel ⓭

222 W. 23rd St. **Map** 8 D4. **C** 243-3700. **M** *23rd St, 34 St.-Penn Station.* **W** www.chelseahotel.com

F EW HOTELS ANYWHERE can match the Chelsea for artistic and literary heritage – and notoriety. Many of its former guests have been commemorated in the brass plaques on the hotel's facade.

They include Tennessee Williams, Mark Twain, Jack Kerouac and Brendan Behan. Dylan Thomas spent his last years here. In 1966, the hotel was the setting for the Andy Warhol movie *Chelsea Girls*, reviving its cult status, and in 1978 punk band member Sid Vicious killed his girlfriend in the hotel. For many, all this adds to the Chelsea's seedy mystique, and it still draws musicians, artists and writers who hope their names will one day be remembered.

Hugh O'Neill Dry Goods Store ⓮

655–671 6th Avenue. **Map** 8 E4. **M** *23rd St.*

T HOUGH THE STORE is long gone, the 1876 cast-iron columned and pilastered facade clearly shows the scale and grandeur of the emporiums that once lined Sixth Avenue from 18th to 23rd streets, the area known as Fashion Row. O'Neill, whose sign can still be seen on the facade, was a showman and super-salesman whose trademark was a shiny fleet of delivery wagons. His customers came in droves via the conveniently close Sixth Avenue El. They were not the "carriage trade" enjoyed by Ladies' Mile *(see p125)*, but their numbers allowed the Row to flourish until the turn of the century, when the retailing district continued its move uptown. The grand buildings remain, and many are now under renovation. All it takes is a look upward to imagine what they were like in their heyday.

Worth Monument ⓯

5th Ave. **Map** 8 F4. **M** *23rd St-Broadway.*

H IDDEN AWAY BEHIND a water meter on a triangle amid city traffic is an obelisk erected in 1857 to mark the grave of the one public figure to be buried under the streets of Manhattan. That honor belongs to General William J. Worth, a hero of the Mexican wars of the mid-1800s. A cast-iron fence of swords embedded in the ground surrounds the monument.

The Worth Monument

A guest's-eye view of the Chelsea Hotel's cast-iron stairwell

THEATER DISTRICT

IT WAS THE move of the Metropolitan Opera House to Broadway at 40th Street in 1883 that first drew lavish theaters and restaurants to this area. In the 1920s, movie palaces added the glamour of neon to Broadway, the signs getting bigger and brighter until the street became known as the "Great White Way."

Lee Lawrie design in Rockefeller Center

After World War II, the pull of the movies waned and glitter was replaced by grime. Now a redevelopment program has brought the public and the bright lights back. Pockets of calm also exist away from the bustle. Explore the Public Library or relax in Bryant Park. For the best of both worlds, though, visit Rockefeller Center.

The heart of the Theater District, around Times Square

SIGHTS AT A GLANCE

Historic Streets and Buildings
New York Yacht Club **5**
New York Public Library **8**
Times Square **10**
Group Health Insurance Building **12**
Paramount Building **13**
Shubert Alley **14**
Alwyn Court Apartments **19**

Museums and Galleries
International Center of Photography **9**
Intrepid Sea-Air-Space Museum **20**

Modern Architecture
Rockefeller Center **1**
MONY Tower **15**

Parks and Squares
Bryant Park **6**

Famous Theaters
Lyceum Theater **3**
New Amsterdam Theater **11**
City Center of Music and Dance **16**
Carnegie Hall **17**

Landmark Hotels and Restaurants
Algonquin Hotel **4**
Bryant Park Hotel **7**
Russian Tea Room **18**

Landmark Stores
Diamond Row **2**

GETTING THERE
Convenient subway routes are the 7th Ave/Broadway 1, 2, 3 and 9 trains to 50th or 42nd St, and N or R trains to 57th or 49th St. Other nearby lines include the 8th Ave A, C or E trains and 6th Ave, B, D, F or Q trains. Bus routes through the area are the M5, M6, M7, M10, M34, M42, M50, M57 and the M58 Street crosstown.

SEE ALSO
- *Street Finder*, maps 8, 11–12
- *Where to Stay* pp274–75
- *Restaurants* pp290–92

KEY

▨	Street-by-Street map
Ⓜ	Subway station
⛴	Riverboat boarding point

0 meters 500
0 yards 500

Mermaid and dolphin fountain in the Channel Gardens

Street by street: Times Square

NAMED FOR THE 25-story New York Times Tower, which opened in 1906, Times Square has been at the heart of the city's theater district since 1899, when Oscar Hammerstein built the Victoria and Republic theaters. Since the 1920s, the glowing neon of theater billboards has combined with the *Times'* illuminated newswire and other advertising to create a spectacular lightshow. After a period of decline starting in the 1930s, which saw sex shows taking over many of the grand theatres, rejuvenation of the district began in the 1990s. Old-style Broadway glamour again rubs shoulders with modern entertainment in this enticing part of the city.

Paramount Hotel
This hotel *(see p278),* designed by Philippe Starck, is the hip haunt of the theatre crowd, in the Whiskey Bar for a late-night drink.

MTV Studios
Crowds gather outside at 3pm Monday through Friday to watch interviews being filmed in the second-floor studios. Roving cameras often seek reactions on the street.

★ **E Walk**
This vast entertainment and retail complex is home to a state-of-the-art multiplex cinema, restaurants, a hotel, the BB King Blues Club, and the high-tech Broadway City Arcade.

Sardi's
In Times Square since 1921, Sardi's walls are lined with caricatures of Broadway stars of yesterday and today.

★ **New Victory Theater**
Renovated in 1995, this classic Broadway theater reopened as a dedicated young people's performance space.

★ **Times Square** ❿
Every New Years Eve at midnight, the famed silver ball drops from the top of One Times Square. There are great views from the front of this New York landmark.

0 kilometres/metres   100

0 miles/yards   100

Electronic Ticker Tape
The figures on the Morgan Stanley LED tickertape are 10 feet (3 m) high. It is only one of the eye-catching lighting displays that illuminate Times Square day and night. City ordinances require office buildings to carry neon advertising.

STAR SIGHTS

★ **E Walk**

★ **Times Square**

★ **New Victory Theater**

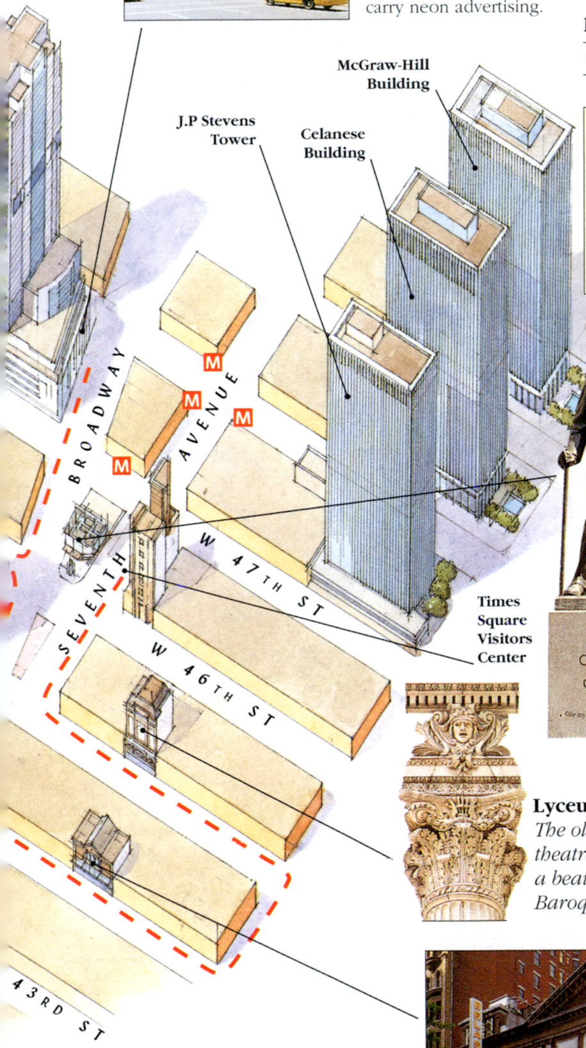

McGraw-Hill Building

J.P Stevens Tower

Celanese Building

Duffy Square
A statue of actor, composer, and writer George M Cohan, responsible for many of Broadway's hits, stands proud in this small square. Duffy Square is named for World War I hero, "Fighting" Father Duffy, immortalized in a statue. It is also home to the TKTS booth, where cut-price tickets are sold daily.

BROADWAY

SEVENTH AVENUE

W 47TH ST

W 46TH ST

43RD ST

Times Square Visitors Center

GEORGE
· M ·
COHAN
1878–1942

Lyceum Theater
The oldest Broadway theatre, the Lyceum has a beautifully ornate, Baroque façade. ❸

Belasco Theater
Built in 1907 by producer David Belasco, it was the most technically advanced theater of its time. Original Tiffany glass and Everett Shinn murals decorate the interior. It is rumored that Belasco's ghost still treads the boards some nights.

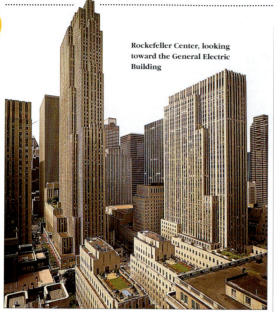

Rockefeller Center, looking toward the General Electric Building

Rockefeller Center ❶

Map 12 F5. **M** *47th-50th Sts.*

WHEN THE New York City Landmarks Preservation Commission unanimously voted to declare Rockefeller Center a landmark in 1985, they rightly called it "the heart of New York . . . a great unifying presence in the chaotic core of midtown Manhattan."

It is the largest privately owned complex of its kind and the inspiration for many cities to emulate its perfect urban mix. The Art Deco design was by a team of top architects headed by Raymond Hood. Works by 30 artists can be found in foyers, on facades, and in the gardens.

The site, once a botanic garden owned by Columbia University, was leased in 1928 by John D. Rockefeller, Jr., as an ideal central home for a new opera house. When the 1929 Depression scuttled the plans,

Rockefeller, stuck with a long-term lease, went ahead with his own development. The 14 buildings that were erected between 1931 and 1940 provided jobs for 225,000 people during the worst of the Depression. More development between 1957 and 1973 brought the Center to a total of 19 buildings in all.

In December 1932, Radio City Music Hall opened within the complex. It hosts dazzling events; the annual Christmas and Easter shows

***Wisdom* by Lee Lawrie, on the GE Building**

feature the famous Rockettes. In 1999, a complete renovation of the Hall brought back the glitter and sparkle of the original interior.

Diamond Row ❷

47th St. **Map** 12 F5. **M** *47th-50th Sts.* See **Shopping** *p320*.

NEARLY EVERY SHOP window on 47th Street glitters with gold and diamonds. The buildings are filled with booths and workshops where jewelers vie for customers while, upstairs, millions of dollars change hands. The diamond district was born in the 1930s, when the Jewish diamond cutters of Antwerp and Amsterdam fled to America to escape Nazism. Hasidic Jews with black hats, beards and long earlocks are still an integral part of the scene. Although mainly a wholesale district, individual customers are welcome. Bring cash, compare prices, haggle, and stay away if you know nothing about the value of diamonds. In the midst of all this, look for the sign saying "Wise men fish here" – here is the Gotham Book

Diamond Row's main commodity

Mart, a tiny, much-loved treasure house of literary gems *(see p322)*.

Lyceum Theater ❸

149 W 45th St. **Map** 12 E5. **C** *Telecharge 239-6200.* **M** *42nd St-5th Ave.* See **Entertainment** *p330*.

THE OLDEST New York theater still active is a Baroque-style bandbox as frilly as a wedding cake. This 1903 triumph was the first theater by Herts and Tallant, later renowned for their extravagant style. The Lyceum made history with a record run of 1,600 performances of the comedy *Born Yesterday*. It was the first theater to be designated a historic landmark but, though it is safe from change, it is often dark now that the Theater District has shifted westward.

The Rose Room in the Algonquin Hotel

Algonquin Hotel ❹

59 W 44th St. **Map** 12 F5. ☎ 840-6800. Ⓜ 42nd St-5th Ave. See *Where to Stay p278*.

T HE EXTERIOR is a bit fussy – iron bay windows in vertical rows, red brick, too much detail – but it is the ambience, not the 1902 architecture, that makes the Algonquin special. In the 1920s, the Rose Room was home to America's best-known luncheon club, the Round Table, with literary lights such as Alexander Woollcott, Franklin P. Adams, Dorothy Parker, Robert Benchley and Harold Ross. All were associated with the *New Yorker* (Ross was the founding editor), whose 25 West 43rd Street headquarters had a back door opening into the hotel.

A recent renovation has preserved the old-fashioned, civilized feel of the Rose Room, as well as the cozy, paneled lobby where publishing types and theater-goers still like to gather for drinks, settling into comfortable armchairs and ringing a small brass bell to summon the waiters.

New York Yacht Club ❺

37 W 44th St. **Map** 12 F5. Ⓜ 42nd St-5th Ave. ⬤ to the public (access to members only).

A WHIMSICAL 1899 creation, this private club has the carved sterns of 16th-century Dutch galleons in the three bay windows. The prows of the ships are borne up by sculpted dolphins and waves spilling over the windowsills and splashing down to the pavement. (The building, just over 100 years old, has been spruced up for its next century.)

This is the birthplace of the America's Cup yacht race, which was based in the US from 1857 to 1983. That was the year the much coveted prize was taken from the table where it had stood for more than a century, when the *Australia II* sailed to a historic victory.

The America's Cup, the coveted yachting prize

Bryant Park ❻

Map 8 F1. Ⓜ 42nd St-5th Ave.

I N 1853, WITH the New York Public Library site still occupied by Croton Reservoir, Bryant Park (then Reservoir Park) housed a dazzling Crystal Palace, built for the World's Fair of that year *(see p23)*.

In the 1960s the park was a hangout for drug dealers and other undesirables. In 1989 the city closed and renovated it, reclaiming it for workers and visitors to relax in. In spring and fall, world-famous fashion shows take place here; in the summer, there are free classic movie screenings.

Over seven million books lie in storage stacks beneath the park.

Statue of poet William Cullen Bryant in Bryant Park

Bryant Park Hotel ❼

40 W 40th St. **Map** 8 F1. Ⓜ 42nd St-Grand Central. .

T HE AMERICAN Radiator building (now the Bryant Park Hotel) was the first major New York work by Raymond Hood and John Howells, who went on to design the Daily News Building *(see p153)*, the McGraw-Hill building, and Rockefeller Center. The 1924 structure is reminiscent of one of Hood's best-known Gothic buildings, Chicago's Tribune Tower. Here, the design is sleeker, giving the building the illusion of being taller than its actual 23 stories. The black brick facade is set off by gold terra-cotta trim, evoking images of flaming coals: a comparison that would have suited its original owners well, since they made heating equipment.

The building is now a luxury hotel right in the heart of Midtown, across the street from the New York Public Library, Bryant Park and Fifth Avenue.

The Bryant Park Hotel, formerly the American Radiator Building

The New York Public Library **8**

5th Ave and 42nd St. **Map** 8 F1. **C**
869-8089. **M** *42nd St–Grand Central.*
◯ *Mon–Sat; hours vary.* ● *public hols.*
◯ ♿ ✉ **Lectures, workshops,
readings.** ◻ **W** www.nypl.org

**The doorway leading to the Main
Reading Room**

IN 1897 THE COVETED JOB of
designing New York's main
public library was awarded to
architects Carrère & Hastings.
The library's first director
envisaged a light, quiet, airy
place for study, where millions
of books could be stored and
yet be available to readers as
promptly as possible. In the
hands of Carrère & Hastings,
his vision came true, in what
is considered the epitome of
New York's Beaux Arts period.

Built on the site of the
former Croton Reservoir *(see
p22),* it opened in 1911 to
immediate
acclaim,
despite
having
cost the
city $9
million.

**Barrel vaults of carved
white marble over the
stairs in the Astor Hall**

The vast, paneled Main
Reading Room stretches
two full blocks and is
suffused with daylight
from the two interior
courtyards. Below it
are 88 miles (140 km)
of shelves, holding over
seven million volumes.
A staff of over 100 and
a computerized dumb-
waiter can supply any
book within 10 minutes.

The Periodicals Room
holds 10,000 current
periodicals from 128
countries. On its walls
are murals by Richard
Haas, honoring New York's
great publishing houses. The
original library combined the
collections of John
Jacob Astor and James
Lenox. Its collections
today range from
Thomas Jefferson's
handwritten copy of
the Declaration of
Independence to
T.S. Eliot's typed
copy of "The
Waste Land." More
than 1,000 queries

**One of the library's two stone lions, named
Patience and Fortitude by Mayor LaGuardia**

**The Main Reading Room, with its
original bronze reading lamps**

are answered daily, using the
vast database of the CATNYP
computer catalog.

This library is the hub of a
network of 82 branches, with
nearly seven million users.
Some branches are very well
known, such as the New York
Public Library for the Performing Arts at the Lincoln Center
(see p210) and the Schomburg
Center in Harlem *(see p227).*

International Center of Photography **⑨**

1133 Avenue of the Americas (43rd St)
Map 8 F1. **📞** *860 1777* **Ⓜ** *42nd St-Times Sq.* **🕐** *10am–5pm Tue–Thu, 10am–8pm Fri, 10am–6pm Sat & Sun*
♿ 📷 🖥 🅦 *www.icp.org*

T HIS MUSEUM was founded by Cornell Capa in 1974 to conserve the work of such photojournalists as his brother Robert, who was killed on assignment in 1954. The ICP's collection of 12,500 original prints contains work by many top photographers, including Ansel Adams and Henri Cartier-Bresson. Special exhibitions are organized from the contents of the archive, as well as from outside sources. There are also films, lectures, and classes.

Times Square **⑩**

Map 8 E1. **Ⓜ** *42nd St-Times Sq.*
ℹ *Times Square Visitors Center, 1560 Broadway (46th St) 8am–8pm daily.* **☑** *noon Fri.* **🅦** *www.timessquarebid.org*

T HE 1990s saw a huge transformation in Times Square, reversing a decline that began during the Depression – the square is now a safe and vibrant place for theatergoers and tourists, where Broadway traditions comfortably coexist with modern innovations.

Although the *New York Times* has moved on from its original headquarters at the south end of the square, the silver ball still drops at midnight on New Years Eve, as it has since the building opened with fanfare and fireworks in 1906. Exciting new buildings, such as the Bertlesmann building and the fashionably minimalist Condé Nast offices, sit comfortably alongside the classic Broadway theaters.

Broadway's fortunes have also revived. Many theaters, such as the New Victory and the New Amsterdam, have been reclaimed and renovated.

They are again housing new productions, and theatergoers throng the area's bars and restaurants each evening.

The newest landmark is the 57-story skyscraper designed by Miami architects Arquitectonica, that tops the E-Walk entertainment and retail complex at 42nd Street and Eighth Avenue *(see p140)*. Other new attractions include an outpost of Madame Tussaud's Wax Museum at 42nd Street, between Seventh and Eighth Avenue, and Lazer Park, a huge lazer tag arena, at 46th Street and Broadway.

W.C. Fields (far left) and Eddie Cantor (holding top hat, right) in the 1918 *Ziegfeld Follies* at the New Amsterdam Theater

New Amsterdam Theater **⑪**

214 W 42nd St. **Map** 8 E1. **📞** *282-2907* **Ⓜ** *42nd St-Times Sq.* **☑** *10am-5pm Mon, 10am-12pm Tues.*

T HIS WAS the most opulent theater in the United States when it opened in 1903, and the first to have an Art Nouveau interior. It was owned for a time by Florenz Ziegfeld, who produced his famous *Follies* revue here between 1914 and 1918 – with Broadway's first $5 ticket price. He remodeled the roof garden into another theater, the Aerial Gardens. This is one of the fine early theaters on 42nd Street that fell on hard times. With the rehabilitation of Times Square its fortunes rose again, and it is once more in Show Business.

The Art Deco top of the Paramount Building

Group Health Insurance Building **⑫**

330 W 42nd St. **Map** 8 D1. **Ⓜ** *42nd St.* **🕐** *office hours.*

T HIS 1931 design by Raymond Hood was the only New York building selected for the influential International Style survey of 1932 *(see p41)*. Its unusual design gives it a stepped profile seen from east and west, but a slab effect viewed from north or south. The exterior's horizontal bands of blue-green terra-cotta have earned it the nickname "jolly green giant." Step inside to see the classic Art Deco lobby of opaque glass and stainless steel.

One block west is Theater Row, a pleasant group of Off-Broadway theaters and cafés.

Paramount Building **⑬**

1501 Broadway. **Map** 8 E1. **Ⓜ** *34th St.*

T HE FABULOUS ground-floor movie theater where bobby-soxers stood in line in the 1940s to hear Frank Sinatra perform is gone, but there's still a theatrical feel to the massive building designed by Rapp & Rapp in 1927. On each side are symmetrical setbacks, 14 in all, rising like building blocks to an Art Deco crown – a tower, clock and globe. In the heyday of the "Great White Way," the tower was lit, with an observation deck at the top.

Shubert Alley ⑭

Between W 44th and W 45th St.
Map 12 E5. **M** *42nd St-Times Sq.*

THE PLAYHOUSES on the streets west of Broadway are rich in theater lore – and in notable architecture. Two classic theaters built in 1913 are the Booth (22 West 45th Street), named after actor Edwin Booth, and the Shubert (221 West 44th), after theater baron Sam S. Shubert. They form the west wall of Shubert Alley, where aspiring actors lined up, hoping for a casting in a Shubert play.

A Chorus Line ran at the Shubert until 1990, for a record 6,137 performances; Katharine Hepburn starred earlier in The Philadelphia Story. Across from the 44th Street end of the alley is the St. James, where Rodgers and Hammerstein made their debut with Oklahoma! in 1941, followed by The King and I. Nearby is Sardi's, the restaurant where actors waited for opening night reviews. Irving Berlin staged The Music Box Revue opposite the other end of the alley in 1921. His Music Box Theater has since housed many famous shows.

The tiled Moorish facade of the City Center of Music and Drama

MONY Tower ⑮

1740 Broadway. **Map** 12 E4.
M *57th St.* ● *to the public.*

BUILT IN 1950, the head office of the Mutual of New York insurance company (now MONY Financial Services) has a weather vane that tells you everything except the wind direction. The mast turns green for fair, orange for cloudy, flashing orange for rain and white for snow. Lights moving up the mast mean warmer weather; lights going down mean get out your overcoat!

City Center of Music and Dance ⑯

131 W 55th St. **Map** 12 E4.
C *581-1212.* **M** *57th St.* Ø &
See **Entertainment** *p334.* W
www.citycenter.org

THIS HIGHLY ornate Moorish structure with its dome of Spanish tiles was designed in 1924 as a Masonic Shriners' Temple. It was saved from the developers by Mayor La Guardia, becoming home to the New York City Opera and Ballet in 1943. When the troupes moved to Lincoln Center, City Center lived on as a major venue for dance. Renovation work has preserved the delightful excesses of the architecture.

Carnegie Hall ⑰

154 W 57th Street. **Map** 12 E3.
C *903-9765.* **M** *57th St, 59th St.*
Museum ○ *11am–4:30pm daily &
after concerts.* ● *Wed.* Ø & ✗
▣ See **Entertainment** *p338.*
W www.carnegiehall.org

FINANCED BY millionaire philanthropist Andrew Carnegie, New York's first great concert hall opened in 1891 in what was then a suburb of the city. The terra-cotta and brick Italian Renaissance–style building is said to have among the best acoustics in the world. On opening night, when Tchaikovsky was a guest conductor, all of New York's

Auditorium of the Shubert Theater, built by Henry Herts in 1913

finest families attended; many waited an hour before they could alight from their horse-drawn carriages.

For many years Carnegie Hall was home to the New York Philharmonic, under such conductors as Arturo Toscanini, Leopold Stokowski, Bruno Walter and Leonard Bernstein. Playing Carnegie Hall quickly became an international symbol of success for both classical and popular musicians.

A campaign led by violinist Isaac Stern in the late 1950s saved the building from redevelopment as offices, and in 1964 the hall was made a national landmark. Interior renovation in 1986 brought the bronze balconies and the ornamental plaster back to their original splendor. The corridors are lined with memorabilia of artists who have performed here. In 1991, a museum opened adjacent to the first-tier level, telling the story of the illustrious first 100 years of "The House that Music Built."

Millionaire Andrew Carnegie

Today, top orchestras and performers from around the world still fill Carnegie Hall with their wonderful music. Tours of the hall are also available to visitors.

Russian Tea Room ⑱

150 W 57th St. **Map** 12 E3.
⟨ 974-2111. Ⓜ 57th St.
See **Restaurants and Bars** p303.
ⓦ www.russiantearoom.com

THIS RESTAURANT is a New York classic, and its location next to Carnegie Hall couldn't be better. After many delays, the restaurant reopened in 1999. The interiors display a the owner's vision of St. Petersburg on the Hudson, complete with bears, gilded trees with glass eggs, lavishly decorated

The new Russian Tea Room's opulent first-floor restaurant

private rooms, an aquarium, and modernized Russian food.

Alwyn Court Apartments ⑲

180 W 58th St. **Map** 12 E3. Ⓜ 57th St. ● to the public.

YOU CAN'T miss it – not with the fanciful crowns, dragons and other French Renaissance-style terra-cotta carvings covering the exterior of this 1909 Harde and Short apartment building. The ground floor has been altered and lost its cornice in the process, but the rest of the building is intact, an intricate stone tapestry, and one of a kind in the city.

The facade follows the style of François I, whose reign saw the building of some of the finest Loire Valley châteaux, and whose symbol, a crowned salamander, can be seen above the entrance to the building at 58th Street.

Residents and their guests are fortunate to be able to enjoy the visual delights of

Salamander on Alwyn Court

the interior courtyard, which features a dazzling display of the illusionistic skills of artist Richard Haas, in which plain walls are transformed into "carved" stonework.

Flight deck of the _Intrepid_

Intrepid Sea-Air-Space Museum ⑳

Pier 86, W 46th St. **Map** 11 A5. Ⓕ 245-0072. Ⓜ M42, M16, M50. ●
Apr–Sep: 10am–5pm daily; 10am–6pm Sat-Sun; Oct–Mar:10am–4pm Wed–Sun
Ⓖ Ⓓ ⓦ www.intrepidmuseum.org

ON THE _Intrepid_, a World War II US aircraft carrier, the exhibits range from fighter planes from the 1940s to the A-12, fastest spy plane in the world. The _Growler_, a guided-missile submarine, and the destroyer _Edson_ are also open.

Pioneers Hall traces the development of flying and the workings of today's super-carriers; Technologies Hall looks at ocean exploration and the rockets of the future. Mission Control offers live coverage of NASA shuttle missions via satellite.

LOWER MIDTOWN

FROM BEAUX ARTS to Art Deco, this section of midtown boasts some fine architecture. Quiet, residential Murray Hill was named for a country estate that once occupied the site. By the turn of the century, it was home to many of New York's first families, including the financier J.P. Morgan, whose library,

Brass door, Fred F. French Building

now a museum, reveals the grandeur of the age. The commercial pace quickens at 42nd Street, near Grand Central Terminal, where tall office buildings line the streets. However, few of the newer buildings have equaled the Beaux Arts Terminal itself or such Art Deco beauties as the Chrysler Building.

SIGHTS AT A GLANCE

Historic Streets and Buildings
Grand Central Terminal pp154–5 ❷
Home Savings of America ❸
Chanin Building ❹
Chrysler Building ❺
Daily News Building ❻
Tudor City ❼
Helmsley Building ❽
Fred F. French Building ⓬
Sniffen Court ⓯

Museums and Galleries
Pierpont Morgan Library pp162–3 ⓮
Japan Society ⓫

Modern Architecture
MetLife Building ❶
Nos. 1 and 2 United Nations Plaza ❾
United Nations pp158–61 ❿

Churches
Church of the Incarnation ⓭

GETTING THERE
By subway, take the Lexington Avenue 4, 5 or 6 trains to 42nd Street–Grand Central. Buses M15, M101/102, M1, M2, M3 and M4 run along the area's avenues, while the M34 and M42 are the crosstown buses.

Flower box in Sniffen Court

SEE ALSO

• *Street Finder*, maps 9, 12, 13
• *Where to Stay* pp274–5
• *Restaurants* pp290–92

KEY

▰	Street-by-Street map
Ⓜ	Subway station

0 meters   500
0 yards   500

The stainless-steel–coated spire of the Chrysler Building

Street by Street: Lower Midtown

A WALK IN THE neighborhood allows you to see an eclectic mix of New York's architectural styles. Step back to appreciate the contours of the tallest skyscrapers, and step inside to experience the many fine interiors, from modern atriums such as those in the Philip Morris Building and Ford Foundation buildings to the ornate details of the Home Savings Bank and the soaring spaces of Grand Central Terminal.

MetLife Building
This skyscraper, built by Pan Am in 1963, towers above Park Avenue. ❶

★ **Grand Central Terminal**
The vast, vaulted interior is a splendid reminder of the heyday of train travel ❷

The Philip Morris Building is the headquarters of a tobacco company. It houses a branch of the Whitney Museum, which specializes in modern American art.

Grand Central-42nd St. subway (lines S, 4, 5, 6, 7)

Chanin Building
Built for self-made real estate mogul Irwin Chanin in 1922, this building has a fine Art Deco lobby ❹

STAR SIGHTS

★ **Grand Central Terminal**

★ **Chrysler Building**

★ **Home Savings of America**

★ **Daily News Building**

Brass door, Home Savings Bank

★ **Home Savings of America**
Formerly the headquarters of the Bowery Savings Bank, this is one of the finest bank buildings in New York. Architects York & Sawyer designed it to resemble a Romanesque palace ❸

The Mobil Building has a self-cleaning stainless steel facade that is embossed in geometric patterns to prevent it from warping. It was built in 1955.

PARK AVENUE

E 41ST ST

LEXINGTON AVENUE

Helmsley Building

Its ornate entrance symbolized the wealth of the New York Central Railroad, the first occupants. It straddles Park Avenue near Grand Central **8**

Mailbox in the Chrysler Building

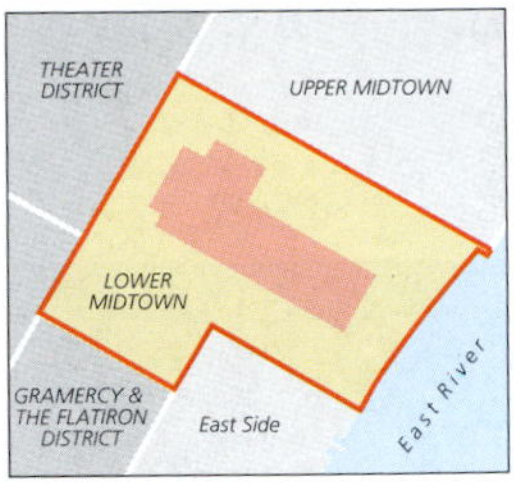

LOCATOR MAP
See Manhattan Map pp12–13

KEY

– – – Suggested route

0 meters 100

0 yards 100

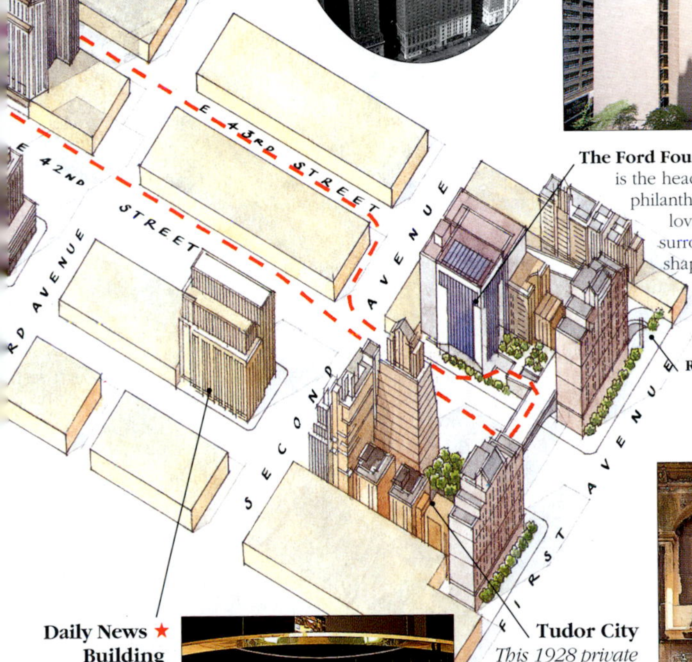

★ Chrysler Building

Ornamented with automotive motifs, this Art Deco delight was built in 1930 for the Chrysler car company **5**

Worker resting during construction of the Chrysler Building

The Ford Foundation Building
is the headquarters of Ford's philanthropic arm. It has a lovely interior garden surrounded by a cube-shaped building made of pinkish gray granite, glass and steel.

Ralph J. Bunche Park

E 43RD STREET

E 42ND STREET

3RD AVENUE

SECOND AVENUE

FIRST AVENUE

Daily News ★ Building

The Art Deco former home of the newspaper has a revolving globe in the lobby **6**

Tudor City

This 1928 private residential complex has 3,000 apartments. Built in the Tudor style, it features fine stonework details **7**

MetLife Building ❶

200 Park Ave. **Map** 13 A5.
Ⓜ *42nd St-Grand Central.*
◯ *office hours.* 🍸 🍴

Lobby of the MetLife Building

Once, the sculptures atop the Grand Central Terminal stood out against the sky. Then this colossus, formerly called the Pan Am Building and designed by Walter Gropius, Emery Roth and Sons and Pietro Belluschi, rose up in 1963 to block the Park Avenue view. It dwarfed the terminal and aroused universal dislike. At the time it was the largest commercial building in the world, and the dismay over its scale helped thwart a later plan to build a tower over the terminal itself.

It is ironic that the New York skies were blocked by Pan Am, a company that had opened up the skies as a means of travel for millions of people. When the company began in 1927, Charles Lindbergh, fresh from his solo trans-atlantic flight, was one of their pilots and an adviser on new routes. By 1936, Pan Am managed to introduce the first trans-Pacific passenger route, and in 1947 they introduced the first round-the-world route.

The building's famous roof-top heliport was abandoned in 1977 after a freak accident showered debris on to the surrounding streets. Now Pan Am itself has gone, too, and in 1981 the entire building was sold to the Metropolitan Life organization.

Grand Central Terminal ❷

See pp154–5.

Home Savings of America ❸

110 E 42nd St. **Map** 9 A1.
Ⓜ *42nd St-Grand Central.* ◯
banking hours.

Many consider this 1923 building the best work of the best bank architects of the 1920s. York & Sawyer chose the style of a Romanesque basilica for the uptown offices of the venerable Bowery Savings Bank (now Home Savings of America). An arched entry leads into the vast banking room, with a high beamed ceiling, marble mosaic floors and marble columns that support the stone arches that soar overhead.

Facade of Home Savings of America building

Between the columns are unpolished mosaic panels of marble from France and Italy. The rich detailing includes symbolic animal motifs, such as a squirrel representing thrift and a lion for power.

Chanin Building ❹

122 E 42nd St. **Map** 9 A1.
Ⓜ *42nd St-Grand Central.*
◯ *office hours.*

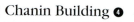

Stonework detail on the Chanin Building

Once the headquarters of Irwin S. Chanin, one of New York's leading real estate developers, the 56-story tower was the first skyscraper in the Grand Central area, a harbinger of things to come. It was designed by Sloan & Robertson in 1929 and is one of the best examples of the Art Deco period. A wide bronze band, patterned with birds and fish, runs the full length of the facade; the terra-cotta base is decorated with a luxuriant tangle of stylized leaves and flowers. Inside, Radio City's sculptor René Chambellan worked on the reliefs and the bronze grills, elevator doors, mailboxes, clocks and pattern of waves in the floor. The vestibule reliefs chart the career of Chanin, who was a self-made man.

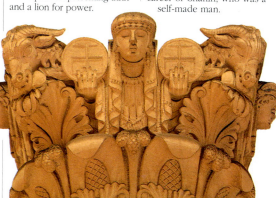

Carved detail in the banking hall of Home Savings of America

Chrysler Building ❺

405 Lexington Ave. **Map** 9 A1.
☎ 682-3070. **M** 42nd St-Grand
Central. ⬜ office hours, lobby only.
📷 ♿

**Stainless steel
gargoyle on the
Chrysler Building**

WALTER P. CHRYSLER began
his career in a Union
Pacific Railroad machine
shop, but his passion for the
motor car helped him
rise swiftly to the top
of the new industry,
to found, in 1925, the
corporation bearing
his name. His wish for
a headquarters in New
York that symbolized
his company led to a
building that will
always be linked with
the golden age of
motoring. Following
Chrysler's wishes, the
stainless-steel Art
Deco spire resembles
a car radiator grill; the
building's series of
stepped setbacks are
emblazoned with
winged radiator caps,
wheels and stylized
automobiles; and there
are gargoyles modeled
on hood ornaments
from the 1929
Chrysler Plymouth.

Though it lost the
title of tallest building
in the world to the
Empire State Building
only a few months
after its completion in
1930, William Van
Alen's 77-story Chrysler
Building and its shining
crown are still among the
city's best-known and most-
loved landmarks.

The crowning spire was
kept a secret until the last
moment, when, having been
built in the fire shaft, it was
raised into position through
the roof, ensuring that the
building would be higher
than the Bank of Manhattan,
then just completed down-
town by Van Alen's great
rival, H. Craig
Severance.

Van Alen was
poorly rewarded
for his labors.
Chrysler accused him
of accepting bribes from
contractors and refused to
pay him. Van Alen's career
never recovered from the slur.

The stunning lobby, once
used as a showroom for
Chrysler cars, was perfectly
restored in 1978. It is lavishly
decorated with patterned
marbles and granite from
around the world and has
chromed steel trim. A vast
painted ceiling by Edward

Elevator door at the Chrysler Building

Trumball shows transportation scenes of the late 1920s.

Although the Chrysler Corporation never occupied the
building as their headquarters,
their name remains, as firm a
fixture as the gargoyles.

Entrance to the News Building

Daily News
Building ❻

220 E 42nd St. **Map** 9 B1.
M 42nd St-Grand Central.
⬜ 8am–6pm Mon–Fri.

THE *DAILY NEWS* was founded
in 1919, and by 1925 it
was a million-seller. It was
known, rather scathingly, as
"the servant girl's bible," for
its concentration on scandals,
celebrities and murders, its
readable style and heavy use
of illustration. Over the years
it has stuck to what it does
best, and the formula paid off
handsomely. It revealed
stories such as the romance of
Edward VIII and Mrs.
Simpson, and has become
renowned for its punchy
headlines that sum up the
mood of the moment. Its
circulation figures are still
among the highest in the
United States.

Its headquarters, designed by
Raymond Hood in 1930, has
rows of brown and black brick
alternating with windows to
create a vertical striped effect.
Hood's lobby is familiar to
many as that of the *Daily
Planet* in the 1980s *Superman*
movies. It includes the world's
largest interior globe, and
bronze lines on the floor
indicate the direction of world
cities and the position of the
planets. At night, the intricate
detail over the front entrance of
the building is lit from within
by neon. The newspaper's
offices are now on West 43rd
Street, and the future of the
building is in some doubt.

Grand Central Terminal ❷

Iᴺ 1871 CORNELIUS VANDERBILT opened a
railway station on 42nd Street. Although
often revamped, it was never large enough
and was finally demolished. The present
station opened in 1913. This Beaux Arts
gem has been a gateway to and symbol of
the city ever since. Its glory is the soaring
main concourse and the way it separates
pedestrian and train traffic. The building
has a steel frame covered with plaster and
marble. Reed & Stern were in charge of
the logistical planning; Warren & Wetmore
for the overall design. The restoration by
architects Beyer
Blinder Belle
is awesome.

42nd Street colonnaded facade

Statuary on the 42nd Street Facade
*Jules-Alexis Coutans sculptures of Mercury,
Hercules and Minerva crown the main entrance.*

Main Concourse Level

Circumferential Road

Cornelius Vanderbilt
*The railroad magnate was
known as the "Commodore."*

Subway

Commuters use the terminal.
Half a million people pass
through it each day. An escalator
leads up into the MetLife
Building, where there are
specialty shops and restaurants.

Vanderbilt Hall, adjacent
to the Main Concourse, is a
good example of Beaux Arts
architecture. It is decorated
with gold chandeliers and
pink marble.

Grand Central Oyster Bar
*This popular spot (see p294),
with its yellow Guastavino
tiles, is one of the many
eateries in the station. The
dining concourse is
enormous, with food,
snacks, and drinks to suit
all tastes.*

Sᴛᴀʀ Sɪɢʜᴛs

★ **Grand Staircases**

★ **Main Concourse**

★ **Central Information**

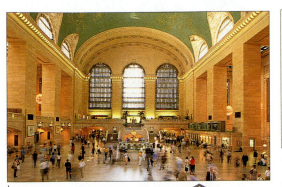

VISITORS' CHECKLIST

E 42nd St at Park Ave.
Map 13 A5. 532-4900.
4, 5, 6, 7, S to Grand Central
M104, M42. 5:30am–
1:30am daily. Wed
12:30pm (free). 935-3960.
Fri 12:30pm (free). 697-
1245. Baggage
check; lost & found
W www.grandcentralterminal.com

★ **Main Concourse**
This vast pedestrian area with its high vaulted ceiling is dominated by three

great arched windows, 75 ft (23 m) high on each side.

Vaulted Ceiling
A medieval manu-script provided the basis for French artist Paul Helleu's zodiac design containing over 2,500 stars. Lights pinpoint the major constellations.

The Lower Level
is linked to the other levels by stairways, ramps and brand new escalators.

★ **Grand Staircase**
There are now two of these double flights of marble steps, styled after the staircase in Paris' Opera House, and a vivid reminder of the glamorous days of early rail travel.

★ **Central Information**
This four-faced clock tops the travel information booth on the main concourse.

Tudor City **7**

E. 42nd St. **Map** 9 B1.
Ⓜ *42nd St–Grand Central.* Ⓦ
www.tudorcity.com

T HIS EARLY URBAN renewal
effort, developed between
1925 and 1928 by the Fred
F. French Company, was
designed as a middle-class
city within the city. Rents
were modest, thanks to the
"large-scale production." There
are 12 buildings containing
3,000 apartments, a hotel,
shops, restaurants, a post office
and two small private parks, all
built in the Tudor Gothic style.
  In the mid-19th century the
area was the haunt of gangs
and criminals and was known
as Corcoran's Roost, after
Paddy Corcoran, the leader of
the notorious "Rag Gang." The
East River shore was lined
with glue factories, slaughter-
houses, breweries and a
gasworks. Some were still
there when Tudor City was
planned, so its buildings have
only a few outward-facing
windows from which residents
might enjoy what is
now a great view
of the river.

Upper stories of Tudor City

Helmsley Building **8**

230 Park Ave. **Map** 13 A5.
Ⓜ *42nd St–Grand Central.* ◻ *office
hours.*

O NE OF THE GREAT New
York views looks south
down Park Avenue to the
Helmsley Building straddling
the busy traffic flow beneath.
There is just one flaw – the
monolithic MetLife Building
(which was built by Pan Am
as its corporate headquarters

Performance at the Japan Society

in 1963) that towers behind it,
replacing the building's
former backdrop, the sky.
  Built by Warren & Whetmore
in 1929, the Helmsley Building
was originally the headquarters
of the New York Central Railroad Company. Its current
owner is Leona Helmsley,
wife of the late
Harry Helmsley, a
billionaire who
began his career
as a New York
office boy for
$12 per week.
Leona was a
prominent
feature in all the
advertise-
ments for
their hotel
chain – until her imprisonment in 1989 for tax evasion
on a grand scale. Many
observers believe that the
extravagant glitter of the
building's face-lift is due to
Leona's over-blown
taste in decor.

1 & 2 United Nations Plaza **9**

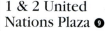

Map 13 B5. Ⓜ *42nd St.-
Grand Central.*

T HESE TWO
GREAT columns
of lovely blue-
green mirrored
glass are set at an
angle to each other;
the play of light and reflections
on their gleaming sides and
sloping setbacks make them
seem an ever-changing,
giant work of modern art.
The marble and mirrored
interiors are also stunning.
They house streamlined
modern offices and, in
No. 1, the Regal
United Nations
Plaza Hotel *(see
p280)*. Here,
the guest list
frequently includes many UN
delegates from all over the
world as well as a number of
visiting heads of state. Even
the stresses of international
diplomacy must ease when
one is floating lazily in the
glassed-in swimming pool,
enjoying the bird's-eye views
of the city and the United
Nations itself.

United Nations **10**

See pp158–61.

Japan Society **11**

333 E 47th St. **Map** 13 B5.
Ⓒ *832-1155.* Ⓜ *42nd St.-Grand
Central.* **Gallery** ◻ *11am–6pm
Tue–Sun.* ⦸ & Ⓦ
www.japansociety.org

T HE HEADQUARTERS of the
Japan Society, founded in
1907 to foster understanding
and cultural exchange
between Japan and
the US, was under-
written by
John D.
Rockefeller

Roman gods reclining against the Helmsley Building clock

III at a cost of some $4.3 million. The striking black building with its delicate sun grilles was designed by Tokyo architects Junzo Yoshimura and George Shimamoto in 1971. It includes an auditorium, a language center, a research library, a museum gallery and serene, traditional Oriental gardens.

Changing exhibits include a variety of Japanese arts, from swords to kimonos to scrolls. The society offers programs of Japanese performing arts, lectures, language classes and many business workshops for American and Japanese executives and managers.

Fred F. French Building ⑫

521 5th Ave. **Map** 12 F5.
Ⓜ *42nd St.-Grand Central.* ☐ *office hours.*

BUILT IN 1927 to house the best-known real estate firm of the day, this is a fabulously opulent creation. It was designed by French's chief architect, H. Douglas Ives, in collaboration with Sloan & Robertson, whose

Tiffany stained-glass window in the Church of the Incarnation

other work included the Chanin Building *(see p152).* They handsomely blended Near Eastern, ancient Egyptian and Greek styles with early Art Deco forms.

Multicolored faïence ornaments decorate the upper facade, and the water tower is hidden in a false top level of the building. Its disguise is an elaborate one, with reliefs showing a rising sun flanked by griffins and bees and symbols of virtues such as integrity and industry. Winged Assyrian beasts ride on a bronze frieze over the entrance. These exotic themes continue into the vaulted lobby, with its elaborate polychrome ceiling decoration and 25 gilt-bronze doors.

This was the first building project to employ members of the Native Canadian Caughnawaga tribe as construction workers. They did not fear heights and soon became highly sought-after scaffolders for many of the city's most famous skyscrapers.

Church of the Incarnation ⑬

205 Madison Ave. **Map** 9 A2.
☎ *689-6350.* Ⓜ *42nd St.-Grand Central.* ☐ *11:30am–2pm Mon–Wed Fri.* ✝ *8:30am, noon Sun.* ☐ ♿ *By appointment.* ☐ Ⓦ *www.churchoftheincarnation.org*

THIS EPISCOPAL church and parish house date from 1864, when Madison Avenue was home to the elite. Its patterned sandstone and brownstone exterior is representative of the period.

The interior has an oak communion rail by Daniel Chester French; a chancel mural, *Adoration of the Magi,* by John La Farge; and stained-glass windows by La Farge, Tiffany, William Morris and Edward Burne-Jones.

Pierpont Morgan Library ⑭

See pp162–3.

Sniffen Court ⑮

150–158 E 36th St. **Map** 9 A2.
Ⓜ *33rd St.*

HERE IS a delightful, intimate courtyard of ten brick Romanesque revival carriage houses, built by John Sniffen in the 1850s.

They are perfectly and improbably preserved off a busy block in modern New York. The house at the south end was used as a studio by the American sculptor Malvina Hoffman, whose plaques of Greek horsemen decorate the exterior wall.

Lobby of the Fred F. French Building

Malvina Hoffman's studio

United Nations ⑩

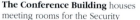

Flag of the
United Nations

F OUNDED IN 1945 near the end of World War
II with 51 members, the United Nations
now numbers some 188 nations. Its
aims are to preserve world peace,
promote self-determination and to aid
economic and social well-being around
the globe. New
York was chosen
as the UN headquarters,
and John D. Rockefeller, Jr. donated
$8.5 million for the purchase of the
East River site. The chief architect
was American Wallace Harrison, who
worked with an international Board
of Design Consultants. The 18-acre
(7-ha) site is not on US territory. It is
an international zone and has its
own stamps and post office. Daily
guided tours show visitors the
various council chambers and
General Assembly hall.

**United Nations
headquarters**

Secretariat
building

The Conference Building houses
meeting rooms for the Security
Council, the Trusteeship Council and
the Economic and Social Council.

Trusteeship
Council

★ **Security Council**
*Delegates and their
assistants confer around
the horseshoe-shaped
table while verbatim
reporters and other UN
staff members sit at the
long table in the center.*

Economic
and Social
Council

STAR FEATURES

★ **General Assembly**

★ **Security Council**

★ **Peace Bell**

★ **Reclining Figure**

★ **Peace Bell**
*Cast from the coins of
60 nations, this gift
from Japan hangs on a
cypress pagoda shaped
like a Shinto shrine.*

Rose Garden
*Twenty-five varieties of roses
adorn the manicured
gardens on the East River.*

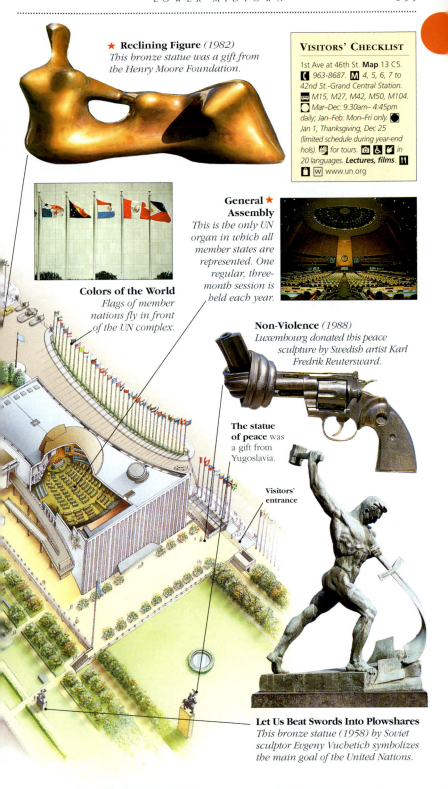

★ **Reclining Figure** (1982)
This bronze statue was a gift from the Henry Moore Foundation.

VISITORS' CHECKLIST

1st Ave at 46th St. **Map** 13 C5.
963-8687. 4, 5, 6, 7 to
42nd St.-Grand Central Station.
M15, M27, M42, M50, M104.
Mar–Dec: 9:30am– 4:45pm
daily; Jan–Feb: Mon–Fri only.
Jan 1, Thanksgiving, Dec 25
(limited schedule during year-end
hols). for tours. in
20 languages. **Lectures, films**.
www.un.org

General ★
Assembly
This is the only UN organ in which all member states are represented. One regular, three-month session is held each year.

Colors of the World
Flags of member nations fly in front of the UN complex.

Non-Violence (1988)
Luxembourg donated this peace sculpture by Swedish artist Karl Fredrik Reutersward.

The statue of peace was a gift from Yugoslavia.

Visitors' entrance

Let Us Beat Swords Into Plowshares
This bronze statue (1958) by Soviet sculptor Evgeny Vuchetich symbolizes the main goal of the United Nations.

The Work of the United Nations

T HE GOALS of the United Nations are pursued by three UN councils and a General Assembly comprising all member nations. The Secretariat carries out the administrative work of the organization. Guided tours allow visitors to see the Security Council Chamber and General Assembly Hall.

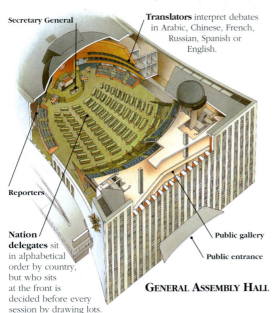

Secretary General

Translators interpret debates in Arabic, Chinese, French, Russian, Spanish or English.

Reporters

Nation delegates sit in alphabetical order by country, but who sits at the front is decided before every session by drawing lots.

Public gallery

Public entrance

GENERAL ASSEMBLY HALL

GENERAL ASSEMBLY

T HE GENERAL ASSEMBLY is the governing body of the UN and has regular sessions each year from mid-September to mid-December. Special sessions are also held when the Security Council or a majority of members request one. All member states are represented with an equal vote, regardless of size. The General Assembly may discuss any international problem raised by the members or by other UN bodies. Although it cannot enact laws, recommen-dations strongly influence world opinion; these require a two-thirds majority vote.

Lots are drawn before each session to determine the seating in the chamber for the delegations. All 1,898 seats in the chamber are equipped with earphones that offer simultaneous translations in several languages. The General Assembly also appoints the Secretary General (on the recommendation of the Security Council), approves the UN budgets and elects the non-permanent members of

Foucault's Pendulum **(Holland); its slowly rotating swing is proof of the earth's rotation on its axis**

the Councils. Together with the Security Council, it also appoints the judges of the International Court of Justice, based in the Netherlands.

SECURITY COUNCIL

T HE MOST POWERFUL part of the UN is the Security Council. It strives to achieve

Mural symbolizing peace and freedom by Per Krohg (Norway)

international peace and security and intervenes in crises such as the fighting in Kuwait, the former Yugo-slavia and Kosovo. It is the only body whose decisions member states are obliged to obey as well as the only one in continuous session.

Five of its members – China, France, the Russian Federation, the United Kingdom and the United States – are permanent. The other nations are elected by the General Assembly to serve two-year terms.

When international conflicts arise, the Council first tries to seek agreement by mediation. If fighting breaks out, it may issue cease-fire orders and impose military or economic sanctions. It could also decide to send UN peace-keeping missions into troubled areas to separate opposing factions until issues can be resolved through diplomatic channels.

Military intervention is the Council's last resort. UN forces may be deployed, and peace-keeping forces are resident in such places as Cyprus and the Middle East.

TRUSTEESHIP COUNCIL

T HE SMALLEST OF the councils, this is the only UN body whose workload is decreasing. The council was established in 1945 with the goal of fostering peaceful independence for non–self-governing territories or colonies. Since then, more than 80 colonies have gained self-rule, and the number of people living in dependent territories has been reduced from 750 million to about 3 million. The council currently consists of the five permanent members of the Security Council.

Zanetti mural (Dominican Republic) in the Conference Building depicting the struggle for peace

Trusteeship Council Chamber

ECONOMIC AND SOCIAL COUNCIL

THE 54 MEMBERS OF this Council work to improve the standard of living and social welfare around the world, goals that consume 80% of the UN's resources. It makes recommendations to the General Assembly, to each member nation and to the UN's specialized agencies. The Council is assisted by commissions dealing with regional economic problems, human rights abuses, population, narcotics and women's rights. It also works with the International Labor Organization, the World Health Organization, UNICEF and other global welfare organizations.

SECRETARIAT

AN INTERNATIONAL STAFF of 16,000 works for the Secretariat to carry out the day-to-day work of the United Nations, providing services to all UN councils, commissions and agencies. The Secretariat is headed by the Secretary General, who

plays a key role as a spokesperson in the organization's peace-keeping efforts. The Secretary General is appointed by the General Assembly for a five-year term.

IMPORTANT EVENTS IN UN HISTORY

Soviet premier Krushchev speaking to the General Assembly in 1960

WITH NO PERMANENT police force to deal with disputes, the UN depends on voluntary compliance and

military support from members. As a result, it has had successes and failures in its efforts to keep the peace. In 1948, the UN declared South Korea the legitimate government of Korea; two years later, it played a leading role in defending South Korea against the invading North Korean armies. In 1949, the UN helped negotiate a cease-fire between Indonesia and the Netherlands and set up a conference that led to the Dutch granting independence to Indonesia. In 1974, the People's Republic of China – long refused membership in favor of Taiwan – gained UN membership, restoring it to the international community.

The most persistent problems have been in the Middle East. When Israel was invaded by five Arab nations after it was declared a state in 1948, the UN negotiated a cease-fire; UN forces have been present in the area since 1974, but the Palestinians' status is unresolved.

The UN was instrumental in negotiating the independence of Cyprus from Britain in 1957, and in 1964 it created a UN military force in Cyprus to keep peace between the Greeks and Turks.

WORKS OF ART AT THE UN

The UN Building has acquired numerous works of art and reproductions by major artists; many have been gifts from member nations. Most of them have either a peace or international friendship theme. The legend on Norman Rockwell's *The Golden Rule* reads "Do unto others as you would have them do unto you." Marc Chagall designed a large stained-glass window as a memorial to former Secretary General Dag Hammarskjöld, who was accidentally killed while on a peace mission in 1961. A Henry Moore sculpture graces the grounds. There are many other sculptures and paintings by the artists of many nations.

The Golden Rule (1985), a large mosaic by Norman Rockwell

Morgan Library ⑭

THE MORGAN LIBRARY came into being as the private collection of banker Pierpont Morgan. In 1902, architects McKim, Mead & White designed a magnificent palazzo-style building to house it. Morgan's son, J.P. Morgan, Jr., established the library as a public institution in 1924. Today it has one of the world's finest collections of rare manuscripts, prints, books and fine bindings displayed in a complex that includes the original library and J.P. Morgan, Jr.'s home.

Exterior of the original library building

★ Garden Court
This three-story skylit garden area links the library with the Morgan house.

Morgan House

KEY TO FLOOR PLAN
☐ Exhibition space
☐ Non-exhibition space

Forecourt Gallery

The Song of Los (1795)
Mystic poet William Blake designed and engraved this plate for one of his most innovative works.

The Nursery Alice
Lewis Carroll's characters are immortalized in John Tenniel's classic illustrations (c. 1865).

Exhibition Room

STAR EXHIBITS

★ **The West Room**

★ **The Rotunda**

★ **Garden Court**

★ **Manuscript of Mozart's Horn Concerto in E-flat Major**

Gutenberg Bible (1455)
Printed on vellum, this volume is one of only eleven surviving copies.

VISITORS' CHECKLIST

29 E. 36th St. **Map** 9 A2.
☎ 685-0008. Ⓜ 6 to 33rd St;
4, 5, 6, 7 to Grand Central; B, D,
F, Q to 42nd St. 🚌 M2, M3, M4
○ 10:30am–5pm Tue–Thu,
10:30am–8pm Fri, 10:30am–6pm
Sat, noon–6pm Sun. ● Mon &
hols. 🅿 🚫 ♿ 🎥 📷 🎬
Concerts, lectures, film/video.
Ⓦ www.morganlibrary.org

LIBRARY GUIDE

Mr. Morgan's Study and the original library contain some of his favorite paintings, objets d'art and rare acquisitions. Changing exhibitions provide visitors access to some of the world's most significant cultural artifacts.

★ Mozart's Horn Concerto in E-flat Major

The six surviving leaves of this score are written in different colored inks.

West Room (Mr. Morgan's study)

Rotunda

East Room

The walls are lined from floor to ceiling with triple tiers of bookcases. Murals show historical figures and their muses, and signs of the zodiac.

Main entrance

★ The Rotunda (1504)

The entrance foyer of the Library has marble columns and pilasters; the marble floor is modeled on the floor in Villa Pia in the Vatican gardens.

★ The West Room

Renaissance art and an antique, Florentine wooden ceiling adorn this room.

PIERPONT MORGAN

Pierpont Morgan (1837–1913) was not only a leading financier but also one of the great collectors of his time. Rare books and original manuscripts were his passion, and inclusion in his collection was an honor. In 1909, when Morgan requested the donation of the manuscript of *Pudd'nhead Wilson*, Mark Twain responded, "One of my high ambitions is gratified."

UPPER MIDTOWN

UPSCALE NEW YORK in all its diversity is here, in this area of churches, synagogues, clubs, museums, luxury hotels, famous stores, trend-setting skyscrapers and pockets of luxury living. For almost 30 years from 1833, it was home to society names

1946 Cisitalia in the MoMA

such as Astor and Vanderbilt. In the 1950s, architectural history was made when the Lever and Seagram buildings were erected. These first great modern towers marked mid-town Park Avenue's change from a residential street to a prestigious office address.

SIGHTS AT A GLANCE

Historic Streets and Buildings
Villard Houses ⑩
General Electric Building ⑫
Sutton Place and Beekman Place ⑱
Roosevelt Island ⑲
Fuller Building ㉑

Modern Architecture
Trump Tower ②
IBM Building ③
Lever House ⑭
Seagram Building ⑮
Citigroup Center ⑯

Museums and Galleries
Museum of Modern Art (MoMA) pp170–73 ⑤
American Craft Museum ⑥
American Folk Art Museum ⑦

Museum of Television and Radio ⑧

Churches and Synagogues
St. Thomas' Church ④
St. Patrick's Cathedral pp176–7 ⑨
St. Bartholomew's Church ⑪
Central Synagogue ⑰

Landmark Hotels
Waldorf–Astoria ⑬
Plaza Hotel ㉒

Landmark Stores
Fifth Avenue ①
Bloomingdale's ⑳

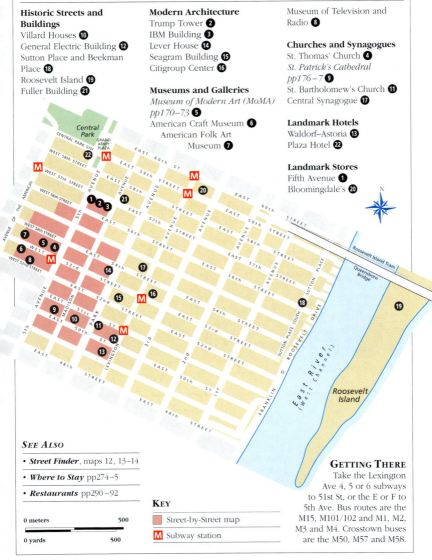

SEE ALSO

- *Street Finder*, maps 12, 13–14
- *Where to Stay* pp274–5
- *Restaurants* pp290–92

KEY

▨	Street-by-Street map
M	Subway station

0 meters   500
0 yards   500

GETTING THERE
Take the Lexington Ave 4, 5 or 6 subways to 51st St, or the E or F to 5th Ave. Bus routes are the M15, M101/102 and M1, M2, M3 and M4. Crosstown buses are the M50, M57 and M58.

◁ **View down Fifth Avenue**

Street by Street: Upper Midtown

THE LUXURY STORES that are synonymous with Fifth Avenue first blossomed as society moved on uptown. In 1917, Cartier's acquired the mansion of banker Morton F. Plant in exchange for a string of pearls, setting the style for other retailers to follow. But this stretch of midtown is not simply for shoppers. There are three distinctive museums and an equally diverse assembly of architectural styles to enjoy, too.

Fifth Avenue
Today's carriage rides offer a taste of past elegance **1**

The University Club was built in 1899 as an elite club for gentlemen.

American Craft Museum
This is a showcase for crafts – from ceramics to furniture **6**

St. Thomas' Church
Much of the interior carving was designed by sculptor Lee Lawrie **4**

★ **Museum of Modern Art**
This is one of the finest collections of modern art in the world **5**

Museum of Television and Radio
Exhibitions, seasons of special screenings, live events and a vast library of historic broadcasts are offered at this media museum **8**

Fifth Avenue subway (lines E, F)

Saks Fifth Avenue has offered goods in impeccable taste to generations of New Yorkers. *(See p.311.)*

★**St. Patrick's Cathedral**
This, the largest Catholic cathedral in the United States, is a magnificent Gothic Revival building **9**

Olympic Tower combines offices, apartments and a skylit atrium within its sleek walls.

Villard Houses
Five handsome brownstone houses now form part of the New York Palace Hotel **10**

STAR SIGHTS

★ **Museum of Modern Art**

★ **St. Patrick's Cathedral**

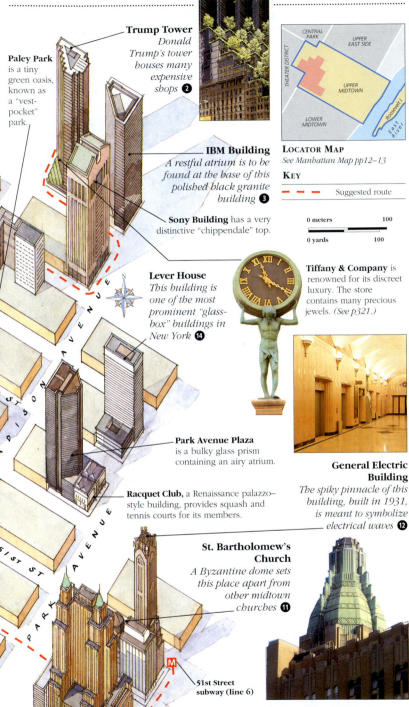

Trump Tower
Donald Trump's tower houses many expensive shops ❷

Paley Park
is a tiny green oasis, known as a "vest-pocket" park.

IBM Building
A restful atrium is to be found at the base of this polished black granite building ❸

Sony Building has a very distinctive "chippendale" top.

LOCATOR MAP
See Manhattan Map pp12–13

KEY

— — — 　　Suggested route

0 meters 　　　　　100
0 yards 　　　　　100

CENTRAL PARK
UPPER EAST SIDE
THEATER DISTRICT
UPPER MIDTOWN
LOWER MIDTOWN
East River
Roosevelt I.

Lever House
This building is one of the most prominent "glass-box" buildings in New York ⓮

Tiffany & Company is renowned for its discreet luxury. The store contains many precious jewels. *(See p321.)*

Park Avenue Plaza
is a bulky glass prism containing an airy atrium.

General Electric Building
The spiky pinnacle of this building, built in 1931, is meant to symbolize electrical waves ⓬

Racquet Club, a Renaissance palazzo–style building, provides squash and tennis courts for its members.

St. Bartholomew's Church
A Byzantine dome sets this place apart from other midtown churches ⓫

MADISON AVENUE

51ST ST

PARK AVENUE

Ⓜ **51st Street subway (line 6)**

Waldorf-Astoria
Old-world elegance has attracted many famous guests to this hotel, including the late Duke and Duchess of Windsor ⓭

Window display at Bergdorf Goodman *(see p311)*

Fifth Avenue ❶

Map 4 F1–16 E1. **M** *5th Ave-53rd St.*

Iᴺ 1883, ᴡʜᴇɴ William Henry Vanderbilt built his mansion at Fifth Avenue and 51st Street, he started a trend that resulted in palatial residences stretching as far as Central Park, built for top families such as the Astors, Belmonts and Goulds. Only a few remain to attest to the grandeur of the era.

One of these is the Cartier store at 651 Fifth Avenue, originally the home of Morton F. Plant, millionaire and commodore of the New York Yacht Club. As retailers swept north up the avenue – a trend that began in 1906 – society gradually moved to better locations uptown. In 1917, Plant moved to a new mansion at 86th Street, and legend has it that he traded his old home to Pierre Cartier for a perfectly matched string of pearls.

Fifth Avenue has been synonymous with luxury goods ever since. From Cartier at 52nd Street to Tiffany and Berg-dorf Goodman at 57th, you will find a range of famous brands symbolizing wealth and social standing today, just as Vanderbilt and Astor did more than a century ago.

Trump Tower ❷

725 5th Ave. **Map** 12 F3.
C *832-2000.* **M** *5th Ave-53rd St.*
Garden level, shops ◯ *10am–6pm Mon–Sat, noon–5pm Sun.* ***Building*** ◯ *10am–7pm daily. See* ***History*** *p31.* ◎ ⬤ ***Concerts.*** 🍴 💻 🛍
ⓦ www.trumponline.com

Aɢʟɪᴛᴛᴇʀɪɴɢ, exorbitantly expensive apartment and office tower rises above a lavish six-story atrium with layers of exclusive shops and cafés. Designed in 1983 by Der Scutt of Swanke, Hayden, Connell & Partners, the public space has pink marble, a waterfall, mirrors and glitz. It is the most opulent example of the new urban trend toward vertical shopping centers. The tower is a flamboyant monument to affluence by the developer Donald Trump, a symbol of the excesses of the 1980s. Next door, 727 Fifth Avenue is a complete contrast: the location of Tiffany & Co., the prestigious jewelers founded in 1837. Famed for its exquisite window displays, the store uses understated but elegant blue packaging as a status symbol in itself. Tiffany's was immortalized in New York culture by Truman Capote's

Entrance to Tiffany and Co., the exclusive jewelry emporium

IBM Building ❸

580 Madison Ave. **Map** 12 F3.
C *745-5994.* **M** *5th Ave.* ***Garden Plaza*** ◯ *8am–10pm daily.* ◎ ⬤
Newseum/NY **C** *317-7503.* ◯ *10am– 5:30pm Mon–Sat.* ⓦ www.newseum.org

Tʜɪs 43-sᴛᴏʀʏ tower was designed by Edward Larrabee Barnes. Completed in 1983, it is a sleek, five sided prism of gray-green polished granite, with a cantilevered corner at 57th Street. The Garden Plaza is open to the public. Near the atrium is a work by American sculptor Michael Heizer, entitled *Levitated Mass.* Inside a low, stain-less steel tank is a huge slab of granite which seems to float on air while beneath it, a sheet of water flows.

A new photo-journalism gallery, Newseum/NY, features exhibits, films, and lectures designed to further the public's under-standing of First Amendment issues and journalism.

Interior of the Trump Tower atrium

St. Thomas' Church ❹

1 W 53rd St. **Map** 12 F4.
📞 757-7013. **M** 5th Ave-53rd St.
🕐 7am–6pm daily. 🚻 frequent. 📷
♿ 📷 after 11am service & concerts
W www.saintthomaschurch.org

T HIS IS THE FOURTH home for this parish and the second on this site. Today's church was built between 1909 and 1914 to replace an earlier structure destroyed in a fire in 1905. The previous building had provided the setting for most of the glittering high society weddings of the late 19th century. The most lavish of these was in 1895 when heiress Consuela Vanderbilt married the English duke of Marlborough.

The limestone building, in French–Gothic style, has a single asymmetrical tower and an off-center nave, novel solutions to the architectural problems posed by its corner position. The richly carved, shimmering white screens behind the altar were designed by architect Bertram Goodhue and sculptor Lee Lawrie. Carvings in the choir stalls, dating from the 1920s, include modern inventions such as the telephone, Presidents Roosevelt and Wilson, and Lee Lawrie himself.

Silver chalice at the Craft Museum

Museum of Modern Art ❺

See pp170–73.

American Craft Museum ❻

40 W 53rd St. **Map** 12 F4.
📞 956-3535. **M** 5th Ave-53rd St.
🕐 10am– 6pm Tue–Sun, 10am–8pm
Thu. 📷 📷 ♿ 📷 **Lectures, films**.
W www.americancraftmuseum.org

T HERE IS NO BETTER place to experience the vitality of the contemporary American crafts movement than this, the showcase home of the American Crafts Council. On

display are handmade quilts, ceramics, glass, textiles, wood, silver, furniture, paper and metalwork drawn from the museum's extensive collection of crafts, which date from 1900 to the present day. Founded in a brownstone on this site in 1956, the museum reopened in 1987 in the three-story atrium of an office tower. The reception desk is itself a work of art, designed and hand-carved in maple by James Schneider. The displays are not for sale.

American Folk Art Museum ❼

45 W 53 St. **Map** 12 F4.
📞 585-9533.
M 5th Ave-53rd St.
🕐 10am–6pm Tue–Sun, 10am–8pm Fri. ♿ 📷
W www.folkartmuseum.org

T HE PERMANENT home for the appreciation and study of American folk art is here, in the first free-standing art museum built in New York since 1966. Designed by the innovative architectural firm of Tod Williams Billie Tsien & Associates and built in 2001, the structure is clad in panels of white tombasil, a white bronze alloy. The museum has 30,000 sq ft (2,787 sq m) of exhibition space on eight levels. The museum still retains the Eva and Morris Feld Gallery at the Lincoln Square location (see p213).

Museum of Television and Radio ❽

25 W 52nd St. **Map** 12 F4.
📞 621-6800. **M** 5th Ave-53rd
St. 🕐 noon–6pm Tue–Sun (8pm
Thu). Theaters and screening rooms
close 9pm Fri. ⬤ public hols. 📷 📷
♿ 📷 🚹 **W** www.mtr.org

I N THIS one-of-a-kind repository museum, visitors can watch and listen to news and a collection of entertain-

Beatles Paul, Ringo and John on the "Ed Sullivan Show" in 1964

ment and sports documentaries from radio and television's earliest days to the present. Pop fans can see the early Beatles or a young Elvis Presley making his television debut. Sports enthusiasts can relive classic Olympic competitions. World War II footage might be chosen by students of history or by those who lived through the war. Six choices at any one time can be selected from a computer catalogue that covers a library of over 50,000 programs. The selections are then played on small private areas. There are larger screening areas and a theater for 200, where retrospectives of artists, directors and topics are shown. There are also photo exhibits, posters and memorabilia.

The museum was the brainchild of William S. Paley, a former head of the CBS TV network. It opened in 1975 as the Museum of Broadcasting on East 53rd Street. It proved so popular that in 1991 it moved into this hi-tech $50 million home in a building reminiscent of an antique radio set.

1960s television star Lucille Ball

Museum of Modern Art ❺

Museum facade on West 53rd Street

Tʜᴇ ᴍᴜꜱᴇᴜᴍ of Modern Art contains one of the world's best and most comprehensive collections of modern art. Founded in 1929, it set the standard for other museums of its kind. MoMA is currently undergoing a $650 million building project, and the museum in Midtown is closed from mid-2002 to 2004 (though the shop will remain open). Highlights of MoMA's exhibits are housed in Queens *(see p245).*

Sculpture Garden
Now closed for renovation and construction but will reopen in 2004.

Christina's World
(1948) Andrew Wyeth contrasts an overwhelming horizon with the minutely-studied surroundings of his handicapped neighbor.

Sᴛᴀʀ Pᴀɪɴᴛɪɴɢꜱ

★ **The Starry Night by Vincent Van Gogh**

★ **Les Demoiselles d'Avignon by Pablo Picasso**

Gᴀʟʟᴇʀʏ Gᴜɪᴅᴇ

Changing exhibitions are displayed on the first floor. Painting and sculpture are exhibited on the second and third floors. Photography is on the second floor, prints are on the third floor. Architecture and design collections are on the fourth. Films are shown on the lower level.

Bird in Space *(c. 1928)*
Constantin Brancusi's elegant bronze sculpture captures the sheer essence of flight.

Main entrance

Sculpture Garden

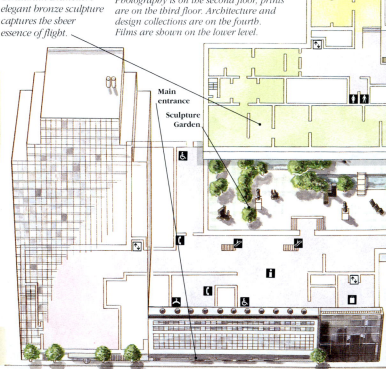

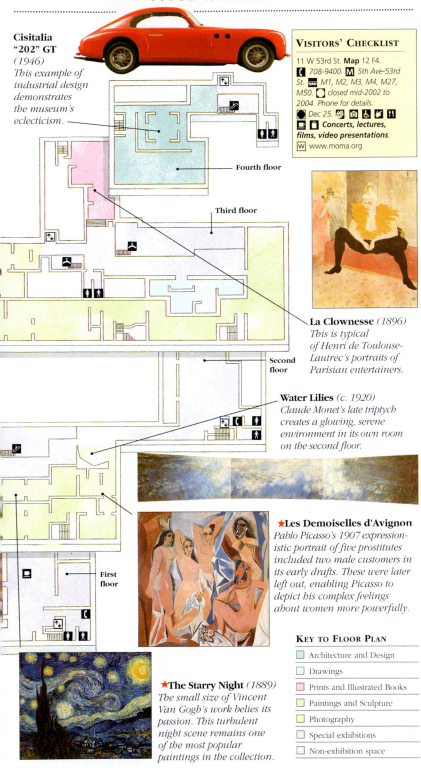

Cisitalia "202" GT *(1946)*
This example of industrial design demonstrates the museum's eclecticism.

Fourth floor

Third floor

La Clownesse *(1896)*
This is typical of Henri de Toulouse-Lautrec's portraits of Parisian entertainers.

Second floor

Water Lilies *(c. 1920)*
Claude Monet's late triptych creates a glowing, serene environment in its own room on the second floor.

★**Les Demoiselles d'Avignon**
Pablo Picasso's 1907 expressionistic portrait of five prostitutes included two male customers in its early drafts. These were later left out, enabling Picasso to depict his complex feelings about women more powerfully.

First floor

★**The Starry Night** *(1889)*
The small size of Vincent Van Gogh's work belies its passion. This turbulent night scene remains one of the most popular paintings in the collection.

KEY TO FLOOR PLAN

- Architecture and Design
- Drawings
- Prints and Illustrated Books
- Paintings and Sculpture
- Photography
- Special exhibitions
- Non-exhibition space

Exploring the Collection

THE MUSEUM OF MODERN ART houses approximately 100,000 works of art – ranging from a collection of Post-Impressionist classics to an unrivaled collection of modern American art, from fine examples of design to early masterpieces of photography and film.

1880s TO 1940s
PAINTING AND SCULPTURE

The Persistence of Memory by the Surrealist Salvador Dalí (1931)

PAUL CEZANNE'S monumental *The Bather* and Vincent van Gogh's passionate and transcendent *The Starry Night* are two of the seminal works in the museum's collection of late 19th-century painting. Both Fauvism and Expressionism are well represented with works by Matisse, Derain, Kirchner and others, while Pablo Picasso's *Les Demoiselles d'Avignon* marks a transition to a new style of painting.

The museum also has an unparalleled collection of Cubist paintings, providing an overview of a movement that radically challenged our perception of the world. Among the vast display are Picasso's *Girl with a Mandolin*, Georges Braque's *Man with a Guitar* and *Soda*, and *Guitar and Flowers* by Juan Gris. Works by the Futurists, who brought color and movement to Cubism to depict the dynamic modern world, include Gino Severini's *Dynamic Hieroglyphic of the Bal Tabarin* and *Dynamism of a Soccer Player* by Umberto Boccioni, plus works by Balla, Carrà and Villon.

The geometric abstract art of the Constructivists is included in a strong display of Malevich, Lissitzky and Rodchenko: De Stijl's influence is seen in paintings by Piet Mondrian, including *Broadway Boogie Woogie*. An entire room is devoted to work by Matisse, such as *Dance I* and *The Red Studio*. Dalí, Miró and Ernst feature among the collection of bizarre, strangely beautiful Surrealist works.

POSTWAR PAINTING AND SCULPTURE

AN EXTENSIVE display of postwar art begins on the third floor, with a series of works by Bacon, Dubuffet and others. The collection of Abstract Expressionist art includes Jackson Pollock's *One [Number 31, 1950]*, Willem de Kooning's *Woman, I*, Arshile Gorky's *Agony* and *Red, Brown, and Black* by Mark Rothko. The following

Dog (1952), an oil painting by British artist Francis Bacon

galleries exhibit works such as Jasper Johns' *Flag* and Robert Rauschenberg's *First Landing Jump*, composed from urban refuse, and *Bed*, composed of bed linen. The Pop Art on show includes Roy Lichtenstein's *Girl with Ball* and *Drowning Girl*, Andy Warhol's famous *Gold Marilyn Monroe* and Claes Oldenburg's *Giant Soft Fan*.

Works after about 1965 are displayed on a rotating basis and can include pieces by Judd, Flavin, Serra and Beuys among many others.

DRAWINGS AND OTHER WORKS ON PAPER

Man with a Hat by Pablo Picasso (1912), in collage and charcoal

THE MUSEUM of Modern Art has one of the most comprehensive collections of modern drawings anywhere in the world. This collection has a range of works in traditional mediums – pencil, ink and charcoal – and also in watercolor, gouache and collage. Some are early studies for famous paintings; Picasso's *Head of the Medical Student* is a study for *Les Demoiselles d'Avignon*. Special strengths are the works representing the School of Paris, Dada and Surrealism. The rotating exhibition in the department's second-floor galleries may include the works of Matisse, Ernst, Klee, Pollock, Dubuffet and Rauschenberg. At various times some of this collection is shown outside the drawings department to complement the museum's other exhibitions.

PRINTS AND ILLUSTRATED BOOKS

The Game of Solitaire by Jacques Villon (1903 but dated 1904)

WIDE-RANGING examples of historical and contemporary printmaking include works in such traditional techniques as lithography, etching, screenprinting and woodcuts, as well as in more experimental techniques. There are fine examples of portraiture, notably a *Self-portrait with Grimace* by Marc Chagall. The collection is strong in the works of Redon, Munch, Klee, Matisse, Picasso, Dubuffet, Villon and Johns. Prints by these and other artists are always displayed in the constantly rotating exhibition in the department's second-floor galleries.

At the entrance to the Print galleries is a reading room containing catalogs and books about prints. The first gallery has a changing survey of printed art from the 1880s up to the 1950s. The next displays art from the 1960s onward, introducing recent and contemporary work.

PHOTOGRAPHY

THE PHOTOGRAPHY collection begins with the invention of the medium around 1840. It includes pictures by fine artists, journalists, scientists and entrepreneurs, as well as amateur photographers. The first of the department's third-floor galleries is devoted to temporary exhibitions. The other galleries offer an ever-changing chronological series of the collection's highlights. Included in these are photographs by Atget, Stieglitz, Lange, Arbus, Steichen,

FILM DEPARTMENT

With a collection of some 10,000 films and four million stills, the museum offers a wide range of programs, including retrospectives of individual directors and actors, films in specific genres and experimental work, as well as a broad range of other exhibitions. Film conservation is a key part of the department's work. Today's top directors are now donating copies of their films to help fund this expensive but vital work.

Film still of Charlie Chaplin and Jackie Coogan in *The Kid* (1921)

Cartier-Bresson and Kertesz, plus a range of contemporary photographers, most notably Friedlander, Sherman and Nixon. There is an extensive variety of subject matter – covering delicate landscapes, scenes of urban desolation, abstract imagery and stylish portraiture, including some

Sunday on the Banks of the Marne, photographed by Henri Cartier-Bresson in 1939

beautiful silver-gelatin print nudes by the French Surrealist Man Ray. Together, they form a complete history of photographic art and represent one of the finest collections in existence.

ARCHITECTURE AND DESIGN

THE MUSEUM of Modern Art was the first art museum to include utilitarian objects in its collection. These range from household appliances, stereo equipment, furniture, lighting, textiles and glassware to industrial ball bearings and silicon chips. Architecture is represented in the displays of scale models, drawings and photographs. Graphic design is shown in typography and posters. Architectural models and drawings are displayed in the first gallery, and selections from the design collection follow. Pinin Farina's Cisitalia car and the Bell helicopter are on permanent display in the fourth-floor galleries.

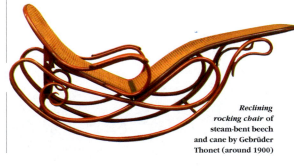

Reclining rocking chair of steam-bent beech and cane by Gebrüder Thonet (around 1900)

St. Patrick's Cathedral 9

See pp176–7.

Villard Houses 10

457 Madison Ave (New York Palace Hotel). **Map** 13 A4. 935-3960. 51st St. **Urban Center** 11am–5pm Mon–Wed, Fri, Sat. W www.mas.org

Henry Villard was a Bavarian immigrant who became publisher of the *New York Evening Post* and founder of the Northern Pacific Railroad. In 1881, he bought the land opposite St. Patrick's Cathedral and hired McKim, Mead & White to design town houses, one for himself, the rest for sale. The inspired result has six four-story houses built around a central court opening to the street and the church. The south wing was Villard's, but financial difficulties forced him to sell before it was finished.

Ownership passed to the Roman Catholic Archdiocese, but the houses were threatened when the church outgrew its space in the 1970s. The problem was solved when the Helmsley chain purchased air rights for the 51-story Helmsley (now New York) Palace Hotel. The south wing became the formal entrance to the hotel and the grand public rooms of the Villard suite, now restored to their former glory, house French restaurant, Le Cirque 2000. The Urban Center occupies the north wing, and its bookshop is the best place in New York to find architectural books on the city.

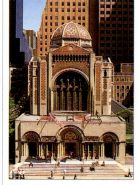

St. Bartholomew's Church

St. Bartholomew's Church 11

109 E 50th St. **Map** 13 A4. 751-1616. 51st St. 7:30am–6pm daily. frequent Lectures, concerts. after 9 & 11am Sunday services. W www.stbarts.org

Known fondly to New Yorkers as "St. Bart's," this Byzantine structure with its ornate detail, pinkish brick, open terrace and a polychromed gold dome brought color and variety to Park Avenue in 1919.

Architect Bertram Goodhue incorporated into the design the Romanesque entrance portico created by Stanford White for the original 1903 St. Bartholomew's on Madison Avenue, and marble columns from the earlier church were used in the chapel.

St. Bartholomew's musical programs are well known, their Jazz Nativity being a favorite. They concentrate on classical, choral and organ music.

General Electric Building 12

570 Lexington Ave. **Map** 13 A4. Lexington Ave. to the public.

In 1931 architects Cross & Cross were commissioned to design a skyscraper that would be in keeping with its neighbor, St. Bartholomew's Church. Not an easy task, but the result won unanimous acclaim. The colors were chosen to blend and contrast, and the design of the tower complemented the church's polychrome dome.

The General Electric Building on Lexington Avenue

View the pair from the corner of Park and 50th to see how well it works. However, the General Electric is no mere backdrop but a work of art in its own right and a favorite part of the city skyline. It is an Art Deco gem from its chrome and marble lobby to its spiky "radio waves" crown.

Walk one block north on Lexington Avenue to find a place much cherished by movie fans. It is right at this spot that Marilyn Monroe, in a billowing white frock, stood so memorably in the breeze from the Lexington Avenue subway grating in the movie *The Seven-Year Itch*.

Villard Houses, now the entrance to the New York Palace Hotel

Waldorf–Astoria  ❶❸

301 Park Ave. **Map** 13 A5. **C** 355-3000. **M** *Lexington Ave, 53rd St. See* **Where to Stay** *p281*
W www.waldorf.com

T HIS ART DECO classic, which covers an entire city block, was designed by Schultze & Weaver in 1931. The original Hotel at 34th Street was demolished to make way for the Empire State Building.

Winston Churchill and New York philanthropist Grover Whalen at the Waldorf–Astoria in 1946

Still deservedly one of New York's most prestigious hotels, the Waldorf–Astoria serves, too, as a reminder of a more glamorous era in the city's history. The 625-ft (190-m) twin towers, where the Duke and Duchess of Windsor lived, have hosted numerous celebrities, including every US president since 1931. The giant lobby clock, executed for the Chicago World's Fair of 1893, is from the original hotel, and the piano in the Peacock Alley cocktail lounge belonged to Cole Porter when he was a resident of the hotel's exclusive Towers.

Lever House ❶❹

390 Park Ave. **Map** 13 A4. **C** 888-1260. **M** *5th Ave-53rd St.* **Lobby and building** ● *to the public. Call for additional information.*

I MAGINE A PARK AVENUE lined with sturdy, residential buildings – and then imagine the sensation when they were suddenly reflected here in the first of the city's glass-walled skyscrapers, one of the most influential buildings of the modern era. The design, by Skidmore, Owings & Merrill, is simply two rectangular slabs of stainless steel and glass, one laid horizontally, the other stacked to stand tall above it, to allow light in from every side. The crisp and bright design was always intended to symbolize many of the Lever Brothers' products – they make soaps and other cleaning products. Revolutionary though it was in 1952, Lever House is now dwarfed by the many imitators that have grown up around it, but its importance as an architectural pacesetter remains undiminished.

Lever House on Park Avenue

Seagram Building ❶❺

375 Park Ave. **Map** 13 A4. **C** 572-7000. **M** *5th Ave-53rd St.* ● *9am–5pm Mon–Fri.* ● *3pm Tue.* ∏

S AMUEL BRONFMAN, the late head of Seagram distillers, was prepared to put up an ordinary commercial building until his architect daughter, Phyllis Lambert, intervened and persuaded him to go to the best – Mies van der Rohe.

The pool at the Four Seasons in the Seagram Building

The result, which is widely considered the best of the many Modernist buildings of the 1950s, consists of two rectangles of bronze and glass that let the light pour in.

Within is the exclusive Four Seasons Restaurant *(see p293)*, a landmark in its own right. Designer Philip Johnson has created two linked rooms, with the centerpiece of one a pool, and the other a bar that is topped by a quivering Richard Lippold sculpture.

Office workers at lunch in the spacious Citigroup atrium

Citigroup Center ❶❻

153 E 53rd St. **Map** 13 A4. **M** *53rd St-Lexington Ave.* **Open** *7am–11pm daily.* ∏ ● *St. Peter's Lutheran Church* **C** 935-2200. ● *9am–9pm daily* ● *8:45am, 11am Sun.* **Jazz vespers** *5pm Sun.* **Concerts** *daily except Mon.* **Theater at St. Peter's Church** **C** 935-5800.
W www.saintpeters.org

A N ALUMINUM-CLAD spire built on ten-story stilts with a sliced-off roof, Citigroup Center is unique; it caused a sensation when it was completed in 1978. The unusual base design had to incorporate St. Peter's Lutheran Church. The church is separate both in space and design, a granite sculpture below a corner of the tower. Step inside to see the striking interior and the Erol Beker Chapel by sculptor Louise Nevelson. The church is well known for its organ concerts, jazz vespers, and theater presentations. Citigroup's slanting top never functioned as a solar panel as intended, but it is an unmistakable landmark on the skyline.

Saint Patrick's Cathedral 9

THE ROMAN CATHOLIC Church originally intended this site for use as a cemetery, but in 1850 Archbishop John Hughes decided to build a cathedral instead. Many thought that it was foolish to build so far beyond the (then) city limits, but Hughes went ahead anyway. Architect James Renwick built New York's finest Gothic Revival building, the largest Catholic cathedral in the United States. The cathedral, which seats 2,500 people, was completed in 1878, though the spires were added from 1885 to 1888.

Fifth Avenue facade

Lady Chapel ★
This chapel honors the Blessed Virgin. The stained-glass windows portray the mysteries of the rosary.

Pièta
American sculptor William O. Partridge created this statue of the Pièta in 1906; it stands at the side of the Lady Chapel.

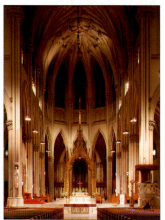

★ **Baldachin**
The great baldachin rising over the high altar is made entirely of bronze. Statues of the saints and prophets adorn the four piers supporting the canopy.

Cathedral Facade
The exterior wall is built of white marble. The spires rise 330 ft (101 m) above the pavement.

STAR FEATURES

★ **Baldachin**

★ **Great Bronze Doors**

★ **Lady Chapel**

★ **Great Organ and Rose Window**

Stations of the Cross
Carved of Caen stone in Holland, these reliefs won first prize in the field of religious art at the Chicago World's Fair in 1893.

VISITORS' CHECKLIST

5th Ave and 50th St. **Map** 12 F4.
753-2261. M 6 to 51st St.;
E, F to Fifth Ave. M1, M2,
M3, M4. 7:30am–8:30pm
daily. frequent Mon–Sat; 7,
8, 9, 10:15am & 12 noon, 1, 4 &
5:30pm Sun.
Concerts & lectures.
W www.stpatrickscathedral.org

Shrine of St. Elizabeth Ann Seton
The bronze statue and screen depict the life of the first American to be canonized a saint. She founded the Sisters of Charity (see p76).

Great Organ ★ and Rose Window
Measuring 26 ft (8 m) in diameter, the rose window shines above the great organ, which has more than 7,000 pipes.

Main entrance

Great Bronze Doors ★
The massive doors weigh 20,000 lb (9,000 kg) and are adorned with important religious figures in New York.

Central Synagogue ⑰

652 Lexington Ave. **Map** 13 A4.
C *838–5122.* **M** *51st St, Lexington Ave.* ⬛ *by appt.* ✪ *Fri. evening, Sat. morning.*
W www.centralsynagogue.org

THIS IS NEW YORK'S oldest building in continuous use as a synagogue. It was designed in 1870 by Silesian-born Henry Fernbach, America's first prominent Jewish architect. He also designed some of SoHo's finest cast-iron buildings. Now completely restored after a 1999 fire, the Synagogue considered the city's best example of Moorish-Islamic Revival architecture. The congregation was originally founded in 1846 as Ahawath Chesed (Love of Mercy) by 18 newly arrived immigrants, most of them from Bohemia, on Ludlow Street on the Lower East Side.

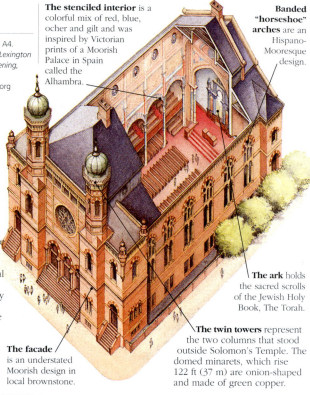

The stenciled interior is a colorful mix of red, blue, ocher and gilt and was inspired by Victorian prints of a Moorish Palace in Spain called the Alhambra.

Banded "horseshoe" arches are an Hispano-Mooresque design.

The ark holds the sacred scrolls of the Jewish Holy Book, The Torah.

The facade is an understated Moorish design in local brownstone.

The twin towers represent the two columns that stood outside Solomon's Temple. The domed minarets, which rise 122 ft (37 m) are onion-shaped and made of green copper.

Sutton Place and Beekman Place ⑱

Map 13 C3, 13 C5. **M** *59th St.*

SUTTON PLACE IS A posh and pleasant neighborhood, delightfully devoid of busy traffic, made up of elegant low-rise apartment houses and town houses designed by noted architects. The arrival of New York society in the 1920s transformed an area that had once been the province of factories and tenements. Three Sutton Square is the residence of the secretary-general of the United Nations.

Look beyond Sutton Square and 59th Street for a glimpse of Riverview Terrace, a private street of five ivy-covered brownstones fronting on the river. The tiny parks at the end of 55th Street and jutting out at 57th Street offer views of the river and the Queensboro Bridge.

Smaller than Sutton Place, and even more tranquil, is Beekman Place, a virtually private two-block enclave of 1920s town houses and some small-scale apartments. Famous residents here have included Gloria Vanderbilt, Rex Harrison, Irving Berlin and members of the large Rockefeller family.

After much neighborhood opposition, Bridgemarket opened in 2000. Located between the huge vaults under the Queensboro Bridge, there is an upscale Terence Conran's for housewares, two Guastavino's restaurants, and a Food

Park at Sutton Place, looking toward Queensboro Bridge and Roosevelt Island

Emporium. A fountain-blessed plaza is being considered.

At Turtle Bay Gardens, two rows of brownstone houses dating from the 1860s hide a charming Italianate garden. Among the residents enticed by this privacy have been the film stars Tyrone Power and Katharine Hepburn, composer Stephen Sondheim, and writer E.B. White.

Roosevelt Island ⑲

Map 14 D2. Ⓜ *59th St. Tram, Roosevelt Island station (Q, B).* Ⓦ *www.rioc.com*

SINCE 1976 a Swiss cable car has offered a quick ride across the East River to Roosevelt Island, with eagle's-eye views of the city and the Queensboro Bridge.

Near the tram station are the remains of the Blackwell farmhouse, which stood from 1796 to 1804 and gave the island its name until the 1920s, when real estate development began. From the 1920s to the 1970s, the island housed a succession of hospitals, an almshouse, a jail, a workhouse and an insane asylum, and became known as Welfare Island.

In 1927, Mae West was held in the penitentiary here for eight days after a "lewd performance." She requested, and got, her silk lingerie to wear under her prison uniform. The ruins of 19th-century hospitals still remain, as does an 1872 lighthouse built by an asylum inmate.

The tram departs from 2nd Avenue at 60th Street and affords a thrilling ride and some fine city views.

Bloomingdale's store sign

Bloomingdale's ⑳

1000 3rd Ave. **Map** 13 A3. Ⓒ 355-5900. Ⓜ 59th St. Ⓞ 10am–8:30pm Mon–Fri, 10am–7pm Sat, 11am–7pm Sun. See **Shopping** p311.

FOR A WHILE in the booming 1980s, "Bloomies" was synonymous with the good life. Founded by Joseph and Lyman Bloomingdale in 1872, this famous department store had a bargain-basement image until the 3rd Avenue El was taken down in the 1960s. Then came the store's transformation to the epitome of trendy, sophisticated shopping. But the late 1980s brought new ownership and eventual bankruptcy. While not as flashy as in the past, Bloomingdale's is open every day and remains one of the city's best-stocked stores.

Fuller Building ㉑

41 E 57th St. **Map** 13 A3. *Peter Findlay Gallery.* Ⓒ 644-4433; *James Goodwin Gallery.* Ⓒ 583-3737. Ⓞ 10am–6pm Tue–Sat. Ⓜ 59th St.

THIS SLIM-TOWERED black, gray and white 1929 beauty by Walker & Gillette is a prime example of geometric Art Deco design. The striking statues on either side of the clock above the entry are by Elie Nadelman. Step inside to see the intricate mosaic tile floors; one panel shows the Fuller Company's

The clock statues above the Fuller Building entrance

former home in the Flatiron Building. The Fuller Building is a hive of exclusive art galleries, most of which are open to the public daily.

French Renaissance–style facade of the Plaza Hotel

Plaza Hotel ㉒

5th Ave.& Central Park South **Map** 12 F3. Ⓒ 759-3000. Ⓜ 59th St. See **Where to Stay** p281.

THE CITY'S grande dame of hotels was designed by Henry J. Hardenbergh, known for the Dakota *(see p216)* and the original Waldorf–Astoria. Completed in 1907 at the exorbitant cost of $12.5 million, the Plaza was proclaimed "the best hotel in the world," with 800 rooms, 500 baths, a two-story ballroom, five marble staircases, and 14- to 17-room apartments for such families as the Vanderbilts and the Goulds *(see p49)*.

The 18-story cast-iron structure resembles a French Renaissance château on a larger scale. Much of the interior decoration came from Europe. The Palm Court still has mirrored walls and Italian carvings of the four seasons as supporting columns.

Former owner Donald Trump restored the hotel's original glitter (too much of it for some) with elaborate new Bavarian glass chandeliers, lush carpet and miles of gold leaf. Public areas have been refurbished without losing their original ambience.

UPPER EAST SIDE

African urn, Metropolitan Museum of Art

AT THE TURN of the century, New York society moved to the Upper East Side – and stayed. Many of the Beaux Arts mansions are now museums and embassies, but the well-to-do still occupy grand apartment buildings on Fifth and Park avenues. Chic shops and galleries line Madison Avenue. Farther east, the area includes what is left of German Yorkville in the East 80s, Hungarian Yorkville to the south and little Bohemia, with its Czech population, below 78th Street. Many of these ethnic groups have left the area, but their churches, restaurants, and shops still remain.

Looking down into the lobby of the Guggenheim Museum

SIGHTS AT A GLANCE

Historic Streets and Buildings
Seventh Regiment Armory ⑩
Henderson Place ⑭
Gracie Mansion ⑯

Museums and Galleries
Neue Galerie New York ❶
Jewish Museum ❷
Cooper-Hewitt National
Design Museum ❸
National Academy of
Design ❹
*Solomon R. Guggenheim
Museum pp186–87* ❺
*Metropolitan Museum
of Art pp188–95* ❻
*Whitney Museum of
American Art pp198–99* ❼
Frick Collection pp200–1 ❽
Asia Society ❾
Society of Illustrators ⑫
Mount Vernon Hotel
Museum and Garden ⑬
Museum of the City of
New York ⑲

Churches and

Synagogues
Temple Emanu-El ⑪
Church of the Holy Trinity ⑰
St. Nicholas Russian
Orthodox Cathedral ⑱

Parks and Squares
Carl Schurz Park ⑮

GETTING THERE
The Lexington Ave 4 and
5 express trains stop at 59th
and 86th streets. The local
(No. 6) also stops at 68th, 77th
and 96th streets. Buses include:
M1, M2, M3 and M4 on Fifth/
Madison Aves, M101/102 on
Lexington/Third and M15 on
First/Second. The crosstown
buses are the M66, M72, M79,
M86 and M96.

SEE ALSO

KEY

Street-by-Street map

M Subway station

Ferry terminal

Heliport

0 meters   500

0 yards   500

**Statue of Diana, National
Academy of Design**

Street by Street: Museum Mile

MANY OF NEW YORK'S museums are clustered on the Upper East Side, in homes ranging from the former Frick and Carnegie mansions to the modernistic Guggenheim, designed by Frank Lloyd Wright. The displays are as varied as the architecture, running the gamut from old masters to photographs to decorative arts. Presiding over the scene is the vast Metropolitan Museum of Art, America's answer to the Louvre. Many of the museums stay open late on Tuesday evenings, and some offer free admission.

Jewish Museum
The most extensive collection of Judaica in the world is housed here. It includes coins, archaeological objects and ceremonial and religious artifacts ❷

Cooper-Hewitt Museum ★
The decorative arts, including ceramics, glass, furniture and textiles, are well represented here ❸

The Church of the Heavenly Rest was built in 1929 in the Gothic style. The madonna in the pulpit is by sculptor Malvina Hoffman.

National Academy of Design
The Academy, founded in 1825, moved here in 1940. Its fine collection includes paintings and sculptures by its members ❹

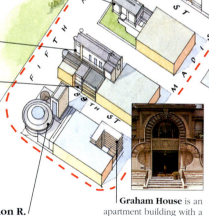

Graham House is an apartment building with a splendid Beaux Arts entrance. It was built in 1892.

★ **Solomon R. Guggenheim Museum**
Floodlit at dusk, architect Frank Lloyd Wright's building looks purple. It is in the form of a spiral. Take the elevator to the top and walk down to see one of the world's best collections of modern art ❺

STAR SIGHTS

★ **Solomon R. Guggenheim Museum**

★ **Cooper-Hewitt Museum**

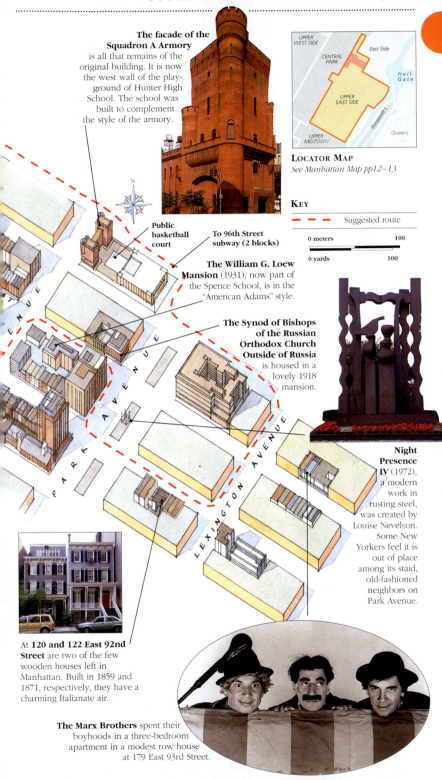

The facade of the Squadron A Armory is all that remains of the original building. It is now the west wall of the playground of Hunter High School. The school was built to complement the style of the armory.

LOCATOR MAP
See Manhattan Map pp12–13

KEY

- - - - Suggested route

| 0 meters | | 100 |
| 0 yards | | 100 |

Public basketball court

To 96th Street subway (2 blocks)

The William G. Loew Mansion (1931), now part of the Spence School, is in the "American Adams" style.

The Synod of Bishops of the Russian Orthodox Church Outside of Russia is housed in a lovely 1918 mansion.

PARK AVENUE

LEXINGTON AVENUE

Night Presence IV (1972), a modern work in rusting steel, was created by Louise Nevelson. Some New Yorkers feel it is out of place among its staid, old-fashioned neighbors on Park Avenue.

At **120 and 122 East 92nd Street** are two of the few wooden houses left in Manhattan. Built in 1859 and 1871, respectively, they have a charming Italianate air.

The Marx Brothers spent their boyhoods in a three-bedroom apartment in a modest row house at 179 East 93rd Street.

Neue Galerie New York ❶

1048 5th Ave at E 86th St. **Map** 16 F3.
📞 628-6200. Ⓜ 86th St, 96th St.
🕐 11am–7pm Fri–Mon. 📷 🚫
🍴 Breakfast, lunch, tea Wed–Mon
📷 ♿ Ⓦ www.neuegalerie.org

T HIS MUSEUM was founded by art dealer Serge Sabarsky and philanthropist Ronald Lauder. The objective of this newest museum in the New York spectrum is to collect, research and exhibit the fine and decorative arts of Germany and Austria from the early 20th century.

The Louis XIII-style Beaux-Arts structure was completed in 1914 by Carrere & Hastings, who also designed and built the New York Public Library. The building has been designated a landmark and is considered to be one of the most distinguished buildings ever erected on Fifth Avenue. Once occupied by Mrs. Cornelius Vanderbilt III, the mansion was purchased by Lauder and Sabarsky in 1994. The ground floor houses the entrance, a bookshop, and the Café Sabarsky, which draws its inspiration from the Viennese cafés of old. The second floor is devoted to the works of Klimt, Schiele, and Wiener Werkstätte objects. The upper floors feature works from Der Blaue Reiter (artists such as Klee, Kandinsky), the Bauhaus (Feininger, Schlemmer) and Die Brücke (Mies van der Rohe, Breuer).

Jewish Museum ❷

1109 5th Ave. **Map** 16 F2.
📞 423-3200. Ⓜ 86th St, 96th St.
🕐 11am–5:45pm Sun–Thu;
11am–8pm Tue. ● Fri, Sat, public & Jewish hols. 📷 🚫 ♿ 📷 📷 📷
Ⓦ www.jewishmuseum.org

T HE EXQUISITE château-like residence of Felix M. Warburg, financier and leader of the Jewish community, was designed by C.P.H. Gilbert in 1908. It now houses one of the world's largest collections of Jewish fine and ceremonial art, and historical Judaica. Renovation has almost doubled the display space. The stonework in the new extension is by the stonemasons of St. John the Divine (see pp224–5).

Objects have been brought here from all over the world, some at great risk of persecution to the donors. Covering 4,000 years, artifacts include Torah crowns, candelabras, kiddush cups, plates, scrolls and silver ceremonial objects.

There is a Torah ark from the Benguiat Collection, the exquisite faience entrance wall of a 16th-century Persian synagogue and the powerful *Holocaust* by sculptor George Segal. Changing exhibitions reflect Jewish life and experience around the world.

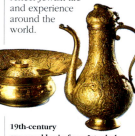

19th-century ewer and basin from Istanbul at the Jewish Museum

Cooper-Hewitt National Design Museum ❸

2 E 91st St. **Map** 16 F2. 📞 849-8300, 849-8387. Ⓜ 86th St. 🕐 10am–9pm Tue, 10am–5pm Wed–Sat, noon–5pm Sun. ● public hols. 📷
♿ 📷 📷 Ⓦ www.si.edu/ndm

O NE OF THE largest design collections in the world, this museum occupies the former home of industrialist Andrew Carnegie. The collection was amassed by the Hewitt sisters, Amy, Eleanor and Sarah. The museum opened in 1897 at Cooper Union (see p118); the Smithsonian Institution acquired the collections in 1967, and the Carnegie Corporation offered the mansion.

Carnegie asked for "the most modest, plainest and most roomy house in New York," but the house set new trends

Cooper-Hewitt Museum entrance

with central heating, private elevator, and air-conditioning. Note the wooden staircase, rich paneling and carving, and the sunny solarium.

National Academy of Design ❹

1083 5th Ave. **Map** 16 F3.
📞 369-4880. Ⓜ 86th St. 🕐 noon–5pm Wed–Sun, 10am–6pm Fri. 📷 except 5–6pm Fri. 🚫 ♿ 📷
Ⓦ www.nationalacademy.org

M ORE THAN 6,000 paintings, drawings and sculptures, including works by Thomas Eakins, Winslow Homer, Raphael Soyer and Frank Lloyd Wright, comprise the collection of the National Academy of Design, founded in 1825 by a group of artists. The group's mission was (and is) to train artists and exhibit their work. In 1940, Archer Huntington, an art patron and philanthropist, donated his house, an attractive building with patterned marble floors and decorative plaster ceilings. The grand entrance foyer has a statue of Diana by sculptor Anna Hyatt Huntington.

Statue of Diana in the National Academy of Design entrance foyer

Solomon R. Guggenheim Museum ❺

See pp186–7.

Metropolitan Museum of Art ❻

See pp188–95.

Whitney Museum of American Art ❼

See pp198–9.

Frick Collection ❽

See pp200–1.

Asia Society ❾

725 Park Ave. **Map** 13 A1.
📞 *288-6400.* Ⓜ *68th St.*
🕐 *10am–6pm Tue–Sat.*
📷 *except 12–5pm Sun.*
🚫 ♿ 🎟 🏛
Ⓦ *www.asiasociety.org*

FOUNDED BY John D. Rockefeller III in 1956 to in-crease American understanding of Asian culture, the society is a forum for 30 countries from Japan to Iran, Central Asia to Australia.

The 1981 eight-story building was designed by Edward Larrabee Barnes and is made of red granite. After a complete renovation in 2001, the museum has greatly increased gallery space. One gallery is permanently devoted to Rockefeller's own collection of Asian sculptures, amassed by him and his wife on frequent trips to the East.

Changing exhibits show a wide variety of Asian arts, and the society has a full program of films, dance, concerts, and lectures and well-stocked bookshop.

Entrance Hall of the Seventh Regiment Armory

Seventh Regiment Armory ❿

643 Park Ave. **Map** 13 A2.
📞 *452-3067.* Ⓜ *68th St.*
🕐 *Mon–Fri by appt only.*
🌑 *public hols.* 🚫 ♿ 🎟

FROM THE WAR of 1812 through two world wars, the Seventh Regiment has played a vital role. They were an elite corps of "gentlemen soldiers" from prominent families, and their armory is unlike any other in the US. Within the stern fortresslike exterior are extraordinary rooms filled with lavish furnishings of the Victorian era, objets d'art and regimental memorabilia.

The design by Charles W. Clinton, a veteran of the regiment, had offices facing Park Avenue, with a vast drill hall stretching behind to Lexington Avenue. The reception rooms include the Veterans' Room and the Library by Louis Comfort Tiffany. The drill hall is now the site of the Winter Antiques Show *(see p53)* and a favorite place to hold the city's many charity balls.

South Asian sculpture at the Asia Society

Temple Emanu-El ⓫

1 E 65th St. **Map** 12 F2.
📞 *744-1400.* Ⓜ *68th St, 60th St.*
🕐 *10am–4:30pm Sun–Fri, 12:30pm–4:45pm Sat (last adm on Fri 3:30pm)*
🌑 *Jewish hols.* ✡ *5:30pm Sun–Thu, 5:15pm Fri, 10:30am Sat.* 📷 ♿ 🎟
🏛 Ⓦ *www.emanuelnyc.org*

THIS IMPRESSIVE limestone edifice of 1929 is one of the largest synagogues in the world, seating 2,500 in the main sanctuary alone. It is home to the oldest Reform congregation in New York. Among the many fine details are the bronze grille doors of the Ark, and stained glass showing the Shield of David and the Lion of Judah. The dominant feature of the Fifth Avenue exterior is the great recessed arch enclosing a magnificent wheel window. The Beth-El Chapel is a twin-domed structure with a Byzantine influence.

The synagogue stands on the site of the palatial home of the legendary society hostess Mrs. William Astor. She left her midtown mansion when her nephew, who was feuding with her, built the Waldorf Hotel next door. The formidable Mrs. Astor moved to the Upper East Side, taking society with her, while her son built the Astoria Hotel on the site of her previous home.

The Ark at Temple Emanu-El

The Solomon R. Guggenheim Museum ⑤

HOME TO ONE of the world's finest collections of modern and contemporary art, the building itself is perhaps the museum's greatest masterpiece. Designed by architect Frank Lloyd Wright, the shell-like facade is a New York landmark. The spiral ramp curves down and inward from the dome, passing works by major 19th- and 20th-century artists. A downtown site opened in 1992, the Guggenheim SoHo *(see p105)*. There are plans for a new Guggenheim, designed by Frank Gehry, to be built on the East River. This museum will house the postwar collection and two theaters.

Fifth Avenue facade

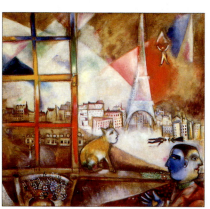

Paris Through the Window
The vibrant colors of Marc Chagall's 1913 masterpiece illumine the canvas, conjuring up images of a magical and mysterious city where nothing is quite what it appears to be.

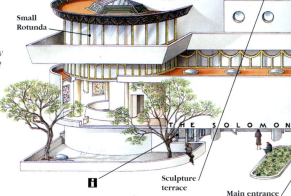

Small Rotunda

Sculpture terrace

Main entrance

Woman Ironing *(1904)*
A work from Pablo Picasso's Blue Period, this painting is his quintessential image of hard work and fatigue.

Yellow Cow *(1911)*
Franz Marc's work was influenced by a German back-to-nature movement.

Nude *(1917)*
This sleeping figure is typical of Amedeo Modigliani's stylized work.

MUSEUM GUIDE

The Great Rotunda features special exhibitions. The Small Rotunda shows some of the museum's celebrated Impressionist and Post-Impressionist holdings. The new Tower galleries feature exhibitions of work from the permanent collection as well as contemporary pieces. A fifth-floor sculpture terrace overlooks Central Park. Not all of the collection is on display at any one time.

Tower

Great Rotunda

VISITORS' CHECKLIST

1071 5th Ave at 89th St. **Map** 16 F3. 📞 423-3500. Ⓜ 4, 5, 6 to 86th St. 🚌 M1, M2, M3, M4. 🕐 9am–6pm Sun–Wed, 9am–8pm Fri, Sat. 🔴 Dec 25, Jan 1. 🎟 ⬛ ♿ ✔ **Concerts, lectures, performing art series.** 📷 📹 ⓦ www.guggenheim.org

Before the Mirror *(1876) In trying to capture the flavor of 19th-century society, Edouard Manet often used the image of the courtesan.*

Woman Holding a Vase *Fernand Léger incorporated elements of Cubism into this work from 1927.*

Black Lines *(1913) This is one of Vasily Kandinsky's earliest examples of his work in "non-objective" art.*

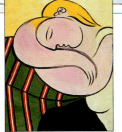

Woman with Yellow Hair *(1931) The gentle, voluptuous figure of Picasso's mistress often appears in his work.*

FRANK LLOYD WRIGHT

During his lifetime, Wright was considered the great innovator of American architecture. Characteristic of his work are Prairie-style homes and office buildings of concrete slabs, glass bricks and tubing. Wright received the Guggenheim commission in 1942 and it was completed after his death in 1959, his only New York building.

Interior of the Guggenheim's Great Rotunda

Metropolitan Museum of Art ❻

FOUNDED IN 1870 by a group of artists and philanthropists who dreamed of an American arts institution to rival those of Europe, this collection is thought to be the most comprehensive in the Western world. Works date from prehistoric times to the present. It moved to its current site in 1880 and houses collections from all continents, including ancient Egyptian art and American sculpture and decorative art since colonial times.

The entrance of the Metropolitan Museum of Art

★ Gertrude Stein *(1905–6) This portrait of the American writer Gertrude Stein is by Pablo Picasso. The masklike face is evidence of his debt to African and Roman art.*

Robert Lehman Collection

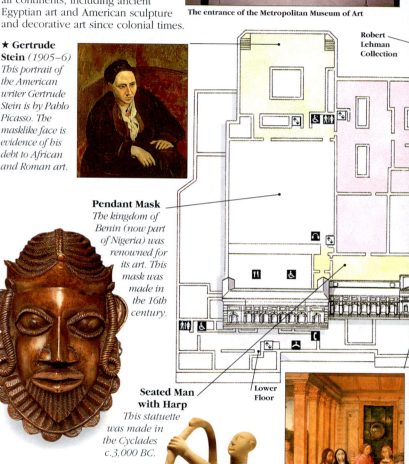

Pendant Mask *The kingdom of Benin (now part of Nigeria) was renowned for its art. This mask was made in the 16th century.*

Seated Man with Harp *This statuette was made in the Cyclades c.3,000 BC.*

Lower Floor

GALLERY GUIDE

Most of the collections are housed on the two main floors. Works from 19 curatorial areas are in the permanent galleries, with designated galleries for temporary exhibitions. Central on the first and second floors are European painting, sculpture and decorative art. Other collections can be found radiating out from the center on both levels.

The Marriage Feast at Cana *This rare 16th-century panel painting by Juan de Flandes is part of the Linsky Collection.*

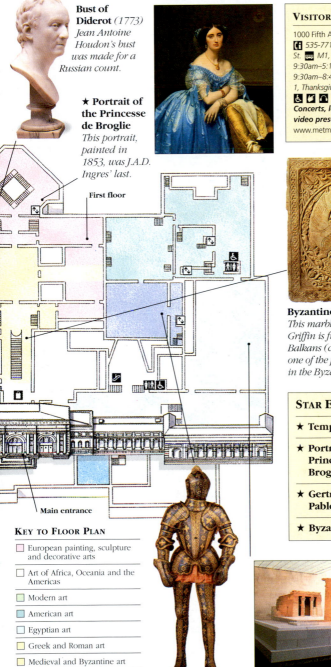

**Bust of
Diderot** *(1773)
Jean Antoine
Houdon's bust
was made for a
Russian count.*

★ **Portrait of
the Princesse
de Broglie**
*This portrait,
painted in
1853, was J.A.D.
Ingres' last.*

First floor

Main entrance

VISITORS' CHECKLIST

1000 Fifth Ave. **Map** 16 F4.
535-7710. M 4, 5, 6 to 86th
St. M1, M2, M3, M4.
9:30am–5:15pm Sun & Tue–Thu,
9:30am–8:45pm Fri, Sat. Jan
1, Thanksgiving, Dec 25.
*Concerts, lectures, film &
video presentations.* W
www.metmuseum.org

Byzantine Galleries
*This marble panel with a
Griffin is from Greece or the
Balkans (c.1250). It is just
one of the pieces on display
in the Byzantine Galleries.*

STAR EXHIBITS

★ **Temple of Dendur**

★ **Portrait of the
Princesse de
Broglie by Ingres**

★ **Gertrude Stein by
Pablo Picasso**

★ **Byzantine Galleries**

KEY TO FLOOR PLAN

- European painting, sculpture and decorative arts
- Art of Africa, Oceania and the Americas
- Modern art
- American art
- Egyptian art
- Greek and Roman art
- Medieval and Byzantine art
- Arms and armor
- Costume Institute
- Special exhibitions
- Non-exhibition space

English Armor
*This was made for
Sir George Clifford
around 1580.*

★ **Temple of Dendur** *(15 BC)
The Roman emperor Augustus built
this three-room temple. He is shown
in its reliefs making offerings.*

Metropolitan Museum of Art: Upper Levels

Marrakech
This 1964 work is one of Frank Stella's "Moroccan" paintings. Within a square format, fluorescent strips form the painting's main focus.

Sculpture Garden
These modern sculptures, on top of the Modern Art wing, are changed annually.

Card Players *(1890)*
Paul Cézanne departed here from his traditional landscapes, still lifes and portraits to paint this scene of peasants intently playing cards.

Islamic art

Second floor

First floor

★ **Cypresses** *(1889)*
Vincent Van Gogh painted this the year before he died. The heavy brushstrokes and the swirling style mark his later work.

STAR EXHIBITS

★ **Self-portrait of 1660 by Rembrandt**

★ **George Washington Crossing the Delaware by Leutze**

★ **Cypresses by Vincent Van Gogh**

★ **Diptych by Jan van Eyck**

Eagle-headed Winged Being Pollinating the Sacred Tree *(about 900 BC)*
This relief comes from an Assyrian palace.

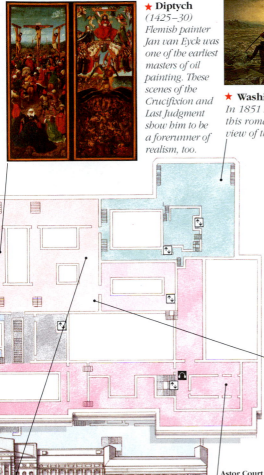

★ **Diptych**
(1425–30)
Flemish painter
Jan van Eyck was
one of the earliest
masters of oil
painting. These
scenes of the
Crucifixion and
Last Judgment
show him to be
a forerunner of
realism, too.

★ **Washington Crossing the Delaware**
In 1851 Emanuel Gottlieb Leutze painted
this romanticized – and inaccurate –
view of the famous crossing.

KEY TO FLOOR PLAN

☐ European painting, sculpture and decorative arts

☐ Ancient Near Eastern and Islamic art

☐ Twentieth-century art

☐ American art

☐ Asian art

☐ Greek and Roman art

☐ Musical instruments

☐ Drawings, prints and photographs

☐ Special exhibitions

▨ Non-exhibition space

The Death of Socrates *(1787)*
Jacques-Louis David shows
Socrates about to take poison
rather than renounce his beliefs.

Astor Court

★ **Self-portrait** *(1660)*
Rembrandt painted almost
100 self-portraits. This one
shows him at the age of 54.

THE ASTOR COURT

In 1979, 27 crafts-people from China, responsible for the care of Souzhou's historic gardens, came to New York to replicate a Ming-style scholar's garden in the Metropolitan Museum. They used centuries-old techniques and handmade tools that had been passed down for generations. It was the first cultural exchange between the United States and the People's Republic of China. The result is a quiet garden for meditation, a Western parallel to Souzhou's Garden of the Master of the Fishing Nets.

Exploring the Metropolitan

T HE TREASURES OF "THE MET" include a vast collection of American art and more than 2,500 European paintings, including masterpieces by Rembrandt and Vermeer. There are also many Islamic exhibits, plus the greatest collection of Egyptian art outside Cairo.

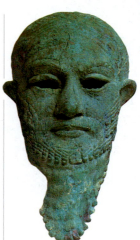

Mysterious in identity and origin, a rare 5,000-year-old copper head from the Near East

AFRICA, OCEANIA AND THE AMERICAS

A painted gold funerary mask (10th–14th century) from the necropolis of Batán Grande, Peru

N ELSON ROCKEFELLER built the Michael C. Rockefeller Wing in 1982 in memory of his son, who lost his life on an art-finding expedition in New Guinea. The wing showcases a superb collection of over 1,600 objects from Africa, the islands of the Pacific and the Americas.

Among the African works, the ivory and bronze sculptures from the royal kingdom of Benin (Nigeria) are outstanding, as is the wooden sculpture by the Dogon, Bamana and Senufo peoples of Mali. From the Pacific come carvings by the Asmat people of New Guinea and decorations and masks from the Melanesian and Polynesian islands. From Mexico and Central and South America come pre-Columbian gold, ceramics and stonework. The wing also contains fine Native American artifacts by the Inuit and other groups.

AMERICAN ART

G ILBERT STUART'S first portrait of George Washington, George Caleb Bingham's *Fur Traders Descending the Missouri*, John Singer Sargent's notorious portrait of *Madame X,* and the monumental *Washington Crossing the*

Delaware by Emanuel Leutze are among the icons of the American Wing. It holds one of the world's finest collections of American painting, including several works by Edward Hopper, and sculpture and decorative arts from colonial times to this century.

Period rooms, with original woodwork and furnishings, range from the saloon hall in which George Washington celebrated his last birthday to the elegant prairie-style living room from the Little house in Minnesota, designed by Frank Lloyd Wright in 1912.

Engelhard Court is an indoor sculpture garden with large-scale architectural elements, including the lovely stained-glass and mosaic loggia from Louis Comfort Tiffany's Long Island estate and the facade of an 1824 United States Branch Bank that stood on Wall Street.

***The Lighthouse at Two Lights** (1929) by Edward Hopper*

ANCIENT NEAR EASTERN AND ISLAMIC ART

M ASSIVE STONE SCULPTURES of human-headed winged lions, once guardians of the 9th-century BC Assyrian

palace of Assurnasirpal II, sit at the entrance to the Ancient Near Eastern galleries. Inside is a collection spanning 8,000 years, rich in Iranian bronzes, Anatolian ivories, Sumerian sculptures, and Achaemenian and Sassanian works in silver and gold. An adjacent gallery area displays the diversity of Islamic art from the 7th to the 19th century; glass and metal-work from Egypt, Syria and Mesopotamia; royal miniatures from the courts of Persia and Mughal India; rugs of the 16th and 17th centuries; and an 18th-century room from Syria.

ARMS AND ARMOR

M OUNTED KNIGHTS in full armor charge at each other across the equestrian court here. These galleries are a favorite with children and anyone moved by medieval romance or thrilled by power.

There are suits of armor, rapiers and sabers with hilts of precious stones and gold, firearms inlaid with ivory and mother-of-pearl, plus colorful heraldic banners and shields.

The pistol of Holy Roman Emperor Charles V (16th century)

Highlights include the armor of gentleman-pirate Sir George Clifford, a favorite of Queen Elizabeth I. The rainbow-colored armor of a 14th-century Japanese shogun and a collection of Wild West revolvers that once belonged to gunmaker Samuel Colt are also exhibited here.

ASIAN ART

The Old Plum, a Japanese paper screen from the early Edo period (about 1650)

MANY OUTSTANDING galleries contain masterpieces of Chinese, Japanese, Korean, Indian and Southeast Asian art, dating from the second millennium BC to the 20th century. A full-scale Ming-style Chinese scholar's garden was built by craftspeople from Souzhou as part of the first cultural exchange between the United States and the People's Republic of China. The museum also has one of the finest collections of Sung and Yuan paintings in the world, Chinese Buddhist monumental sculptures, fine Chinese ceramics and jade and an important display of the arts of ancient China.

The full range of Japanese arts is represented in a breathtaking suite of 11 galleries featuring chronological and thematic displays of Japanese lacquer, ceramics, painting, sculpture, textiles and screens. Indian, Southeast Asian and Korean galleries display superb sculptures and other arts from these regions.

COSTUME INSTITUTE

THERE IS ALWAYS a portion of the 75,000-piece collection of costumes, dating from the 17th century to the present, on display in these new state-of-the-art galleries. Here, the Institute maintains a definitive compendium of fashionable dress, from the elaborately embroidered dresses of the late 1600s to the shocking-pink evening dresses of Elsa Schiaparelli, complete with hats, scarves, gloves, handbags and other accessories. There are also the designs of Worth, Quant and Balenciaga, as well as gowns from the Napoleonic and Victorian eras, the costumes of the Ballets Russes and even David Bowie's sequined jockstrap.

The regional portion of the collection is rich with folk costumes from Europe, Asia, Africa and the Americas.

The Institute is so sophisticated in its understanding of conservation techniques that it has been called upon to advise NASA on the cleaning of astronauts' spacesuits.

A 17th-century European silk-and-satin doublet

DRAWINGS, PRINTS AND PHOTOGRAPHS

A NEW GALLERY regularly displays selections from the museum's incredible holdings of drawings, prints, etchings and photographs.

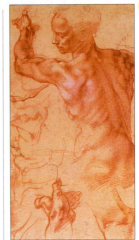

Michelangelo's studies of a Libyan Sibyl for the ceiling of the Sistine Chapel (1508)

The drawings collection is especially rich in Italian and French art from the 15th to the 19th century. Specific exhibits of the drawings in this collection are shown on a rotating basis because of the light-sensitive nature of works on paper.

Highlights among the 11,000 drawings include works by Michelangelo, Leonardo da Vinci, Raphael, Ingres, Goya, Rubens, Rembrandt, Tiepolo and Seurat. The encyclopedic print collection of nearly 1.5 million images and the 14,000 illustrated books includes major works by virtually every master printmaker, from an early German woodcut called *Virgin and Child* to some of Dürer's most accomplished works and Goya's *The Giant*.

Influential gallery-owner Alfred Stieglitz's donation of his own extensive collection of photographs brought here such gems as Edward Steichen's *The Flatiron*. It formed the core of a photography collection that is now also particularly strong in Modernist works dating from between the world wars.

Ephemera such as posters and advertisements form another part of this collection.

EGYPTIAN ART

ONE OF THE MUSEUM'S finest and best-loved areas is the ancient Egyptian wing, which displays every one of its thousands of holdings – from the prehistoric period to the 8th century AD. Objects range from the fragmented jasper lips of a 15th-century BC queen to the massive Temple of Dendur. Other amazing archaeological finds, most of them from museum-sponsored expeditions undertaken early in the 20th century, include sculptures of the notorious Queen Hatshepsut, who seized the Theban throne in the 16th century BC; 100 carved reliefs of Amenhotpe IV's reign; and tomb figures like the blue faïence hippo that has become the museum's mascot.

**Queen Tiye, wife of
Amenhotpe III (1417–1379 BC)**

EUROPEAN PAINTING, SCULPTURE AND DECORATIVE ARTS

THE HEART of the museum is its awe-inspiring collection of 3,000 European paintings. The Italian works include

**Young Woman with a Water Jug
(1660) by Jan Vermeer**

Botticelli's *Last Communion of Saint Jerome* and Bronzino's *Portrait of a Young Man*. The Dutch and Flemish canvases are among the finest in the world, with Brueghel's *The Harvesters*, several works by Rubens and Van Dyck, over a dozen Rembrandts and more Vermeers than any other museum. The collection also has masterpieces by Spanish artists El Greco, Velázquez and Goya, and by French artists Poussin and Watteau. Some of the finest Impressionist and Post impressionist canvases reside here: 34 Monets, including *Terrace at Sainte-Adresse;* 18 Cézannes; and Van Gogh's *Cypresses*. In the Kravis wing and adjacent galleries are works from the 60,000-object collection of European sculpture and decorative arts, such as Tullio Lombardo's marble statue of Adam; a bronze statuette of a rearing horse, after a model by Leonardo; and dozens of pieces by Degas and Rodin. Period settings include the patio from a 16th-century

Spanish castle and a series of ornate 18th-century French domestic interiors known as the Wrightsman Rooms. The Petrie European Sculpture Court features French and Italian sculpture in a beautiful garden setting reminiscent of Versailles in France.

GREEK AND ROMAN ART

A ROMAN SARCOPHAGUS from Tarsus, donated in 1870, was the first work of art in the Met's collections. It can still be seen in the museum's superbly restored Greek and Roman galleries, along with breathtaking wall panels from a villa that was buried under the lava of Vesuvius in AD 79, Etruscan mirrors, Roman portrait busts, exquisite objects in glass and silver and hundreds of Greek vases. A monumental 7th-century BC statue of a youth shows the movement toward naturalism in sculpture, and the Hellenistic *Old Market Woman* demonstrates how the Greeks had mastered realism by the 2nd century BC.

**An amphora by Exekias, showing
a wedding (6th century BC)**

LEHMAN COLLECTION

WHAT HAD BEEN one of the finest private art collections in the world, that of investment banker Robert Lehman, came to the museum in 1969. The Lehman Wing is a dramatic glass pyramid housing an extraordinarily varied collection rich in Old Masters and 19th-century French paintings, drawings,

EGYPTIAN TOMB MODELS

In 1920, a Met researcher's light illuminated a room, hitherto undiscovered for 2,000 years, in the tomb of the nobleman Mekutra. Within were 24 tiny, perfect replicas of his daily life, to ensure his comfort in the next world – his house and garden, fleet of ships and herd of cattle. Mekutra himself is there, too, on his boat, inhaling a lotus's scent and enjoying the music of his singer and harpist.

A panel from the stained-glass *Death of the Virgin* window, from the 12th-century cathedral of Saint Pierre in Troyes, France

bronzes, Renaissance majolica, Venetian glass, furniture and enamels. Among the canvases are works by north–European masters; Dutch and Spanish paintings, French masterworks, Post impressionists and Fauves.

MEDIEVAL ART

THE METROPOLITAN'S medieval collection includes works dating from the 4th to the 16th century, roughly from the fall of Rome to the beginning of the Renaissance. It is split between the main museum and its uptown branch, the Cloisters *(see pp234–7)*. In the main building are a chalice once thought to be the Holy Grail, six silver Byzantine plates showing scenes from the life of David, a 1301 pulpit by Giovanni Pisano in the shape of an eagle, several monumental sculptures of the Virgin and Child, plus a huge choir screen from Spain. Other exhibits include Migration jewelry, liturgical vessels, stained glass, ivories and 14th- and 15-century tapestries.

MUSICAL INSTRUMENTS

THE WORLD'S OLDEST piano, Andrés Segovia's guitars and a sitar shaped like a peacock are some of the features of a broad and sometimes quirky collection of musical instruments that spans six continents and dates from prehistory to the present. The instruments illustrate the history of music and performance, and most of them are conserved to remain in playable condition. Worth particular mention are instruments from the European courts of the Middle Ages and the Renaissance; rare violins; spinets and harpsichords; instruments inlaid with precious materials; a fully equipped traditional violin-maker's workshop; there are also African drums, Asian *pi-pas*, or lutes; and Native American flutes. Visitors can use audio equipment to hear many of the instruments playing the music of their day.

Stradivari violin from Cremona, Italy (1691)

MODERN ART

SINCE ITS FOUNDATION in 1870, the museum has been acquiring contemporary art, but it was not until 1987 that a permanent home for 20th-century art was built – the Lila Acheson Wallace Wing. Other museums in New York have larger collections of modern art, but this display space is considered among the finest. European and American works from 1900 onward are featured on three levels, starting with Europeans such as Picasso, Kandinsky and Bonnard. The collection's greatest strength lies in its collection of modern American art, with works by New York school "The Eight," including John Sloan; such Modernists as Charles Demuth and Georgia O'Keeffe; American Regionalist Grant Wood; Abstract Expressionists Willem de Kooning; and such Color Field painters as Clyfford Still.

Grant Wood's view of *The Midnight Ride of Paul Revere* (1931)

Special areas of the wing house Art Nouveau and Art Deco furniture and metalwork; a large collection of works on paper by Paul Klee; and the Sculpture Gallery, with its large-scale sculptures and canvases.

Gems of the collection include Picasso's portrait of Gertrude Stein, Matisse's *Nasturtiums* and *"Dance,1"* Demuth's *I Saw the Figure 5 in Gold*, Jackson Pollock's *Autumn Rhythm* and Andy Warhol's last self-portrait.

Each year the Cantor Roof Garden at the top of the wing features a new installation of contemporary sculpture, especially dramatic against the backdrop of the New York skyline and Central Park.

Book cover (1916) by illustrator N.C. Wyeth

Society of Illustrators ⑫

128 E 63rd St. **Map** 13 A2. 🅲 838-2560. Ⓜ Lexington Ave. ◯ 10am–5pm Wed–Fri, 10am–8pm Tue, noon–4pm Sat. 🄰 ♿ restricted. 🖉 🄵
Ⓦ www.societyillustrators.org

Established in 1901, this society was formed to promote the illustrator's art. Its notable roster included Charles Dana Gibson, N.C. Wyeth and Howard Pyle. It was at first concerned with education and public service, and held occasional exhibits. In 1981, the Museum of American Illustration opened in two galleries. Changing thematic exhibitions show the history of book and magazine illustration, with an annual exhibition of the year's finest American illustrations.

Mount Vernon Hotel Museum ⑬

421 E 61st St. **Map** 13 C3. 🅲 838-6878. Ⓜ Lexington Ave, 59th St. ◯ 11am–4pm Tue–Sun (Tues in Jun & Jul: to 9pm). ◯ Aug, public hols. 🄰 🖉 🄵

Built in 1799, the Mount Vernon Hotel Museum and Garden was once a country day hotel for New Yorkers who needed a quite escape from the crowded city, then only at the south end of the island. The stone building sits on land once owned by Abigail Adams Smith, daughter of President John Adams.

It was acquired by the Colonial Dames of America in 1924 and turned into a charming re-creation of a Federal home. Costumed guides show visitors through the rooms, pointing out the treasures, including Chinese porcelain, Aubusson carpets, Sheraton chests and a Duncan Phyfe sofa. In one bedroom there is even a baby's cradle and children's toys. An 18th-century-style garden has been planted around the house.

Henderson Place ⑭

Map 18 D3. Ⓜ 86th St.

Queen Anne row houses at Henderson Place

Now surrounded by modern apartment blocks, this enclave of 24 red-brick Queen Anne row houses was built in 1882. The row houses were commissioned by John C. Henderson, a hat-maker, as a self-contained community. The elegant Lamb & Rich design has gray slate roof gables, pediments, parapets, chimneys and dormer windows. forming patterns, and a turret marking the corner of each block.

Carl Schurz Park promenade

Carl Schurz Park ⑮

Map 18 D3. Ⓜ 86th St.

Laid out in 1891, this park along the East River has a wide promenade over the East River Drive. It offers fine vistas of the river and the turbulent waters of Hell Gate, where the river meets Long Island Sound. It is named after Carl Schurz, a native who became Secretary of the Interior (1869–75). The first part of the promenade is the John Finlay Walk, named for an editor of the *New York Times* known for his hiking prowess. One of the city's most pleasant green escapes, the park's grassy areas are filled with basking New Yorkers on sunny days.

Gracie Mansion ⑯

East End Ave at 88th St. **Map** 18 D3. 🅲 570-4751. Ⓜ 86th St. ◯ Apr–mid Nov:10am, 11am, 1pm, 2pm Wed for prebooked guided tours only. 🄰 🖉 ♿ 🄵

This gracious, balconied wooden 1799 country home is the official mayor's residence. Built by wealthy merchant Archibald Gracie, it is one of the best Federal houses left in New York.

The house was acquired by the city in 1887 and was the first home of the Museum of the City of New York. In 1942 it became the official Mayoral Residence, and when Mayor Fiorello La Guardia moved in

Front view of Gracie Mansion

after nine years in office, preferring it to a 75-room palace on Riverside Drive – he said that even the modest Gracie Mansion was much too fancy for him. La Guardia, "the Little Flower" (from Fiorello), fought corruption and reformed the city.

Church of the Holy Trinity ⑰

316 E 88th St. **Map** 17 B3.
☎ 289-4100. Ⓜ 86th St. ◷ 9am–5pm Mon–Fri, 7:30am–2pm Sun. ⛪ winter: 8am, 9am, 11am, 6pm Sun; 6:30pm Wed; summer: 8am, 10am. ⓞ

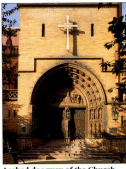

Arched doorway of the Church of the Holy Trinity

DELIGHTFULLY PLACED in a serene garden setting, this church was constructed in 1889 of glowing golden brick and terra-cotta in French Renaissance style. It boasts one of New York's best bell towers, which holds a handsome wrought-iron clock with brass hands. The arched doorway is richly decorated with carved images of the saints and prophets.

The complex was donated by Serena Rhinelander in memory of her father and grandfather. The land was part of the Rhinelander farm, which the family had owned for 100 years.

Farther down at 350 E. 88th Street is the Rhinelander Children's Center, also a gift, and the headquarters of the Children's Aid Society.

St. Nicholas Russian Orthodox Cathedral ⑱

15 E 97th St. **Map** 16 F1.
☎ 289-1915. Ⓜ 96 St. ◷ by appt. ⛪ 6pm Sat, 10:00am Sun (Russian).
ⓞ ⓦ www.stnicholasronyc.com

THIS REALLY IS "Moscow on the Hudson." Built in Muscovite Baroque style in 1902, it has five onion domes crowned with crosses, and blue and yellow tiles on a red brick and white stone facade. Among the early worshipers were White Russians who had fled the first uprisings at home, mostly intellectuals and aristocrats who soon became a part of New York society. Later, there were more waves of refugees, dissidents and defectors.

The cathedral now serves a scattered community, and the congregation is small. Mass is celebrated in Russian with great pomp and dignity.

The cathedral is filled with the scent of incense. The high central sanctuary has marble columns with blue and white trim above. Ornate wooden screens trimmed with gold enclose the altar. It is unique, an unexpected find on a side street in this staid part of Manhattan.

Facade and domes of St. Nicholas Russian Cathedral

Facade of the Museum of the City of New York

Museum of the City of New York ⑲

5th Ave at 103rd St. **Map** 21 C5.
☎ 534-1672. Ⓜ 103rd St. ◷ 10am–5pm Wed–Sat, 12–5pm Sun. ◉ public hols. **Donations welcome**.
ⓞ ♿ ⓕ ⓕ ⓦ www.mcny.org

FOUNDED IN 1923 and at first housed in Gracie Mansion, this museum is dedicated to New York's development from its earliest beginnings, shown in costumes, paintings, furnishings, toys and a range of fascinating memorabilia.

Housed in this handsome Georgian Colonial building since 1932, it is noted for its period rooms from actual homes, including John D. Rockefeller's bedroom and dressing room, and for its wonderful collection of toys, dolls and dollhouses dating from 1769. Start with *The Big Apple* video, then visit the exhibition, "Broadway! 125 Years of Musical Theater." The second floor has a magnificent collection of silver objects dating from 1678 to 1984. The Alexander Hamilton Gallery contains furniture and paintings that once belonged to the first Secretary of the Treasury.

The impressive collection housed in the basement includes antique fire equipment, paintings, maps and prints all relating to city history.

Whitney Museum of American Art ❼

THE WHITNEY MUSEUM is the foremost showcase for American art of this century. It was founded in 1930 by sculptor Gertrude Vanderbilt Whitney after the Metropolitan Museum of Art turned down her collection of works by living artists including George Bellows and Edward Hopper. In 1966 the museum moved to the present inverted pyramid building designed by Marcel Breuer. The Whitney Biennial show is the most significant survey of new trends in American art.

The cantilevered facade of the Whitney Museum

Green Coca-Cola Bottles
Andy Warhol's 1962 work is a commentary on mass production and monopoly.

The White Calico Flower
Georgia O'Keeffe's enlarged flower paintings have an abstract quality, as in this 1931 example.

Little Big Painting
The 1965 work by Roy Lichtenstein is a comic critique of Abstract Expressionist painting.

Early Sunday Morning (1930)
Edward Hopper's paintings often convey the emptiness of American city life.

MUSEUM GUIDE
There are no permanent displays here; the only item always on exhibit is Alexander Calder's sculpture Circus, situated on the first floor. Changing exhibitions occupy the second, third and fourth floors.

Dempsey and Firpo
In 1924, George Bellows depicted one of the most famous prizefights of the century.

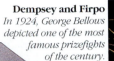

VISITORS' CHECKLIST

945 Madison Ave. **Map** 17 A5.
570-3600. 6 to 77th St.
M1, M2, M3, M4, 30, 72 .
11am–6pm Tue–Thu,
Sat–Sun, 1–9pm Fri. public
hols. **Lectures,
film/video presentations.**
W www.whitney.org

Three Flags *(1958)*
Jasper Johns's use of familiar objects in an abstract form was influential in the development of Pop art.

Owh! In San Paõ *(1951)*
In this painting by Stuart Davis, abstract forms are combined with lettering to create a unique and distinctive American style.

Circus *(1926–31)*
Alexander Calder's fanciful creation is always on display.

Tango *(1919)*
This is considered Polish-born Elie Nadelman's greatest wood sculpture.

Hudson River Landscape *(1951)*
This steel sculpture is one of David Smith's most influential works.

Frick Collection **8**

THE PRICELESS ART collection of steel magnate Henry Clay Frick (1849—1919) is exhibited in a residential setting amid the furnishings of his opulent mansion, providing a rare glimpse of how the extremely wealthy lived in New York's gilded age. Frick intended the collection to be a memorial to himself and bequeathed the entire house to the nation on his death. The collection includes old master paintings, French furniture, Limoges enamels and Oriental rugs.

Fifth Avenue facade of the Frick Collection

Colonnade Garden Court

The Harbor of Dieppe *(1826)*
J.M.W. Turner was criticized by some skeptical contemporaries for depicting this northern European port suffused with light.

The White Horse *(1819)*
John Constable based this painting on a familiar scene from his Suffolk home.

Library

West Gallery

Limoges Enamel
The collection of enamels includes The Seven Sorrows of the Virgin *(1500–50).*

Living Hall

STAR PAINTINGS

★ **Sir Thomas More by Hans Holbein**

★ **Mall in St. James's Park by Thomas Gainsborough**

★ **Officer and the Laughing Girl by Jan Vermeer**

★ **Lady Meux by James A.M. Whistler**

★ **Sir Thomas More** *(1527)*
Holbein's portrait of Henry VIII's Lord Chancellor was painted eight years before More's execution for treason.

GALLERY GUIDE
Of special interest are the skylit West Gallery, offering oils by Vermeer, Hals and Rembrandt; the East Gallery, featuring Whistler; the Library and Dining Room, devoted to English works; and the Living Hall with works by Titian, Bellini and Holbein.

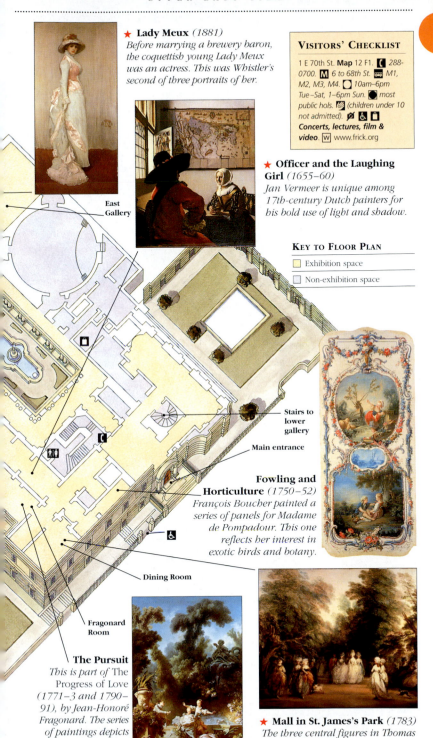

★ **Lady Meux** (1881)
Before marrying a brewery baron, the coquettish young Lady Meux was an actress. This was Whistler's second of three portraits of her.

East Gallery

★ **Officer and the Laughing Girl** (1655–60)
Jan Vermeer is unique among 17th-century Dutch painters for his bold use of light and shadow.

KEY TO FLOOR PLAN

☐ Exhibition space
☐ Non-exhibition space

Stairs to lower gallery

Main entrance

Fowling and Horticulture (1750–52)
François Boucher painted a series of panels for Madame de Pompadour. This one reflects her interest in exotic birds and botany.

Dining Room

Fragonard Room

The Pursuit
This is part of The Progress of Love (1771–3 and 1790–91), by Jean-Honoré Fragonard. The series of paintings depicts the events of an idealized courtship.

★ **Mall in St. James's Park** (1783)
The three central figures in Thomas Gainsborough's London landscape may be the daughters of George III.

CENTRAL PARK

THE CITY'S "BACKYARD" was created by Frederick Law Olmsted and Calvert Vaux in 1858 on an unpromising site of quarries, pig farms, swampland and shacks. Ten million cartloads of stone and earth turned it into the lush 843-acre (340-ha) park of today. There are scenic hills, lakes and lush meadows, dotted throughout with outcrops of Manhattan bedrock and planted with more than 500,000 trees and shrubs. Over the years the park has blossomed, with playgrounds and skating rinks, plus ball fields and spaces for everything from chess and croquet to concerts and events. Cars are banned on weekends, giving bicyclists, in-line skaters and joggers the right-of-way.

Statues, Delacorte Theater (see p206)

SIGHTS AT A GLANCE

Historic Buildings
The Dairy ❶
Belvedere Castle ❸

Monuments and Statues
Strawberry Fields ❷
Bethesda Fountain and Terrace ❺
Bow Bridge ❹

Lakes and Gardens
Conservatory Water ❻
Central Park Wildlife Center ❼
Conservatory Garden ❽

SEE ALSO

• **Street Finder**, maps 12, 16

• **Restaurants** pp290–92

Ⓦ www.centralparknyc.org

GETTING THERE

Subway lines B and C run the length of the park on the Upper West Side, with stops at 59th, 72nd, 81st, 86th, 96th and 103rd Sts. The 59th St/Columbus Circle stop is served by the 1 and 9 Broadway/7th Ave lines, the 8th Ave lines; the N and R Broadway local trains stop at 57th St and 5th Ave at the southern end of the park. Bus routes M1, M2, M3 and M4 run along the eastern edge of the park.

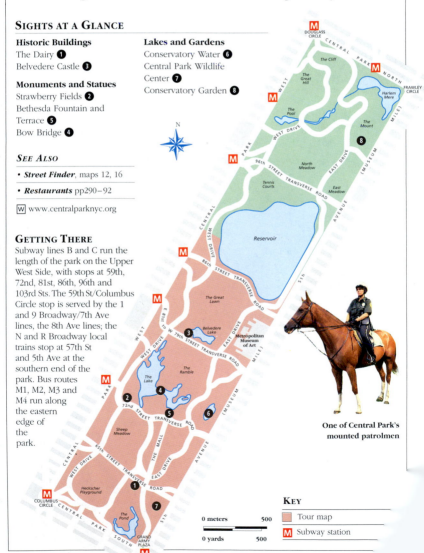

One of Central Park's mounted patrolmen

KEY

Tour map

Ⓜ Subway station

0 meters 500
0 yards 500

Bird's-eye view of the park

A Tour of Central Park

ON A SHORT VISIT, a walking tour from 59th to 79th streets takes in some of Central Park's loveliest features, from the dense wooded Ramble to the open formal spaces of Bethesda Terrace. Along the way, you will see artificial lakes and some of the 30 graceful bridges and arches, no two alike, that link some 58 miles (93 km) of footpaths, bridle paths and roads in the park. In summer the park is often several degrees cooler than the city streets around it, and thus is a favorite retreat.

★ **Strawberry Fields**
One of the park's most visited spots, this peaceful area was created in memory of John Lennon, who lived nearby ❷

★ **Bethesda Fountain and Terrace**
The richly ornamented formal terrace overlooks the Lake and the wooded shores of the Ramble ❺

Wollman Rink was restored in the 1980s for future generations of skaters by tycoon Donald Trump.

Central Park Wildlife Center
Three climate zones are home to over 100 species of animals ❼

The Pond

Plaza Hotel
(see p179)

C E N T R A L   P A R

SHEEP MEADOW

THE MALL

CENTRAL PARK SOUTH

TRANSVERSE

65TH ST

FIFTH

The Dairy
*Victorian Gothic building
...s the Visitor Center. Make it
...rst stop and pick up a
...r of park events* ❶

Frick Collection
(see pp200–1)

Hans Christian Andersen's statue is a favorite Central Park landmark for children. It is on the west side of Conservatory Water and is a popular site for storytelling in the summer.

Bow Bridge
This cast-iron bridge links the Ramble with Cherry Hill by a graceful arch, 60 ft (18 m) above the Lake ❹

LOCATOR MAP
See Manhattan Map pp12–13

Alice in Wonderland is immortalized in bronze at the northern end of Conservatory Water, along with her friends the Cheshire Cat, the Mad Hatter and the Dormouse. Children love to slide down her toadstool seat.

STAR SIGHTS

★ **The Dairy**

★ **Strawberry Fields**

★ **Belvedere Castle**

★ **Bethesda Fountain**

★ **Conservatory Water**

akota uilding *(see p216)*

San Remo Apartments *(see p212)*

American Museum of Natural History *(see pp214–15)*

GREAT LAWN

M

W E S T

86TH ST TRANSVERSE

79TH ST

A V E N U E

Metropolitan Museum *(see pp188–95)*

Obelisk

The Ramble is a wooded area of 37 acres (15 ha), crisscrossed by paths and streams. It is a paradise for bird-watchers – over 250 species have been spotted in the park, which is on the Atlantic migration flyway.

Reservoir

Guggenheim Museum *(see pp186–87)*

★ **Belvedere Castle**
From the terraces there are unequaled views of the city and surrounding park. Within the stone walls is the Central Park Learning Center ❸

★ **Conservatory Water**
From March to November, this is the scene of model boat races each Saturday. Many of the tiny craft are stored in the boathouse that adjoins the Lake ❻

The Carousel, part of the park's Children's District

The Dairy ❶

Map 12 F2. 📞 794-6564.
Ⓜ *Fifth Ave.* ◷ *Apr–Oct: 10am–5pm Tue–Sun; Nov–Mar: 10am–4pm Tue–Sun.* **Slide show.** 📷
🌐 www.centralparknyc.org

NOW USED AS the park information center, this charming building of natural stone was planned as part of the "Children's District" of the park, which included a playground, the Carousel, a Children's Cottage and stable. In 1873, there were cows grazing on the meadows in front of the Dairy, a ewe and her lambs feeding nearby, and chickens, guinea fowl and peacocks roaming the lawn. City children could get fresh milk and other refreshments here. Over the years, the Dairy deteriorated, being used as a shed until restoration in 1979, done according to original photographs and drawings. The Dairy is the place to begin exploring the lush and leafy park; maps and details of events can be obtained here. The less energetic can rent chess and checkers sets for use on the pretty inlaid boards of the *kinderberg*, the charming little "children's hill" nearby.

Strawberry Fields ❷

Map 12 E1. Ⓜ *72nd St.*

THE RESTORATION of this tear-drop-shaped section of the park was Yoko Ono's tribute in memory of her slain husband, John Lennon. They lived in the Dakota apartments over-looking this spot *(see p216).* Gifts for the garden came from all over the world. A mosaic set in the pathway, inscribed with the word *Imagine* (named for Lennon's famous song), was a gift from the city of Naples in Italy.

This broad expanse of the park's landscape was designed by Vaux and Olmsted. Now it is an international peace garden, with 161 species of plants (one from every country of the world), including jetbead, roses, witch hazel, birches – and strawberries.

Belvedere Castle ❸

Map 16 E4. 📞 772-0210.
Ⓜ *81st St.* ◷ *10am–5pm Tue–Sun.*
📷 ♿ *to main floor only.*

THIS STONE CASTLE atop Vista Rock, complete with tower and turrets, offers one of the best views of the park and the city from its lookout on the rooftop. Inside is the Henry Luce Nature Observatory, with a delightful exhibit telling inquisitive young visitors about the surprising variety of wildlife to be found in the park.

The view to the north from the castle allows you to look down into

Belvedere Castle with its lookout over the park

the Delacorte Theater, home to the free productions of Shakespeare in the Park every summer, featuring big-name stars *(see p335).* The theater was the gift of George T. Delacorte. Publisher and founder of Dell paperbacks, Delacorte was a delightful philanthropist who was responsible for many of the park's pleasures.

Bow Bridge ❹

Map 16 E5. Ⓜ *72nd St.*

THIS IS ONE of the park's seven original cast-iron bridges and is considered one of the finest. It was designed by Vaux as a bow tying together the two large sections of the lake. In the 19th century, when the Lake was used for ice skating, a red ball was hoisted from a bell tower on Vista Rock to signal that the ice was safe. The bridge offers expansive views of the park and the buildings bordering it on both the east and west sides.

A tranquil scene in Central Park, overlooked by exclusive apartments

An 1864 print of Bethesda Fountain and Terrace

Bethesda Fountain and Terrace ⑤

Map 12 E1. Ⓜ *72nd St.*

SITUATED BETWEEN the Lake and the Mall, this is the architectural heart of the park, a formal element in the naturalistic landscape. The fountain was dedicated in 1873. The statue, *Angel of the Waters*, marked the opening of the Croton Aqueduct system in 1842, bringing the city its first supply of pure water; its name refers to a biblical account of a healing angel at the pool of Bethesda in Jerusalem. The Spanish-style detailing, such as the sculptured double staircase, tiles and friezes, is by Jacob Wrey Mould.

The terrace is one of the best spots to relax and take in some people-watching.

Conservatory Water ⑥

Map 16 F5. Ⓜ *77th St.*

BETTER KNOWN as the Model Boat Pond, this stretch of water is home to model yacht races every weekend.

At the north end of the lake, a sculpture of Alice in Wonderland is a delight for children. It was commissioned by George T. Delacorte in honor of his wife. He himself is immortalized in caricature as the Mad Hatter. On the west bank, free story hours are held at a statue of Hans Christian Andersen, portrayed reading from his own story, "The Ugly Duckling," while its hero waddles at his feet. Like that of Alice, this statue is climbed on by small children, who especially like to snuggle in the author's lap.

Conservatory Water's literary links continue into adolescence: it is here that J.D. Salinger's Holden Caulfield comes to tell the ducks his troubles in *The Catcher in the Rye*.

Central Park Wildlife Center ⑦

Map 12 F2. Ⓒ *439-6500.* Ⓜ *Fifth Ave.* ◯ *Year round 10am–5pm Mon–Fri, 10:30am–5:30pm Sat, Sun, & hols.* 🅿 📷 ♿ 🚇 🚻 Ⓦ *www. wcs.org/zoos; centralparkzoo.com*

REOPENED IN 1988 after four years of reconstruction, this imaginative zoo won plaudits for its creative and humane use of small space. More than 100 species of animals are represented in three climate zones, the Tropics, the Polar Circle and the California coast. An equatorial rain forest is home to monkeys and free-flying birds, while penguins and polar bears populate an Arctic landscape that allows views both above and under water.

Near the entrance to the Tisch Children's Zoo is the much-loved Delacorte Clock, another example of the whimsical generosity of George T. Delacorte. Every half hour, bronze musical animals (such as a goat playing pan pipes) circle the clock playing nursery rhymes. Toward Willowdell Arch is another children's favorite – the memorial to Balto, lead dog of a team of huskies that made a heroic journey across Alaska to deliver serum for a diphtheria epidemic.

Statue of Balto, the heroic husky sled dog

Conservatory Garden ⑧

Map 21 B5. Ⓜ *Central Pk N, 103rd St.* Ⓒ *860-1382.*

THE VANDERBILT GATE on Fifth Avenue is the entry to three formal gardens filled with thousands of flowering trees and shrubs. The Central Garden has a large lawn with yew hedges and ends in a semicircle of hedges and shrubs crowned by a wisteria pergola. On either side are blooming Siberian crabapple trees. The South Garden spills over with perennials. The bronze statue in the reflecting pool is of Mary and Dickon, from Frances Hodgson Burnett's *The Secret Garden*. Beyond is a slope featuring thousands of native wildflowers, spreading into the park beyond. The North Garden, centered around the bronze *Fountain of the Three Dancing Maidens*, puts on a brief but brilliant display of an each summer

Polar bear in the Wildlife Center

UPPER WEST SIDE

Indian mask, Museum of Natural History

THIS AREA became residential only in the 1870s, when the Ninth Avenue El (see pp24-5) made commuting to midtown possible for the first time. When the Dakota, New York's first luxury apartment house, was built between 1880 and 1884, the city finally began to grade and level the streets. Buildings soon sprang up along Broadway and Central Park West, and today the area is bustling and diverse. The cross streets, dating mainly from the 1890s, boast many fine brownstone row houses. Many cultural institutions are here, including Lincoln Center and the American Museum of Natural History.

SIGHTS AT A GLANCE

Historic Streets and Buildings
Twin Towers of Central Park West ❶
The Dakota ❾
Pomander Walk ❸
Riverside Drive and Park ❹
The Dorilton ❼

Museums and Galleries
American Folk Art Museum ❼
New-York Historical Society ❿
American Museum of Natural History pp214–15 ⓫
Hayden Planetarium ⓬
Children's Museum of Manhattan ⓯

Famous Theaters
Lincoln Center for the Performing Arts ❷
New York State Theater ❸
Metropolitan Opera House ❹
Lincoln Center Theater ❺
Avery Fisher Hall ❻

Landmark Hotels and Restaurants
Hotel des Artistes ❽
The Ansonia ⓰

GETTING THERE
By subway, take the 6th Ave B or D, the 7th Ave/Broadway 1/9, 2 and 3, or the 8th Ave A, C and E trains. By bus, the M10 (Central Park West), M7, M11, M104 and M5 or the M66, M72, M79, M86 and M96 crosstown buses.

SEE ALSO

Stone figure on the facade of the Hotel des Artistes

KEY
Street-by-Street map
M Subway station

The facade of 14 Riverside Drive

0 meters 500
0 yards 500

Street by Street: Lincoln Center

LINCOLN CENTER was conceived when both the Metropolitan Opera House and the New York Philharmonic required homes, and a large tract on Manhattan's west side was in dire need of revitalization. The notion of a single complex where different performing arts could exist side by side seems natural today, but in the 1950s it was considered both daring and risky. Today Lincoln Center has proved itself by drawing audiences of five million each year. Proximity to its halls prompts both performers and arts lovers to live nearby.

★ **Lincoln Center for the Performing Arts**
Dance, music and theater come together in this fine contemporary complex. It is also a great place to sit around the reflecting fountain and people-watch ❷

Lincoln Center Theater
The Vivian Beaumont and the Mitzi E. Newhouse theaters are both housed in this building ❺

Composer Leonard Bernstein's
famous musical *West Side Story,* which was based on the Romeo and Juliet theme, was set in the impoverished streets around what is now Lincoln Center. Bernstein was later instrumental in setting up the large music complex.

The Guggenheim Bandshell
in Damrosch Park is the site of free concerts.

The New York State Theater
This is the home of the New York City Ballet, as well as an opera company. The theater seats 2,737 people ❸

Metropolitan Opera House
Lincoln Center's focus is the Opera House. The café at the top of the lobby offers wonderful plaza views ❹

The College Board Building is an Art Deco delight that now houses condominiums and the administrative offices of the College Board, developers of the college entrance exam.

Early American quilt

American Folk Art Museum
Quilting and naïve painting are some of the arts displayed here ❼

James Dean once lived in a one-room apartment on the top floor at 19 West 68th Street.

LOCATOR MAP
see Manhattan Map pp12–13

KEY

— — — Suggested route

| 0 meters | | 100 |
| 0 yards | | 100 |

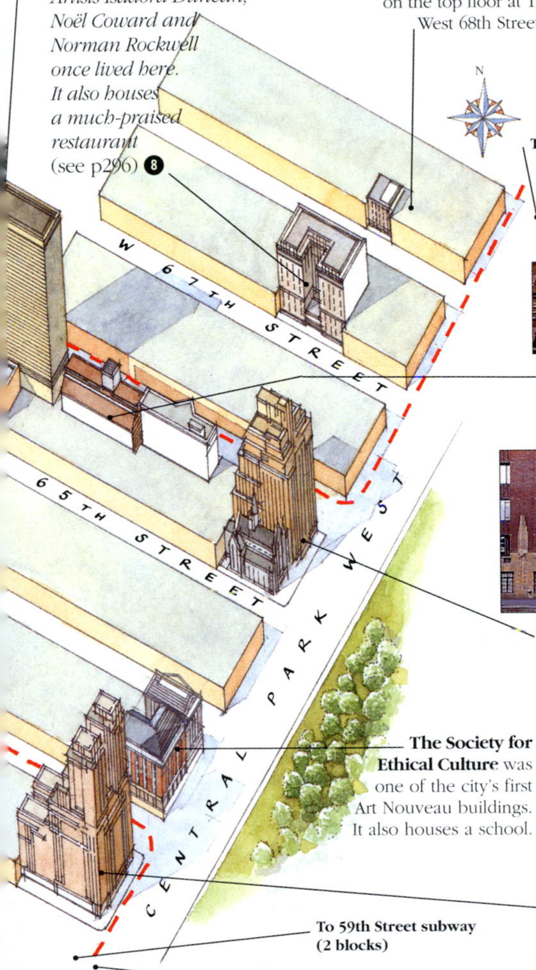

To 72nd Street subway (4 blocks)

★ **Hotel des Artistes**
Artists Isadora Duncan, Noël Coward and Norman Rockwell once lived here. It also houses a much-praised restaurant (see p296) ❽

An ABC-TV sound stage for soap operas is housed in this castle-like building, formerly an armory.

55 Central Park West is the Art Deco apartment building that featured in the film *Ghostbusters*.

The Society for Ethical Culture was one of the city's first Art Nouveau buildings. It also houses a school.

To 59th Street subway (2 blocks)

Central Park West is home to many celebrities, who like the privacy of its exclusive apartments.

Century Apartments
The Century's twin towers are visible from the park, making it a New York landmark ❶

STAR SIGHTS

★ **Lincoln Center**

★ **Hotel des Artistes**

The San Remo, a twin-towered apartment house designed by Emery Roth

Twin Towers of Central Park West ❶

Map 12 D1, 12 D2, 16 D3, 16 D5.
Ⓜ *59th St–Columbus Circle, 72nd St.*
⬤ *to public.*

AMONG THE MOST familiar landmarks on the New York skyline are the five twin-towered apartment houses on Central Park West. Built from 1929 and 1931, just before the Great Depression halted all luxury construction, they are now among the most highly sought-after residences in New York.

Admired today for their grace and architectural detail, they were designed in response to a city planning law allowing taller apartments if set backs and towers were used.

Emery Roth designed the San Remo (145 CPW), whose tenants have included Dustin Hoffman, Paul Simon and Diane Keaton. Madonna was turned down by the residents' committee and lives close by at 1 West 64th Street, next door to the New York Society for Ethical Culture. The towers on the Eldorado (300 CPW), also designed by Roth, are crowned by futuristic pinnacles. Celebrities here have included Groucho Marx, Marilyn Monroe and Richard Dreyfuss. The Majestic (115 CPW) and the Century (25 CPW) are both sleek classics by Art Deco designer Irwin S. Chanin.

Lincoln Center for the Performing Arts ❷

Map 11 C2. Ⓒ 546-2656. Ⓜ *65th St.* ♿ 🅿 875-5350. 🍴 🚻 *See* ***Entertainment*** *pp338–9.*
🅦 www.lincolncenter.org

IN MAY 1959, President Eisenhower traveled to New York to turn a shovelful of earth, Leonard Bernstein lifted his baton, the New York Philharmonic and the Juilliard Choir broke into the *Hallelujah Chorus* – and New York's most important cultural center was born.

It soon covered 15 acres (6 ha) on the site of the slums that had been the setting for Bernstein's classic musical *West Side Story*. The plaza fountain is by Philip Johnson, and the sculpture in the reflecting pool, *Reclining Figure*, is by Henry Moore.

Guided tours are the best way to see the complex.

New York State Theater ❸

Lincoln Center. **Map** 11 D2. Ⓒ 870-5570. Ⓜ *66th St.* ♿ 🅿 🍴 🚻 *See* ***Entertainment*** *pp334–5.* 🅦
www.nycballet.com; www.nyco.com

THE HOME BASE for the highly acclaimed New York City Ballet and the New York City Opera, a troupe devoted to presenting opera at popular prices, is a Philip Johnson design. It was inaugurated in 1964.

Gargantuan white marble sculptures by Elie Nadelman dominate the vast four-story foyer. The theater seats 2,800 people. Because of its rhinestone lights and chandeliers both inside and out, some have described the theater as "a little jewel box."

Metropolitan Opera House ❹

Lincoln Center. **Map** 11 D2. Ⓒ 362-6000. Ⓜ *66th St.* ♿ 🅿 🍴 🚻 *See* ***Entertainment*** *pp338–9.* 🅦
www.metopera.org; www.abt.org

HOME TO THE Metropolitan Opera Company and the American Ballet Theater, "the Met" is certainly the most spectacular of Lincoln Center's buildings and the focal point of the plaza. Five great arched windows offer views of the opulent foyer and two radiant murals by Marc Chagall. (You can't see them in the mornings when they are protected from the sun.)

Central plaza at Lincoln Center

Inside there are curved white marble stairs, miles of plush red carpeting and exquisite starburst crystal chandeliers

Free open-air concerts are held at the Guggenheim Bandshell

that are raised to the ceiling just before each performance. All the greats have sung here, including Maria Callas, Jessye Norman and Luciano Pavarotti. First nights are glittering, star-studded occasions.

The Guggenheim Bandshell, in Damrosch Park next to the Met, is a popular concert site featuring music from opera to jazz. The high point of the season is the Lincoln Center Out-of-Doors Festival that takes place in August.

Lincoln Center Theater ❺

Lincoln Center. **Map** 11 C2.
📞 362-7600 (Beaumont and Newhouse), 870-1630 (Library).
Ⓜ 66th St. ♿ 🚻 🎫 See *Entertainment* pp338–9. Ⓦ www.lct.org

TWO THEATERS MAKE up this innovative complex, presenting eclectic and often experimental drama.

The theaters are the 1000-seat Vivian Beaumont and the smaller, more intimate 280-seat Mitzi E. Newhouse.

Works by some of New York's best modern playwrights have been featured at the Beaumont. The theater's inaugural performance in 1962 was Arthur Miller's *After the Fall*.

The size of the Newhouse suits workshop-style plays, but it can still make the news with theatrical gems such as Robin Williams and Steve Martin in a production of

Samuel Beckett's *Waiting for Godot*. The New York Public Library for the Performing Arts (closed for renovation until spring 2001) houses exhibits including cylinders of early Met performances and original scores and playbills.

Avery Fisher Hall ❻

Lincoln Center. **Map** 11 C2. 📞 875-5030. Ⓜ 66th St. ♿ 🎫 🚻 🎫
See *Entertainment* p338–9.
Ⓦ www.newyorkphilharmonic.org

HOME TO THE New York Philharmonic, America's oldest orchestra as well as Lincoln Center's own Great Performers; Mostly Mozart Festival; and Jazz at Lincoln Center, Avery Fisher Hall opened in 1962 as Philharmonic Hall. While critics initially complained about the acoustics, several structural modifications, including one in 1992, have rendered the Hall an acoustic gem, comparing favorably with the great concert halls of the world. For a small fee, the public can attend rehearsals on Thursday mornings.

American Folk Art Museum (Eva and Morris Feld Gallery) ❼

Lincoln Sq. **Map** 12 D2.
📞 977-7170. Ⓜ 66th St. ◯ 11:30am–7:30pm daily. 🚫 ♿ 🎫
Ⓦ www.folkartmuseum.org

THIS GALLERY opened here in 1989 to show American folk art. Exhibits include quilts, carvings and paintings from the museum's permanent collection (*see p169*) as well as changing displays. There are also special demonstration programs and craft workshops. The new

American Folk Art Museum, located on West 53rd Street, is now the parent home, exhibiting folk art from the 18th and 19th centuries to the work of contemporary artists. The popular weathervane, named after legendary American Indian chief Tammany, is now on display in the new museum.

Copper weathervane from the Museum of American Folk Art

Hotel des Artistes ❽

1 W 67th St. **Map** 12 D2.
📞 362-6700. Ⓜ 72nd St.

BUILT IN 1918 by George Mort Pollard, these two-story apartments were intended as working artists' studios but have attracted a variety of interesting tenants, including Alexander Woollcott, Norman Rockwell, Isadora Duncan, Rudolph Valentino and Noël Coward. The Café des Artistes is well known for its misty, romantic Howard Chandler Christy murals and its fine cuisine.

Decorative figure on the Hotel des Artistes

American Museum of Natural History ⓫

THIS IS THE largest natural history museum in the world. Since the original building opened in 1877, the complex has grown to cover three city blocks, and today holds over 32 million artifacts. The most popular areas are the dinosaurs, meteors and the Hall of Minerals and Gems, which contains jewels valued at nearly $50 million. The spectacular Rose Center for Earth and Space (*see p216*) adjoins the Museum.

The entrance on 77th Street

see p216

STAR EXHIBITS

★ **Barosaurus**

★ **Blue Whale**

★ **Haida Canoe**

★ **Star of India**

★ **Star of India**
This 563-carat gem is the world's largest blue star sapphire. Found in Sri Lanka, it was given to the museum by J.P. Morgan in 1901.

GALLERY GUIDE

Enter at Central Park West onto the second floor to view the barosaurus exhibit, African, Asian, Central and South American peoples and animals. First floor exhibits include ocean life, meteors, minerals and gems., and the new Hall of Biodiversity. North American Indians, birds and reptiles occupy the third floor. Dinosaurs, fossil fishes and early mammals are on the fourth floor.

★ **Blue Whale**
The blue whale is the largest of all animals, living or extinct. Its weight can exceed 150 tons. This replica is based on a female captured off the southern US coast in 1925.

★ **Haida Canoe**
This 32-ft (9.7-m) seafaring war canoe of the Haida Indians was carved from the trunk of a single cedar. It stands in the 77th Street foyer.

Entrance on W. 77th St

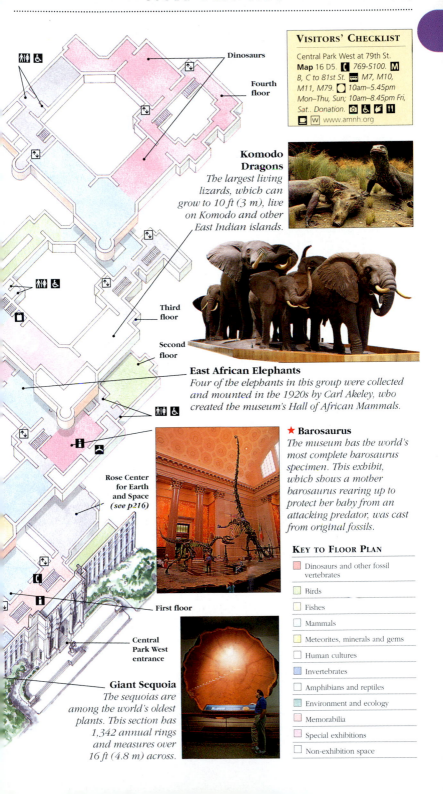

Dinosaurs

Fourth floor

VISITORS' CHECKLIST

Central Park West at 79th St.
Map 16 D5. [phone] 769-5100. [M]
B, C to 81st St. [bus] M7, M10,
M11, M79. [clock] 10am–5.45pm
Mon–Thu, Sun; 10am–8.45pm Fri,
Sat.. Donation. [icons]
[W] www.amnh.org

Komodo Dragons
The largest living lizards, which can grow to 10 ft (3 m), live on Komodo and other East Indian islands.

Third floor

Second floor

East African Elephants
Four of the elephants in this group were collected and mounted in the 1920s by Carl Akeley, who created the museum's Hall of African Mammals.

Rose Center for Earth and Space (*see p216*)

★ **Barosaurus**
The museum has the world's most complete barosaurus specimen. This exhibit, which shows a mother barosaurus rearing up to protect her baby from an attacking predator, was cast from original fossils.

First floor

Central Park West entrance

KEY TO FLOOR PLAN

- Dinosaurs and other fossil vertebrates
- Birds
- Fishes
- Mammals
- Meteorites, minerals and gems
- Human cultures
- Invertebrates
- Amphibians and reptiles
- Environment and ecology
- Memorabilia
- Special exhibitions
- Non-exhibition space

Giant Sequoia
The sequoias are among the world's oldest plants. This section has 1,342 annual rings and measures over 16 ft (4.8 m) across.

The Dakota ❾

1 W 72nd St. **Map** 12 D1. Ⓜ *72nd St.* ⬤ *to the public.*

THE NAME AND STYLE reflect the fact that this apartment building was truly "way out West" when Henry J. Hardenbergh, the architect responsible for the Plaza Hotel, designed it in 1880–84. It was New York's first luxury apartment house and was originally surrounded by squatters' shacks and wandering farm animals. Commissioned by Edward S. Clark, heir to the Singer sewing machine fortune, it is one of the city's most prestigious addresses.

The Dakota's 65 luxurious apartments have had many famous owners, including Judy Garland, Lauren Bacall, Leonard Bernstein and Boris Karloff, whose ghost is said to haunt the place. It was the setting for the film *Rosemary's Baby,* and the site of the tragic murder of former Beatle John Lennon. His widow, Yoko Ono, still lives here.

Carved Indian head over the entrance to the Dakota

New-York Historical Society ❿

170 Central Park West/77th St. **Map** 16 D5. Ⓒ 873-3400. Ⓜ *81st St.* **Galleries** ◯ *11am–5pm Tue–Sun.* **Library** ◯ *11am–5pm Tue–Sat.* ⬤ *public hols.* 🚫 *for galleries.* 🚫 ♿ 📷 📷 Ⓦ *www.nyhistory.org*

AUDUBON'S ORIGINAL *Birds of America* prints and over 150 Tiffany lamps are among the treasures of New York's

The Rose Center for Earth and Space

oldest museum. Founded in 1804, the Society has a wide collection of paintings and decorative arts dating back to the 17th century. The portrait collection includes Gilbert Stuart's *George Washington.* There is fine furniture from the Federal period, plus an exceptional silver display.

American Museum of Natural History ⓫

See pp214–15.

Hayden Planetarium ⓬

Central Park West at 81st St. **Map** 16 D4. Ⓒ 769-5900, for Space Show tickets: 769-5200. Ⓜ *81st St.* Ⓦ *www.amnh.org/rose*

ADJOINING THE American Museum of Natural History is the Hayden Planetarium, the centerpiece of the spectacular new Rose Center for Earth and Space, designed by Polshek and Partners. Housed within an 87-ft sphere, the Planetarium contains a technologically advanced Space Theater, the Cosmic Pathway, a 350-ft spiral ramp with a timeline chronicling 13 billion years of evolution, and a Big Bang Theater. The Hall of Planet Earth, built around rock samples and using state-of-the-art computer and video displays explaining how the Earth works, explores our geologic history. Exhibits in the Hall of the Universe present the discoveries of modern astrophysics. Four zones feature hands-on

interactive exhibits and educational programming. Seen from the street at night, the Rose Center is simply breathtaking; the exhibits inside prove that, as Carl Sagan said, "We are starstuff."

Pomander Walk ⓭

261–7 W 94th St. **Map** 15 C2. Ⓜ *72nd St.*

LOOK THROUGH the gate for a delightful surprise – a double row of tiny town houses built in 1921 to look like the London mews setting of a popular play of the time.

Appropriately, it was much favored as a home by movie actors, including Rosalind Russell, Humphrey Bogart and the Gish sisters.

Facade of Pomander Walk town house

Riverside Drive and Park ⓮

Map 15 B4. Ⓜ *103rd St.*

RIVERSIDE DRIVE is one of the city's most attractive streets – broad, with shaded, and lovely views of the Hudson River. It is lined with the opulent original town houses as well as newer apartment buildings. At 40–46, 74–77, 81–89 and 105–107 Riverside Drive are houses designed at the end of the 19th century by local architect Clarence F. True.

The curved gables, bays and arched windows seem to suit the curves of the road and the flow of the river.

The bizarrely named Cliff Dwellers' Apartments at 243 is a 1914 building with a frieze showing early Arizona cliff dwellers, complete with masks, buffalo skulls, mountain lions and rattlesnakes.

Riverside Park was designed by Frederick Law Olmsted in 1880. He also laid out Central Park *(see pp202–5).*

Soldiers' and Sailors' monument in Riverside Park

Children's Museum of Manhattan ⑮

212 W 83rd St. **Map** 15 C4. 📞 721-1223. Ⓜ *86th St.* ◐ *10am–5pm Wed–Sun.* ● *Jan 1, Dec 25, Thanksgiving* 📷 ⬛ 📱 Ⓦ *www.cmom.org*

Ⓣ HIS PARTICULARLY imaginative participatory museum was founded in 1973 on the premise that children learn best through play. The Body Odyssey shows kids what they're made of in a fun-filled scientific ride through the body. The HP Inventor Center transports kids to this digital domain where they can rethink, revise, and reshape design solutions. The Time Warner Center for Media transforms children into

Children's Museum entrance

budding camera operators, newscasters, animators and technicians in a state-of-the-art TV studio. On weekends and holidays there are guest performers from puppeteers to storytellers in the 150-seat theater. There is also a gallery for free play and a special Word Play area for early language acquisition.

The Ansonia ⑯

2109 Broadway. **Map** 11 C1. Ⓜ *72nd St.* ● *to the public.*

Ⓣ HIS BEAUX ARTS gem was built in 1899 by William Earl Dodge Stokes, heir to the Phelps Dodge Company fortune, who brought French architect Paul E.M. Duboy to design a building to rival the Dakota. The hotel was converted to a condominium in 1992. The most prominent features are the round corner tower and the two-story mansard roof adorned with single and double dormers. The building had a roof garden (complete with Dodge's menagerie: ducks,

Distinctive rounded turret of the Ansonia Hotel

chickens and a tame bear) and two swimming pools.

The hotel's thick, sound-muffling walls soon made it a favorite with the musical stars of yesteryear. Florenz Ziegfeld, Arturo Toscanini, Enrico Caruso, Igor Stravinsky and Lily Pons were once regular guests there.

The Dorilton ⑰

171 W 71st St. **Map** 15 C5. Ⓜ *72nd St.* ● *to the public.*

Ⓞ PULENT DETAIL and an impressive high mansard roof adorn this apartment house. On the West 71st Street side of the building is a nine-story-high gateway. To the modern eye, the Dorilton is gloriously elaborate, but when it was first built in 1902 it provoked this reaction, reported by the *Architectural Record*: "The sight of it makes

Balcony on the Dorilton, supported by groaning figures

strong men swear and weak women shrink affrighted."

What would the critics have made of the Alexandria Condominium, at 135 West 70th Street, just a block away? Built in 1927 as the Pythian Temple, its current name stems from the lavish Egyptian-style motifs that adorned this former Masonic lodge. Many were stripped away when the building was converted to a condominium, but you can still see what the polychrome designs were like. There are lotus leaves, hieroglyphics, ornately carved columns, mythical beasts, and, in majestic splendor on the roof, two seated pharaohs.

MORNINGSIDE HEIGHTS AND HARLEM

MORNINGSIDE HEIGHTS, near the Hudson River, is home to Columbia University and two of the city's finest churches. Farther east is Hamilton Heights, situated on the border of Harlem, America's most famous black community. One way to see its highlights, which are spread over a large area, is

St. Francis of Assisi, Museo del Barrio

with one of the various tours offered, including a Sunday morning tour *(see p353)*. Many tours start in Hamilton Heights, move east to the St. Nicholas Historic District, stop to enjoy the gospel choir at the Abyssinian Baptist Church, and end with a southern-style brunch at Sylvia's, Harlem's best-known restaurant.

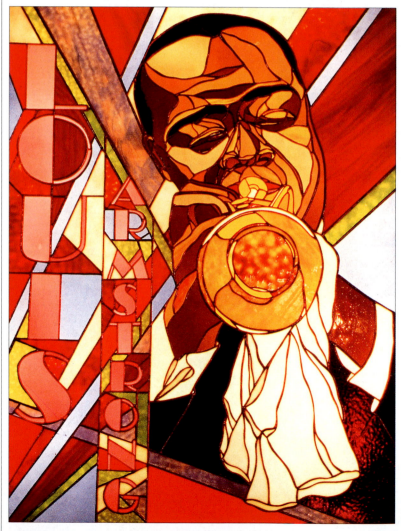

Louis Armstrong in a stained-glass window at the new Cotton Club

Sights at a Glance

Historic Streets and Buildings
Columbia University ❶
St. Paul's Chapel ❷
Low Library ❸
Grant's Tomb ❻
City College of the City University of New York ❼
Hamilton Grange National Memorial ❽
Hamilton Heights Historic District ❾
St. Nicholas Historic District ❿
Mount Morris Historical District ⓱

Museums and Galleries
Schomburg Center for Research into Black Culture ⓬
Studio Museum in Harlem ⓰
Museo del Barrio ⓳

Famous Theaters
Harlem YMCA ⓭
Apollo Theater ⓯

Churches
Cathedral of St. John the Divine pp224–25 ❹
Riverside Church ❺
Abyssinian Baptist Church ⓫

Parks and Squares
Marcus Garvey Park ⓲

Landmark Restaurants
Sylvia's ⓮

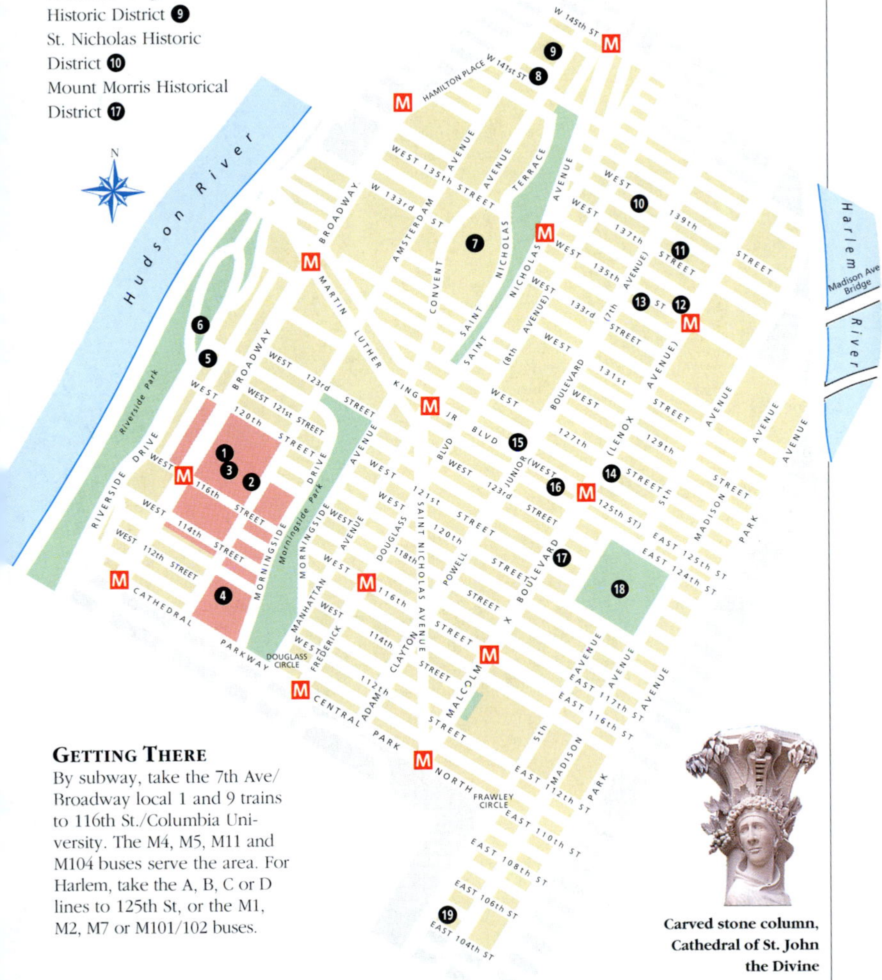

Carved stone column, Cathedral of St. John the Divine

Getting There

By subway, take the 7th Ave/ Broadway local 1 and 9 trains to 116th St./Columbia University. The M4, M5, M11 and M104 buses serve the area. For Harlem, take the A, B, C or D lines to 125th St, or the M1, M2, M7 or M101/102 buses.

See Also

- ***Street Finder***, maps 19–21
- ***Where to Stay*** pp174–75
- ***Restaurants*** pp290–92

0 meters 500
0 yards 500

Key

Street-by-Street map
M Subway station

Street by Street: Columbia University

A GREAT UNIVERSITY is as much spirit as buildings. After admiring the architecture, linger awhile on Columbia's central quadrangle in front of the Low Library, where you will see the jeans-clad future leaders of America meeting and mingling between classes. Across from the campus on both Broadway and Amsterdam Avenue are the coffeehouses and cafés where students engage in lengthy philosophical arguments, debate the topics of the day or simply unwind.

Alma Mater was sculpted by Daniel Chester French in 1903 and survived a bomb blast in the 1968 student demonstrations.

116th St./Columbia University subway (lines 1, 9)

The School of Journalism is one of Columbia's many McKim, Mead & White buildings. Founded in 1912 by publisher Joseph Pulitzer, it is the home of the Pulitzer Prize awarded for the best in letters and music.

Butler Library is Columbia's main library.

Low Library
With its imposing facade and high dome, the library dominates the main quadrangle. McKim, Mead & White designed it in 1895–97 ❸

★ **Central Quadrangle**
Columbia's first buildings were designed by McKim, Mead & White and built around a central quadrangle. This view looks across the quad toward Butler Library ❶

St. Paul's Chapel

Designed by the architects Howells & Stokes in 1907, this church is known for its fine woodwork and magnificent vaulted interior. It is full of light and has fine acoustics ❷

The Sherman Fairchild Center was built in 1977 to house the university's life sciences departments.

LOCATOR MAP
See Manhattan Map pp12–13

KEY

– – – – –   Suggested route

0 meters   100

0 yards   100

Student demonstrations put Columbia University in the news in 1968. The demonstrations were sparked by the university's plan to build a gymnasium in nearby Morningside Park. The protests forced the university to build elsewhere.

The Eglise de Notre Dame was built for a French-speaking congregation. Behind the altar is a replica of the grotto at Lourdes, France, the gift of a woman who believed her son was healed there.

Cathedral of St. John the Divine
If this Neo-Gothic cathedral is ever finished, it will be the largest in the world. Although one third of the structure has not yet been built, it can hold 10,000 parishioners ❹

Carved stonework decorates the facade of the Cathedral.

STAR SIGHTS

★ **Columbia University**

★ **Cathedral of St. John the Divine**

W 116TH ST

MORNINGSIDE DRIVE

Alma Mater statue at Low Library, Columbia University

Columbia University ❶

Main entrance at W 116th St. **Map** 20 E3. 854-4900. 116th St-Columbia Univ. www.columbia.edu

THIS IS THE third location of one of America's oldest and finest universities. Founded in 1754 as King's College, it was first situated close to where the World Trade Center now stands.

In 1814, when a move uptown was proposed, the university approached the authorities for funding but was instead given a plot of land valued at $75,000, on which to build a new home. The university never built on the land itself, but leased it out and spent the years from 1857 to 1897 in buildings nearby. It finally sold the plot in 1985 to the leaseholders, Rockefeller Center Inc., for the sum of $400 million.

The present campus was begun in 1897 on the site of the Bloomingdale Insane Asylum. Architect Charles McKim placed the university on a terrace, serenely above street level. Its spacious lawns and plazas still create a sense of contrast in the busy city.

At last count there were over 20,000 students at this campus. Columbia, an Ivy League School, is noted for its law, medicine and journalism schools. Its highly distinguished faculty and alumni, past and present, include over 50 Nobel laureates. Famous alumni include Isaac Asimov, J.D. Salinger, James Cagney and Joan Rivers.

St. Paul's Chapel ❷

Columbia University. **Map** 20 E3. 854-1487 concert info. 116th St-Columbia Univ. 10am–11pm Mon–Sat (term time), 10am–4pm (breaks). Sun.

Interior brick vaulting of St. Paul's Chapel dome

COLUMBIA'S MOST outstanding building, built in 1904, is a mix of Italian Renaissance, Byzantine and Gothic. The interior Guastavino vaulting is of intricate patterns of aged red brick; the whole chapel is bathed in light from above.

The free organ concerts are an exceptionally fine way to appreciate the beauty and acoustics of this church. The Aeolian-Skinner pipe organ is renowned for its fine tone.

Facade of St. Paul's Chapel

Low Library ❸

Columbia University. **Map** 20 E3. 116th St-Columbia Univ.

A CLASSICAL, columned building atop three flights of stone stairs, the library was donated by Seth Low, a former mayor and college president. The statue in front of it, *Alma Mater* by Daniel Chester French, became familiar as the backdrop to the many 1968 anti–Vietnam War student demonstrations. The building is now used as offices, and its rotunda for a variety of academic and ceremonial purposes. The books were moved in 1932 to Butler Library, across the quadrangle. The university's library collections total some six million volumes.

Cathedral of St. John the Divine ❹

See p224–5.

Riverside Church ❺

490 Riverside Dr at 122nd St. **Map** 20 D2. 870-6700. 116th St-Columbia Univ. 9am–5pm daily. 10:45am Sun. with prior permission. **Carillon bell concerts** 870-6784. noon, 3pm Sun. **Theater** 864-2929. www.theriversidechurch.org

A 21-STORY STEEL frame with a Gothic exterior, the church design was inspired by the cathedral at Chartres. It was lavishly funded by John D. Rockefeller, Jr., in 1930. The Laura Spelman Rockefeller Memorial Carillon (in honor of Rockefeller's mother) is the largest in the world, with 74

Columbia University's main courtyard and the Low Library

bells. The 20-ton Bourdon, or hour bell, is the largest and heaviest tuned carillon bell ever cast. The organ, with its 22,000 pipes, is among the largest in the world.

At the rear of the second gallery is a figure by Jacob Epstein, *Christ in Majesty*, cast in plaster and covered in gold leaf. Another Epstein statue, *Madonna and Child*, stands in the court next to the cloister. The panels of the chancel screen honor eight men and women whose lives have exemplified the teachings of Christ. They range from Socrates and Michelangelo to Florence Nightingale and Booker T. Washington.

For quiet reflection, enter the small, secluded Christ Chapel, patterned after an 11th-century Romanesque church in France. For views, take the elevator to the 20th floor and then walk the 140 steps to the top of the 392-ft (120-m) bell tower for a fine panorama of Upper Manhattan from the windy observation deck. (This is definitely not recommended when the bells are tolling.)

Mosaic mural in Grant's Tomb showing Grant (right) and Robert E. Lee

Grant's Tomb ❻

W 122nd St and Riverside Dr. **Map** 20 D2. ☎ 666-1640. Ⓜ 116th St-Columbia Univ. ◗ 9am– 5pm daily. ● Jan 1, Thanksgiving, Dec 25. ⬛ ◩ ⬛ ⬛ Ⓦ www.nps.gov/gegr

T**HIS GRANDIOSE** monument honors America's 18th president, Ulysses S. Grant, the commanding general of the Union forces in the Civil War.

The mausoleum contains the coffins of General Grant and his wife, in accordance with the president's last wish that they be buried together. After Grant's death in 1885, more than 90,000 Americans contributed $600,000 to build the sepulcher, which was inspired by Mausoleus's tomb at Halicarnassus, one of the Seven Wonders of the Ancient World. The

General Grant on a Civil War campaign

tomb was dedicated on what would have been Grant's 75th birthday, April 27, 1897. The parade of 50,000 people, along with a flotilla of 10 American and 5 European warships, took more than seven hours to pass in review.

The interior was inspired by Napoleon's tomb at Les Invalides in Paris. Each sarcophagus weighs 8.5 tons. Two exhibit rooms feature displays on Grant's personal life and his presidential and military career.

Surrounding the north and east sides of the building are 17 sinuously curved mosaic benches that seem totally out of keeping with the formal architecture of the tomb. They were designed in the early 1970s by the Chilean-born Brooklyn artist Pedro Silva and built by 1,200 local volunteers under his supervision. The benches were inspired by the Spanish architect Antonio Gaudi's work in Barcelona. The mosaics depict subjects ranging from the Inuits to New York taxis to Donald Duck.

A short walk north of Grant's Tomb is another monument. An unadorned urn on a pedestal marks the resting place of a young child who fell from the riverbank and drowned. His grieving father placed a marker that reads simply "Erected to the memory of an amiable child, St. Clair Pollock, died 15 July 1797 in his fifth year of his age."

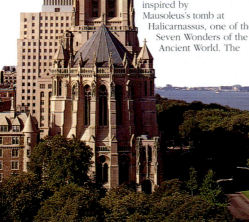

The 21-story Riverside Church, from the north

Cathedral of St. John the Divine ❹

Cram's Gothic West Front

Sᴛᴀʀᴛᴇᴅ ɪɴ 1892 and still only two-thirds finished, this will be the largest cathedral in the world. The interior is over 600 ft (180 m) long and 146 ft (45 m) wide. It was originally designed in Romanesque style by Heins and LaFarge; Ralph Adams Cram took over the project in 1911, devising a Gothic nave and west front. Medieval construction methods, such as stone supporting buttresses, continue to be used to complete the cathedral, which is also a venue for theater, music and avant-garde art.

Choir
Each of the choir's columns is 55 ft (17 m) tall and made of polished gray granite.

Nave
Rising to a height of over 100 ft (30 m), the piers of the nave are topped by graceful stone arches.

Rose Window ★
Completed in 1933, the stylized motif of the Great Rose is symbolic of the many facets of the Christian Church.

★ **West Front Entrance**
The portals of the cathedral's west front are adorned with many fine stone carvings. Some are recreations of medieval religious sculpture, but others have modern themes. This apocalyptic vision of New York's skyline, by local stonemason Joe Kinkannon, seems almost to predict the events of September 11, 2001 (see p54).

Sᴛᴀʀ Fᴇᴀᴛᴜʀᴇs

★ **Rose Window**

★ **West Front Entrance**

★ **Bay Altars**

★ **Peace Fountain**

★ **Peace Fountain**
The sculpture is the creation of Greg Wyatt and represents nature in its many forms. It stands within a granite basin on the Great Lawn, south of the cathedral.

Baptistry
The Gothic Baptistry has Italian, French and Spanish influences.

THE FINISHED DESIGN

Crossing tower

South transept

West towers

It will cost approximately $400 million to complete the cathedral. The south transept, crossing tower and west towers have yet to be finished. When the money is raised, the proposed design will take at least another 50 years to complete.

Pulpit

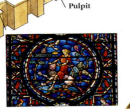

★ **Bay Altars**
The bay altar windows are devoted to human endeavor. The sports window shows feats of skill and strength.

Bishop's Chair
This is a copy from the Henry VII chapel in Westminster Abbey.

St. Ambrose Chapel
Named after a 4th-century Italian bishop, the chapel is decorated with Renaissance-style ironwork.

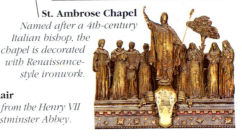

TIMELINE

1823 Cathedral planned for Washington Square

1891 Site chosen and designated Cathedral Parkway

1909 Pulpit designed by Henry Vaughan

1911 Cram design replaces earlier ones

1967 Bronze lamps from former Penn Station installed on front steps

1800   1850   1900   1950

1873 Charter granted

1888 Competition to design cathedral won by Heins & LaFarge

1892 December 27 (St. John's Day), cornerstone laid

1916 Ground broken for nave

1941 Work halted by World War II and does not resume until 1978

1978 Third phase of building begins, and Stonemasons' Yard opened

City College of the City University of New York ❼

Main entrance at W. 138th St. and Convent Ave. **Map** 19 A2. ☎ 650-7000. Ⓜ *137th St-City College.* Ⓦ www.ccny.cuny.edu

Sᴇᴛ ʜɪɢʜ on a hill adjoining Hamilton Heights, the original Gothic quadrangle of this college, built between 1903 and 1907, is very impressive. The material used for the buildings is Manhattan schist, a stone that had been excavated in building the IRT subway. Later, contemporary buildings were added to the school, which enrolls nearly 15,000 students.

Once free to all residents of New York, City College still offers an education at low tuition rates. Three-quarters of the students are from minority groups, and a large number of them are the first in their families to attend college.

Shepard Archway at City College of the City University of New York

Hamilton Grange National Memorial ❽

287 Convent Ave. **Map** 19 A1. ☎ 283-5154. Ⓜ *137th St-City College.* ◯ 9am–5pm Fri–Sun. ⬙ ⬙ *hourly.* Ⓦ www.nps.gov/hagr

Sǫᴜᴇᴇᴢᴇᴅ ʙᴇᴛᴡᴇᴇɴ a church and apartments is one of the city's most historic buildings, the 1802 columned wooden country home of Alexander Hamilton. He was one of the architects of the federal government system, the first secretary of the treasury and founder of the

Statue of Alexander Hamilton at Hamilton Grange

National Bank. It is his face that appears on the $10 bill. Hamilton lived here for the last two years of his life. He was killed in a duel with political rival Aaron Burr in 1804.

The house was acquired by St. Luke's Episcopal Church in 1889 and moved two blocks to this "temporary" site, where it is open and always awaiting relocation and renovation.

Hamilton Heights Historic District ❾

W 141st–W 145th St. and Convent Ave. **Map** 19 A1. Ⓜ *137th St-City College.*

Oʀɪɢɪɴᴀʟʟʏ ᴛʜɪs was a setting for the impressive country estates of the wealthy. Also known as Harlem Heights, it was developed during the 1880s following the extension of the El line (*see p24*) into the neighborhood. The privacy of the enclave, on a high hill above Harlem, made it a very desirable location.

The section known as Sugar Hill was highly favored by Harlem's elite – US Supreme Court Justice Thurgood Marshall, notable jazz musicians Count Basie, Duke

Ellington and Cab Calloway, and world champion boxer Sugar Ray Robinson have all lived there.

The handsome three- and four-story stone row houses were built between 1886 and 1906 mixing Flemish, Romanesque and Tudor influences. In fine condition, many are used as residences by the faculty of City College.

Row houses in Hamilton Heights

St. Nicholas Historic District ❿

202–250 W 138th & W 139th St. **Map** 19 B2. Ⓜ *135th St (B, C).*

A sᴛᴀʀᴛʟɪɴɢ ᴄᴏɴᴛʀᴀsᴛ to the rundown surroundings, the two blocks here, known as the King Model Houses, were built in 1891 when Harlem was considered a neighborhood for New York's gentry. They still comprise one of the city's most distinctive examples of row townhouses.

The developer, David King, chose three leading architects, who succeeded in blending their different styles to create a harmonious whole. The most famous of these was the firm of McKim, Mead & White,

Houses in St. Nicholas district

Adam Clayton Powell, Jr. (in dark suit) during a civil rights campaign

designers of the Pierpont Morgan Library (see pp162-3) and Villard Houses (see p174), who were responsible for the northernmost row of solid brick Renaissance palaces. Their homes featured ground floor entrances rather than the typical New York brownstone stoops. Also, the elaborate parlor floors have ornate wrought-iron balconies below, as well as carved decorative medallions above their windows.

The Georgian buildings designed by Price and Luce are built of buff brick with white stone trim. James Brown Lord's section of buildings, also Georgian in architectural style, feels much closer to Victorian, with outstanding red brick facades and bases constructed of brownstone.

Successful blacks were attracted here in the 1920s and 1930s, giving it the nickname Strivers' Row. Among them were celebrated musicians W. C. Handy and Eubie Blake.

Abyssinian Baptist Church ⑪

132 W. 138th St. **Map** 19 C2.
📞 862-7474. Ⓜ 135th St (B, C, 2, 3). ✝ 9am, 11am Sun. Groups of 10 or more need reservations.

NEW YORK'S OLDEST black church, founded in 1808, became famous through its charismatic pastor Adam Clayton Powell, Jr. (1908–72), a congressman and civil rights leader. Under his leadership it became the most powerful black church in America. A room in the church houses memorabilia from his life.

The church, a fine 1923 Gothic building, welcomes properly dressed visitors to Sunday services and to hear its superb gospel choir.

Schomburg Center for Research into Black Culture ⑫

515 Malcolm X Blvd. **Map** 19 C2.
📞 491-2200, 491-2265 for tours. Ⓜ 135th St. (2, 3). 🕐 10am–6pm Mon–Sat, 1–5pm Sun (exhibition hours vary). ⚫ public hols. ♿ 📷 📅 ⧠ www.schomburgcenter.org

HOUSED IN a sleek contemporary complex opened in 1991, this is the largest research center of black and African culture in the United States. The immense collection was assembled by the late Arthur Schomburg, a black man of Puerto Rican descent, who was told by a teacher that there was no such thing as "black history." The Carnegie

Kurt Weill, Elmer Rice and Langston Hughes at the Schomburg Center

Corporation bought the collection in 1926 and gave it to the New York Public Library; Schomburg was made curator in 1932.

The library was the unofficial meeting place for writers involved in what later became known as the black literary renaissance of the 1920s, including Langston Hughes, W.E.B. Du Bois, Zora Neale Hurston and many other great writers of the day. It also hosted many literary gatherings and poetry readings.

The Schomburg Library has excellent facilities for conserving and making available the archive's treasures, which include rare books, photos, movies, art and recordings. The library was planned and designed to double as a cultural center and includes a theater and two art galleries, which feature changing shows of art and photography.

Harlem YMCA ⑬

180 W 135th St. **Map** 19 C3.
📞 281-4100. Ⓜ 135th St (2, 3).

Sociologist W.E.B. Du Bois

PAUL ROBESON and many others made their first stage appearances here in the early 1920s. The Krigqa Players, organized by W.E.B. Du Bois in the basement in 1928, was founded to counter the derogatory images of blacks often presented in Broadway reviews of the time. The "Y" also provided temporary lodgings for some notable new arrivals in Harlem, including writer Ralph Ellison.

Gospel singers performing at Sylvia's during Sunday brunch

Sylvia's ⑮

328 Lenox Ave. **Map** 21 B1.
📞 996-0660. Ⓜ *125th St (2,3).*
ⓦ www.sylviassoulfood.com

Harlem's best-known soul food restaurant serves up southern-fried or smothered chicken, spicy ribs, black-eyed peas, collard greens, candied yams, sweet potato pie and other Southern delicacies

Sylvia's

(see p287). Sunday brunch is served to the accompaniment of Gospel singers.

Take some time to explore the market at the corner of 125th Street and Lenox Avenue (opposite Sylvia's), extending for a block or more in either direction. This isn't a food market: it sells African clothing, jewelry and art of varying quality.

Apollo Theater ⑯

253 W 125th St. **Map** 21 A1.
📞 531-5305, 749-5838. Ⓜ *125th St (A, B, C, D).* ⬛ *at showtimes. See* ***Entertainment*** *p341.*
ⓦ www.showtimeattheapollo.com

The Apollo opened in 1914 as a whites-only opera house. Its great fame came when Frank Schiffman, a white entrepreneur, took over in 1934. He then opened the

theater to all races and turned it into Harlem's best-known showcase, with legendary artists such as Bessie Smith, Billie Holiday, Duke Ellington, and Dinah Washington.

Amateur nights on Wednesdays,

Apollo Theater

with winners determined by audience applause, were famous, and there was a long waiting list for performers.

These amateur nights launched the careers of Sarah Vaughan, Pearl Bailey, James Brown and Gladys Knight, among others, and they still attract hopefuls.

The Apollo was *the* place during the swing band era; following World War II, a new generation of musicians, such as Charlie "Bird" Parker, Dizzy Gillespie, Thelonius Monk and Aretha Franklin, continued the tradition.

Rescued from decline and refurbished in the 1980s, the Apollo once again features top black entertainers.

Studio Museum in Harlem ⑰

144 W 125th St. **Map** 21 B2.
📞 *864-4500.* Ⓜ *125th St (2, 3).*
⬤ *10am–5pm Wed–Fri, 1–6pm Sat, Sun.* ● *Jan 1, Thanksgiving, Dec 25.*
🚫 ♿ ✓ *except Sat.* **Lectures, children's programs, films.**
ⓦ www.StudioMuseuminHarlem.org

The museum was founded in 1967 in a loft on upper Fifth Avenue with the mission of becoming the premier center for the collection and exhibition of the art and artifacts of African-Americans.

The present premises, a five-story building on Harlem's main commercial street, was donated to the museum by the New York Bank for Savings in 1979. The new museum opened in 1982. There are galleries on two levels for changing exhibitions featuring artists and cultural themes, and three galleries are devoted to the permanent collection of works by major black artists.

The photographic archives comprise one of the most

Exhibition space at the Studio Museum in Harlem

complete records in existence of Harlem in its heyday. A side door opens onto a small sculpture garden.

In addition to its excellent exhibitions, the Studio Museum also maintains a national artist-in-residence program, and offers regular lectures, seminars, children's programs and film festivals. An excellent small shop sells a range of books and African crafts.

Mount Morris Historical District ⑱

W 119th–W 124th Sts. **Map** 21 B2.
Ⓜ *125th St (2, 3).*

Y OU CAN PLAINLY see that the late 19th-century Victorian-style town houses near Marcus Garvey Park were once grand. This was a favorite neighborhood of German Jews moving up in the world from the Lower East Side. Time has not been kind, and this district shows how the area has deteriorated.

A few impressive churches, such as St. Martin's Episcopal Church, remain. There are also some interesting juxta-positions of faiths to be seen: the columned Mount Olivet Baptist Church, at 201 Lenox Avenue, was once Temple Israel, one of the most imposing synagogues in the

St. Martin's Episcopal Church on Lenox Avenue

city; and at the Ethiopian Hebrew Congregation, 1 West 123rd Street, housed in a former mansion, the choir sings in Hebrew on Saturdays.

Marcus Garvey Park ⑲

120th–124th Sts. **Map** 21 B2.
Ⓜ *125th St (2,3).*

The flamboyant black nationalist leader Marcus Garvey

T HIS HILLY, ROCKY, two-block square of green is the site of New York's last fire watchtower, an open cast-iron structure built in 1856, with spiral stairs leading to the observation deck. The bell below the deck sounded the alarm. It may be best to view it from a distance, however, if you have any doubts about your safety. Previously known as Mount Morris Park, it was renamed in 1973 in honor of Marcus Garvey. He came to Harlem from Jamaica in 1916 and founded the Universal Negro Improvement Association, which promoted self-help, racial pride and a back-to-Africa movement.

Museo del Barrio ⑳

1230 5th Ave. **Map** 21 C5. 📞 *831-7272.* Ⓜ *103rd St (6).* ⭘ *11am–5pm Wed–Sun.* **Donation expected.**
Ⓧ ♿ ☐ Ⓦ www.elmuseo.org

F OUNDED IN 1969, this is North America's only museum devoted to Latin American art, specializing in the culture of Puerto Rico. Exhibitions feature contemporary painting and sculpture, folk art and historical artifacts. The stars of the permanent collection are about 240 wooden Santos, carvings of the saints by folk artisans and a reconstructed *bodega* or Latino corner grocery. Exhibits change often, but some of the Santos are always on display. The pre-Columbian collection contains rare artifacts from the Caribbean. Situated at the far end of Museum Mile, this unusual museum attempts to bridge the gap between the lofty Upper East Side and the cultural heritage of El Barrio (Spanish Harlem).

Folk art at the Museo del Barrio: one of the *Three Wise Men* (left) and the *Omnipotent Hand*

FARTHER AFIELD

THOUGH OFFICIALLY part of New York City, the boroughs outside Manhattan are quite different in feel and spirit. They are residential and don't have the famous skyscrapers that are associated with New York. The difference is evident even in the way residents describe a trip to Manhattan as "going into the city." Yet the outlying areas boast many attractions, including the city's biggest zoo, botanical gardens, museums, beaches and sports arenas. For a guided walk around Brooklyn see pages 264–65.

SIGHTS AT A GLANCE

Historic Streets and Buildings
Morris-Jumel Mansion **2**
George Washington Bridge **3**
Wave Hill **5**
Yankee Stadium **10**
Grand Army Plaza **18**
Park Slope Historic District **19**
Historic Richmond Town **24**
Alice Austen House **27**

Museums and Galleries
Audubon Terrace **1**
The Cloisters pp234–37 **4**
Van Cortlandt House Museum **6**
New York Hall of Science **13**

American Museum of the Moving Image and Kaufman Astoria Studio **14**
Museum of Modern Art (MoMA), Queens **15**
Brooklyn Children's Museum **16**
Brooklyn Museum of Art pp248–51 **21**
Jacques Marchais Museum of Tibetan Art **25**
Snug Harbor Cultural Center **26**

Parks and Gardens
New York Botanical Garden pp240–41 **8**
Bronx Zoo pp242–43 **9**

Flushing Meadow-Corona Park **12**
Prospect Park **20**
Brooklyn Botanic Garden **22**

Famous Theaters
Brooklyn Academy of Music **17**

Cemeteries
Woodlawn Cemetery **7**

Beaches
City Island **11**
Coney Island **23**
Jamaica Bay Wildlife Refuge Center **28**
Jones Beach State Park **29**

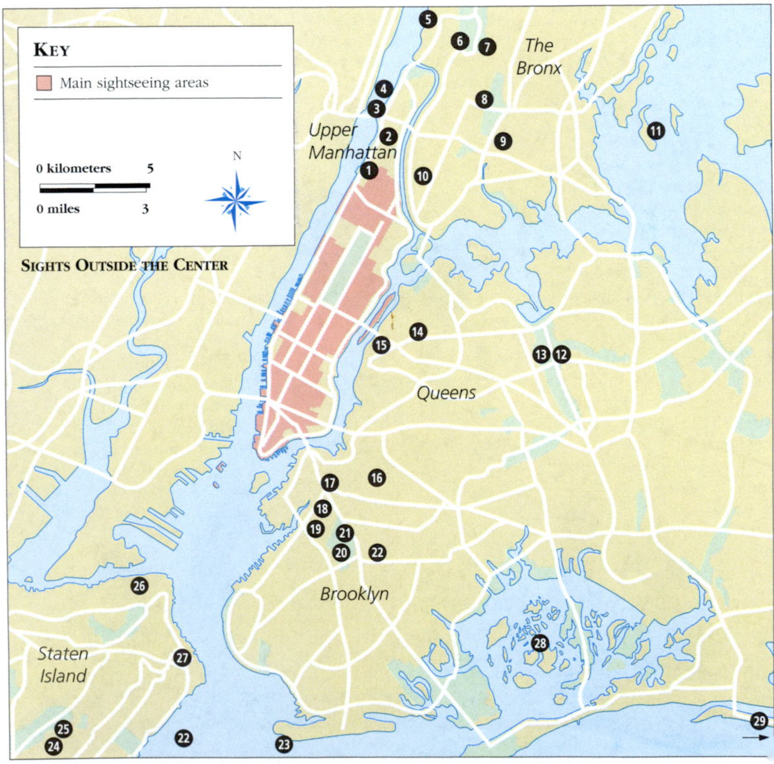

SIGHTS OUTSIDE THE CENTER

KEY

Main sightseeing areas

0 kilometers 5

0 miles 3

The Bronx

Upper Manhattan

Queens

Brooklyn

Staten Island

Jamaica Bay

Upper Manhattan

IT WAS IN UPPER Manhattan that the 18th-century Dutch settlers established their farms. Now a suburban area with little of the bustle of downtown Manhattan, it is a good place to escape the inner city for some relaxed museum and landmark sightseeing. The Cloisters (*see pp234–37*) displays a magnificent collection of medieval art, housed within original European buildings of the period. A piece of New York history is found at the Morris-Jumel Mansion in north Harlem. From his headquarters here, George Washington mounted the defense of Manhattan in 1776.

Audubon Terrace ❶

Broadway at 155th St. **M** *157th St.*
American Numismatic Society **C** *234-3130.* ◯ *9:30am–4:30pm Tue–Fri.* ⦸ 🛗 📷 **W** www. amnumsoc.org ***American Academy of Arts and Letters*** **C** *368-5900.* ◯ *during exhibitions.* ⦸ ***Hispanic Society of America*** **C** *926-2234.* ◯ *10am–4:30pm Tue – Sat, 1– 4pm Sun.* ⬤ *public hols.* **Donations.** 📷 🛗 **W** www.hispanicsociety.org

THIS 1908 complex of Classical Revival buildings by Charles Pratt Huntington is named after naturalist John James Audubon, whose estate once included this land. Audubon is buried in nearby Trinity Cemetery. His gravestone, a Celtic

Facade of the American Academy of Arts and Letters

cross, bears the symbolic images of this adventurous artist's career: the birds he painted, his palette and brushes, and his rifles.

The complex was funded by the architect's cousin, civic benefactor Archer Milton Huntington. His dream was that it should be a center of culture and study. A central plaza contains statues by his wife, the sculptress Anna Hyatt Huntington.

Audubon Terrace contains several theme museums that are worth seeking out. The American Numismatic Society is the leading American museum devoted to coinage and medals, and has one of the world's best collections,

with half a million photos and illustrations of coins. A permanent exhibition called "The World of Coins" traces the historical and political role of money, and there is a vast library.

The American Academy of Arts and Letters was set up to honor American writers, artists, and composers, and 75 honorary members from overseas. On the roll are writers John Steinbeck and Mark Twain, painters Andrew Wyeth and Edward Hopper, and the composer Aaron Copland. Exhibitions feature members' work. The library (for scholars, by appointment) has old manuscripts and first editions.

Bronze door at the academy

The Hispanic Society of America is a public museum and library based upon the personal collection of Archer M. Huntington. The Spanish Renaissance-style main gallery holds works by Goya, El Greco and Velázquez. There are one-month exhibitions from March through May, and on one Sunday in late October the building is open to the public.

Statue of El Cid by Anna Hyatt Huntington at Audubon Terrace

Morris-Jumel Mansion ❷

Corner W 160th St and Edgecombe Ave. **☎** 923-8008. **M** 163rd St. **🕐** 10am–4pm Wed–Sun. **●** public hols. **♿ 📷 🎫** by appt. **▯** **W** www. morrisjumel.org

THIS IS ONE of New York's few pre-Revolutionary buildings. Now a museum, it was built in 1765 for Roger Morris. His former military colleague George Washington used the house as temporary headquarters while defending Manhattan in 1776.

The house was bought and updated in 1810 by Stephen Jumel, a merchant of French-Caribbean descent, and his wife Eliza. The pair furnished the house with souvenirs of their many visits to France. Her boudoir contains her bed and "dolphin" chair, reputedly bought from Napoleon. Eliza's social climbing and love affairs scandalized New York society. It was rumored that she let her husband bleed to death in 1832 so she could inherit his fortune. She later married Aaron Burr, aged 77, and divorced him three years later on the day he died.

The exterior of this wood-sided Georgian house with its classical portico and octagonal wing – the earliest in the colonies – has been restored. The museum exhibits include many original Jumel pieces.

The 3,500-ft (1,065-m) span of the George Washington Bridge

George Washington Bridge ❸

M 175th St. **W** www.panynj.gov

FRENCH ARCHITECT Le Corbusier called this "the only seat of grace in the disordered city." While not as famous a landmark as its Brooklyn equivalent, this bridge by engineer Othmar Ammann and his architect Cass Gilbert has its own character and history. Plans for a bridge linking Manhattan to New Jersey had been in the pipeline for more than 60 years before the Port of New York Authority raised the $59 million needed to fund the project. It was

The lighthouse under Washington Bridge

Ammann who suggested a road bridge rather than the more expensive rail link. Work began in 1927 and the bridge was finally opened in 1931: first across were two young roller skaters from the Bronx. Today the bridge is a vital link for commuter traffic and is in constant use.

Cass Gilbert had plans to clad the two towers with masonry but funds did not permit it, leaving an elegant skeletal structure 600 ft (183 m) in height and 3,500 ft (1,065 m) long. Ammann had also allowed for a second deck in his original plan, and this lower deck was added in 1962, increasing the bridge's capacity enormously. Now the eastbound toll collection shows a traffic level of over 53 million cars per year.

Below the eastern tower is a lighthouse that was saved from possible demolition in 1951 by sheer force of public pressure. The reason for this unlikely protest has become part of the city's mythology. Many thousands of young New Yorkers and children all around the world have loved the bedtime story *The Little Red Lighthouse and the Great Gray Bridge*, and wrote letters to save the lighthouse. Author Hildegarde Hoyt Swift wove the tale around her two favorite New York landmarks.

The Cloisters ❹

See pp234–37.

Morris-Jumel Mansion, built in 1765, with its original colossal portico

The Cloisters ❹

The Cloisters seen from Fort Tryon Park

THIS WORLD-FAMOUS museum of medieval art resides in a building constructed from 1934 to 1938, incorporating medieval cloisters, chapels and halls. Sculptor George Grey Barnard founded the museum in 1914; John D. Rockefeller, Jr. funded the Metropolitan Museum of Art's 1925 purchase of the collection and donated the site at Fort Tryon Park and also the land on the New Jersey side of the Hudson, directly across from the Cloisters.

Tomb Effigy of Jean d'Alluye
This tomb immortalizes the 13th-century Crusader.

Pontaut Chapter House

★ **Unicorn Tapestries**
The set of beautifully preserved tapestries, woven in Brussels around 1500, depicts the quest and capture of the mythical unicorn.

Boppard Stained-Glass Lancets *(1440–47)*
Below the lancet of Saint Catherine, angels display the arms of the coopers' guild, of which Catherine was patron.

Bonnefont Cloister

Trie Cloister

STAR EXHIBITS
★ **Unicorn Tapestries**
★ **Belles Heures de Jean, Duc de Berry**
★ **Annunciation Altarpiece by Robert Campin**

★ **Annunciation Altarpiece** *(about 1425)*
The Campin Room is the location of this Robert Campin of Tournai small triptych, a magnificent example of early Flemish painting.

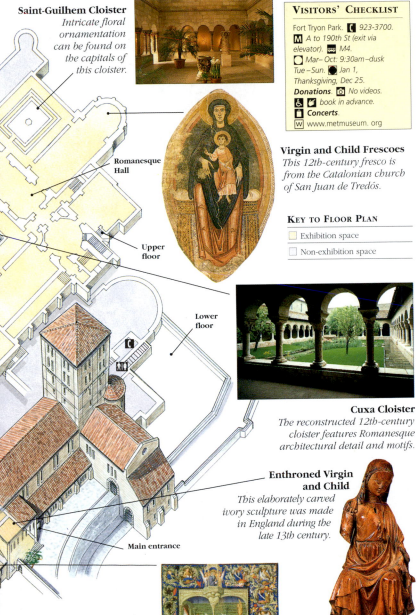

Saint-Guilhem Cloister
Intricate floral ornamentation can be found on the capitals of this cloister.

Romanesque Hall

Upper floor

Lower floor

Main entrance

Virgin and Child Frescoes
This 12th-century fresco is from the Catalonian church of San Juan de Tredós.

KEY TO FLOOR PLAN

Exhibition space

Non-exhibition space

Cuxa Cloister
The reconstructed 12th-century cloister features Romanesque architectural detail and motifs.

Enthroned Virgin and Child
This elaborately carved ivory sculpture was made in England during the late 13th century.

GALLERY GUIDE
The museum is organized roughly in chronological order. It starts with the Romanesque period (1000 AD) and moves to the Gothic (1150 to 1520). Sculptures, stained glass, paintings and the gardens are on the lower floor. The Unicorn Tapestries are on the upper floor.

★ **Belles Heures**
This book of hours, commissioned by Jean, Duc de Berry, for his devotions, is illuminated by 94 miniatures in tempera and gold.

Exploring The Cloisters

Known particularly for its Romanesque and Gothic architectural sculpture, The Cloisters collection also includes illuminated manuscripts, stained glass, metalwork, enamels, ivories and paintings. Among its tapestries is the renowned *Unicorn* series. The Cloisters' splendid medieval complex is unrivaled in North America.

A 16th-century Flemish boxwood rosary bead from the Treasury

ROMANESQUE ART

A lifesized 12th-century Spanish crucifix portraying Christ as the King of Heaven

Fanciful beasts and people, acanthus blossoms and scrollwork, top the columns around The Cloisters. Many are in the Romanesque style that flourished in the 11th and 12th centuries. The museum has numerous masterpieces of Romanesque art and architecture, showing the style's powerful rounded arches and intricate details. Highly embellished capitals and warm, pink marble typify the 12th-century Cuxa Cloister from the Pyrenees in France. A griffin, a dragon, a centaur and a basilisk are among the creatures parading over the Narbonne Arch nearby. In the Romanesque Hall, a golden-crowned Christ is depicted as triumphant over death.

In a more solemn style, the apse from the church of Saint-Martín in Fuentidueña, Spain, is a massive rounded vault constructed from 3,000 blocks of limestone. It is decorated with a 12th-century fresco of the Virgin and Child.

More than 800 years ago, Benedictine and Cistercian monks sat on the cold stone benches in the Pontaut Chapter House. By the 19th century it had become so neglected that it was used as a stable. Its ribbed vaulting is a foretaste of the Gothic style to come.

GOTHIC ART

Where Romanesque art was solid, the Gothic style that followed (from 1150 to around 1520) was open, with pointed arches, glowing stained-glass windows and three-dimensional sculpture. Gothic depictions of the Virgin and Child display exquisite craftsmanship.

The Gothic Chapel's brilliantly colored windows show scenes and figures from biblical stories. Lifesized tomb sculptures include the effigy of the Crusader knight Jean d'Alluye. During the 1790s,

Vaulted ceiling of the Pontaut Chapter House

the statue's original home, La Clarté-Dieu Abbey in France, was vandalized, and the statue was used to bridge a stream.

In the Boppard Room, the lives of the saints are told in marvellous late Gothic stained glass from Germany.

Robert Campin's Flemish masterwork, the *Annunciation* altarpiece, is the focus of the Campin Room. It is an intimate room with furnishings that might have belonged to a wealthy 15th-century family.

MEDIEVAL GARDENS

More than 250 varieties of plants grown in the Middle Ages can be found in The Cloisters' gardens. The Bonnefont Cloister has herbal, medicinal and cooking plants. The Trie Cloister features plants shown in the *Unicorn Tapestries* and reveals the use of flowers in medieval symbolism: roses (for the Virgin Mary), pansies (the Holy Trinity) and daisies (the eye of Christ).

Bonnefont Cloister

THE TAPESTRIES

THE CLOISTERS' tapestries are full of rich imagery and symbolism, and are among the museum's most highly prized treasures. The four *Nine Heroes Tapestries* bear the coat of arms of Jean, Duc de Berry, who was a brother of the King of France and one of the greatest art patrons of the Middle Ages. These tapestries are one of only two sets that survived from the late 14th century; the other set belonged to Jean's brother, Louis, Duc d'Anjou.

Nine great heroes of the past – three pagan, three Hebrew, three Christian – are shown with members of the medieval court, from cardinals, knights and damsels to musicians.

In an adjacent room is the magnificent *Hunt of the Unicorn*, a series of seven tapestries woven in Brussels around 1500. It depicts the symbolic hunt of the mythical unicorn and capture by a maiden.

Although they were misused in the 19th century to protect fruit trees from frost damage,

the tapestries are remarkably well preserved. They are also astonishing in detail, with

Julius Caesar, entertained by court musicians, in a *Nine Heroes* tapestry

literally hundreds of minutely observed plants and animals. Their story can be read as a tale of courtly love, but the series is also an allegory for the Crucifixion and the Resurrection of Christ.

THE TREASURY

IN MEDIEVAL TIMES, precious objects were stored in sanctuaries for safekeeping. At the Cloisters, they are to be found in the Treasury.

The collection includes several Gothic illuminated "books of hours." These were used for the private devotions of the nobility, such as the Limbourg brothers' *Belles Heures*, made for Jean, Duc de Berry, in 1410, and the tiny, palm-sized version by Gothic master Jean Pucelle for the Queen of France, around 1325.

Other religious artifacts range from a 13th-century English ivory Virgin to the 14th-century silver gilt and enamel reliquary shrine thought to have belonged to Queen Elizabeth of Hungary, along with censers, chalices, candlesticks and crucifixes.

Curiosities here include the "Monkey Cup," an enameled beaker probably made for the 15th-century Burgundian court, showing mischievous monkeys robbing a sleeping peddler; an intricately carved rosary bead the size of a walnut; a 13th-century shaped, jeweled sa... one of the oldes... playing cards ...

Hunting images and symbols depicted on a 15th-century deck

The west parlor of the Van Cortlandt House Museum

The Bronx

ONCE A prosperous suburb with a famous Grand Concourse lined with apartment buildings for the wealthy, the Bronx has now become an unfortunate symbol of urban decay. Still, diverse ethnic communities, unique resources and charming areas, such as Riverdale at the northern end, remain. Two major, outstanding attractions are the Bronx Zoo and the New York Botanical Garden. New Yorkers still flock to see baseball at Yankee Stadium, now more than 50 years old. *(see p239)*.

Wave Hill ❺

W 249th St. and Independence Ave, Riverdale. **C** (718) 549-3200. **M** 231st St. then bus Bx7, 10, 24. ❍ ?am–5:30pm Tue–Sun (9am–4:30pm Oct to mid-May). 🎫 *Sat, Sun;* ?– Mar. **W** www.wavehill.org

?TY concrete begins ?helm, come to ?a) oasis of ?ith its fine ? Jersey ?lson

Arturo Toscanini. Perkins also owned neighboring estates, underneath which he built a subterranean recreation center complete with bowling alley, and a tunnel leading into the main building.

The house and the grounds are open to the public. The house is frequently used for concerts. They often take place in the grand Armor Hall, designed in 1928 for Bashford Dean, who was then the curator of the collection of arms and armor at the Metropolitan Museum of Art.

The gardens were originally designed by Viennese landscape gardener, Albert Millard. There are also greenhouses, lawns, an herb garden and woodlands. Exhibitions range from sculpture to horticulture.

The adjoining Riverdale Park has attractive woodland and paths along the river.

?rior of the grand Armor ?e Hill

Van Cortlandt House Museum ❻

Van Cortlandt Park. **C** *(718) 543-3344.* **M** *242nd St, Van Cortlandt Park.* ❍ *10am–3pm Tue–Fri, 11am–4pm Sat, Sun (last adm: 30 mins before closing).* ● *most public hols.* 🎫. 📷 🎥 🔒 *See* ***The History of New York** pp18–19.* **W** *www.nycparks.org*

The facade of Van Cortlandt House

A RESTORED 1748 Georgian Colonial country manor built of rough stone, this was originally the family home of Frederick Van Cortlandt, a New Yorker who inherited great wealth and was related to many of the influential and rich families of his day.

The dining room was used as one of General George Washington's headquarters; the ground behind the house was once the scene of skirmishing during the Revolutionary War.

The interior has American period furnishings as well as a superb collection of delftware and a complete 17th-century Dutch bedroom.

On the exterior, look for the carved faces in the keystones over the windows.

Woodlawn Cemetery ❼

Jerome and Bainbridge Aves. (718) 920-0500. M Woodlawn. 9am–4:30pm daily. Office public hols.

FOR A GLIMPSE into another kind of social history, visit Woodlawn Cemetery, the burial place of many a wealthy and distinguished New Yorker.

Memorials and tombstones are set in beautiful grounds. F.W. Woolworth and many members of his family are interred in a mausoleum only a little less ornate than the building that carries the family name. The pink marble vault of meat magnate Herman Armour is oddly reminiscent of a ham.

Entrance to the Woolworth mausoleum

Other New York notables buried here include Mayor Fiorello La Guardia, Roland Macy, the founder of the great department store, author Herman Melville and jazz legend Duke Ellington.

New York Botanical Garden ❽

See pp240–41.

Bronx Zoo/ Wildlife Conservation Park ❾

See pp242–43.

Yankee Stadium ❿

E 161st St at River Ave, Highbridge. (718) 293-6000. M 161st St. See **Entertainment** pp344–45. by appt (718) 579-4531 www.yankees.com

THIS IS THE HOME of the New York Yankees baseball team. Among Yankee heroes are two of the greatest players of all time: Babe Ruth and Joe DiMaggio (who was also famous for marrying, in 1954, the legendary actress Marilyn Monroe).

The stadium was completed in 1923 by Jacob Ruppert, the owner of the Yankees. It became known as "the house that Ruth built" after the famous left-hander Babe Ruth. The Stadium had a face-lift in the mid-1970s, and now seats up to 54,000 people who come for sports, concerts and other events. For a great New York experience though, get tickets for a Yankees game.

Joe DiMaggio in action at Yankee Stadium in 1941

City Island ⓫

M 6 to Pelham Parkway, then Bx29 to City Island. **Museum** 190 Fordham St www.cityisland.com

SITUATED JUST off the northeast shore of the Bronx and surrounded by Long Island Sound, City Island is a small nautical outpost with a very New England feel – it seems a world apart from New York City, and offers a refreshing change of pace. Its scenic marinas are filled with sailboats, and

Diving helmet at the City Island Museum

its seafood restaurants would satisfy any sailor's appetite. Several America's Cup winners have been built in its boatyards.

The City Island Museum is located in one of the island's most historic buildings, the old Public School 17, which was built on an Indian burial ground at a high point on the island. Several of the old schoolrooms now serve as galleries. The Nautical Room is dedicated to the island's maritime history; the Walsh Room displays more than 60 paintings of City Island; and the School Room shows what life was like for school children in the 1830s. City Island is linked to the Bronx by bridge. To the north on the mainland is Orchard Beach, a crescent of white sand edged with 1930s bathing huts. The beach is very popular with area residents, and it can be uncomfortably crowded and dirty.

An old tugboat moored at one of City Island's piers

New York Botanical Garden ❽

Hibiscus

THE NEW YORK Botanical garden is 250 acres of dazzling beauty and hands-on enjoyment. From the nation's most glorious Victorian glasshouse to the 12-acre Everett Children's Adventure Garden it is alive with things to discover. One of the oldest and largest botanical gardens in the world, the Garden has 28 specialty gardens and plant collections, and 40 acres of uncut forest. The spectacular Enid A. Haupt conservatory has been restored as *A World of Plants*, with misty tropical rain forests and dramatic deserts.

Entrance to Enid A. Haupt Conservatory

Display gallery

Old World Desert

Americas' Deserts

Rock Garden
Giant boulders, ledges, streams and a waterfall create an alpine habitat for plants from the world's rocky and mountainous regions ④

Botanical Garden Forest
One of New York City's last surviving natural forest areas includes red oak, white ash, tulip trees and maples ⑤

Children's Adventure Garden
Kids can discover the wonders of ecology and the plant world ⑧

Rose Garden
Over 2,700 roses have been planted in the Peggy Rockefeller Rose Garden, laid out in 1988 according to the original 1915 design ⑦

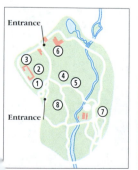

Entrance

③ ②
①

⑥

④ ⑤

⑧

⑦

Entrance

LOCATOR MAP

Palms of the Americas
One hundred of these majestic palms soar into a 90-ft glass dome. A tranquil reflecting pool is surrounded by tropical plants.

The Enid A. Haupt Conservatory consists of 11 interconnecting glass galleries housing *A World of Plants*, including rain forests, deserts, aquatic plants, and seasonal displays ①

Demonstration Gardens
Colorful displays are designed to inspire visitors with ideas for their own gardens ③

Jane Watson Irwin Perennial Garden
Flowering perennials are arranged in dramatic patterns according to height, shade, color and blooming time ②

Tropical pool

Tropical flora

Tropical Lowland Rainforest

Aquatic plants

Main entrance

Tropical New World Upland Rainforest

Garden Café
Abigail Kirsch's new Garden Café is a delightful spot to enjoy a full lunch or light refreshments and snacks. You can eat indoors, or enjoy the food outside on terraces that overlook the Demonstration Gardens ⑥

Bronx Zoo ⑨

Opened in 1899, the Bronx Zoo is the largest urban zoo in the US, home to some 7,166 animals of 531 species, living in realistic representations of their natural habitats. The Park is a leader in the perpetuation of endangered species, such as the Indian rhinoceros and the snow leopard. Its 265 acres of woods, streams and parklands include a children's zoo (seasonal), a butterfly zone, and a shuttle train that transports visitors around the sprawling park. Visitors are also free to walk around. For the best overview of the different areas of the park take the Skyfari cable car (open seasonally).

★ **The Congo Gorilla Forest**
This award winning replica of central African rain forest is home to gorillas, monkeys, and a host of other animals.

Skyfari cable car

Mouse-House

**Wild...
Mars...**

World of Darkness

Carter Giraffe Building

★ **African Plains**
Zebras, lions, cheetahs and gazelles roam the African Plains. Predators and prey are separated by a moat.

Africa
Oryxes find shelter under an African hut.

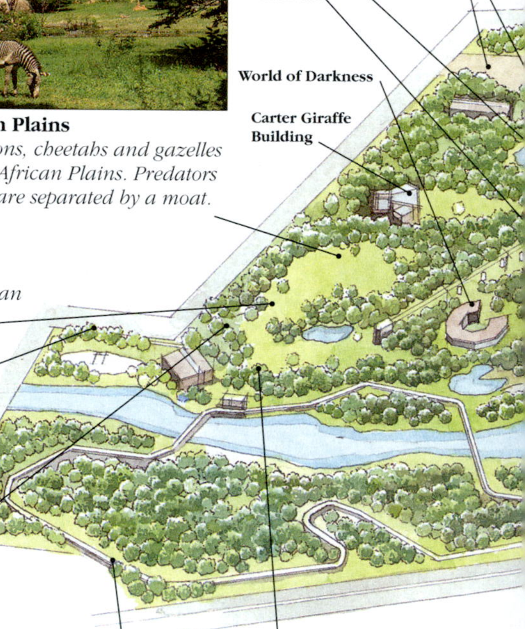

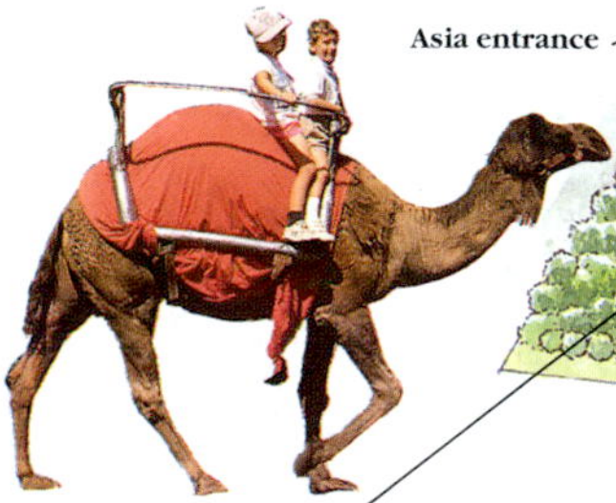

Asia entrance

Camel Rides
Children enjoy such seasonal experiences as camel rides and other attractions.

Bengali Express monorail

★ **JungleWorld**
A climate-controlled tropical rain forest harbors mammals, birds and reptiles from South Asia. The animals are kept apart from visitors by ravines, streams and cliffs.

Monkeys in JungleWorld

Baboon Reserve
Visitors walk along a dry riverbed to see wildlife in an Ethiopian mountain habitat.

Children's Zoo
Kids can crawl through a prairie dog tunnel, climb on a spiderweb, try on a turtle shell, and pet and feed the animals.

STAR FEATURES

★ **Wild Asia**

★ **African Plains**

★ **JungleWorld**

★ **World of Birds**

★ **Congo Gorilla Forest**

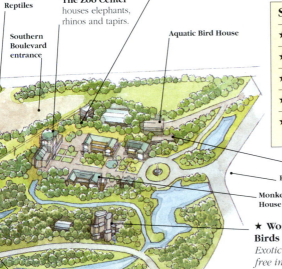

World of Reptiles

The Zoo Center houses elephants, rhinos and tapirs.

Southern Boulevard entrance

Aquatic Bird House

Aitken Aviary

Rainey Gate entrance

Monkey House

Bronxdale entrance

★ World of Birds

Exotic birds soar free in the lush surroundings of a rain forest. An artificial waterfall rushes down a 50-ft (15-m) fiberglass cliff in this walk-through habitat.

Greater hornbill

Himalayan Highlands
Endangered species, such as snow leopards and red pandas, are kept here.

★ Wild Asia

The Bengali Express monorail journeys through forests and meadows of an Asian habitat, where elephants, rhinoceroses and Siberian tigers roam free.

Queens

A BIG, SPRAWLING borough, Queens has a wide variety of attractions and residential and commercial areas, including Long Island City, where exciting new museums and restaurants are springing up all over. Development of the borough accelerated after 1909, when the construction of Queensboro Bridge made commuting easier. The city's main airports are here, and there are many different ethnic enclaves including the Greek neighborhood of Astoria and the various Asian communities in Flushing.

A 1900 Mutoscope at the Museum of the Moving Image

Flushing Meadow–Corona Park ⑫

M *Willets Point-Shea Stadium. See* **Entertainment** *pp344–45.*

T HE SITE of New York's two World's Fairs now offers expansive waterside picnic grounds and a multitude of attractions. These include the 50,000-seat Shea Stadium, the home of the New York Mets baseball team and a popular site for rock concerts. Flushing Meadow is also home to the US Tennis Center, where the prestigious United States Open is played. The courts are open for would-be Agassis, Grafs and Everts for the remainder of the year. In the 1920s this area was known as the Corona Dump, a nightmarish place of salt marshes and great piles of smoldering trash. In *The Great Gatsby*, author F. Scott Fitzgerald dubbed it the "valley of ashes." It reeked of rotting garbage and glowed red at night. New York's Parks' Commissioner Robert Moses was the driving force behind its transformation. A whole mountain of rubbish was removed and the river was totally re-channeled. The marsh was drained and sewage works were built, helping to restore the area. This site was to serve as the site for the 1939 World's Fair, at which a world on the brink of war saluted the elusive notion of world peace.

The Unisphere, symbol of the 1964 fair, still dominates the remains of the fairground. This giant hollow ball of green steel, built by the US Steel Corporation, is 12 stories high and weighs a massive 350 tons.

The 1964 World's Fair Unisphere at Flushing Meadow-Corona Park

New York Hall of Science ⑬

46th Ave and 111th St Flushing Meadows, Corona Park. **C** *(718) 699-0005.* **M** *111th St.* 9:30am–2pm Mon–Wed, 9:30am–5pm Thu–Sun. *public hols.* www.nyhallsci.org

T HE SCIENCE PAVILION built for the 1964 World's Fair was designed with stained glass set in concrete panels. It is now a hands-on museum for science and technology, with exhibits on color, light and physics. Children love to watch the giant video screens that can magnify a drop of water, and the interactive video and laser optical exhibits.

The concrete curtain wall of the New York Hall of Science

American Museum of the Moving Image and Kaufman Astoria Studio ⑭

35th Ave at 36th St, Astoria. **Museum C** *(718) 784-4520.* **Studio C** *(718) 392-0077.* **M** *36th St.* **Museum** *noon–5pm Tue–Fri, 11am–6pm Sat, Sun.* **Studio** *to public.* www.ammi.org

I N NEW YORK'S filmmaking heyday, Rudolph Valentino, W.C. Fields, the Marx Brothers and Gloria Swanson all made films here in the city's largest studio, opened by Paramount Pictures in 1920. When the movies went west, the army took over, making training films here from 1941 to 1971. The complex stood empty until the 1970s when Astoria Motion Picture and Television Foundation was founded to preserve it. *The Wiz*, a musical starring Michael Jackson and

Poster at the Museum of the Moving Image

again in full use. *The Cotton Club* and Woody Allen's *Radio Days* were filmed here.

In 1981 one of the studio buildings was transformed into the American Museum of the Moving Image, with interactive displays on production and theaters for the screening of movies and television.

There is a lot of memorabilia on display, from Ben Hur's chariot to Star Trek costumes. The main gallery draws from the permanent collection, containing over 85,000 movie artifacts. The Museum offers seminars, and a 200-seat theater presents film and video programs, from early silent movies to the most avant-garde. Silent films are presented with live music.

Diana Ross, was made here, helping to pay for restoration. Today, the studios house the largest moviemaking facilities on the East Coast and are

Museum of Modern Art, Queens ⓕ

45-20 33rd St at Queens Blvd. Ⓒ *(212) 708-9400.* Ⓜ *7 IRT to 33rd St.* ◯ *10:30am–5:45pm Thu-Tue; 10:30am–8:15pm Fri.* ● *Wed.* ♿ 🅟 Ⓦ *www.moma.org*

THE MUSEUM OF MODERN ART celebrates the opening of its temporary exhibition space in Long Island City with several world-famous masterpieces, including van Gogh's *The Starry Night*. A former factory, MoMA QNS, provides 25,000 sq ft (2,322 sq m) of exhibition space in a dramatic two-level building, designed by architect Michael Maltzan. A major exhibit on Matisse and Picasso (2003) and other shows will be presented here until late 2004, when MoMA moves back to its multimillion-dollar renovated facility in Manhattan *(see p170)*.

Brooklyn

The bandstand at Prospect Park *(see p246)*

IF BROOKLYN were a separate city, it would be the country's fourth largest. It has a character all of its own. Many entertainment greats – Mel Brooks, Phil Silvers, Woody Allen and Neil Simon among them – celebrate their birthplace with great affection and humor. Brooklyn is the ultimate melting pot, with West Indians, Hasidic Jews, Russians, Italians and Arabs living side by side. Among the diverse neighborhoods are the historic residential districts of Park Slope and Brooklyn Heights.

Brooklyn Children's Museum ⓖ

145 Brooklyn Ave. Ⓒ *(718) 735-4432.* Ⓜ *Kingston.* ◯ *2–5pm Wed–Fri, 10am–5pm Sat, Sun. Jul; Aug; 10am–5pm Mon, noon–6:30pm Wed–Sun.* ● *Jan 1, Thanksgiving, Dec 25.* **Donation expected.** ♿ 🅟 Ⓦ *www.bchildmus.org*

THE BROOKLYN Children's Museum was the first to be designed especially for children and was founded in 1899. Since then, it has been a model, inspiration and consultant to the development of more than 250 museums for children across the country and all over the world. Housed in a high-tech, specially designed underground building dating from 1976, it is one of the most imaginative children's museums anywhere.

The layout of the building is a maze of complex interconnected passageways running off

the main "people tube" – a huge drainage pipe that connects the four levels. This is not a passive place where children are meant to stand around and stare – the emphasis is on involvement and hands-on exhibits. Everywhere you look there are curiosities to be discovered, experienced, made or played with. There is even a walk-on piano like the one in the film *Big* – children of every age find it quite irresistible.

Special exhibitions and events are designed to help children learn about the planet, resolve their fears or problems, understand other cultures and discover the past. The squeals of laughter and delight that are always heard are a sign of this well-designed and clever museum's success in teaching children and the young at heart.

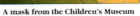

A mask from the Children's Museum

The facade of the Brooklyn Academy of Music

Brooklyn Academy of Music ⑰

30 Lafayette Ave. ☎ (718) 636-4100.
Ⓜ Atlantic Ave. 🎭 🚫 ♿ 🏠
Ⓦ www.bam.org
See **Entertainment** pp338–9.

Ⓗ OME TO THE Brooklyn Philharmonic, the Academy (known as BAM) is Brooklyn's leading cultural venue and the oldest, founded in 1858. It offers outstanding performances, often tending toward the innovative and avant-garde.

The classic 1908 building was designed by Herts & Tallant, and inaugurated with a production of Gounod's opera *Faust* featuring the legendary Neapolitan tenor Enrico Caruso. The list of the greats who have performed here is endless and includes actress Sarah Bernhardt, ballerina Anna Pavlova, musicians Pablo Casals and Sergei Rachmaninoff, poets Edna St. Vincent Millay and Carl Sandburg, and statesman Winston Churchill. Many international touring groups have made appearances here, including Britain's Royal Shakespeare Company.

The BAM Next Wave Festival has presented a number of well-known contemporary artists, including musicians Philip Glass and David Byrne, performance artist Laurie Anderson, and choreographers Pina Bausch and Mark Morris. The Brooklyn Academy of Music also runs the Harvey Theater nearby, once a movie theater and now used for dance, drama and music events.

Grand Army Plaza ⑱

Plaza St at Flatbush Ave.
☎ (718) 965-8951. Ⓜ Grand Army Plaza. **Arch** ⬜ for occasional exhibitions.

The Soldiers' and Sailors' Arch at Grand Army Plaza

Ⓕ REDERICK LAW OLMSTED and Calvert Vaux laid out this grand oval in 1870 as a gateway to Prospect Park. The Soldiers' and Sailors' Arch and its sculptures were added in 1892 as a tribute to the Union Army. The bust of John F. Kennedy here is the only official New York monument to him.

In June, the plaza is the center of the Welcome Back to Brooklyn Festival for the famous – and not-so-famous – people born in Brooklyn.

Park Slope Historic District ⑲

Streets from Prospect Park W below Flatbush Ave, to 8th/7th/5th avenues.
Ⓜ Grand Army Plaza.

Relief work on the Montauk Club

Ⓣ HIS WONDERFUL enclave of beautiful Victorian town houses was developed on the edge of Prospect Park in the 1880s. It served the upper-middle-class professionals who were able to commute into Manhattan after the Brooklyn Bridge was opened in 1883. The shady streets are lined with two- to five-story houses in every architectural style popular in the late 19th century, some with the towers, turrets and curlicues so representative of the era. Particularly fine examples are in Romanesque Revival style, with rounded entry arches.

The Montauk Club at 25 Eighth Avenue combines the style of Venice's Ca' d'Oro palazzo with the friezes and gargoyles of the Montauk Indians, after whom this popular 19th-century gathering place was named.

Prospect Park ⑳

☎ (718) 965-8969. 🎫 (718) 965-8999. Ⓜ Grand Army Plaza. 🎭 (718) 788-8500. Ⓦ www.prospectpark.org

Ⓓ ESIGNERS OLMSTED and Vaux considered this park, opened in 1867, better than their earlier Central Park. The Long Meadow, a sweep of broad lawns and grand vistas, is the longest unbroken swath of green space in New York.

Olmsted's belief was that "a feeling of relief is experienced by entering them [the parks] on escaping from the cramped, confining and controlling circumstances of the streets of the town." That

The facade of the Brooklyn Public Library on Grand Army Plaza

vision is still as true today as it was a century ago.

Among the many notable features are Stanford White's colonnaded Croquet Shelter, and the pools and weeping willows of the Vale of Cashmere. The Music Grove bandstand shows Japanese influences and hosts both jazz and classical music concerts throughout the summer.

A favorite feature of the park is the Camperdown Elm, an ancient and twisted tree planted in 1872. The Friends of Prospect Park raise money to keep it and all the park trees healthy. This old elm has inspired many poems and paintings. Prospect Park has a wide variety of landscapes, from classical gardens dotted with statues to rocky glens with running brooks. A guided tour with a ranger is the best way to see the park.

Carousel horse in Prospect Park

Brooklyn Museum of Art ㉑

See pp248–51.

Brooklyn Botanic Garden ㉒

900 Washington Ave. 【 (718) 623-7200. Ⓜ Prospect Pk, Eastern Pkwy. **Grounds** ◯ Apr–Sep: 8am–6pm Tue–Fri (10am Sat & Sun); Oct–Mar: 8am–4:30pm (10am Sat & Sun). ◑ Jan 1, Thanksgiving, Dec 25. 🎫 for Japanese Garden, free Tue & Sat. ◙ ♿ 🛍 🍴 🅿 �W www.bbg.org

T**HOUGH IT** is not vast in size, you will find that this 50-acre (20-ha) garden holds many delights. The area was designed by the Olmsted Brothers in 1910 and features a traditional Elizabethan-style "knot" herb garden and one of North America's largest collections of roses.

The central showpiece is a Japanese hill-and-pond garden, complete with both a teahouse and Shinto shrine. In late April and early May the park promenade is aglow with delicate Japanese cherry blossoms, which have prompted an annual festival featuring typical Japanese culture, food and music.

April is also the time for tourists to appreciate Magnolia Plaza, where some 80 trees display their beautiful, creamy blossoms against a backdrop of daffodils on Boulder Hill.

The Fragrance Garden is planted in raised beds, where the heavily scented, textured and flavored plants are all labeled in Braille, giving blind visitors an opportunity to identify them as well.

The new conservatory now houses one of America's largest bonsai collections and some rare rain forest trees, which are providing scientists with medicinal extracts to produce life-saving drugs.

A beluga whale at the New York Aquarium

Coney Island ㉓

Ⓜ Stillwell Ave, Coney Island. **New York Aquarium** Boardwalk and W 8th St, Coney Island. 【 (718) 265-3400. ◯ 10am–6pm daily. �W www.nyaquarium.com

I**N THE MID-19TH** century, Brooklyn poet Walt Whitman composed many of his works on Coney Island, accompanied by the roar of the surf. At that time it was untamed Atlantic coastline, the tip of the nose on the great "whale" to which the poet compared Long Island.

By the 1920s, Coney Island was starting to bill itself as the "World's Largest Playground." It had grown from three huge fairgrounds built between 1887 and 1904 (Luna Park, Dreamland and Steeplechase Park), providing a popular combination of hair-raising rides and nearby beaches. The subway arrived in 1920, and the addition of the boardwalk in 1921 ensured Coney Island's popularity throughout the Depression. Here was an escape from the city that cost little more than a few nickels.

A main attraction is the New York Aquarium, moved from Batt in 1955 a vis Is

Brooklyn Botanic Garden lily

Brooklyn Museum of Art ㉑

When it opened in 1897, the Brooklyn Museum building, designed to be the largest cultural edifice in the world, was the greatest achievement of New York architects McKim, Mead & White. Though only one-fifth completed, the museum is today one of the most impressive cultural institutions in the United States, with a permanent encyclopedic collection of some 1.5 million objects, which are housed in a grand structure of 560,000 sq ft (41,805 sq m).

North facade, designed by Stanford White

Chinese Jar
Cobalt blue fishes and water plants adorn this 14th-century Yuan dynasty blue-and-white ceramic jar.

Key to Floor Plan

- [ ] Arts of Africa, the Pacific, and the Americas
- [ ] Asian art
- [ ] Prints, drawings and photographs
- [ ] Classical and Egyptian art
- [ ] Decorative arts
- [ ] Painting and sculpture
- [ ] Williamsburg murals
- [ ] Special exhibitions
- [ ] Non-exhibition space

★ **Paracas Textile**
Over 2,000 years old, a woven mantle from Peru still glows with color.

Mother and Child
Figurines like this are carved by the Luluwa tribe of Zaire as amulets for pregnant or nursing women.

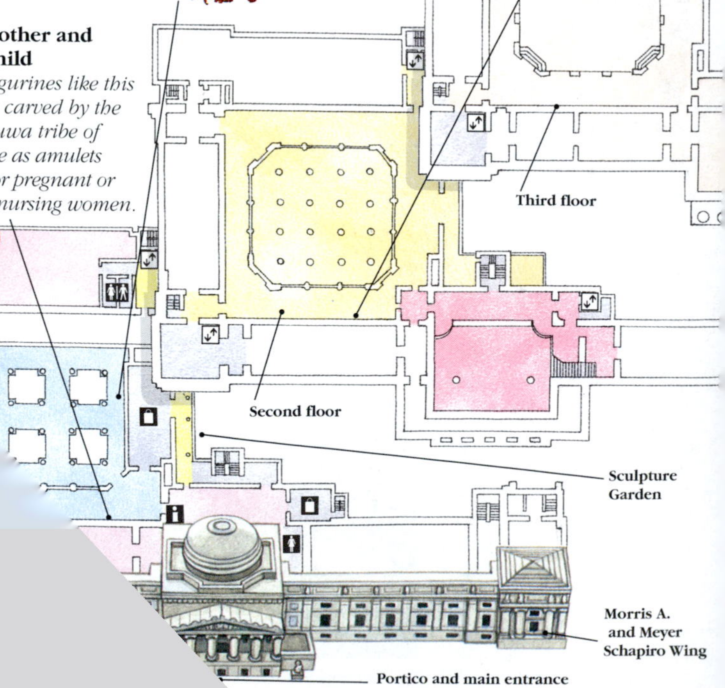

Third floor

Second floor

Sculpture Garden

Morris A. and Meyer Schapiro Wing

Portico and main entrance

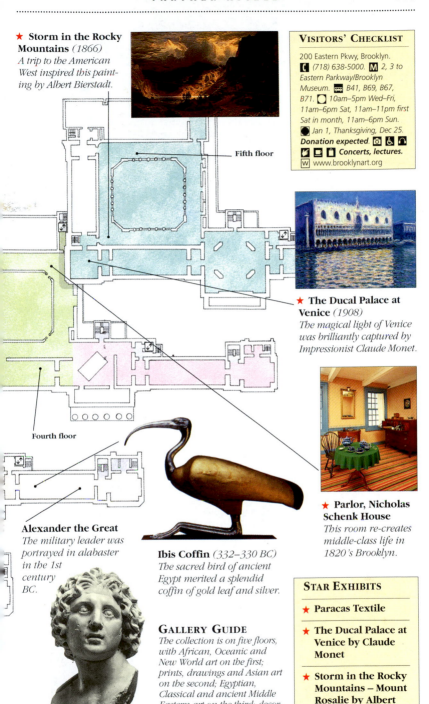

★ **Storm in the Rocky Mountains** *(1866)*
A trip to the American West inspired this painting by Albert Bierstadt.

Fifth floor

VISITORS' CHECKLIST

200 Eastern Pkwy, Brooklyn.
C (718) 638-5000. **M** *2, 3 to Eastern Parkway/Brooklyn Museum.* **B41, B69, B67, B71.** ☐ *10am–5pm Wed–Fri, 11am–6pm Sat, 11am–11pm first Sat in month, 11am–6pm Sun.* ● *Jan 1, Thanksgiving, Dec 25.* **Donation expected.** 🅿 ♿ 🏪 📷 🎨 📖 🎭 *Concerts, lectures.* **W** *www.brooklynart.org*

★ **The Ducal Palace at Venice** *(1908)*
The magical light of Venice was brilliantly captured by Impressionist Claude Monet.

Fourth floor

Alexander the Great
The military leader was portrayed in alabaster in the 1st century BC.

Ibis Coffin *(332–330 BC)*
The sacred bird of ancient Egypt merited a splendid coffin of gold leaf and silver.

★ **Parlor, Nicholas Schenk House**
This room re-creates middle-class life in 1820's Brooklyn.

GALLERY GUIDE
The collection is on five floors, with African, Oceanic and New World art on the first; prints, drawings and Asian art on the second; Egyptian, Classical and ancient Middle Eastern art on the third; decorative art on the fourth; and American, European and contemporary art on the fifth. There is special exhibition space on the first and fourth floors.

STAR EXHIBITS

★ **Paracas Textile**

★ **The Ducal Palace at Venice by Claude Monet**

★ **Storm in the Rocky Mountains – Mount Rosalie by Albert Bierstadt**

★ **Parlor, Nicholas Schenk House**

Exploring the Collection

THE BROOKLYN MUSEUM houses one of the finest, and the second largest, art collections in the United States. Its strengths include an outstanding collection of Native American art from the Southwest; 28 American period rooms; exquisite examples of ancient Egyptian and Islamic art; and many important American and European paintings.

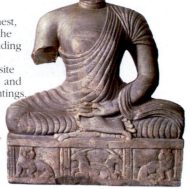

Seated Buddha torso in limestone, from India (late 3rd century AD)

ARTS OF AFRICA, THE PACIFIC, AND THE AMERICAS

THE BROOKLYN Museum set a precedent in the United States in 1923 by exhibiting African objects as works of art rather than artifacts. Since then, the African art collection has grown steadily in both importance and size.

Exhibits include a rare intricately carved ivory gong from the Benin kingdom of 16th-century Nigeria, one of only five in existence.

The museum also has a notable collection of Native American work, including totem poles, textiles and pottery. A 19th-century deerskin shirt, once worn by a chief of the Blackfoot tribe, depicts his brave and daring exploits in battle.

Ancient American artistic traditions are represented by Peruvian textiles, Central American gold and Mexican sculpture. A beautifully preserved tunic from Peru, dating from AD 600, is so tightly woven that its vibrant symbolic designs appear to have been painted onto the cloth rather than woven in the traditional manner.

The Oceanic collection includes sculpture from the Solomon Islands, Papua New Guinea and New Zealand.

ASIAN ART

CHANGING EXHIBITIONS from the museum's permanent collection of Chinese, Japanese, Korean, Indian, Southeast Asian and Islamic art are always on display. Japanese and Chinese paintings, Indian miniatures and Islamic calligraphy complement the Asian sculpture, textiles and ceramics. The collections of Japanese folk art, Chinese cloisonné (enamel work) and Oriental carpets are of particular note. Good examples of Buddhist art range from a variety of Chinese, Indian and Southeast Asian Buddhas to a mandala-patterned temple banner from 14th-century Tibet, painted in rich, luminous watercolors.

Blackfoot tribe deerskin shirt, decorated with porcupine quills and glass beads (19th century)

DECORATIVE ARTS

THE FOCUS of the decorative arts department is a very stylish assembly of 28 superb American period rooms.

The earliest is from a 17th-century Brooklyn Dutch house. It served as a parlor, dining room and sleeping area, with the enclosed "bed boxes" built against the wall opposite the fireplace. The Moorish Smoking Room, from John D. Rockefeller's brownstone house, is an opulent example of elegant New York living during the 1880s. In complete contrast, the most recent room is a 1928–30 Art Deco study from a Park Avenue apartment, including a walk-in bar that was hidden behind paneling during the Prohibition era (see pp28-29).

Normandie **chrome pitcher, by Peter Müller-Munk (1935)**

Also on exhibit is a wide selection from the museum's vast collection of furniture, ceramics, glass, pewter, silver and metalware, including a 1930s pitcher whose shape was inspired by the stacks of the ocean liner *Normandie*.

EGYPTIAN, CLASSICAL AND ANCIENT MIDDLE EASTERN ART

RECOGNIZED AS among the world's finest, the Egyptian collection holds many masterpieces. It begins with an early female figure dating from 3500 BC, and encompasses sculptures, statues, tomb paintings and reliefs as well as funerary paraphernalia. Of the latter, the most unusual is the coffin of an ibis, probably recovered from the vast animal cemetery of Tuna el-Gebel in Middle Egypt. The ibis was a sacred bird representing the god Thoth, and this coffin is made of solid silver and wood overlaid with gold leaf, with rock crystal for the bird's eyes. These galleries have been renovated into a state-of-the-art, high-tech installation.

Among the artifacts from the Greek and Roman civilizations are statuary, pottery, bronzes, jewelry and mosaics.

Among the Ancient Near and Middle Eastern exhibits are an extensive collection of pottery and 12 alabaster reliefs from the Assyrian palace of King Ashur-nasir-pal II. These date from around 883-859 BC and depict the king fighting, overseeing his crops and purifying the "sacred tree," a major icon in Assyrian religion.

PAINTING AND SCULPTURE

THIS SECTION contains works from the 14th century to the present, including a well-known and outstanding 19th-century French art collection with works by Degas, Rodin, Monet, Cézanne, Matisse and Pissarro. It also boasts one of the largest holdings of Spanish

Pierre de Wiessant (about 1886) by Auguste Rodin, from his *Burghers of Calais* group

Colonial paintings and one of the best collections of North American paintings to be found in the United States.

The museum's 20th-century American collection includes, appropriately, *Brooklyn Bridge* by Georgia O'Keeffe.

The Sculpture Garden has a collection of architectural ornamentation taken from demolished New York buildings, including statues that were rescued from the original Penn Station.

PRINTS, DRAWINGS AND PHOTOGRAPHS

THE PRINTS section displays examples by many masters, ranging from a rare woodcut print by Dürer entitled *The Great Triumphal Chariot* and works by Piranesi to an excellent Impressionist and Post-Impressionist collection. This includes works by Toulouse-Lautrec and Mary Cassatt, the only American woman associated with the Impressionist movement. There are lithographs by James McNeill Whistler, Winslow Homer engravings, and a superb selection of

Rotherbide, an etching by James McNeill Whistler (1860)

drawings by Fragonard, Paul Klee, Van Gogh, Picasso and Gorky, among others, many of them in black and white.

The photography collection consists mainly of works by major 20th-century American photographers, including a 1924 portrait of Mary Pickford by Edward Steichen and work by Margaret Bourke-White, Berenice Abbott and Robert Mapplethorpe. All of these artworks are constantly rotated for conservation purposes.

Sandstone reliefs from Thebes in Egypt (around 760–656 BC), depicting the great god Amun-Re and his consort Mut

Staten Island

APART FROM the famous ferry ride, Staten Island and its attractions are not well known to New Yorkers in general. Residents feel so ignored, they've talked about seceding from the city. Visitors who venture beyond the ferry terminal, however, will be pleasantly surprised to find hills, lakes and greenery, with expanses of open space, amazing harbor views and well-preserved early New York buildings. One of the biggest surprises here is a cache of Tibetan art hidden away in a replica of a Buddhist temple.

Historic Richmond Town ㉔

441 Clarke Ave. **C** *(718) 351-1611.*
S74 from ferry.
○ *Sep–Jun: 1–5pm, Wed–Sun;*
Jul–Aug: 10am–5pm Wed–Fri; Sat &
Sun 1–5pm..
📷 🔲 🔲 🔲 🔲 🔲
W www.historicrichmondtown.org

Cologne at the
General Store

THERE ARE now 29 buildings, 14 of which are open to the public, in New York's only restored village and outdoor museum. The village was first named Coccles-town, after the local shellfish, but was soon corrupted to "Cuckoldstown," much to the annoyance of the residents. By the end of the Revolutionary War the new name of Richmondtown had been adopted. It was the county seat until Staten Island was made part of the city in 1898, and has been preserved as an example of an early New York settlement.

The Voorlezer House, built in the Dutch era before 1696, is the oldest elementary school to be found in the country. The Stephens General Store, which opened in 1837, doubled as the local post office. It has been well restored, right down to the contents of the shelves. The complex, set on 100 acres (40 ha), includes wagon sheds, a courthouse built in 1837, houses, several shops and a tavern. There are also seasonal workshops where traditional rural crafts are demonstrated to visitors. St. Andrew's Church (1708) and its old graveyard are just across the Mill Pond stream, and the Historical Society Museum is in the County Clerk's and Surrogate's Office. The toy room is a delight.

Jacques Marchais Museum of Tibetan Art ㉕

338 Lighthouse Ave. **C** *(718) 987-3500.* **S74 from ferry.** ○
Apr–Nov: 1–5pm Wed–Sun;
(4:45pm: last adm) Dec–Mar: 1–5pm
Wed–Fri. ● *public hols.* 📷 🔲
🔲 🔲

A HILLTOP provides a very tranquil setting for one of the largest collections of privately owned Tibetan art outside Tibet. The main building is a replica of a mountain temple with an authentic altar

Sacred sculpture at the Jacques
Marchais Center of Tibetan Art

The Voorlezer House at Richmond Town

in three tiers, crowded with gold, silver and bronze figures.

Another building is used as a library. The garden has some stone sculptures, including life-size Buddhas. The museum was built in 1947 by Mrs. Harry Klauber, a dealer in Asian art trading under the name of Jacques Marchais. The Dalai Lama paid his first visit here in 1991.

A gazebo at the Snug Harbor
Cultural Center

Snug Harbor Cultural Center ㉖

1000 Richmond Terrace. **C** *(718) 448-2500.* **S40 from ferry to Snug Harbor Gate.** **Grounds** ○ *dawn–dusk daily.* **Gallery and Children's Museum** ○ *noon–5pm Tue–Sun.* ●
Jan 1, Thanksgiving, Dec 25. 🔲
limited. 🔲 🔲 **W** www.sibg.org

FOUNDED IN 1801 as a haven for aged sailors, Snug Harbor is now an arts center complex of 28 historical buildings in various stages of restoration. There are five stately Greek Revival gems, dating from 1831 to 1880. The oldest, the Main Hall, is the Newhouse Center for Contemporary Art, but the ships at sea in the stained-glass windows are a reminder of its origins.

Other buildings house the award-winning Staten Island Children's Museum and the Veterans Memorial Hall, a restored chapel now used for indoor performances.

An annual sculpture festival and summer shows are held on the lawns. The grounds include the Staten Island Botanical Garden, with its noted orchid collection and a beautiful rose garden.

Snug Harbor is the legacy of a Scottish sailor, Robert Richard Randall, who became rich during the Revolutionary War, some say by piracy, and bequeathed his wealth to care for less fortunate seamen. His estate's trustees bought the property so that the sailors could enjoy its harbor views.

Clear Comfort, Alice Austen's lifetime residence

Alice Austen House ❷❼

2 Hylan Blvd. ☎ *(718) 816-4506.*
🚌 *S 51 from ferry to Hylan Blvd.*
⏱ *noon–5pm Thu–Sun.* ⬤ *Jan, Feb, public hols.* 💷 **Donation**
📷 ♿ *limited.* 🚻 🎁
W www.aliceausten.8m.com

CLEAR COMFORT is a delightfully named small cottage built around 1710. This was the home of the photo-

grapher Alice Austen. Born in 1866, she lived in this house for most of her life. She documented life on the island, in Manhattan, and also on trips to other parts of the country and on her travels to Europe. She lost all her money in the stock market crash of 1929, and her poverty forced her into a public poorhouse at the age of 84. One year later, her photographic talent was finally recognized by *Life* magazine, which published an article about her, earning her enough money to enter a nursing home. She left 3,500 negatives dating from 1880 to 1930. Today, the Friends of Alice Austen House mounts exhibitions of her best work.

Even Farther Afield

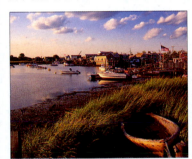

The village of Broad Channel at Jamaica Bay

Jamaica Bay Wildlife Refuge Center ❷❽

Cross Bay Blvd at Broad Channel.
☎ *(718) 318-4340.* M *Broad Channel.* ⏱ *8:30am–5pm daily.* ✗

THE MARSHES and uplands of the Refuge cover an area almost the size of Manhattan. Over 300 species of birds live here either seasonally or all year round. Situated on the main Atlantic migratory path, the Refuge is at its best in spring and autumn, when the skies are filled with skeins of geese and ducks. The park rangers conduct hikes and nature walks for weekend visitors – be sure to wear

suitable shoes and clothes, and take along a zoom lens camera or binoculars to get the best from your visit. The only village at Jamaica Bay is named Broad Channel, a small collection of houses on pilings along the Cross Bay Boulevard. The Refuge and a 10-mile (16-km) stretch of beach and boardwalk at nearby Rockaway, are accessible by subway straight from the heart of Manhattan.

Jones Beach State Park ❷❾

☎ *(516) 785-1600.* 🚆 *Long Island Railroad from Penn Station to Jones Beach.* **Operates** *late May–Labor Day.* ☎ *(718) 217-5477.* **Jones Beach Theater** ☎ *(516) 221-1000.* **Beaches** ⏱ *late May –Labor Day.* W www.nysparks.state.ny.us/parks

JONES BEACH was the creation of New York's Parks' Commissioner Robert Moses *(see p244),* who transformed this narrow spit of land into Long Island's most accessible

and popular beach in 1929. There are sand dunes, surf on the Atlantic side and sheltered water in the bay. There is also miniature golf, swimming pools, restaurants and the Jones Beach Theater, which hosts a variety of open-air concerts in the summer.

Robert Moses State Park is on the next island to the east, Fire Island, which is over 30 miles (48 km) long, yet less than 900 yds (800 m) across. Areas of the island are totally unspoiled and unpopulated, with long stretches of white sands, making it a great place for walking and bicycling in peaceful surroundings.

Fire Island's communities are small and very varied – some are favored by singles looking for the company of the opposite sex, others are sedate and family-orientated, others are favorites with New York's large gay community.

Sunbathers basking at Jones Beach

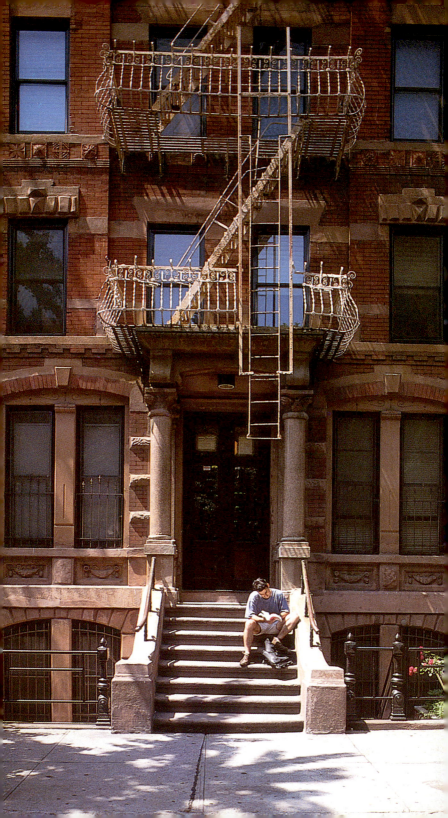

FOUR GUIDED WALKS

WALKING IN NEW YORK is an excellent way to discover the human scale of the city. The following ten pages explore the unique character and charm of New York through four thematic walks. These range from an exploration of Greenwich Village and SoHo's literary and artistic connections (*see pp258–9*) to a trip across the Brooklyn Bridge for spectacular views and a glimpse of 19th-century New York (*see pp264–5*).

In addition, each of the 15 areas of Manhattan described in the *Area by Area* section of this book has a short

Sculpture outside US Custom House, Lower Manhattan

walk on its *Street-by-Street* map, taking you past many of the interesting sights in that area. Various organizations and enthusiasts run walking tours of the city. These range from serious appraisals of architectural history to a guide to the ghosts of Broadway. Details of tour organizers are listed on page 353, or you can consult *Time Out New York* magazine. As in any major city, take extra care of your personal belongings while walking (*see p356–7*). Plan your route ahead; walk only during daylight hours; and, whenever possible, go in a group.

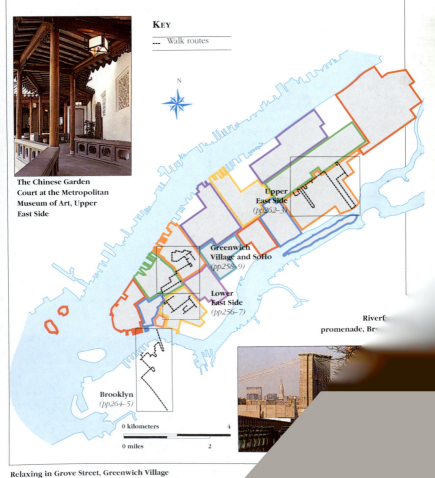

KEY

--- Walk routes

The Chinese Garden Court at the Metropolitan Museum of Art, Upper East Side

Upper East Side (*pp262–3*)

Greenwich Village and SoHo (*pp258–9*)

Lower East Side (*pp256–7*)

Riverfront promenade, Br

Brooklyn (*pp264–5*)

0 kilometers 4

0 miles 2

Relaxing in Grove Street, Greenwich Village

A 90-Minute Walk in the Lower East Side

THIS WALK PASSES through some of the old immigrant neighborhoods that have given New York its unique texture, and gives you the chance to experience a taste of the character, cultures, and cuisine of some of New York's most vibrant communities. Sunday is the best day for local outdoor activity. For more details on sights in the Lower East Side see pages 92–9.

The Lower East Side

Begin at the Lower East Side Tenement Museum ① at 97 Orchard Street between Delancey and Broome. This original tenement building is being restored to show how immigrants lived at the turn of the century. It features a gallery of exhibits on the immigrant experience, giving insights for the remainder of your walk.

Orchard Street itself ② was the center of the Jewish Lower East Side. The pushcarts that once lined the block are gone, but the shops selling fashionable merchandise at discount prices still remain. The stores close on Saturday, the Jewish

An 1885 iron from the Lower East Side Tenement Museum ①

Sabbath, and so Sunday is the traditional shopping day.

Much of the Jewish population has moved, but reminders are many. Turn left at Grand Street and right at Essex to 35 Essex, Guss' Pickle Company ③, the pickle store in the film *Crossing Delancey*. Barrels of pickles are outside, and people line up to buy. Just a few steps down Hester Street brings you to Kadouri Import (dried fruits, nuts and lots of spices) and Gertel's, an old Jewish bakery.

Go back up Essex, cross Delancey, and at Rivington, turn right for tours and tastings at Schapiro's Winery ④ at 126 Rivington. At 150 is Streit's Matzoh, the largest manufacturer of unleavened bread in New York.

A cultural mixture

Go back along Rivington Street. Have a look at the Spanish *bodegas* and the Chinese grocers supplying the new restaurants in this once-Jewish area. This is a rather gritty street and requires caution, but it shows a true picture of the new immigrant life. Walk across the street. At the corner of Forsyth, a synagogue has been converted to a Spanish church ⑤. Once back on Rivington Street, turn right on to Eldridge

which is a typical tenement street. At the junction of Grand and Eldridge streets you will find the hub of the textile area, good for discount towels and linens. Just beyond Canal Street is the Eldridge Street Synagogue ⑥, which was the first Eastern European synagogue in New York. It is once again open after extensive restoration.

KEY

— Walk route

- Detour route

✲ Good viewing point

M Subway station

Clothes vendors at Orchard Street market ②

Guss' Pickle Company ③

Chinatown

Return to Canal Street and turn left. At the entry to the Manhattan Bridge, you'll see the distant towers of the financial district, framed by the nearby tenements. Cross the Bowery; you'll see many jewelry shops, the remnants of the original Diamond District ⑦. As you continue, the shops give way to stalls selling an exotic array of vegetables, and butcher shops with rows of

cuisine, all offering a chance to taste unusual fare. For spiritual sustenance. visit the Eastern States Buddhist Temple ⑧.

At Bayard Street, turn left to see all the Chinese political posters and messages on the Wall of Democracy, then turn back and to the right, to Mulberry Street. The curve next to Columbus Park was Mulberry Bend ⑨, once notorious for gang murders and mayhem.

An Italian deli in Little Italy ⑩

Little Italy

Turn and walk the other way on Mulberry Street and you are suddenly in Little Italy ⑩. Small in area though it is, and encroached on by Chinatown, this is still a wonderful neighborhood full of old-world restaurants and stores selling homemade pasta, sausages, breads and pastries. The Italian population has dwindled over the years, as the younger generation has moved out. But a staunch community still remains, as does the area's Italian atmosphere.

The big event of the year is the Feast of San Gennaro, named for the patron saint of Naples. For eleven nights every September, Mulberry Street is jammed with thousands of locals and visitors enjoying the parades and Italian food, with rows of stalls selling sizzling sa

Little Italy's foothol to Mulberry on Hes then from Hester Mulberry. If you to Grand Street find yourself Chinese gr

Pretzel seller on Orchard Street ②

roast ducks in the windows. At 200 Canal Street is Kam Man Food Products. One of the largest Chinese markets in the area, it is a fascinating place to explore.

Turn left from Canal to Mott Street and you'll know you are right in the heart of Chinatown by all the Chinese neon signs. Even the banks and phone booths are shaped like pagodas. There are hundreds of restaurants here, from holes-in-the-wall to haute

Kam Man Food Products at 200 Canal Street

A 90-Minute Walk in Greenwich Village and SoHo

A STROLL THROUGH the patchwork quilt of streets in Greenwich Village takes you to where New York's best-known writers and artists have lived, worked and played, and ends with a tour of SoHo's galleries and museums, where today's artists show their work. For more details on sights in Greenwich Village, see pages 106–13, and for SoHo sights, see pages 100–5.

Facade in Washington Mews ⑬

Author Mark Twain, who lived on 10th Street

West 10th Street

The junction of 8th Street and 6th Avenue ① has many book, music and clothing stores nearby. Walk up Sixth to West Ninth Street to see (on the left) Jefferson Market Courthouse ② and (on the right) Balducci's gourmet market.

Turn right at West 10th Street ③ to the Alexander Onassis Center for Hellenic Studies. A passageway at the front once led up to the Tile Club, a gathering place for the artists of the Tenth Street Studio,

TIPS FOR WALKERS

Starting point: *8th St/6th Ave.*
Length: *2 miles (3.2 km).*
Getting there: *Take subway train A, B, C, D, E or F to West Fourth Street-Washington Square station (Eighth Street exit). Fifth Avenue buses M2 and M3 stop at Eighth ?reet. From here, walk one block ? to Sixth. The M5 bus loops ? Washington Square back Avenue and Eighth Street.*
-off points: The Pink ? Grove Street, is good SoHo Kitchen & ? Street, is a typical ?e, also known ?on of wines.

where Augustus Saint-Gaudens, John LaFarge and Winslow Homer lived. Mark Twain lived at 24 West 10th Street, and Edward Albee at 50 West 10th.

Back across Sixth Avenue is Milligan Place ④, a cluster of 19th-century houses, and Patchin Place ⑤, where the poets e e cummings and John Masefield both lived.

Farther on is the Ninth Circle bar ⑥ which, when it first opened in 1898, was known as "Regnaneschi's." It was the subject of John Sloan's painting *Regnaneschi's Saturday Night.* Playwright Edward Albee first saw the question "Who's afraid of Virginia Woolf?" scrawled on a mirror here.

The doorway of Chumley's ⑩

Greenwich Village

Turn left at Waverly Place past the Three Lives Bookstore, a typical Village literary gathering spot, to Christopher Street and to the triangular Northern Dispensary ⑦.

Follow Grove Street along Christopher Park to Sheridan Square, the busy hub of the

Village. The Circle Repertory Theater ⑧, which premiered plays by Pulitzer Prizewinner Lanford Wilson, is now closed.

Cross Seventh Avenue and bear left on to Grove Street. At the corner of Bedford Street, you can't miss "Twin Peaks" ⑨, a home for artists in the 1920s. Turn right to see Bedford: the unmarked door is Chumley's ⑩, a saloon not much changed since 1928 when it was a speakeasy *(see p28).* Writers Dylan Thomas, Simone de Beauvoir, Ernest Hemingway, William Faulkner, J.D. Salinger, Jack Kerouac and many others drank here. Covers of their books line the walls. 75 Bedford is the narrowest house in the Village, once the home of feminist poet Edna St. Vincent Millay.

Walk up Carmine to Sixth Avenue and turn right at Waverly Place. At 116 Waverly ⑪, Anne Charlotte Lynch, an English teacher, held weekly gatherings in her town house for such eminent friends as Herman Melville and Edgar Allan Poe, who gave his first reading of *The Raven* here.

A detour left of half a block will bring you to MacDougal Alley ⑫, a lane of carriage houses in which Gertrude Vanderbilt Whitney had her studio. She opened the first Whitney Museum here in 1932, just behind the studio.

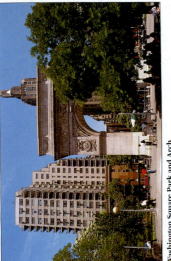

Washington Square Park and Arch

Washington Square

Back on MacDougal, turn left to Washington Square North, to see the finest Greek Revival houses in the United States. Built of red brick, they have marble balustrades and entrances flanked by columns. Writer Henry James set his *Washington Square* in No. 18, his grandmother's home.

Pause at Fifth Avenue to look back at Washington Square Park, with its famous Washington Square Arch. Go across to Two Fifth Avenue; opposite is Washington Mews ⑬, an elegant carriage house complex. John Dos Passos, Edward Hopper and Rockwell Kent lived in the studio at No. 14a at various times.

Go back up Washington Square North, past some elegant houses. Writer Edith Wharton lived at Seven Washington Square North. Walk beneath the arch and across Washington Square Park. On the left as you leave the park, is the fine Judson Memorial Church and Tower ⑭ by Stanford White and the NYU Loeb Student Center. T Center was once a board' house, known as the ' of genius," and is Theodore Drei *American T*

SoHo

Walk south on Thompson, a typical Village street lined with clubs, cafés and shops. Turn left at Houston, SoHo's northern limit, and right on West Broadway, lined with some of the city's most famous galleries along with chic and arty boutiques.

Turn left at Spring Street for yet more tempting shops, then right at Greene Street ⑮, the heart of the Cast-Iron Historic District. Many of these fine buildings now house clusters of galleries. Turn left at the end of Greene Street to Canal Street, the end of SoHo, to see how quickly New York can change. This noisy street is full of hawkers and discount electronics stores. You can explore bargains for the next two blocks and then turn left up Broadway, soon finding yourself on the cutting edge of art, at the New Museum of Contemporary Art at 583 Broadway and the Guggenheim Museum SoHo ⑯ found at 575 Broadway (see p105).

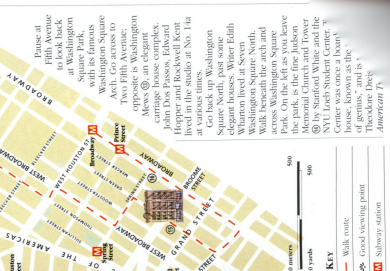

KEY

— Walk route

❀ Good viewing point

Ⓜ Subway station

0 meters   500
0 yards   500

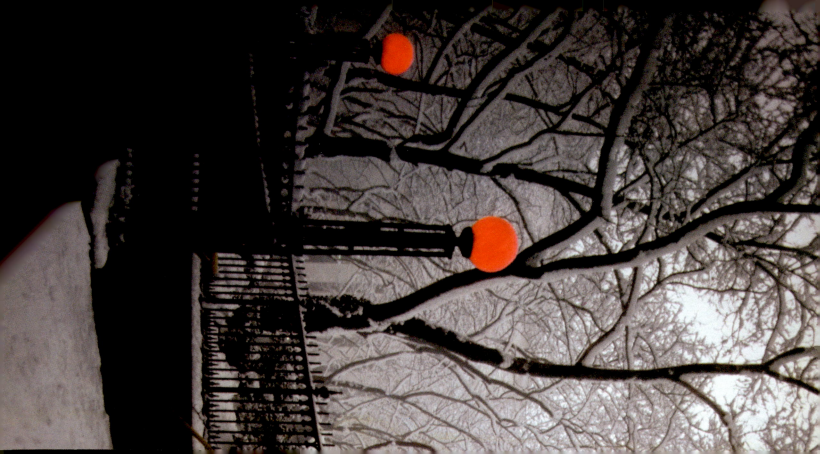

A Two-Hour Walk in the Upper East Side

A PROMENADE ALONG upper Fifth Avenue and its
environs will take you past the best remaining
examples of New York's turn-of-the-century gilded age.
A detour through the old German district of Yorkville
leads to a riverside stroll to Gracie Mansion, official
residence of the city's mayor, dating from 1799. For
details on Upper East Side sights, see pages 180–201.

| 0 meters | 500 |
| 0 yards | 500 |

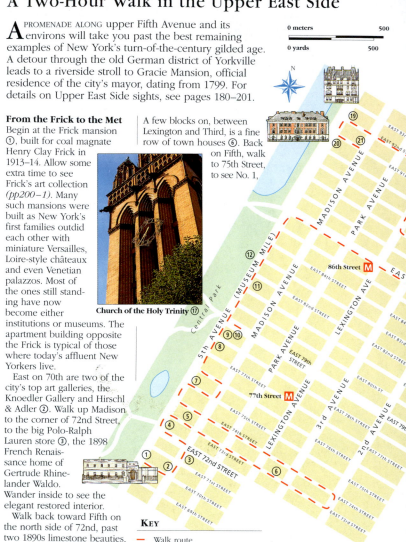

From the Frick to the Met
Begin at the Frick mansion
①, built for coal magnate
Henry Clay Frick in
1913–14. Allow some
extra time to see
Frick's art collection
(pp200–1). Many
such mansions were
built as New York's
first families outdid
each other with
miniature Versailles,
Loire-style châteaux
and even Venetian
palazzos. Most of
the ones still stand-
ing have now
become either
institutions or museums. The
apartment building opposite
the Frick is typical of those
where today's affluent New
Yorkers live.

East on 70th are two of the
city's top art galleries, the
Knoedler Gallery and Hirschl
& Adler ②. Walk up Madison
to the corner of 72nd Street,
to the big Polo-Ralph
Lauren store ③, the 1898
French Renais-
sance home of
Gertrude Rhine-
lander Waldo.
Wander inside to see the
elegant restored interior.

Walk back toward Fifth on
the north side of 72nd, past
two 1890s limestone beauties,
now the Lycée Français de
New York ④. Continue along
Fifth Avenue to 73rd Street.
Turn east to 11, Joseph
Pulitzer's former
home ⑤.

A few blocks on, between
Lexington and Third, is a fine
row of town houses ⑥. Back
on Fifth, walk
to 75th Street,
to see No. 1,

Church of the Holy Trinity ⑰

KEY

—	Walk route
☆	Good viewing point
Ⓜ	Subway station

the former residence
of Edward S. Hark-
ness, son of
a founder of
Standard Oil.
It is now the
Common-
Fund ⑦.
At 1 East
78th, the
tobacco
millionaire
James B.

Duke's 18th-century
French-style château is now
the New York University
Institute of Fine Arts ⑧. At
79th Street and Fifth, the
former home of financier
Payne Whitney, is the
French Embassy ⑨ and 2
East 79th is the Ukrainian
Institute of America ⑩. On
the southeast corner of 82nd
is Duke-Semans House ⑪,
one of the few grand Fifth
Avenue residences still
privately owned. Save another
full day for The Metropolitan
Museum of Art ⑫ at 82nd.

Ukrainian Institute of America ⑩

Carl Schurz Park Promenade

TIPS FOR WALKERS

Starting point: Frick Collection.
Length: 3 miles (4.8 km).
Getting there: Take subway train 6 to 68th Street and Lexington, then walk left (left) three blocks to Fifth Avenue. Or take the M1, M2, M3 or M4 bus up Madison Avenue to 70th Street and walk one block west.
Stopping-off points: The cafés at the Whitney and Guggenheim museums are pleasant. M.Rohr's Cafe is at 303 E85/2nd Ave and Mocca Hungarian is at 1588 2nd Ave/82nd, or try the Heidelberg Café on Second Avenue off 86th Street. Madison Avenue between 92nd and 93rd has many places to eat, including Sarabeth's Kitchen, with its excellent weekend brunch.

Yorkville

Turn east on 86th Street for the vestiges of German Yorkville – Bremen House ⑬, cross Second Avenue, then turn right to the

Heidelberg Café and German deli, Schaller & Weber ⑭. For a restful stop, try Mocca Hungarian or M.Rohr's cafe on Second Avenue.

East River and Gracie Mansion

Henderson Place ⑮ at East End Avenue is a cluster of 24 red-brick Queen Anne town houses. Carl Schurz Park opposite was named after the city's most prominent German immigrant, editor of *Harper's Weekly* and the *New York Post*. The park promenade atop the east River Drive leads to a view of Hell Gate, where the Harlem River, Long Island Sound and New York harbor meet. From the walkway you can see the back of Gracie Mansion ⑯, the mayor's official residence. The path west along the fence leads to a better view. Walk west on 88th Street past the Church of the Holy Trinity ⑰ and at Lexington Avenue go to 92nd Street and west past two of the few wooden houses left in Manhattan ⑱.

The Cooper-Hewitt Museum ⑳

Carnegie Hill

Back on Fifth Avenue, turn downtown past the Felix Warburg Mansion of 1908, now the Jewish Museum ⑲, and continue to 91st Street and the huge Andrew Carnegie home, now the Cooper-Hewitt Museum ⑳. Built in 1902 in the style of an English country manor, it gave the area the unofficial name of Carnegie Hill. T James Burden House East 91st Street, bui Vanderbilt heires in 1905, has a under a stai that was "the sta East Ka

Wooden houses on 92nd Street ⑱

A Three-Hour Walk in Brooklyn

A TRIP ACROSS New York's most famous crossing leads to Brooklyn Heights, the city's first suburb. This neighborhood has a 19th-century feel, mixed with a hint of Middle Eastern cultures. The riverfront promenade has unrivaled views of Manhattan. For more details on sights in Brooklyn, see pages 245–51.

Brooklyn Bridge Worth Street
550yards/500m

Fire Station on Old Fulton Street

Fulton Ferry Landing

About 3,580 ft (1 km) long, the Brooklyn Bridge span yields thrilling views of the lower New York skyline and prize photo opportunities. Take a taxi, or, if feeling energetic, walk across to Brooklyn.

On the far side, follow the Tillary Street sign to the right, turn right at the bottom of the stairs, then take the first path through the park and walk down Cadman Plaza West ① under the Brooklyn-Queens Expressway; here Cadman becomes Old Fulton Street. You can see the bridge on the right as you head to the river at Water Street and the Fulton Ferry landing ②. During the Revolutionary War, George

Washington's troops fled to Manhattan from here. In 1814, this was the depot for the ferry connecting Brooklyn and Manhattan Island. This transformed Brooklyn Heights from a predominantly farming area to a residential district. The area is full of character and is still a very popular place to live. To the right is the River Café ③. This restaurant's fine cuisine and spectacular views of the Manhattan skyline make it one of New York's most exceptional dining spots.

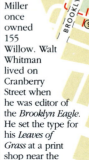

Eagle Warehouse ④

Brooklyn Heights

From the landing, turn right to steep Everitt Street up Columbia Heights, past the former Eagle Warehouse ④ of 1893 to Middagh Street and along the streets of Brooklyn Heights. 24 Middagh ⑤ is one of the oldest, built in 1824.

Next turn right on Willow and left on Cranberry; here the town houses range from wooden clapboards to brick Federal-style to brownstones. Except for cars and a few modern buildings, you could be in the 19th century.

Many famous people have lived here. Truman Capote wrote *Breakfast at Tiffany's* and *In Cold Blood* in the basement of 70 Willow, and Arthur

Miller once owned 155 Willow. Walt Whitman lived on Cranberry Street when he was editor of the *Brooklyn Eagle*. He set the type for his *Leaves of Grass* at a print shop near the corner of Cranberry and Fulton. The town houses now on the site are called Whitman Close.

Turn right along Hicks. The Hicks family, local farmers, inspired the name "hick" for a yokel. Turn left on Orange Street to the Plymouth Church ⑥, home of Henry Ward Beecher, an antislavery preacher. His sister, Harriet Beecher Stowe,

Truman Capote with feathered friend

wrote *Uncle Tom's Cabin*. At Clark Street are marquees of once-luxurious hotels, such as the Towers. Follow Clark Street to 142 Columbia Heights, where Norman Mailer lives ⑦. Invalid Washington Roebling lived at 110 – using a telescope, he directed the construction of Brooklyn Bridge from his room.

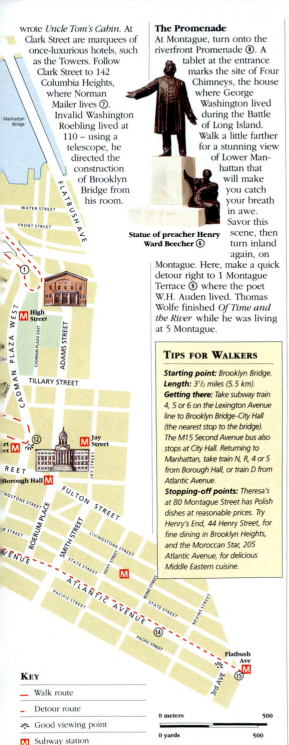

Statue of preacher Henry Ward Beecher ⑥

The Promenade

At Montague, turn onto the riverfront Promenade ⑧. A tablet at the entrance marks the site of Four Chimneys, the house where George Washington lived during the Battle of Long Island. Walk a little farther for a stunning view of Lower Manhattan that will make you catch your breath in awe. Savor this scene, then turn inland again, on Montague. Here, make a quick detour right to 1 Montague Terrace ⑨ where the poet W.H. Auden lived. Thomas Wolfe finished *Of Time and the River* while he was living at 5 Montague.

TIPS FOR WALKERS

Starting point: Brooklyn Bridge.
Length: 3¹/₂ miles (5.5 km).
Getting there: Take subway train 4, 5 or 6 on the Lexington Avenue line to Brooklyn Bridge-City Hall (the nearest stop to the bridge). The M15 Second Avenue bus also stops at City Hall. Returning to Manhattan, take train N, R, 4 or 5 from Borough Hall, or train D from Atlantic Avenue.
Stopping-off points: Theresa's at 80 Montague Street has Polish dishes at reasonable prices. Try Henry's End, 44 Henry Street, for fine dining in Brooklyn Heights, and the Moroccan Star, 205 Atlantic Avenue, for delicious Middle Eastern cuisine.

The old Montague Street trolley, which led to the river and the ferry

Montague and Clinton Streets

Once back on Montague Street, walk to the heart of Brooklyn Heights, with all its cafés and boutiques. The baseball team, the Brooklyn Dodgers, got their name from dodging the trolley cars that once ran down the street. Walk to the intersection of Montague and Clinton to see the stained glass of the 1834 Church of St. Ann and the Holy Trinity ⑩. Walk a block left on Clinton to Pierrepont Street for the Brooklyn Historical Society ⑪. A block farther, at Court Street, is the 1849 Borough Hall ⑫, and the subway taking you back to Manhattan.

Brooklyn's Dodgers, who got their name from dodging trolley cars

Atlantic Avenue

Another option is to stay on Clinton and walk five short blocks to Atlantic Avenue. A left turn here leads to a whole string of Middle Eastern emporia ⑬, such as Sahadi Imports at 187 Atlantic Avenue, with a huge selection of foods. The Damascus Bakery at 195 makes the most delicious filo pastries. Various shops sell Arabic books, tapes, publications, and CDs. Two blocks on are numerous antique shops ⑭. At Flatbush Avenue, look left to the Brooklyn Academy of Music ⑮ and the grand front Williamsburg Savings Watch for signs to the back to Manhattan.

KEY

— Walk route

- Detour route

☆ Good viewing point

Ⓜ Subway station

0 meters   500
0 yards   500

TRAVELERS' NEEDS

WHERE TO STAY

With over 65,000 hotel rooms available, New York offers something for everyone. The top hotels are not quite as expensive as those in Paris or London, but the best news for visitors is the increase in budget hotels. While many of these are basic rather than charming, they offer good value. Other budget options are furnished apartments and studios and bed and breakfast in private homes, as well as youth hostels and YMCAs. From an inspection of over 200 hotels in New York, we have selected the best of their kind. *Choosing a Hotel (pp272–83)* contains detailed descriptions of the hotels, which will help you select the one best suited to your needs. Many of the hotels have a website address to enable you to book a room via the internet.

Cole Porter's piano, in the Waldorf–Astoria bar (see p280)

Bathroom at the Paramount Hotel (see p277)

WHERE TO LOOK

The East Side, roughly between 59th and 77th streets, is the traditional location for luxury hotels, but the renovation of certain landmark midtown properties, such as the St. Regis, and new hotels in famous chains from the Far East, such as the Peninsula Group, have increased competition in this price range.

Business travelers tend to favor midtown, especially the moderately priced hotels lining Lexington Avenue near Grand Central Terminal.

Those seeking relative quiet with access to midtown should look in the Murray Hill area, while theater lovers should note the revival of the Times Square area. Hotels within walking distance of theaters offer an advantage, since performances tend to end at the same time and cabs are hard to come by.

There are a number of good, inexpensive hotels around Herald Square, which is convenient for shopping. The Upper West Side hotels are also less expensive. This popular residential area is convenient for Lincoln Center and offers easy access to public transportation.

The **New York Convention and Visitors Bureau** publishes a free, annually updated leaflet called "The New York Hotel Guide," listing current rates, toll-free numbers and fax numbers. Staff will offer advice about hotels but do not make reservations.

HOTEL PRICES

Some hotels offer seasonal promotional rates and other off-peak reductions. For example, business travelers vacate hotels at the end of the working week, and you can take advantage of bargain weekend deals, even in luxury hotels, as prices drop *(see Special Breaks p270)*. There is a growing number of all-suite hotels available in every price category. Suites offer extra space plus cooking facilities and a refrigerator. Most suites can accommodate up to four people, which makes them popular with families.

Café Botanica at the Essex House Hotel (see p277)

HIDDEN EXTRAS

When calculating the cost of hotels in New York, it is not enough simply to take into consideration the quoted room price. Hotel rooms have long been subject to extra taxes, but the former sliding scale, which favored rates under $100, has now given way to a blanket 13.25% hotel tax, plus $2 per night per room fee.

Several hotels now include continental breakfast in the room price. This is a big

Lobby phones, to reach a guest staying in the hotel.

Suite at the Millennium *(see p278)*

saving, since standard hotel continental breakfast prices, before tax and tip, start at about $5 and soar to around $15 in some of the luxury hotels. To save money, head for the nearest deli or coffee shop and leave the hotel to business people having power breakfasts.

Hotel telephone charges are always high; it is much less expensive to use the pay phone in the lobby, particularly when you are calling overseas.

Tips are expected. Staff who take your luggage to the room are usually tipped a minimum of $1 per bag – more in a luxury hotel. The concierge need not be tipped for normal services such as arranging transportation or making dinner reservations, but should be rewarded for exceptional services.

When you order from room service, check the menu to see whether a service charge will also be included in the bill; if not, a 15% tip is customary. Solo travelers will find that single room rates are usually

at least 80% of the double rate and are sometimes the same as for two people.

FACILITIES

ALTHOUGH you'd expect hotel rooms in New York City to be noisy, most windows are double- or even triple-glazed to keep out the noise. Air-conditioning is a standard feature, so there is no need to open the windows in hot weather. Even so, some rooms are obviously quieter than others, if they are at the back of the hotel or overlooking a courtyard – check when reserving.

Television, radio and at least one telephone are usually provided in every room, even in modest lodgings, and most hotel bedrooms have private bathrooms. In budget and

mid-priced hotels a shower, rather than a tub is the norm. Many mid-range hotels now offer fax outlets and machines in each room, a health club or exercise room and a full concierge service. Luxury facilities include mini-bars in the room, dual phones, private phone message systems and electronic checkout.

The hotels listed here are all within a few minutes' walk of a large number of shops and restaurants. Very few hotels have their own parking, but valets may park your car in areas reserved for guests' use in nearby garages. A reduced (but still expensive) daily parking fee is normally offered. If there is no concierge at the hotel, front desk staff will be able to help with tourist information and to answer any queries.

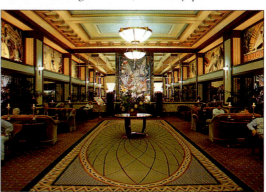

The Art Deco lobby of the Edison Hotel *(see p276)*

DIRECTORY

TOURIST OFFICE

New York Convention and Visitors Bureau
810 7th Ave, NY, NY 10019. **Map** 12 E4.
📞 484-1222. Publications available at JFK Airport.
🌐 www.nycvisit.com

SUITE HOTELS

Manhattan East Suite Hotels
One reservation number serves all of the following suite hotels:

📞 465-3690.
🌐 www.mesuite.com

Beekman Tower
3 Mitchell Pl. **Map** 13 C5.

Dumont Plaza
150 E 34th St. **Map** 9 A2.

Eastgate Tower
222 E 39th St. **Map** 9 B1.

Lyden Gardens
215 E 64th St. **Map** 13 B2.

Lyden House
320 E 53rd St. **Map** 13 B4.

Plaza Fifty
155 E 50th St. **Map** 13 B4.

Shelburne–Murray Hill
303 Lexington Ave.
Map 9 A2.

Southgate Tower
371 7th Ave. **Map** 8 E3.

Surrey
20 E 76th St. **Map** 17 A5.

RESERVATION AGENCIES

Assured Accommodations
Suite 714, 225 Lafayette St, NY, NY 10012. **Map** 4 F2.
📞 431-0569.
FAX 431-7088.
🌐 www.assurednyc.com

Hotel Reservations A Meegan Services
JFK International Airport, Jamaica, NY 11430.

📞 (718) 995-9292.
FAX (718) 917-6278.

DISCOUNT RESERVATION SERVICE

Express
📞 (303) 440-8481.
FAX (303) 440-0166.
🌐 www.express-res.com

Hotel con-x-ions
📞 840-8686.
FAX 221-8686. 🌐
www.hotelconxions.com

Quikbook
📞 840-8686.
🌐 www.quikbook.com

How to Reserve

IT IS ADVISABLE to make hotel reservations at least one month in advance. While it's unlikely that the hotel will be fully booked, you may well find that the best rooms and suites have been taken, especially if a major convention is taking place. The busiest periods are at Easter, the New York Marathon week in late October or early November, Thanksgiving and Christmas.

Reserve directly with the hotel by telephone, letter or fax. Written confirmation of your telephone booking will be required, probably with a deposit as a guarantee of your arrival; any cancellation fees may be deducted from this. You can pay by credit card, international bank draft or money order, or US traveler's check. Advise the staff if you are going to arrive at the hotel after 6pm or you will lose your reservation, unless you have prepaid with a credit card.

You can also book a hotel through your travel agent or airline. Most hotels have a toll-free telephone number for use in the United States, but these numbers do not work from Europe and the UK. If the hotel is part of an international chain, an affiliated hotel in your country should be able to reserve a room for you.

Special Rates

HOTELS ARE BUSIEST during the week, when business travelers are in the city, so most of them offer budget packages to encourage more weekend business. It's often possible to move from a standard to a luxury room for the weekend at the same rate.

A lower corporate rate is usually available to employees of large companies. Quite often, reservation clerks will grant corporate discounts on request without asking for a company affiliation.

Some reservation agencies offer discount rates. A good travel agent should be able to get the best current rates, but compare prices by contacting directly a discount reservation service such as Express or Quikbook *(see p269)*, which offers discounts between 20% and 50%, depending on the time of year. You reserve by credit card and receive a voucher, which you present to the hotel.

Lobby of the St. Regis Hotel *(see p278)*

Package tours can also provide savings on the usual price. These rates may not oblige you to stay with a tour group, only to use their air and hotel arrangements. These packages may also include airport transfers, an additional saving. Airlines frequently have their own special deals, particularly during slow travel seasons. Again, a knowledgeable travel agent should be able to tell you the current best deals, but newspapers often advertise special, limited offers that can be booked directly. At off-peak times you may net even bigger savings than with the package plans.

DISABLED TRAVELERS

BY LAW, NEW hotels must provide facilities for disabled visitors, and many older buildings have been renovated to comply, too. Guide dogs are allowed in most hotels, but it is advisable to check when reserving.

This guide's disabled access information is based upon each hotel's own assessment of its suitability. Let the hotel know of any specific needs when booking. The **Mayor's Office for People With Disabilities** also offers information about hotels.

TRAVELING WITH CHILDREN

AMERICAN HOTELS generally have a very welcoming attitude toward children. Cots or cribs and lists of baby-sitters are normally widely available, and most hotel restaurants are happy to cater to young guests.

Traveling with children can be cheaper than anticipated. Many hotels do not charge for children if they stay in their parents' room, or make only a small charge for an extra bed. There is usually a limit of one or two children per room in these cases, and most hotels stipulate that the children must be under a certain age, often 12. Parents of older children are expected to pay the full price, although the age limit is occasionally extended to 18. Ask about family rates when reserving.

BED-AND-BREAKFAST

THERE IS AN increasing number of bed-and-breakfast accommodations to be had in private apartments. This varies from a room in an apartment with an owner-host in residence to an entire apartment to yourself, with its own kitchen and bathroom, yours while the owner is away.

Staying in a private apartment enables you to feel at home in a New York neighborhood and to visit local restaurants, usually far more reasonably priced than

Entrance to the Peninsula Hotel *(see p281)*

those in tourist areas. Bed-and-breakfast lodgings can be found through many free booking services. Some booking agencies have a two-night minimum. Rates for unhosted apartments vary from about $70 to $200, and for a double room range from $60 to $90 a night, depending on whether you have a private bathroom. There is a wide range of apartments, from spacious and luxurious to cramped and dowdy. Your costs will rise if the address is remote, requiring frequent cabs. Ask about location and amenities when you reserve.

YOUTH AND BUDGET ACCOMMODATIONS

A YOUTH HOSTEL and many YMCA dormitories offer lodgings for those on a tight budget. For the longer-term visitor, the **92nd Street Y**, a nonsectarian hostel and lively cultural center situated in the Upper East Side, has good-value rooms from about $30 to $50 a night.

There are no campsites in Manhattan, and, sadly, youth hostels are not as prevalent in New York as they are in large European cities.

Sky-high swimming pool at a luxury hotel

Choosing a Hotel

THESE HOTELS have been selected across a wide price range for their good value, facilities, and location; they are listed area by area, starting with Lower Manhattan and moving on to hotels farther outside the city. Within each area, the hotels are listed by price category, from the least expensive to the most expensive. For map references, see pages 388–409.

		CREDIT CARDS	NUMBER OF ROOMS	RESTAURANT	AIR CONDITIONING	QUIET LOCATION

LOWER MANHATTAN

EMBASSY SUITES NEW YORK W www.embassysuites.com $$$
102 North End Ave., NY, NY 10281. **Map** 1 A2. 212-945-0100. FAX 212-945-3012.
This all-suite hotel towers over Battery Park City, just steps from the World Trade Center. Large, comfortable accommodation boasts high-speed internet connection. Modern art dresses up the chain-standard design. Harbor views and discounted weekend rates.
AE DC JCB MC V | 463 | ● | ▦ | ●

HOLIDAY INN WALL STREET W www.holidayinnwsd.com $$$
15 Gold St., NY, NY 10038. **Map** 2 D2. 212-232-7800. FAX 212-269-9569.
Wall Street's most technologically mature hotel was designed with business travelers in mind. Standard features include a desk and personal computer with CD/DVD drive, fax/copier/color printer, ergonomic chair, portable phones, even supplies like paper clips. SMART rooms feature laptops. Good buffet breakfast.
AE DC JCB MC V | 138 | ● | ▦

REGENT WALL STREET W www.regenthotels.com $$$$$
55 Wall St., NY, NY 10005. **Map** 1 C3. 212-845-8600. FAX 212-845-8601.
The Financial District's finest hotel occupies a stunning 1842 Greek Revival building. The grand Neoclassical interiors have been beautifully preserved and smartly updated. With gorgeous, amenity-laden rooms, facilities include an excellent spa. Weekend rates are a bargain.
AE DC JCB MC V | 144 | ● | ▦ | ●

SOHO AND TRIBECA

COSMOPOLITAN HOTEL – TRIBECA W www.cosmohotel.com $
95 W. Broadway, NY, NY 10007. **Map** 1 B1. 212-566-1900. FAX 212-566-6909.
In the heart of hip TriBeCa is one of Manhattan's best budget hotels. Rooms are petite but well maintained and pleasantly furnished; with tiny but pristine bathrooms. The location is super-convenient, and a wealth of first-rate restaurants are within walking distance. Highly recommended.
AE DC JCB MC V | 113 | | ▦

HOLIDAY INN DOWNTOWN/SOHO W www.holiday-inn.com $$$
138 Lafayette St., NY, NY 10013. **Map** 4 F5. 212-966-8898. FAX 212-966-3933.
The hotel itself is nothing special, but travelers with an eye for trends will love the bustling edge-of-Chinatown location. Boutique-lined SoHo is just steps away, as is Nolita, downtown's hip neighborhood of the moment. Rooms are rather bland but comfortable enough. A well-regarded Cantonese restaurant is on site.
AE DC JCB MC V | 227 | ● | ▦

60 THOMPSON W www.60thompson.com $$$$
60 Thompson St., NY, NY 10012. **Map** 4 D4. 212-431-0400. FAX 212-431-0200.
Despite its chic modernist lines, this smallish newcomer boasts a warm, and surprisingly domestic, ambiance. Done in a soothing celadon-and-mahogany palette, rooms are plush and well equipped, with DVD and CD players, Internet access, and marble baths. Location is first rate.
AE DC JCB MC V | 100 | ● | ▦

TRIBECA GRAND HOTEL W www.tribecagrand.com $$$$$
2 Sixth Ave., NY, NY 10013. **Map** 3 E5. 212-519-6600. FAX 212-519-6700.
Smart design is the key at this chic luxury hotel just south of SoHo. Sumptuous textiles, clean-lined custom furnishings, and cutting-edge technology unite luxury and utility in the ultra-modern rooms. A soaring central atrium is home to a celebrity-studded lounge scene.
AE DC JCB MC V | 203 | ● | ▦

LOWER EAST SIDE

OFF SOHO SUITES HOTEL W www.offsoho.com $
11 Rivington St., NY, NY 10002. **Map** 5 A3. 212-979-9808. FAX 212-979-9801.
It used to be that this budget hotel was in no-man's-land – but hip downtown has expanded so much as to practically embrace it. Decor is nonexistent and beds are a bit too firm, but rooms are well tended. Deluxe suites have a fully outfitted kitchen and bath, while economy suites share facilities.
AE DC JCB MC V | 38 | ● | ▦

<table>
<thead>
<tr><th></th><th>Credit Cards</th><th>Number of Rooms</th><th>Restaurant</th><th>Air Conditioning</th><th>Quiet Location</th></tr>
</thead>
</table>

Price categories for a standard double room per night, inclusive of breakfast, service charges and any additional taxes such as VAT:

$ under $150
$$ $150–$250
$$$ $250–$350
$$$$ $350–$450
$$$$$ over $450

RESTAURANT
Hotel restaurant or dining room usually open to non-residents unless otherwise stated.

AIR CONDITIONING
In-room units or central AC.

QUIET LOCATION
Quiet residential location or quiet street in a busy area.

CREDIT CARDS
Indicates which credit cards are accepted: *AE* American Express; *DC* Diners Club; JCB; *MC* MasterCard/Access; *V* VISA.

EAST VILLAGE

ST. MARK'S HOTEL W www.stmarkshotel.qpg.com $
2 St. Mark's Place, NY, NY 10003. **Map** 4 F1. 212-674-2192. **FAX** 212-420-0854.
In a city where ancient carpet and dingy walls are the norm in budget hotels, this bright and clean hotel offers welcome relief. Oak-and-marble hallways lead to sparse but neat rooms with small bathrooms. Shop-lined St. Mark's Place features a constant parade of tattooed youth, so don't expect quiet.

Credit Cards: AE DC JCB MC V — *Number of Rooms:* 70 — *Air Conditioning*

UNION SQUARE INN W www.unionsquareinn.com $$
209 E. 14th St., NY, NY 10003. **Map** 4 F1. 212-614-0500. **FAX** 212-614-0512.
Here's a wonderful find for discerning travelers who want standard comforts at a reasonable price. Rooms are small but boast high-quality mattresses and brand-new bathrooms. There are no views and services are minimal, but the value is tops. A basic breakfast is included.

Credit Cards: AE DC JCB MC V — *Number of Rooms:* 40 — *Air Conditioning*

GREENWICH VILLAGE

ABINGDON GUEST HOUSE W www.abingdonguesthouse.com $$
13 Eighth Ave., NY, NY 10014. **Map** 3 C1. 212-243-5384. **FAX** 212-807-7473.
This absolutely lovely guest house is located in the brownstone-lined, boutique-dotted West Village, one of the city's most charming neighborhoods. Each artfully decorated room is outfitted with first-rate comforts. Best for independent-minded travelers, since there is no resident innkeeper. No breakfast included, but a coffee bar is downstairs.

Credit Cards: AE DC JCB MC V — *Number of Rooms:* 9 — *Air Conditioning*

WASHINGTON SQUARE HOTEL W www.wshotel.com $$
103 Waverly Place, NY, NY 10011. **Map** 4 D2. 212-777-9515. **FAX** 212-979-8373.
This hotel faces Washington Square Park in the heart of New York University territory. A surprisingly smart marble lobby leads to small but recently freshened rooms. Rates are a bit high, but the bustling location is great for bar-hoppers and live-music fans. The restaurant is very good.

Credit Cards: AE DC JCB MC V — *Number of Rooms:* 170 — *Restaurant* — *Air Conditioning*

GRAMERCY & THE FLATIRON DISTRICT

HOTEL 17 W www.hotel17.citysearch.com $
225 E. 17th St., NY, NY 10003. **Map** 9 B5. 212-475-2845. **FAX** 212-677-8178.
A hip reputation belies this budget hotel's essential austerity. Rooms are tiny, dark, and basic, with a TV, sink, and hairdryer rounding out the amenities. Still, the location and the price are right. Weekly rates are a bargain. Best for young travelers.

Credit Cards: AE DC JCB MC V — *Number of Rooms:* 160 — *Air Conditioning*

MURRAY HILL INN W www.murrayhillinn.com $
143 E. 30th St., NY, NY 10016. **Map** 9 A3. 212-683-6900. **FAX** 212-545-0103.
Rooms are small, simple, and utterly unstylish, but this well-managed walk-up hotel overflows with good value. Rooms with private bathrooms are nicest, but shared bathrooms (spotless) are fine for shoestring travelers.

Credit Cards: AE DC JCB MC V — *Number of Rooms:* 50 — *Air Conditioning* — *Quiet Location*

GERSHWIN HOTEL W www.gershwinhotel.com $$
7 E. 27th St., NY, NY 10016. **Map** 8 F3. 212-545-8000. **FAX** 212-684-5546.
This Andy Warhol-inspired hotel sets a postmodern tone with lipstick colors, cartoonish furniture, and remarkably high-quality pop art. Rooms are attractive, bright, and stylishly outfitted.

Credit Cards: AE DC JCB MC V — *Number of Rooms:* 121 — *Restaurant* — *Air Conditioning*

GRAMERCY PARK HOTEL W www.gramercyparkhotel.com $$
2 Lexington Ave., NY, NY 10010. **Map** 9 A4. 212-475-4320. **FAX** 212-505-0535.
Huge rooms and an appealing old-world ambiance are the keynotes here. Accommodation is stuck in the 1970s, but even standard rooms are large enough for families; suites and park-view rooms have small kitchenettes. An extra-special amenity: guests have access to Gramercy Park, off-limits to everyone else save a few area residents.

Credit Cards: AE DC JCB MC V — *Number of Rooms:* 509 — *Restaurant* — *Air Conditioning* — *Quiet Location*

For key to symbols see back flap

Price categories for a standard double room per night, inclusive of breakfast, service charges and any additional taxes such as VAT:

$ under $150
$$ $150–$250
$$$ $250–$350
$$$$ $350–$450
$$$$$ over $450

RESTAURANT
Hotel restaurant or dining room usually open to non-residents unless otherwise stated.

AIR CONDITIONING
In-room units or central AC.

QUIET LOCATION
Quiet residential location or quiet street in a busy area.

CREDIT CARDS
Indicates which credit cards are accepted: *AE* American Express; *DC* Diners Club; JCB; *MC* MasterCard/Access; *V* Visa.

	CREDIT CARDS	NUMBER OF ROOMS	RESTAURANT	AIR CONDITIONING	QUIET LOCATION
QUALITY HOTEL EASTSIDE W www.applecorehotels.com $$ 161 Lexington Ave., NY, NY 10016. **Map** 9 A3. 212-545-1800. **FAX** 212-790-2760. This unremarkable hotel is notable for its better-than-budget facilities and often heavily discounted rates. Rooms are small and spartan. Always ask for a better rate – if you're quoted more than $175, stay elsewhere. 🔲 1 TV 📶 🍽 🔲 ♿	AE DC JCB MC V	95		■	
THIRTY THIRTY W www.thirtythirty-nyc.com $$ 30 E. 30th St., NY, NY 10016. **Map** 9 A3. 212-689-1900. **FAX** 212-689-0023. This stylish hotel is ideal for travelers who want a great value and a dash of panache. A sleek lobby leads to small but comfortable rooms that boast smart modern decor. A good number of twin-bedded rooms are available, and a few larger rooms have kitchenettes. 🔲 1 TV 📶 🍽	AE DC JCB MC V	240		■	
ROGER WILLIAMS HOTEL W www.rogerwilliamshotel.com $$$ 131 Madison Ave., NY, NY 10016. **Map** 9 A3. *212-448-7000.* **FAX** *212-448-7007.* This stylish hotel boasts attractive rooms with blond-wood, modern furnishings, VCRs, and CD players. A great staff and a wealth of free goodies – continental breakfast, all-day serve-yourself cappuccino and cookies, video and CD lending – makes it even more attractive. 🔲 🔲 TV 📶 🍽 🔲 ♿	AE DC JCB MC V	200		■	
HOTEL GIRAFFE W www.hotelgiraffe.com $$$$ 365 Park Ave. South, NY, NY 10016. **Map** 9 A4. 212-685-7700. **FAX** 212-685-7701. The Flatiron District's finest hotel brims with inspired elegance – rich textiles and custom furnishings. Amenities include CD players and granite bathrooms; deluxe rooms have French doors onto a juliet balcony. Complimentary breakfast, plus a stylish Euro-Asian fusion restaurant. 🔲 🔲 TV 📶 🍽 🔲 ♿	AE DC JCB MC V	73	●	■	
INN AT IRVING PLACE W www.innatirving.com $$$$ 56 Irving Place, NY, NY 10003. **Map** 9 A5. 212-533-4600. **FAX** 212-533-4611. This impeccably run ultra-Victorian inn, housed in adjoining brownstones, is outfitted in high period style. Each room boasts high-quality antiques and a beautiful bathroom, plus VCR and CD player. Complimentary breakfast is served in the salon, which also presents the city's best high tea. 🔲 🔲 TV 📶 🍽	AE DC JCB MC V	12	●	■	●

CHELSEA & THE GARMENT DISTRICT

	CREDIT CARDS	NUMBER OF ROOMS	RESTAURANT	AIR CONDITIONING	QUIET LOCATION
AMERICANA INN W www.newyorkhotel.com $ 69 W. 38th St., NY, NY 10018. **Map** 8 F1. 212-840-6700. **FAX** 212-840-1830. Linoleum floors lend an institutional feel, but otherwise this is a winner in the budget-basic price category. Rooms – which have private sinks – and baths are bright and spotless. The location is central, and the friendly, professional service is of a higher caliber than most in this price range. 1 🔲 TV 📶 🍽 ♿	AE DC JCB MC V	50		■	
CHELSEA INTERNATIONAL HOSTEL W www.chelseahostel.com $ 251 W. 20th St., NY, NY 10011. **Map** 8 D5. 212-647-0010. **FAX** 212-727-7289. A warren of low-rise buildings framing a central square comprise one of the city's best hostels. Private doubles and dorm beds are available. Facilities include two well-equipped kitchens, TV lounges, and laundry machines. The trendy neighborhood makes an excellent base. 1	AE DC JCB MC V	57			
CHELSEA LODGE W www.chelsealodge.com $ 318 W. 20th St., NY, NY 10011. **Map** 8 D5. 212-243-4499. **FAX** 212-243-7852. A beautifully restored townhouse in the Chelsea Historic District hides this delightful budget hotel. A private sink and stall shower are in the room, so guests only have to share toilets. The impeccably maintained rooms are small but overflow with country charm. A real find! 🔲 1 TV 📶	AE DC JCB MC V	22		■	
COLONIAL HOUSE INN W www.colonialhouseinn.com $ 318 W. 22nd St., NY, NY 10011. **Map** 8 D4. 212-243-9669. **FAX** 212-633-1612. This lovely brownstone caters to a gay crowd but welcomes everybody. Rooms are small and simple but nicely maintained; almost half have private baths, and a few have working fireplaces. Continental breakfast is included. 🔲 1 TV	AE DC JCB MC V	20		■	

Hotel Wolcott ⓦ www.wolcott.com $
4 W. 31st St., NY, NY 10001. **Map** 8 F3. ☎ 212-268-2900. **FAX** 212-563-0096.
Extensive facilities, large rooms, and low rates make this a good option for
value-conscious travelers, especially families. Rooms are plain but fine;
internet access on your TV is a bonus for those who use email. The staff is
helpful, and there are coin-operated laundry machines. 🖼 🗄 📺 ⬆ ☂ 🚻 ⛨

| | AE DC JCB MC V | 250 | | ▪ | |

Chelsea Inn ⓦ www.chelseainn.com $$
46 W. 17th St., NY, NY 10011. **Map** p 8 F5. ☎ 212-645-8989. **FAX** 212-645-1903.
Two 19th-century brownstones house an eclectic mix of rooms and suites,
about two-thirds of which have private bathrooms. Mix-and-match furnishings
and well-worn textiles add a tenement feel, but everything is clean. Rooms
with shared bath often price around $100. 🗄 📺

| | AE DC JCB MC V | 26 | | ▪ | |

Chelsea Savoy Hotel ⓦ www.chelseasavoy.qpg.com $$
204 W. 23rd St., NY, NY 10011. **Map** 8 E4. ☎ 212-929-9353. **FAX** 212-741-6309.
This modern hotel has won a committed clientele with its generic but consistent comforts. Built from scratch a few years back, its hallways are wide,
rooms pleasant. Rates include continental breakfast. 🖼 ① 🗄 📺 ⬆ ☂ 🚻 ♿

| | AE DC JCB MC V | 90 | | ▪ | |

Comfort Inn Manhattan ⓦ www.comfortinnmanhattan.com $$
42 W. 35th St., NY, NY 10001. **Map** 8 F2. ☎ 212-947-0200. **FAX** 212-594-3047.
Recently bestowed with a hospitality award for outstanding service by its head
office, this characterless but reliably comfortable chain hotel is just a few
strides from the Empire State Building and other major midtown attractions.
Rooms are well-kept, nicely appointed, and remarkably large by city
standards. Rates include continental breakfast. 🖼 🗄 📺 ⬆ ☂ 🚻

| | AE DC JCB MC V | 131 | ● | ▪ | |

Hotel Chelsea ⓦ www.hotelchelsea.com $$
222 W. 23rd St., NY, NY 10011. **Map** 8 E4. ☎ 212-243-3700. **FAX** 212-675-5531.
This legendary artists' haven has housed famous names from Sandra
Bernhardt to Sid Vicious, who killed girlfriend Nancy Spungen here in a
seminal moment of punk history. About 100 rooms are available to short-term
visitors with a bohemian spirit. Rooms are large and eccentrically outfitted
with generally older furnishings. 🖼 ① 🗄 📺 ⬆ ☂

| | AE DC JCB MC V | 400 | ● | ▪ | |

Hotel Metro ⓦ www.hotelmetronyc.com $$
45 W. 35th St., NY, NY 10001. **Map** 8 F2. ☎ 212-947-2500. **FAX** 212-279-1310.
This Art Deco delight is midtown's best mid-priced hotel. Rooms are larger
and much more attractive than most in this price range, and comforts are first-
rate. The restaurant is very good, rates include breakfast, and the roof terrace
boasts views of the Empire State Building. Excellent for families. 🖼 🗄 📺 ⬆
☂ 🚻 ♿

| | AE DC JCB MC V | 179 | ● | ▪ | |

Inn on 23rd ⓦ www.bbonline.com/ny/innon23rd $$
131 W. 23rd St., NY, NY 10011. **Map** 8 E4. ☎ 212-463-0330. **FAX** 212-463-0302.
This wonderful inn offers a just-right blend of bed-and-breakfast charm and
real-hotel amenities. Rooms and suites are impeccably outfitted, including
pillowtop beds and plush Turkish terry towels in the bathrooms. The
innkeepers serve a generous continental breakfast. 🖼 🗄 📺 ⬆ ☂ ♿

| | AE DC JCB MC V | 11 | | ▪ | |

Red Roof Inn ⓦ www.redroof.com $$
6 W. 32nd St., NY, NY 10001. **Map** 8 F3. ☎ h 212-643-7100. **FAX** 212-643-7101.
This premier urban outpost of the middle-America motel chain is a rousing
success thanks to comfortable, freshly outfitted rooms and professional
service. On-screen internet access is a bonus. It is located in a safe, bustling
block, lined with affordable Korean restaurants and convenient to sightseeing
and shopping. Rates include breakfast. 🖼 🗄 📺 ⬆ ☂ 🍸 🚻 ⛨ 🚻 ♿

| | AE DC JCB MC V | 172 | | ▪ | |

Holiday Inn/Martinique on Broadway ⓦ www.holiday-inn.com $$$
49 W. 32nd St., NY, NY 10001. **Map** 8 F3. ☎ 212-736-3800. **FAX** 212-277-2703.
This fine branch of the reliable Holiday Inn chain is housed in a landmark
French-Renaissance building. Rooms are chain standard once you move past the
marble lobby. The Little Korea location offers affordable Asian dining at all
hours. Rates are high, so ask for discounts. 🖼 🗄 📺 ⬆ ☂ 🍸 🍸 🚻 ⛨ 🚻 ♿

| | AE DC JCB MC V | 532 | ● | ▪ | |

THEATER DISTRICT

Big Apple Hostel ⓦ www.bigapplehostel.com $
119 W. 45th St., New York, NY 10036 **Map** 12 E5 ☎ 212-302-2603 **FAX** 212-302-2605
New York's best hostel caters to a world of young travelers with super-clean
accommodation and a prime location. Most beds are in dormitories, but a few
private doubles are available. Everything is newer and nicer than at most
hostels. Book well in advance. ① 🗄 ⬆

| | AE DC JCB MC V | 39 | | | |

Price categories for a standard double room per night, inclusive of breakfast, service charges and any additional taxes such as VAT:

$ under $150
$$ $150–$250
$$$ $250–$350
$$$$ $350–$450
$$$$$ over $450

RESTAURANT
Hotel restaurant or dining room usually open to non-residents unless otherwise stated.

AIR CONDITIONING
In room units or central AC.

QUIET LOCATION
Quiet residential location or quiet street in a busy area.

CREDIT CARDS
Indicates which credit cards are accepted: *AE* American Express; *DC* Diners Club; *JCB*; *MC* MasterCard/Access; *V* Visa.

	Credit Cards	Number of Rooms	Restaurant	Air Conditioning	Quiet Location
PARK SAVOY HOTEL $ 158 W. 58th St., New York, NY 10019 Map 12 E3 *h* 212-245-5755 FAX 212-765-0668 This plain-Jane hotel offers basic accommodation in an excellent location: the best part of midtown, a block from Central Park. Rooms are spartan and not well maintained, but everything is clean. Some are big enough to accommodate four. The front desk is friendly but keeps service to a minimum.	AE DC JCB MC V	70		■	
BELVEDERE HOTEL W www.newyorkhotel.com $$ 319 W. 48th St., New York, NY 10036 Map 12 D5 *C* 212-245-7000 FAX 212-245-4455 This pleasing mid-range hotel is much smarter than most hotels in this price category and area. Rooms are good-sized, comfortable, and attractive. On site is a festive and hugely popular Brazilian steakhouse, but good restaurants abound in the area. A good choice for families.	AE DC JCB MC V	400	●	■	
BEST WESTERN PRESIDENT HOTEL W www.bestwestern.com $$ 234 W. 48th St., New York, NY 10036 Map 12 E5 *C* 212-632-9000 FAX 212-974-3922 This well-run chain hotel boasts small but just-fine rooms in a good location. Executive rooms feature a large desk and a new bathroom, but standard rooms do the job for most. Junior suites have a fold-out sofa for children. Two high-priced penthouse suites seem totally out of place.	AE DC JCB MC V	334	●	■	
BROADWAY INN W www.broadwayinn.com $$ 264 W. 46th St., New York, NY 10036 Map 12 D5 *C* 212-997-9200 FAX 212-768-2807 Part B&B, part hotel, the Broadway Inn is a haven of tranquility and good taste in the heart of the Theater District. Rooms are simply but tastefully decorated with an Art-Deco flair. Breakfast is served in the charming library-style sitting room. Service is unparalleled in this price category.	AE DC JCB MC V	41		■	
COMFORT INN MIDTOWN W www.comfortinn.com $$ 129 W. 46th St., New York, NY 10036 Map 12 E5 *C* 212-221-2600 FAX 212-790-2760 A recent renovation has transformed a formerly dour hotel into an attractive mid-priced option in a prime location. A marble-and-mahogany lobby leads to petite but pleasant guestrooms that have cheerful Americana-style decor; they are best suited to two travelers at most.	AE DC JCB MC V	79		■	
DAYS HOTEL MIDTOWN W www.daysinn.com $$ 790 Eighth Ave., New York, NY 10019 Map 12 D5 *C* 212-581-7000 FAX 212-974-0291 The tone is generic at this somewhat institutional hotel. The value is best when rates are $125 or lower. A decent New York-style coffee shop/deli is on site, and good affordable restaurants abound.	AE DC JCB MC V	367	●	■	
HOTEL EDISON W www.edisonhotelnyc.com $$ 228 W. 47th St., New York, NY 10036 Map 12 E5 *C* 212-840-5000 FAX 212-596-6850 This mammoth hotel has raised rates too high to qualify as a bargain, but it continues to be a good choice for travelers who want a comfortable room in a prime location. Quad rooms suit families well. Facilities include a cheap and perennially popular coffee shop/deli.	AE DC JCB MC V	850	●	■	
HUDSON W www.hudsonhotel.com or www.ianschragerhotels.com $$ 356 W. 58th St., New York, NY 10019 Map 12 D3 *C* 212-554-6000 FAX 212-554-6000 This creation from the Ian Schrager/Philippe Starck team brims with riotous, eye-popping design. Rooms are beautiful but tiny – best for those who value style and scene over space. Public spaces often overflow with revelers. Expect more in the way of attitude than service.	AE DC JCB MC V	1000	●	■	
MAYFAIR HOTEL W www.mayfairnewyork.com $$ 242 W. 49th St., New York, NY 10019 Map 12 D5 *C* 212-586-0300 FAX 212-307-5226 Beware – rooms are miniscule at the Mayfair. But they're also comfortable and modern, service is extra-friendly, and the location is prime for theatergoing. Rates climb too high in the fall, but rooms are excellent value until then. The French bistro is worth enjoying even if you don't stay.	AE DC JCB MC V	78	●	■	

WYNDHAM $$
42 W. 58th St., New York, NY 10019 Map 12 F3 [212-753-3500 FAX 212-754-5638
Extra-large rooms at low, low prices. The individually decorated rooms and suites swing wildly between tacky and gorgeous, but they're all well maintained. The location (near Fifth Avenue and Central Park) is stellar.

AE DC JCB MC V | 212

ALGONQUIN W www.algonquinhotel.com $$$
59 W. 44th St., NY, NY 10036. Map 12 F5. [212-840-6800. FAX 212-944-1419.
This fully restored legend – home to Dorothy Parker's literary "Round Table" of the 1920s – is one of Midtown's most evocative hotels. Rooms are smallish but comfortable; the literary-themed suites make a worthy splurge. Off the glorious mahogany-paneled lobby – still ideal for socializing – is the Oak Room for star-quality cabaret.

AE DC JCB MC V | 165

CASABLANCA HOTEL W www.casablancahotel.com $$$
147 W. 43rd St., New York, NY 10036 Map 8 E1 [212-869-1212 FAX 212-391-7585
This stylish, Moroccan-themed hotel is enchanting – and the location is ideal for theatergoers. Rooms are not large, but are nicely outfitted in polished rattan and boast high-quality details. Breakfast and all-day cappuccino are served in the fireplace lounge.

AE DC JCB MC V | 48

DOUBLETREE GUEST SUITES W www.nyc.doubletreehotels.com $$$
1568 Broadway, New York, NY 10036 Map 12 E5 [212-719-1600 FAX 212-921-5212
This all-suite hotel towing over Times Square more than compensates for its lack of personality with first-rate facilities and a central location. Some suites are designed for families, others are ideally suited to business travelers. A "Kids Club" playroom adds to the family appeal.

AE DC JCB MC V | 400

GORHAM W www.gorhamhotel.com $$$
136 W. 55th St., New York, NY 10019 Map 12 E4 [212-245-1800 FAX 212-582-8332
Excellent package deals – often including Broadway show tickets – regularly make this good value even better. The spacious rooms are well appointed and have kitchenettes. Suites are well priced, but two queen beds make even standard rooms large enough for families.

AE DC JCB MC V | 115

HILTON TIMES SQUARE W www.timessquare.hilton.com $$$
234 W. 42nd St., New York, NY 10036 Map 8 E1 [212-840-8222 FAX 212-840-5516
This Hilton surpasses its chain-hotel status with larger-than-standard rooms and a sophisticated air throughout. Rooms don't begin until the 23rd floor, so they're quiet despite the location. A pleasing restaurant from famous-name chef Larry Forgione adds to the appeal.

AE DC JCB MC V | 444

MANSFIELD W www.mansfieldhotel.com $$$
12 W. 44th St., New York, NY 10036 Map 12 E5 [212-944-6050 FAX 212-764-4477
This 1905 hotel fuses romance and modernism in rooms that are smallish but very inviting. Natural-fiber rugs cover ebony-stained floors and sleighbeds wear Belgian linens. All-day cappuccino included.

AE DC JCB MC V | 124

PARAMOUNT W www.ianschragerhotels.com $$$
235 W. 46th St., New York, NY 10036 Map 12 D5 [212-764-5500 FAX 212-354-5237
Hotelier Ian Schrager set the high design/low price standard here a decade ago, and it's still going strong. The miniscule rooms are all whites and grays, with compact stainless-steel bath and gilt-framed classic work doubling as art and headboard. Weekend rates often hover around $150.

AE DC JCB MC V | 618

SOFITEL NEW YORK W www.sofitel.com $$$
45 W. 44th St., New York, NY Map 12 F5 [212-354-8844 FAX 212-782-3002
This smart hotel is a welcome addition to the Theater District, with its dramatic blend of classic and modern. Rooms are spacious and beautifully designed; thoughtful touches include soft lighting and soundproofing. Executive suites have an excellent work area, plus terraces in some.

AE DC JCB MC V | 398

ESSEX HOUSE – A WESTIN HOTEL W www.westin.com $$$$
160 Central Park South, New York, NY 10019 Map 12 E3 [212-247-0300 FAX 212-315-1839
This ornate tower overlooking Central Park sparkles in full Art-Deco splendor. The reason to stay is the Westin Heavenly Bed, offering a genuinely celestial sleeping experience. Alain Ducasse (see p295) is one of New York's most coveted restaurant reservations.

AE DC JCB MC V | 600

LE PARKER MERIDIEN W www.parkermeridien.com $$$$
118 W. 57th St., New York, NY 10019 Map 12 E3 [212-245-5000 FAX 212-708-1776
The rooms here are modern, attractive, and functional, and facilities are excellent: two terrific restaurants, a creative cocktail bar, and one of the best hotel gyms in town (with spa services).

AE DC JCB MC V | 731

<table>
<tr><td colspan="3">
Price categories for a standard double room per night, inclusive of breakfast, service charges and any additional taxes such as VAT:

$ under $150
$$ $150–$250
$$$ $250–$350
$$$$ $350–$450
$$$$$ over $450
</td></tr>
</table>

RESTAURANT
Hotel restaurant or dining room usually open to non-residents unless otherwise stated.

AIR CONDITIONING
In-room units or central AC.

QUIET LOCATION
Quiet residential location or quiet street in a busy area.

CREDIT CARDS
Indicates which credit cards are accepted: *AE* American Express; *DC* Diners Club; JCB; *MC* MasterCard/Access; *V* Visa.

	CREDIT CARDS	NUMBER OF ROOMS	RESTAURANT	AIR CONDITIONING	QUIET LOCATION

MICHELANGELO W www.summithotels.com $$$$
152 W. 51st St., New York, NY 10019 **Map** 12 F4 📞 212-765-1900 **FAX** 212-541-6604
This elegant hotel exudes Italian style, from the Vivaldi in the lobby to the Baci chocolates at bedtime. Each oversized room is warmly dressed in either Art Deco, Neoclassical, or country French style; bathrooms have Italian marble.
AE DC JCB MC V — **178** ● ■

MILLENNIUM BROADWAY W www.millennium-hotels.com $$$$
145 W. 44th St., New York, NY 10036 **Map** 12 E5 📞 212-768-4400 **FAX** 212-768-0847
Large rooms are outfitted in a smart deco style with comfy club chairs. The real perks come in the Premier tower, whose designer rooms manage to be both sleek and cozy. Club-level and Premier rooms include breakfast and cocktails served in a private lounge.
AE DC JCB MC V — **752** ● ■

MUSE W www.themusehotel.com $$$$
130 W. 46th St., New York, NY 10036 **Map** 12 E5 📞 212-485-2400 **FAX** 212-485-2900
If you want the intimate tone and personal service of a boutique hotel without the hard-edged modern design that often accompanies it, check into this classic-meets-contemporary newcomer, where the emphasis is on comfort, functionality, and service.
AE DC JCB MC V — **200** ● ■

ROYALTON W www.ianschragerhotels.com $$$$
44 W. 44th St., New York, NY 10036 **Map** 12 F5 📞 212-869-4400 **FAX** 212-869-8965
This super-stylish hotel may be the best effort from hotel pioneer Ian Schrager. An fashionable lounge scene occupies the lobby. Rooms are gorgeously designed on a loose cruise-ship theme (white cotton, mahogany, slate) complete with porthole windows.
AE DC JCB MC V — **205** ● ■

TIME W www.thetimeny.com $$$$
224 W. 49th St., New York, NY 10019 **Map** 12 D5 📞 212-320-2900 **FAX** 212-320-2926
Rooms are decorated in a black-and-cream Cubist scheme accented with one of three vivid colors: red, yellow, or blue. Rooms are efficient, but some are small. Rates are high, but specials are common.
AE DC JCB MC V — **200** ● ■

W TIMES SQUARE W www.whotels.com $$$$
1567 Broadway, New York, NY 10036 **Map** 12 E5 📞 212-407-2975 **FAX** 212-407-2975
Design-conscious travelers looking for a heart-of-Times Square location in addition to high style will enjoy this new addition to the fashionable "W" hotel chain.
AE DC JCB MC V — **562** ● ■

CHAMBERS W www.chambers-ahotel.com $$$$$
15 W. 56th St., New York, NY 10019 **Map** 12 F3 📞 212-974-5656 **FAX** 212-974-5657
Situated in the heart of midtown, this place radiates downtown style from tip to toe with a sleek urban vibe. Expect Tibetan rugs, cashmere throws, and mood-setting candles as well as cutting-edge art. Town restaurant has received excellent notices.
AE DC JCB MC V — **77** ● ■

RITZ-CARLTON, NEW YORK W www.ritzcarlton.com $$$$$
50 Central Park South, New York, NY 10019 **Map** 12 F3 📞 212-308-9100 **FAX** 212-877-6465
This reliable luxury chain's first midtown hotel debuts in 2002. Expect all of the classic Ritz-Carlton hallmarks, which blend traditional stylings and premier comforts: state-of-the-art technology, a full-service spa, and staff who never say "no."
AE DC JCB MC V — **287** ● ■

ST. REGIS NEW YORK W www.stregis.com $$$$$
2 E. 55th St., New York, NY 10022 **Map** 12 F4 📞 212-753-4500 **FAX** 212-787-3447
This Beaux-Arts jewel is awash in luxury: crystal chandeliers, oriental carpets, gilt-framed oils, Louis XIV antiques. Service is formal but impeccable. Lespinasse (*see p297*) is one of only a fistful of *New York Times* four-star-winning restaurants.
AE DC JCB MC V — **408** ● ■

LOWER MIDTOWN

HOTEL GRAND UNION W www.hotelgrandunion.com $
34 E. 32nd St., New York, NY 10016 **Map** 9 A3 212-683-5890 FAX 212-689-7397
The Grand Union is justifiably popular with value-minded travelers. Rooms
verge on ugly, but they boast all the required comforts, and the maintenance
level is very high. Some are large enough for families. The staff is more
helpful than most in this price range. ⛏ 1 🎫 TV ↻

| | AE DC JCB MC V | 95 | ● | ■ | |

CLARION HOTEL FIFTH AVENUE W www.hotelchoice.com $$$
3 E. 40th St., New York, NY 10016 **Map** 8 F1 212-447-1500 FAX 212-213-0972
This freshly renovated chain hotel offers excellent value in a busy neigh-
borhood. Rooms are outfitted in comfort with a hint of smart Art-Deco
style. The location – near New York Public Library and Grand Central
Terminal – is convenient for the Theater District but cleaner and quieter.
⛏ 🎫 TV ↻ 🍽 🍷 🔒 ♿

| | AE DC JCB MC V | 189 | ● | ■ | |

DUMONT PLAZA W www.mesuite.com $$$
150 E. 34th St., New York, NY 10016 **Map** 9 A2 212-481-7600 FAX 212-889-8856
This all-suite hotel is great for those who value space and comfort over high
style. Trappings include fully appointed kitchens with microwave (the staff
will even do your shopping). New in 2002 are executive workstations for
work-minded travelers. ⛏ 🎫 TV ↻ 🍽 🍷 🍴 🔒 🏋 ♿

| | AE DC JCB MC V | 248 | ● | ■ | |

DYLAN W www.dylanhotel.com $$$
52 E. 41st St., New York, NY 10017 **Map** p 9 A1 212-338-0500 FAX 212-338-0569
This recently unveiled boutique hotel prizes form over function a bit too
much. Still, rooms are spacious by city standards. The excellently reviewed
French restaurant Virot is appeal enough. ⛏ TV ↻ 🍽 🍷 🍴 🔒 ♿

| | AE DC JCB MC V | 197 | ● | ■ | |

LIBRARY HOTEL W www.libraryhotel.com $$$
299 Madison Ave., New York, NY 10017 **Map** 9 A1 212-983-4500 FAX 212-499-9099
The best among the bevy of new boutiques is this charmer, an understated
but beautiful haven. Each room boasts a unique theme, ranging from Fairy
Tales to Erotic Literature. Breakfast and all-day snacks are laid out in a cozy
lounge that doubles as – what else? – a well-stocked library. ⛏ TV ↻ 🍽 🍷 🔒

| | AE DC JCB MC V | 60 | ● | ■ | |

FITZPATRICK GRAND CENTRAL HOTEL W www.fitzpatrickhotels.com $$$$
141 E. 44th St., New York, NY 10017 **Map** 13 A5 212-351-6800 FAX 212-308-0572
This lovely hotel is steps from Grand Central Terminal. Rooms surpass the
business-hotel standard with luxury fabrics and colors, and half-canopied
beds. The Liam Neeson penthouse offers marble-adorned luxury. A genuine
pub is on site. ⛏ 24 TV ↻ 🍽 🍷 🔒

| | AE DC JCB MC V | 155 | ● | ■ | |

MORGANS W www.ianschragerhotels.com $$$$
237 Madison Ave., New York, NY 10016 **Map** 9 A2 212-686-0300 FAX 212-779-8352
Opened in 1984, Ian Schrager's first boutique hotel is still going strong,
catering to a chic clientele that likes a low profile. Beware, though – some
rooms can be mighty small. Rates include breakfast. ⛏ 24 TV ↻ 🍽 🍷 🍴 🔒

| | AE DC JCB MC V | 154 | ● | ■ | |

W THE COURT/W THE TUSCANY $$$$
120-130 E. 39th St., New York, NY 10016 **Map** 9 A1 W www.whotels.com
Court: 212-685-1100 FAX 212-889-0287 Tuscany: 212-685-1600 FAX 212-779-9822
This matched set of boutique-style hotels boasts beautifully designed rooms
that excel at both form and function. The Court is home to the super-trendy
bar-and-lounge scene, while the Tuscany features a more relaxed ambiance
and slightly larger rooms. ⛏ 🎫 24 TV ↻ 🍽 🍷 🍴 🔒 ♿

| | AE DC JCB MC V | 320 | ● | ■ | |

BRYANT PARK W www.bryantparkhotel.com $$$$$
40 W. 40th St., New York, NY 10018 **Map** 8 F1 212-869-0100 FAX 212-869-4446
This hotel occupies the stunning American Radiator Building in an
appealing midtown pocket: across from the charming Bryant Park, around
the corner from the New York Public Library. Appointments bespeak
cutting-edge luxury, and 24-hour butler service is among the perks.
⛏ 🎫 24 TV ↻ 🍽 🍷 🍴 🔒 ♿

| | AE DC JCB MC V | 151 | ● | ■ | |

KITANO W www.kitano.com or www.summithotels.com $$$$$
66 Park Ave., New York, NY 10016 **Map** 9 A1 212-885-7000 FAX 212-885-7100
This elegant Japanese-owned hotel is a sea of tranquility in the bustle, chaos,
and excitement of the city. Hotel rooms are elegantly appointed havens of
restful Japanese luxury. The Kaiseki cuisine in the restaurant is exceptional,
and the service is flawless. ⛏ 1 🎫 TV ↻ 🍽 🍷 🍴 🔒 ♿

| | AE DC JCB MC V | 149 | ● | ■ | ● |

		CREDIT CARDS	NUMBER OF ROOMS	RESTAURANT	AIR CONDITIONING	QUIET LOCATION

Price categories for a standard double room per night, inclusive of breakfast, service charges and any additional taxes such as VAT:

$ under $150
$$ $150–$250
$$$ $250–$350
$$$$ $350–$450
$$$$$ over $450

RESTAURANT
Hotel restaurant or dining room usually open to non-residents unless otherwise stated.

AIR CONDITIONING
In-room units or central AC.

QUIET LOCATION
Quiet residential location or quiet street in a busy area.

CREDIT CARDS
Indicates which credit cards are accepted: *AE* American Express; *DC* Diners Club; JCB; *MC* MasterCard/Access; *V* VISA.

UPPER MIDTOWN

HABITAT HOTEL [W] www.habitatny.com $
130 E. 57th St., New York, NY 10022 **Map** 13 A3 [C] 212-753-8841 FAX 212-829-9605
The Habitat successfully fuses budget rates and designer comforts, but beware – most rooms are narrow, with a bed and pull-out trundle in lieu of a real double or twins. Most share hall baths but have in-room sinks. The location is great for shoppers. Ask about discounts for European travelers.

		CREDIT CARDS	NUMBER OF ROOMS	RESTAURANT	AIR CONDITIONING	QUIET LOCATION
		AE DC JCB MC V	300	●	▣	

PICKWICK ARMS [W] www.pickwickarms.com $
230 E. 51st St., New York, NY 10022 **Map** 13 B4 [C] 212-355-0300 FAX 212-755-5029
Despite its location in a prestigious neighborhood, the Pickwick remains a beacon for budget travelers (although refurbishment is bringing in higher prices). Some rooms are tiny, but everything is clean and management is professional. About two-thirds of rooms have private baths.

		AE DC JCB MC V	320	●	▣	

KIMBERLY HOTEL [W] www.kimberlyhotel.com $$$
145 E. 50th St., New York, NY 10022 **Map** 13 A5 [C] 212-755-0400 FAX 212-486-6915
This low-profile hotel boasts mostly apartment-style one- and two-bedroom suites featuring home comforts, such as a full-size kitchen, dining area, and large, well-appointed rooms. Excellent for families and business travelers staying a while. Check for discounts and packages.

		AE DC JCB MC V	186	●	▣	●

METROPOLITAN HOTEL [W] www.metropolitanhotelnyc.com $$$
569 Lexington Ave., New York, NY 10022 **Map** 13 A4 [C] 212-752-7000 FAX 212-752-3817
Previously Loews New York, the hotel continues to keep prices reasonable and caters to value-minded business travelers and child-toting families with equal aplomb.

		AE DC JCB MC V	722	●	▣	

ROGER SMITH [W] www.rogersmith.com $$$
501 Lexington Ave., New York, NY 10017 **Map** 13 A5 [C] 212-755-1400 FAX 212-758-4061
This pleasant hotel infuses creature comforts with a few artsy twists. Rooms are generous and individually decorated, mostly in a classic Americana style. Suites have microwaves and VCRs, and VIP rooms have whirlpool tubs. Rates include breakfast. Popular with up-and-coming rockers.

		AE DC JCB MC V	130	●	▣	

SWISSÔTEL NEW YORK – THE DRAKE [W] www.swissotel.com $$$
440 Park Ave., New York, NY 10022 **Map** 13 A3 [C] 212-421-0900 FAX 212-371-4190
Built in 1929, this Park Avenue dowager boasts a loyal following due to a great location, sophisticated European ambiance, and rooms that are excellent value. Printer/fax/copiers come standard for laptop-toters. For the ultimate luxury, ask for a room with a terrace.

		AE DC JCB MC V	495	●	▣	

BENJAMIN [W] www.thebenjamin.com $$$$
125 E. 50th St., New York, NY 10022 **Map** 13 A4 [C] 212-715-2500 FAX 212-715-2525
This low-key hotel boasts well-outfitted rooms decorated in a Neoclassical-meets-modern style. Each has a gourmet kitchenette, and a work desk wired for high-tech travelers. The pillow menu will guarantee a good night's sleep. Facilities include a restaurant and a spa.

		AE DC JCB MC V	209	●	▣	

OMNI BERKSHIRE PLACE [W] www.omnihotels.com $$$$
21 E. 52nd St., New York, NY 10022 **Map** 12 F4 [C] 212-753-7800 FAX 212-754-5018
This refined hotel is first-rate on all fronts, from the comfortable decor to the impeccable service. Extensive business facilities serve corporate travelers, the neighborhood is great for shoppers, and the hotel caters to families, too. Check for discounted weekend rates.

		AE DC JCB MC V	396	●	▣	

WALDORF-ASTORIA/WALDORF TOWERS [W] www.hilton.com $$$$
301 Park Ave., New York, NY 10022 **Map** 13 A5 [C] 212-355-3000 FAX 212-872-7272
This New York legend is as great as ever. Rates are very reasonable in the main hotel, considering the glamorous air, extra-large rooms, and first-class dining and amenities. The exclusive Waldorf Towers has 24-hour butler service and a solid reputation for discretion.

		AE DC JCB MC V	1242	●	▣	

NEW YORK PALACE [W] www.newyorkpalace.com $$$$$ | AE DC JCB MC V | 722 | ● |
455 Madison Ave., New York, NY 10022 **Map** 13 A4 [C] 212-888-7000 [FAX] 212-303-6000
This splendid hotel is housed in the landmark 1882 Villard Houses and a 55-story modern tower. The main hotel overflows with opulent old-world style, while the more exclusive tower boasts a refined contemporary-Deco style and around-the-clock butler service. Excellent on-site dining includes legendary Le Cirque 2000 *(see p296)*.

PENINSULA – NEW YORK [W] www.peninsula.com $$$$$ | AE DC JCB MC V | 241 | ● | ■ |
700 Fifth Ave., New York, NY 10019 **Map** 12 F4 [C] 212-956-2888 [FAX] 212-903-3949
A stunning Beaux-Arts structure houses New York's best ultra-luxury hotel. Huge rooms are done in an Art Nouveau style, with big work desks and 21st-century technology. The rooftop spa offers pampering and relaxation.

PLAZA HOTEL [W] www.fairmont.com $$$$$ | AE DC JCB MC V | 805 | ● | ■ |
768 Fifth Ave., New York, NY 10019 **Map** 12 F3 [C] 212-759-3000 [FAX] 212-546-5256
The star of countless Hollywood films – and stage for even more high-society affairs – this 1907 French Renaissance palace continues to reign as New York's most glamorous address. The refined Fairmont hotels group has freshened the opulent period interiors and added a terrific new spa, but tourist crowds often undermine the elegance.

UPPER EAST SIDE

FRANKLIN [W] www.franklinhotel.com $$$ | AE DC JCB MC V | 48 | | ■ |
164 E. 87th St., New York, NY 10128 **Map** 17 A3 [C] 212-369-1000 [FAX] 212-369-8000
The modern Franklin is more subway-convenient than sister hotel the Wales (below), but beware: rooms are miniscule. Sleekly designed and luxuriously equipped – with pillowtop beds wearing romantic sheer canopies, plus VCRs and CD players – they're nevertheless best for light packers and short-term stays. Continental breakfast and all-day cappucino included.

HOTEL WALES [W] www.waleshotel.com $$$ | AE DC JCB MC V | 87 | ● | ■ |
1295 Madison Ave., New York, NY 10128 **Map** 17 A2 [C] 212-876-6000 [FAX] 212-860-7000
This quirky Victorian-style hotel offers pleasant relief in an expensive neigh-borhood. Comforts include beds dressed in Belgian linens, VCRs, and CD players. Rates include breakfast and self-serve cappuccino all day. Sarabeth's is a favorite for homestyle cooking and afternoon tea.

SURREY HOTEL [W] www.mesuite.com $$$$ | AE DC JCB MC V | 130 | ● | ■ |
20 E. 76th St., New York, NY 10021 **Map** 17 A5 [C] 212-288-3700 [FAX] 212-628-1549
Experience the high life for less at this lovely all-suite hotel. The Old World suites are spacious and pleasing from tip to toe; each one has a fully equipped kitchen. In-suite dining, from Cafe Boulud *(see p295)*, one of New York's finest restaurants, is reason enough to stay.

CARLYLE $$$$$ | AE DC JCB MC V | 180 | ● | ■ |
35 E. 76th St., New York, NY 10021 **Map** 17 A5 [C] 212-744-1600 [FAX] 212-717-4682
One of New York's most legendary and refined hotels, the Carlyle epitomizes Upper East Side elegance. Drawn in by the low-profile luxury and faultless service, generations of movie stars and world leaders have stayed in the beautifully appointed rooms and suites.

PIERRE [W] www.fourseasons.com $$$$$ | AE DC JCB MC V | 202 | ● | ■ | ● |
2 E. 61st St., New York, NY 10021 **Map** 12 F3 [C] 212-838-8000 [FAX] 212-940-8109
Live like a royal at this elegantly residential, very European hotel, with opulent classical interiors. The old-world ambiance is extremely formal – with doormen and gloved elevator operators – but not uninvitingly so. Business travelers are better off elsewhere.

SHERRY-NETHERLAND [W] www.sherrynetherland.com $$$$$ | AE DC JCB MC V | 77 | ● | ■ |
781 Fifth Ave., New York, NY 10022 **Map** 12 F3 [C] 212-355-2800 [FAX] 212-319-4306
No other hotel simulates genteel New York apartment living as well the Sherry. Mammoth rooms and suites are elegantly outfitted, and the service is impeccable. Rates include breakfast at exclusive Cipriani's, a favorite among power brokers.

STANHOPE [W] www.hyatt.com $$$$$ | AE DC JCB MC V | 185 | ● | ■ | ● |
995 Fifth Ave., New York, NY 10028 **Map** 16 F4 [C] 212-774-1234 [FAX] 212-988-7439
This bright and elegant member of the Park Hyatt chain is ideal for museum lovers, since the Metropolitan Museum of Art is just across the street. The Versailles-inspired lobby displays Louis XIV antiques and museum-quality tapestries. Excellent through and through.

ories for a standard
m per night, inclusive
st, service charges and
ional taxes such as VAT:

der $150
$150–$250
$ $250–$350
$$$ $350–$450
$$$$$ over $450

RESTAURANT
Hotel restaurant or dining room usually open to non-residents unless otherwise stated.

AIR CONDITIONING
In-room units or central AC.

QUIET LOCATION
Quiet residential location or quiet street in a busy area.

CREDIT CARDS
Indicates which credit cards are accepted: *AE* American Express; *DC* Diners Club; JCB; *MC* MasterCard/Access; *V* VISA.

	CREDIT CARDS	NUMBER OF ROOMS	RESTAURANT	AIR CONDITIONING	QUIET LOCATION

UPPER WEST SIDE

	CREDIT CARDS	NUMBER OF ROOMS	RESTAURANT	AIR CONDITIONING	QUIET LOCATION
AMSTERDAM INN W www.amsterdaminn.com $ 340 Amsterdam Ave., New York, NY 10023 **Map** 15 C5 C 212-579-7500 FAX 212-579-6127 Rooms are narrow and basic, but everything is fairly new and well maintained at this walk-up hotel. Bathrooms, both shared and private, are some of the nicest around for the money. Note that some "doubles" have single beds with a pull-out trundle rather than a real bed for two. 1 TV	AE DC JCB MC V	25		■	
GERSHWIN 97 HOTEL W www.gershwin97.com $ 258 W. 97th St., New York, NY 10025 **Map** 15 C1 C 212-665-7434 FAX 212-684-5546 This budget hotel/hostel is sister to the Flatiron's Gershwin (see p273). Expect clean and colorful accommodation, whether you opt for a private room (with TV and full bath) or a dorm bed. Facilities include a TV lounge with microwave, lockers, and laundry. The neighborhood is terrific. 1	AE DC JCB MC V	56		■	
HOSTELLING INTERNATIONAL – NEW YORK W www.hinewyork.org $ 891 Amsterdam Ave., New York, NY 10025 **Map** 20 E5 C 212-932-2300 FAX 212-932-2574 This mammoth, square-block-sized hostel feels like an international college dormitory, complete with coffee bar and cafeteria, game room, a common kitchen, coin-operated laundry, a lounge with Internet-access machines, and a large yard with picnic tables. Travelers must be 18 years or older. 1	AE DC JCB MC V	628	●	■	
HOTEL NEWTON W www.newyorkhotel.com $ 2528 Broadway, New York, NY 10025 **Map** 15 C2 C 212-678-6500 FAX 212-678-6758 This clean, attractive, and professionally run hotel is a front-runner in the budget category. Rooms are large, with good, firm beds and nice bathrooms; some rooms are large enough for four. 1 24 TV	AE DC JCB MC V	110	●	■	
HOTEL OLCOTT W www.hotelolcott.com $ 27 W. 72nd St., New York, NY 10023 **Map** 12 D1 C 212-877-4200 FAX 212-580-0511 This old-world apartment house is just steps from the ritzy Dakota and Central Park. The studios and suites are huge and bargain-priced; each has a kitchenette and large bath. TV	AE DC JCB MC V	200	●	■	
JAZZ ON THE PARK W www.jazzhostel.com $ 36 W. 106th St., New York, NY 10025 **Map** 21 A5 C 212-932-1600 FAX 212-932-1700 This funky, artsy hostel brings a downtown vibe to the Upper West Side. A coffeehouse with live music most evenings lends a party atmosphere. Dorm rooms are hostel-basic, and bathrooms are decent. Expect a young, energetic, international crowd. Continental breakfast is a value-added touch. 1	AE DC JCB MC V	220	●	■	
BELLECLAIRE HOTEL W www.hotelbelleclaire.com $$ 250 W. 77th St., New York, NY 10024 **Map** 15 C5 C 212-362-7700 FAX 212-362-1004 This recently renovated hotel has sparsely equipped but rather stylish rooms, with simple contemporary furnishings, cushioned headboards, and small bathrooms. A handful of rooms with shared baths go for as little as $80. Two-bedroom/one-bath family suites are also available. TV	AE DC JCB MC V	189		■	
EXCELSIOR HOTEL W www.excelsiorhotelny.com $$ 45 W. 81st St., New York, NY 10024 **Map** 16 D4 C 212-362-9200 FAX 212-721-2994 This hotel offers high-quality comforts in a celebrity-dotted residential neighborhood, directly across from the Museum of Natural History and steps from Central Park. Rooms are attractive and comfortable, with pretty bathrooms and fax/copier/printers for business travelers. TV	AE DC JCB MC V	196		■	
HOTEL BEACON W www.beaconhotel.com $$ 2130 Broadway, New York, NY 10023 **Map** 15 C5 C 212-787-1100 FAX 212-724-0839 The Beacon is one of the city's best-value hotels, especially for families. The rooms won't win style awards, but each has a modern kitchenette and most accommodate four. One-bedroom and two-bedroom/two-bath suites are good value. Washer/dryers are another family-friendly plus. 1 TV	AE DC JCB MC V	236	●	■	

MILBURN W www.milburnhotel.com $$
242 W. 76th St., New York, NY 10023 Map 15 C5 212-362-1006 FAX 212-721-5476
This well-priced all-suite hotel is an excellent choice for families, or any
traveler who desires the comforts of home. Suites compensate for their lack of
style with a wealth of amenities, including modern bathrooms and well-
equipped kitchenettes. A helpful staff, laundry facilities, and a better-than-
average exercise room add to the value.

AE DC JCB MC V — 114

ON THE AVE W www.ontheave-nyc.com $$
2178 Broadway, New York, NY 10024 Map 15 C5 212-362-1100 FAX 212-787-9521
Travelers with an eye for modern design and a mid-range budget will like this
stylish hotel. Rooms feature Scandinavian-style modular furniture, natural-
hued textiles, and attractive art. Beds should be a bit more plush, but
accommodation is comfortable overall. Cheaper rooms are smallish; the
deluxe category offers the best space-for-money ratio.

AE DC JCB MC V — 251

QUALITY HOTEL ON BROADWAY $$
W www.bestnyhotels.com or www.hotelchoice.com
215 W. 94th St., New York, NY 10025 Map 15 C2 212-866-6400 FAX 212-866-1357
This nicely renovated chain hotel offers a subway-convenient location and good-
sized, if generic, guestrooms. Bathrooms are spacious by New York standards.
Some rooms have refrigerators and/or kitchenettes. The formerly sketchy neigh-
borhood is now one of Uptown's most pleasant, and affordable dining options
abound. Rates sometimes plummet, so ask for discounts.

AE DC JCB MC V — 350

LUCERNE W www.newyorkhotel.com $$$
201 W. 79th St., New York, NY 10024 Map 15 C4 212-875-1000 FAX 212-579-2408
A distinctive 1903 building houses one of the city's best mid-priced hotels.
Service is the key note. The extremely well-kept rooms are outfitted in a
comfortable and attractive colonial Americana style; suites have kitchenettes
and minibars. A stylish grill hosts live jazz and blues. Rates, which include
continental breakfast, often drop well below $250.

AE DC JCB MC V — 250

MAYFLOWER HOTEL W www.mayflowerhotel.com $$$
15 Central Park West, New York, NY 10023 Map 12 D3 212-265-0060 FAX 212-265-0227
The prime location – in an upscale residential neighborhood at Central Park
West, just a shout from Lincoln Center and the Theater District – is the best
feature of this perfectly fine but otherwise undistinctive hotel. Rooms are
extra-large, traditionally styled, and comfortable. Extensive facilities include a
pleasant restaurant overlooking the park.

AE DC JCB MC V — 365

INN NEW YORK CITY W www.innnewyorkcity.com $$$$$
266 W. 71st St., New York, NY 10023 Map 11 C1 212-580-1900 FAX 212-580-4437
Expect ultra-luxury at this sparkling gem of a guesthouse, housed in a
gorgeous late 19th-century brownstone that has been restored to better-than-
new. Each spectacularly appointed suite has its own theme – Opera, Library,
Vermont, or Spa. Brilliant touches include bounteous in-suite breakfast
cupboards. Ridiculously expensive, but worth it.

AE DC JCB MC V — 4

TRUMP INTERNATIONAL HOTEL & TOWER W www.trumpintl.com $$$$$
1 Central Park West, New York, NY 10023 Map 12 D3 212-299-1000 FAX 212-299-1150
Housed in a freestanding tower overlooking Central Park, this luxuriously
modern hotel is one of the city's finest. Smartly designed rooms are softened
with soothing Tuscan hues; floor-to-ceiling windows allow for unobstructed
city or park views. Each guest is assigned a personal concierge, making
service unparalleled. Jean Georges just may be New York's best restaurant.

AE DC JCB MC V — 167

MORNINGSIDE HEIGHTS & HARLEM

SUGAR HILL INTERNATIONAL HOUSE W www.sugarhillhostel.com $
722 St. Nicholas Ave., New York, NY 10031 Map 19 A1 212-926-7030
This quiet, well-run, all-nonsmoking hostel offers two-dozen dorm beds to
shoestring travelers. Bunks fill spacious, high-ceilinged rooms; a few double
rooms are available to early arrivals. Security is good, the neighborhood is quiet,
there is a common kitchen, and the kind owners are happy to offer advice.

AE DC JCB MC V — 25

ELLINGTON W www.nycityhotels.net $$
610 W. 111th St., New York, NY 10025 Map 20 E4 212-864-7500 FAX 212-749-5852
Smart Art-Deco accents disguise the fundamental austerity of this budget hotel.
Still, it makes a reasonable choice for wallet-watching travelers who want a
private bathroom and a few extras (like hairdryers), especially when rates
drop below $150, which they often do. A basic continental breakfast is
included. Always check for discounts.

AE DC JCB MC V — 85

Restaurants and Bars

Nᴇᴡ ʏᴏʀᴋᴇʀꜱ love to eat well, and there are over 25,000 restaurants in the five boroughs catering to their wishes. City dwellers avidly read restaurant reviews in magazines such as *New York* to ensure that they are seen in the latest fashionable eatery. "In" places and cuisine change with great regularity, while some favorite places simply remain

The classic Manhattan cocktail

popular. The restaurants in our listings have been selected as the best that New York can offer. *Choosing a Restaurant* on pages 288–91 will help narrow down your choice, and the information on pages 288–303 will fill out all the details. For lighter refreshment and casual meals, see *Light Meals and Snacks* on pages 304–305.

Restaurant Menus

Mᴇᴀʟꜱ ɪɴ ᴍᴏꜱᴛ of the better restaurants consist of three courses: the appetizer (or starter), an entrée (the main course) and a dessert. Virtually all New York restaurants, except fast-food places, serve you rolls or bread and butter just after you're seated, at no extra charge – it's all part of the expected service. In some fine restaurants you may be offered a complimentary appetizer, such as a small

Street-corner hot dog stand

dollop of mousse or a tiny triangle of quiche. Appetizers at the better restaurants are often the chef's most creative dishes – many diners request two appetizers and no entrée. Italian menus offer a pasta dish as a course before the main course, but in many places pasta is considered a main course. Coffee or tea and a dessert ordinarily conclude the meal in restaurants above the coffee-shop level. Your coffee cup may be refilled until you refuse any more. The cheeseboard used to be a rarity in New York restaurants, although some of the better establishments now feature one on the menu.

Prices

Yᴏᴜ ᴡɪʟʟ ᴀʟᴡᴀʏꜱ find a restaurant in New York to suit your budget. At inexpensive coffee shops, diners and fast food chains, $10 will buy you a filling meal. There are also hundreds of acceptable, even first-rate, restaurants where you can eat well at a moderate cost – around $25 per person for a filling and decent meal, not including drinks – in attractive surroundings. For dinner at a trendy New American venue with a star chef, the bill could be upward of $70 to $100 per person, excluding drinks. Many top restaurants do, however, offer fixed-price (or, as they are known in New York, prix-fixe) meals. These are normally much cheaper than items on the à la carte menu. Lunch is also less expensive than dinner in such places, and because of the profusion of business diners, lunch is also the busiest period of the day.

Taxes and Tipping

Nᴇᴡ ʏᴏʀᴋ ᴄɪᴛʏ sales tax of 8.25% will be added to your bill. Service is not usually included. Tipping can run from 10% at a coffee shop to 20% at the fanciest places, with 15% an average fair tip. Many people just double the sales tax for a tip.

The bill is known as the "check" in New York, as all

A typical New York deli *(see p304)*

over the US. Commonly accepted credit cards are VISA, MasterCard and American Express. Traveler's checks are also taken in many restaurants. Luncheonettes and coffee shops accept cash only. In fast-food chains, you order at the counter and pay cash in advance.

Dining on a Budget

Dᴇꜱᴘɪᴛᴇ ᴛʜᴇ ᴛᴀʟᴇꜱ of $200 business lunches, there are ways to stretch a meal budget in New York.

Order fewer courses than you would normally. American portions are huge, and an appetizer is often big enough for a light main course. You could share one with your companion or choose two appetizers and no entrée.

"Specials of the day" may be more expensive than items on the printed menu, so be sure to check prices.

Ask your waiter if there is a prix-fixe menu. Many expensive restaurants offer

Interior of Zen Palate, Manhattan

this at lunch and dinner – in the early evening it may often be called the pre-theater menu. Or try a prix-fixe lunch buffet. These are popular in

Indian restaurants and other places and are very reasonably priced meals.

Go to bars featuring "happy hours." They often offer a variety of hors d'oeuvres, like Spanish *tapas*, which can make a meal in themselves. If you want to simply see inside the restaurants every visitor has heard about, just go to have a drink and soak up the atmosphere. Avoid breakfast in your hotel. Even its coffee shop is likely to be more expensive than an out-side coffee shop or deli. Many restaurants post their menus or will let you see them before you are seated, good for checking prices in advance.

HOURS

BREAKFAST HOURS are usually from 7 to 10:30 or 11am. Sunday brunch is a popular meal, served at most better restaurants between about 11am and 3pm. Lunch runs from 11:30am or noon to 2:30pm at most places, but the busiest time of the day

Poolside dining at the Four Seasons Hotel

is 1pm. Dinner is usually served from 5:30 to 6pm onward. The most popular time is around 7:30 to 8pm.

Some restaurants stop serving at 10pm during the week, or 11pm on Friday and Saturday. Certain informal restaurants, especially Chinese, are open from 11:30am to 10pm. Coffee shops are open long hours, from 7am to midnight or even 24 hours.

DRESS CODES

FEW RESTAURANTS demand that male diners dress formally, though a jacket is required at classy restaurants, and jacket and tie at the very best. At most places, for both men and women, "casual but

Waiting in style at the Oyster Bar in Grand Central Terminal

chic" suffices. Women tend to dress up when dining at the expensive restaurants. If unsure, check the dress code when making a reservation.

RESERVATIONS

IT IS PRUDENT to make reservations at any restaurant above the luncheonette/fast food level, especially on week-ends. A few of the trendiest restaurants won't even accept reservations except for groups of six or more. It is essential to make reservations for lunch at a midtown restaurant. But you may still have to wait at the bar, even if you have booked a table.

SMOKING

SMOKING IS now illegal in restaurants with 35 or more seats. Many places provide separate rooms for smokers, but phone ahead for details.

CHILDREN

WHEN EATING out with children, ask if there's a child's menu with half-portions. The prices are reduced, some-times by half. Children are accepted in most New York restaurants, but if yours are unpredictable stick to casual spots, Chinatown Chinese or family-run Italian restaurants, burger bars, delis, cafés, fast food chains and luncheonettes. A few of the better restaurants have facilities for babies or toddlers; others may not be so well equipped. Dining out in the more formal New York restaurants is certainly not a family affair.

WHEELCHAIR ACCESS

WHILE MANY restaurants may be able to accom-modate a wheelchair, it is always best to mention your requirements when making your reservation. Many smaller places cannot cater to disabled customers because of lack of space.

What to Eat in New York

Hot dog

THE VARIETY OF FOOD found in New York is as varied as its cultural and ethnic makeup, and you can find virtually any food you want. For a hearty simple meal, such as marinated vegetables, pasta or salami and cheese, visit one of the Italian restaurants found in every neighborhood. For a more sophisticated meal try a Japanese restaurant for sushi and sashimi – as good in New York as anywhere in Japan. Or try such traditional Jewish foods as pastrami, blintzes and bagels, found in most delis and coffee shops. Spicy curries can be found in the many Indian restaurants around Manhattan. If you are really hungry, visit a steakhouse for juicy steaks, fresh seafood and some especially wicked desserts.

Bagel
This chewy Jewish bread roll is most popularly served with lox (smoked salmon) and cream cheese.

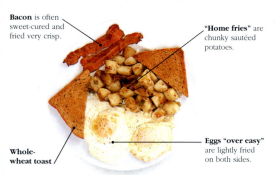

Pancakes
Thick, sweet pancakes are usually served with maple syrup as breakfast. Fresh or dried fruit may be mixed into the batter before cooking.

Bacon is often sweet-cured and fried very crisp.

"Home fries" are chunky sautéed potatoes.

Whole-wheat toast

Eggs "over easy" are lightly fried on both sides.

Breakfast or Brunch
Breakfast (or brunch if eaten midmorning) can consist of anything from home fries, eggs, bacon and toast to sweet pancakes or croissants, often with unlimited coffee.

French Toast
A breakfast dish of sliced bread dipped in egg then fried and often served with syrup.

Egg Cream
This drink is made with milk, chocolate syrup and carbonated soda water.

Corned Beef on Rye
Cured beef is served on rye bread with mild mustard and a pickled dill gherkin.

Burger and Fries "To Go"
A hamburger and french fries may come with salad and onion rings.

Giant Pretzel
This savory bread twist is sold on many street corners.

Pork ribs are barbecued in a rich, sweetened sauce.

Corn bread muffins

Boiled, spiced collard greens

Black-eyed peas

Clam Chowder
The Manhattan version of this shellfish soup is made with tomatoes and garnished with crackers.

Soul Food
The cuisine of Harlem stems from America's Deep South. Simple foods are cooked with spices for a unique flavor.

Pizza
The street food of Italian festivals is available all over the city – this uptown version is topped with artichoke hearts.

Sushi
Japanese cuisine, like this ultrafresh raw fish and rice, is a New York favorite.

Dim Sum
Tiny steamed dumplings, stuffed with fish, meat or vegetables, are a speciality of Chinese cuisine.

Waldorf Salad
Created in the 1930s at the Waldorf Hotel, it's made out of apples, nuts and lettuce.

Cappuccino and Cookies
Frothy coffee sprinkled with chocolate is served with cookies in New York cafés.

Apple Pie à la Mode
This traditional American dessert is only "à la mode" when served with ice cream.

New York Cheesecake
This thick, baked Jewish dessert may be served plain or glazed with fruit.

Banana Split
Some New York ice cream concoctions will feed a family. No one will mind if you order extra spoons and share.

Choosing a Restaurant

THE RESTAURANTS in this section have been selected for their good value or exceptional food. The chart highlights some factors that may influence your choice. For details see pages 293–303. Details of *Light Meals and Snacks* are on pages 304–6 and for some of New York's best *Bars* see pages 307–9.

		Page Number	Fixed-Price Menu	Late Opening	Children's Facilities	Tables Outside	Sunday Night Opening	Vegetarian Dishes	Seafood Specialties
LOWER MANHATTAN									
American Park at the Battery *(Seafood)*	$$$$	300			●	■			●
14 Wall Street Restaurant *(French)*	$$$$	296							
Bayard's *(French)*	$$$$$	295							
SEAPORT AND THE CIVIC CENTER									
Cabana *(Latin American/Carribean)*	$$	302		■	●		●		
Bridge Café *(American)*	$$$	291		■	●		●	■	
LOWER EAST SIDE									
Golden Unicorn *(Chinese)*	$	303			●		●		
Grand Sichuan *(Chinese)* ★	$	303					●		
Da Nico *(Italian)*	$$	297	●	■	●	■	●		
Il Palazzo *(Italian)*	$$	298			●	■	●	■	
Joe's Shanghai *(Chinese)*	$$	303			●				
Canton *(Chinese)* ★	$$$	303					●		
Prune *(American)*	$$$	293	●				●	■	
Sammy's Famous Roumanian *(European)*	$$$	300		■					
71 Clinton Fresh Food *(American)*	$$$	293			●			■	
The Tasting Room *(American)*	$$$	293	●				●		
SOHO AND TRIBECA									
Tennessee Mountain *(American Regional)*	$	294	●	■	●		●		
Kin Khao *(Thai)*	$$	303		■			●	■	
Le Jardin Bistro *(French)*	$$$	296			●	■	●		
Le Zinc *(French)*	$$$	296		■					
Lupa *(Italian)* ★	$$$	299			●		●	■	
Provence *(French)*	$$$	297			●	■	●	■	
Alison on Dominick Street *(French)*	$$$$	295							
Aquagrill *(Seafood)* ★	$$$$	301					●	■	●
Montrachet *(French)*	$$$$	297	●						
Bouley Bakery *(French)*	$$$$$	295	●				●		
Chanterelle *(French)*	$$$$$	295	●						
Danube *(European)*	$$$$$	299	●					■	
GREENWICH VILLAGE									
Café de Bruxelles *(European)*	$$$	299			●		●		
Rio Mar *(European)*	$$$	299		■			●		
Home *(American)*	$$	292	●		●	■	●		
Il Bagatto *(Italian)*	$$	298			●		●	■	
Pearl Oyster Bar *(Seafood)*	$$	301			●				●
Blue Hill *(American)*	$$$	291			●		●	■	
Blue Ribbon Bakery *(American)*	$$$	291		■					
Da Silvano *(Italian)*	$$$$	297				■	●		
Babbo *(Italian)* ★	$$$$$	297					●		
Gotham Bar & Grill *(American)*	$$$$$	292			●			■	
Il Mulino *(Italian)* ★	$$$$$	298						■	
One if by Land, Two if by Sea *(American)*	$$$$$	293	●				●	■	

Price categories include a three-course meal for one, half a bottle of house wine, and all unavoidable extra charges such as sales tax and service.
$ under $25
$$ $25–$35
$$$ $35–$50
$$$$ $50–$70
$$$$$ over $70

★ Means highly recommended.

FIXED-PRICE MENU A fixed price for a set meal that is less expensive than normal menu prices.
LATE OPENING Last orders at or after 11:30pm excluding Sunday.
CHILDREN'S FACILITIES High chairs and/or child portions.
QUIET RESTAURANT No piped music; peaceful atmosphere.
VEGETARIAN DISHES Vegetarian restaurant, or restaurant with good vegetarian selection.

Restaurant	Price	Page Number	Fixed-Price Menu	Late Opening	Children's Facilities	Tables Outside	Sunday Night Opening	Vegetarian Dishes	Seafood Spec
EAST VILLAGE									
Great Jones Café (American Regional)	$	294		■	●			■	●
First (American)	$$$	292		■	●		●	■	●
Iso (Japanese)	$$$	303		■			●		
GRAMERCY AND THE FLATIRON DISTRICT									
Craft (American)	$$	291	●				●	■	
Bolo (European)	$$$	299	●				●		
Chicama (Latin American/Caribbean)	$$$$	302		■				■	
Eleven Madison Park (American)	$$$$	291	●				●	■	
I Trulli (Italian) ★	$$$$	298				■	●	■	
Mesa Grill (American Regional) ★	$$$$	294					●	■	
Patria (Latin American) ★	$$$$	302	●	■			●		
Periyali (Greek)	$$$$	300							
Union Square Café (American) ★	$$$$	293			●		●	■	
Gramercy Tavern (American) ★	$$$$$	292	●				●	■	
Union Pacific (American)	$$$$$	293	●					■	
Veritas (American)	$$$$$	293	●				●	■	
CHELSEA AND THE GARMENT DISTRICT									
Rocking Horse Café (Latin American)	$$	302		■				■	
Bottino (Italian)	$$$	297			●	■	●	■	
The Red Cat (American)	$$$	293					●	■	
AZ (American) ★	$$$$	291	●	■			●	■	
Da Umberto (Italian)	$$$$	298						■	
Le Madri (Italian)	$$$$	298					●	■	
THEATER DISTRICT									
Virgil's Real Barbecue (American Regional)	$	294			●		●		
Becco (Italian) ★	$$	297	●	■	●		●	■	
Joe's Shanghai (Chinese) ★	$$	303			●		●	■	
Churrasccaria Plataforma (Latin American) ★	$$$	302	●	■			●	■	
Jezebel (American Regional)	$$$	294						■	
Molyvos (Greek) ★	$$$	300		■					
Orso (Italian) ★	$$$	299					●		
Esca (Seafood)	$$$	301				■			●
Beacon (American)	$$$$	291					●	■	
Osteria del Circo (Italian)	$$$$	299						■	
Russian Tea Room (European)	$$$$	300	●				●		
Le Bernardin (Seafood) ★	$$$$$	301							●
Alain Ducasse at the Essex House (French)	$$$$$	295							
LOWER MIDTOWN									
The Oyster Bar and Restaurant (Seafood) ★	$$$	301			●			■	
Asia de Cuba (Latin American/Caribbean)	$$$$	301		■			●		
Michael Jordan's – The Steak House (American)	$$$$	293			●		●		
UPPER MIDTOWN									
La Bonne Soupe (French)	$$	296	●	■	●	■	●		
Dawat (Indian)	$$$	303			●		●	■	

For key to symbols see p285

...ategories include a
...ourse meal for one, half
...le of house wine, and all
...oidable extra charges such
...ales tax and service.
...under $25
...$ $25–$35
...$$ $35–$50
...$$$ $50–$70
...$$$$ over $70.

★ Means highly recommended.

FIXED-PRICE MENU
A fixed price for a set meal that is less expensive than normal menu prices.
LATE OPENING
Last orders at or after 11:30pm excluding Sunday.
CHILDREN'S FACILITIES
High chairs and/or child portions.
QUIET RESTAURANT
No piped music; peaceful atmosphere.
VEGETARIAN DISHES
Vegetarian restaurant, or restaurant with good vegetarian selection.

Restaurant	Price	Page Number	Fixed-Price Menu	Late Opening	Children's Facilities	Tables Outside	Sunday Opening	Vegetarian Dishes	Seafood Specialities
Rosa Mexicano (*Latin American*)	$$$	302					●	■	
Shun Lee Palace (*Chinese*) ★	$$$	303	●		●		●	■	
Felidia (*Italian*)	$$$$	298	●		●		●		
Guastavino Restaurant and Club (*French*)	$$$$	296	●				●		
Inagiku (*Japanese*)	$$$$	303		■			●		
Aquavit (*European*) ★	$$$$$	299	●				●		●
Four Seasons (*American*)	$$$$$	292	●						
La Grenouille (*French*) ★	$$$$$	296							
Lespinasse (*French*) ★	$$$$$	297							
March (*American*)	$$$$$	292	●				●	■	
Oceana (*Seafood*)	$$$$$	301	●						●
UPPER EAST SIDE									
Mocca Hungarian Restaurant (*European*)	$	299	●		●		●		
Cabana (*Latin American/Caribbean*)	$$	302		■	●		●		
Maya (*Latin American*)	$$$	302			●		●		
Orsay (*French*)	$$$	297			●		●		
The Dining Room (*American*)	$$$$	291		■			●	■	
Erminia (*Italian*)	$$$$	298						■	
Aureole (*American*)	$$$$$	291				■			
Café Boulud (*French*)	$$$$$	295					●	■	
Cello (*Seafood*)	$$$$$	301	●						●
Le Cirque 2000 (*French*) ★	$$$$$	296					●		
Daniel (*French*) ★	$$$$$	295	●						
UPPER WEST SIDE									
Gennaro (*Italian*)	$$	298			●				
Santa Fe (*American Regional*)	$$	294					●		
Café Fiorello (*Italian*)	$$$	297		■		■	●		
Café Luxembourg (*French*)	$$$	295	●			■			
Calle Ocho (*Latin American/Caribbean*)	$$$	302		■			●		
Pasha (*Turkish*)	$$$	300			●		●	■	
Rosa Mexicano (*Latin American/Caribbean*) ★	$$$	302			●		●	■	
Café des Artistes (*French*)	$$$$	295			●			■	
Jean George (*French*)	$$$$$	296	●						
Picholine (*European*) ★	$$$$$	299	●				●		
MORNINGSIDE HEIGHTS AND HARLEM									
Copeland's (*American Regional*)	$	294		■	●		●	■	
Terrace in the Sky (*European*)	$$$$	300							
BROOKLYN									
Gage & Tollner (*American*)	$$$	292			●				
Peter Luger (*American*)	$$$$	293			●		●		
River Café (*American*) ★	$$$$$	293	●			■	●	■	
QUEENS									
Elias Corner (*Seafood*)	$	301			●	■			●
S'Agapo (*Greek/Middle Eastern/Afghan*)	$$$	300		■		■			

Price categories include a three-course meal for one, half a bottle of house wine, and all unavoidable extra charges such as sales tax and service.
$ under $25
$$ $25–$35
$$$ $35–$50
$$$$ $50–$70
$$$$$ over $70.

LATE OPENING
Last orders at or after 11:30pm excluding Sunday.
BAR DINING
Snacks, light meals or appetizers, served at the bar or at tables in the bar area.
FIXED-PRICE MENU
A fixed price for a set meal that is usually less expensive that normal menu prices.
SUNDAY OPENING
Brunch and/or dinner served on Sunday.
TABLES OUTSIDE
Garden or courtyard with outside tables.

	LATE OPENING	BAR DINING	FIXED-PRICE MENU	SUNDAY OPENING	TABLES OUTSIDE

AMERICAN

AUREOLE $$$$$
34 East 61st St. (212) 319-1660 W www.aureolerestaurant.com
Chef Charlie Palmer has won numerous awards for his New American fare, served in a flower-filled duplex townhouse setting that does justice to the elegant cuisine. A charming garden is an option on sunny days. Aureole ranks among New York's top restaurants. ○ L Mon–Fri; D Mon–Sat. ▮ ▨ AE, MC, V

| | | | | | ● |

AZ $$$$
21 West 17th St. (212) 691-8888 W www.aznyc.com
The New American/Asian fusion creates magic at this innovative star, where every dish is delicious. The triplex building features a wall of water and a chic and charming rooftop space beneath a greenhouse. The prix-fixe lunch is an excellent buy. ○ L Mon–Fri, Sun; D daily. ⬥ ★ ▨ AE, MC, V

| | ● | | ● | ▪ | |

BEACON $$$$
25 West 56th St. (212) 332-0500 W www.beaconnyc.com
The spare, tri-level space is striking, the American menu highly praised, especially the rustic dishes from the wood-burning oven. Moods change with the levels, busy at the bar, intimate upstairs, and cozy near the open kitchen. ○ L Mon–Fri; D Mon–Sat. ⬥ ▨ AE, MC, V

| | | ▪ | | | |

BLUE HILL $$$
75 Washington Pl. (212) 539-1776, W www.bluehillnyc.com
This intimate Greenwich Village restaurant is known for inventive New American fare that uses garden-fresh produce of the season, from two chefs who trained under David Bouley. Given the caliber of the food, the prices are reasonable. ○ D daily. ▨ AE MC, V

| | | | | ▪ | |

BLUE RIBBON BAKERY $$$
33 Downing St. (212) 337-0404
More than a bakery, this bi-level Village favorite has an enormous, eclectic menu that ranges from old-fashioned American comfort foods to sophisticated French-inspired fare, plus sandwiches on bread freshly baked in their brick oven, a notable cheese selection, and many "small plates" if you want to do some sampling. ○ L, D Tue–Sun. ⬥ ▨ AE, MC, V

| | ● | | | ▪ | |

BRIDGE CAFÉ $$$
279 Water St. (212) 227-3344 W www.bridgecafe.citysearch.com
Hidden in the shadows of the Brooklyn Bridge is city's oldest continuously operating tavern, a quaint wooden building circa 1794, with checked tablecloths, authentic old New York ambience, and a surprisingly sophisticated American menu. The Sunday brunch is also highly recommended. ○ L Mon–Fri; D Mon–Sun. ⬥ ▨ AE, MC, V

| | ● | | | ▪ | |

CRAFT $$
43 East 19th St. (212) 780-0880 W www.craftrestaurant.com
Talented Tom Colicchio of Gramercy Tavern has a new place around the corner where the emphasis is on simple preparation of highest quality, and absolutely fresh ingredients from small, specialized local farms and purveyors. The results have critics cheering. ○ L Mon–Fri; D Mon–Sun. ⬥ ▨ AE, MC, V

| | | ▪ | ● | ▪ | |

THE DINING ROOM $$$$
154 East 79th St. (212) 327-2500 W www.screeningroom.com/tlr
Excellent American cuisine and a comfortable upstairs setting with privacy conducive to conversation make this sibling of the downtown Screening Room a prime choice, and it has been booked constantly almost from the day it opened. The glazed red snapper is a favorite. ○ D daily. ⬥ (Main floor) ▨ AE, MC, V

| | ● | | | ▪ | |

Price categories include a three-course meal for one, half a bottle of house wine, and all unavoidable extra charges such as sales tax and service.
$ under $25
$$ $25–$35
$$$ $35–$50
$$$$ $50–$70
$$$$$ over $70.

LATE OPENING
Last orders at or after 11:30pm excluding Sunday.
BAR DINING
Snacks, light meals or appetizers, served at the bar or at tables in the bar area.
FIXED-PRICE MENU
A fixed price for a set meal that is usually less expensive that normal menu prices.
SUNDAY OPENING
Brunch and/or dinner served on Sunday.
TABLES OUTSIDE
Garden or courtyard with outside tables.

	LATE OPENING	BAR DINING	FIXED-PRICE MENU	SUNDAY OPENING	TABLES OUTSIDE

ELEVEN MADISON PARK $$$
11 Madison Ave. 【 *(212) 889-0905*
*V*Restaurateur Danny Meyer has single-handedly made Madison Square Park chic with this soaring, three-story, Art Deco setting in the old Metropolitan Life Building. His typically imaginative New American cuisine is offered. The ambience is elegant but never stuffy. ◯ L Mon–Fri; D daily.
🍷 ♿ 🖃 *AE, MC, V*

| | | ■ | ● | ■ | |

FIRST $$$
87 First Ave. 【 *(212) 674-3823* W *www.first.citysearch.com*
Where do chefs go when they get off work? For many the answer is this late-opening café, where the black-clad East Village crowd is not alone in discovering Sammy DeMarco's great New American fare.
◯ D daily; Brunch Sun. ♿ 🖃 *AE, MC, V*

| | ● | | | ■ | |

FOUR SEASONS $$$$$
99 East 52nd St. 【 *754-9494* W *www.fourseasonsrestaurant.com*
Restaurants come and go, but this gracious New York institution with landmark decor by Philip Johnson seems to go on forever, always among the top-rated for American/Continental food. The Grill Room is still the prime place for power lunches, and the Pool Room is a perfect setting for special-occasion dinners. ◯ L, Mon–Fri; D Mon–Sat. 🍷 ♿ 🖃 *AE, MC, V*

| | | ■ | ● | | |

GAGE & TOLLNER $$$
372 Fulton St, Brooklyn. 【 *(718) 875-5181* W *www.gageandtollner.com*
The old-world ambience is real in this landmark, in business since 1879. Recent restoration, with gas lights and brocade walls, make it a special experience worth the subway ride to Brooklyn. The reliable menu features traditional seafood and steak, with a few contemporary additions. The crabcakes are highly recommended. ◯ L Mon–Fri; D Mon–Sat. ♿ 🖃 *AE, MC, V*

GOTHAM BAR AND GRILL W *www.gothambarandgrill.com* $$$$$
12 East 12th St between 5th Ave and University Pl. 【 *(212) 620-4020*
Chef Alfred Portale has long been known for his "vertical food," artful layers of delicious and elegant New American fare. The lofty columned space manages to convey a mood that is both sophisticated and casual. The $20.01 three-course lunch is a great buy. ◯ L Mon–Fri; D Sat, Sun. 🍷 🖃 *AE, MC, V*

GRAMERCY TAVERN $$$$$
42 East 20th St. 【 *(212) 477-0777* W *www.gramercytavern.com*
Another Danny Meyer success, this is perhaps New York's most unpretentious fine dining, with the beams, antiques, and comfortable rustic ambience of a country inn, and a hospitable, knowledgeable staff. Tom Colicchio's inventive American cuisine is universally praised. No reservations needed for the less expensive Tavern Room. ◯ L Mon–Fri, Sat, Sun in Tavern; D daily.
🍷 ♿ ★ 🖃 *AE, MC, V*

| | | ■ | ● | ■ | |

HOME $$
20 Cornelia St. 【 *(212) 243-9579*
Food like Mom used to make (provided she was a terrific cook) keeps this small, narrow café crowded. Entrees are lovingly prepared, many seasoned with the signature homemade catsup. The patio behind is a breath of fresh air in summer. ◯ L, D daily. ♿ 🖃 *AE*

| | | | | ■ | |

MARCH $$$$$
405 East 58th St. 【 *(212) 754-6272*
Another elite dining spot, featuring a romantic setting in a gracious townhouse and a creative menu from star chef Wayne Nish. The recently expanded restaurant now has a skylit downstairs dining room. Menus make the most of the season's fresh produce, and the four-to-seven course prix-fixe dinners are memorable. ◯ D Mon–Sun. 🍷 ♿ 🖃 *AE, MC, V*

| | | | ● | ■ | |

MICHAEL JORDAN'S – THE STEAK HOUSE $$$$
Grand Central Terminal, West Balcony ((212) 655-2300
The basketball great has scored again with this steak house and cigar bar
overlooking the grand spaces of freshly renovated Grand Central Terminal.
Order a steak with light-as-air french fries and creamed spinach, and revel in
an All-American classic dinner. But don't come on a hot summer day; the
terminal is not air-conditioned. ☐ L, D daily. 🍷 ♿ 🗭 AE, MC, V

ONE IF BY LAND, TWO IF BY SEA $$$$$
17 Barrow St. ((212) 228-0822 W www.oneifbyland.com
Romance is in the air in this charming, landmark Greenwich Village
townhouse. Elegant New American/Continental fare comes with firelight,
flickering candles, flowers and a tinkling piano. If you want to propose or
celebrate a special anniversary, this is the place. ☐ D daily. 🍷 🗭 AE, MC, V

PETER LUGER $$$$
178 Broadway, Williamsburg, Brooklyn. ((718) 387-7400 W www.peterluger.com
There's nothing more all-American than a great steak, and nobody does it
better than Peter Lugar. The gritty beer-hall ambience and remote location
don't discourage beef lovers. Don't even think about coming without a
reservation--and still expect a wait. ☐ L, D daily. ♿

PRUNE $$$
54 East 1st St. ((212) 677-6221
Short on space but long on creativity, this unpretentious East Village café
serves original, reasonably priced American home cooking with multi-cultural,
sometimes quirky touches. Reservations are hard to come by, but it's worth
the effort. ☐ D Tue–Sun. 🗭 AE, MC, V

THE RED CAT $$$
227 Tenth Ave. ((212) 242-1122 W www.theredcat.com
Red banquettes and red accent plates are just the start of the warmth at this
modern neighborhood place, stylish but still friendly and with first-rate
American fare with Mediterranean accents. Don't miss the parmesan frites with
mustard aioli. ☐ L Tue–Sat., dinner daily. 🗭 AE, MC, V

RIVER CAFÉ $$$$$
One Water St, Brooklyn. ((718) 522-5200 W www.rivercafe.com
New York's most spectacular view is from this Brooklyn standout, and the
New American fare is worthy of the romantic setting. The signature Chocolate
Duo dessert includes a chocolate marquise mini-Brooklyn Bridge. If you can't
afford the dinner tab, come for drinks and light fare on the terrace. (No jeans,
please.) ☐ L Mon–Sat; Brunch, Sun.; D Daily. 🍷 ♿ ★ 🗭 AE, MC, V

71 CLINTON FRESH FOOD $$$
71 Clinton St. ((212) 614-6960
A sure sign of the changes on the Lower East Side is this hot and hip (albeit
cramped) storefront café gaining fame for the exciting creations of chef Wylie
Dufresne, formerly of Jean George, and drawing food lovers from all over
town. ☐ D Mon–Sat. 🍷 🗭 AE, MC, V

THE TASTING ROOM $$$
72 East 1st St. ((212) 358-7831
The praise is universal for this small New American entry in the East Village,
where the friendly, unhurried ambience is set by hostess Renee Alevras, and
the seasonal dishes of her husband, chef Colin Alevras, can be accompanied
by a choice of 300 American wines. Tasting portions are available for each
main course. ☐ L Wed, D Mon–Sat. 🍷 ♿ 🗭 AE, MC, V

UNION PACIFIC $$$$$
111 East 22nd St. ((212) 995-8500 W www.unionpacificrestaurant.com
A waterfall at the entrance and a lofty vaulted-ceiling dining room set the
stage for a dramatic evening. Rocco DiSpirito's bold New American menu with
Pacific Rim influences is a big reason why this neighborhood is becoming a
major food destination. ☐ L Tue–Fri; D Mon–Sat. 🍷 ♿ 🗭 AE, MC, V

UNION SQUARE CAFÉ $$$$
21 East 16th St. ((212) 243-4020 W www.unionsquarecafe.com
Restaurant entrepreneur Danny Meyer's first venue has been one of New
York's most popular since 1985, loved for delicious fare served in comfortable,
casual surroundings by a friendly staff. Chef Michael Romano's new takes on
American standards include the freshest ingredients from the neighboring
Union Square Greenmarket. ☐ L Mon–Sat; D Sun. 🍷 ♿ ★ 🗭 AE, MC, V

e categories include a
e-course meal for one, half a
tle of house wine, and all
unavoidable extra charges such
s sales tax and service.
$ under $25
$$ $25–$35
$$$ $35–$50
$$$$ $50–$70
$$$$$ over $70.

LATE OPENING
Last orders at or after 11:30pm excluding Sunday.
BAR DINING
Snacks, light meals or appetizers, served at the bar or at tables in the bar area.
FIXED-PRICE MENU
A fixed price for a set meal that is usually less expensive that normal menu prices.
SUNDAY OPENING
Brunch and/or dinner served on Sunday.
TABLES OUTSIDE
Garden or courtyard with outside tables.

	LATE OPENING	BAR DINING	FIXED-PRICE MENU	SUNDAY OPENING	TABLES OUTSIDE
VERITAS $$$$$ 43 East 20th St. (212) 353-3700 W www.veritas-nyc.com A wine list offering 1,300 selections and helpful sommeliers are the biggest draws, but the New American cuisine is quite outstanding on its own at this chic and sleek restaurant. Just 55 seats, so be sure to reserve ahead. L Mon–Fri; D daily. AE, MC, V		■	●	■	
AMERICAN REGIONAL					
COPELAND'S $ 549 West 145th St. (212) 234-2357 Take your pick of Southern fried chicken, Maryland crab cakes, or Louisiana gumbo. You can't go wrong at this popular Harlem spot where folks like Bill Cosby and Danny Glover have been spotted, and the Sunday gospel brunch is the best around. Jazz adds to the atmosphere. D Tue–Sun; Brunch Sun. AE, MC, V	●			■	
GREAT JONES CAFÉ $ 54 Great Jones St. (212) 674-9304 Cajun food lovers hie to this hole-in-the-wall NoHo neighborhood café for spicy gumbo made with andouille sausage, jambalaya, corn-meal fried catfish, and other delicious New Orleans fare. Don't expect atmosphere, but do expect a young, hip, local crowd. D daily.	●				
JEZEBEL $$$ 630 Ninth Ave. (212) 582-1045 W www.jezebelny.com A setting of porch swings, antiques, and palms add up to just the place to sample soul food favorites like fried chicken, catfish, grits, and okra – and be sure to save room for the scrumptious homemade pies. The location near the Theater District is another plus. L Tue–Thu; D Tue–Sat; Brunch Sun. AE					
MESA GRILL $$$$ 102 Fifth Ave. (212) 807-7400 W www.mesagrill.com Celebrity chef Bobby Flay is a master of Southwestern cookery, and his creative menus, from roasted pumpkin and smoked chile soup to cumin crusted chicken, have kept the customers coming in droves for a decade. Even the corn muffins are delicious. Sit upstairs for less of the perpetual din. L Mon–Fri, D daily, Brunch Sat-Sun. ★ AE, MC, V		■		■	
SANTA FE $$ 72 West 69th St. (212) 724-0822 A relaxing setting amid peach-colored walls adorned with colorful rugs, and the location near Lincoln Center, are among the reasons this Southwestern standby has been a favorite for years. Some of the best dishes are the Masa shrimp appetizer and chipotle chicken with rice, steamed vegetables, and grated cheese over refried beans. L, D daily. AE, DC, MC, V				■	
TENNESSEE MOUNTAIN $ 143 Spring St. (212) 431-3993 W www.tnmountain.com Housed in a landmark farmhouse built in 1807, Tennessee Mountain is famous for its huge portions of barbecued and smoked chicken and ribs and its recently added steak menu. Southern-style pulled pork and Texas-style smoked brisket are also provided, plus a broad range of lighter snacks and appetizers. Monday and Tuesday nights have an excellent-value all-you-can-eat special. L, D daily. AE, MC, V	●		●	■	●
VIRGIL'S REAL BBQ $ 152 West 44th St. (212) 921-9494 This big, boisterous Theater District restaurant offers a tour of barbecue styles throughout the South, Memphis to Carolina to Texas, 10 different platters of beef, pork, or chicken with a variety of sauces. On the side come flaky buttermilk biscuits with honey-butter, collard greens, and other delicious Southern standards. L, D daily. AE, MC, V				■	

FRENCH

ALAIN DUCASSE AT THE ESSEX HOUSE $⑤⑤⑤⑤⑤
155 West 58th St. █ *(212) 265-7300* Ⓦ *www.alain-ducasse.com*
The celebrated French chef has come to New York in grand style, with a
limited schedule in a posh, intimate 65-seat home with just one seating at
each meal – and New York's most expensive menu. No one questions the
quality of the food, only whether it is worth the stratospheric prices.
◯ L Wed-Thu; D Mon-Fri. █ █ █ *AE, MC, V*

ALISON ON DOMINICK STREET $⑤⑤⑤⑤
38 Dominick St. █ *(212) 727-1188* Ⓦ *www.alisonondominick.com*
Many a proposal takes place in this romantic, candlelit favorite tucked away in
SoHo. The seasonal menu is country French, a mix of seafood and meats,
always beautifully presented. A typical creative combination: poached chicken
breast with roasted pears, turnip, almond, and millet ragout, braised greens,
and a fig balsamic vinaigrette. ◯ D daily. █ *AE, MC, V*

BAYARD'S $⑤⑤⑤⑤⑤
1 Hanover Sq. █ *(212) 514-9454* Ⓦ *www.bayards.com*
Formerly the New York Cotton Exchange and private club for traders, this
mansion has been beautifully restored in Old-World style, furnished with
period antiques and nautical paintings. The highly regarded chef uses only the
freshest and finest ingredients, and the wine list is extensive. A special
experience. ◯ D Mon-Sat. █ █ █ *AE, MC, V*

BOULEY BAKERY $⑤⑤⑤⑤⑤
120 West Broadway. █ *(212) 964-2525* Ⓦ *www.bouley.net*
There is, indeed, a bakery, but there is also a rather simple dining room
overseen by master chef David Bouley, and his New French cuisine will make
you forget everything but your happy palate. The attached bakery café serves
breakfast, brunch, and lunch sandwiches on Bouley's heavenly breads.
◯ L, D daily. █ █ █ *AE, MC, V*

CAFÉ BOULUD $⑤⑤⑤⑤
20 East 76th St. █ *(212) 772-2600* Ⓦ *www.danielnyc.com*
Since Daniel Boulud opened his Midtown palace, his first restaurant has
become a bit more casual. The food is superbly prepared, serious French, and
the tab is also serious. Menus feature classic dishes, specialties of the season,
"Le Potager," a celebration of vegetables, and "Le Voyage," dishes with more
exotic flavors. ◯ L Tue–Sat; D daily. █ █ *AE, MC, V*

CAFÉ DES ARTISTES $⑤⑤⑤
1 West 67th St. █ *(212) 877-3500* Ⓦ *www.cafedesartistesnyc.com*
Once a haunt of artists who lived in the building, the café has long been a
favorite for the romantic floor-to-ceiling murals of naked nymphs by Howard
Christy. Some say the food has slipped, but the regulars, everyone from Peter
Jennings to Itzhak Perlman, don't seem to mind. ◯ L Mon–Fri; D daily;
Brunch Sat, Sun. █ █ █ *AE, MC, V*

CAFÉ LUXEMBOURG $⑤⑤
200 W. 70th St. █ *(212) 873-7411*
A neighborhood favorite for nearly 20 years, this is a classic art deco Parisian
bistro with a zinc-topped bar, antique mirrors, and a loyal, hip clientele that
sometimes includes movie stars. The steak *frite* can't be beat. ◯ L Mon–Sat; D
nightly, Brunch Sun. █ *AE, MC, V*

CHANTERELLE $⑤⑤⑤⑤⑤
2 Harrison St. █ *(212) 966-6960* Ⓦ *www.chanterellenyc.com*
A classic for two decades, this understated Tribeca dining room still ranks high
for its flawless New French food and gracious service. Chanterelle is ideal for
special occasions or any time you want to linger over a memorable three-hour
dinner. ◯ L Tue-Sat; D Mon-Sat. █ █ █ *AE, MC, V*

DANIEL $⑤⑤⑤⑤⑤
60 East 65th St. █ *(212) 288-0033* Ⓦ *www.danielnyc.com*
A shining star of the New York food world, Daniel Boulud presides in a
flower-filled, Venetian Renaissance-inspired dining room worthy of his
extraordinary food. Seasonal menus with choices such as roasted squab with
spiced pineapple or black truffle-crusted cod are divine. Lunch is a less
astronomical opportunity to sample the master. ◯ L, D Mon-Sat.
█ █ ★ █ *AE, MC, V*

Price categories include a three-course meal for one, half a bottle of house wine, and all unavoidable extra charges such as sales tax and service.
$ under $25
$$ $25–$35
$$$ $35–$50
$$$$ $50–$70
$$$$$ over $70.

LATE OPENING
Last orders at or after 11:30pm excluding Sunday.
BAR DINING
Snacks, light meals or appetizers, served at the bar or at tables in the bar area.
FIXED-PRICE MENU
A fixed price for a set meal that is usually less expensive that normal menu prices.
SUNDAY OPENING
Brunch and/or dinner served on Sunday.
TABLES OUTSIDE
Garden or courtyard with outside tables.

	LATE OPENING	BAR DINING	FIXED-PRICE MENU	SUNDAY OPENING	TABLES OUTSIDE
14 WALL STREET RESTAURANT $$$$					
GUASTAVINO RESTAURANT AND CLUB $$$$		■	●	■	
JEAN GEORGES $$$$$			●		
LA BONNE SOUPE $$	●			■	●
LA GRENOUILLE $$$$$					
LE CIRQUE 2000 $$$$$		■		■	
LE JARDIN BISTRO $$$				■	●
LE ZINC $$$	●			■	

14 WALL STREET RESTAURANT $$$$
14 Wall St. (212) 233-2780 W www.14wallstreetrestaurant.com
Once J.P. Morgan's private dining room, this penthouse with wonderful views is a Wall Street expense-account favorite. The room with high ceilings, dark wood trim, and vintage French posters is a handsome setting for generally fine French cuisine. The service is impeccable, and there's a convivial bar for after dinner. L, D Mon-Fri. AE, MC, V

GUASTAVINO RESTAURANT AND CLUB $$$$
409 East 59th St. (212) 980-2455, Club (212) 421-6644 W www.guastavino.com
Under the savvy guidance of London's Terence Conran, this has emerged as one of the city's great settings, beneath the 59th Street Bridge, with formal French dining upstairs in the Club beneath the arched Guastavino tiles, and a huge, usually packed brasserie and bar in the lofty spaces downstairs.
L Mon-Sat; D Mon-Sun; Brunch Sun. AE, MC, V

JEAN GEORGES $$$$$
Trump International Hotel, 1 Central Park West. (212) 299-3900 W www.jean-georges.com
Jean-George Vongerichten in his namesake restaurant turns out food that is among the very best in New York, transformed by the French master's delicate sauces and creative combinations. Adam Tihany has designed a polished, almost austere setting that does not upstage the four-star chef.
L Mon-Fri; D Mon-Sat. ★ AE, MC, V

LA BONNE SOUPE $$
48 West 55th St. (212) 586-7650 W www.labonnesoupe.com
This cozy midtown haven for the thrifty, nearing its 30th birthday, exudes comfortable, old-fashioned French charm. Besides filling soups, including a classic onion soup, specials include fondues, quiches, omelets, and reasonably priced "plats du jour," steak *pomme frites* to *poulet* to sweetbreads.
L, D daily. AE, MC, V

LA GRENOUILLE $$$$$
3 East 52nd St. (212) 752-1495;
La Grenouille maintains the highest standards of elegant French dining in a beautiful dining room with silk on the walls, velvet banquette,s and glorious flower bouquets everywhere. A classic since 1962, it remains one of the city's best restaurants year after year. L, D Tue-Sat. ★ AE, MC, V

LE CIRQUE 2000 $$$$$
455 Madison Ave. (212) 303-7788 W www.lecirque.com
Some love the bright neon and the playful curving furniture by Adam Tihany, although some find it jarring amid the gilded old world splendor of the landmark Villard Houses. But no one doubts that Le Cirque is one of the city's better French restaurants and for many the place to see and be seen.
L Mon-Sat; D Mon-Sun. ★ AE, MC, V

LE JARDIN BISTRO $$$
25 Cleveland Pl. (212) 343-9599 W www.lejardinbistro.com
When the weather is warm, dining beneath an umbrella in this leafy SoHo garden is delightful. The reasonably priced menu of simple French favorites such as bouillabaise, coq au vin, or mussels is never a disappointment, the staff is pleasant, and the ambience is delightful in the small indoor café as well as in the garden. L, D daily. AE, MC, V

LE ZINC $$$
139 Duane St. (212) 513-0001 W www.lezincnyc.com
The proprietors of the very haute Chanterelle have opened a welcome informal bistro, open to 4am. The spare decor features creamy walls, bare tables, and wine bottles adorning the walls. Onion fritters and skate are recommended. L Mon-Sat; D daily; Brunch Sun. AE, MC, V

LESPINASSE $$$$$
2 East 55th St, St. Regis Hotel ((212) 339-6719 w www.stregis.com
Opulent Louis XV surroundings, Waterford crystal, Limoges china, and sumptuous formal French fare put this firmly in the top ranks of New York restaurants, but be forewarned that the tab can be a painful ending to a wonderful meal. ☐ L, D Tue-Sat. ★ AE, MC, V

MONTRACHET $$$$
239 West Broadway. ((212) 219-2777 w www.montrachet.net
This first of Drew Nieporent's restaurant empire, nearly two decades old, continues to rank among the city's best, known for its comfortable, casual decor, modern French cuisine, and exceptional wine list. The Friday-only $20.01 prix-fixe lunch is worth planning for. ☐ L Fri; D Mon-Sat. ★ AE, MC, V

ORSAY $$$
1057-59 Lexington Ave. ((212) 517-6400 w www.orsayrestaurant.com
Replacing the late Mortimer's, society's favorite hangout, isn't easy, but this chic French café has succeeded, drawing back the upscale clientele and many others with authentic bistro fare served with flair by very French waiters. ☐ L, D daily. AE, MC, V

PROVENCE $$$
28 MacDougal St. ((212) 475-7500 w www.provence.citysearch.com
Popular for its Provençal atmosphere, outdoor garden, and reasonable prices, this picturéque French café in SoHo is a romantic find. The menu features traditional dishes such as bouillabaisse and roasted duck as well as more "nouveau" additions. ☐ L, D daily. AE

ITALIAN

BABBO $$$$$
110 Waverly Pl. ((212) 777-0303
The setting in a century-old duplex Greenwich Village townhouse, with grand stairway and skylight, and the inventive, rustic Italian country fare of notable chef Mario Batali, make this one of the most popular of the many Italian restaurants in the city; reserve well in advance. Sit upstairs for less crowded surroundings. ☐ D nightly. ★ AE, MC, V

BOTTINO $$$
246 10th Ave. ((212) 206-6766 w www.bottinonyc.com
A 100-year-old hardware store amid the booming Chelsea gallery scene has been transformed into sleek minimalist modern space with Eames, Knoll, and Bertoia furnishings. Bottino attracts a stylish crowd both day and night for good Northern Italian fare and a lovely garden that is tented in winter. ☐ L Tue-Sat; D daily. AE, MC, V

BECCO $$
355 West 46th St. ((212) 397-7597 w www.lydiasitaly.com
A best-bet in the Theater District, popular Becco has bargain prix-fixe menus, your choice of a generous antipasto with unlimited portions of three pastas of the day, or Caesar salad with a main course, all well prepared under the watchful eyes of the Bastianiches, who also own the upscale Felidia. ☐ L Mon-Sat; D nightly. ★ AE, MC, V

CAFÉ FIORELLO $$$
1900 Broadway. ((212) 595-5330
The bountiful antipasto bar alone is enough reason to visit: you can have a seat on a stool and sample enough for a whole meal before heading for Lincoln Center, just across the street. But the thin crust pizzas are equally tempting, and there is a full Italian menu as well. ☐ L, D daily. AE, MC, V

DA NICO $$
165 Mulberry St. ((212) 343-1212 w www.littleitalynyc.com/danico
A rustic setting and a wonderful courtyard garden make this family-run restaurant one of the favorites in Little Italy. Take your pick of southern or northern Italian standards, an antipasto bar, and 16 kinds of pizza, and don't miss the tiramisu for dessert. ☐ L, D daily. AE, MC, V

DA SILVANO $$$$
260 Sixth Ave. ((212) 982-2343
Try for a table outside where you can watch for the celebrities, who are often regulars at this neighborhood trattoria where chef/owner Silvano Marcetta has presided for 25 years. The northern Italian fare is consistent, and the buzz is even better. ☐ L, D daily. AE, MC, V

			LATE OPENING	BAR DINING	FIXED-PRICE MENU	SUNDAY OPENING	TABLES OUTSIDE

Price categories include a three-course meal for one, half a bottle of house wine, and all unavoidable extra charges such as sales tax and service.
$ under $25
$$ $25–$35
$$$ $35–$50
$$$$ $50–$70
$$$$$ over $70.

LATE OPENING
Last orders at or after 11:30pm excluding Sunday.
BAR DINING
Snacks, light meals or appetizers, served at the bar or at tables in the bar area.
FIXED-PRICE MENU
A fixed price for a set meal that is usually less expensive that normal menu prices.
SUNDAY OPENING
Brunch and/or dinner served on Sunday.
TABLES OUTSIDE
Garden or courtyard with outside tables.

DA UMBERTO $$$$
107 West 17th St. ☎ (212) 989-0303
Sophisticated Tuscan fare has kept them coming for years to this unpretentious restaurant where a long list of daily specials uses the freshest ingredients of the season. A regional wine list complements the food, and the tiramisu is worth the calories. ◯ L Mon-Fri; D Mon-Sat. 🍷 📋 AE

ERMINIA $$$$
150 East 83rd St. ☎ (212) 879-4284
Romance is in the air in this tiny, candlelit Italian with brick walls, beamed ceilings, and a fireplace. The well-prepared, authentic Italian classics and caring service add to the special feeling, and the homemade napoleon dessert is a great way to end the meal. ◯ D Mon-Sat. 📋 AE

FELIDIA $$$$
243 East 58th St. ☎ (212) 758-1479 ⓦ www.lydiasitaly.com
Exposed brick, wood paneling, and extravagant flowers in an East Side townhouse make a cozy setting for fine Northern Italian fare overseen by a popular TV chef, Lidia Bastianich. The wide-ranging seasonal menu includes creative pastas and risottos, along with seafood and meat dishes. The wine list offers more than 1,000 labels. ◯ L Mon-Fri; D Mon-Sat. 🍷 📋 AE, MC, V

GENNARO $$
665 Amsterdam Ave. ☎ (212) 665-5348
This tiny café serves the best Italian food on the Upper West Side, prepared to order by the owner/chef and at fair prices, which explains the constant lines (no reservations, but a current expansion should help). The antipasto is a meal in itself. ◯ D daily. ♿

IL BAGATTO $$
192 East 2nd St. ☎ (212) 228-0977
Even uptowners head for this East Village hangout between Avenues A & B, where the Italian food is good and the price is right. Expect a wait to get in and rushed service, but fans say it's worth it, and you can meet some neighborhood types while you wait. ◯ D Tue-Sun

---

IL MULINO $$$$$
86 West 3rd St. ☎ (212) 673-3783
Call weeks ahead if you hope for a reservation at the Greenwich Village restaurant many call Manhattan's best Italian. The Tuscan menu is not innovative, but the high quality is consistent, the portions large, the brick-walled, lamp-lit room is inviting, and the service warm and caring. The odds of a table are much better for lunch. ◯ L Mon-Fri; D Mon-Sat. 🍷 ♿ 🍴 ★ 📋 AE, MC, V

IL PALAZZO $$
151 Mulberry St. ☎ (212) 343-7000 ⓦ www.littleitalynyc.com/ilpalazzo
One of the better choices on Mulberry Street: cozy, candlelit, and non-touristy. The menu includes all the Italian favorites, including tempting pastries. The serene garden with a fountain out back is a summer delight. ◯ L, D daily. 📋 AE, MC, V

I TRULLI $$$$
122 East 27th St. ☎ (212) 481-7372 ⓦ www.itrulli.com
Reviewers rave about this Gramercy favorite specializing in the Southern food of Puglia, accompanied by a notable wine list. (There's even more wine at the Enoteca I Trulli next door). With a cozy fireplace in winter and a summer garden, this is a winner for all seasons. ◯ L Mon-Fri; D Mon-Sat. 🍷 ★ 📋 AE, MC, V

LE MADRI $$$$
168 West 18th St. ☎ (212) 727-8022 ⓦ www.lemadri.citysearch.com
Casually elegant and known for flavorful Northern Italian cooking, this Chelsea old-timer attracts a well-heeled crowd who enjoy lusty dishes such as osso buco, and an Italian wine list with more than 200 choices. ◯ L, D daily (closed for lunch weekends July, Aug). 🍷 📋 AE, MC, V

LUPA $$$
170 Thompson St. ▐ *(212) 982-5089*
Informal and much less expensive than his Babbo, Mario Batali's rustic,
candle-lit Roman trattoria serves elegant fare at affordable prices: appetizers
like heavenly prosciutto with figs, and pastas such as squid ink tagliarini with
spicy calamari. You may have to wait for a seat, but you won't be sorry you
came. ◖ L, D daily. ♿ ★ 🗩 *AE, MC, V*

ORSO $$$
322 West 46th St. ▐ *(212) 489-7212* Ⓦ *www.orsorestaurant.com*
If you are lucky enough to snag a reservation, you'll enjoy some of the Theater
District's best dining, with a splendid Italian menu that ranges from thin-crusted
pizzas to formal entrees, served in a sophisticated contemporary setting. Save
room for dessert; it's too good to miss. ◖ L, D daily. ♿ ★ 🗩 *AE, MC, V*

OSTERIA DEL CIRCO $$$$
120 West 55th St. ▐ *(212) 265-3636* Ⓦ *www.osteriadelcirco*
The sons of Le Cirque 2000 owner Sirio Maccioni have created their own
whimsical circus motif with banners, jugglers, and saucy monkeys. They serve
tasty Tuscan fare from mother Egidiana's recipes, adding up to a lively (albeit
noisy) Theater District favorite. ◖ L, Mon-Sat; D daily. ♿ 🗩 *AE, MC, V*

EUROPEAN

AQUAVIT $$$$$
13 West 54th St. ▐ *(212) 307-7311* Ⓦ *www.savvydiner.com/newyork/aquavit*
A midtown townhouse decorated with contemporary Swedish art is the setting
for New York's top Scandinavian restaurant, serving Swedish-inspired cuisine
as interpreted an inventive chef, Marcus Samuelsson, whose presentation is as
exciting as his menus. The herring plate and the arctic char are highly
recommended. ◖ L Mon-Sat; D daily, Brunch Sun. 🍴 ★ 🗩 *AE, MC, V*

BOLO $$$$
23 East 22nd St. ▐ *(212) 228-2200* Ⓦ *www.bolo.citysearch.com*
A vibrant room filled with paintings is the venue for the Mesa Grill's creative
chef Bobby Flay, whose contemporary take on Spanish cuisine draws a
packed house. Grilled meats and rice dishes such as black squid ink risotto
and a tasty paella are specialties, and roast suckling pig is the feature every
Wednesday night. ◖ L Mon-Fri; D Mon-Sun. ♿ 🗩 *AE, MC, V*

CAFÉ DE BRUXELLES $$
118 Greenwich Ave. ▐ *(212) 206-1830*
Ten kinds of mussels, crispy frites, and fabulous Belgian beer can't be beat at
this comfortable Greenwich Village restaurant, established long before the
current Belgian fad began in New York. Stews and seafood are also excellent,
and the Belgian chocolate desserts make all others seem inadequate.
◖ L, D daily. 🗩 *AE, MC, V*

DANUBE $$$$$
30 Hudson St. ▐ *(212) 791-3771* Ⓦ *www.bouley.net*
The chemistry is just right at David Bouley's unusual Tribeca restaurant, offering light-as-air, "nouveau Austrian" food in an intimate new spin on an old-
world setting. It's all so warm and wonderful, nobody wants to leave. Wiener
schnitzel and spaetzle never had it so good. ◖ L, D Mon-Sat. ♿ ★ 🗩 *AE, MC, V*

MOCCA HUNGARIAN RESTAURANT $
1588 Second Ave. ▐ *(212) 734-6470*
Mocca brings to mind a simple European café with flowery china on the wall,
lace curtains, and old-fashioned lighting. Chicken paprikash, beef goulash,
stuffed cabbage, dumplings, and schnitzels are among the traditional choices.
All are reasonable, and the prix-fixe dinners are a real bargain. ◖ L, D daily

PICHOLINE $$$$$
35 West 64th St. ▐ *(212) 724-8585*
For fine dining in the Lincoln Center area, the top choice is Terrance
Brennan's elegant Mediterranean restaurant, where the chef's blending of
subtle flavors transforms every dish. The cheese course is famous – be sure to
save room. ◖ L Tue-Sat; D Mon-Sun. 🍴 ★ 🗩 *AE, MC, V*

RIO MAR $$
7 Ninth Ave at Little West 12th St. ▐ *(212) 242-1623*
The generous free tapas at the bar of this hip Spanish taverna in the trendy
Meatpacking District just might fill you up, but upstairs you can enjoy big
helpings of classics like paella or arroz con pollo and sangria in a shabby-chic
dining room. ◖ L, D daily. 🗩 *AE*

Price categories include a three-course meal for one, half a bottle of house wine, and all unavoidable extra charges such as sales tax and service.
$ under $25
$$ $25–$35
$$$ $35–$50
$$$$ $50–$70
$$$$$ over $70.

LATE OPENING
Last orders at or after 11:30pm excluding Sunday.
BAR DINING
Snacks, light meals or appetizers, served at the bar or at tables in the bar area.
FIXED-PRICE MENU
A fixed price for a set meal that is usually less expensive that normal menu prices.
SUNDAY OPENING
Brunch and/or dinner served on Sunday.
TABLES OUTSIDE
Garden or courtyard with outside tables.

	LATE OPENING	BAR DINING	FIXED-PRICE MENU	SUNDAY OPENING	TABLES OUTSIDE
RUSSIAN TEA ROOM $$$$			●	■	
SAMMY'S ROUMANIAN $$$	●				
TERRACE IN THE SKY $$$$					
MOLYVOS $$$	●				
PASHA $$$				■	
PERIYALI $$$$		■			
S'AGAPO $$	●				●
AMERICAN PARK AT THE BATTERY $$$$					●

RUSSIAN TEA ROOM $$$$
150 West 52nd St. 📞 (212) 757-0168
Opulent to the max in glitzy red and gold with faux Fabergé eggs, a dancing bear, and live fish tank, this reincarnated old favorite has added a talented new chef; the chicken Kiev and duck Tabaka are better than ever.
🕐 L, D daily. 🚻 💳 AE, MC, V

SAMMY'S ROUMANIAN $$$
157 Chrystie St. 📞 (212) 673-0330
It looks like a Jewish wedding every night, with balloons everywhere and diners dancing the *hora* in the aisles. The skirt steaks, chopped liver, and *shmaltz* (chicken fat) on the table will freak your cholesterol level, and you'll enjoy every minute. 🕐 D daily. 🚻 💳 AE, MC, V

TERRACE IN THE SKY $$$$
400 West 119th St. 📞 (212) 666-9490 🌐 www.terraceinthesky.com
Way off the beaten path, this dimly lit, elegant rooftop restaurant near Columbia University is so romantic that many weddings are held here. The view from the dining room is fine, from the terrace divine, the harpist adds to the ambience, and the Continental fare lives up to the setting.
🕐 D Tue-Sat. 🚻 💳 AE, MC, V

GREEK/MIDDLE EASTERN/AFGHAN

MOLYVOS $$$
871 Seventh Ave. 📞 582-7500 🌐 www.molyvos.com
Owner John Livanos (also of the upscale Oceana) comes from the fishing village of Molyvos, and he has done his hometown proud with this handsome Theater District restaurant in warm Mediterranean hues, where traditional Greek cooking is elevated to haute cuisine. 🕐 L, D daily. 🚻 ★ 💳 AE, MC, V

PASHA $$$
70 West 71st St. 📞 (212) 579-8751
All is serene in this spacious, skylit, Turkish restaurant a few blocks from Lincoln Center. Tiny appetizer lamb dumplings with mint are delicious, as is the chicken stuffed with rice, pistachios, and currants, served on spinach, and many eggplant dishes, including the lamb with eggplant and tomatoes.
🕐 D daily. 💳 AE, MC, V

PERIYALI $$$$
35 West 20th St. 📞 (212) 463-7890 🌐 www.periyali.com
A billowing, canopied ceiling and white stucco walls set the scene for ultra-sophisticated Greek dining. The double grilled lamb chop and creative fish dishes put Greek food into gourmet territory, and the list of Greek wines is incomparable. Periyali was the first to elevate Greek cuisine to fine dining and continues to set the standard. 🕐 L Mon-Fri; D Mon-Sat. 🍴 💳 AE, MC, V

S'AGAPO $$
34-21 34th Ave near 35th St, Astoria, Queens. 📞 (718) 626-0303
The name means "I love you" in Greek, and it's apt for this cheerful spot with wonderful Greek food, especially grilled fish. There is music on weekends and a terrace for summer evenings. The American Museum of the Moving Image and MoMA QNS are nearby. 🕐 L, D daily. 💳 MC, V

SEAFOOD

AMERICAN PARK AT THE BATTERY $$$$
Battery Park, opposite 17 State St. 📞 (212) 809-5508 🌐 www.americanpark.com
A great location at the tip of the Battery with wall-to-wall harbor views makes this a popular choice. If you can sit on the expansive terrace on a sunny day, you won't mind if the generous seafood selection doesn't quite equal the view. 🕐 L Mon-Fri; D Mon-Sat. 🚻 💳 AE, MC, V

AQUAGRILL $$$$
210 Spring St. [(212) 274-0505
Yellow walls, seashell lighting fixtures, and cushy banquettes are the setting
for a trendy SoHo seafood haven with a spacious raw bar featuring oysters
flown in daily. The fish is always the freshest, the warm octopus salad is a
classic, and those who like their seafood prepared simply can order anything
on the menu grilled, poached, or roasted. ⬤ L Mon-Fri; D daily; Brunch Sat,
Sun. ♀ ★ 🄴 AE, MC, V

CELLO $$$$$
53 East 77th St. [(212) 517-1200 [w] www.cellorestaurant.com
Admirers say French chef Laurent Tourondel, formerly of Le Bernardin, turns
out superb seafood to rival his much-praised former kitchen. The crowd at
this Upper East Side townhouse restaurant is elegantly appointed; the $35
prix-fixe lunch is the best way to break bread without breaking the bank.
⬤ L Mon-Fri; D Mon-Sat. ♀ & 🕇 🄴 AE, MC, V

ELIAS CORNER $
24-02 31st St at 24th Ave, Astoria, Queens. [(718) 932-1510
The largest Greek community outside the motherland is a 15-minute subway
ride from Manhattan in Astoria, where Elias Corner serves wonderful fish
simply grilled with oil and oregano seasoning. On a summer evening in the
garden, with the hum of Greek conversation all around you, it might as well
be Athens. ⬤ D daily. &

ESCA $$$
402 West 43rd St. [(212) 564-7272
Chef Mario Batali, best known for Italian restaurants such as Babbo and
Lupa in the Village, has staged a Theater District smash hit by serving the
freshest of seafood, deliciously prepared with a Southern Italian accent. The
patio dining is a plus in warm weather. The only problem is getting a
reservation. ⬤ L, D Mon-Sat. & 🄴 AE, MC, V

LE BERNARDIN $$$$$
155 West 51st St. [(212) 489-1515 [w] www.le-bernardin.com
Seafood doesn't come any better than at this quietly luxurious French
restaurant lauded for revolutionizing the way fish is served in New York and
considered one of America's best restaurants. Chef Eric Lipert seems to have
no critics. Perfection has its price, but the meal will be memorable.
⬤ L Mon-Fri; D Mon-Sat. ♀ ★ 🄴 AE, MC, V

OCEANA $$$$$
55 East 54th St. [(212) 759-5941 [w] www.oceanarestaurant.com
Fitted with the look and intimacy of a posh private yacht, Oceana is a first-
class passage all the way, food to decor, reflected in a high tab, even for the
prix-fixe lunch. Upstairs is more masculine, with paneling, posters, and a
seafood bar serving raw oysters as well as main courses. ⬤ L Mon-Fri;
D Mon-Sat. ♀ 🄴 AE, MC, V

THE OYSTER BAR AND RESTAURANT $$$
Grand Central Station, lower level, 42nd St and Lexington Ave. [(212) 490-6650
A New York classic beneath a vaulted ceiling of Guastavino tiles, this big,
bustling, 90-year-old restaurant serves only the finest seafood, from the formal
menu with as many as 30 choices, to the long raw bar with two dozen kinds
of oysters. ⬤ L Mon-Fri; D Mon-Sat. ♀ & ★ 🄴 AE, MC, V

PEARL OYSTER BAR $$
18 Cornelia St. [(212) 691-8211
New England-style informality is the mood, and Maine lobster rolls rival
oysters as the favorite dish at this Greenwich Village seafood haven whose
only fault may be that it is too popular. If you don't want to stand in line,
come for lunch. ⬤ L Mon-Fri; D Mon-Sat. & 🄴 MC, V

LATIN AMERICAN/ CARIBBEAN

ASIA DE CUBA $$$$
Morgans Hotel, 237 Madison Ave. [(212) 726-7755 [w] www.asiadecuba.com
Sit on the balcony to enjoy people-watching, or join the downstairs communal
table for 36. Either way, you'll enjoy Philippe Starck's ultra-hip interior, and
the buzz that hasn't let up since the restaurant opened. As the name suggests,
the unusual menu is a blend of Asian and Caribbean flavors. ⬤ L Mon-Fri;
D daily. 🄴 AE, MC, V

Price categories include a three-course meal for one, half a bottle of house wine, and all unavoidable extra charges such as sales tax and service.
$ under $25
$$ $25–$35
$$$ $35–$50
$$$$ $50–$70
$$$$$ over $70.

LATE OPENING
Last orders at or after 11:30pm excluding Sunday.
BAR DINING
Snacks, light meals or appetizers, served at the bar or at tables in the bar area.
FIXED-PRICE MENU
A fixed price for a set meal that is usually less expensive that normal menu prices.
SUNDAY OPENING
Brunch and/or dinner served on Sunday.
TABLES OUTSIDE
Garden or courtyard with outside tables.

	LATE OPENING	BAR DINING	FIXED-PRICE MENU	SUNDAY OPENING	TABLES OUTSIDE

CABANA W www.cabananewyorkcity.citysearch.com $$
1032 Third Ave. ((212) 980-5678. **Also at**
Pier 17, South Street Seaport ((212) 406-1155
Latin flavor and background music enliven this favorite with two locations, serving a Cuban/Caribbean menu that features sizzling platters and dishes such as coconut shrimp, empanadas, arroz con pollo, and Jamaican jerk chicken. Order a pina colada or margarita and pretend you're in the islands.
L Mon-Sat; D daily. & AE, MC, V
(LATE OPENING ●, SUNDAY OPENING ■)

CALLE OCHO ((212) 873-5025 $$$
446 Columbus Ave.
Every night feels like a party at this loud and lively spot named for the Cuban area of Miami, always filled with beautiful people and pulsing with Latin rhythm. The chef is Cuban, but his sophisticated modern dishes are inspired by Latin cuisine from Peru to Puerto Rico. D daily, Brunch Sun. &
(LATE OPENING ●, SUNDAY OPENING ■)

CHICAMA $$$$
35 East 18th St. ((212) 505-2233 W www.chicamarestaurant.com
Chef Douglas Rodriguez, who began the "nouveau Latin" craze at Patria, has succeeded again. His bold Pan-Latin, Peruvian-inspired menu, featuring dishes like ceviche and roast pig from a eucalyptus-burning oven-grill, is served in a rustic wood-beamed room with gala South American decor, making for a colorful and satisfying experience. L, D daily. ▮ & AE, MC, V
(LATE OPENING ●, BAR DINING ■)

CHURRASCCARIA PLATAFORMA W www.churrasccariaplataforma.com $$$
318 West 49th St, Belvedere Hotel ((212) 245-0505
A Brazilian carnival for carnivores, with carvers offering all-you-can-eat servings of prime rib, suckling pig, lamb, chicken – 20 choices in all – plus a 40-foot salad bar with anything from carpaccio to sushi, along with exotic greens, all for a reasonable prix-fixe tab. L, D daily. & ★ AE, MC, V
(LATE OPENING ●, FIXED-PRICE MENU ●, SUNDAY OPENING ■)

MAYA ((212) 585-1818 $$$
1191 First Ave.
A major reason that Mexican cuisine is being treated with new respect, Maya chef Richard Sandoval serves up sophisticated and delicate main courses and wonderful side dishes in a lovely peach-hued setting. The only drawback is the sound level; dine early to avoid the din. D daily. & AE, MC, V
(SUNDAY OPENING ■)

PATRIA $$$$
250 Park Ave South. ((212) 777-6211 W www.patrianyc.com
Latin American gone gourmet, creative dishes beautifully presented in a festive setting of mosaic murals and terrazzo floors, draws crowds despite the steep prix-fixe tab. Come for the $20 lunch to sample the excellent fare at an affordable price. L Mon-Fri; D Mon-Sun. ▮ ★ AE, MC, V
(LATE OPENING ●, BAR DINING ■, FIXED-PRICE MENU ●, SUNDAY OPENING ■)

ROCKING HORSE CAFÉ $$
182 Eighth Ave. ((212) 463-9511 W www.rockinghorsecafe.com
The place rocks all right, always packed with diners even after a recent expansion. They come for the great margaritas and excellent Mexican food, with new takes on the traditional, all at reasonable prices.
L, D daily. AE, MC, V
(LATE OPENING ●)

ROSA MEXICANO $$$
1063 First Ave. ((212) 753-7407; 51 Columbus Ave. ((212) 977-7700
New York's first gourmet Mexican restaurant, now with a festive West Side sibling, has colorful decor and food that would do credit to a French chef. But while the food is wonderful, what many people remember most here are the guacamole made at the table and the power-packed margaritas.
D daily. & ★ AE, DC, V
(SUNDAY OPENING ■)

ASIAN

CANTON $$$
45 Division St. ((212) 226-4441

Those who prefer the milder tastes of Cantonese food will find it at its best here. Refined atmosphere and service lure many local diners as well as visitors, even though the prices are a bit high for Chinatown. Let the waiter guide your choices and you'll have an excellent meal. ☐ L, D Wed-Sun. ★

GOLDEN UNICORN $
18 East Broadway. ((212) 941-0911

Dim sum is the star here, but all the dishes are well prepared in this third-floor restaurant in typical Hong Kong style, which means big, flashy, crowded, and noisy. The larger the group the better, so you can taste more of the specialties. ☐ L, D daily. & ✎ AE, MC, V

GRAND SICHUAN $
125 Canal St. ((212) 625-9212.

For those who favor the spicy seasonings of China's Szechwan province, this is a Chinatown find, a no-frills storefront with little ambience but authentic specialties of the region at reasonable prices. The good reputation has spawned two uptown siblings at 229 Ninth Avenue and 745 Ninth Avenue. ☐ L, D daily. ★ ✎ AE, MC, V

INAGIKU $$$$
Waldorf-Astoria Hotel, 301 Park Ave. ((212) 355-0440.

Specialties at this beautifully formal Japanese restaurant are the tempura and the traditional Kaiseki, a full-course dinner with dozen or so dishes served in a designated order. ☐ L, D daily. & ✎ AE, MC, V

ISO $$$
175 2nd Ave. ((212) 777-0361

This Japanese restaurant combines walls hung with modern art, the freshest sushi imaginable, and a casual East Village ambience. Moderate prices make this a neighborhood favorite. ☐ D Mon-Sat. ● one week in summer.
✎ AE, MC, V

JOE'S SHANGHAI $$
9 Pell St. ((212) 233-8888; 24 West 56th Street ((212) 333-3868

Both the Chinatown and Midtown locations are branches of a Flushing restaurant famous for its soup dumplings (look for "steamed buns" on the menu) with delicious broth that spurts out when you take a bite. The rest of the moderately priced Shanghai menu is admirable as well. ☐ L, D daily. ★

KIN KHAO $$
171 Spring St. ((212) 966-3939

The name means "eat rice" in Thai but that's only the beginning of a vast menu offering regional Thai and Bangkok cuisine. Be sure to make reservations; the Soho location is very popular especially on weekends. Save room for the sticky-rice and papaya dessert. ☐ L, D daily. ✎ AE, MC, V

SHUN LEE PALACE $$$
155 East 55th St. ((212) 371-8844 W www.shunleepalace.com

For decades this handsome dining room has been considered New York's premiere Chinese restaurant. Owner Michael Tong sets the elegant mood, and the Cantonese/Szechuan blend menu never disappoints. Casseroles are among the specialties, along with Beijing duck and dishes such as crispy prawn with passion fruit. Choices include a spa menu. ☐ L, D daily. & ★ ✎ AE, MC, V

INDIAN

DAWAT $$$
210 East 58th St. ((212) 355-7555 W www.restaurant.com/dawat

One of the more attractive and upscale Indian dining places in the city, Dawat features recipes inspired by Madhur Jaffrey, a noted Indian cookbook author. It is known for generous portions and signature dishes such as salmon rubbed in coriander chutney and steamed in a banana leaf. ☐ L Mon-Sat; D Mon-Sun.
& ✎ AE, MC, V

Light Meals and Snacks

YOU CAN GET A SNACK almost anywhere and anytime in Manhattan. New Yorkers seem to eat endlessly – on street corners, in bars, luncheonettes, delis, before and after work, and long into the night. Casual eating in New York might include soft pretzels or char-roasted chestnuts from a corner stand; a huge sandwich from a deli; a Greek *gyro* sandwich (roasted lamb in pita bread) from street vendors; a pretheater snack at a café or coffee bar; or a post-party binge at an all-night diner or bistro. While street fare is generally cheap, the quality and culinary skills vary greatly.

DELIS

DELICATESSENS are a New York institution, a great source for a hefty lunchtime sandwich. Try the wonderful corned beef and pastrami sandwiches at the famous **Carnegie Delicatessen**, considered by many to be New York's best deli.

Some delis, such as **Katz's Deli**, cater to those who enjoy traditional kosher food. Most deli business is, however, takeout and as such delis are bustling places serving huge sandwiches at relatively cheap prices. Counter staff are typically surly and impatient, and rudeness has almost become a trademark of the **Stage Deli**, which is now more of a tourist stop than the showbiz favorite it used to be.

For New York ethnic Jewish flavor, try the **Second Avenue Delicatessen**, well-known for its homemade soups, pickles, corned beef sandwiches, chopped liver, and other kosher goodies. **Zabar's** is a takeout heaven for yuppies who put up with the crowds for superb smoked fish, pickles, and salads.

Aficionados say the best pastrami sandwiches and other favorites are to be found at the **Pastrami King** in Queens.

CAFÉS, BISTROS AND BRASSERIES

CAFÉS, BISTROS, and the larger brasseries have become "in" places in New York in recent years. Try **Balthazar** on Spring St. for "brilliantly faux" everything except the menu, which is stellar. The **Café Centro**, above Grand Central, is particularly busy and noisy during lunchtime, and is a favorite with business types. The Provençal/ Mediterranean fare includes fish soups and some succulent desserts. **The Brasserie**, a longtime landmark, has reliable French food and is open 24 hours a day. **Bistro du Nord** on Madison Ave serves a variety of good French/American fare with an inventive flair. Downtown, **Odeon** is a TriBeCa favorite for its brasserie menu and late hours. **Raoul's** in SoHo is a French bistro with a relaxed ambience that keeps artists and other habitués coming back for reliable, informal food. **Elephant and Castle**, a minimally decorated café, is a Greenwich Village standby for soup-salad-omelette lunches and other light snacks. Its real forte is breakfast and brunch, served in ample portions at modest prices. The bar scene is lively too. Tiny **Chez Jacqueline** is also a favored Village spot. Its French bistro fare and proximity to several off-Broadway theaters make it popular with the young, hip, and international crowd for a moderately priced dinner or late supper.

In the Theater District, try the Cuban **Victor's Café 52**. Large, lively, and Latin, it is known for authentic Cuban food served in giant portions at medium prices. **Chez Josephine** is an exuberant bistro-cabaret with live jazz piano playing. The scene is the main attraction here, and the French food is excellent.

La Boite en Bois, small but delightfully French, serves delicious French bistro food and is conveniently close to Lincoln Center. In the same vicinity is **Vince and Eddie's**, a tiny gem known for reliable, often superb American food.

Sarabeth's, on the Upper West Side, defies categorizing, but might best be dubbed a café. The best time to visit is for breakfast or weekend brunch, when families wolf down waffles, French toast, pancakes, and omelettes. There are two other branches, one of which is located in the Whitney Museum of Art.

The Gramercy Park area's **Les Halles** is about as all-out French bistro as New York gets. At its late-night peak, the decibel level is high, but regulars think the *frites* and beef dishes are worth the noise and crowds.

PIZZERIAS

PIZZA IS AVAILABLE all over New York, from street stands and fast-food places that sell it by the slice for a few dollars, to a traditional Neapolitan pizzeria.

Some pizzerias offer something more. **Arturo's Pizzeria** uses a coal oven for crisp, thin-crusted bases with the added inducement of live jazz. **Mezzogiorno** has a Tuscan menu and wonderful pizzas with unusual toppings. The crowded **Mezzaluna** also specializes in brick-oven, thin-crusted pizza, as does **John's Pizzeria**, whose many fans (including Woody Allen) consider it to be Manhattan's best.

Brooklyn boasts a top pizzeria in Coney Island's **Totonno Pizzeria**, which is well worth the trip for real pizza aficionados.Generally, pizza parlors are good places to go for a cheap, simple meal, especially with children. Most places won't take reservations, so the popular ones may have long lines.

HAMBURGER PLACES

YOUR NOSE may lead you to some of the cheaper burger and hot dog stands on the street. However, there are many places in New York where you can buy a better quality burger, even though prices for a top grade all-beef burger can go up to $10.

Hamburger Harry's offers reasonably priced, large, juicy, and mesquite-grilled burgers, with a choice of over a dozen toppings and a huge fresh salad. **Hard Rock Café** is a well-known chain which serves hearty portions in a lively atmosphere.

Bright and basic, the five outlets of **Jackson Hole** offer fat, juicy, meaty burgers in 28 varieties popular with kids. Adults might prefer less glare and smarter décor, but they will like the low prices. It's also a good place to try the quintessential New York drink, the egg cream *(see p286)*.

The **Beer Bar** at Café Centro is where professional types like to hang out. Besides an unusual beer menu, the burgers are delicious.

New York's best burgers may well be found at the **Corner Bistro** in Greenwich Village. Not only are the burgers tasty and reasonably priced, but the beer selection is good, too, and the 4am closing makes this a great late-night stop.

DINERS AND LUNCHEONETTES

DINERS and luncheonettes, also called sandwich or coffee shops, can be found all over town. Food is usually indifferent but served in huge, cheap platefuls. Despite the name luncheonette, such places are usually open from breakfast until late evening, and you can stop in at almost any hour for coffee and something basic and filling to eat.

A recent trend with diners has seen 1990s replicas of the old 1930s cheap-eats places. One such retro-diner is the chic Empire Diner *(see p136)*. The **Broadway Diner** in Midtown is a faithful re-creation of a 1940s diner. It offers a good American breakfast, including thick-cut fries and homemade corned beef hash with poached eggs.

Jerry's attracts a SoHo art and celebrity crowd who love the inventive sandwiches, salads, desserts and huge breakfasts. Also attracting a hip art crowd is **Florent**, a West Village diner with reliable French food served around the clock. **Big Nick's** is the best place for a pizza, hamburger, or breakfast on the Upper West Side. **The Coffee Shop** in Union Square serves Brazilian-American fare and is open all night.

On the Upper East Side, Eli Zabar's **E.A.T.** sells top quality, but pricey Jewish favorites – like mushroom-barley soup and *challah* bread, as well as some sinful desserts.

Devotees swear by **Viand**, a spic-and-span East Side luncheonette, with cheap, ample American breakfasts, good burgers, egg creams, and the best turkey sandwiches in town. **Veselka** is not the usual New York sandwich shop – what makes it special is the Polish/Ukrainian food, all at rock-bottom prices.

TEAROOMS

ABOUT THE ONLY PLACE you can be absolutely sure of getting a cup of real, brewed tea is at a formal, prix fixe afternoon tea in a lounge at one of New York's pricier hotels, from 3pm to 5pm.

Afternoon tea in the **Plaza Hotel**'s Palm Court has cream cakes and hot buttered scones galore. For an extra stylish tea, on Chippendale furniture, visit the **Carlyle** hotel. The **Hotel Pierre** offers one of the better buys in hotel prix fixe teas. Tea at the **Waldorf–Astoria** comes with Devonshire cream, while the elegant tea at the **Stanhope** hotel is abundant enough to carry you through to a late dinner.

A variation on tea themes can be found in a new chain of teahouses called **Saint's Alp**. These delightful spots serving frothy, flavored, colorful tea drinks poured over crushed ice can be found at 51 Mott Street near Chinatown and in the new Times Square area. Teatime, Japanese style, can be enjoyed at **The Tea Box** located in the Takashimaya department store.

COFFEE AND CAKES

YOU CAN GET a decent cup of coffee for as little as 75 cents, with endless free refills, at most diners, luncheonettes, and coffee shops. There is a new trend for coffee bars that serve a variety of gourmet and specialty coffees, such as cappuccino, espresso and caffè latte. Some ice cream parlors and patisseries also serve good coffee, along with decadently luscious pastries.

Some of the most charming coffee houses are in Little Italy, such as **Caffè Biondo**, which serves cappuccino and sinful sweets, and **Caffè Vivaldi** with relatively cheap coffees, teas, and desserts served on marble tables. **Caffè Ferrara**, going strong since 1892, has moderately priced Italian pastries, good coffee, and outdoor seating. **Caffè Dante** is a favorite with students who like to sit outside in warm weather.

The European-style outdoor **Fledermaus Café**, in the South Street Seaport, serves fine coffee and is a good place to watch the passing scene.

The **Candy Bar and Grill**, in Chelsea, offers a selection of excellent Viennese pastries and coffees *mit schlag* (with whipped cream) in a cozy turn-of-the-century setting. The modern Austrian dishes make this a worthwhile dinner stop as well. At **Caffè Bianco**, uptown, desserts are fabulous, the coffee is good, and prices are low. The much pricier **Café Guy Pascal** has delicious French pastries as does **Payard Patisserie**. **Sant' Ambroeus** is a luxurious outpost of the Milanese *pasticceria*, with decadent desserts and an espresso bar. **Dessert Delivery** is the FTD of the dessert world. In addition to home delivery of pies, cakes, or cakes, they have a nifty cafe where you can taste the pastries and enjoy coffee. Try **Serendipity 3**, famous for its Victoriana, elaborate ice cream creations, coffee, and mid-afternoon snacks. **Barnes & Noble Café** is a happy refuge for coffee and a pastry while browsing at one of New York's largest bookstores.

DIRECTORY

LOWER EAST SIDE

Caffè Biondo
141 Mulberry St.
Map 4 F5.

Caffè Ferrara
195 Grand St.
Map 4 F4.

Fledermaus Café
199 Water St.
Map 2 E2.

Katz's Deli
205 E Houston St.
Map 5 A3.

Saint's Alp
51 Mott St
Map 4 F 4.

SOHO AND TRIBECA

Jerry's
101 Prince St.
Map 4 D3.

Mezzogiorno
195 Spring St.
Map 4 D4.

Odeon
145 W Broadway.
Map 1 B1.

Raoul's
180 Prince St.
Map 4 D3.

GREENWICH VILLAGE

Arturo's Pizzeria
106 W Houston St.
Map 4 E3.

Balthazar
80 Spring St.
Map 3 E4.

Caffè Dante
79 MacDougal St.
Map 4 D3.

Caffè Vivaldi
32 Jones St. **Map** 3 C2.

Chez Jacqueline
73 MacDougal St.
Map 4 D2.

Corner Bistro
331 W 4th St.
Map 3 C1.

Elephant and Castle
68 Greenwich Ave.
Map 3 C1.

Florent
69 Gansevoort St
Map 3 B1.

EAST VILLAGE

Second Avenue Delicatessen
156 2nd Ave.
Map 4 F1.

Veselka
144 2nd Ave.
Map 4 F1.

GRAMERCY AND THE FLATIRON

The Coffee Shop
29 Union Sq.
Map 9 A5.

Les Halles
411 Park Ave.
Map 9 A3.

CHELSEA AND THE GARMENT DISTRICT

Candy Bar and Grill
131 8th Ave.
Map 8 D2.

THEATER DISTRICT

Broadway Diner
1726 Broadway.
Map 12 E4.

Carnegie Delicatessen
854 7th Ave.
Map 12 E4.

Chez Josephine
414 W 42nd St.
Map 7 B1.

Hamburger Harry's
145 W 45th St.
Map 12 E4.

Hard Rock Café
221 W 57th St.
Map 12 E3.

Stage Deli
834 7th Ave.
Map 12 E4.

Victor's Café 52
236 W 52nd St.
Map 11 B4.

EAST SIDE MIDTOWN

Beer Bar at Café Centro
MetLife Building,
200 Park Ave. **Map** 9 A2.

UPPER MIDTOWN

Barnes & Noble Café
Citicorp Building,
160 E. 54th St. **Map** 13 A4.

The Brasserie
100 E 53rd St. **Map** 13 A4.

Plaza Hotel
Palm Court, 768 5th Ave.
Map 12 F3.

The Tea Box
Takashimaya, 693 5th Ave.
Map 12 F2.

Waldorf–Astoria
301 Park Ave.
Map 13 A5.

UPPER EAST SIDE

Bistro du Nord
1312 Madison Ave.
Map 17 A2.

Caffè Bianco
1486 2nd Ave.
Map 17 B5.

Carlyle
35 E 76th St.
Map 17 A5.

Café Guy Pascal
1231 Madison Ave.
Map 17 A3.

Dessert Delivery
350 E. 55th St.
☎ 838-5411
Map 13 B4.

E.A.T.
2 E 61st St.
Map 12 F3.

Hotel Pierre
2 E 61st St.
Map 12 F3.

Jackson Hole
232 E 64th St.
Map 13 B2.

John's Pizzeria
408 E 64th St.
Map 13 C2.
One of several branches.

Mezzaluna
1295 3rd Ave.
Map 17 B5.

Payard Patisserie
1032 Lexington Ave.
Map 13 A1.

Sant' Ambroeus
1000 Madison Ave.
Map 17 A5.

Serendipity 3
225 E 60th St.
Map 13 B5.

Stanhope
995 5th Ave.
Map 17 A4.

Viand
1011 Madison Ave.
Map 17 A5.

UPPER WEST SIDE

Big Nick's
2175 Broadway at 77th.
Map 15 C5.

La Boite en Bois
75 W 68th St.
Map 11 C1.

Sarabeth's
423 Amsterdam Ave.
Map 15 C4.

Whitney Museum
945 Madison Ave
Map 17 A5.

Vince and Eddie's
70 W 68th St.
Map 11 C1.

Zabar's
2245 Broadway.
Map 15 C2.

BROOKLYN

Totonno Pizzeria
1524 Neptune Ave.
Map 7 C5.

QUEENS

Pastrami King
124 Queens Blvd,
Kew Gardens.

New York Bars

NEW YORK BARS play a huge role in the life and culture of the city. Many New Yorkers spend the evening in a succession of bars, because each usually offers something more than just alcohol. There may be additional inducements, like excellent food, live music, dancing, or a particularly large selection of beers. Brew pubs, which serve meals and brew beer on the premises, are a recent phenomenon. Bars suiting every taste and budget are to be found all over the city.

RULES AND CONVENTIONS

BARS GENERALLY stay open from around 11am to midnight. Some stay open to 2 or 4am, when they must close by law. Many bars have a "happy hour" between 5pm and 7pm, when they offer twofers (two drinks for the price of one) and a variety of free snacks. Bartenders also have the right to refuse to serve anyone they consider having had too much to drink.

The legal minimum drinking age is 21; if the bartender suspects you are younger, you'll be "carded," or asked to show some identification to prove your age. Children are not usually taken into bars.

It is common to "run a tab" and pay your bill just before you leave. Tipping the bartender is expected – 10% of the bill or about 50 cents for a single drink. Shots are not premeasured, so if you want a bigger drink, it can help to "belly up" to the bar and tip the bartender accordingly for his or her generosity. If you sit at a table, you'll be served there and be charged more.

A round of drinks can be expensive. A good way to save money is by buying a quart (95 cl) or a half gallon (190 cl) pitcher of beer.

Avoid the "free drinks for ladies" bars, which are often just pick-up joints. Some of New York's pubs did not admit women until forced by law to do so, a few years ago. Even today, many women feel uncomfortable drinking alone in certain places. Safer bets for single women are hotel bars or singles bars, although it may still be difficult to avoid harassment.

WHAT TO DRINK

YOU CAN GET almost any alcoholic drink you want in New York bars; the most popular drink is ice-cold beer. Mainstream bars serve standard beers from big producers like Budweiser, Coors, and Miller, and high-profile imports such as Bass ale, Becks and Heineken, and even draft Guinness. Some bars, especially the old pubs and certain chic new bars, have a much wider variety of beers, imported and small domestics. These include locally made products by some of New York's microbreweries, and the popular Brooklyn Lager. There is a vogue now, especially among the young, for microbrewery products. A microbrewery is a small producer of flavorful beers often based on traditional European (German/ Belgian/English) styles.

Other popular drinks include cocktails; rum and coke; dry martinis; Scotch or bourbon, either "straight up" (without ice) or on the rocks (with ice); vodka-and-tonic and gin-and-tonic. Wine is also widely available at bars, although the "wine bar" concept has been replaced by the "olive bar."

FOOD

ALL BARS SERVE some sort of food throughout the day. It is usually convenience food like burgers, fries, salads, sandwiches and small snacks like delicious spicy chicken wings. Happy hour is an excellent time to fill up on free snacks and hot hors d'oeuvres in New York bars. Most bar kitchens stop serving food just before midnight.

FASHIONABLE BARS

YOU MAY have to line up to watch the bored and beautiful at **BB's** (formerly the Bowery Bar) – one of the hippest bars on the current scene. The bar's pretentiousness belies its humble beginnings as a gas station.

Much more fun is the funky late night scene at **Bar Six**, a West Village hangout for the cool and quirky, with microbrewery beers and food that has a Moroccan accent. Also downtown is **SoHo Kitchen and Bar**, a handsome loftlike space with tiered dining areas, a long brick bar, good pizzas, a lengthy wine list containing some 400 wines, and a good range of beers. The **Odeon** on Broadway is another good place to catch the lively SoHo–TriBeCa scene.

On the Upper East Side, the bar at **Swifty's** is a place to observe what passes these days for high society without paying steep prices for the restaurant's ordinary food.

There is a new vogue for cigar bars that encourage smokers. **The Cigar Room at Trumpets** has a 36 premium cigar menu and a large single malt Scotch list. Its attached *intime* dining room is also cigar-friendly. At **Bar and Books** you can inhale, sip, and nibble snacks before a fireplace in a club-like library setting, with live jazz on weekends. In the same venue is the Beekman Bar and Book.

BARS WITH VIEWS

TAKE THE ELEVATOR to the 26th floor of the Art Deco **Beekman Tower** for unsurpassed views of the city plus piano music to set the mood. Also spectacular is the **Pentop Bar and Terrace** at the Peninsula Hotel; though expensive, it has marvelous Midtown views. In warm weather **BP Café**, a friendly outdoor café, is the latest Midtown scene. The **Tavern on the Green** has magical views of Central Park. Inside, the glitz may overwhelm you, but the garden is a pure delight.

HISTORIC AND LITERARY BARS

IF YOU SAMPLE only one New York bar, it should probably be **McSorley's Old Alehouse**, an Irish saloon, often dubbed "McSurly's" because of the staff. It's been on the same site since 1854, making it one of New York's oldest bars. It offers a good choice of beers and a tasty lunch. Try the chili.

The Ear Inn dates from 1812 when the first tavern opened on this SoHo site. Now the haunt of poets and writers, its dark, cramped interior and long wooden bar ooze authenticity.

Greenwich Village has some of the city's oldest bars, such as **Chumley's**, which retains its character as a Prohibition-era speakeasy. It's particularly snug in winter, when an open fire burns in the hearth.

Dylan Thomas's old favorite, the **White Horse Tavern**, is an unpretentious 1880s landmark still going strong and crowded with literary and collegiate types. There's an outdoor café used in warm weather.

Peculier Pub is a beer-lover's paradise, with over 360 varieties of beer from all over the world. You must, however, be willing to tolerate the sometimes snappish and uninformed staff.

A good, though rather touristy, place for a drink in the financial district is the atmospheric **Fraunces Tavern**, first built in 1719 *(see p76)*. Another oldie, dating to 1864, is **Pete's Tavern**, a prime hangout in the Gramercy Park area that is busy until 2am. It is known for its Victoriana, its house brew called Pete's Ale, and the many beers on tap. In the same area, the **Old Town Bar** has been a typically Irish pub since 1892 and is now favored largely by advertising types.

No longer the celebrity scene it once was, **Sardi's** is still a hangout for *New York Times* reporters and is worth a stop to inspect the "who's who" celebrity caricatures lining the walls and for the generous drinks served in the second floor bar.

After work, crowds head to **P. J. Clarke's**, a long time favorite New York saloon dating back to the 1890s, with Irish bartenders and an incredibly bustling *après*-office scene. **Elaine's**, also on the East Side, remains a haunt of New York and visiting literary types. Sit close to Elaine's table where the meeting-and-greeting action takes place. The food is nothing much.

Near Carnegie Hall is the unobtrusive **P. J. Carney's**, which has been a watering hole for musicians and artists since 1927. It serves Irish ales and a good shepherd's pie.

YOUNG HANGOUTS

BREW PUBS, where the house beer is brewed on the premises, are currently the rage with the 20s-to-30s crowd, as are bars with sizable beer lists that feature a variety of microbrewery and imported beers. **The Chelsea Brewing Company** is a large, fun-filled brewpub situated in the Chelsea Piers sports complex, overlooking the Hudson River. In the nearby Gramercy neighborhood you will find the **Heartland Brewery**, which is the busiest, and, some think, best of the new brew pubs, with five beers, including the outstanding India Pale Ale, and many seasonals, such as cranberry and pumpkin ales.

The **Westside Brewing Company** uptown is a favorite youth and neighborhood hangout, popular for its house ales and fruit beers. Also popular is the **Yorkville Brewery & Tavern**, which has a sports bar feel in what used to be a German neighborhood. The beer list is extensive, and there is typical pub fare served at the bar.

Brews in the Garment District has a huge beer list, good grub, and an upstairs club with live music, making it a pub-crawlers' favorite.

For homesick Brits, the **Manchester** is a name to reckon with. In a cozy publike setting, you'll find Watneys or Newcastle Brown Ale on tap, just two of 18 draft beers and 40 bottled ones not widely available in New York.

In the East Village is bustling **d.b.a.**. Depending on whom you ask, the initials might stand for "don't bother to ask" or "draft beer available." There are 14 draft beers on tap, along with scores of microbrews and 50 single malt whiskies to choose from.

A popular beer stop uptown for the college-age crowd is the loud and noisy **Brother Jimmy's BBQ**, where you can snack on old-fashioned southern barbequed ribs.

Park Slope Brewery Company, in two Brooklyn locations, is another brew pub favored by the young for its 12 home brews and seasonal beers, as well as its decent pub grub and lively ambience.

SINGLES BARS

THE CHANCE TO MEET new people is offered in singles bars, which are still extremely popular. These are located all over the city, with a large concentration in midtown on the East Side. Prices in such places can be inflated, with beer costing $3 and up.

The Art Deco styled **Beer Bar**, with its interesting beer list and beer-tasting menus, is currently new and "with it." There is a frenetic singles scene at **Live Bait**, which is good for model-gazing and for its passable southern food.

GAY AND LESBIAN BARS

GAY BARS CAN be be found in Greenwich Village, with many also in SoHo, the East Village, Chelsea, and Murray Hill. Lesbian bars are mostly in Greenwich Village and the East Village. For current listings, check the *Native* newspaper and the *Village Voice* or call the Gay and Lesbian Switchboard *(see p343)*.

HOTEL BARS

CENTRALLY LOCATED in midtown, the Algonquin Hotel *(see p143)* was a famous literary haunt in the 1920s and early 1930s. Its Lobby Bar and Blue Bar are both good places for a quiet pre-dinner or pretheater drink.

The round bar in the handsome lobby lounge of the trendy **Royalton Hotel** is a perfect spot for a drink while watching the theatrical crowds drifting in and out. This is a favorite meeting place for Conde-Nast staffers. Also in the Theater District, the **Whiskey Bar** in the Paramount Hotel has floor-to-ceiling windows and is usually frequented by fashion and theater types. In Lower Midtown is the **Sun Garden**, a glassed-in, tiered space, particularly pleasant on bright afternoons when the sun streams through the glass.

The **Bull and Bear** in the Waldorf–Astoria, dating back to the Prohibition era, exudes comfort and a sense of history. There are many exotic drinks and Bull and Bear ale on tap.

Uptown, the **Oak Room** at the Plaza Hotel is a posh place to impress people, drink, and converse in earnest tones – but at a high price. The **King Cole Room** at the St. Regis Hotel is named after the mural behind the bar, by Maxfield Parrish, which adds color to a stylish room.

For nostalgic British visitors and anglophile New Yorkers, **Journeys** in the Essex House Hotel has an English club ambience, with hunting prints and mahogany paneling.

Drinks are a bargain at **Randolf's** in the Warwick Hotel, especially during happy hour, when free, delicious snacks are served.

For a trip back into the 1930s and 1940s, head uptown to the Waldorf-Astoria and its **Starlight Roof**. Once New York's most glamorous nightclub, it has been restored to its original Art Deco splendor.

SHOPPING

A VISITOR to New York will inevitably include shopping in his or her action plan. The city is the consumer capital of the world: a shopper's paradise that is a constant source of entertainment, with dazzling window displays and a staggering variety of goods for sale. Everything is available here, from high fashion to rare children's

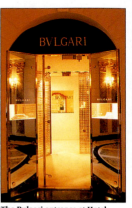

Tiffany's clock

books, state-of-the-art electronics and a mouthwatering array of exotic food. Whether you are looking for a personal Hovercraft, read-in-the-dark eyeglass attachments, a designer bed for your pet gerbil or a Wurlitzer jukebox, this is the city of your dreams. Whether you have $50,000 or $5, New York is the place to spend it.

BEST BUYS

N EW YORK is a bargain hunter's dream, with huge discounts on anything from household goods to designer clothes. Some of the best shops are on Orchard Street and Grand Street on the Lower East Side, where designer goods are sold at

The 1920s-style Henri Bendel store *(see p311)*

20–50% below the retail price. You can find just about every imaginable item of clothing here, in addition to tableware, shoes, home furnishings and electronics. Shops in this area are closed on Saturday – the Jewish Sabbath – but are usually open all day Sunday.

Another great area for fashion bargain hunters is the trendy Garment District, roughly between Sixth and Eighth avenues from 30th to 40th Street. The hub of it – Seventh Avenue – was renamed as Fashion Avenue in the early 1970s. Here, many different designers and manufacturers have showrooms, some of which are open to the public. They also have sales of many of their samples, announced on notices posted around the

area. Often the best time to go and visit these stores is just before one of the major gift-giving holidays.

SALES

O NE WORD you are likely to see all over the city, no matter what time of year you visit, is "Sale." So before you pay full price for anything, check the sale goods first. The best sales are during New York's sale seasons, which run from mid-June until the end of July and from December 26 until February. For information, look for ads in the local papers. A word of warning: along midtown Fifth Avenue there are signs announcing "Lost Our Lease" sales. But many of the shops have had these signs up for years and are best avoided.

HOW TO PAY

M OST SHOPS accept major credit cards, although there will often be a minimum purchase price. If you want to use your traveler's checks, identification is needed. Personal checks drawn in another currency will be refused. Some stores only take cash, especially during sales.

Designer dress at a New York sale

The Bulgari entrance at Hotel Pierre *(see p282)*

OPENING HOURS

M OST SHOPS in New York are normally open from 10am to 6pm, Monday to Saturday. Many department stores, though, are open all day Sunday and until 9pm at least two nights a week. The best time to avoid crowds is weekday mornings. The most crowded times are lunch hours (noon to 2:30pm), Saturday mornings, sales and holidays.

TAXES

T HERE IS NO city 8.25% sales tax on clothing and shoes under $110, but you may still be asked to pay duty on goods at customs if you exceed the allowance. However, if the goods are sent direct, you won't have to pay sales tax.

SHOPPING TOURS

IF YOU CAN'T face the thought of braving the stores by yourself, why not go on one of the many shopping tours available in New York? Apart from visiting the main department stores, options include a visit to private designer showrooms, auction houses and fashion shows. Some operators will customize tours to suit your requirements.

Convention Tours Unlimited
545-1160.

Doorway to Design
221-1111.

Guide Service of New York
408-3332.

The Intrepid New Yorker
534-5071.

A magnificent display offering household goods

experience of a lifetime.

Barney's New York is a favorite among young professional New Yorkers. It specializes in excellent, but expensive, designer clothes. A branch for men only is located in the glittering World Financial Center.

Bergdorf Goodman is luxurious, very elegant and understated. It carries high-quality contemporary fashions at high prices, specializing in European designers. The men's store is right across the street.

Almost every visitor to New York includes **Bloomingdale's** *(see p179)* on their sight-seeing list. Bloomingdale's is the Hollywood film star of the department stores, with many eye-catching displays and seductive goods. Its ambience is that of a luxurious wonderland, filled with young and old New Yorkers seeking out the newest in fashion. The linen and fine china depart-

ments have an undisputed reputation for quality. Check out the gourmet food section– it has a shop devoted entirely to caviar. Extensive shopping services and amenities include a noted restaurant, Le Train Bleu, with its view of the Queensboro Bridge

Everything found in **Henri Bendel's**, from the Art Deco jewels to beautiful handmade shoes, is displayed as though each were a priceless work of art. The store, which is laid out in a series of 1920s-style boutiques, is exclusive and sophisticated, and has a good selection of creative and innovative women's fashions.

Lord & Taylor is renowned for its classic and much more conservative fashions for men and women. The store places an emphasis on US designers.

Window displays at Bloomingdale's *(see p179)*

DEPARTMENT STORES

MOST OF New York's large department stores are in midtown Manhattan. Be sure to allow plenty of time to explore the ones you are interested in, because all these stores tend to be enormous, with an amazing range of goods. If at all possible, avoid going at weekends and around vacation times – the crowds can be overwhelming. Prices are often high, but you can get bargains during sales.

Stores such as Saks Fifth Avenue, Bloomingdale's and Macy's provide a diverse and extraordinary range of shopping services, including doing the shopping for you. But then you would miss out on what may be the shopping

You need comfy shoes and lots of spare time to wander.

Macy's, the self-proclaimed largest store in the world *(see p132–3),* sprawls over an entire city block. It has ten floors and sells everything imaginable from can openers to massive antiques.

Saks Fifth Avenue is synonymous with style and elegance. It has long been considered one of the city's high-quality department stores, with service to match. It sells stunning designer clothes for men, women and children.

ADDRESSES

Barney's New York
660 Madison Ave.
Map 13 A3.
826-8900.
Upper Level, 2 World Financial Center.
Map 1 A2.
945-1600.

Bergdorf Goodman
754 5th Ave. **Map** 12 F3.
753-7300.

Bloomingdale's
1000 3rd Ave. **Map** 13 B3.
705-2000.

Henri Bendel
712 5th Ave. **Map** 12 F4.
247-1100.

Lord & Taylor
424 5th Ave. **Map** 8 F1.
391-3344.

Macy's
151 W 34th St. **Map** 8 E2.
695-4400.

Saks Fifth Avenue
611 5th Ave. **Map** 12 F4.
753-4000.

New York's Best: Shopping

Designer shoes from Madison Avenue

IN A CITY where you can literally shop 24 hours a day, the best plan is to shop the way New Yorkers do, by neighborhood. Each has its own character and specialties. Here are highlights of the best shopping districts – where they are and what you will find in each. If time is very tight, head for one of the huge department stores *(see p311)*, or if window shopping is your preference, stroll along Fifth Avenue, home to Manhattan's most glittering stores *(see opposite)*. For great bargains in a truly ethnic area, try the Lower East Side.

Greenwich and East Villages

Explore around Eighth Street and St. Mark's Place for shoes and avant-garde fashions, books, ethnic goods and flea markets. Move to lower Broadway for antiques (often "retro" 20th century). (See pp108–9 and pp116–17.)

SoHo

The area bordered by Sixth Avenue, Lafayette, Houston and Canal streets is bustling with contemporary art galleries, antiques, crafts, exclusive or unusual gifts and fashions. Weekend brunchtime gallery-hopping is very popular. (See pp102–3.)

Lower East Side

Sunday is the day when New Yorkers and visitors flock to Canal, Delancey, Orchard and Essex streets for great bargains in fashions, shoes, jewelry, electronics and household goods. (See pp94–95.)

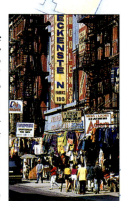

South Street Seaport

This is a browser's paradise of crafts, gifts, toys, souvenirs, antiquarian and new books, and antiques with a seafaring connection. (See pp82–83.)

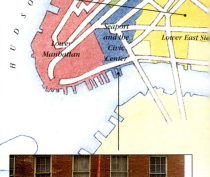

Chel and Garm Distr

Greenwich Village

SoHo and TriBeCa

E Vill

Lower Manhattan

Seaport and the Civic Center

Lower East Sir

HUDSON RIVER

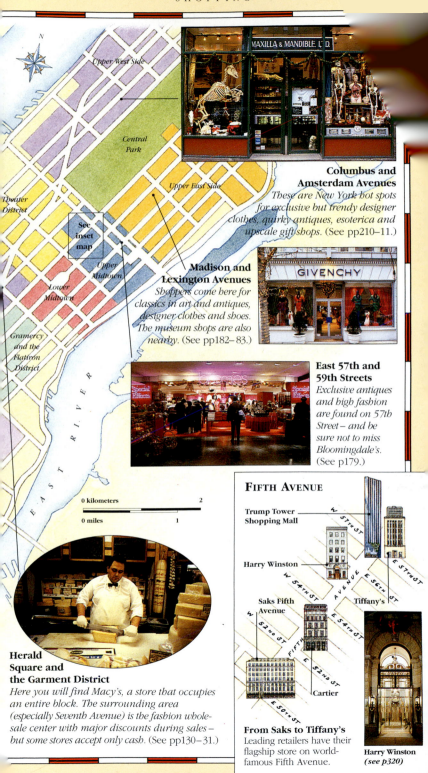

Columbus and Amsterdam Avenues
These are New York hot spots for exclusive but trendy designer clothes, quirky antiques, esoterica and upscale gift shops. (See pp210–11.)

Madison and Lexington Avenues
Shoppers come here for classics in art and antiques, designer clothes and shoes. The museum shops are also nearby. (See pp182–83.)

East 57th and 59th Streets
Exclusive antiques and high fashion are found on 57th Street – and be sure not to miss Bloomingdale's. (See p179.)

Herald Square and the Garment District
Here you will find Macy's, a store that occupies an entire block. The surrounding area (especially Seventh Avenue) is the fashion whole-sale center with major discounts during sales – but some stores accept only cash. (See pp130–31.)

FIFTH AVENUE

Trump Tower Shopping Mall

Harry Winston

Saks Fifth Avenue

Tiffany's

Cartier

From Saks to Tiffany's
Leading retailers have their flagship store on world-famous Fifth Avenue.

Harry Winston
(see p320)

...rk Originals

...RK IS A CITY where just about any kind of ..., no matter how esoteric, will always attract ...rs. Dozens of tiny shops scattered around the ...ecialize in unusual merchandise, from butterflies ...ones to traditional Tibetan treasures and ...nrock sprigs from Ireland. Coming across these in ...ne tucked-away corner is what makes shopping in ...ew York such an entertaining experience.

SPECIALTY SHOPS

FOR BEAUTIFUL BRASS, onyx and pewter chess sets, and the opportunity to play a decent game, make a move to the **Chess Shop**. For every type of pen **Arthur Brown & Bros.** stocks an enormous range, including such names as Mont Blanc and Schaeffer. **Big City Kites and Darts** has kites in different kinds of weird and wonderful shapes from fiery dragons to cuddly teddy bears, plus enough accessories to satisfy even the most dedicated kite flyer. For those with a bit more energy, **Blades** sells and rents out skates and also the trendiest skateboards plus all the safety equipment to go with them.

If you're looking for different or unusual buttons, a visit to **Tender Buttons**, which stocks millions, is a must. Whether you want enamel, wood or Navajo silver buttons – or perhaps want your own buttons made into cuff links or earrings – here you'll find just what you want – and more.

Leo Kaplan Ltd. is the place to go if you are a keen collector of paperweights and **Rita Ford's Music Boxes**, a 19th-century style shop, stocks a tuneful and extensive range of music boxes.

The **New York Firefighter's Friend** sells an intriguing range of items related purely to fire-fighting, including toy fire engines, firemen's jackets, badges, scaled-down uniforms for children, stuffed toy dalmatians and a wide selection of T-shirts including a popular one with NYFD (New York Fire Department) on one side and "Keep back 200 feet" on the other.

For the true romantic who wants to impress, everything sold by **Only Hearts** is heart-shaped, including pillows, soap and jewelry. If you are artistic, or if you wish to buy a present for someone who is, visit the **Pearl Paint Co.**, which stocks everything you could need. The **Magickal Childe** is an occult emporium full of potions, tarot cards and fragrant incense (note: there's no phone here and hours are erratic). Step straight into the space age at **Star Magic** to buy celestial maps, holograms, prisms and scientific toys.

Cologne made especially for George Washington and the official soap of the White House during the Eisenhower era are just some of the many fascinating items for sale at **Caswell-Massey Ltd.**, the oldest pharmacy in the city.

Guitar gurus will want to visit **Rudy's**, Manny's or Sam Ash's guitar shop. Not only is there a chance you'll bump into Eric Clapton or Lou Reed – both have their guitars made in this area – but you'll find the widest and best choice of instruments in the city.

Bibliophiles will find a range of gifts in both the **New York Public Library Shop** (see p144) (such as bookends of the lions guarding the main entrance) and the **Pierpont Morgan Library shop** (see pp162–3), including book-marks and writing paper.

University logos and college colors dominate the many knickknacks and accessories are at **The Yale Club** gift shop and **The Princeton Club**.

Hebrew Religious Articles carries one of the largest selections of Jewish religious items in the city.

The Cathedral Shop at the Cathedral of St. John the Divine is a large store selling books, artworks, herbs, jewelry and religious items made locally.

MEMORABILIA

AT LINCOLN CENTER, the **Metropolitan Opera Shop** has records, cards, librettos, small binoculars and many other opera-related items. The **Performing Arts Shop** downstairs is a real treasure trove of theater, opera, ballet and music memorabilia. For ballet fans, everything from Nureyev T-shirts to dance records can be found at the **Ballet Shop**. For thousands of rare and classic film stills and posters visit **Jerry Ohlinger's Movie Material Store**.

If you're looking for an old Wurlitzer jukebox or a Coke machine, go to **Back Pages Antiques**. The **Carnegie Hall Shop** carries musically themed cards, T-shirts, games, posters, tote bags and much more. For something truly original and very American, be sure to visit **Lost City Arts** and **Urban Archaeology** in SoHo. Between these two shops, you'll unearth all sorts of relics from America's past, from Barbie Doll lunch boxes to furniture from traditional ice-cream parlors.

TOYS, GAMES AND GADGETS

FOR CHILDREN'S GIFTS, don't miss the legendary **F.A.O. Schwarz**. This is a massive store crammed from floor to ceiling with luxury toy cars, enormous stuffed animals and every kind of electronic toy imaginable. There are shoulder-to-shoulder crowds at Christmas, when you might have to line up to get in.

The **Children's General Store** is one of the city's newest – and cleverest – children's toy stores.

The **Enchanted Forest** (see p102) is a magical experience for children. Its handmade toys are artfully displayed among the trees of the delightful interior, built by a theatrical set designer.

Penny Whistle Toys sells a huge selection of quality toys, games and all kinds of different dolls.

For games for both children and adults, the **Game Show** has puzzles and games galore, from real classics like Monopoly to the latest yuppie favorite. **Red Caboose** is for fans of model railways. **Toys 'R' Us** doesn't have Schwarz's style but it does stock over a million toys for all ages at reasonable prices.

Dinosaur Hill on Second Avenue offers handmade puppets and toys, mobiles, and beautifully made children's clothes. It's expensive but worth it.

MUSEUM SHOPS

SOME OF NEW YORK'S best souvenirs can be found in the city's many museum shops. In addition to the usual range of books, posters and cards, there are reproductions of the exhibits on display, including jewelry and sculpture. The **American Craft Museum** (see p169) has an excellent selection of American crafts as well as original works for sale. In addition to realistic model dinosaurs, rubber animals, minerals, and rocks, the **American Museum of Natural History** (see pp214–15) has a variety of

recycled products and earth-awareness gifts, which include posters, bags and T-shirts with environmental messages, and a large selection Native American handicrafts. There is also a kids' shop with reasonably priced items such as shell sets, magnets and toys.

The **Asia Society Bookstore and Gift Shop** (see p185) has a striking selection of Oriental prints, posters, art books, toys and jewelry. Items related to interior design are offered at the **Cooper-Hewitt** (see p184). One of New York's largest collections of Jewish ceremonial objects, including menorahs and Kiddush cups, books and jewelry, is found in the small shop at the **Jewish Museum** (see p184).

For reproduction prints of famous paintings and other exquisite gifts a visit to the **Metropolitan Museum of Art** (see pp188–95) gift shop is a must. There is also an enormous book department and a children's gift shop. The traditional **American Folk Art Museum** (see p213) prides itself on its American country crafts, including wooden toys, quilts and

weathervanes, which are mostly original. Works by craftspeople who currently have pieces on display in the museum are also sold.

The **Museum of the City of New York** (see p197), specializes in pictures of old New York. The **Museum of Modern Art/MOMA Design Store** (see pp170–73) has a highly praised selection of innovative home furnishings, toys and kitchenware inspired by international designers such as Frank Lloyd Wright and Le Corbusier. The store will remain open during the reconstruction.

For a selection of nautical items, including charts, maps, model ships and scrimshaw, go to the **South Street Seaport Museum Shops** (see pp82–85). The **Whitney Museum's Store Next Door** (see pp198–9) stocks only American-made items, including jewelry, wooden toys and books and posters complementing current exhibitions. The **Museum of Jewish Heritage** (see p77) has an interesting gift shop with an unusual array of gifts, souvenirs and educational material about Jewish life. Open to ticketed visitors only.

THE BEST OF THE IMPORTS

NEW YORK is a massive melting pot of different nationalities, cultures and ethnic groups, all of which have made their mark on New York's diverse culture in one way or another. Many ethnic shops specialize in food or goods of a particular group. Some of the most interesting and unusual shops include **Alaska on Madison**, which has a huge collection of Eskimo art, and the **Chinese Porcelain Company,** for exquisite Chinese decorative arts and furniture. **Back From Guatemala** has jewelry and decorative arts from Central and South America, and **Himalayan Crafts and Tours** stocks everything

from paintings to Tibetan rugs. **Sweet Life**, on the Lower East Side, is a tiny but charming old-fashioned candy shop with delicacies from around the world. **Things Japanese** has beautifully made crafts and unusual books. **Surma** is a Ukrainian general store that sells hand painted eggs and linens. **Common Ground** sells Native American arts, and **Astro Gems** has a large collection of jewelry and mineral specimens from Africa and Asia.

ADDRESSES

Alaska on Madison
937 Madison Ave. **Map** 17 A1.
(879-1782.

Astro Gems
185 Madison Ave. **Map** 9 A2.
(889-9000.

Back From Guatemala
306 E 6th St. **Map** 5 A2.
(260-7010.

Chinese Porcelain Company
475 Park Ave. **Map** 13 A3.
(838-7744.

Common Ground
19 Greenwich Ave. **Map** 1 B1.
(989-4178.

Himalayan Crafts and Tours
2007 Broadway. **Map** 11 C1.
(787-8500.

Sweet Life
63 Hester St.
Map 5 B4.
(598-0092.

Surma
11 E 7th St. **Map** 4 F2.
(477-0729.

Things Japanese
127 E 60th St.
Map 13 A3.
(371-4661.

DIRECTORY

SPECIALTY SHOPS

Arthur Brown & Bros.
2 W 46th St.
Map 12 F5.
(575-5555.

Big City Kites and Darts
1210 Lexington Ave.
Map 17 A4.
(472-2623.

Blades
120 W 72nd St.
Map 11 C1.
(787-3911.
One of several branches.

Caswell-Massey Ltd.
518 Lexington Ave.
Map 13 A5.
(755-2254.

The Cathedral Shop
Cathedral of St. John the Divine, 1047 Amsterdam Ave. **Map** 20 E4.
(222-7200.

Hebrew Religious Articles
45 Essex St.
Map 5 B4.
(674-1770.

Leo Kaplan Ltd.
967 Madison Ave.
Map 17 A5.
(249-6766.

Magickal Childe
35 W 19th St.
Map 8 F5.

New York Firefighter's Friend
263 Lafayette St.
Map 4 F3.
(226-3142.

New York Public Library Shop
5th Ave at 42nd St.
Map 8 F1.
(930-0678.

Only Hearts
386 Columbus Ave.
Map 15 D5.
(724-5608.

Pearl Paint Co
308 Canal St.
Map 4 E5
(431-7932

Pierpont Morgan Library Shop
Madison Ave at 36th St.
Map 9 A2.
(685-0610.

The Princeton Club
15 W 43rd St. **Map** 8 F1.
(596-1200.

Rita Ford's Music Boxes
19 E 65th St. **Map** 12 F2.
(535-6717.

Rudy's
169 W 48th St. **Map** 12 E5.
(391-1699.

Star Magic
745 Broadway. **Map** 4 E2.
(228-7770.

Tender Buttons
143 E 62nd St.
Map 13 A2.
(758-7004.

The Chess Shop
230 Thompson St.
Map 4 D3.
(475-9580.

The Yale Club
50 Vanderbilt Ave.
Map 13 A5.
(661-2070.

MEMORABILIA

Back Pages Antiques
125 Greene St.
Map 4 E4.
(460-5998.

Ballet Company
1887 Broadway.
Map 12 D2.
(246-6893.

The Carnegie Hall Shop
881 7th Ave.
Map 12 E3.
(903-9610.

Jerry Ohlinger's Movie Material Store
242 W 14th St.
Map 3 C1.
(989-0869.

Lost City Arts
18 Cooper Sq.
Map 4 F2.
(375-0500.

Metropolitan Opera Shop
Metropolitan Opera House, Lincoln Center, 136 W 65th St.
Map 11 C2.
(580-4090.

Performing Arts Shop
Metropolitan Opera House, Lincoln Center, 136 W 65th St.
Map 11 C2.
(580-4356.

Urban Archaeology
143 Franklin St.
Map 4 D5.
(431-6969.

TOYS, GAMES AND GADGETS

The Children's General Store
2473 Broadway.
Map 15 C4.
(580-2723.

The Enchanted Forest
85 Mercer St.
Map 4 E4.
(925-6677.

Dinosaur Hill
306 E 9th/2nd Ave.
Map 4 F1.
(473-5850.

F.A.O. Schwarz
767 5th Ave.
Map 12 F3.
(644-9400.

Game Show
474 6th Ave.
Map 12 E5.
(633-6328.

Penny Whistle Toys
448 Columbus Ave.
Map 16 D4.
(873-9090.
One of several branches.

Red Caboose
23 W 45th St.
Map 12 F5.
(575-0155.

Toys 'R' Us
Herald Center,
1293 Broadway.
Map 8 E2.
(594-8697.

MUSEUM SHOPS

American Craft Museum
40 W 53rd St. **Map** 12 F4.
(956-3535.

American Folk Art Museum
45 W 53rd St. **Map** 12 F4.
(496-2966.

American Museum of Natural History
W 79th St at Central Park West. **Map** 16 D5.
(769-5150.

Asia Society Bookstore and Gift Shop
725 Park Ave. **Map** 13 A1.
(288-6400.

Cooper-Hewitt
2 E 91st St. **Map** 16 F2.
(860-6878.

Jewish Museum
1109 5th Ave. **Map** 16 F2.
(423-3200.

Metropolitan Museum of Art
5th Ave at 82nd St.
Map 16 F4.
(535-7710.

Museum of the City of New York
5th Ave at 103rd St.
Map 21 C5.
(534-1672.

Museum of Jewish Heritage
18 First Place,
Battery Park City.
Map 1 B4.
(968-1800.

Museum of Modern Art/MOMA Design Store
44 W 53rd St.
Map 12 F4.
(767-1050.

South St. Seaport Museum Shops
207 Front St. **Map** 2 D2.
(748-8600.

The Whitney Museum's Store Next Door
943 Madison Ave.
Map 13 A1.
(606-0200.

Fashion

WHETHER YOU'RE LOOKING for a secondhand pair of 501s or the kind of ballgown Ivana Trump would be proud to wear, you're sure to find it in New York. The city is the fashion capital of America and an important center of clothing manufacture and design. New York's clothing stores, like its restaurants, reflect the city's dramatically different styles and cultures. To save time it's probably best to visit one area at a time and wander from store to store. Alternatively, visit one of the major department stores for an excellent selection of fashion for everyone.

AMERICAN DESIGNERS

MANY AMERICAN designers sell their creations in boutiques within the large department stores, or have exclusive shops of their own. One of the most famous is Geoffrey Beene, known for sophisticated looks that are casual and comfortable. Bill Blass is the king of American fashion whose clothes feature loads of different colors, wild patterns, innovative shapes and a lot of wit. Liz Claiborne's designs are always elegantly simple, casual and reasonably priced, including everything you could possibly need from tennis whites to casual professional wear for women.

The late Perry Ellis's style lives on with clothes designed by Marc Jacobs, known for his sportswear. James Galanos is an exclusive designer for the rich and famous, making one-of-a-kind *couture* clothes, and Betsey Johnson is popular with women able to wear figure-hugging fashions in fabulous fabrics.

In recent years, Donna Karan has become a name that appears everywhere. Her simple, stylish and great-looking designs work for everything from work-out clothes to black tie wear. Calvin Klein now has his name on place settings and sunglasses in addition to underwear, jeans and a whole range of clothes. He is renowned for comfortable, sensuous and well-fitting – as well as very hip – looks. Ralph Lauren is well known for his aristocratic and expensive clothes, a "look" favored by the exclusive and posh Ivy League, horsey set. For those with a taste for more experimental designs, Joan Vass specializes in moderately priced but exciting, colorful and innovative knitwear.

DISCOUNT DESIGNER CLOTHES

IF YOU'RE on the lookout for discount designer clothes, **Designer Resale**, **Encore** and **Michael's** sell a wide range. Oscar de la Renta, Ungaro and Armani are just some of the leading labels available. Clothes are either new or worn but near-perfect.

MEN'S CLOTHES

IN THE CENTER of midtown, you'll find two of the city's most highly regarded mens-wear stores: **Brooks Brothers** and **Paul Stuart**. Brooks Brothers is something of a New York institution, famous for its traditional, conservative clothing such as smart button-down shirts and Chinos. There's an ultra-conservative woman's line too. Paul Stuart prides itself on its very British look and offers a stylish array of superbly tailored fashions.

Go to the high-quality department store **Bergdorf Goodman Men** to find beautifully made Turnbull & Asser shirts and marvelous suits by Gianfranco Ferré or Hugo Boss.

Barney's New York has one of the most comprehensive men's departments in America, with a truly massive range of clothes and accessories. A smaller Barney's, at the World Financial Center, specializes in even smarter business clothes and suits for professionals. The **Polo/Ralph Lauren** department store is packed from floor to ceiling with the so-called king of American Sportswear's simple and timeless fashions as well as his many stylish accessories.

A. Sulka sells very expensive, Italian-made but American-designed clothing and furnishings. **Rothman's** offers international styles at great bargain prices.

The Custom Shop Shirtmakers specializes in custom-made suits and shirts in beautiful materials. Go to **Burberry Limited** if you are looking for classic British trenchcoats.

J. Press sells classic, conservative yet elegant clothes. Uptown designer menswear boutiques include the renowned **Beau Brummel** with a selection of very stylish European clothes and for superb designer bargains, check out **Moe Ginsburg** for one of New York's largest selections of men's Italian clothing. Many of these men's stores also carry striking women's fashions. Watch for the new Hickey-Freeman store on 5th Avenue for a wife range of men's traditional clothing.

CHILDREN'S CLOTHES

IN ADDITION to an excellent selection within the large department stores, there are several shops around the city that sell children's clothing exclusively. A good example is **Bonpoint**, which has a world of French-style charm.

GapKids and **BabyGap** shops, often in the **Gap** shops, have comfortable, long-lasting cotton overalls, sweat pants, denim jackets, sweatshirts and leggings. The wonderfully named **Peanut Butter & Jane** sells trendy but particularly comfortable togs. **Space Kiddets** has everything from booties to Western wear.

WOMEN'S CLOTHES

WOMEN'S FASHION is subject to design trends, and New York stores keep pace with them all. Most of the city's most fashionable shops are found in the midtown area around Madison and Fifth avenues. These include some of the major department stores *(see p311)*, which stock a range of American designers, including Donna Karan, Ralph Lauren and Bill Blass.

Leading international names such as **Chanel**, **Fendi**, and **Valentino** also have shops here, as does one of the outstanding American designers, **Geoffrey Beene**. There is also a handful of popular ready-to-wear stores, including **Ann Taylor**, which is much favored by young, busy professionals looking for stylish, comfortable clothing.

Right at the heart of this area stands the pink-marbled Trump Tower, which houses a selection of exclusive shops.

Madison Avenue is packed with designers for the smart set, who have everything you could ever need, including **Givenchy** who sells show-stopping formal gowns at phenomenal prices, Valentino who has classic Italian clothes and **Emanuel Ungaro** who is relatively unintimidating and has something to suit most tastes and physiques from beautifully tailored jackets to more matronly full-figured and boldly patterned print dresses. **Missoni** is famous for richly textured sweaters in sumptuous wools and colorful patterns. **Yves St Laurent Rive Gauche** has evening gowns, one-of-a-kind jackets, silks and extravagant blouses and beautifully cut pants suits.

Sophisticated Italian looks are also available from Italian style kings **Giorgio Armani** and **Gianni Versace**. **Dolce & Gabbana** sells only unique, one-of-a-kind Italian clothing. **Gucci**, one of the oldest Italian shops in America, is only for the wealthy and status-conscious.

The Upper West Side has many shops competing for attention with contemporary fashions, including **Betsey Johnson's** shop, with her whimsical, relatively inexpensive designs. **Calvin Klein** now has a store on the East Side, specializing in ultra-hip, casual fashions. **French Connection** is known for its affordable separates, both casual and for the office. **Variazioni** is *the* place to get a little black dress.

The villages – the East Village in particular – are the best places to go for second-hand clothing and 1950s rock 'n' roll gear, with ever-changing interesting shops run by new and young designers and art school graduates. For a range of affordable, well-cut clothes from classic to casual, try **APC**.

Cheap Jack's carries a huge selection of second-hand Levi's as well as hundreds of denim and leather jackets. **Loehmann's** offers discounted fashion clothes, and it's the place to shop if you want top-of-the-line fashions at unbelievable discounts. **Big Drop** has a great selection of perfectly fitting little black dresses. **Screaming Mimi's** is where you could unearth that pair of velvet bell-bottoms or go-go boots you've always dreamed of having. A more mainstream shop is **The Gap**, a chain store selling lots of moderately-priced, casual and comfortable clothes for men, women and children.

Recently SoHo has come to rival Madison Avenue for designer boutiques specializing in expensive but interesting clothes – the fashions here are far more avant-garde. You'll find **Yohji Yamamoto**, among other exclusive stores. **Comme des Garçons** sells minimalist Japanese chic.

More accessible is one of SoHo's most famous stores, the **Canal Jean Co.**, which has all the latest SoHo looks at affordable prices.

What Comes Around Goes Around is the place to go for vintage jeans.

SIZE CHART

For Australian sizes follow the British and American conversions.

Children's clothing

American	2-3	4-5	6-6x	7-8	10	12	14	16 (size)
British	2-3	4-5	6-7	8-9	10-11	12	14	14+ (years)
Continental	2-3	4-5	6-7	8-9	10-11	12	14	14+ (years)

Children's shoes

American	7½	8½	9½	10½	11½	12½	13½	1½	2½
British	7	8	9	10	11	12	13	1	2
Continental	24	25½	27	28	29	30	32	33	34

Women's dresses, coats and skirts

American	4	6	8	10	12	14	16	18
British	6	8	10	12	14	16	18	20
Continental	38	40	42	44	46	48	50	52

Women's blouses and sweaters

American	6	8	10	12	14	16	18
British	30	32	34	36	38	40	42
Continental	40	42	44	46	48	50	52

Women's shoes

American	5	6	7	8	9	10	11
British	3	4	5	6	7	8	9
Continental	36	37	38	39	40	41	44

Men's suits

American	34	36	38	40	42	44	46	48
British	34	36	38	40	42	44	46	48
Continental	44	46	48	50	52	54	56	58

Men's shirts

American	14	15	15½	16	16½	17	17½	18
British	14	15	15½	16	16½	17	17½	18
Continental	36	38	39	41	42	43	44	45

Men's shoes

American	7	7½	8	8½	9½	10½	11	11½
British	6	7	7½	8	9	10	11	12
Continental	39	40	41	42	43	44	45	46

DIRECTORY

DISCOUNT DESIGNER CLOTHES

Designer Resale
324 E 81st St.
Map 17 B4.
(734-3639.

Encore
1132 Madison Ave.
Map 17 A4.
(879-2850.

Michael's
1041 Madison Ave.
Map 17 A5.
(737-7273.

MEN'S CLOTHES

A. Sulka
301 Park Ave.
Map 13 A4.
(980-5200.

Barney's New York
660 Madison Ave.
Map 13 A3.
(593-7800.

Beau Brummel
421 West Broadway.
Map 4 E3.
(219-2666.
One of several branches.

Bergdorf Goodman Men
754 5th Ave.
Map 12 F3.
(753-7300.

Brooks Brothers
346 Madison Ave.
Map 9 A1.
(682-8800.

Burberry Limited
9 E 57th St.
Map 12 F3.
(371-5010.

The Custom Shop Shirtmakers
618 5th Ave. **Map** 12 F4.
(245-2499.
One of several branches.

J. Press
7 E 44th St. **Map** 12 F5.
(687-7642

Moe Ginsburg
162 5th Ave.
Map 8 F4.
(242-3482.

Paul Stuart
Madison Ave at 45th St.
Map 13 A5.
(682-0320.

Polo/Ralph Lauren
Madison Ave at 72nd St.
Map 13 A1.
(606-2100.

Rothman's
200 Park Ave South.
Map 9 A5.
(777-7400.

CHILDREN'S CLOTHES

Bonpoint
1269 Madison Ave.
Map 17 A3.
(722-7720.

GapKids
60 W 34th St. **Map** 8 F2.
(643-8995.
One of several branches.

Peanut Butter & Jane
617 Hudson St.
Map 3 B1.
(620-7952.

Space Kiddets
46 E 21st St. **Map** 8 F4.
(420-9878.

WOMEN'S CLOTHES

Ann Taylor
645 Madison Ave.
Map 13 A3.
(832-2010.
One of several branches.

APC
131 Mercer St.
Map 4 E3.
(966-9685.

Betsey Johnson
248 Columbus Ave.
Map 16 D4.
(362-3364.
One of several branches.

Big Drop
174 Spring St.
Map 3 C4.
(966-4299.

Calvin Klein
654 Madison Ave.
Map 13 A3.
(292-9000.

Canal Jean Co
504 Broadway.
Map 4 E4.
(226-0737.

Chanel
15 E 57th St.
Map 12 F3.
(355-5050.

Cheap Jack's
841 Broadway.
Map 4 E1.
(777-9564.

Comme des Garçons
520 W 22nd St.
Map 8 F3.
(604-9200.

Emanuel Ungaro
792 Madison Ave.
Map 13 A2.
(249-4090.

Fendi
720 5th Ave.
Map 12 F3.
(767-0100.

French Connection
304 Columbus Ave.
Map 12 D1.
(496-1470.
One of several branches.

The Gap
250 W 57th St.
Map 12 D3.
(315-2250.
One of many branches.

Geoffrey Beene
783 5th Ave.
Map 12 F3.
(935-0470.

Gianni Versace
815 Madison Ave.
Map 13 A2.
(744-6868.

Giorgio Armani
760 Madison Ave.
Map 13 A2.
(988-9191.

Givenchy
710 Madison Ave.
Map 13 A1.
(772-1040.

Gucci
685 5th Ave.
Map 12 F4.
(826-2600.

Loehmann's
101 Seventh Ave.
Map 8 E1.
(352-0856.

Missoni
836 Madison Ave.
Map 13 A1.
(517-9339.

Dolce & Gabbana
434 W Broadway.
Map 4 E3.
(965-8000.

Saks Fifth Avenue
611 Fifth Ave.
Map 12 F4.
(753-4000.

Screaming Mimi's
382 Lafayette St.
Map 4 F2.
(677-6464.

Valentino
747 Madison Ave.
Map 13 A2.
(772-6969.

Variazioni
309 Columbus Ave.
Map 16 D2.
(874-7474.

What Comes Around Goes Around
351 West Broadway.
Map 4 E4.
(431-8848.

Yohji Yamamoto
103 Grand St.
Map 4 E4.
(966-9066.

Yves St Laurent Rive Gauche
855 Madison Ave.
Map 13 A1.
(472-5299.

Accessories

IN ADDITION TO the following shops, all of the major Manhattan department stores have extensive accessory departments stocking a range of hats, gloves, bags, jewelry, watches, scarves, shoes and umbrellas.

JEWELRY

MIDTOWN FIFTH AVENUE is where to find the most dazzling jewelers. By day, windows glisten with gems from around the world; by night they are empty – the jewels safely locked away. The most sensational shops are all within a couple of blocks of one another and include the museum-like **Harry Winston**, which showcases its coveted jewels from around the world. **Buccellati** is well respected for its innovative Italian creations and excellent workmanship. **Bulgari** has an impressive collection that ranges in price from a mere couple of hundred to over a million dollars.

Housed in a Renaissance-style palazzo, **Cartier** is a jewel in itself and sells its beautiful baubles at unthinkable prices. **Tiffany & Co.** has ten floors of glittering crystal, diamonds and other jewels just waiting to be packed up for you and taken away in the store's signature sky blue boxes.

Diamond Row, a one-block area on 47th Street (between Fifth and Sixth avenues), is lined with shops displaying hundreds of thousands of dollars worth of diamonds, gold, pearls and other exotic jewels from around the world. Try not to miss the **Jewelry Exchange**, a complex where 60 different crafts-people sell their ware direct to the public. Boisterous bargaining is very much alive here, so be prepared to play the game.

HATS

NEW YORK'S OLDEST hat shop is **Worth & Worth**, which also has the largest collection of hats in the city. You can get everything you could possibly want here, ranging from original Australian bush hats to silk toppers, to slouch hats and boaters. Check out **Larisa/L&R Design Studios** for custom-designed hats for women and strange cold-weather hats for men. **Suzanne Millinery** is the hat-maker to the stars, as she has proved very popular with celebrities such as Whoopi Goldberg and Ivana Trump.

UMBRELLAS

THE MINUTE IT STARTS to rain in New York, hundreds of street vendors selling umbrellas seem to sprout like mushrooms. Their umbrellas, which sell at just a few dollars, are without doubt the cheapest in the city, but unlikely to last much longer than the downpour itself. For good-quality umbrellas, you'll find a fine selection of Briggs of London at **Worth & Worth**. There is a wide range of different sizes, trendy patterns and traditional tartans and stripes at **Barney's New York**, and there's always Macy's for the usual sizes and styles. World-famous **Gucci** has umbrellas to match its ties. There are expensive and telescopic ones found at **Hanae Mori**, and doorman-sized ones in solid black or in the university's traditional colors of black and orange at **The Princeton Club**. **The Yale Club** has blue ones emblazoned with a white "Y".

HANDBAGS AND BRIEFCASES

TWICE A YEAR, during the January and August sales, a serpentine line of buyers wraps around the corner of 48th Street and Madison Avenue waiting to get into **Crouch & Fitzgerald**. An old New York institution, selling handbags, briefcases and luggage. All the well-known brands are sold here, including Judith Leiber, Ghurka, Dooney & Bourke and Louis Vuitton, as well as the firm's own line. Elsewhere in the city are such exclusive shops as **Bottega Veneta** and **Prada**, where handbags are displayed like precious art, with prices to match. Younger and trendier places include **Furla**, well-respected for its Italian designs, and the stylish **Il Bisonte**. Current must-have designer Rafé Totengco's soft suede pastel pouches are found at **TG-170** and **Big Drop**. **The Coach Store** is known for its simple, classic leather handbags.

For discount designer handbags go to the legendary **Fine & Klein**, and for bargain briefcases from slim envelopes to thick lawyer's bags, a visit to the **Altman Luggage Company** is a must.

SHOES AND BOOTS

MANHATTAN SHOE stores are famous for their extensive selections of shoes and boots, and if you shop around you are sure to find what you want at a reasonable price.

Most of the large department stores in New York also have shoe departments where you can find designer-label shoes in addition to other brands. **Bloomingdale's** (see p179) has a huge women's footwear department, and **Brooks Brothers** has one of the best selections of traditional men's shoes in the city.

For both men's and women's shoes, the most exclusive shops are around the midtown area. **Martinez Valero** has beautiful shoes made from suede and leather, in various elegant styles. **Ferragamo** sells classic styles crafted in Florence. Go to **Botticelli** for whimsical shoe fashions. The best new place is **Jeffrey's** for excellent selection. For stylish shoes at decent prices, head for **Sigerson Morrison** in Little Italy. For cowboy boots, head for **Billy Martin's**. There's an enormous selection of handmade boots, from basic, no-frills "ropers," which real American cowboys wear, to crocodile leather boots that sell for thousands of dollars. Billy Martin's stocks western garb and accessories, so you dress in western gear from head to toe. For beautiful custom-made boots, try **Buffalo Chips Bootery**.

For the latest and best in children's shoes, **East Side Kids** stocks the trendiest fashions for kids. **Little Eric**

has unusual, eye-catching footwear and **Shoofly** has imported shoes in all styles. **Harry's** carries a wonderful selection of sensible shoes.

For discounted shoes, the greatest concentration of shops is around West 34th Street and West 8th Street between Fifth and Sixth Avenues, and Orchard Street on the Lower East Side.

LINGERIE

EXPENSIVE imports from Europe, which are sexy yet elegant, can be found at **La Petite Coquette**.

More affordable is **Victoria's Secret**, which offers two floors of beautifully made lingerie in satin, silk and many other fine fabrics.

DIRECTORY

JEWELRY

Buccellati
46 E 57th Ave.
Map 12 F3.
308-2900.

Bulgari
730 5th Ave.
Map 12 F3.
315-9000.

Cartier
653 5th Ave.
Map 12 F4.
753-0111.

Harry Winston
718 5th Ave.
Map 12 F3.
245-2000.

Jewelry Exchange
15 W 47th St.
Map 12 F5.

Tiffany & Co
5th Ave at 57th St.
Map 12 F3.
755-8000.

HATS

Larisa Designs
342 7th Ave/29th St.
Map 8 E3.
695-8989.

Suzanne Millinery
700 Madison Ave.
Map 13 A3.
593-3232.

Worth & Worth
101 W 55th St, Suite 3N
Map 12 E4.
265-2887.

UMBRELLAS

Barney's New York
See p311.

Gucci
685 5th Ave.
Map 12 F4.
826-2600.

Hanae Mori
27 E 79th St.
Map 16 F5.
472-2352.

The Princeton Club
15 W 43rd St.
Map 8 F1.
596-1200.

Worth & Worth
See Hats.

The Yale Club
50 Vanderbilt Ave.
Map 13 A5.
661-2070.

HANDBAGS AND BRIEFCASES

Altman Luggage Company
125 Orchard St.
Map 5 A3.
254-7275.

Big Drop
174 Spring St.
Map 4 F4.
966-4299.

Il Bisonte
120 Sullivan St.
Map 4 D4.
966-8773.

Bottega Veneta
635 Madison Ave.
Map 13 A3.
371-5511.

The Coach Store
595 Madison Ave.
Map 13 A3.
754-0041.

Crouch & Fitzgerald
400 Madison Ave.
Map 13 A5.
755-5888.

Fine & Klein
119 Orchard St.
Map 5 A3.
674-6720.

Furla
727 Madison Ave.
Map 13 A3.
755-8986.
One of two branches.

Prada
45 E 57th St. Map 12 F3.
308-2332.

TG-170
170 Ludlow St.
Map 5 A3.
995-8660.

SHOES AND BOOTS

Billy Martin's
220 E 60th St.
Map 13 B3.
861-3100.

Botticelli
620 5th Ave. Map 12 F4.
582-6313.

Bloomingdale's
See p311.

Brooks Brothers
See p319.
Buffalo Chips Bootery
355 W Broadway Map 4 E4.
625-8400.

East Side Kids
1298 Madison Ave.
Map 17 A2.
360-5000.

Ferragamo
661 5th Ave.
Map 12 F3.
759-3822.

Harry's
2299 Broadway.
Map 15 C2.
874-2035.

Jeffrey's
449 W 14th St.
Map 3 B1.
206-1272.

Little Eric
1331 3rd Ave.
Map 17 B5.
288-8987.

Shoofly
465 Amsterdam Ave.
Map 15 C4.
580-4390.

Martinez Valero
1029 Third Ave.
Map 13 B3.
753-1822.

Sigerson Morrison
28 Prince St.
Map 4 F3.
219-3893.

LINGERIE

La Petite Coquette
51 University Place.
Map 4 E1.
473-2478.

Victoria's Secret
34 E 57th St.
Map 12 F3.
758-5592.

Books and Music

As THE PUBLISHING CAPITAL of America, it's not surprising that New York has the country's best selection of bookstores. These range from vast general interest stores to hundreds of esoteric bookstores specializing in everything from sci-fi to suspense, selling new books and old. Music lovers will also find sounds for all tastes at reasonable prices, plus thousands of rare recordings.

GENERAL INTEREST BOOKSTORES

One OF THE MOST well-known of New York's bookstores – for best prices as well as selection of titles – is **Barnes & Noble** on Fifth Avenue, reputedly the world's largest bookstore and packed high with over three million books on every imaginable subject. There are branches all over the City, plus the sales annex across the street, with amazing bargains.

Several blocks away is the main branch of New York's famous **Strand Book Store**. The Strand, as those in the know refer to it, has an aston-ishing two million copies of new and secondhand books at some of the best prices in town. There is also a large rare book room for first editions.

Gryphon Bookshop is as comprehensive as its music counterpart, as it stocks an enormous collection of used books and country/bluegrass LPs. **Coliseum Books** has a vast selection of paperbacks. The two branches of **Borders Books & Music** offer a choice of CDs and books of all genres. In midtown, **Rizzoli** has an enormous selection of photo-graphy, foreign language, music and art books plus children's books and videos. **Gotham Book Mart**, a New York institution, is a tiny shop with hundreds of out-of-print books and limited editions. **Shakespeare & Co.** offers a sensational selection of titles and is open late every night.

SPECIALTY BOOKSTORES

For THE BEST selection of art books in the city, visit **Hacker Art Books**. **Urban Center Books** has titles on urban planning and other conservation issues. The city's largest selection of theatrical books and publications is found at **Drama Book Shop**. Jewish books and music abound at **J. Levine Judaica**. Rare books, books out-of-print and old books about New York are the *raison d'être* of **JN Bartfield Books**. The **Biography Bookshop** is the only midtown store specializing in diaries, letters, biographies and auto-biographies. Theater buffs should try **Applause Theater & Cinema Books**.

For hundreds of titles on science, business, technology and computers visit **McGraw-Hill Bookstore**.

Books on murder and suspense are the focus of two shops: **Murder Ink** and **Mysterious Bookshop**. Try **Forbidden Planet** for old and new science fiction books and comics. The **Village Comics** has thousands of old and new comics to suit all tastes.

Bank Street Book Store has one of the best selections of current children's books. Visit **Books of Wonder** for a variety of hardcover and rare children's books.

Travelers' Choice specializes in travel guides, maps, videos and travel accessories. **The Complete Traveler** also stocks a wide selection of brand-new and antique travel books and guides for your trip, on everywhere from Alabama to Zimbabwe. The staff is very knowledgeable and more than helpful. **The Civilized Traveler** carries travel accessories, from portable high-tech gadgets to an array of leather bags. There are also travel videos for rent, an ongoing schedule of lectures and seminars on worldwide travel issues, some by well-known travelers, and special interest trip services.

For an excellent range of maps visit the large **Rand McNally Map & Travel Store** and the **Hagstrom Map & Travel Store**. Cookbooks are on the menu at **Kitchen Arts & Letters**, with many out-of-print books and first editions.

Radicals should head for **Revolution Books** or **St. Mark's Bookstore,** which also has an excellent selection of literary and art titles.

The **Oscar Wilde Memorial Bookshop** has a wide selection of gay and lesbian texts.

RECORDS, TAPES AND COMPACT DISCS

THE BEST MANHATTAN record-store chain is **Tower Records**, whose three stores have everything from bebop to rap. **HMV** and **Virgin** follow a close second. **J&R Music World** is a complete home entertainment store with one of the best CD selections in the city. **Record Explosion** carries many budget CDs.

For out-of-print records, go to **Gryphon Records**, a treasure trove for collectors with an excellent choice of classical, jazz and opera recordings. **Footlight Records** is for lovers of Broadway musicals and film soundtracks, and **House of Oldies** has a massive stock of deleted and rare records to suit all tastes. **Bleecker Bob's Golden Oldies** Record Shop has everything from imports, rock and punk to rare jazz. Try **Midnight Records** for imports, reissues, American garage rock and psychedelia.

SHEET MUSIC

JUST BEHIND Carnegie Hall is one of the best stores for classical sheet music, **Joseph Patelson Music House Ltd**. The **Frank Music Company** has a huge collection of classical music scores. **Charles Colin Publications** specializes in jazz. For chart music and pop tunes try **Colony Record and Music Center** in the Brill Building.

DIRECTORY

GENERAL INTEREST BOOKSTORES

Barnes & Noble
105 5th Ave. **Map** 8 F5.
807-0099.
One of many branches.

Borders Books & Music
461 Park Avenue.
Map 17 A3.
980-6785.
One of two branches.

Coliseum Books
1771 Broadway.
Map 12 D3.
757-8381.

Gotham Book Mart
41 W 47th St. **Map** 12 F5.
719-4448.

Gryphon Bookshop
2246 Broadway.
Map 15 C4.
362-0706.

Rizzoli
31 W 57th St.
Map 12 F3.
759-2424.
One of several branches.

Shakespeare & Co
716 Broadway.
Map 4 E2.
529-1330.

939 Lexington Ave.
Map 13 A1.
570-0201.

Strand Book Store
828 Broadway.
Map 4 E1.
473-1452.

SPECIALTY BOOKSTORES

Applause Theater & Cinema Books
211 W 71st St.
Map 11 C1.
496-7511.

Drama Book Store
723 7th Ave.
Map 12 E5.
944-0595.

Bank Street Book Store
610 W 112th St.
Map 21 A4.
678-1654.

Biography Bookshop
400 Bleecker St.
Map 3 C2.
807-8655.

Books of Wonder
16 W 18th St.
Map 8 E5.
989-3270.

The Civilized Traveler
2003 Broadway.
Map 11 C1.
875-0306.

The Complete Traveler
199 Madison Ave.
Map 9 A2.
685-9007

Forbidden Planet
840 Broadway.
Map 4 E1.
473-1576.

Hacker Art Books
45 W 57th St.
Map 12 F3.
688-7600.

Hagstrom Map & Travel Store
57 W 43rd St.
Map 8 F1.
398-1222.

J. Levine Judaica
5 W 30th St.
Map 8 F3.
695-6888.

JN Bartfield Books
30 W 57th St.
Map 12 F3.
245-8890.

Kitchen Arts & Letters
1435 Lexington Ave.
Map 17 A2.
876-5550.

McGraw-Hill Bookstore
1221 6th Ave.
Map 12 E4.
512-4100.

Murder Ink
2486 Broadway.
Map 15 C2.
362-8905.

Mysterious Bookshop
129 W 56th St.
Map 12 E3.
765-0900.

Oscar Wilde Memorial Bookshop
15 Christopher St.
Map 3 C2.
255-8097.

Rand McNally Map & Travel Store
150 E 52nd St.
Map 13 A4.
758-7488.

Revolution Books
9 W 19th St.
Map 7 C5.
691-3345.

St. Mark's Bookshop
31 3rd Ave.
Map 5 A2.
260-7853.

Travelers' Choice
2 Wooster St.
Map 4 E4.
941-1535.

Urban Center Books
457 Madison Ave.
Map 13 A4.
935-3592.

Village Comics
214 Sullivan St.
Map 4 D2.
777-2770.

RECORDS, TAPES, COMPACT DISCS

Bleecker Bob's Golden Oldies
118 W 3rd St.
Map 4 D2.
475-9677.

Footlight Records
113 E 12th St.
Map 4 F1.
533-1572.

Gryphon Records
233 W 72nd St.
Map 11 D1.
874-1588.

HMV
57 W 34 St.
Map 8 E2.
629-0900.
One of several branches.

House of Oldies
35 Carmine St.
Map 4 D3.
243-0500.

J&R Music World
15, 23, 27 & 33 Park Row.
Map 1 C2.
732-8600.

Midnight Records
263 W 23rd St.
Map 8 D4.
675-2768.

Record Explosion
507 5th Ave. **Map** 8 F1.
661-6642.
One of several branches.

Tower Records
692 Broadway.
Map 4 E2.
505-1500.
One of three branches.

Virgin Megastore
45th & Broadway.
Map 12 E5.
921-1020.

SHEET MUSIC

Charles Colin Publications
315 W 53rd St.
Map 12 D4.
581-1480.

Colony Record and Music Center
1619 Broadway.
Map 12 E4.
265-2050.

Frank Music Company
244 W 54th St.
Map 12 D4.
582-1999.

Joseph Patelson Music House Ltd
160 W 56th St.
Map 12 E4.
757-5587.

Art and Antiques

Any art-loving visitor to New York could easily spend several days gallery-hopping around the several hundred galleries found throughout New York. Antique lovers can find an exciting variety of goods, including Americana and many bargains, at the many flea markets; or they can browse through European and American fine antiques in one of the more exclusive antiques centers. To find out what's happening, pick up the free monthly *Art Now Gallery Guide*, available at most galleries, or check the local papers.

ART GALLERIES

One of the most well known galleries in New York is **Leo Castelli**, an important showcase for Pop Art during the early 1960s and now spotlighting new artists. **Mary Boone Gallery** features Neo-Expressionist artists such as Julian Schnabel. **Pace Wildenstein Gallery** exhibits current stars, especially well-known painter-photographers, and the trendy gallery **Gorney, Bravin & Lee** deals in contemporary art and sculpture. The **John Weber Gallery** features new talent but is famous for its many Minimalists and Conceptualists. **Postmasters** is a treasure trove of conceptual pieces.

The venerable **Swann Galleries** has prints, rare books, maps, posters, autographs and photographs; **Marian Goodman Gallery** features the European avant-garde. **Holly Solomon Gallery** in Chelsea has European and American contemporary painting, drawing and sculpture.

Along the Upper East Side is **Knoedler & Company**, which exhibits contemporary paintings by modern masters. **Gagosian Gallery** has great works by Lichtenstein and Johns, and the **Hirschl & Adler Galleries** feature a good selection of European and American fine art.

AMERICAN FOLK ART

If you're in the market for American folk art, go to **Susan Parrish Antiques** for a selection of hooked rugs and other Americana. Similar goods are at **Brian Windsor**.

Laura Fisher sells everything from decoys to hooked rugs.

ANTIQUES CENTERS AND SECONDHAND ANTIQUES

In addition to hundreds of small shops selling everything from tiger teeth to multimillion-dollar paintings, Manhattan is home to **The Manhattan Art & Antiques Center**, which has dozens of dealers under one roof. **Chelsea Antiques** is home to more than 100 galleries and even has a small cafe. **Irving Barber Shop Antiques** is filled with fabulous secondhand finds at astoundingly good prices.

AMERICAN FURNITURE

For furniture from the 17th-, 18th- and 19th-centuries, try **Bernard & S. Dean Levy**, **Eagles Antiques**, **Leigh Keno American Furniture** or the highly regarded **Israel Sack**. **Judith & James Milne** sell early American country furniture and a splendid collection of quilts. Go to **Woodard & Greenstein American Antiques & Quilts** for a truly wonderful selection of Shaker pieces.

Collectors of Art Deco or Art Nouveau furniture should pay a visit to **Alan Moss**, which is full of furniture and decorative items. **Macklowe Gallery & Modernism** has a massive collection of fine Art Nouveau furniture. **Minna Rosenblatt** and **Lillian Nassau** have Tiffany lamps and many Art Nouveau and Art Deco pieces.

New York has a handful of retro shops, though numbers are growing all the time. Two of the best are **Depression Modern** and **Mood Indigo**, which have treasures from the 1930s and 1940s.

INTERNATIONAL ANTIQUES

If you're looking for English antiques, try **Florian Papp** and **Kentshire Galleries**. For European pieces, you'll have plenty of choices; try **Betty Jane Bart Antiques**, **Kurt Gluckselig Antiques**, **The Little Antique Shop**, **Linda Horn Antiques**, **La Belle Epoque**, and **Les Pierres**. Oriental dealers include **Doris Leslie Blau**, **E. & J. Frankel** and **Flying Cranes Antiques**.

FLEA MARKETS

New York has a number of year-round weekend markets. The best time to go is at the crack of dawn. Most flea markets officially open at 9 or 10am, but the haggling starts as early as 6am. If you arrive early, you may be lucky enough to unearth some valuable piece of cultural Americana like a Barbie lunch box or a Soupy Sales record.

Visit the **Annex Antiques Fair and Flea Market** for everything from secondhand clothing to antique furniture. The weekend **Canal Street Flea Market** has bric-a-brac; the **Columbus Avenue Flea Market** has new and secondhand clothing and furniture. For information on all street fairs and flea markets, check Friday's *The New York Times*.

AUCTION HOUSES

Manhattan's two most celebrated auction houses are **Christie's** and **Sotheby's**, selling collectibles ranging from coins, jewels, and vintage wines to fine and decorative arts. **William Doyle Galleries** and **Phillips Fine Art Auctioneers** are both well-respected names for fine art, jewelry, and antiques. Items for sale are previewed several days before the auctions, so check the Friday and Sunday *Times*.

DIRECTORY

ART GALLERIES

Gagosian Gallery
980 Madison Ave.
Map 17 A5.
📞 744-2313.

Hirschl & Adler Galleries
21 E 70th St. **Map** 12 F1.
📞 535-8810.
One of several branches.

Holly Solomon
222 W 23rd St. at Chelsea Hotel, #425. **Map** 8D4.
📞 243-3700.

Gorney, Bravin & Lee
534 W 26 St. **Map** 7 C4.
📞 352-8372.

John Weber Gallery
529 W 20th St. **Map** 7 C5.
📞 691-5711.

Knoedler & Company
19 E 70th St. **Map** 13 A1.
📞 794-0550.

Leo Castelli
59 E 79th St.
Map 17 A4.
📞 249-4470.

Marian Goodman Gallery
24 W 57th St. **Map** 12 F3.
📞 977-7160.

Mary Boone Gallery
745 5th Ave.
Map 12 F3.
📞 752-2929.

Pace Wildenstein Gallery
142 Greene St.
Map 4 E2 📞 431-9224.

Postmasters
459 W 19th St. **Map** 9 D5
📞 727-3323.

Swann Galleries
104 E 25th St. **Map** 9 A4.
📞 254-4710.

AMERICAN FOLK ART

Brian Windsor
272 Lafayette St.
Map 4 F4.
📞 274-0411.

Laura Fisher
Manhattan Art & Antiques Center, 1050 2nd Ave.
Map 13 B4.
📞 838-2596.

Susan Parrish Antiques
390 Bleecker St.
Map 3 C2.
📞 645-5020.

ANTIQUE CENTERS AND SECOND-HAND ANTIQUES

Chelsea Antiques
110 W 25th St.
Map 8 E4.
📞 929-0909.

Irving Barber Shop Antiques
210 E 21st St.
Map 9 A4.
no phone.

The Manhattan Arts & Antiques Center
1050 2nd Ave.
Map 13 A3.
📞 355-4400.

AMERICAN FURNITURE

Alan Moss
436 Lafayette St.
Map 4 F2.
📞 473-1310.

Bernard & S. Dean Levy
24 E 84th St.
Map 16 F4.
📞 628-7088.

Depression Modern
150 Sullivan St.
Map 4 D3.
📞 982-5699.

Eagles Antiques
1097 Madison Ave.
Map 17 A5.
📞 772-3266.

Israel Sack
730 5th Ave.
Map 12 F3.
📞 399-6562.

Judith & James Milne
506 E 74th St. **Map** 17 C5.
📞 472-0107.

Leigh Keno American Furniture
980 Madison Ave.
Map 17 A5.
📞 734-2381.

Lillian Nassau
220 E 57th St. **Map** 13 B3.
📞 759-6062.

Macklowe Gallery & Modernism
667 Madison Ave.
Map 13 A3.
📞 644-6400.

Minna Rosenblatt
961 Madison Ave.
Map 17 A5.
📞 288-0250.

Mood Indigo
181 Prince St.
Map 4 E3.
📞 254-1176.

Woodard & Greenstein American Antiques
506 E 74th St.
Map 17 A5.
📞 988-2906.

INTERNATIONAL ANTIQUES

La Belle Epoque
280 Columbus Ave.
Map 12 D1.
📞 362-1770.

Betty Jane Bart Antiques
1225 Madison Ave.
Map 17 A3.
📞 410-2702.

Doris Leslie Blau
724 5th Ave.
Map 12 F3.
📞 586-5511.
By appointment only.

E & J Frankel
1040 Madison Ave.
Map 17 A5.
📞 879-5733.

Florian Papp
962 Madison Ave.
Map 17 A5.
📞 288-6770.

Flying Cranes Antiques
1050 2nd Ave.
Map 13 B4.
📞 223-4600.

Kentshire Galleries
37 E 12th St. **Map** 4 E1.
📞 673-6644.

Kurt Gluckselig Antiques
200 E 58th St.
Map 13 B4.
📞 758-1805.

Linda Horn Antiques
1015 Madison Ave.
Map 17 A5.
📞 772-1122.

The Little Antique Shop
44 E 11th St.
Map 4 E1.
📞 673-5173.

Les Pierres
362 Bleecker St.
Map 3 C2.
📞 243-7740.

FLEA MARKETS

Annex Antiques Fair and Flea Market
24th to 27th Sts at 6th Ave.
Map 8 E4.
📞 243-5343.
Open Sat and Sun.

Canal Street Flea Market
335 Canal St.
Map 4 E5.
Open every weekend Mar–Dec.

Columbus Avenue Flea Market
Columbus Ave, between 76th and 77th St.
Map 16 D5.
📞 721-0900.
Open Sun.

AUCTION HOUSES

Christie's
20 Rockefeller Plaza.
Map 12 F5.
📞 636-2000.

Sotheby's
1334 York Ave.
Map 13 C1.
📞 606-7000.

William Doyle
175 E 87th St.
Map 17 A3. 📞 427-2730.

Phillips Fine Art
406 E 79th St.
Map 17 C4. 📞 570-4830.

Food and Household Goods

N EW YORK'S STRIKING cultural and ethnic diversity is celebrated in its food – the city's food shops provide a truly international feast. There is also a dazzling array of household goods, electronics and photographic equipment available almost everywhere you turn.

GOURMET GROCERIES

S CATTERED AROUND town are several famous food emporiums that are tourist attractions in themselves. Remember, too, to visit the department stores, which often rival the specialty food stores.

Balducci's in Greenwich Village is a real Italian delight, with its own brands of cold meats, pastas, salami and fish. Food has been elevated to an art form at **Dean & DeLuca**, a chic delicatessen – don't miss the huge selection of take-out food. **Russ & Daughters** is one of the oldest gourmet shops, known as an "appetizing" store, full of ethnic food and famous for smoked fish, cream cheese, chocolates and bagels. **The Gourmet Garage** sells all kinds of delicious fresh food, in particular organic produce. **Zabar's** is perhaps the finest food store in the world, with huge crowds jostling for the excellent smoked salmon, bagels, caviar, cheese and coffee.

William Poll offers picnic hampers as well as a great variety of prepared dishes. For pâté de foie gras, Scottish smoked salmon, and caviar, go to **Caviarteria**.

SPECIALTY FOOD AND WINE SHOPS

F ABULOUS BREAD and cake shops abound but one of the best is **Poseidon Greek Bakery**, renowned for its filo pastry. **H & H Bagels** bakes 60,000 of the best bagels every day. **Vesuvio** has Italian bread and some unusual pepper biscuits. Try **Fung Wong** for delicious Chinese pastries or purchase a traditional Sicilian loaf from **A. Zito & Sons Bakery**.

Great confectionery shops include **Li-Lac** for handmade chocolates and **Mondel**

Chocolates for chocolate animals. **Economy Candy** has a huge selection of dried fruit but for a real treat go to **Teuscher**, which has fresh champagne truffles flown in direct from Switzerland.

Myers of Keswick imports English food. For something more exotic, **Kam Man Food Products** is an Oriental grocery selling Chinese, Thai, and other oriental products. The **Italian Food Center** has great olive oils, dried pastas and sausages, and try **Raffeto's Corporation** for every kind of pasta. Go to **Jefferson Market** for meat and fish, and **Citarella** for its fine seafood. **Angelica's Herbs and Spices** has a selection of 2,000 varieties of herbs and spices.

For fine burgundies, **Acker, Merrall & Condit** is a good choice. Go to **Garnet Liquors** for fine wines and champagnes at bargain prices. **SoHo Wines and Spirits** has an extensive selection of single-malt Scotch whisky. **Sherry-Lehmann** is New York's leading wine merchant.

New York also has many fine coffee stores. Among the best are **Oren's**, **The Sensuous Bean** and **Porto Rico Importing Company**, each with a mouth-watering selection. For fruit and vegetables at reasonable prices, visit a farmers' market, but get there early. Among the most popular are **City Hall**, **Upper West Side**, **St. Mark's in-the-Bowery**, and **Union Square**. For information about the city's markets, phone: 788-7900.

HOUSEHOLD GOODS

M OST OF THE department stores offer a wide range of household goods. For a specialized shop, try **Broadway Panhandler**, a cook's heaven with outstand- ing baking and pastry-making

equipment. **Bridge Kitchen- ware** is a household name among most restaurateurs. **Williams-Sonoma** has many cooking utensils and cook- books. **Zabar's** has a great selection of cooking utensils.

Baccarat, **Daum**, **Lalique** and **Villeroy & Boch** are where you'll find the finest crystal, china and silverware. Other fashionable shops include **Orrefors Kosta Boda** and **Tiffany & Co**. Go to **Avventura** for crystal and china and, for the best of inexpensive, utilitarian American china, visit **Fishs Eddy**. Also visit **Ceramica**, which stocks lovely handmade Italian pottery, and **La Terrine** and **Steuben Glass** for hand- painted ceramics.

Inexpensive linens can be found in most department stores, but for silk sheets and luxurious linens, visit **Port- hault** and **Pratesi**. **ABC Carpet & Home** has an enviable reputation for home furnishings as does **Bed, Bath & Beyond** for its bed linens, kitchen and bath accessories. For the lowest prices, shop- hop on Grand Street on the Lower East Side.

ELECTRONICS AND PHOTOGRAPHIC EQUIPMENT

P ERHAPS THE MOST competitive retailers in New York are the ones that sell electronics, and it pays to shop around. If you're buying electrical goods to take to Europe, make sure they have compatible voltages and formats (many in the US are made to different standards).

B & H Photo is where amateur and professional photographers can find everything they need. Another place for computer equipment is **CompUSA**. **J&R Music World** sells competitively priced equipment and has the best jazz CD selection in the city. **The Wiz** offers a wide range of equipment and games. Check the newspapers for **Willoughby's**; they have good sales on photographic equipment and supplies.

DIRECTORY

GOURMET GROCERIES

Balducci's
424 Ave of the Americas.
Map 4 D1.
☎ 673-2600.

Caviarteria
502 Park Ave. **Map** 13 A3.
☎ 759-7410.

Dean & DeLuca
560 Broadway. **Map** 4 E3.
☎ 226-6800.

Gourmet Garage
453 Broome St. **Map** 4 E4.
☎ 941-5850.
One of several branches.

Russ & Daughters
179 E Houston St.
Map 5 A3.
☎ 475-4880.

William Poll
1051 Lexington Ave.
Map 17 A5.
☎ 288-0501.

Zabar's
2245 Broadway.
Map 15 C4.
☎ 787-2000.

SPECIALTY FOOD AND WINE SHOPS

A Zito & Sons Bakery
259 Bleecker St. **Map** 3 C2.
☎ 929-6139.

Acker, Merrall & Condit
160 W 72nd St.
Map 11 C1.
☎ 787-1700.

Angelica's Herbs and Spices
147 1st Ave.
Map 5 A1.
☎ 677-1549.

Citarella
2135 Broadway.
Map 15 C5.
☎ 874-0383.

City Hall Green Market
Centre St and Chambers St.
Map 1 C1.

Economy Candy
108 Rivington St.
Map 5 A3.
☎ 254-1531.

Fung Wong
44 Mott St. **Map** 4 F3.
☎ 267-4037.

Garnet Liquors
929 Lexington Ave.
Map 13 A1.
☎ 772-3211.

H & H Bagels
2239 Broadway.
Map 15 C4. **☎** 595-8000.
One of two branches.

Italian Food Center
186 Grand St. **Map** 15 C4.
☎ 925-2954.

Jefferson Market
450 Ave of the Americas.
Map 12 E5. **☎** 533-3377.

Kam Man Food Products
200 Canal St. **Map** 4 F5.
☎ 571-0330.

Li-Lac
120 Christopher St.
Map 3 C2. **☎** 242-7374.

Mondel Chocolates
2913 Broadway.
Map 20 E3. **☎** 864-2111.

Myers of Keswick
634 Hudson St.
Map 3 C2.
☎ 691-4194.

Oren's
1144 Lexington Ave.
Map 17 A4. **☎** 472-6830.

Porto Rico Importing Company
201 Bleecker St. **Map** 3 C2.
☎ 477-5421.

Poseidon Greek Bakery
629 9th Ave. **Map** 12 D5.
☎ 757-6173.

Raffeto's Corporation
144 West Houston St.
Map 4 D3. **☎** 777-1261.

St. Mark's in-the-Bowery Greenmarket
E 10th St at 2nd Ave.
Map 4 F1.

The Sensuous Bean
66 W 70th St. **Map** 12 D1.
☎ 724-7725.

Sherry-Lehmann
679 Madison Ave.
Map 13 A3.
☎ 838-7500.

SoHo Wines and Spirits
461 W Broadway.
Map 4 E4.
☎ 777-4332.

Teuscher Chocolates
25 E 61st St. **Map** 12 F3.
☎ 751-8482.
620 5th Ave. **Map** 12 F4.
☎ 246-4416.

Union Square Greenmarket
E 17th St and Broadway.
Map 8 F5.

Upper West Side Greenmarket
Columbus Ave at 77th St.
Map 16 D5.

Vesuvio Bakery
160 Prince St. **Map** 4 E3.
☎ 925-8248.

HOUSEHOLD GOODS

ABC Carpet & Home
888 Broadway.
Map 8 F5.
☎ 473-3000.

Bed, Bath & Beyond
620 Ave of the Americas
Map 8 F5.
☎ 255-3550.

Avventura
463 Amsterdam Ave.
Map 15 C4.
☎ 769-2510.

Baccarat
625 Madison Ave.
Map 13 A3.
☎ 826-4100.

Bridge Kitchenware
214 E 52nd St.
Map 13 B4.
☎ 688-4220.

Broadway Panhandler
477 Broome St.
Map 4 E4.
☎ 966-3434.

Ceramica
59 Thompson St.
Map 4 D4.
☎ 941-1307.

Daum Boutique
694 Madison Ave.
Map 13 A3.
☎ 355-2060.

Fishs Eddy
2176 Broadway.
Map 15 C5.
☎ 873-8819.

Lalique
680 Madison Ave.
Map 13 A3.
☎ 355-6550.

Orrefors Kosta Boda Crystal
685 Madison Ave.
Map 13 A3.
☎ 752-1095.

Porthault
18 E 69th St.**Map** 12 F1.
☎ 688-1660.

Pratesi
829 Madison Ave.
Map 13 A2.
☎ 288-2315.

Steuben Glass
667 Madison Ave. **Map** 13 A3. **☎** 752-1441.

La Terrine
1024 Lexington Ave.
Map 13 A1.
☎ 988-3366.

Tiffany & Co
See p321.

Villeroy & Boch
901 Broadway.
Map 8 F5.
☎ 535-2500.

Williams-Sonoma
E 59th St at Lex.Ave. **Map** 13 A3. **☎** (917) 369-1131. One of three.

Zabar's
See Gourmet Groceries.

ELECTRONICS AND PHOTOGRAPHIC EQUIPMENT

B & H Photo
420 9th Ave. **Map** 8 D2.
☎ 444-6630.

J&R Music World
See p322.

The Wiz
555 5th Ave. **Map** 12 F5.
☎ 557-7770.
One of several branches.

CompUSA
420 5th Ave. **Map** 8 F1.
☎ 764-6224.

Willoughby's
138 W 32nd St. **Map** 8 E3.
☎ 564-1600.

ENTERTAINMENT IN NEW YORK

N EW YORK CITY IS a non-stop entertainment extravaganza, every day, all year round. Whatever your taste, you can be sure the city will satisfy it on both a grand and an intimate scale. The challenge is to take advantage of as many of the entertainments as possible. If it's theater, you can enjoy a mainstream success on Broadway or take a chance on an experimental production

Performance by the New York City Ballet

in a loft. If it's music, there's the magnificence of opera at the Met or a jazz group blowing in a club in the Village. You can catch a spectacle of avant-garde dance in a café or try your own avant-garde dancing in one of the city's warehouse-sized clubs. Movie theaters abound. But perhaps best of all is wandering and watching the vast show that is New York.

PRACTICAL INFORMATION

F IND OUT what you can choose from in the arts and leisure listings of the *New York Times* and the *Village Voice* newspapers and *Time Out New York* (referred

TKTS discount ticket booth

to as TONY) and *The New Yorker* magazines. These briefly describe the entertainment and tell you which credit cards are accepted. At your hotel ask for *Where*, a free weekly magazine containing maps and information on the many different attractions.

Hotel staff may be able to answer some of your questions and should also carry a wide selection of brochures and leaflets. They may also be willing to reserve tickets for you. Some hotel TVs have a New York visitor information channel.

The New York Convention and Visitors Bureau, now known as **NYC & Company**, is the city's official source for everything to do and see in the city. Touch-screen kiosks provide information and sell general admission

tickets to the city's top attractions. Multilingual counselors, discount coupons, free maps, brochures, tour information and ATMs are available. **NYC On Stage** is a telephone hotline for theater, dance and music; **Broadway Line** gives brief descriptions of current shows, schedules and the different prices; **Moviefone** gives recorded information on all the films; and **ClubFone** (777-2582) has information on nightlife.

BOOKING TICKETS

P OPULAR SHOWS may be sold out for weeks ahead, so buy your seats well in advance. Box offices are open daily, except Sundays, from 10am until one hour after the performance begins. Call in person, or phone the box office or a ticket agency

and order your seats by credit card. The biggest agencies are **Telecharge**, **Ticketmaster** and **Ticket Central**; a small fee of a few dollars will be charged. An independent ticket agent may also be able to find seats – try **Prestige Entertainment**; others are listed in the Yellow Pages. Fees vary according to demand. **Broadway Ticket Center** in the Times Square Visitors Center sells full-price tickets.

DISCOUNT TICKETS

E STABLISHED in 1973 to the advantage of theaters and theater-goers alike, the non-profit TKTS company sells unsold tickets on the day of the performance for all Broadway shows. Discounts range from 25% to 50%, but the price will include a small handling fee and must be paid for in cash or by traveler's check.

The TKTS booth on Broadway sells matinée tickets from 10am to 2pm every Wednesday and Saturday; evening tickets are sold from 3pm to 8pm, and Sunday tickets from 11am until 7pm. Queues at the booth get very long very quickly, particularly during the vacation season, so it is advisable to get there early.

You can purchase day-of-performance tickets from **Ticketmaster** at discounts of 10% to 25% (with a small commission charge) by telephone.

Bobby Short singing at the Café Carlyle (p343)

The Booth Theater on Broadway *(see p333)*

The **Hit Show Club** sells vouchers that can be exchanged at theater box offices for discounted tickets. Some shows offer standing-room tickets on the day at a bargain price. It's often the only way to catch a sold-out show on short notice.

"SCALPERS" AND TOUTS

IF YOU BUY from a "scalper" (a ticket tout), tickets for the wrong day or wrong price, counterfeit tickets and outrageous prices are among the risks. The police often monitor sports and theater venues for scalpers and their customers.

FREE TICKETS

FREE TICKETS to TV shows, concerts and special events are sometimes offered at the **NYC & Company Visitor Information Center,** which is open from 8:30am to 6pm Monday to Friday and 9am to 5pm on weekends. Free or deeply discounted tickets to film or theater premieres are often advertised in the *New York Times*, *Daily News* or *Time Out New York*. The "Cheap Thrills" section in the *Village Voice* lists poetry readings, recitals and experimental films. The New York Shakespeare Festival at the **Delacorte Theater** in Central Park offers free tickets – one ticket per person – on a first-come, first-

served basis. The line forms at noon on the day of the performance. Take a picnic basket and blankets.

Free tickets for TV video-taping sessions are available by writing to the networks or from their on-street agents at **Rockefeller Center.**

Royale Theater at night *(see p333)*

HANDICAPPED ACCESS

BROADWAY THEATERS reserve a few spaces and cut-price tickets for the disabled. Call **Ticketmaster** or **Telecharge** well in advance for information about shows and also to reserve tickets. For Off-Broadway theaters, call their box offices. Some theaters offer useful equipment for the hearing-impaired. **Tap** can arrange sign language for Broadway theaters, and **Hands On** for Off-Broadway.

USEFUL ADDRESSES

Broadway Line
C 563-2929.

Delacorte Theater
Entrance via 81st St at Central Park W. **Map** 16 E4. **C** 861-7277. **W** www.publictheater.org
Summer time only.

Hands On
C 672-4898 (Voice/TDD).

Hit Show Club
8th floor, 630 9th Ave. **Map** 12 D5. **C** 581-4211.

Moviefone
(see p337)
C 777-FILM.

Prestige Entertainment
C 697-7788.

Network Tickets
ABC.
67th St and Columbus Ave.
C 456-3537.

CBS.
524 W 57th St.
C 975-2476

New York Convention Center & Visitors Bureau (NYC & Co.)
810 7th Ave **Map** 12 E4.
C 484-1222
W www.newyork.citysearch.com
W www.nycvisit.com

NYC On Stage
1501 Broadway. **Map** 12 D2
C 768-1818.

Tap (Theatre Access Project)
C 221-1103 (Voice),
719-4537 (TDD).

Telecharge
C 239-6200.
W www.telecharge.com

Ticket Central
C 279-4200.
W www.ticketcentral.org

Ticketmaster
C 307-4100.
W www.ticketmaster.com

TKTS
Broadway at W 47th St.
Map 12 E5.

New York's Best: Entertainment

Greenwich Village jazz club

NEW YORK is one of the great entertainment capitals of the world. Top names in every branch of the arts are drawn here to perform and often to live and work. Major sports events are also constant, and as for nightlife, New York lives up to its reputation as "the city that never sleeps." From the huge choice offered, there are some venues and events that stand out as classics of their kind; this selection has been chosen from the listings on pages 332 to 347 as among those not to be missed. Even if you experience only one of them, you will have been part of something as essentially New York as the Empire State Building.

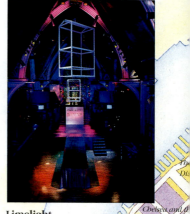

Limelight
Nightclubs come and go, but this converted church has become a firm favorite with New York's night owls. (See p342.)

Madison Square Garden
Top sporting action is found at "the Garden," including home games for basketball's New York Knicks and ice hockey's Rangers, plus the Golden Gloves boxing tournament. (See p344.)

Film Forum
At New York's most stylish arts movie theater you can see the latest foreign and American independent releases or catch up with a classic in a wide range of retrospectives. (See p336.)

Village Vanguard
The jazz clubs of Greenwich Village have played host to all the great names in jazz. Fans can catch the stars of today and tomorrow at the world-famous Village Vanguard and the Blue Note. (See p340.)

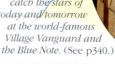

Upper
West Side

Central
Park

Upper
East
Side

Upper
Midtown

nercy
the
iron
rict

EAST RIVER

0 kilometers   2

0 miles   1

Philharmonic Rehearsals

*The Thursday-morning
rehearsals at Avery Fisher
Hall are often open to
the public at a fraction of
the normal ticket price.
(See p338.)*

Metropolitan Opera House

*Reserve well ahead and prepare
to pay high prices to see the giants
of the opera world. (See p338.)*

Shakespeare in
Central Park

*If you are a
summer visitor,
set aside a time
to get one of
the rare free
tickets for the
Delacorte
Theater's open-air Shakespeare
featuring top Hollywood and
Broadway names. (See p332.)*

The Nutcracker

*The Christmas event for children of
every age is performed each year at
Lincoln Center by the New York City
Ballet. (See p334.)*

The Fantasticks

*The tiny Sullivan
Street Playhouse
has been home to
America's longest-
running play since
May 1960. New
Yorkers who saw it
when they were
young are now
taking their own
children to the
show. (See p332.)*

Carnegie Hall

*Conveniently situated in the
Theater District, Carnegie Hall is
famous the world over as a showcase for the best in the musical arts.
A backstage tour gives a fascinating insight into "the house that
music built." (See p338.)*

Theater and Dance

NEW YORK IS FAMOUS for its extravagant musicals and its ferocious critics. It is one of the world's greatest theater and dance centers, featuring every kind of production imaginable. Whether your preference is for the glitz and glamour of a Broadway blockbuster or something truly experimental, you'll find it here.

BROADWAY

BROADWAY HAS long been synonymous with New York's Theater District, but the majority of Broadway theaters are actually scattered between 41st and 53rd streets and from Sixth to Ninth Avenues, with a few around the much-improved Times Square. Most were built between 1910 and 1930, during the heyday of vaudeville and the famous Ziegfeld Follies. The **Lyceum** (see p142) is the oldest theater still in operation (1903), the **American Airlines Theater**, now the permanent home of the Roundabout Theater Co., is the newest (2000). Many Broadway theaters experienced a slump during the 1980s but are now enjoying a revival because of cutting costs, using big names to draw in the crowds and benefiting from the Times Square renewal.

This is where you will find the "power productions" – the big, highly publicized dramas, musicals and revivals starring many Hollywood luminaries in (it is hoped) sure-fire money earners. Recent hits have included such international imports as *Les Misérables;* New York originals like *Cats* and *The Producers,* the popular children's favorite *The Lion King,* and great revivals like *42nd Street.*

OFF-BROADWAY AND OFF-OFF-BROADWAY

THERE ARE about 20 Off-Broadway stages and 300 Off-Off-Broadway stages whose works will sometimes transfer to Broadway. Off-Broadway theaters have from 100 to 499 seats, and Off-Off-Broadway showplaces have fewer than 100. Both range from the well-appointed to the improvised, sited in lofts,

churches and even garages. Off-Broadway became very popular during the 1950s as a reaction to the commercialism of Broadway. It was also an ideal place for more cautious producers to try out works considered too avant-garde or unsuitable for Broadway at much lower operating costs. During the last two decades, Off-Off-Broadway theaters have become the venue for the more experimental pieces by these same producers.

Off-Broadway theaters are found all over Manhattan – from Greenwich Village's **Sullivan Street Playhouse** (where the longest-running show in New York, *The Fantasticks,* plays) to Central Park's open-air **Delacorte Theater**. Some are even in the traditional Broadway district, such as the **Manhattan Theater Club**. Farther afield are the **Brooklyn Academy of Music (BAM)** (see p246), the **Manhattan Theater Club** and the **92nd Street Y**. In these venues you will always find lively, unusual and experimental showcases for new talent as well as lots of uninhibited productions.

The Off-Broadway theatres mounted the first productions in New York of the works of playwrights Sean O'Casey, Tennessee Williams, Eugene O'Neill, Samuel Beckett, Jean Genet, Eugene Ionesco and David Mamet. They host new and very often irreverent treatments of the classics, and every imaginable theatrical presentation is floated.

Sometimes a more intimate, smaller Off-Broadway stage suits a production better than a larger more established theater would, as proved by such long-running successes as *The Fantasticks* and the *Threepenny Opera.* Of course, there are flops occasionally – but that's show business.

PERFORMANCE THEATER

THIS EXTREMELY avant-garde art form can be found in several Off- and Off-Off-Broadway locations. Accurate descriptions and categorizations are almost impossible, but expect the bizarre and outlandish. The most likely venues to find this are **La MaMa**, **P.S. 122**, **HERE**, **92nd Street Y**, **Symphony Space** and the Joseph Papp **Public Theater** (see p118). The latter is perhaps the most influential theater in New York. It was founded in the 1950s by the late director Joseph Papp, who introduced neighborhood tours to bring theater to people who had never seen it before.

The Public Theater created hits like *Hair* and *A Chorus Line;* it is most famous for its free summer performances of Shakespeare at the Delacorte Theater in Central Park (see p206). It usually has several productions running, and at 6pm on the day of performance, "Quiktix" tickets (limited to two per person) are sold in the Public Theater lobby.

THEATER SCHOOLS

NEW YORK is the best place in the country to see actors learning their trade. Foremost among the acting schools is **The Actors' Studio**. The late Lee Strasberg, the advocate of method acting – in which the actor aims for complete identification with the character being played – was its guru. His students included Dustin Hoffman, Al Pacino and Marilyn Monroe. "In progress" productions feature trainees and are usually open to the public. Sandy Meisner trained many actors, including the late Lee Remick, at the **Neighborhood Playhouse School of the Theater**. Its plays are not open to the public. The **New Dramatists** began in 1949 to develop new playwrights, helping the careers of the likes of William Inge. Play readings are open to the public and free.

BROADWAY THEATERS

① Ambassador
215 W 49th St.
239-6200.

② Barrymore
243 W 47th St.
239-6200.

③ Belasco
111 W 44th St.
239-6200.

④ Booth
222 W 45th St.
239-6200.

⑤ Broadhurst
235 W 44th St.
239-6200.

⑥ Broadway
1681 Broadway.
239-6200.

⑦ Brooks Atkinson
256 W 47th St.
307-4100.

⑧ CORT
139 W 48th St.
239-6200.

⑨ Eugene O'Neill
230 W 49th St.
239-6200.

⑩ Gershwin
222 W 51st St.
307-4100.

⑪ John Golden
252 W 45th St.
239-6200.

⑫ Helen Hayes
240 W 44th St.
307-4100.

⑬ Imperial
249 W 45th St.
239-6200.

⑭ Longacre
220 W 48th St.
239-6200.

⑮ Lunt–Fontanne
205 W 46th St.
307-4100.

⑯ Lyceum
149 W 45th St.
239-6200.

⑰ Majestic
245 W 44th St.
239-6200.

⑱ Marquis
1535 Broadway.
307-4100.

⑲ Martin Beck
302 W 45th St.
239-6200.

⑳ Minskoff
Broadway at 45th St.
307-4100.

㉑ Music Box
239 W 45th St.
239-6200.

㉒ Nederlander
208 W 41st St.
307-4100.

㉓ Neil Simon
250 W 52nd St.
307-4100.

㉔ Palace
1564 Broadway.
307-4100.

㉕ Plymouth
236 W 45th St.
239-6200.

㉖ Richard Rodgers
226 W 46th St.
307-4100.

㉗ American Airlines Theater
227 W 42nd St (between
7th & 8th). 719-1300.

㉘ Royale
242 W 45th St.
239-6200.

㉙ St. James
246 W 44th St.
239-6200.

㉚ Shubert
225 W 44th St.
239-6200.

㉛ Virginia
245 W 52nd St.
239-6200.

㉜ Walter Kerr
219 W 48th St.
239-6200.

㉝ Winter Garden
1634 Broadway.
239-6200.

For other theaters see p335.

BALLET

At the heart of the dance world is Lincoln Center *(see p212)*, where the New York City Ballet performs pieces in the **New York State Theater**. This company was created by the legendary brilliant choreographer George Balanchine *(see p46)* and is probably still the best in the world. The current director, Peter Martins, was one of Balanchine's best dancers and continues the strict policy of ensemble dancing rather than "star turns." The season runs from November to February and late April to early June. The ballet school at the **Juilliard Dance Theater** also presents a spring workshop every year, and this is a good chance to see budding stars.

The American Ballet Theatre appears at the **Metropolitan Opera House**, which also hosts many visiting foreign companies, such as the Kirov, Bolshoi and Royal ballets. Its repertoire includes 19th-century classics, such as *Swan Lake,* and works by modern choreographers like Twyla Tharp and Paul Taylor.

CONTEMPORARY DANCE

New York is the center of many of the most important movements in modern dance. The **Dance Theater of Harlem** is world famous for its modern, traditional and ethnic productions. Other havens of experimental dance include the **92nd Street Y** and the **Merce Cunningham Studio** in Greenwich Village. The unusual **Dance Theater Workshop** has a packed program as well as an art gallery. **The Kitchen**, **La MaMa**, **Symphony Space** and **P.S. 122** are all multimedia venues with the latest in contemporary dance, performance art and avant-garde music. Choreographer Mark Morris's company performs at the brand new **Mark Morris Dance Center** in Brooklyn; **City Center** *(see p146)* is a favorite spot for dance fans. It used to house the New York City Ballet and the American Ballet Theater

before Lincoln Center was built. As well as featuring the Joffrey Ballet, City Center has held performances by all the great contemporary artists, including Alvin Ailey's blend of modern, jazz and blues and the companies of modern dance masters Merce Cunningham and Paul Taylor. Avoid the mezzanine as the view is restricted.

The city's single most active venue for dance is probably the **Joyce Theater,** where such well-established companies as the Feld Ballet, along with bold newcomers and visiting troupes, perform.

Each spring the Festival of Black Dance at the **Brooklyn Academy of Music (BAM)** *(see p246)* features everything from ethnic dance to hip-hop. During autumn the "Next Wave" festival of music and dance is held, celebrating international and American avant-garde dance and music. During winter the American Ballet Festival is held here.

During June, **New York University** *(see p113)* holds a Summer Residency Festival with lecture-demonstrations, rehearsals and performances, and **Dancing in the Streets** organizes summertime dance performances all over the city. Throughout the month of August, **Lincoln Center Out of Doors** has a program of free dance events on the plaza, with such experimental groups as the American Tap Dance Orchestra.

The new **Duke Theater** presents many contemporary dance companies and participates in events such as the New York Tap Festival.

At different times of the year, **Radio City Music Hall** holds several spectacular shows, with different companies from all over the world. At Christmas and Easter, it features the famously precise Rockettes dance troupe.

Choreographers and dance companies frequently present works-in-progress and recitals to the public. Among the most interesting venue for these is **Alvin Ailey's Repertory Ensemble**. The **Hunter College Dance Company** performs new works by its

student choreographers, and the **Isadora Duncan Dance Foundation** re-creates her original dances. For contemporary choreographers the best place to go is **Juilliard Dance Theater**.

PRICES

Theater is extremely expensive to produce, and ticket prices tend to reflect this. Even Off- and Off-Off-Broadway tickets are not cheap anymore. At one time, all tickets to previews of new plays sold at a much-reduced price, but not so today. Preview tickets are easier to get hold of, though, and it's fun to see a show before the reviews are in so you're able to make up your own mind.

For Broadway theater you can expect to pay $80 or more; for musicals, up to $99; Off-Broadway, $25 to $40. For dance, $20 to $50 is the usual range, with up to $115 for the American Ballet Theatre. The **Music and Dance Booth** *(see p329)* in Bryant Park sells half-price day-of-performance tickets, worth the wait.

TIMES OF PERFORMANCE

The general rules for theater hours are: closed on Mondays (except for most musicals), with matinees on Wednesdays, Saturdays and sometimes Sundays. Matinees usually begin at 2pm, with evening performances at 8pm. Be sure to check the correct dates and times of the performance beforehand.

BACKSTAGE TOURS AND LECTURES

For those interested in the mechanics and anecdotes of the theater, your best bet is to go on one of the theater tours. The **92nd Street Y** organizes insider's views of the theater, with famous directors, actors and choreographers taking part. Writers are invited along to read or discuss their current works. **Radio City Music Hall** also holds tours.

DIRECTORY

OFF-BROADWAY

92nd Street Y
Lexington Ave.
Map 17 A2.
[415-5420.

Actors' Playhouse
100 Seventh Ave S.
Map 3 C1.
[463-0060.

American Place
111 W 46th St.
Map 12 E5.
[840-3074.

**Brooklyn
Academy of Music**
30 Lafayette St., Brooklyn.
[(718) 636-4100.

HERE Art Center
145 6th Ave.
Map 4 D4.
[647-0202.

**Circle in the
Square**
50th St. west of B'way.
Map 12 E4.
[239-6200.

Delacorte Theater
Central Park. (81st St.)
Map 16 E4.
[861-7277.
Summer time only.

John Houseman
450 W 42nd St.
Map 7 C1.
[967-9077.

Lambs Theater
130 W 44th St.
Map 12 F5.
[997-1780.

**Manhattan
Theater Club**
311 W 43rd St.
Map 8 D1.
[399-3030.

**New York Theater
Workshop**
79 E 4th St.
Map 4 F2.
[460-5475.

Public Theater
425 Lafayette St.
Map 4 F2.
[539-8500.

**Sullivan Street
Playhouse**
181 Sullivan St.
Map 4 D3.
[674-3838.

Symphony Space
2537 Broadway.
Map 15 C2.
[864-5400.

Vivian Beaumont
Lincoln Center.
Map 11 C2.
[362-7600.

OFF-OFF-BROADWAY

**Bouwerie Lane
Theater**
330 Bowery. **Map** 4 F2.
[677-0060.

The Kitchen
512 W 19th St. **Map** 7 C5.
[255-5793.

Living Theater
[865-3957.
Touring group. Call for info.

**Performing
Garage**
33 Wooster St.
Map 4 E4.
[966-3651.

**Theater at St.
Peter's Church**
Citigroup Center, 619
Lexington Ave.
Map 13 A4.
[935-5824.

PERFORMANCE
THEATER

La MaMa
74a E 4th St. **Map** 4 F2.
[475-7710.

P.S. 122
150 First Ave. **Map** 5 A1.
[477-5288.

Public Theater
See Off-Broadway.

THEATER SCHOOLS

**The Actors'
Studio**
432 W 44th St.
Map 11 C5.
[757-0870.

New Dramatists
424 W 44th.
Map 11 C5.
[757-6960.

DANCE

92nd Street Y
See Off-Broadway.

**Alvin Ailey American
Dance Center**
211 W 61st St. **Map** 11 3C.
[767-0590.

**Brooklyn Academy
of Music**
See Off-Broadway.

City Center
131 W 55th St.
Map 12 E4. [581-7907.

**Dance Theater of
Harlem**
466 W 152nd St.
[690-2800.

**Dance Theater
Workshop**
219 W 19th St.
Map 8 E5.
[924-0077.

**Dancing in the
Streets**
55 6th Ave. *(offices)*
[625-3505.

**Hunter College
Dance Company**
695 Park Ave.
Map 13 A1.
[772-4490.

**Isadora Duncan
Dance Foundation**
141 W 26th St.
Map 20 D2.
[691-5040.

Joyce Theater
175 Eighth Ave at 19th St.
Map 8 D5.
[242-0800.

**Juilliard Dance
Theater**
60 Lincoln Center Plaza,
W 65th St.
Map 11 C2.
[769-7406.

PERFORMANCE
VENUES

Duke Theater
229 W 42nd St.
Map 8 E1.
[996-1100.

The Kitchen
See Off-Off Broadway.

La MaMa
See Performance Theater.

**Lincoln Center
Out of Doors**
Lincoln Center, Broadway
at 64th St. **Map** 11 C2.
[362-6000.

Manhattan Center
311 W 34th St.
Map 8 D2. [307-4100.

Mark Morris
3 Lafayette St.
(Brooklyn)
[(718) 624-8400.

**Merce Cunning-
ham Studio**
55 Bethune St.
Map 3 B2.
[255-8240.

**Metropolitan
Opera House**
Lincoln Center,
Broadway at 65th St.
Map 11 C2.
[362-6000.

**Music and Dance
Booth**
See page 329.

**New York State
Theater**
Lincoln Center, Broadway
at 65th St. **Map** 11 C2.
[870-5570.

**New York
University**
Tisch School of the Arts
(TSOA), 111 2nd Ave.
Map 4 F1. [998-1920.

P.S. 122
See Performance Theater.

**Radio City Music
Hall**
50th St at Ave of the
Americas. **Map** 12 F4.
[247-4777.

Symphony Space
See Off-Broadway.

BACKSTAGE TOURS

92nd Street Y
See Off-Broadway.

**Radio City Music
Hall**
[247-4777.

[w] **EVENTS GUIDE**
www.culturefinder.com
www.broadway.org
www.stagebill.org
www.newyork.citysearch.
com

Movies

NEW YORK is a film buff's paradise. Apart from new US releases, which show months in advance of other countries, many classic and foreign films are screened here.

The city has always been the testing ground for new developments in films, and it continues to be a hotbed of new and innovative talent. Many of the movies' most famous directors – Spike Lee, Martin Scorsese and Woody Allen – were born and raised in New York, and the city's influence can be seen in many of their films. They, and others, can often be seen filming on the streets of the city; many of New York's landmarks have become famous after appearing in films. Most of the TV networks based in New York offer free tickets to the taping of their shows. Watching a show, such as *The David Letterman Show,* is popular with visitors.

FIRST-RUN MOVIES

NEW YORK REVIEWS and box office returns are so vital to a film's success that most major American films have their premieres in Manhattan's theaters. First-run films are shown mainly at the City Cinema chains, Loews, United Artists and Cineplex Odeon, which are scattered around the city. Some theaters have recorded information giving the names and duration of the different films showing, with starting times and ticket prices.

Programs start at 10am or 11am and are repeated every two to three hours until midnight. You should expect to line up for most evening and weekend performances of the more popular films. Making reservations using a credit card is possible at some theaters for an additional charge of about $1 per ticket. Matinées (usually before 4pm) are easier to get into. Senior citizens pay a reduced price for tickets: the required age may be over 60, 62 or 65 depending on the policy of the theater.

NEW YORK FILM FESTIVAL

A HIGH POINT of the year for film buffs is the New York Film Festival, now in its third decade. Organized by the **Film Society of Lincoln Center**, the festival starts in late September and continues for two weeks at the many Lincoln Center theaters. Outstanding new films from the United States and abroad are entered in a competition that has no prizes except for the huge prestige of winning an award. Many of the films shown during the festival are later released and can usually be seen only in art houses.

FOREIGN FILMS AND ART HOUSES

FOR THE LATEST foreign and independent films, go to the **Angelika Film Center**, which has six screens and an upscale coffee bar. Other good places are the 4-screen **Rose Cinemas** at the Brooklyn Academy of Music, the stylish **Film Forum,** and **Lincoln Plaza Cinema**. The Plaza has a busy program of foreign and art films. For

FILM RATINGS

Films in the United States are graded as follows:
G General audiences; all ages admitted.
PG Parental guidance suggested; some material unsuitable for children.
PG-13 Parents strongly cautioned; some material inappropriate for children under age 13.
R Restricted. Children under 17 need to be accompanied by a parent or an adult guardian.
NC-17 No children under 17 admitted.

ON LOCATION

Many New York locations have played starring roles in films. Here are a few:

The Brill Building (1141 Broadway) contained Burt Lancaster's penthouse in *Sweet Smell of Success.*

The Brooklyn Bridge was a great backdrop in Spike Lee's *Mo' Better Blues.*

Brooklyn Heights and the **Metropolitan Opera** appeared in *Moonstruck.*

Central Park has shown up in countless films, including *Love Story* and *Marathon Man.*

55 Central Park West will be remembered as Sigourney Weaver's home in *Ghostbusters.*

Chinatown played a major role in *Year of the Dragon.*

The Dakota was where Mia Farrow lived in the classic *Rosemary's Baby.*

The Empire State Building is still standing after *King Kong*'s last battle. The observation deck is where Cary Grant waited in vain in *Affair to Remember;* here Meg Ryan finally met Tom Hanks in *Sleepless in Seattle.*

Grand Central Station is famous for Robert Walker's meeting with Judy Garland in *Under the Clock* and the magical ballroom sequence in *The Fisher King.*

Harlem hosted the jazz musicians and dancers in *The Cotton Club.*

Katz's Deli was the setting for the café scene between Billy Crystal and Meg Ryan in *When Harry Met Sally…*

Little Italy appeared in *The Godfather I* and *II.*

Madison Square Garden was the setting for the dramatic climax of *The Manchurian Candidate.*

Tiffany & Co. was Audrey Hepburn's favorite shop in *Breakfast at Tiffany's.*

The United Nations Building featured in *North by Northwest.*

Washington Square Park was where Robert Redford and Jane Fonda walked *Barefoot in the Park.*

Asian, Indian and Chinese films, you should visit the **Asia Society**. The **French Institute** screens many French films with English subtitles and plays host to the Asian American International Film Festival. The **Quad Cinema** shows a wide selection of foreign films, often quite rare. **Cinema Village** runs special film events, such as the Festival of Animation.

The **Walter Reade Theater** houses the Film Society of the Lincoln Center, offering retrospectives of international movies as well as celebrations of contemporary works, such as the popular annual Spanish Cinema Now festival.

CLASSIC FILMS AND MUSEUMS

Retrospectives of films by particular directors or featuring specific actors are shown at the **Public Theater** and the **Whitney Museum of American Art** *(see pp198–9)*. The extensive **Museum of Modern Art** *(see pp170 -3)* is one of the best places to see a wide range of classic and silent movies, and films on art and cultural subjects. The **American Museum of the**

Moving Image *(see p244)* screens old films and also has many exhibits of memorabilia from the film industry. The **Museum of Television & Radio** *(see p169)* has regular screenings of classic films; you can also see or hear specific television or radio programs. Students interested in classic, new and experimental movies will appreciate the huge wealth of material at the **Anthology Film Archives.**

The sky shows at the **Rose Center for Earth and Space** at the **American Museum of Natural History** are well worth a whole day's visit.

On summer evenings in Bryant Park, you can watch free classic movies, and on Saturday mornings, take your young filmgoers to the **Film Society of Lincoln Center,** where special children's shows are held.

TELEVISION SHOWS

A number of TV programs originate in New York. By writing several months in advance, you may be able to see one or more of them as they are being taped for broadcast. The popular David Letterman show is almost impossible to get tickets for,

however. To request free tickets from **ABC** and **CBS**, write to each company individually. Another good source of free tickets is the Times Square Visitors Information Bureau *(see p352)*. On weekday mornings on Fifth Avenue around **Rockefeller Plaza**, free tickets for a number of TV programs are sometimes distributed by the program's production staff. There's absolutely no way that you can plan for this. It's simply a matter of good luck and being in the right place at the right time.

For those who want to get a glimpse behind the scenes of TV, NBC organizes tours around the studios, usually from 9am to 4pm on Monday to Saturday.

CHOOSING WHAT TO SEE

If you feel bewildered by the huge range of films offered in New York, check the listings in *New York* magazine, the *New York Times*, the *Village Voice* and *The New Yorker*. The following Internet guides give show times and locations:
- w www.moviefone.com
- w www.movietickets.com.

FILM HOUSES

ABC
See p329.

American Museum of the Moving Image
35th Ave and 36th St
Astoria, Queens.
(718) 784-0077.

American Museum of Natural History
Central Park W at 79th St.
Map 16 D5.
769-5650.

Angelika Film Center
18 W Houston St.
Map 4 E3. 995-2000.

Anthology Film Archives
32 2nd Ave at 2nd St.
Map 5 C2.
505-5181.

Asia Society
725 Park Ave.
Map 13 A1.
517-2742.

Rose Cinemas
Brooklyn Academy of Music.
(718) 623-2770

CBS
See p329.

Cinema Village
22 E 12th St.
Map 4 F1.
924-3363.

Film Forum
209 W Houston St.
Map 3 C3.
727-8110.

French Institute
55 E 59th St.
Map 12 F3.
355-6160.

Lincoln Plaza Cinema
1886 Broadway.
Map 12 D2.
757-2280.

Moviefone
777-FILM.

Museum of Modern Art
11 W 53rd St.
Map 12 F4.
708-9480.

Museum of Television & Radio
25 W 52nd St.
Map 12 F4.
621-6600.

New York Film Festival
875-5600.

Public Theater
425 Lafayette St.
Map 4 F4.
539-8500.

Quad Cinema
34 W 13th St.
Map 4 D1.
225-8800.

Rockefeller Plaza
47th–50th St, 5th Ave.
Map 12 F5.

Walter Reade Theater/Film Society of the Lincoln Center
70 Lincoln Center Plaza.
Map 12 D2.
875-5600.

Whitney Museum of American Art
945 Madison Ave.
Map 13 A1.
570-3600.

Classical and Contemporary Music

N EW YORKERS HAVE A voracious appetite for music. Live concerts by the world's most celebrated musical performers may be enjoyed at famous halls throughout the year, and younger, newer artists and exotic imports always find receptive audiences.

TICKETS

F IND OUT WHAT you can choose from in New York by checking out the listings in the *New York Times* and the *Village Voice* and in *Time Out New York* and *The New Yorker* magazines.

CLASSICAL MUSIC

T HE ORCHESTRA in residence at **Avery Fisher Hall** in Lincoln Center (*see p213*) is the New York Philharmonic. It is also the annual site for the popular "Mostly Mozart" series and Young People's Concerts. **Alice Tully Hall**, in Lincoln Center, is an acoustic gem and home to the Chamber Music Society.

One of the world's premier concert halls is the revamped **Carnegie Hall** (*see p146*). Upstairs in the Weill Recital Hall there are quality performances for reasonable prices.

The **Brooklyn Academy of Music (BAM)** (*see p246*) is the home of the Brooklyn Philharmonic. The **New Jersey Performance Arts Center** in Newark is the newest star in the music venue crown. Classical music, dance, opera, jazz and world music all find an audience here.

The **Merkin Concert Hall** is host to some top chamber ensembles and soloists. For really excellent acoustics, go to the **Town Hall**. The **92nd Street Y's** Kaufmann Concert Hall also offers a lively menu of music and dance. There's also the **Frick Collection**

and **Symphony Space**, both of which offer a varied program ranging from gospel to Gershwin, classical to ethnic. The beautiful Grace Rainey Rogers Auditorium in the **Metropolitan Museum of Art** is for chamber music and soloists, while the **Florence Gould Hall**, at the Alliance Française, presents a varied program of chamber music and orchestral pieces.

The **Juilliard School of Music** and the **Mannes College of Music** are both considered excellent. Their students and faculties give free recitals, and there are shows by leading orchestras, chamber music groups and opera companies. The **Manhattan School of Music** offers an excellent program of over 400 events per year, from classical to jazz.

At 9:45am on the Thursdays of the New York Philharmonic concerts, the evening show is rehearsed at **Avery Fisher Hall** in Lincoln Center. Audiences are often admitted to listen, and rehearsal tickets are available at low prices. The **Kosciuszko Foundation** hosts the annual Chopin Competition. **Corpus Christi Church** has an active concert schedule, presenting such groups as the Tallis Scholars.

OPERA

D OMINATING the city's operatic scene is **Lincoln Center** (*see p212*), home to the New York City Opera, and the **Metropolitan Opera House**, which has its own opera company. The Met is the jewel in the crown, offering top international performers. More accessible and dynamic is the New York City Opera. Its performances range from *Madame Butterfly* to *South Pacific*, with subtitles above the stage to help the audience understand the plot.

Lower-priced quality performances are staged by the up-and-coming singers at the **Village Light Opera Group**, the **Amato Opera Theater**, the **Kaye Playhouse** at Hunter College, and the students at the **Juilliard Opera Center** in Lincoln Center.

CONTEMPORARY MUSIC

N EW YORK is one of the most important places in the world for contemporary music. Exotic, ethnic and experimental music is played in many first-rate venues. The **Brooklyn Academy of Music (BAM)** is the standard-bearer of the avant-garde. Each autumn the Academy holds a festival of music and dance called "Next Wave," which has helped launch many musical careers.

An annual festival of serious modern music called "Bang on a Can" is performed at the **Ethical Culture Society Hall** and features works by Steve Reich, Pierre Boulez and John Cage. Experimentalists, such as Davie Weinstein with his "audio-visual acid test" music – a mix of CD players, amplified instruments, keyboards and sound effects – perform at the **Dance Theater Workshop**.

Other venues include the **Asia Society** (*see p185*), with its jewel of a theater for many visiting Asian performers, and **St. Peter's Church**.

BACKSTAGE TOURS

B EHIND-THE-SCENES tours are offered by **Lincoln Center** and **Carnegie Hall**.

RELIGIOUS MUSIC

F EW EXPERIENCES are more moving than an Easter concert in the vast **Cathedral of St. John the Divine** (*see pp224–5*). Seasonal music is also offered at many of the city's museums and in almost every other available space – from Grand Central Terminal's main concourse (*see pp154–5*) to bank and hotel lobbies. For jazz vespers in a stunning modern building, visit **St.**

CLASSICAL RADIO

New York has three FM radio stations that broadcast classical music: WQXR at 96.3, the National Public Radio station WNYC at 93.9 and WKCR 89.9.

Peter's Church (see p175). Most of these concerts are free, but you are encouraged to contribute.

ALFRESCO

FREE OUTDOOR summer concerts occur in **Bryant Park**, **Washington Square** and **Lincoln Center's Damrosch Park**. The annual concerts on Central Park's Great Lawn and in Brooklyn's Prospect Park are performed by the New York Philharmonic and the Metropolitan Opera. In good weather, strolling musicians perform at South Street Seaport, on the steps of the **Metropolitan Museum of Art** (see pp188–95), and in the area around Washington Square.

MUSIC FOR FREE

THROUGHOUT the year free musical performances are given at the **Citigroup Atrium** (see p175), **The Cloisters** (see pp234–7) and the **Whitney Museum's** Philip Morris Building (see p150). Sunday-afternoon recitals are held at **The Dairy** in Central Park (see p206). You will also find music in the **Federal Hall** (see p68), while at **Lincoln Center,** don't miss the exciting free performances held in the **Juilliard School of Music**. Other very popular venues include the **Greenwich House Music School** (free student recitals) and the **Theodore Roosevelt Birthplace** (see p125). Numerous free concerts and talks take place in the city's churches, including **St. Paul's Chapel** and **Trinity Church Wall Street**. (see p68).

W INTERNET EVENTS GUIDE

www.culturefinder.com
www.nytoday.com
www.newyork.citysearch.com

MUSIC VENUES

92nd Street Y
1395 Lexington Ave.
Map 17 A2.
996-1100.

Amato Opera Theater
319 Bowery at 2nd St.
Map 4 F2. 228-8200.

Asia Society
725 Park Ave.
Map 13 A1.
288-6400.

Brooklyn Academy of Music
30 Lafayette Ave, Brooklyn.
(718) 636-4100.

Bryant Park
Map 8 F1. 983-4143.

Carnegie Hall
881 7th Ave. **Map** 12 E3.
247-7800.

Cathedral of St. John the Divine
Amsterdam Ave and 112th St. **Map** 20 E4.
316-7400.

Citigroup Atrium
Lexington Ave at 53rd St.
Map 13 A4.
559-6892.

The Cloisters
Fort Tryon Park.
923-3700.

Corpus Christi Church
529 W 121st St.
Map 20 E2. 666-9350.
W www.mb1800.org

The Dairy
Central Park.
Map 12 F2.
794-6564.

Dance Theater Workshop
See Dance p335.

Ethical Culture Society Hall
2 W 64th St.
Map 12 D2.
874-5210.

Federal Hall
Broad St at Wall St.
Map 1 C3.
866-2086.

Florence Gould Hall (at the Alliance Française)
55 E 59th St.
Map 13 A3. 355-6160.

Frick Collection
1 E 70th St.
Map 12 F1.
288-0700.

Greenwich House Music School
46 Barrow St.
Map 3 C2.
242-4770.

Kaye Playhouse (Hunter College)
695 Park Ave.
Map 13 A1
772-4448.

Kosciuszko Foundation
15 E 65th St. **Map** 12 F2
734-2130.

Lincoln Center
155 W 65th St.
Map 11 C2.
546-2656.

Tours for all venues at Lincoln Center can be arranged by calling:
875-5350.

Alice Tully Hall
875-5050.

Avery Fisher Hall
875-5030.

Damrosch Park
875-5596.

Juilliard Opera Center
769-7406.
Juilliard School of Music
799-5000.

Metropolitan Opera House
362-6000.

Manhattan School of Music
120 Claremont Ave.
Map 20 E2.
749-2802.

Mannes College of Music
150 W 85th St.
Map 15 D3.
580-0210.

Merkin Hall
129 W 67th St.
Map 11 D2.
501-3330.

Metropolitan Museum of Art
5th Ave at 82nd St.
Map 16 F4.
570-3949.

New Jersey Performance Arts Center
1 Center St, Newark, NJ.
888-466-5722.

NYC On Stage
1501 Broadway.
Map 12 D2.
768-1818.

St. Paul's Chapel
Broadway at Fulton St.
Map 1 C2.
602-0876.

St. Peter's Church
54th St at Lexington Ave.
Map 13 A4.
935-2200.

Symphony Space
2537 Broadway.
Map 15 C2.
864-5400.

Theodore Roosevelt Birthplace
28 E 20th St. **Map** 8 F5.
260-1616.

Town Hall
123 W 43rd St. **Map** 8 E1.
840-2824.

Trinity Church
Broadway at Wall St.
Map 1 C3.
602-0876.

Village Light Opera Group
227 W 27th St. **Map** 8 E3.
243-6281.

Washington Square
Map 4 D2.

Whitney Museum
120 Park Ave at 42nd St.
Map 9 A1. 878-2550.

Rock, Jazz and World Music

THERE'S EVERY IMAGINABLE form of music in New York, from international stadium rock to the sounds of the 1960s, from Dixieland jazz or country blues, soul and world music to talented street musicians. The city's music scene changes at a dizzying pace, with many new arrivals (and departures) almost daily, so there's no way to predict what you may find when you arrive. Musical standards also vary.

PRICES AND PLACES

AT CLUBS, EXPECT a cover charge and possibly a one- or two-drink minimum (at $5 or more) requirement. The prices for concerts range from $8 to $75 for the major venues, with about $12 to $25 the norm. Many of the smaller concert venues are arranged for seating in certain areas and dancing in others – often with different prices for each.

The top international bands are usually to be found in the huge arenas at **Shea Stadium** in Flushing Meadows or at the **Meadowlands** and **Madison Square Garden** *(see p133)*. Here the likes of Elton John, Bruce Springsteen and the Stones perform. Tickets for these events sell out very fast, so buy as many as you need as soon as you hear of a concert, unless you don't mind paying a lot for them through an agent or a scalper. During the summer, big outdoor concerts are held at Jones Beach *(see p253)* and **Central Park SummerStage**.

Medium-sized venues for mainstream bands include the Art Deco palace of **Radio City Music Hall** and the **Beacon Theater**, by far the most popular live-music venue in the Upper West Side area.

Many leading rock venues are basically bars with music. They will often book different bands every night, so check the listings in the *New York Times*, *Village Voice* or *Time Out New York* or phone the place to find out what's happening and at what time during that particular week.

ROCK MUSIC

ROCK COMES IN many forms: gothic, industrial, techno, psychedelic, post-punk funk, indie and alternative music are among the latest crazes. If you prefer to see more of a band than a giant video screen, the following venues have a much more intimate, friendly atmosphere. **CBGB**, New York's sleazy, dungeon-like cradle of new wave, launched such bands as Talking Heads and Blondie in the 1970s and is still a show-case for new indie bands.

The **Knitting Factory** has live jazz and new music. The **Limelight** is a good bet for the latest sounds and the newest groups. **The Mercury Lounge** is another of the most happening music spots, featuring hot new bands being groomed for MTV. **Irving Plaza** is where relatively unknown and sometimes known rock groups play, as do the occasional famous country and blues musicians.

Mega-star Bruce Springsteen played his first recorded concert in the 1970s at the **Bottom Line**, and it still remains a record industry showcase for new bands.

Bands appearing at the **Acme Underground** are mostly up-and-coming acts, given a chance to find fame in the rock music world. Located in the old meat-packing district, **The Cooler** is a hip new home for ravers. Alternative rock, avant-garde jazz and innovative DJs make this a great place to dance. The subterranean space is huge and wild.

The **Hammerstein Ball-room** at the Manhattan Center in midtown hosts techno, progressive and alternative bands. **Roulette** has avant-garde sounds performed by such appropriately named groups such as Woof, Quack and Miaow.

JAZZ

THE ORIGINAL Cotton Club and Connie's Inn, which were once crucibles of jazz, are long gone, as are the former speakeasies of West 52nd Street. But living legends such as Maynard Ferguson still play, while others carry on the old traditions of Dave Brubeck, Les Paul, Duke Ellington, Count Basie and other big bands.

In Greenwich Village, jazz temples from the 1930s survive and continue to foster great music. Foremost among them is the **Village Vanguard**, where some of the most highly revered jazz memories linger and newer ones are being fashioned by such groups as the McCoy Tyner and Branford Marsalis trios. **Blue Note** hosts big bands at high prices but has an excellent atmosphere.

The **Knitting Factory** and the well-known **Bottom Line** feature contemporary and avant-garde jazz; **Small's** offers three live jazz shows every night, with some top-flight musicians. Note that Small's has no liquor license.

Birdland features ex-Mingus alumni and musicians such as Bud Shank. Expect the great sounds of Dixieland jazz or small unknown groups in **Cajun**, a friendly New Orleans–style restaurant.

Café Carlyle, an East Side spot famed for mellow jazz pianist and singer Bobby Short, now also features clarinetist-filmmaker Woody Allen playing with Eddy Davis and his New Orleans Jazz Band

Sweet Rhythm, (once Sweet Basil and one of the top four jazz clubs in New York during the 1980s and '90s) presents a good mix of world music and jazz. A sophisticated club and restaurant **Iridium** features progressive jazz. **Fez under Time Café** presents the Mingus Big Band workshop every Thursday. If you're in New York in June, don't miss the annual **JVC Jazz Festival**, where such famous jazz and blues icons as Oscar Peterson,

Nina Simone and B.B. King play at various clubs all around Manhattan.

Jazz at Lincoln Center events are scheduled throughout the year, including concerts by the renowned Lincoln Center Jazz Orchestra under the direction of Wynton Marsalis. The music ranges from Duke Ellington's New York sounds to Johnny Dodds' traditional New Orleans-style jazz. Friday night at the **Rose Center** (at **AMNH**) offers live jazz concerts.

FOLK AND COUNTRY MUSIC

FOLK, ROCK MUSIC and R&B (rhythm and blues) can be found at the famed but much-

faded **Bitter End**, which once showcased James Taylor and Joni Mitchell but now specializes in new talent as does **Kenny's Castaways**.

The **Sun Music Company** offers "open mike" night every Tuesday for folk and bluegrass newcomers. Also worth checking out is the **Sidewalk Café**.

BLUES, SOUL AND WORLD MUSIC

FOR BLUES, soul and world music, options include the **Apollo Theater** in Harlem (see p228). For nearly 60 years the near-legendary Wednesday Amateur Nights have been responsible for discovering and launching stars such as James Brown

and Dionne Warwick. The **Cotton Club** is no longer located in its original spot, but it offers good blues, jazz and a Sunday real Gospel brunch on Harlem's main street. **Chicago B.L.U.E.S.** is now considered to be best blues club in the city and you'll hear more than Chicago sounds there. Don't miss "Mambo Mondays" with Nestor Torres at **SOB's** (Sounds of Brazil), a world music club specializing in Afro-Latin rhythms. **Terra Blues**'s bar doubles as an interesting music venue. The blues artists that appear can range from authentic Chicago acoustic players to more modern blues acts. Finally, there's **The Wetlands**, for classic soul and 60's sounds.

DIRECTORY

MUSIC VENUES

Beacon Theater
2124 Broadway.
Map 15 C5. (496-7070.

Central Park SummerStage
Rumsey Playfield.
Map 12 F1. (360-2777.

Madison Square Garden
7th Ave 33rd St.
Map 8 E2. (465-6741.

Meadowlands
50 Route 120
East Rutherford, N J.
((201) 935-3900.

Radio City Music Hall
See Dance p335.

Shea Stadium
126th St at Roosevelt Ave.
Flushing, Queens.
((718) 507-8499.

ROCK MUSIC

Acme Underground
9 Great Jones St.
Map 4 F2. (677-6963.

Bottom Line
15 W 4th St. **Map** 4 D2.
(228-6300.

CBGB
315 Bowery. **Map** 4 F2.
(982-4052.

The Cooler
416 W 14th St. **Map** 3 B1.
(229-0785.

Knitting Factory
74 Leonard St. **Map** 4 E5.
(219-3055.

Limelight
660 W 6th Ave. **Map** 8 F4.
(807-7780.

Mercury Lounge
217 E Houston St.
Map 5 A3. (260-4700.

Hammerstein Ballroom
311 W 34th St. **Map** 8 D2.
(564-4882.

Roulette
228 W Broadway. **Map** 4 E5.
(219-8242.

Irving Plaza
17 Irving Pl. **Map** 9 A5.
(777-6800.

JAZZ

Birdland
315 W 44th St.
Map 12 D5.
(581-3080.

Blue Note
131 W 3rd St.
Map 4 D2.
(475-8592.

Café Carlyle
35 E 76th St.
Map 17 A5.
(570-7189.

Cajun
129 8th Ave. **Map** 8 D5.
(691-6174.

Fez under Time Café
380 Lafayette St. **Map** 4 F2.
(533-7000.

Iridium
48 W 63rd St. **Map** 12 D2.
(582 2121.

Jazz at Lincoln Center
(259-9800.

JVC Jazz Festival
(501-1390.

Knitting Factory
See Rock Music.

Rose Center Jazz
79th St at CPW. **Map** 16 D5.
(769-5100.

Small's
183 W 10th St. **Map** 3 C2.
(920-7565.

Sweet Rhythm
88 7th Ave S. **Map** 8 E5.
(242-1785.

Village Vanguard
178 7th Ave South.
Map 3 C1. (255-4037.

FOLK AND COUNTRY

Bitter End
147 Bleecker St. **Map** 4 E3.
(673-7030.

Kenny's Castaways
157 Bleecker St.
Map 4 E3.
(473-9870.

Sidewalk Café
94 Ave A.
Map 5 B2. (473-7373.

Sun Music Company
340 E 71st St. **Map** 13 B1.
(396-9521.

BLUES, SOUL AND WORLD MUSIC

Apollo Theater
253 W 125th St.
Map 19 A1.
(531-5305.

Chicago B.L.U.E.S.
73 8th Ave.
Map 3 C1.
(924-9755.

Cotton Club
656 W 125th St.
Map 22 F2. (663-7980.

SOB's
204 Varick St.
Map 4 D3. (243-4940.

Terra Blues
149 Bleecker St.
Map 4 E3. (777-7776.

The Wetlands
161 Hudson St. **Map** 4 D5.
(966-4225.

Clubs, Dance Halls and Piano Bars

NEW YORK'S NIGHTLIFE and club scene is legendary, and deservedly so. Whatever your preference – be it for a noisy disco, stand-up comedy or the soothing melodies of a Harry Connick, Jr., sound-alike in a piano bar – you'll be really amazed at the choice. There was a rash of big discos in the 1980s, but relatively few of these have survived the recent trend toward the comfort and style of supper clubs.

WHEN AND WHERE

THE BEST and hippest time for clubbing is during the week – it's also a lot cheaper. Take a fair amount of money and some ID to prove you're old enough to drink (which is over 21) – but beware, all the drinks are very expensive.

The trendiest clubs roll on until 4am or later. Fashions and club nights change all the time, so go to Tower Records on Broadway for all the latest leaflets, check club details in the listings magazines *(see p328)* and read the *Village Voice.* The most interesting places nowadays are often popularized by word of mouth. Your best bet is to go somewhere like the **Limelight** and hope someone will tell you where to go on to – often invitations to other clubs are given out there as well.

DANCING

NEW YORKERS thrive on music and dancing. The dance floors available all around the city range from the ever-popular **SOB's** – for jungle, reggae, soul, jazz, and salsa – to a few huge basketball-court-sized places, such as **Roseland**. This has ballroom dancing every Thursday and Sunday and is New York's classic Broadway ballroom, revealing a tantalizing glimpse of older Broadway culture. It also has a good megasize, 700-seater, restaurant with a fully stocked bar.

For mainstream danceable music, the venerable **Rainbow Room** is still *the* place to dine and dance, just like in the old days. If you want to sample something really different, try **Barbetta**, where Boris and Yvgeny play

a combination of gypsy music and Viennese waltzes. The **Copacabana**, which when it originally opened starred the likes of Dean Martin and Frank Sinatra, is now a disco alternating with live bands. It also stages wild parties on the last Thursday of every month, with go-go boys, drag queens and disco divas.

The **Limelight**, which is a mixed venue with ground-floor dancing and spectator seats up in the balconies, was renovated in 1998, and the new, improved club is well worth a visit. It always advertises upcoming events. To reserve tickets ahead, call Ticketmaster *(see p329).*

Some of the most popular clubs for dancing, which also feature the latest music groups, are Ritz, Acme Underground, Marquee, CBGB, Tramps, and the Knitting Factory *(see p340).* Few of these have strict membership policies. Be sure to get there early and be prepared to line up for entry.

NIGHTCLUBS

NIGHTCLUBS are the places to see a show. New York shows are less flashy than in the 1940s and 1950s but they still boast a wide variety of acts. Expect to pay a cover charge; many of the clubs also require that you have at least two drinks.

The **Rainbow Grill** on the 65th floor of the RCA Building has a fine piano bar. **Maxim's** usually has one room open that features revues, plus another with singers. The chic **Supper Club** surrounds you with gold lamé draperies and features big band music downstairs. Cabaret singers perform upstairs in their

intimate Blue Room. **Joe's Pub** at the Public Theater has very decent food and offers the likes of John Hammond and Mo Tucker. Central Park has an indoors/outdoors club, **Tavern on the Green**, which offers jazz in its Chestnut Room, and **Feinstein's at the Regency** is the epitome of classic cabaret.

GAY AND LESBIAN VENUES

THE PAST TWO decades have seen the arrival of clubs and restaurants specifically geared to gay and lesbian clientele. Although the entertainment is varied, transvestite revues predominate. Though all the clubs are open to heterosexuals and often to the opposite sex, too, some can make "interlopers" feel extremely uncomfortable. The current popular gay cabarets include the **Duplex**, which has a mix of stand-up comics, comedy sketches and singers. The very fashionable nightclubs and bars for men include the trendy uptown **Town House**, a piano bar with restaurant, and **Julius**, known as Greenwich Village's top neighborhood bar. **Don't Tell Mama** is a long-established gay bar that presents good musical revues and spoofs.

Henrietta Hudson and **Crazy Nanny's** cater solely to women, as does **Grolier**. **Marie's Crisis** piano bar is a mixed venue, and **Splash** is open daily with a happy hour between 5pm and 9pm.

The *Village Voice* has good listings of what's happening in the gay communities, and the *Gay Yellow Pages* covers the gay scene. If you need more information, phone the **Gay and Lesbian Switchboard**.

COMEDY SHOWCASES

MANY OF New York's best current comedy clubs or showcases have evolved from earlier "improvisational" comedy. Leading the pack are the **Boston Comedy Club**, the **Original Improv** and **Caroline's**. Also good for a visit are the **Comic Strip**, **Stand-Up New York**, **NY Comedy Club**, **55 Grove St.**, **Dangerfield's**, and **Comedy Cellar**. Each club presents a nightly batch of comics.

PIANO BARS AND HOTEL "ROOMS"

CABARETS HAVE become a New York institution. Such cozy, just-for-listening places are often called "rooms" and are located in hotels. Most operate from Tuesday to Saturday (usually with a cover charge or drink minimum), and most take credit cards.

The **Algonquin's** Oak Room has song stylists. For a classic piano lounge with a panoramic Manhattan view, visit the **Beekman Tower**. The "long-distance hummer" award goes to Bobby Short, who has played his piano for over 25 years at the Café Carlyle in the **Carlyle Hotel**. Woody Allen plays there on Mondays with Eddy Davis's New Orleans Jazz Band. Also in the Carlyle is Bemelman's Bar, with its whimsical murals; it attracts a relaxed crowd who enjoy first-class crooners.

Hear tinkling keys and fine songs in the lounge of the **Drake Swissôtel**. Performers such as Barbara Cook play the **Hilton Hotel's** Lobby Lounge, and Café Pierre's singer-pianist Kathleen Landis holds court at the **Pierre Hotel**. There's also piano music at the Ambassador Lounge in the **Regal UN Plaza Hotel**.

Sports and Fitness

Nᴇᴡ ʏᴏʀᴋᴇʀs ᴀʀᴇ sᴘᴏʀᴛs ᴄʀᴀᴢʏ, and there are activities to suit every taste. If you're a doer not a viewer, you can choose from health clubs and horseback riding to pumping iron and swimming, playing tennis or jogging. Spectator sports are provided by two professional baseball teams, two hockey teams, a basketball team and two football teams, while for tennis fans there are the US Open and Virginia Slims tournaments.

Tickets

Tʜᴇ ᴇᴀsɪᴇsᴛ ᴡᴀʏ to get hold of your tickets is through Ticketron or Ticketmaster (*see p329*). For the big games, you may need a ticket agent.

Football

Tʜᴇ ᴄɪᴛʏ's two professional football teams are the New York Giants and the New York Jets. They both play their home games across the river at **Giants Stadium** in New Jersey. Tickets for the Giants are almost impossible to obtain, but they may be available for the Jets.

Baseball

Tᴏ ᴄᴀᴘᴛᴜʀᴇ the essence of this American institution, first time spectators should go to **Yankee Stadium**, home of the New York Yankees. **Shea Stadium**, the Mets' base, is also convenient. The season runs from April to September.

Basketball

Tʜᴇ ɴᴇᴡ ʏᴏʀᴋ ᴋɴɪᴄᴋs play their home games from October to April at **Madison Square Garden**; you may also catch the ever-popular Harlem Globetrotters there.

Bicycling

Tʜᴇ ʙᴇsᴛ ᴘʟᴀᴄᴇ to cycle is in Central Park during the weekend, when it is closed to cars. Bikes may be rented from **Metro Bikes**.

Boxing

Pʀᴏғᴇssɪᴏɴᴀʟ boxing matches are more often seen on Paramount's wide TV screen than in the flesh at **Madison Square Garden**.

Fitness Centers, Gyms and Health Clubs

Mᴏsᴛ ᴍᴀᴊᴏʀ ʜᴏᴛᴇʟs have fitness centers. Check out the **Chelsea Piers Sports & Entertainment Complex;** there's something for everyone at this enormous facility. Many of the commercial gyms and health clubs are open only to those with an annual membership, but it is possible to use the facilities at a **Y** if you are a member.

Golf

Pʀᴀᴄᴛɪᴄᴇ ʏᴏᴜʀ swing at the **Randalls Island Golf Center, Chelsea Golf Club** or play mini-golf at the **Wollman Memorial Rink**. The city owns several courses in the boroughs, such as **Pelham Bay Park** in the Bronx and **Silver Lake** on Staten Island. To make a reservation, phone 225-GOLF.

Horseback Riding and Racing

Tʜᴇ ᴏɴʟʏ riding stable in Manhattan is **Claremont Riding Academy**. You can ride in its indoor arena or go trotting in Central Park.

Harness racing, in which horses pull sulkies (small carts), takes place year-round at **Yonkers Raceway**. Flat races are held daily, except Tuesday, October to May at the **Aqueduct Race Track**, and May to October at the **Belmont Park Race Track**.

Ice Hockey

Tʜᴇ ɪᴄᴇ ғʟɪᴇs, as do the players' fists, when the New York Rangers meet their competition at **Madison Square Garden**. The season runs from October to April.

Ice-Skating

Tʜᴇʀᴇ ᴀʀᴇ ᴛʜʀᴇᴇ good places to go ice skating out of doors. One is the **Rockefeller Plaza Rink**, which looks beautiful at Christmas. The others are in Central Park: **Wollman Rink** and **Lasker Rink**. For indoor sites, try the **Sky Rink** at Chelsea Piers.

Indoor Sports

Cʜᴇʟsᴇᴀ Pɪᴇʀs has it all: roller rinks, bowling, indoor soccer, basketball, rock-climbing walls, fitness centers, golf, a field house for gymnastics, sports medicine and spa centers, and of course, swimming pools. This huge complex, spread over four old West Side piers, is open to all. As the ads say, "You gotta see this place!"

Jogging

Sᴏᴍᴇ ᴘᴀʀᴋs are safe for joggers, others are not, so be guided by your concierge. None is safe after dark, at dusk or before dawn. The most popular route is around the reservoir in Central Park. The **International Running Center** has weekly running clinics and races, as does **Chelsea Piers**.

Marathon

Tᴏ ʙᴇ ᴏɴᴇ of the 25,000 who enter the New York Marathon, you have to sign up six months in advance. The race is held on the first Sunday in November. Phone 860-4455 for information.

Sports Bars

Tᴏᴘ ʙᴀʀs include **The Sporting Club** or **Mickey Mantle's**, both of which have giant scoreboards and multiple video screens.

Swimming

Mᴀɴʏ ᴍᴀɴʜᴀᴛᴛᴀɴ hotels have pools with free access during your stay. You can also swim and surf at the

Surfside 3 Maritime Center at Chelsea Piers. For a day trip, go to Jones Beach State Park (*see p253*) along Long Island's shoreline.

TENNIS

T HE TOP TENNIS tournament in New York is the US Open, played each August at the **National Tennis Center**. Also good is the women's Virginia Slims Championships in November at **Madison Square Garden** (*see p133*).

If you want to play tennis rather than watch it, look in the telephone directory under "Tennis Courts: Public and Private." For private courts,

you can expect to pay up to about $50 an hour. For public courts, you will need a $50 permit, available from the **NY City Parks & Recreation Department**. You will also need an identity card and a reservation. **Crosstown Tennis** and the **Manhattan Plaza Tennis Center** are two possibilities.

TRACK AND FIELD

T HE MILLROSE GAMES are normally held in early February, and the Amateur Athletic Union (AAU) championships, where most of the top athletes usually appear, are held in late February at

Madison Square Garden. Chelsea Piers also has a complete track and field complex.

OTHER ACTIVITIES

I N CENTRAL PARK, options include renting rowboats from **Loeb Boathouse** or playing chess – pick up the pieces from The Dairy (*see p206*). Bowling is available at **Chelsea Piers** and a few other lanes throughout the city. **Slate Billiards** and many bars offer pool and darts.

If you want something completely different, go to **Sheepshead Bay**, Brooklyn, and try deep-sea fishing.

SPORTS ADDRESSES

Aqueduct Race Track
Ozone Park, Queens.
((718) 641-4700.

Belmont Park Race Track
Hempstead Turnpike,
Long Island.
((718) 641-4700.

Chelsea Piers Sports & Entertainment Complex:
Piers 59- 62 at 23rd St and 11th Ave (Hudson River).
Map 7 B4-5.
(336-6666. W
www.chelseapiers.com

Claremont Riding Academy
175 W 89th St.
Map 15 C3.
(724-5100.

Crosstown Tennis
14 W 31st St.
Map 8 F3.
(947-5780.

Giants Stadium
Meadowlands
East Rutherford, N.J.
((201) 935-8222.
New York Giants.
((201) 935-8500.
New York Jets.

International Running Center
9 E 89th St.
Map 17 A3.
(860-4455.

Lasker Ice Rink
Central Park Drive East at 108th St.
Map 21 B4.
(534-7639.

Loeb Boathouse
Central Park. Map 16 F5.
(517-4723.

Madison Square Garden
7th Ave at 33rd St.
Map 8 E2.
(465-67411.
W www.thegarden.com

Manhattan Plaza Racquet Club
450 W 43rd St. Map 7 C1.
(594-0554.

Metro Bikes
231 W 96th St .
Map 15 C2.
(663-7531.

Mickey Mantle's
42 Central Park South.
Map 12 E3.
(688-7777.

National Tennis Center
Flushing Meadow Park,
Queens.
((718) 760-6200.
W www.usta.com

NY City Parks & Recreation Department
Arsenal Building
64th St and 5th Ave.
Map 12 F2. (408-0100.

Pelham Bay Park
The Bronx.
((718) 885-3368

Plaza Rink
1 Rockefeller Plaza, 5th Ave.
Map 12 F5.
(332-7654.

Printing House Fitness & Racquet Center
421 Hudson St. Map 3 C3.
(243-3777.

Randalls Island Golf Center
Randalls Island.
Map 22 F2.
(427-5689.

Shea Stadium
126th St at Roosevelt Ave,
Flushing, Queens.
((718) 507-TIXX or
(718) 507-8499.

Sheepshead Bay
(*For information on fishing trips call Mike's Tackle & Bait Shop.*)
((718) 646-9261.

Silver Lake
915 Victory Blvd
Staten Island.
((718) 447-5686 or
(718) 225-4653.

Slate Billiards
54 W 21st St.
Map 8 E4.
(989-0096.

The Sporting Club
99 Hudson St.
Map 4 D5.
(219-0900.

Wollman Memorial Rink
Central Park, 5th Ave at 59th St.
Map 12 F2.
(396-1010.

Yankee Stadium
River Ave at 161st St
The Bronx.
((718) 293-6000.

YMCA 47th St
224 E 47th St.
Map 13 B5.
(756-9600

Y at 92nd St
1395 Lexington Ave.
Map 17 A2.
(427-6000.

YMCA West Side
5 W 63rd St.
Map 12 D2.
(875-4100.

Yonkers Raceway
Yonkers
Westchester County.
((914) 968-4200.

Late-Night New York

NEW YORK IS INDEED a city that never sleeps. If you wake up in the middle of the night – with a craving for fresh bread, a need to be entertained or an urge to watch the sun rise over the Manhattan skyline – there are always plenty of options to choose from.

BARS AND CLUBS

THE BEST and friendliest bars are often the Irish ones. **O'Flanagan's** or **Scruffy Duffy's** are both loud, have late-night dancing, and cater to regulars. Go for a late-night dry martini at the **Temple Bar**. The best piano bars are in the hotels: try the Café Carlyle in the **Carlyle Hotel**, Feinstein's at the **Regency**, or the Oak Room in the **Algonquin Hotel**.

For hot American jazz until 4am, go to **Joe's Pub** or the **Blue Note**. Traditional jazz and swing entertain the diners and dancers at the **Rainbow Room**. **Cornelia Street Café** is a snug and lively nook for prose, poetry and theater readings. Poetry, theater and Latin music can be found at the **Nuyorican Poets Café**. If you're in the Village, stop in at **Rose's Turn** for open mike, piano bar, and late-night ambience.

MIDNIGHT MOVIES

SPECIAL MIDNIGHT showings and a youthful crowd can be found the Angelika Film Center and the Film Forum (see pp336–7). New multiplexes often show movies at midnight on weekends

SHOPS

SHAKESPEARE & Company Booksellers on Broadway and the St. Mark's Bookshop are open until late. The Upper West Side branch of HMV is open until midnight, the East Side branch until 10pm. Both Tower Records branches shut at midnight, as does Gryphon Records. Bleecker Bob's Golden Oldies Record Shop stays open until 3am on weekends (see Shopping pp322-3). Check out **Mrs. Hudson's Video** on Hudson if you've forgotten to rent a movie

tape. Among the many Village clothing stores that stay open late on weekends are the **Antique Boutique** (open until midnight) and **Trash and Vaudeville** (open till 8pm on Fridays and Saturdays). For aspirin and other health essentials, two **Duane Reade** drugstores and **Rite Aid Pharmacy** are open 24 hours. **Love Drugstores** are usually open until midnight

TAKE-OUT FOOD AND GROCERIES

A FEW TAKE-OUT food stores are open 24 hours a day, including the **Delmonico Gourmet Food Market** and the **West Side Supermarket**. Many Korean greengrocers also stay open all night. The **Food Emporium** is a supermarket chain usually open until midnight. On Saturdays, **Zabar's** stays open until midnight. Liquor stores are usually open until 10pm and many deliver.

For the best in bagels, go to **H & H Bagels**, **Bagels On The Square** and **Jumbo Bagels and Bialys**. There are many pizzerias and Chinese restaurants that stay open late, and most deliver.

DINING

CLUBBERS AND the trendy set often frequent **La Jumelle**, **Florent** and **Les Halles** for good French dishes. Twentysomethings will seek out the **Coffee Shop** for late-night beer and Brazilian food. You'll find delicious and legendary sandwiches at the **Carnegie Deli**. **Caffè Reggio** in Greenwich Village has been a favorite for late-night coffee and desserts since 1927. It is also possible to find good food in dinner clubs. **Le Bar Bat** is popular for its bat cave décor and Vietnamese

cuisine. **The Dead Poet** is a real Upper West Side neighborhood hangout, with live music, a lively bar: bring your own food. The other end of the scale is the glitzy **Rainbow Room** or **Rainbow Grill**. Cipriani's magic touch, good music, and the New York ambience make these two spots extra-special.

SPORTS

THERE IS round-the-clock play at **Slate Billiards** or until 5am at the **Billiard Club** on weekends. Have late-night beers and burgers with the New York University crowd at **Bowlmore Lanes** bowling alley.

SERVICES

MIDNIGHT EXPRESS CLEANERS picks up garments in Manhattan until midnight and has them ready the next day. Note that this service does not pick up or deliver to major hotels. On Thursdays hairdresser **George Michael of Madison Avenue/Madora Inc** is open until 10pm and will also make house calls.

TOURS AND VIEWS

ONE OF NEW YORK's most enjoyable walks is along the Hudson River at the World Financial Center's **Battery Park City**, open (and safe) at all hours. Piers 16 and 17 at South Street Seaport attract strollers and revelers all night long and the **Harbour Lights** restaurant on Pier 17 is open until 4am for a middle of the night pick-me-up. Enjoy the city lights by taking a **Circle Line** two-hour tour of the nighttime harbor.

Try the Riverview Terrace at Sutton Place: the benches offer a peaceful and quiet place to watch the sun rise over the East River, Roosevelt Island and Queens. Two of the most sensational views with the Manhattan backdrop are (looking west) from the **River Café** and (looking east) from **Arthur's Landing** restaurant. Take a trip on the **Staten**

Island Ferry (see p76) to see the Statue of Liberty and the Manhattan skyline in the dawn light, or a take a taxi across Brooklyn Bridge (see pp86–9) to watch the sun rise over New York harbor. Go to the **Beekman Tower Hotel's** Top of the Tower for some panoramas of the city's East Side up to 1am. The ultimate

view is from the **Empire State Building**: its Observation Deck (see pp134–5) stays open until midnight. Have breakfast 107 floors up, at the World Trade Center's **Windows on the World** restaurant, overlooking the city, river and harbor.

Château Stables has rides in horse-drawn carriages and **Liberty Helicopters** run

flights over the city at sunset. If you want something a little bit different, try **Marvelous Manhattan Tours**' escorted evening barhopping walks. And if you still can't sleep, visit the bustling downtown **Fulton Fish Market** at 6am or stroll the Upper West Side and eat two hot dogs at the famous **Gray's Papaya**.

DIRECTORY

BARS AND CLUBS

Algonquin Hotel
See Piano Bars p343.

Blue Note
See Jazz p341.

Carlyle Hotel
See Piano Bars p343.

Cornelia Street Café
29 Cornelia St. Map 4 D2.
[989-9318.

The Dead Poet
450 Amsterdam Map 15 C4. [595-5670.

Joe's Pub
See Jazz p341.

Nuyorican Poets Café
236 E 3rd St. Map 5 A2.
[505-8183.

O'Flanagan's
1215 1st Ave. Map 13 C2.
[439-0660.

Rainbow Room
See Dancing p343.

Rose's Turn
55 Grove St. Map 3 C2.
[366-5438.

Temple Bar
332 Lafayette St.
Map 4 F4. [925-4242.

Scruffy Duffy's
743 6th Ave. Map 12 D5.
[245-9126.

SHOPS

Antique Boutique
712 Broadway.
Map 4 E2.
[460-8830.

Duane Reade Drugstores
224 W 57th (B'way).
Map 12 D3.
[541-9708.

1279 3rd Ave at E 74th St.
Map 17 B5. [744-2668.

Mrs. Hudson's Video
573 Hudson St.
Map 3 C2. [989-1050.

RiteAid Pharmacy
See Survival Guide p357.

Trash and Vaudeville
4 St. Mark's Pl. Map 5 A2.
[982-3590.

TAKE-OUT FOOD AND GROCERIES

Bagels On The Square
7 Carmine St. Map 4 D3.
[691-3041.

Delmonico Gourmet Food Market
55 E 59th St. Map 12 F3.
[751-5559.

Food Emporium
See the Yellow Pages in the phone book for locations.

H & H Midtown Bagels East
1551 2nd Ave. Map 17 B4.
[734-7441.

H & H Bagels
Broadway at 80th St. Map 15 C4. [595-8000.

Jumbo Bagels and Bialys
1070 2nd Ave. Map 13 B3.
[355-6185.

West Side Market
2171 Broadway. Map 15 C5.
[595-2536.

Zabar's
2245 Broadway. Map 15 C4.
[787-2000.

DINING

Caffè Reggio
119 MacDougal St.
Map 4 D2.
[475-9557.

Carnegie Deli
Restaurants and Bars p306.
Coffee Shop
Restaurants and Bars p306.

Florent
Restaurants and Bars p306.

Gray's Papaya
Broadway at 72nd St. Map 11C1. [799-0243.

La Jumelle
55 Grand St.
Map 4 E4.
[941-9651.

Le Bar Bat
311 West 57th St.
Map 12 D3.
[307-7228.

Les Halles
Restaurants and Bars p296.

Rainbow Room
Restaurants and Bars p297.

Rainbow Grill
Restaurants and Bars p297.

SPORTS

Billiard Club
220 W 19th St.
Map 8 E5.
[206-POOL.

Bowlmore Lanes
110 University Pl.
Map 4 E1. [255-8188.

Slate Billiards
See Sport p345.

SERVICES

George Michael of MadisonAvenue/ Madora Inc
420 Madison Ave.
Map 13 A5.
[752-1177.

Midnight Express Cleaners
[921-0111.

TOURS AND VIEWS

Arthur's Landing
Port Imperial Marina, Pershing Circle, Weehawken, NJ.
[(201) 867-0777.

Battery Park City
West St. Map 1 A3.

Beekman Tower Hotel
1st Ave 49th St.
Map 13 C5.
[355-7300.

Château Stables
608 W 48th St.
Map 15 B3.
[246-0520.

Circle Line
W 42nd St. Map 15 B3
[563-3200 .

Marvelous Manhattan Tours
[(877) 898-5551.

Empire State Building
See pp134–5.

Fulton Fish Market Tours
[748-8590.

Harbour Lights
89 South Street Seaport Pier 17 Map 2 D2.
[227-2800.

Liberty Helicopters
[(888) 692-4354.

River Café
See Restaurants and Bars p294.

Staten Island Ferry
See Getting Around New York p76.

Windows on the World
See Restaurants and Bars p295.

CHILDREN'S NEW YORK

Young visitors soon catch the contagious excitement in the air in New York. Attractions for all ages abound, and plenty are designed especially for children. More than a dozen theater companies, two zoos and three imaginative museums are for just the young, backed up with special events at many museums and parks. The chance to visit a TV studio is a treat, and New York's own Big Apple Circus is a perennial delight. With more to do than can ever be squeezed into a single visit, you'll never hear the cry "I'm bored!" Best of all, there's no need to spend a fortune to have fun.

A young visitor making New York his very own playground

PRACTICAL ADVICE

New York is family-friendly. Many of its hotels allow children in parents' rooms free, and will supply cots or cribs if needed. Most museums charge half price or less for children, while others are free. Children under 44 in (112 cm) also ride free on subways and buses when accompanied by an adult. Travel between 9am and 4pm to avoid rush hours.

Supplies such as diapers and medicines are readily available, and the Rite Aid Pharmacy *(see p357)* is open 24 hours a day. Finding changing tables in public toilets is less easy, but no one objects if a counter is used. Best bets are the facilities in libraries, hotels and department stores. Most hotels will arrange baby-sitters; another reliable source is the **Baby Sitters' Guild**.

To find out more about the range of current activities for children, get a copy of the free quarterly calendar of events, available from the New York Convention and Visitors Bureau *(see p352)*. Weekly listings can be found in *New York* magazine.

NEW YORK ADVENTURES

The city can seem like a giant amusement park for youngsters. Elevators whisk you sky-high for bird's-eye views from atop the world's highest buildings. You can set sail on the classic **Circle Line** tour around Manhattan; the sailboat **Pioneer** *(see p84)*, or charter your own paddle-wheeler from the marina at E. 23rd St; or the free round-trip on the Staten Island Ferry *(see p76)*. The Roosevelt Island Tram *(see p179)* is a Swiss cable car offering an airborne ride over the East River. Central Park *(see pp202–7)* is a source of rides of every kind – from the old-fashioned charm of the carousel to real horseback and ponycart rides. Children who prefer a faster pace can join the skate-boarders and in-line skaters who cruise around the traffic-free park every weekend.

Cooling off in a playground in Central Park

MUSEUMS

While many of New York's museums appeal to all ages, some are designed just for the young. High on the list is the imaginative Children's Museum of Manhattan *(see p217)*, a multimedia world in which children can produce their own videos and news-casts. Farther afield are the **Staten Island Children's Museum**, where a huge climb-through anthill is one of the favorite items, and the Brooklyn Children's Museum *(see p245)*. The *Intrepid* Sea-Air-Space Museum *(see p147)* is a real air-craft carrier. Finally, no one should miss the spectacular new Hayden Planetarium and the dinosaur display at the American Museum of Natural History *(see pp214– 15)*.

OUTDOOR FUN

In summer, all of New York comes out to play. Central Park is a child's wonderland, from skating rinks to

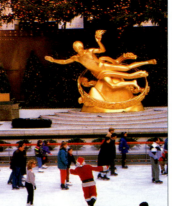

Skating with Santa at Rockefeller Center

boating lakes, bicycle paths to miniature golf. The park has free entertainment galore – such as guided walks by park rangers on Saturdays, toy sailboat races and summer storytelling. The Central Park Wildlife Center and the smaller Tisch Children's Zoo are all-time favorites.

Children of all ages will be fascinated by the Bronx Zoo/Wildlife Conservation Park which is home to over 700 species *(see pp242–3)*.

Rockaway Beach and Coney Island *(see p247)* are just a subway ride away. Winter brings the chance to skate at Rockefeller Center *(see p142)* or in Central Park on a rink fringed with views of skyscrapers.

INDOOR FUN

NEW YORK children's theater is of a quality and variety matching that for adults. Some favorite companies are the **Paper Bag Players** and **Theaterworks USA**, whose shows sell out fast; get schedules and reserve seats early.

The **Swedish Marionette Theater** in Central Park has morning shows Tuesdays through Fridays, and Saturdays until 1pm.

The New York City Ballet's annual Christmas production of *The Nutcracker* at Lincoln Center *(see p212)* opens at about the same time that the **Big Apple Circus** sets up its tent nearby. Ringling Brothers and Barnum & Bailey Circus is in action at Madison Square Garden *(see p133)* for several weeks each spring.

Opportunities for youngsters to work off energy in winter are many, from indoor skating rinks to mini-golf and bowling alleys at **Chelsea Piers**.

Centerpiece clock at toy store F.A.O. Schwarz

SHOPPING

THERE WILL be no complaints about shopping trips if they include **F.A.O. Schwarz**, one of the world's biggest and best toy stores with a vast range of wonderful items. Another favorite among children is **Enchanted Forest**, and youngsters are welcomed for storytelling sessions at **Books of Wonder**.

EATING OUT

HAMBURGER-and-pasta joint **Ottomanelli's Café** is very popular with children, and even adults find it hard to finish their huge burgers. The lively **Hard Rock Café** is another hit, and most children enjoy the foods sold around Chinatown and Little Italy. Drop into the **China-town Ice Cream Factory** for some strange and wonderful flavors. For a quick snack, try pizza-by-the-slice or pretzels and hot dogs from street vendors. There are also scores of fast food places, including White Castle, Burger King or McDonalds.

Storytelling session at South Street Seaport

SURVIVAL GUIDE

PRACTICAL INFORMATION

VISITORS TO New York are treated very much the same as anyone else. While you may not be given special treatment, as long as you follow a few guidelines on personal security *(see pp356–7)* you'll be able to explore the city as freely as any native New Yorker. Buses and subway trains *(pp372–5)*

Visitors resting on the steps of the Metropolitan Museum of Art

are reliable and cheap; there are lots of cash machines *(pp358–9)*, and money can be easily exchanged at banks, hotels and foreign money brokers. The wide range of prices offered by all the many hotels *(pp272–83)*, restaurants *(pp288–304)* and entertainment venues *(pp328–47)* means your New York trip can be both fun and affordable.

SIGHTSEEING TIPS

NEW YORK'S rush hours extend from 8 to 10am, 11:30am to 1:30pm and 4:30 to 6:30pm, Monday to Friday. During these times, every form of public transportation will be crowded, and the streets will be much harder t navigate on foot.

It's worth trying to visit a cluster of sights in the same area – see the *Street-by-Street* plans of each area – instead of exhausting yourself rushing from one distant attraction to another. Buses are a comfortable and reliable way to get around, and you'll see the city as you travel.

It's best to avoid passing through certain areas of the city, especially at particular times *(pp356–7)*. Public toilets in bus stations should be avoided. They attract drug users and the homeless, even when there's an attendant. It is best to find a large hotel, department store, or bookstore if you need a restroom.

If you need help with street directions or feel a need to get off the street, ask a policeman or find a hotel doorman. There is one on duty at the entrance to most hotels 24 hours a day.

OPENING HOURS

BUSINESS HOURS are generally from 9am to 5pm with no lunchtime closing. Only banks close earlier, at 3pm, although some do have longer hours

(8am–6pm) and are open on Saturday mornings. Many museums close on Mondays and major holidays. Some open on Tuesday or Thursday evenings during certain seasons (phone for details).

MUSEUMS

IN NEW YORK, *museum* is used as a blanket term to include institutions that offer diverse holdings. The city's museums are described on pages 34 to 37. Museums either charge admission, starting at around $2, or ask for a "donation," which can be $6 to $9. There are discounts for senior citizens, students and children. The leading museums schedule free guided tours and lectures. Museum Mile *(see pp182–3)*, on and near Fifth Avenue, groups a number of major museums close together. Of these, the Frick Collection and the Cooper-Hewitt are small enough to see in one or two hours, but the larger museums, the Guggenheim, Whitney, and Metropolitan, may take far longer than this.

Hotel doorman

ETIQUETTE

IT IS ILLEGAL to smoke in *any* public place or building in New York. Some restaurants now provide separate rooms for smokers, but it is best to phone ahead for details.

Business travelers need not bring a gift for their hosts. Such tokens are not expected

and may even be considered improper. If you do bring something, it should be something inexpensive and preferably representative of where you live.

Tipping is an integral part of New York life: for taxi drivers leave 10 to 15%; waiters 15 to 20%, cocktail waiters 15%, hotel room service 10% (when not added to the bill); coat check $1; hotel maids $1 or $2 per day after the first day; hotel bellhops about $1 per bag; hair stylists 15 to 20% and barbers 10 to 20%.

TOURIST INFORMATION

ADVICE ON ANY aspect of life in New York City is available from the **New York Convention and Visitors Bureau**, known as **NYC & Co.***(see pp328–9)*. Their 24-hour touch-tone phone service offers help outside office hours. Brochures and information kiosks can also be found at the walk-in office of the **Times Square Visitors Information Bureau**.

Hotel lobbies and museums have free literature racks, and all of the daily newspapers hold a wealth of information about what's going on where.

Useful information

NYC & Co, 810 7th Ave. **Map** 12 E4.
484-1222 www.nycvisit.com
www.ci.nyc.ny.us 8:30am–6pm Mon–Fri; 9am–5pm Sat, Sun.
Times Square Visitors Center
1560 Broadway. **Map** 12 E5.
www.timessquarebid.org
New York State information
www.state.ny.us
On-line guide to everything in NYC:
www.jimsdeli.com

ENTERTAINMENT LISTINGS

A NUMBER of inexpensive or even free publications listing current exhibitions and leisure activities are available at newsstands, hotels or galleries throughout New York.

Among the more popular ones are *New York* magazine, *The New Yorker's* "Goings On About Town" roster and *Time Out New York,* which list offerings at the city's many museums, clubs, theaters, galleries, restaurants, cinemas, colleges and libraries, plus impending auctions. The *Village Voice* focuses on events in SoHo, TriBeCa and Greenwich Village, plus other major cultural activity in the city. *The New York Times* Friday and Sunday editions list current visual and performing arts events in their respective "Weekend" and "Arts and Leisure" sections. *Art News* is a monthly magazine that lists major art events and auctions and reviews exhibits.

There are also various free magazines. The weekly *Where* is distributed through hotel concierges and lists major museums, their opening hours, locations and any exhibitions. *Art Now/New York Gallery Guide* is released in art galleries each month. It lists current exhibitions and has useful maps showing where they are located.

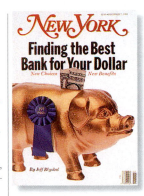

New York **magazine has weekly comprehensive entertainment listings for all of New York**

GUIDED TOURS

Whichever way you want to see New York – with the help of a pre-recorded walk or by an exciting trip in a helicopter, boat or horse-drawn carriage – organized sightseeing trips, planned by someone else, can save a lot of time, effort and often money. There are numerous companies to choose from, each providing plenty of local information.

Boat Tours

Circle Line
Sightseeing Yachts
Pier 83, W 42nd St.
Map 7 A1.
℡ 563-3200.
A three-hour trip circumnavigating Manhattan.

Circle Line Statue of
Liberty Ferry
South Ferry, Battery Park.
Map 1 C4.
℡ 269-5755.

Spirit of New York
W 23rd and 8th Ave.
Map 8 D4.
℡ 741-4266. *Cruises include lunch or dinner.*

Dept. of Transportation
Staten Island Ferry
South Ferry.
Map 2 D4.
℡ 487-5761 or 5766.
Manhattan–Staten Island.

World Yacht, Inc
Pier 81 W 41st St.
Map 2 D5.
℡ 630-8100.
Cruises include lunch, dinner and onboard entertainment.

Carriage Tours

59th St at Fifth Ave and along Central Park S. *Horse-drawn carriages gather outside the Plaza Hotel* (**Map** 12 F3), *days and evenings. The usual itinerary takes in Central Park.*

Bus Tours

Allied Tours
165 W 46th St.
Map 12 E5.
℡ 869-5100.

Gray Line of New York
42nd St and 8th Ave.
Map 8 D1.
℡ 695-0001.

Short Line Tours/American
Sightseeing NY
166 W 46th St.
Map 12 F5.
℡ 800-631-8405.

Bicycle Tours

Bite of the Apple Tours,
2 Columbus Circle, 59th St
& Broadway. **Map** 12 D3.
℡ 541-8759.
*A two-hour spin around
Central Park. $20, or $30
with bike rental. 10am,
1pm, and 4pm.*

Walking Tours

Big Onion Walking Tours
PO Box 250201,
Columbia University.
Map 20 E3.
℡ 439-1090.
Historical and ethnic.

CityWalks
410 W 20th St. **Map** 7 C5.
℡ 989-2456.
*Historic neighborhoods –
Private Tours.*

Harlem Spirituals, Inc.
690 8th Ave. **Map** 8 D1.
℡ 757-0425.
*Harlem's history and
culture. Apr–Oct only.*

Heritage Trails
*Four free do-it-yourself
historical trails begin at
Federal Hall; brochures at
Federal Hall.* **Map** 1 C3.

Museum of the City of
New York
103rd St and Fifth Ave.
Map 21 C5.
℡ 534-1672.
Architecture and history.

NBC Studio Tour
30 Rockefeller Plaza.
Map 12 F5.
℡ 664-7174.

92nd Street Y
1395 Lexington Ave.
Map 17 B5.
℡ 427-6000.
Culture and history.

Talk-a-Walk
30 Waterside Plaza.
Map 9 C4.
℡ 686-0356.
Recorded itineraries.

Carriage ride in Central Park

DISABLED TRAVELERS

DISABLED PEOPLE will find New York more accessible than most cities. All of the city's buses have ramps that can be lowered to help people in wheelchairs board. The buses also "kneel" to help those with restricted mobility.

Hotels, large stores and office buildings are also often well equipped for wheelchair access, and some museums offer tours for the deaf, blind and disabled. Several city theaters have systems to aid hearing-impaired patrons as do a growing number of telephones. *Access Guide to New York City*, free from the **Junior League of the City of New York**, lists buildings accessible to the disabled.

Useful information Junior League of the City of New York, 130 E 80th St. **Map** 17 A4. **(** 288-6220. The Mayor's Office for People with Disabilities. **(** 788-2830.

A New York city bus "kneeling" to help the elderly board

CUSTOMS AND IMMIGRATION

CITIZENS OF Britain, New Zealand, Australia, and 26 other countries do not need visas if they are staying in the US for 90 days or less. Canadians need only proof of citizenship and a photo ID. Students do need proper visas. All travelers need round-trip or onward passage tickets and must show proof they have $500 or more. Check with a US embassy or travel agent if in doubt.

Customs allowances per person when you enter the US

are 200 cigarettes, 50 cigars or 4.4 pounds (2 kilograms) of tobacco; no more than 2 pints (1 liter) of alcohol; gifts worth no more than $100; no meat or meat products (even in cans), seeds, growing plants or fresh fruit.

Upon arrival at one of New York's airports, follow signs stating "other than American passports" to immigration counters where your passport will then be inspected and stamped. Once you have reclaimed your baggage from the appropriate area (again, follow the signs), you will be approached by a Customs officer. He or she will examine the Customs declaration you should have received and filled in on your flight and direct you either toward the exit or to a Customs inspector who will then search your luggage. According to US Customs officials, only 5% of all travelers will have to have their luggage searched. There are no red or green Customs channels – you're cleared and free to go once the Customs officer has seen your fully completed declaration.

STUDENT TRAVELERS

MANY MUSEUMS and theaters allow students a discount on admission. To receive this, however, you will need to carry proof of your student status at all times.

An International Student ID Card can be purchased quite cheaply, provided you have the right credentials, from the **Council Travel**, which has two branches in New York. At the same time, ask for a copy of the *ISIC Student Handbook*. This invaluable booklet identifies places and services throughout the US that offer a range of discounts to card holders. Included are accommodations, various museums, theaters, tours and attractions, nightclubs, restaurants and even Carey

transportation (buses from Manhattan to New York's airports, *see p.363*).

Normally, it is extremely difficult to obtain permission to work in the US; students are an exception. Any branch of the Student Travel Association in the UK, Australia or New Zealand will be able to help you with details of working holidays in New York. In London, contact the **Council on International Educational Exchange**.

STUDENT INFORMATION

Bunac
P.O. Box 430.
((203) 264-0901.
Summertime only.

Council on International Educational Exchange
633 3rd Ave. **Map** 9 B1
(822-2600.

52 Poland St, London W1V 4JQ
(0171-478 2000.

Council Travel
254 Greene St. **Map** 4 E2. Also at 205 E 42nd St. **Map** 9 B1
(254-2525, (800) 226-8624.

CONVERSION CHART

Bear in mind that 1 US pint (0.5 liter) is a smaller measure than 1 UK pint (0.6 liter).

Imperial system:
1 inch = 2.5 centimeters
1 foot = 30 centimeters
1 mile = 1.6 kilometers
1 ounce = 28 grams
1 pound = 454 grams
1 US pint = 0.47 liter
1 US gallon = 3.8 liters

Metric system:
1 millimeter = 0.04 inch
1 centimeter = 0.4 inch
1 meter = 3 feet 3 inches
1 kilometer = 0.6 mile
1 gram = 0.04 ounce

International Student ID Card

New York daily newspapers

A newspaper vending machine

NEWSPAPERS, TELEVISION AND RADIO

You can buy foreign newspapers, usually the previous day's issue, at **Universal News**, airports, hotels and newsstands near international business areas like the World Trade Center or Wall Street.

TV program schedules can be found in the weekly *TV Guide* magazine and the television section of the Sunday edition of *The New York Times*.

The choice of TV stations available in New York is vast. CBS operates on channel 2, NBC on channel 4, ABC on channel 7 and WNYW (Fox) on channel 5. PBS offers cultural and educational fare, including some vintage BBC programs, on channel 13. Cable TV offers everything from the Arts and Entertainment Network (channel 16) to public access programs.

AM radio stations include WCBS News (880AM) and WFAN Sports (660AM). Some FM stations are WNEW rock (102.7FM), WBGO jazz (88.3FM) and WQXR classical (96.3FM).

Useful information Universal News, 234 W 42 **Map** 8 D1. ☎ *221-1809.*

ELECTRICAL APPLIANCES

All American electric current flows at a standardized 110 to 120 volts AC (alternating current). You will need to bring an adapter plug and a voltage convertor that fits standard US electrical outlets. US plugs have two flat prongs.

Most modern New York hotels provide wall-mounted electric hair dryers in bathrooms. In addition, some hotels have wall plugs capable of powering both 110- and 220-volt electric shavers, but little else – not even radios. It can, in fact, be dangerous to connect anything more powerful. If you bring along sophisticated electrical appliances with you, be certain to take a battery pack as well. You will also need an adapter to recharge your spare batteries.

Few New York hotel rooms provide irons or coffee-makers. However, room service should be able to provide you with an iron upon request.

Standard plug

EMBASSIES AND CONSULATES

Australia
150 E 42nd St. **Map** 9 A1.
☎ *351-6500.*
W www.australianyc.org

Britain
845 Third Ave. **Map** 13 B4.
☎ *745-0200.*
W www.britainusa.com/ny

Canada
1251 Sixth Ave at 50th St. **Map** 12 E4. ☎ *596-1628.*
W www.canada-ny.org

Ireland
345 Park Ave. **Map** 13 A4.
☎ *319-2555.* W
www.irelandemb.org

New Zealand
37 Observatory Circle, NW, Washington, DC 20008.
☎ *(202) 328-4800.* W
www.nzemb.org

RELIGIOUS SERVICES

There are some 4,000 places of worship in New York, catering to almost any faith. Most hotels have lists of local organizations and service times. Among the leading churches and temples are:

Baptist
Riverside Church
122nd St at Riverside Dr.
Map 20 D2.
☎ *870-6700.*

Catholic
St. Patrick's Cathedral
Fifth Ave at 50th St.
Map 12 F4.
☎ *753-2261.*

Episcopal
St. Bartholomew's
109 E 50th St. **Map** 13 A4.
☎ *378-0200.*

Jewish
Reform
Temple Emanu-El
Fifth Ave at 65th St.
Map 12 F2.
☎ *744-1400.*

Orthodox
Fifth Avenue Synagogue
5 E 62nd St. **Map** 12 F2.
☎ *838-2122.*

Lutheran
St. Peter's
619 Lexington Ave. **Map** 17 A4.
☎ *935-2200.*

Methodist
Christ Church United Methodist
520 Park Ave. **Map** 13 A3.
☎ *838-3036.*

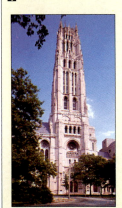

Riverside Church

Personal Security and Health

Police badge

IN 1998, NEW YORK was rated the safest among large US cities with a population of more than one million. This ranks New York 166th among cities with population of over one hundred thousand. The city's police force concentrates on foot and bicycle patrols in tourist areas, and security has been beefed up in midtown, in the transportation system and at airports. While there are places where any traveler would be foolish to tread after dark – and sometimes in daylight – if you keep your wits about you and stick to the following guidelines, you should enjoy a trouble-free visit.

As a general rule, be alert when you walk down the street

LAW ENFORCEMENT

THE NEW YORK police department has around-the-clock foot, horse, bike and car patrols. These are concentrated in specific areas at critical times – for instance, the theater district during show times. There are police who ride the subways and buses, and the recent dramatic drop in crime statistics reflects this.

You may also see youths wearing red berets. As their T-shirts proclaim, they are Guardian Angels. Always unarmed, these safety patrols "police" the subways and midtown streets. Although tolerated by the police and often a welcome sight, they have no official powers.

GUIDELINES ON SAFETY

THE CITY UNDER mayor Giuliani has become a much cleaner, safer place. However, common sense rules, so be alert and walk as

if you know where you're going. Avoid making eye contact and confrontations with down-and-outs. If someone asks you for money, be careful and do not be drawn into conversation.

Avoid deserted streets. At night, if you can't afford a taxi, try to travel with a group and avoid such areas as the Lower East Side, Chinatown, midtown west of Broadway (except Lincoln Center and Times Square) and any place off the beaten path. The Financial District (except for the World Financial Center) is deserted after business hours, and some TriBeCa and SoHo streets can be risky after dark if you are alone.

Parks are often used for drug dealing. They are safest when there is a crowd for a rally, concert or other event. If you want to go for a jog, ask your hotel concierge for a map of safe

routes and follow his or her advice. Keep your wallet in an inconspicuous place and have enough change handy for phone calls and bus fares. It's best not to have to dig into your purse or wallet when standing in line. Never stop to count your money on the street, and be aware of strangers watching at cash machines. Defeat purse snatchers by carrying your bag with the clasp facing toward you and the shoulder strap diagonally across your body.

Leave valuable jewelry at home or stored at your hotel; do not allow anyone except hotel and airport personnel to carry your luggage or parcels; and stow your valuables and camera in a locked suitcase or closet safe when you leave your hotel room.

Mounted police officers

LOST AND FOUND

THE CHANCES are poor of recovering anything lost in New York City. There is no citywide lost and found.

Two armed New York City police officers

Cap and badge worn by city police

The lost-and-found rooms at Grand Central and Penn Station are well-run, well-stocked and very helpful.

USEFUL INFORMATION

Lost and Found Offices
Bus and subway services
☎ 712-4500.

Taxis
☎ 692-8294.

Missing Credit Cards
American Express
☎ (800) 528-4800 (free).

Diners Club
☎ (800) 234-6377 (free).

JCB
☎ (800) 366-4522 (free).

MasterCard
☎ (800) 627-8372 (free).

VISA
☎ (800) 336-8472 (free).

TRAVEL INSURANCE

T RAVEL INSURANCE is highly recommended, mainly because of the high cost of medical care. There are many types of coverage, with prices dependent on the length of your trip and the number of people covered on the policy.

Among the most important features are: accidental death, dismemberment, emergency medical and dental care, trip cancellation, and baggage and travel document loss. There are many policies that include all these items. Your travel agent or insurance company should recommend a suitable policy.

MEDICAL TREATMENT

B E PREPARED to undergo an expensive experience: some of the city's practitioners and facilities are among the best around, and medical fees in the US are unregulated. Be sure to protect yourself well with insurance. A few physicians and dentists may accept credit cards, but they are much more likely to want payment in cash or traveler's checks. Hospitals accept most credit cards *(see p358)*.

A 24-hour pharmacy, one of several in the city

EMERGENCIES

I N THE EVENT of your being involved in a medical emergency, proceed at once to a **Hospital Emergency Room**. Should you need an ambulance, telephone 911 and one will be sent. If your medical insurance is properly in order, you won't have to worry about costs.

Unless you are impoverished, it is better to avoid the city-owned hospitals listed in the telephone book Blue Pages. Instead, choose one of the many private hospitals listed in the Yellow Pages. Dial 411 and ask the operator to give you the number of the nearest public or private hospital. Other options include asking your hotel to call a doctor or dentist to visit you in your room, or finding one yourself through the **NY Hotel Urgent Medical Services** (737-1212), **Dial-A-Doctor** or **NYU Dental Care**. For more general advice and information call **Travelers' Aid**, a national organization geared to helping travelers.

CRISIS INFORMATION

All Emergencies
☎ 911 (or 0). This alerts police, fire and medical services.

Dial-A-Doctor
☎ 971-9692.

Crime Victims Hot Line
☎ 577-7777.

NYU Dental Care
345 E 24th St/1st Ave.
Map 9 B4
☎ 998-9800; 998-9872 (9am–6:30pm Mon–Thu, 9am–4pm Fri), 998-9828 (weekends and after 9pm).

Hospital Emergency Rooms
St. Vincent's.
11th St and Seventh Ave.
Map 3 C1.
☎ 604-7998.

St. Luke's Roosevelt.
58th St and Ninth Ave.
Map 12 D3.
☎ 523-6800.

National Organization for Women (NOW)
☎ 627-9895.

Pharmacy (24-hour)
Rite Aid
50th St./8th Ave
Map 12 D4.
☎ 247-8384.

Poison Control Center
☎ 764-7667.

Sex Crimes Report Line
☎ 267-7273.

Travelers' Aid
JFK Airport, Terminal 410
☎ (718) 656-4870.

New York ambulance

Banking and Currency

NEW YORK IS THE NATION'S banking center. It has a wealth of local, regional and major national banks, plus some retail branches of the leading foreign banks. Fleet Bank and Barclays are well represented in New York; the banks of Australia, Canada, Ireland, Scotland, Tokyo, and Turkey all have offices or branches.

BANKING

NEW YORK banks are generally open weekdays from 9am to 3pm. There are, however, a number of banks that open earlier or close late evening to suit commuters' needs. Tellers are behind a counter. At most banks, all the tellers will cash traveler's checks and exchange your foreign currency.

Automated teller machine (ATM)

AUTOMATED TELLER MACHINES

A CONVENIENT development in banking has been the introduction of the automated teller machine (ATM). These are found in nearly all bank lobbies and enable you to obtain American currency 24 hours a day by electronically tapping into your own bank account. ATMs usually issue American banknotes in $20 denominations.

Before you leave for New York, check with your bank about which New York City banks and ATM systems will accept your bank card and what fees and commissions will be charged on each transaction. Most ATM machines are in either the Cirrus or Plus network. They accept various US bank cards, MasterCard and VISA cards and certain others. Among the many advantages of ATMs is the swift, secure exchange of your money at the wholesale rate used between the banks when they make their million-dollar deals.

On a more cautionary note, be aware of your surroundings when using an unlocked ATM. It is best to use them only in daylight hours or when the streets are crowded.

CREDIT CARDS

MASTERCARD, American Express, VISA, JCB and Diners Card are widely accepted throughout the United States, regardless of which company or bank issues them. These cards can also be used to obtain cash advances from various ATM machines. They may also be upgraded to confer higher spending limits. In the US you can use a credit card to pay for nearly everything imaginable, from groceries to restaurant and hotel bills, and telephone orders for movie and theater tickets. Major expenses such as tours, travel packages and expensive rentals are all best paid for by credit card. Try to avoid carrying huge sums of money around with you.

CASHING CHECKS

DOLLAR TRAVELER's checks issued by American Express and Thomas Cook are widely accepted without a fee by most of New York's department stores, shops, hotels and restaurants. Traveler's checks in other currencies, including sterling, are not universally accepted. They can usually be

Foreign currency exchange counter at Chequepoint USA

exchanged by your hotel cashier, but may require a visit to a bank. Exchange rates are printed daily in the *New York Times* and *Wall Street Journal*, and may be posted in the windows of banks that invite currency-exchange business. American Express checks are always exchanged without a fee at American Express offices. Major hotels have cashiers equipped to exchange your traveler's checks.

Foreign exchange brokers are few. Among the most solidly established are **Thomas Cook Currency Services Inc.** and **CBC Banking Corporation**. The ones listed on the opposite page have late hours. Others are listed in the city's telephone Yellow Pages under *Foreign Money Brokers*. Expect to pay a fee, which will vary widely from one place to the next, plus a commission.

There are scores of hole-in-the-wall check-cashing shops in Manhattan. They are listed in the Yellow Pages classified section. They may not be willing to cash your traveler's checks though, and they are very unlikely to accept or cash foreign checks.

EXCHANGE ADDRESSES

Thomas Cook Currency Services Inc.
1590 Broadway
Map 12 E5. **C** 265-6049.
One of several branches.

CBC Banking Corporation
90 Broad St.
Map 1 C3. **C** 858-3300.

Coins

American coins come in 50-, 25-, 10-, 5- and 1-cent pieces. The new gold-tone $1 coins are now in circulation as are the State quarters, which feature an historical scene on one side. Each value of coin has a popular name: 25-cent pieces are called quarters, 10-cent pieces are called dimes, 5-cent pieces called "nickels" and 1-cent pieces called pennies.

25- cent coin (a quarter)

10- cent coin (a dime)

5- cent coin (a nickel)

1- cent coin (a penny)

An American Eagle from old currency

Bank Notes (Bills)

Units of currency in the United States are dollars and cents. There are 100 cents to a dollar. Notes come in $1, $5, $10, $20, $50 and $100s. All bills are green, so check the amount carefully. The new $5, $10, $20, $50, and $100 bills are now in circulation; they have larger numbers when compared to the old notes.

1- dollar bill ($1)

5- dollar bill ($5)

10- dollar bill ($50)

20- dollar bill ($20)

50- dollar bill ($50)

100- dollar bill ($100)

Using New York's Phones

PUBLIC PAY PHONES can be found at many street corners, in hotel and office lobbies, restaurants, bars, theaters, and department stores. Few use credit cards, but you can now buy prepaid phone cards. Most phones are coin-operated and take 5-, 10- and 25-cent coins. Hotels are free to set their own

Sign for public payphones

rates, and so calls made from your room can be more expensive than using a public pay phone. Avoid this by making calls from a public phone in the lobby.

PUBLIC TELEPHONES

THE STANDARD pay phone has a hand receiver and 12-button key pad and is pillar- or wall-mounted. In some locations the pay phone may belong to an independent company. The independents are often more expensive and less reliable. Regulations require each public pay phone to post information about charges, toll-free numbers and how to make calls using other carriers. Look

Independently operated payphone

for the Verizon logo on the box to be sure the phone will reach all numbers at standard rates. To complain about service, call the **Public Service Commission**.

Useful information

Public Service Commission ☎ *(800) 342-3355 (tollfree number).*

To check e-mail

Times Square Visitors Center,1560 Broadway, **Map** 12 E5; NY Computer Cafe, 247 E 57th St. ☎ *872-1704* **Map** 13 B3; many New York Public Libraries have Internet desks, but there is usually a time limit for use.

PAY PHONE CHARGES

WITHIN the New York boroughs, the standard charge, around 25 cents, buys three minutes' talking time. If your call lasts longer, the operator will request additional payment.

Many newsstands now sell prepaid phone cards for long-distance calls; they can be bought in $5, $10, and $25 amounts. The cards offer substantial savings compared to standard rates. However, the calls are connected over the Internet and so the sound quality may not be as good as calls using a standard carrier.

USING A COIN-OPERATED PHONE

1 Lift the receiver.

3 Dial or press the number.

Coins
Make sure you have the correct coins available before you dial.

5 cents

10 cents

25 cents

2 Insert the necessary coin or coins. The coin drops as soon as you insert it.

4 If you do not want to complete your call or it does not get through, retrieve the coin(s) by pressing the coin return.

5 If the call is answered and you talk longer than the allotted three minutes, the operator will interrupt and ask you to deposit more coins. Pay-phones do not give change.

A typical public pay phone stand

International long-distance rates for calls dialed direct vary from country to country. For calls to the UK, the discount rate starts at 1pm, then drops to an economy rate from 6pm until 7am the next day.

USEFUL NUMBERS

Directory Inquiries
411; 10-10-9000.

Main Post Office
967-8585.

Operator Assistance
0.

Speaking Clock
976-1616.

International Directory Inquiries
00.

REACHING THE RIGHT NUMBER

• Five area codes are used in New York: 212 , 917, 646 for Manhattan; the other boroughs use 718 and 347. 800, 888, and 877 prefixes mean the call will be free.
• To call a number outside your own area, first dial 1. For example, to dial Queens from Manhattan dial 1 (718) (number).
• To call long distance from a pay phone: dial 0 followed by the area code and then the number. The operator will answer and tell you how much money you need to deposit.
• To make an international direct call: dial 011 followed by the country code (New Zealand: 64; Australia: 61; UK: 44), then the city or area code (minus the first 0) and the local number.
• To make an international call via the operator: dial 01 followed by the country code, the city code (minus the first 0) and then the local number.
• International Directory Inquiries are on 00. If you have problems, call international operator assistance on 01.
• **In an emergency, dial 911.**

Sending A Letter

US postal service logo

APART FROM post offices, letters can be mailed at your hotel concierge desk (which usually also sells stamps); in letter slots in office building lobbies; in air, rail and bus terminals; and in the occasional street mailbox. These are always painted blue, or red, white and blue. Mail in most mailboxes is not picked up on weekends. Post offices are shown on the *Street Finder* maps (*see pp378–9*).

POSTAL SERVICES

THE CITY'S main **General Post Office** is open 24 hours a day. Stamps can be bought here or from branch offices (a handy one is in the Empire State Building) or from coin-operated machines in pharmacies, department stores and bus and train stations. All letters go first class.

The post office offers three special delivery services: **Express Mail** service for next-day delivery, **Priority Mail** service for two-day delivery, and **International Express Mail** for overseas. Priority Mail will also pick up letters on weekdays for an extra charge. Private express mail can be arranged through hotel

Colorful US stamps

concierges or with one of the delivery services listed in the telephone book.

Useful information
General Post Office, 421 8th Ave.
Map 8 D2. 967-8585.
(800) 222-1811 Priority and Express Mail.
(800) 463-3339 FedEx.
(800) 225-5345 DHL.
(800) 742-5877 UPS.
Internet guides
w www.bigyellow.com
w www.usps.com

HELD MAIL

MAIL will be held for you for 30 days at the General Post Office's General Delivery window. Mail can be sent to any local post office by giving the zip code or name. Address mail with: Name, General Delivery, US Post Office, New York, NY 10001.

Express Mail   **Priority Mail**

Mailboxes
Mailboxes can be few and far between on New York streets, and it may be easier to find a post office (see Street Finder pp378–9). Instructions on how to use each mailbox are written on the box. If you use Express or Priority services, weigh your letters at a post office to figure out the postage needed.

Standard mailbox

GETTING TO NEW YORK

MANY INTERNATIONAL airlines have direct flights to New York. It is also very well served by charter and domestic services. Price wars between airlines have reduced fares, and domestic flights now prove a viable alternative to bus and train tickets; group tour package prices are often

Grand Central Terminal

unbeatable. The *QE2* is one of several cruise ships that dock in the city. Long-distance trains serving New York are clean and comfortable. Interstate and long distance buses have air-conditioning, video screens and on-board toilets. For information on arriving in New York see the map on pages 366–7.

AIR TRAVEL

NEW YORK CAN be reached by air direct from most major cities. The flight from London takes about eight hours. However, there are no direct flights from Australia or New Zealand. Instead, the airlines fly to the West coast, which takes around 14 hours, land, refuel and then continue on to New York.

Among the main carriers to New York are **Air Canada**, **Delta**, **Continental**, **British Airways**, **American Airlines**, **Virgin Atlantic** and **United Airlines**. All international flights arrive at Newark or JFK airports *(see pp364–5)*.

APEX (Advance Purchase Excursion) tickets for the scheduled airlines are usually the cheapest return fares apart from package tours. But they must be bought in advance and are valid for a stay of 7 to 30 days. Some airlines offer cheaper fares if you limit your stay to specified periods. Senior citizens may also receive discounts on some flights.

AIRLINE NUMBERS

Air Canada **[** *(888) 247-2262.*
[W] www.aircanada.ca

American Airlines **[** *(800) 433-7300.*
[W] www.aa.com

British Airways **[** *(800) 247-9297.*
[W] www.british-airways.com

Continental **[** *(800) 231-0856.*
[W] www.flycontinental.com

Delta **[** *(800) 241-4141.*
[W] www. delta.com

United Airlines **[** *(800) 241-6522*
[W] www.ual.com

Virgin Atlantic **[** *(800) 862-8621*
[W] www.fly.virgin.com

OCEAN TRAVEL

NEW YORK IS a regular port of call for many cruise liners, in addition to the *QE2*, which docks there, via Southampton, 25 times a year. You can also take the *QE2* from New York to Australia and New Zealand. Ocean travel offers an expensive but

Long-distance Greyhound bus

relaxing way of traveling to New York. Ships dock at the Hudson River piers in midtown Manhattan.

LONG-DISTANCE BUSES

ALL LONG-DISTANCE buses such as **Greyhound Lines** arrive in the city at the **Port Authority Bus Terminal**. Buses from here also connect with the three airports. With over 6,000 buses arriving and leaving daily and carrying some 172,000 passengers, the atmosphere is chaotic. Many hotels are also accessible directly from the terminal.
Useful information Greyhound Bus Lines **[** *(800) 231-2222. (24 hrs).*
[W] www.greyhound.com Port Authority Bus Terminal. W 40th St and Eighth Ave. **Map** 8 D1. **[** *564-8484 (24 hrs).* **[W]** www.panynj.gov

TRAIN TRAVEL

AMTRAK TRAINS from Canada, upstate New York, southern, northeastern and western states all stop at Penn Station *(see p376)*. Metro-North lines from upstate New York and Connecticut arrive at Grand Central Terminal.

Ocean liner anchored in Manhattan

New York Airports

THE THREE MAIN airports (Newark, JFK and La Guardia) are all well connected to central Manhattan. Look for uniformed "skycaps" – scarlet-capped porters wearing distinctive badges, who will help you with your luggage. Never trust anyone else to help carry your bags – you may never see them again. Taxi dispatchers will help you into a licensed taxi at the taxi area.

GETTING INTO MANHATTAN

THE GROUND Transportation center at each airport will give you information on the ways you can continue your trip. The most useful services, operating from LaGuardia and JFK, are the **New York Airport Service** and **Gray Line Air Shuttle**. The former stops at Grand Central; the latter will drop you anywhere in Manhattan between 23rd and 63rd streets. New Jersey Transit buses and **Olympia Airport Express** also go to and from each airport into the city. The fare on the Olympia vans is one of the best bargains.

Shared vehicle rides are offered at JFK and LaGuardia by **Classic Airport Share Ride** and **Connecticut Limo**. You can sometimes share a taxi or one of the independent (gypsy) cabs into Manhattan. For the price of a subway ride, the "A" line

Taxi dispatcher

connects with a shuttle bus and takes passengers to and from JFK. The M60 city bus also goes to and from LaGuardia. Most of the car rental firms have courtesy telephones at the baggage-claim areas. Telephone numbers and web addresses for your advance reservations are listed on page 370.

BUS COMPANIES

New York Airport Service
☎ (718) 875-8200.

Classic Airport Share Ride ☎ (631) 567-5100. W
www.classictrans.com

Gray Line Air Shuttle
☎ 315-3006.

Olympia Airport Express
☎ 964-6233.

Connecticut Limo
☎ (800) 472-5466.

LA GUARDIA (LGA)

PRINCIPALLY SERVING business travelers, La Guardia lies 8 miles (13 km) east of Manhattan on the north side of Long Island in Queens.

Upon arrival, you can rent luggage trolleys from the baggage-claim area next to the luggage carousels. Skycaps are on hand to assist you. Baggage can also be left in the Tele-Trip business center on the departure level. Foreign exchange desks are located around the Central Terminal.

Uniformed taxi dispatchers at the airport are on duty at peak hours. Only use yellow taxis licensed by the city. The cost of tolls, plus a small surcharge after 8pm and all day Sunday, will be added to the fare shown on the meter (about $25–$40 to midtown).

Useful information Airport Information Service ☎ (718) 533-3400. W www.laguardiaairport.com W www.panjny.gov

Transatlantic jet

PLAN OF LA GUARDIA AIRPORT

A frequent free bus service runs between each of the terminals and parking areas. Buses and taxis into the city and its suburbs depart from the first floor of the Central Terminal building.

Central Terminal building

Marine Air Terminal

Delta Shuttle Terminal

USAirways Terminal

USAirways Shuttle

Delta Terminal

Grand Central Parkway to New York

KEY

🅿 Parking

🚌 Bus service between terminals

JFK Airport

N EW YORK'S main inter-national airport, JFK, lies 15 miles (24 km) southeast of Manhattan, in the borough of Queens. American Airlines, British Airways, Delta, TWA, and United have their own arrivals buildings, complete with customs and immigration facilities. Other international airlines use Terminals 1, 2 or 4. Note that the terminals have all been recently renumbered.

Luggage trolleys are free

Main Hall at the International Arrivals Building, JFK

for arriving passengers in the meeting area. Foreign ex-change offices are located in all terminals.

The Ground Transportation desk is on the ground level near the baggage-claim. Transportation into Manhattan can be arranged here 24 hours a day. Courtesy phones are provided by the car rental companies. Most have shuttle service to their rental offices. Taxis wait outside the terminals. A trip into Man-hattan normally takes up to an

Airport information signs at JFK

hour; there is a flat fee of $30 plus tolls. The New York Airport Service bus service is reliable, inexpensive, safe, and operates 24 hours a day. For early morning flights there are hotels near the airport. City hotels can be booked at the Meegan Services desk.

A light-rail system, AirTran, is currently under construction at JFK. This service will connect terminals with the close A-train and LIRR stations.

Useful Addresses

Airport Information Service 🔲 *(718) 244-4444*
W www.jfkairport.com
Best Western JFK Airport
138–10 135th Ave, Queens.
◖ *(718) 322-8700.*
Holiday Inn JFK
144–02 135th Ave, Queens.
◖ *(718) 659-0200.*

🔲 Helicopter Flight Services ◖ *355-0801.* W www.heliny.com; Liberty Helicopters ◖ *(888) 692-4354.*

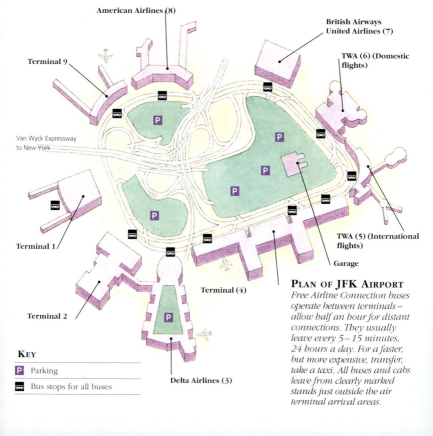

American Airlines (8)

British Airways
United Airlines (7)

TWA (6) (Domestic flights)

Terminal 9

Van Wyck Expressway
to New York

Terminal 1

TWA (5) (International flights)

Garage

Terminal 2

PLAN OF JFK AIRPORT

Free Airline Connection buses operate between terminals – allow half an hour for distant connections. They usually leave every 5 – 15 minutes, 24 hours a day. For a faster, but more expensive, transfer, take a taxi. All buses and cabs leave from clearly marked stands just outside the air terminal arrival areas.

Terminal (4)

Delta Airlines (3)

KEY

🅿 Parking

🚌 Bus stops for all buses

NEWARK AIRPORT

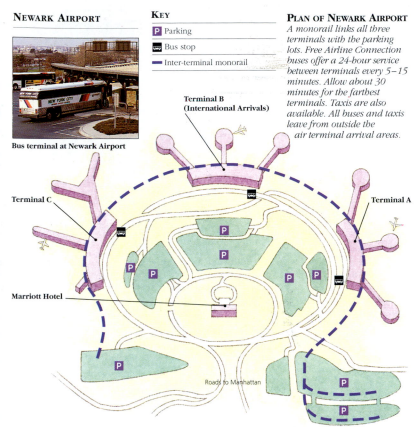

Bus terminal at Newark Airport

KEY

🅿 Parking

🚌 Bus stop

━━ Inter-terminal monorail

PLAN OF NEWARK AIRPORT

A monorail links all three terminals with the parking lots. Free Airline Connection buses offer a 24-hour service between terminals every 5–15 minutes. Allow about 30 minutes for the farthest terminals. Taxis are also available. All buses and taxis leave from outside the air terminal arrival areas.

Terminal B
(International Arrivals)

Terminal C

Terminal A

Marriott Hotel

Roads to Manhattan

Newark, New York's second largest international airport, is located about 16 miles (26 km) southwest of Manhattan, in New Jersey.

All international flights arrive at Terminal "B." Baggage trolleys are free for arriving international passengers. There is no baggage room. Foreign exchange desks are available in each terminal.

The Ground Transportation services desk, open 24 hours a day, is next to the baggage-claim area. Courtesy phones are provided by limousine and car rental firms. Many of these have a free shuttle service to their rental offices.

If you want a taxi, line up at one of the many taxi stands located outside most arrival areas. Uniformed taxi dispatchers will also help you hail a cab. Never accept a ride into town from anyone who approaches you in the terminal: they may not have

insurance and could charge an outrageous fare. The trip into Manhattan takes about 40–60 minutes and will cost you up to $40-$45.

Buses can take anywhere from 40 minutes to over an hour to reach Manhattan, but cost about $10. Electronic boards around the terminal list departure times of all services.

For early morning flights, there are hotels located in and around the airport grounds. City hotels can be booked on arrival through the courtesy phones that are linked directly to various Manhattan

hotels. At Newark, these are located in all three terminals.

USEFUL ADDRESSES

Port Authority at Newark Airport
📞 *(888) 397-4636.*
🌐 *www.newarkairport.com*

Holiday Inn International
1000 Spring St, Elizabeth, N J.
📞 *(800) 465-4329.*

Marriott Hotel
Newark Airport grounds.
📞 *(800) 228-9290.*

Arrival and departure monitors at Newark Airport

Arriving in New York

This map shows the links between New York's three airports and the center of Manhattan. It also illustrates rail connections linking New York to the rest of the United States and Canada. Travel information, including travel times for subway, bus, rail and helicopter services, is listed in each information box. The passenger ship terminal, once New York's key point of arrival for the flood of post-war immigrants, is located a short distance from the center of Manhattan. Port Authority Bus Terminal, on the West Side, provides services across the city.

Ships at the passenger terminal

PASSENGER SHIP TERMINAL
Piers 88–92 for QE2 and other cruise ship arrivals and departures.

Passenger Ship Terminal

KEY

✈	Airport *see pp363–5*
⚓	Seaport *see p362*
🚈	Rail link *see p362*
🚌	Bus station/link *see p362*
M	Subway link *see pp374–5*
⛴	Water shuttle
🚁	Helicopter links *see p364*
▬	New York Airport Service and Gray Line Air Shuttle *see p363*
▬	Water shuttle
▬	Helicopters *see p364*
▬	Long Island Rail Road *see pp376–7*
▬	New Jersey Transit buses *see p363*
▬	Olympia Airport Express *see p363*
▬	Shuttle bus *see p364*
▬	Subway line, A train *see p374*

PORT AUTHORITY BUS TERMINAL
All long-distance buses arrive and depart here; links to all city airports.

Port Authority Bus Terminal

PENN STATION
*Long-distance trains from **Canada** and other US states arrive and depart here; daily commuter train services to **Long Island** and **New Jersey**.*
🚈 *Amtrak, Long Island Rail Road and New Jersey Transit services.*
M *A, C, E, 1, 2, 3, 9.*

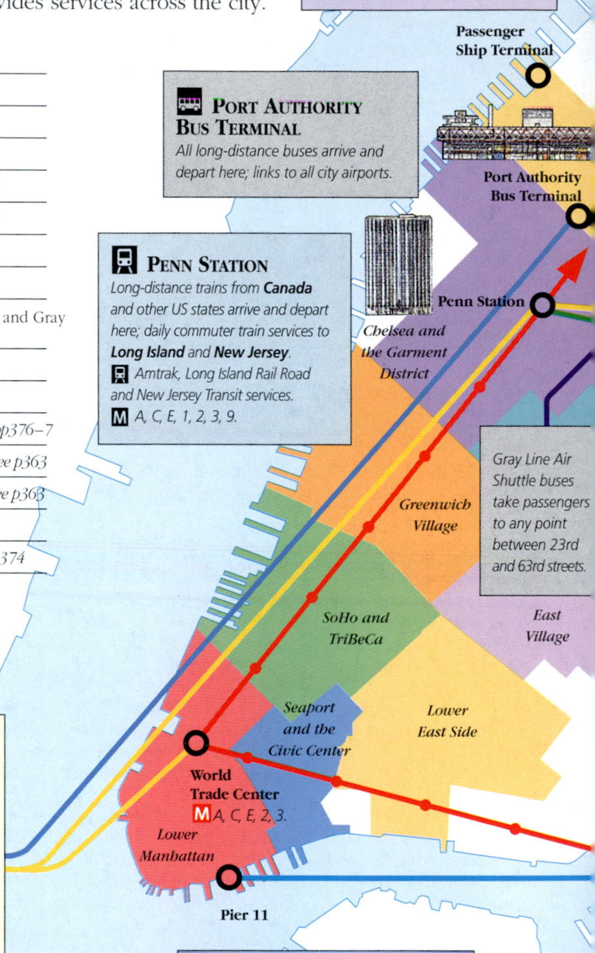

Penn Station

Chelsea and the Garment District

Gray Line Air Shuttle buses take passengers to any point between 23rd and 63rd streets.

Greenwich Village

East Village

SoHo and TriBeCa

Lower East Side

Seaport and the Civic Center

Lower Manhattan

World Trade Center
M *A, C, E, 2, 3.*

Pier 11

✈ NEWARK
Bus to Manhattan every 20–30 mins.
🚌 ***Olympia Airport Express*** *every 20–30 mins to the **World Trade Center**, **Penn Station** and **Grand Central Terminal**.*
🚌 ***New Jersey Transit*** *buses every 15–20 mins to the **Port Authority Bus Terminal**.*
🚁 ***Chartered helicopters*** *to 34th St. heliport.*

The September 2001 attacks on Lower Manhattan have left a question mark over the transport network in that area. Check before starting your journey

Delta Water Shuttle from La Guardia

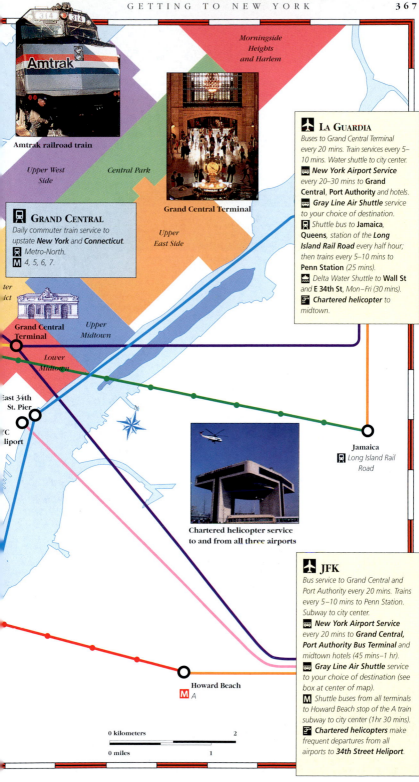

Amtrak railroad train

Morningside Heights and Harlem

Upper West Side

Central Park

Grand Central Terminal

Upper East Side

🚉 LA GUARDIA

Buses to Grand Central Terminal every 20 mins. Train services every 5–10 mins. Water shuttle to city center.

🚌 *New York Airport Service every 20–30 mins to **Grand Central**, **Port Authority** and hotels.*

🚌 *Gray Line Air Shuttle service to your choice of destination.*

🚉 *Shuttle bus to **Jamaica, Queens**, station of the **Long Island Rail Road** every half hour; then trains every 5–10 mins to **Penn Station** (25 mins).*

⛴ *Delta Water Shuttle to **Wall St** and **E 34th St**, Mon–Fri (30 mins).*

🚁 *Chartered helicopter to midtown.*

🚉 GRAND CENTRAL

*Daily commuter train service to upstate **New York** and **Connecticut**.*

🚉 *Metro-North.*

Ⓜ *4, 5, 6, 7.*

Grand Central Terminal

Upper Midtown

Lower Midtown

East 34th St. Pier

7C liport

Jamaica
🚉 *Long Island Rail Road*

Chartered helicopter service to and from all three airports

🛫 JFK

Bus service to Grand Central and Port Authority every 20 mins. Trains every 5–10 mins to Penn Station. Subway to city center.

🚌 *New York Airport Service every 20 mins to **Grand Central, Port Authority Bus Terminal** and midtown hotels (45 mins–1 hr).*

🚌 *Gray Line Air Shuttle service to your choice of destination (see box at center of map).*

Ⓜ *Shuttle buses from all terminals to Howard Beach stop of the A train subway to city center (1hr 30 mins).*

🚁 *Chartered helicopters make frequent departures from all airports to **34th Street Heliport**.*

Howard Beach
Ⓜ *A*

0 kilometers   2

0 miles   1

GETTING AROUND NEW YORK

WITH OVER SIX thousand miles of streets, walking around New York could prove difficult. But the city is a network of districts and many of the major sites can be visited area by area. Taxis are best for door-to-door transit but can be held up in traffic jams, especially during rush hours. The city's bus service is reliable and cheap but often slow. Subways are quick, reliable and cheap, and make stops throughout central Manhattan. There are no weekly or day passes valid for all public transportation, but buses and trains have their own forms of travel passes.

Stretch limousine, the preferred vehicle for New York's glitterati

NEGOTIATING THE AVENUES AND STREETS

MANHATTAN'S avenues run approximately north to south; its streets (except in the older areas) run east to west. Fifth Avenue is used to divide East and West Street addresses; Five West 40th Street is, for example, a few doors west of Fifth Avenue on 40th Street, and Five East 40th is a few doors to the east.

Most streets in midtown are one-way. In general, traffic is eastbound on even-numbered streets and westbound on odd-numbered streets. Avenues also tend to be one-way, alternating northbound or southbound. First, Third (above 23rd Street), Madison, Eighth, Avenue of the Americas (6th Ave) and Tenth avenues, are all northbound, while Second, Lexington, Fifth, Seventh, and Ninth avenues and Broadway below 59th Street are southbound. There is two-way traffic on York, Park, Eleventh and Twelfth avenues and Broadway above 60th Street.

Although most city blocks north of Houston Street are rectangular, they are not very uniform: east–west blocks are three or even four times longer than north–south blocks.

When asking directions from a New Yorker, you may get confused over certain streets. For instance, Avenue of the Americas is also Sixth Avenue, and and Park Avenue South is not the same as Park avenue. Many intersections and plazas have titles commemorating famous people and events. However,

Rush-hour gridlock in Manhattan

FINDING AN ADDRESS

A useful formula has been devised to help pinpoint any **Avenue Address**. By dropping the last digit of the address, dividing the remainder by 2, then adding or subtracting the **Key Number** given here, you will discover the nearest cross street. For example: To find No. 826 Lexington Avenue, first you have to drop the 6; divide 82 by 2, which is 41; then add **22** (the key number). Therefore, the nearest cross street is 63rd Street.

Avenue Address	Key Number
1st Ave	+3
2nd Ave	+3
3rd Ave	+10
4th Ave	+8
5th Ave, up to 200	+13
5th Ave, up to 400	+16
5th Ave, up to 600	+18
5th Ave, up to 775	+20
5th Ave 775–1286, do not divide by 2	-18
5th Ave, up to 1500	+45
5th Ave, up to 2000	+24
(6th) Ave of the Americas	-12
7th Ave below 110th St	+12
7th Ave above 110th St	+20
8th Ave	+10

Avenue Address	Key Number
9th Ave	+13
10th Ave	+14
Amsterdam Ave	+60
Audubon Ave	+165
Broadway above 23rd St	-30
Central Park W, divide full number by 10	+60
Columbus Ave	+60
Convent Ave	+127
Lenox Ave·	+110
Lexington Ave	+22
Madison Ave	+26
Park Ave	+35
Park Ave South	+08
Riverside Drive, divide full number by 10	+72
St Nicholas Ave	+110
West End Ave	+60

MADISON AVENUE

A road sign for Madison Avenue positioned at an intersection with a street

the maps in this guide use the place names that most New Yorkers know and regularly use.

PLANNING YOUR JOURNEY

T HE STREETS and sidewalks are busiest during the rush hours – 8 to 10am, 11:30am to 1:30pm and 4:30 to 6:30pm, Monday to Friday. Throughout these periods it is better to face the crowds on foot than attempt any journey by bus, taxi or subway. At other times of day and during certain holiday periods (see p53), the traffic is often much lighter and you should reach your destination quickly.

There are, of course, a few exceptions. Fifth Avenue should always be avoided on parade days (St. Patrick's Day and Thanksgiving Day are the worst). Celebrity visits or one of the regular demonstrations at City Hall (see p90) can cause major disruption to the traffic. The area around Seventh Avenue, south of 42nd Street, is likely to be busy during the day with the truck and handcart traffic of New York's garment industry.

WALKING

M OST INTERSECTIONS between avenues and streets have lampposts with name-markers and electric traffic signals. The traffic lights show red (stop) and green (go) for vehicles and "Walk–Don't Walk" for pedestrians. You

Pedestrian crossing

Do not cross the street

You may cross the street

will quickly come to realize, however, that most New York pedestrians rely on their eyes and judgment rather than on the numerous "Walk" signs.

Remember that vehicles keep to the right. There are no cautionary "Look Left" signs to alert you to the direction of oncoming traffic. There are, however, numerous one-way streets, so it's best to look both ways before you cross. Beware, too, of cars, trucks and taxis turning the corner behind you as you start to cross the street.

There are pedestrian crossings at some intersections. These are officially designated pedestrian crossing points (at Rockefeller Center for instance) and are closely monitored by the police. The city has a few underground walkways for pedestrians in Central Park.

Staten Island Ferry leaving Battery Park

Circle Line tour boat

FERRIES

There are two ferries of interest to visitors (see also p353): the Circle Line runs a ferry to the Statue of Liberty and Ellis Island several times each day from Battery Park at the southern tip of Manhattan – W www.circleline.com. The 24-hour Staten Island ferry from Battery Park travels the channel and offers splendid views of lower Manhattan, the Statue of Liberty, Ellis Island, the bridges and Governors Island. The round trip is the best bargain in New York; it's free.

CYCLING

F OR VISITORS who want to cycle in New York it is safer on the park pathways (Central Park and along the East and Hudson rivers) in daylight hours. You can rent bikes at Metro Bikes or the Loeb Boathouse in Central Park.
Useful information
Metro Bikes, W 96th St & Broadway. **Map** 15 C2 **(** 663-7531.

Cyclist in Central Park

Driving in New York

Heavy traffic and expensive rental cars make driving in New York a frustrating experience. You must wear a seat belt. The speed limit is 30 mph (48 km/h) – which is difficult to exceed because of Manhattan's potholes and traffic. Most streets are one-way, and there are traffic lights at every corner. Driving is on the right.

Traffic on Sixth Avenue

Renting a Car

To rent a car you must be at least 25 years old, or pay a surcharge. You will need a valid driver's license (for foreign visitors an International Driver's License is useful) and a credit card or you will have to pay a large deposit.

Unless you are adequately covered by your own insurance policy, you should also take out damage and liability protection, as vandalism and theft are common. Refill with gas before you return the car or you'll pay double the normal price for fuel. It is cheaper to rent a car in the city than at the airports.

Traffic Signs

Black-and-white markings on many street crossings mean that pedestrians have right of way. At intersections, they indicate that traffic should keep out when the light is red. Unlike the rest of New York State, you can never turn right on a red light unless there is a sign indicating otherwise.

Traffic flows in a single direction

Parking

Parking in Manhattan is difficult and costly. Parking areas and parking garages post their rates at the entrance. Some hotels include parking charges in their room rates.

In some areas there are meters at the curb for short-term (20–60 minutes) parking. Don't be tempted to park at out-of-order meters – you may receive a parking ticket. Yellow street and curb markings mean no parking.

"Alternate-side" parking applies on most of the city's side streets. Cars may usually be left all day and night but must be moved to the other side of the street before 8am the next day. For specific information call the **Transportation Department.**

Penalties

If you receive a parking ticket, you have seven days to pay the required fine or to appeal against it. If you have any queries about your ticket call the **Parking Violations Bureau** between 8:30am and 7pm on any weekday.

New York's tow-away crews are extremely active, and one-third of cars towed suffer damage. If you cannot find your car at its parking place, first of all call the traffic department's tow-away office. The pound is open 24 hours a day, Monday to Saturday. You can redeem your car for a hefty fine of $150, plus $10 per day storage fee. Traveler's checks, certified checks, money orders and cash are all accepted. There is an ATM machine *(see p358)* on the premises. If you have rented the car, the contract must be produced, and only the authorized driver may redeem the car. If the car is not at the pound, report it to the police.

Useful information Police emergencies only 🔲 911; Parking Violations Bureau 🔲 (718) 422-2800; Traffic Dept, Tow Pound, Pier 76, W 38th St and 12th Ave. **Map** 7 1B; uptown at the 207th St. Pound 🔲 788-7800; Transportation Dept 🔲 225-5368.

Bridge Tolls

Most major access routes in and out of New York City levy tolls. These vary in price from $1.50 for some of the smaller bridges, to $6.00 for the George Washington Bridge between New York and New Jersey. The bridges of the Triborough Bridge Authority charge $3.50 each way. All tolls must be paid in cash. Avoid E-Z Pass lanes, marked with purple signs, which are only for holders of pre-paid passes.

Car Rental Agencies

If you need to rent a car while in New York, agencies are listed in the telephone directory under *Automobile Renting*. The major rental companies include:

Avis 🔲 (800) 331-1212.
🔲 www.avis.com

Budget 🔲 (800) 527-0700.
🔲 www.drivebudget.com

Dollar 🔲 (800) 800-4000.
🔲 www.dollar.com

Hertz 🔲 (800) 654-3131.
🔲 www.hertz.com

National 🔲 (800) 227-7368.
🔲 www.nationalcar.com

Entry prohibited

50 mph (80 km/h) speed limit

Give way to all vehicles

Stop at intersection

New York's Taxis

New York taxi cab

ALL LICENSED TAXI cabs are yellow. If their roof numbers are lit up, they are available and can be flagged down. Occupied cabs have their top lights switched off. Taxis that are not on duty have their "Off-Duty" sign lit. Only licensed cabs are authorized to pick up people who hail them from the street; accepting a ride from anyone else can be dangerous and expensive.

TAKING A CAB

EVERY YELLOW CAB has a meter, and many can issue printed receipts. A taxi can carry up to four passengers with a single fare covering everyone on board.

Taxi stands are scarce; hotels, Penn Station and Grand Central Terminal are by far the best places to seek cabs.

Licensed taxis undergo periodic inspections and are insured against accidents and losses. Non-licensed or "gypsy" cabs are unlikely to have these safeguards, but they can be an alternative.

Once the cab driver accepts a passenger the meter starts ticking at $2. The fare increases 30 cents after each additional 292 yards (267 meters). Surcharges will then be added for waiting time and trips between 8pm and 6am. A few drivers now accept credit cards but most will want to be paid in cash. Tip the driver about 15%.

Cab driving is a traditional occupation of newly arrived immigrants and, as such, communication can be a problem. Although owners of licensed cabs must pass exams in English comprehension and the layout of the city, they will not necessarily understand either. Make sure your driver understands exactly

```
I ♥ NEW YORK
TRIP#    004653
09:11AM 11-15-92
MEDALLION# 6N64
DIST       2.30
FARE $     6.00
TLC:212-221-TAXI
```

A printed receipt available from most taxi cabs

where you want to go before you start your ride.

By law, a driver must take you anywhere in the city unless the off-duty sign is lit and the roof light is off. The driver should not ask you your destination until after you've sat down, and must follow your requests not to smoke, to open or close a window, and to pick up or drop off passengers as you direct. If he or she doesn't comply you can then report them to the **Taxi & Limousine Commission**.

Each yellow cab displays the driver's photograph and registered number next to the meter. Drivers can be sullen, or try to overcharge or not cooperate with some of your requests. Make a note of the driver's number or the license or receipt number (if you have requested one), and report it to the Commission.

Heavy one-way traffic on one of the city's avenues

TAXI NUMBERS

Taxi & Limousine Commission
692-8294 or 676-1000 for general information.

Lost and Found
302-8294.

If you would prefer to use a taxi that has been radio-dispatched, rather than hailing one on the street, call:

Allstate Car & Limousine
(800) 453-4099 (toll free).

Chris Limousines
(718) 356-3232.

Tri-State and Limo Service
777-7171.

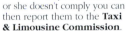

A meter will display your fare as it mounts up. Additional costs are then shown separately.

The roof-light illuminates the cab's number as well as the driver's "Off-Duty" sign.

Charge rates are listed clearly on the outside of the front passenger door.

N.Y.C. TAXI
7B72

Traveling by Bus

THE CITY'S MORE THAN 4,000 blue-and-white buses cover more than 200 routes in the five boroughs. Many run 24 hours a day, every day. The buses are modern, clean and air-conditioned. Traveling by bus is a good way to take in many of New York's sights. Buses are also considered very safe and tend not to get too crowded. Smoking is forbidden on all public buses, and animals (except guide dogs) are not allowed.

The fare box is just inside the entrance doors, next to the driver.

FARE

YOU CAN PAY THE FARE on a bus using a MetroCard (see p374), a token or exact change (these must be in coins only). Bus drivers cannot make change, and fare boxes do not accept bills or pennies. You can buy the MetroCard or tokens at any subway station booth.

If you are need to take more than one bus to reach your destination, you are eligible for a free transfer. If you pay your bus fare with a Metro-Card, a free bus-to-subway, subway-to-bus, or bus-to-bus transfer is electronically placed on the card. If you pay with a token or exact change, be sure to ask the driver for a transfer ticket when you pay.

There are discount fares for senior citizens and the disabled. All buses can "kneel," which may help elderly people to board (see p354), and they are also accessible to wheelchair users via a platform at the rear.

RECOGNIZING YOUR BUS

Each bus stop serves more than one route, so look for the route number posted on the lighted strip above the windshield on the front of the bus. Ask the driver if he or she will be stopping at your destination or close to it.

Exit the bus through the double doors toward the rear.

RIDING THE BUS

BUSES WILL STOP only at the designated bus stops. They follow north–south routes on the major avenues, stopping every two or three blocks. Crosstown buses, running east–west, stop at every block (see p368). Many routes run a 24-hour daily service, which becomes a lot less frequent during the evening and at night; other bus services operate only during the peak hours of 7am to 10pm.

Bus stops are marked by red, white and blue signs and yellow paint along the curb. Most also have bus shelters. A route map and schedule is posted at each stop. When you have identified your bus, enter at the front door and put your MetroCard or token in the fare box. Request a transfer if you will be changing to another bus. The majority of New York's bus drivers are very friendly and will call out your stop if you ask them to.

Bus stops often have three-sided, glass-walled shelters.

This bus map shows the route and main stopping-off points for route M15.

To request a stop when traveling on the bus, press the vertical call strip between the windows. A "Stop Requested" sign near the driver will light up. If the bus is crowded, it is worth starting to move toward the exit door when you are a few blocks from your stop.

Leave through the double door located toward the rear of the bus. The driver will activate the door release as soon as the bus has stopped, but you then have to push the door to open it. If you do not keep a firm grip on the door handle it is liable to swing back and hit you, so take care.

Route numbers appear on the front and side of the bus.

Enter the bus through the doors at the front.

LONG-DISTANCE & COMMUTER BUSES

BUSES TO THE rest of the US and Canada leave from the **Port Authority Bus Terminal**. Another terminal, at the Manhattan end of the George Washington Bridge, is for local buses to northern New Jersey and New York's Rockland County.

Bus tickets at Port Authority are on sale in the main concourse. The long-distance bus companies, Greyhound, Peter Pan, and Adirondack and the commuter Short Line and NJ Transit have their own ticket counters. There are no reservations taken on any of these bus lines.

There are bathrooms open from 6am to 10pm, but caution is advised. The homeless congregate in Port Authority.

A Greyhound bus arriving in New York en route to Port Authority

BUS INFORMATION

Route Maps
Available from MTA, 370 Jay St, Brooklyn, NY 11201 or NYC Visitors Center, 810 7th Ave (212-484-1222).

MTA Travel Information
📞 *(718) 330-1234 (24 hrs).*
🌐 *www.mta.nyc.ny.us*

Port Authority Bus Terminal
West 40th St and Eighth Ave.
Map 8 D1. 📞 *(212) 564-8484.*
🌐 *www.panynj.gov*

George Washington Bridge Terminal
178th St. and Broadway. 📞 *(212) 564-1114.* 🌐 *www.panynj.gov*

Lost Property
📞 *(212) 712-4500.*

SIGHTSEEING BY BUS

For a pleasant and cheap alternative to a tour bus, hop on a city bus and see New York with the New Yorkers. Bus routes M1 and M6 down Fifth and Seventh Avenues to the Battery, returning north via the Wall Street area, Madison Avenue, and Sixth Avenue. Route M5 gives fine views of the Hudson River as buses travel north on Riverside Drive to the George Washington Bridge at 178th Street. Route M104 travels from the United Nations at First Avenue across 42nd Street, through Times Square, then follows Broadway north by Lincoln Center to Columbia University at 125th Street.

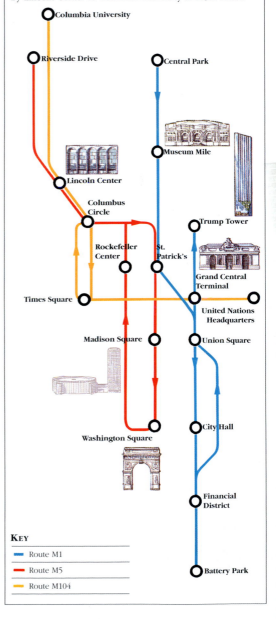

KEY

— Route M1
— Route M5
— Route M104

Using the Subway

New York subway logo

THE SUBWAY is the quickest and most reliable way to travel in the city. The vast system extends over 233 route miles (375 km) and has 468 stations. Most routes operate 24 hours a day throughout the year. Night services are less frequent, and fewer trains run on weekends. In the last few years the subway system has been completely upgraded, and the trains are now air-conditioned, well lit, safer and much more comfortable.

NEW YORK SUBWAY

MANY SUBWAY entrances are marked by illuminated spheres: green where the station booth is manned around the clock, red means restricted entry. Others are marked by a sign bearing the name of the station and the numbers or letters of the routes passing through it.

The subway system runs 24 hours a day, but some routes do have restricted operating times. The basic service is between 6am and midnight.

Bear in mind that there are two types of trains. Local trains stop at all stations, and express trains are faster and stop at fewer stations. Both types of stops are distinguished on every subway map.

In general, the safest, but most crowded, times to travel are between the rush hours of 8am to 6pm. Use common sense, stand in the "Off-Hour Waiting Area" on the platforms, and always be sure of where you are going when you use the subway. It is safe to travel to outer boroughs, although it is not a good idea for anyone to travel alone after midnight. Use the central cars and avoid eye contact with unsavory characters. In an emergency, contact the guard at the station.
Subway information New York City Transit Authority [C] *(718) 330-1234*. Metrocard Customer Service [C] *(212) 638-7622*. [W] *www.mta.nyc.ny.us*

SUBWAY FARE

THE FARE is the same no matter how far you travel on the subway. Since 1997, use of the new MetroCard has greatly increased, and the MTA is phasing out tokens as a means of fare. Many different types of MetroCards exist, providing flexibility for passengers. The price of the MetroCard ranges from $5 to $80 depending on the number of trips you plan to take. Ask at the booth for information.

MetroCard

READING THE SUBWAY MAP

Each route is identified on the subway map *(see inside back cover)* by color, by the names of the stations at each end of the line, and by a letter or number. For instance, the green (6) route links Woodlawn and Utica Avenues, and is served by number 4 trains. Local and express stops and interchange points are identified. The letters and numbers below the station names indicate which routes serve that particular station. A letter or number in heavy type indicates that trains on that route stop there between 6am and midnight; letters in lighter type mean that the route is served by a part-time service only; a boxed letter or number shows the last stop on the line. The maps posted in all the subway stations have a comprehensive guide that explains the trains and timetable of each route.

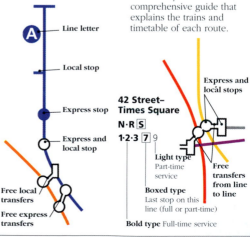

This station's green sphere shows that it is staffed continuously

MAKING A TRIP BY SUBWAY

1 There is a map of the subway system on the back inside cover of this book. Large-scale maps are also positioned in prominent areas in every station, usually very near the token booth.

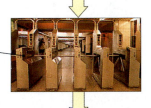

Booth with agent

2 Buy a MetroCard or token from a booth or a vending machine.

Subway map

Vending machine

3 Use the card or token to pass through the turnstile onto the platform.

Entry turnstile

4 Follow the directions for the train you want. For safety, stay in sight of the booth as you wait for your train; at night, stay in one of the yellow off-hours waiting areas.

→ **Uptown Local** **1** **9**

Off-hours waiting area

5 Each train displays its route number or letter in the appropriate color and the names of the terminal stations.

242 St Van Cortlandt Park
Bronx

9

South Ferry
Manhattan

6 Once aboard, you will find a system map next to the door on each side of the car. Use it to follow your progress. Stops are announced on the public address system, and you will also see the station names at each platform. The doors are operated by the driver. For safety, be sure to enter a well-populated car.

Route indicator

Broadway Skip-Stop Express

7 After leaving the train, look for signs giving directions to the exit. If you need to change trains, just follow the signs to the connecting platforms.

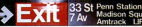

→ **Exit** 33 St Penn Station
7 Av Madison Square Garden
Amtrack LIRR NJ Transit

Traveling by Train

NEW YORK HAS TWO main train stations. Grand Central Terminal is served by commuter trains from New York's suburbs and Connecticut, while Pennsylvania (Penn) Station is the terminal for long-distance services from the rest of the US and also Canada. Most commuter trains have no buffet cars on board, so it's best to buy any food and drink you want before boarding the train. Seat reservations are available only on the long-distance intercity services.

An Amtrak train

GRAND CENTRAL TERMINAL

GRAND CENTRAL Terminal *(see pp154–5)* on Park Avenue between 41st and 42nd streets is the main terminal for **Metro-North Railroad** trains (Hudson, New Haven and Harlem lines), which run north and east of New York and serve southwest Connecticut and Westchester, Dutchess, and Putnam counties. From Grand Central you might travel by train to such destinations as the Bronx Zoo *(see pp242–3)*, the New York

Botanical Garden and President Franklin D. Roosevelt's Hyde Park estate.

The 4, 5 and 6 trains on the green (Lexington) line and number 7 on the purple (Flushing) line serve Grand Central subway station, below the main terminal. A shuttle service links Grand Central to Times Square. Many bus lines stop at Grand Central.

PENN STATION

Long Island Rail Road logo

PENN STATION, between Seventh and Eighth avenues and from 31st to 33rd streets, is a modern terminal that was rebuilt in 1963 underneath the Madison Square Garden complex *(see p133).* Commuter trains, New Jersey Transit trains and **Amtrak** trains from Canada and other parts of the US terminate at this station. There are no luggage trolleys, but redcap porters will help.

You will find taxis at street level. Buses run downtown on Seventh Avenue and uptown on Eighth Avenue. The blue (8th Avenue) subway lines, A, C, and E run on the Eighth Avenue side of the station; the red (Broadway) lines, 1, 2, 3 and 4 run on the Seventh Avenue side of the station. The ticket counters and waiting rooms are one level below; the trains leave from an even lower level.

From Penn Station, you could head for New Jersey and Long Island or farther on Amtrak trains to such destina-

tions as Canada, Philadelphia or Washington. Also in Penn Station are ticket offices and departure points of the **Long Island Rail Road (LIRR)**, mainly a commuter line, but with trains to such Long Island resorts, as the Hamptons and Montauk Point.

PATH TRAINS

PATH TRAINS operate round the clock between New Jersey stations (Harrison, Hoboken, Jersey City and Newark) and Penn Station in Manhattan. They also stop at Christopher Street, the World Trade Center, 9th, 14th, 23rd and 33rd Streets and Avenue of the Americas (6th Avenue).

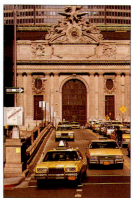

LIRR train at Penn Station

AMTRAK

AMTRAK IS THE US national railroad passenger service linking New York with other US cities and Canada. Some Amtrak trains have cars with reclining seats; others have dining facilities and lounge cars. Sleeper cars are available on all long-distance routes. The new express trains operate on certain Amtrak routes, such as the **Acela** between Boston and Washington via New York.

Tickets can be bought at Penn Station, as well as from Amtrak Travel Centers. Buy your ticket before getting on the train as there is a penalty for buying tickets on board. Senior citizens receive a 15% discount; the conductor will ask for proof of age. There are no student discounts. Seat reservations made by phone with a credit card need to be made at least 10 days in advance of travel if you want the tickets mailed to you.

Amtrak also offers a Great American Vacations package and various promotional fares during the year. Ask for information when you book.

Grand Central Terminal

Information board at Penn Station

TICKETS AND TRAVEL

Ticketing areas at all train stations are well lit and generally crowded at all times of the day. Ticket offices will accept most credit cards, as well as cash. There are a variety of ticket types, most based on a one-way fare; a return fare is twice the single fare. If you are planning a number of trips, Metro-North and LIRR offer weekly passes that will save you money.

Train times, destination and gate numbers are continually updated on numerous large information boards. Watch for signs indicating the major interim stops and transfer points, listed next to the gate for departing trains. Wait for the opening of the gate posted for your train. Metro-North and LIRR cars are all one class, and have no reserved seating. Amtrak trains offer both services. The conductor will ask to see your ticket after the train has left the station.

Penn Station and Grand Central Terminal have good facilities, including bathrooms, banks, shops, bars and restaurants.

TRAIN INFORMATION

Amtrak Travel Centers
12 West 51st St. **Map** 12 F4.
1 East 59th St. **Map** 12 F3.
1 World Trade Center. **Map** 1 B2.
📞 *(800) USA-RAIL or (800) 872-7245.* 🔲 *www.amtrak.com*
Acela
📞 *(800) 523-8720.*
🔲 *www.amtrak.com*
Long Island Rail Road (LIRR)
📞 *(718) 217-LIRR (Information).*
📞 *(212) 643 5228 (Lost property).*
🔲 *www.mta.nyc.ny.us*
Metro-North
📞 *532-4900 (Information).*
📞 *340-2555 (Lost property).*
🔲 *www.mta.nyc.ny.us*
PATH Trains
📞 *(800) 234-7284.*
🔲 *www.panynj.com*

DAY TRIPS BY TRAIN

There are some beautiful places outside New York city, which, if your time allows, are well worth a visit. Below is a list of some recommended sights within 125 miles (200 km) of New York city center. For further details, call the New York Convention and Visitors Bureau *(see p352).*

Phillipsburg Manor, Tarrytown

Stony Brook
Peaceful north shore village. Entrance to the Three Villages historic district.
🚉 *58 miles (93 km) east. Long Island Rail Road from Penn Station. 2 hrs.*

The Hamptons
Chic bars and boutiques in a weathered, historic setting. The Beverly Hills of Long Island.
🚉 *100 miles (161 km) east. Long Island Rail Road from Penn Station. 2 hrs, 50 min.*

Montauk Point
State park on the eastern-most tip of Long Island; windswept ocean views.
🚉 *120 miles (193 km). LIRR from Penn Station. 3 hrs.*

Westbury House, Old Westbury
John Phipps's 1906 re-creation of a Charles II mansion with exquisite English formal gardens.
🚉 *24 miles (39 km) east. Long Island Rail Road from Penn Station. 40 min.*

Tarrytown
Washington Irving's home "Sunnyside" and Jay Gould's mansion.
🚉 *25 miles (40 km) north. Metro-North from Grand Central, then taxi. 40–50 min.*

Hyde Park
Springwood estate of Franklin D. Roosevelt and the Vanderbilt mansion.
🚉 *74 miles (119 km) north. Metro-North from Grand Central to Poughkeepsie, then bus. 2 hrs.*

New Haven, Connecticut
Home of Yale University.
🚉 *74 miles (119 km). Metro-North from Grand Central Terminal. 1 hr, 46 min.*

Hartford, Connecticut
Mark Twain's riverboat-style house, Atheneum Museum and Old State House.
🚉 *112 miles (180 km) north. Amtrak from Penn Station. 2 hrs, 45 min.*

Winterthur, Delaware
Henry du Pont's collection of Early American art, museum and gardens.
🚉 *116 miles (187 km) south. Amtrak from Penn Station to Wilmington, then bus to Winterthur. 2 hrs.*

Yale University in New Haven, Connecticut

STREET FINDER

THE MAP REFERENCES given with all sights, hotels, restaurants, bars, shops and entertainment venues described in this book refer to the maps in this section (*see* How Map References Work *opposite*). These maps cover the whole of Manhattan. A complete index of street names and all the places of interest marked on the maps can be found on the following pages.

The key map *(below)* shows the areas covered by the *Street Finder*, within the various districts. The maps include all of Manhattan's sight-seeing areas (which are color-coded), with all the districts important for hotels, restaurants, bars, shops, theaters and entertainment.

Browsing at South Street Seaport

0 kilometers   2

0 miles   1

Inset on Map 1

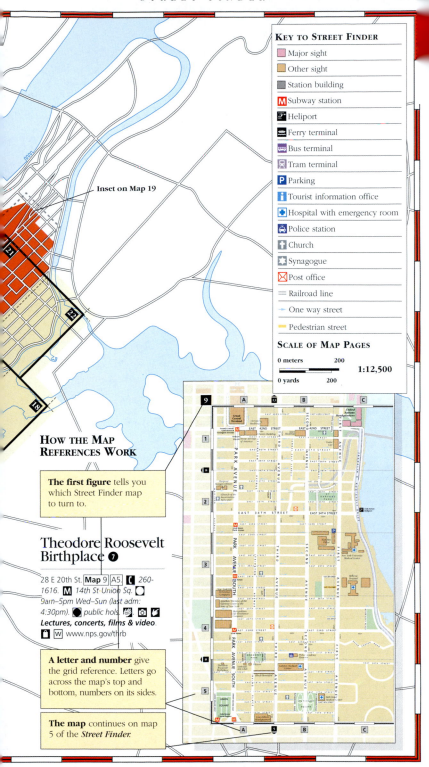

KEY TO STREET FINDER

Major sight

Other sight

Station building

M Subway station

Heliport

Ferry terminal

Bus terminal

Tram terminal

P Parking

i Tourist information office

Hospital with emergency room

Police station

Church

Synagogue

Post office

— Railroad line

One way street

Pedestrian street

SCALE OF MAP PAGES

| 0 meters | 200 | |
| 0 yards | 200 | 1:12,500 |

Inset on Map 19

HOW THE MAP REFERENCES WORK

The first figure tells you which Street Finder map to turn to.

Theodore Roosevelt Birthplace ❼

28 E 20th St. **Map 9** **A5.** 260-1616. **M** *14th St-Union Sq.* 9am–5pm Wed–Sun (last adm: 4:30pm). public hols. Lectures, concerts, films & video. **W** www.nps.gov/thrb

A letter and number give the grid reference. Letters go across the map's top and bottom, numbers on its sides.

The map continues on map 5 of the *Street Finder.*

Street Finder Index

Each place name is followed by its borough (unless in Manhattan) and then by its Street Finder reference

Each place name is followed by its borough (unless in Manhattan) and then by its Street Finder reference

Each place name is followed by its borough (unless in Manhattan) and then by its Street Finder reference

The September 2001 attacks on Lower Manhattan have left a question mark over the transport network in that area (B2 above). Check before starting your journey.

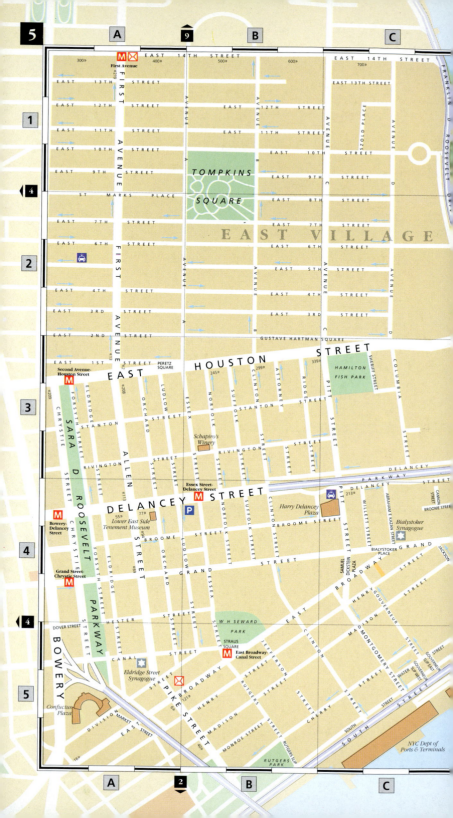

D E F

NORTH 9TH STREET

NORTH 8TH STREET

NORTH 7TH STREET

NORTHE 6TH AVENUE STREET

NORTH 5TH STREET

E A S T

Athletic
Field

NORTH 4TH STREET

KENT AVENUE

WYTHE AVENUE

BERRY STREET

NORTH 3RD STREET

METROPOLITAN AVENUE

#215

NORTH 1ST STREET

RIVER STREET

R I V E R

GRAND STREET

SOUTH 1ST STREET

MANGIN STREET

BARUCH PLACE

SOUTH 2ND STREET

P A R K

SOUTH 3RD STREET

FRANKLIN D

SOUTH 4TH STREET

SOUTH 5TH STREET

Williamsburg Bridge

STREET

SOUTH

SOUTH 6TH STREET

BERRY STREET

#759

DUNHAM PLACE

E A S T

ROOSEVELT DRIVE

□ *Fireboat Station*

BROADWAY

WYTHE AVENUE

SOUTH 7TH STREET

JONES STREET

R I V E R

SOUTH 8TH STREET

SOUTH 9TH ST

STREET

SAMUEL A
SPIEGEL SQUARE

SOUTH 9TH ST

AVENUE

P A R K

CHERRY STREET

Wallabout

SOUTH 11TH ST

CORLEARS
HOOK PARK

Channel

DIVISION AVENUE

STREET

VIADUCT

*Corlears
Hook*

US Naval Reserve
Center

PIER 44

W a l l a b o u t   B a y

D E F

1

2

3

4

5

A ⌃ **15** **B** **C**

1

VERDI
SQUARE
WEST 72ND STREET 🚇 72nd Street
The Dorilton
SHERMAN
WEST 71ST STREET SQUARE

WEST 70TH STREET

W E S T   S I D E

WEST 66TH STREET

2

H u d s o n   R i v e r

CONRAIL
PIERS
(ABANDONED)

WEST 65TH STREET
The
Juilliard
School

Alice
Tully
Hall

Lincoln
Center

WEST 64TH STREET

Metropolitan
Opera House

DAMROSCH
PARK
Guggenheim
Bandshell

Fordham
University

WEST 61ST STREET

WEST 60TH STREET

3

PIER 99

PIER 98

PIER 97

PIER 96

WEST 59TH STREET

Roosevelt
Hospital
Center ✚

WEST 58TH STREET

W E S T   5 7 T H   S T R E E T

WEST 56TH STREET

PIER 95

WEST 55TH STREET

WEST 54TH STREET

PIER 94

WEST 53RD STREET 🅿

4

PIER 92

WEST 52ND STREET

WEST 51ST STREET

N. Y. C. Passenger Ship Terminal
(Port Authority)

PIER 90

WEST 50TH STREET

PIER 88

WEST 49TH STREET

WEST 48TH STREET

WEST 47TH STREET

PIER 86

WEST 46TH STREET

5

Intrepid Sea-Air-Space Museum

WEST 45TH STREET

PIER 84

🅿 WEST 44TH STREET

A **7** **B** **C**

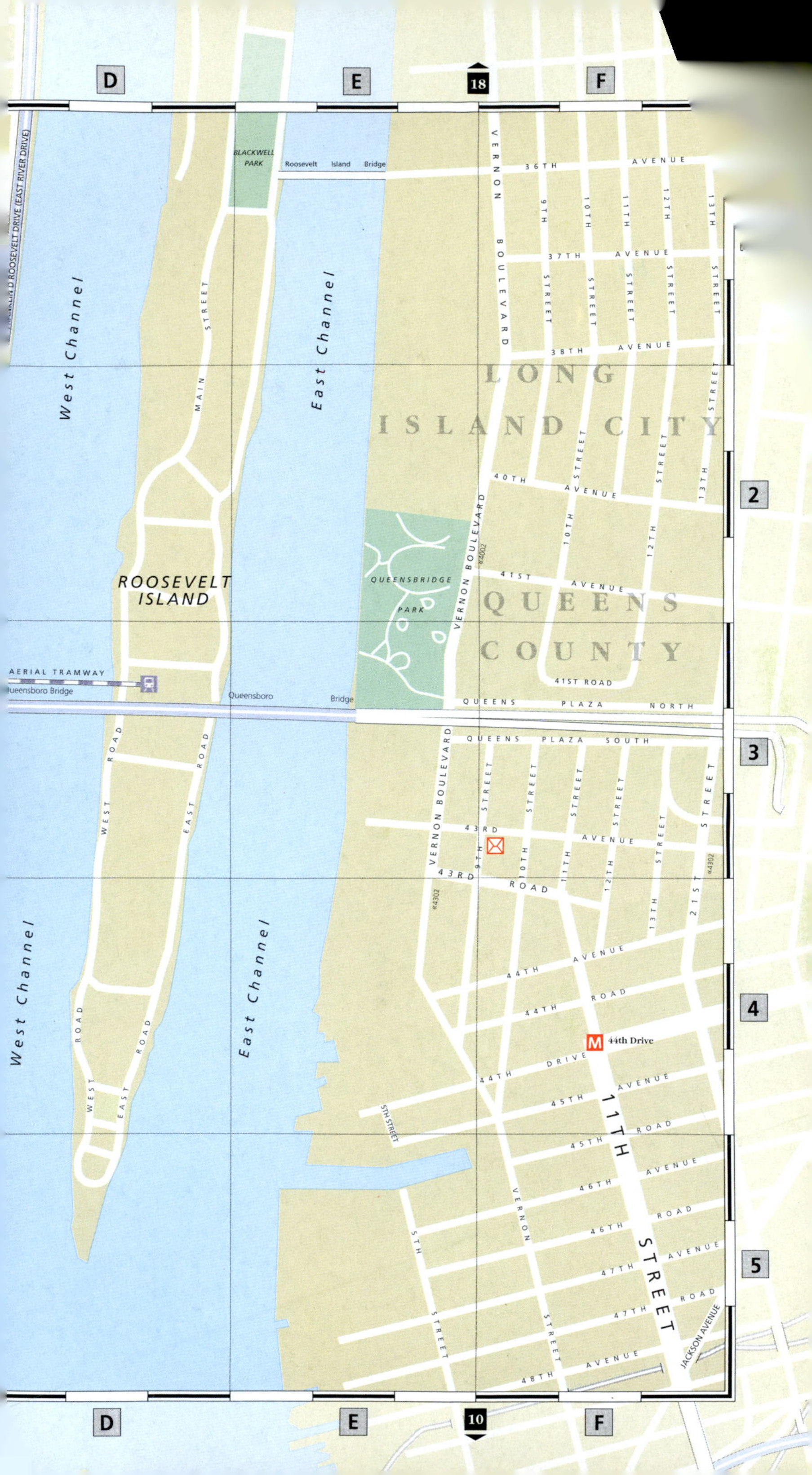

ROAD TO D ROOSEVELT DRIVE (EAST RIVER DRIVE)

BLACKWELL
PARK

Roosevelt   Island   Bridge

VERNON   BOULEVARD

36TH   AVENUE

9TH   STREET
10TH   STREET
11TH   STREET
12TH   STREET
11TH   STREET

37TH   AVENUE

38TH   AVENUE

West Channel

East Channel

MAIN   STREET

L O N G

I S L A N D   C I T Y

40TH   AVENUE

VERNON   BOULEVARD

10TH   STREET
12TH   STREET
13TH   STREET

2

#4002

41ST   AVENUE

QUEENSBRIDGE
PARK

Q U E E N S

C O U N T Y

ROOSEVELT
ISLAND

41ST   ROAD

AERIAL TRAMWAY

WEST   ROAD

EAST   ROAD

Queensboro   Bridge

QUEENS   PLAZA   NORTH

Queensboro Bridge

QUEENS   PLAZA   SOUTH

VERNON   BOULEVARD

9TH   STREET
10TH   STREET
11TH   STREET
12TH   STREET

21ST   STREET

3

43 RD

43RD   ROAD

#4302

AVENUE

#4302

WEST   ROAD

EAST   ROAD

West Channel

East Channel

44TH   AVENUE

44TH   ROAD

13TH   STREET

21ST   STREET

4

M   44th Drive

44TH   DRIVE

5TH   STREET

45TH   AVENUE

11TH   ROAD

45TH   ROAD

1 1 T H   S T R E E T

46TH   AVENUE

VERNON

46TH   ROAD

47TH   AVENUE

5TH   STREET

13TH   STREET

47TH   ROAD

STREET

JACKSON AVENUE

5

48TH   AVENUE

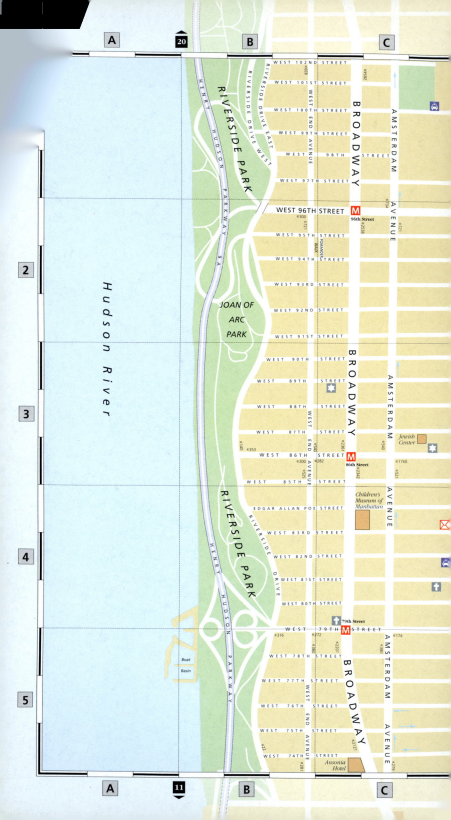

Hudson River

RIVERSIDE PARK

RIVERSIDE DRIVE EAST

RIVERSIDE DRIVE WEST

HENRY HUDSON PARKWAY 9A

WEST 102ND STREET

WEST 101ST STREET

WEST 100TH STREET

WEST 99TH STREET

98TH STREET

WEST 97TH STREET

WEST 96TH STREET   M 96th Street

WEST 95TH STREET

WEST 94TH STREET POMANDER WALK

WEST 93RD STREET

JOAN OF ARC PARK

WEST 92ND STREET

WEST 91ST STREET

WEST 90TH STREET

WEST 89TH STREET

WEST 88TH STREET

WEST 87TH STREET

WEST 86TH STREET   M 86th Street

WEST 85TH STREET

EDGAR ALLAN POE STREET

Children's Museum of Manhattan

RIVERSIDE PARK

WEST 83RD STREET

WEST 82ND STREET

WEST 81ST STREET

WEST 80TH STREET

79th Street

WEST 79TH STREET   M

WEST 78TH STREET

HENRY HUDSON PARKWAY

Boat Basin

WEST 77TH STREET

WEST 76TH STREET

WEST 75TH STREET

WEST 74TH STREET

Ansonia Hotel

B R O A D W A Y

WEST END AVENUE

AMSTERDAM AVENUE

Jewish Center

The Pool

NORTH MEADOW

BALL
FIELD

**EAST
MEADOW**

WEST 101ST STREET
WEST 100TH STREET

EAST 101ST ST

Mount
Sinai
Medical
Center

1

EAST 98TH ST

St Nicholas Russian
Orthodox Cathedral

EAST 97TH ST

WEST 97TH STREET

97TH STREET TRANSVERSE ROAD

17

WEST 96TH STREET   M   96th Street

EAST 96TH ST

C E N T R A L

EAST 95TH ST

WEST 95TH STREET

WEST 94TH STREET

FIFTH

EAST 94TH ST

2

WEST 93RD STREET

SOUTH MEADOW
TENNIS COURTS

EAST 93RD ST

Jewish
Museum

WEST 92ND STREET

EAST 92ND ST

WEST 91ST STREET

Cooper-
Hewitt
Museum

AVENUE

R e s e r v o i r

Eldorado
Apartments
(HENRY J BROWNE BOULEVARD)

EAST 90TH ST

National
Academy
of Design

WEST 89TH STREET

WEST 88TH STREET

Solomon R
Guggenheim
Museum

EAST 88TH ST

WEST 87TH STREET

(MUSEUM

Neue
Gallerie

3

WEST 86TH STREET   M   86th Street

EAST 87TH ST

EAST 86TH ST

WEST 85TH STREET

86TH STREET TRANSVERSE ROAD

EAST 85TH ST

P A R K

EAST 84TH ST

WEST 84TH STREET

**THE GREAT
LAWN**

EAST 83RD ST

WEST 83RD STREET

MILE)

EAST 82ND ST

WEST 82ND STREET

Metropolitan
Museum
of Art

4

WEST 81ST STREET   M   81st Street-
Museum of Natural History

EAST 81ST ST

EAST 80TH ST

Hayden
Planetarium

SHAKESPEARE
GARDEN

Delacorte
Theater

Belvedere Lake

EAST 79TH ST

17

American Museum
of Natural History

Belvedere Castle

79TH STREET TRANSVERSE ROAD

WEST 77TH STREET

CENTRAL PARK WEST

New-York
Historical Society

EAST 78TH ST

EAST 77TH ST

WEST 76TH STREET

**THE
RAMBLE**

Alice in
Wonderland

EAST 76TH ST

5

WEST 75TH STREET

San Remo
Apartments

The Lake

Boat
House

EAST 75TH ST

WEST 74TH STREET

Conservatory
Water

EAST 74TH ST

COLUMBUS AVENUE

Bow Bridge

H a r l e m   R i v e r

Willis Avenue Bridge

EAST 127TH STREET

EAST 126TH STREET

125th Street
(MARTIN LUTHER KING, JR BOULEVARD)
100»   #2206   200»
#2261

Triborough Bridge

LOUIS GUVILLIER PARK

RANDALL'S

ISLAND

PARK

FRANKLIN D ROOSEVELT DRIVE (EAST RIVER DRIVE)

PALADINO

RONALD E MCNAIR PLACE

PLEASANT AVENUE

SYLVAN PL

THIRD   AVENUE

SECOND   AVENUE

FIRST   AVENUE

EAST 120TH STREET

EAST 119TH STREET

EAST 118TH STREET

EAST 117TH STREET   #2254

116th Street
#2120
(LUIS   MUÑOZ   MARIN   BOULEVARD)
100»   #2103   200»   300»   #2238   400»

EAST 115TH STREET

EAST 114TH STREET

JEFFERSON

PARK

EAST 113TH STREET

EAST 112TH STREET

EAST 111TH STREET   #2135

#2002

110th Street   EAST 110TH STREET

#1981

EAST 109TH STREET

EAST 108TH STREET

Benjamin
Franklin
Plaza

RECREATION PIER

EAST 107TH STREET

THIRD   AVENUE

SECOND   AVENUE

FIRST   AVENUE

EAST 106TH STREET

EAST 105TH STREET

H a r l e m

R i v e r

EAST 104TH STREET   #2001

103rd Street   EAST 103RD STREET

Foot Bridge

General Index

Acknowledgments

DORLING KINDERSLEY would like to thank the many people whose help and assistance contributed to the preparation of this book.

MAIN CONTRIBUTOR
Eleanor Berman has lived in New York for almost 40 years. Her travel articles are widely published and she is the author of *Away for the Weekend: New York*, a favorite since 1982. Her other books include *Away for the Weekend* guides for the Mid-Atlantic, New England and Northern California, *Travelling on Your Own* and *Reflections of Washington, DC*.

MUSEUM CONTRIBUTORS
Michelle Menendez, Lucy O'Brien, Heidi Rosenau, Elyse Topalian, Sally Williams.

DORLING KINDERSLEY wishes to thank the following editors and researchers at Websters International Publishers: Sandy Carr, Matthew Barrell, Sara Harper, Miriam Lloyd, Ava-Lee Tanner, Celia Woolfrey.

ADDITIONAL PHOTOGRAPHY
Edward Hueber, Eliot Kaufman, Karen Kent, Dave King, Norman McGrath, Howard Millard, Paul Solomon, Chuck Spang, Chris Stevens.

ADDITIONAL ILLUSTRATIONS
Steve Gyapay, Kevin Jones, Dinwiddie MacLaren, Janos Marffy, Chris D. Orr, Nick Shewring, John Woodcock.

CARTOGRAPHY
Maps Andrew Heritage, James Mills-Hicks, Chez Picthall, John Plumer (Dorling Kindersley Cartography)
Advanced Illustration (Cheshire), Contour Publishing (Derby), Europmap Ltd (Berkshire). Street Finder maps: ERA-Maptec Ltd (Dublin) adapted with permission from original survey and mapping by Shobunsha (Japan).

CARTOGRAPHIC RESEARCH
Roger Bullen, Tony Chambers, Ruth Duxbury, Ailsa Heritage, Jayne Parsons, Laura Porter, Donna Rispoli, Joan Russell, Jill Tinsley, Andrew Thompson.

DESIGN AND EDITORIAL
MANAGING EDITOR Douglas Amrine
MANAGING ART EDITORS Stephen Knowlden, Geoff Manders
SENIOR EDITOR Georgina Matthews
SERIES DESIGN CONSULTANT Peter Luff
EDITORIAL DIRECTOR David Lamb
ART DIRECTOR Anne-Marie Bulat
PRODUCTION CONTROLLER Hilary Stephens
PICTURE RESEARCH Susan Mennell, Sarah Moule
DTP DESIGNER Andy Wilkinson
Keith Addison, Ron Boudreau, Linda Cabasin, Michelle Clark, Carey Combe, Diana Craig, Maggie Crowley, Guy Dimond, Tom Fraser, Alex Gray, Marcus Hardy, Sasha Heseltine, Pippa Hurst, Kim Inglis, Jane Middleton, Helen Partington, Leigh Priest, Nicki Rawson, Marisa Renzullo, Ellen Root, Liz Rowe, Anaïs Scott, Anna Streiffert, Clare Sullivan, Andrew Szudek.

SPECIAL ASSISTANCE
Beyer Blinder Belle, John Beatty at the Cotton Club, Peter Casey at the New York Public Library, Nicky Clifford, Linda Corcoran at the Bronx Zoo, Audrey Manley at the Morgan Library, Jane Fischer, Deborah Gaines at the New York Convention and Visitors Bureau, Dawn Geigerich at the Queens Museum of Art, Peggy Harrington at St. John the Divine, Pamela Herrick at the Van Cortlandt House, Marguerite Lavin at the Museum of the City of New York, Robert Makla at the Friends of Central Park, Gary Miller at the New York Stock Exchange, Laura Mogil at the American Museum of Natural History, Fred Olsson at the Shubert Organization, Dominique Palermo at the Police Academy Museum, Royal Canadian Pancake House, Lydia Ruth and Laura I. Fries at the Empire State Building, David Schwartz at the American Museum of the Moving Image, Joy Sienkiewicz at the South Street Seaport Museum, Barbara Orlando at the Metropolitan Transit Authority, the staff at the Lower East Side Tenement Museum, Msgr. Anthony Dalla Valla at St. Patrick's Cathedral.

RESEARCH ASSISTANCE
Christa Griffin, Bogdan Kaczorowski, Steve McClure, Sabra Moore, Jeff Mulligan, Marc Svensson, Vicky Weiner, Steven Weinstein.

PHOTOGRAPHIC REFERENCE
Duncan Petersen Publishers Ltd.

PHOTOGRAPHY PERMISSIONS
DORLING KINDERSLEY would like to thank the following for their kind permission to photograph at their establishments:
American Craft Museum, American Museum of Natural History, Aunt Len's Doll and Toy Museum, Balducci's, Home Savings of America, Brooklyn Children's Museum, The Cloisters, Columbia University, Eldridge Street Project, Federal Hall, Rockefeller Group, Trump Tower.

PICTURE CREDITS
t = top; tc = top center; tr = top right; cla = center left above; ca = center above; cra = center right above; cl = center left; c = center; cr = center right; clb = center left below; cb = center below; crb = center right below; bl = bottom left; bc = bottom center; br = bottom right.

Works of art have been reproduced with the permission of the following copyright holders:
© ADAGP, Paris and DACS, London 1993: 67cl (*Four Trees*, April 1971–July 1972, by Jean Dubuffet), 105cl, 170bl, 186tl, 187crb, 199crb; *Alice In Wonderland*, 1959 © Jose de Creeft/DACS, New York 1993: 53cl, 205cl; © DACS 1993: 34tr, 113tc, 160tr (donated by the Norwegian Government, 1952), 171cb, 172cr, 186bl, 187cra, 187bl, 188cla; © Estate of STUART DAVIS/DACS, London/VAGA, New York 1993: 199cr; © DEMART PRO ARTE BV/DACS 1993: 172cl; *The American Merchant Mariners Memorial*, 1991, © MARISOL ESCOBAR/DACS, London/VAGA, New York 1993: 55bc; © JASPER JOHNS/DACS, London/VAGA, New York 1993: 199ca; © ROY LICHTENSTEIN/DACS 1993: 173tl,